הלכה

ArtScroll Halachah Series®

Adapted from the Hebrew classic,

פני ברוך/אבלות בהלכה

MOURNING

Translated by
Shlomo Fox-Ashrei

Edited for publication by
Rabbi Meir Zlotowitz

Published by
Mesorah Publications, ltd

אבלות בהלכה/זכרון אבות

IN HALACHAH

THE LAWS AND CUSTOMS
OF THE YEAR OF MOURNING

by Rabbi Chaim Binyamin Goldberg

FIRST EDITION

Thirteen Impressions . . . August 1991 — February 2010

Published and Distributed by
MESORAH PUBLICATIONS, Ltd.
4401 Second Avenue
Brooklyn, New York 11232

Distributed in Europe by
LEHMANNS
Unit E, Viking Business Park
Rolling Mill Road
Jarrow, Tyne & Wear NE32 3DP
England

Distributed in Australia & New Zealand by
GOLDS WORLD OF JUDAICA
3-13 William Street
Balaclava, Melbourne 3183
Victoria Australia

Distributed in Israel by
SIFRIATI / A. GITLER — BOOKS
6 Hayarkon Street
Bnei Brak 51127

Distributed in South Africa by
KOLLEL BOOKSHOP
Ivy Common 105 William Road
Norwood 2192, Johannesburg, South Africa

THE ARTSCROLL HALACHAH SERIES ®
MOURNING IN HALACHAH
© *Copyright 1991, by* MESORAH PUBLICATIONS, Ltd.
4401 Second Avenue / Brooklyn, N.Y. 11232 / (718) 921-9000 / www.artscroll.com

---

ISBN 10: 0-89906-171-0 / ISBN 13: 978-0-89906-171-9 (hard cover)
ISBN 10: 0-89906-172-9 / ISBN 13: 978-0-89906-172-6 (paperback)

Typography by CompuScribe at ArtScroll Studios, Ltd., Brooklyn, NY
4401 Second Avenue / Brooklyn, N.Y. 11232 / (718) 921-9000

Printed in the United States of America by
Noble Book Press Corp., New York, N.Y.
Bound by SeferCraft Quality Bookbinders, Brooklyn, N.Y.

MOURNING
IN
HALACHAH

This volume is dedicated to the memory of

Abe Septimus ה"ע

ר' אברהם חיים ב"ר יוסף דוב ז"ל

נפטר כ"ז תשרי תש"נ

In a family of Jewish aristocracy, he was an aristocrat.
He shunned the limelight, but it sought him out —
for his wisdom, kindness, integrity, idealism, generosity,
love of Torah,
and love of his fellow Jews.

He would never trouble another,
but for him no service to others was ever too much trouble.
His foremost love was the growth of Torah —
and his greatest pride was to see it take luxuriant root in his own family.

תנצב"ה

❀ ❀ ❀

Abraham Blashka ה"ע

ר' אברהם ב"ר משה דוד ז"ל

נפטר י"ט אדר ב' תשמ"א

He was born in the United States
at a time when it was "too hard" to be a Torah Jew —
but for him the right thing was never too hard.

Whether in his profession, in his heartfelt tefillah,
in his duties to family, shul, or fellow Jews,
or in his unyielding allegiance to Torah and mitzvos,
he epitomized the אִישׁ תָּם וְיָשָׁר, a sincere and upright man.
That is what he was and that became his epitaph.

תנצב"ה

זכרון

This volume is dedicated to the memory of

Alter Yisachar Penn ע״ה

ר׳ אלתר יששכר בן ר׳ ישעיהו עמנואל ז״ל

נפטר כ״ג שבט תשמ״א

From a difficult childhood in Poland he made aliyah to Eretz Yisrael,
where he fought in the British Army and became a prisoner of war.
In America he started a third new life,
working hard and dealing honestly.
He was an unassuming, quiet person,
who wished everyone well and was well liked by all.
He raised his sons to lives of Torah and mitzvos
and then lived out his years in Israel.
He earned his epitaph:
נְקִי כַפַּיִם וּבַר לֵבָב, one with clean hands and a pure heart.

תנצב״ה

❀ ❀ ❀

Rabbi Morris Halpern ע״ה

הרב משה צבי יוסף בן ר׳ שלמה ז״ל

נפטר שושן פורים תשל״ב

He came to Montreal as a young talmid chacham of 26,
and in only fifteen years,
he had built a shul of a thousand members
and become president of the Board of Jewish Ministers.
He was a pioneer in bringing people back to Judaism
and in the struggle for Soviet Jews.
No exertion was too great to help a fellow Jew, even a stranger.
At only 41, he was taken — but his rich legacy lives on.

תנצב״ה

৯ **Contents**

◆§ *Haskamos /*
Letters of Approbation to the Hebrew Edition

בית דין צדק לכל מקהלות האשכנזים
ע"י העדה החרדית פרו"ח
(ועד העיר לקהלת האשכנזים)
פעיה"ק ירושלים תובב"א
ת.ד. 5006

פעיה"ק ירושלים ת"ו יום כ' לחדש שבט שנת תשמ"ה

הן הביאו לפנינו, הרבנים גולדבערג נ"י קונטרסים מהספר "פני ברוך" מאביהם
הרב הגאון מוה"ר ברוך פנחס גולדבערג ז"ל אחד מיקירי ירושלים הנודעים לשם
ולתהלה, שסידר על עניני המצוה דבקור חולים והלכותי' המסתעפים מזה לחול
ולשבת, ואמנם גדר בעדינו מבלי תת הסכמה על ספר העוסק בדיני הלכה למעשה
שלא יתפרש כי אנו קבענו הלכה כמות שהוא בהספר עכ"ז היות למען המצוה דבקור
חולים כי רבה היא ומועטים הם הספרים העוסקים בה ובעהמ"ח זה הי' ת"ח ויר"ש
ידוע, אמרינן לפעלא טבא דהרבנים הנ"ל יישר חילם אשר טוב וישר עשו להוציא
לאור הספר אשר אביהם ז"ל יגע עליו, למען עשות נח"ר לנשמתו, ובודאי ימליץ טוב
בעדם ובעד כל זרעם שיחיו.
והננו לברך אותם בהצלחה גמורה במעשי ידיהם, כעתירת המצפים לישועה
בקרוב.

הביד"ץ דפעיה"ק ת"ו

נאם משה ארי' פריינד
ראב"ד פה עיה"ק ת"ו

נאם ישראל משה בלאאמו"ר
הגה"צ מהרי"ץ זצוק"ל דושינסקי

נאם אברהם דוד הורוויץ

הרב ישראל יעקב פישר

רב דזכרון משה וחבר הביד"צ העדה החרדית בעיה"ק ירושלים תובב"א
רחוב חפץ חיים 4

ב"ה יום כ"ד אייר תשמ"ו

הן הובא לפני קונטרסין מספר פני ברוך חלק ב' אשר סדרו וחברו הרב הגאון מו"ה
חיים בנימין שליט"א בן הרב הגאון מו"ה ברוך פינחס גולדברג זצ"ל ובו נאספו כל
דיני קריעה ואבילות בחול ובשבת ויו"ט וראיתי ברא כרעא דאבוה דכמעשהו של
האב בראשון כך מעשהו של הבן בשני. שליקט כל ההלכות הנפזרות והעיר הערות
להלכה ולמעשה וכבר שקלו וטרו בעניני הספר בקונטרס אהל חנה אשר נספח לחלק
הראשון ונתקבל באהבה בקרב צבור שוחרי התורה, ובודאי גם חלק הזה שנסדר ע"י
בנו שליט"א יתקבל ויהיה תועלת גדול לרבים, ...

הכותב וחותם למען כבוד התורה ולומדיה
נאם ישראל יעקב פישר

הרב אברהם דוד הורוויץ

אבד"ק שטראסבורג
רחוב רבינו גרשום 37 ירושלים עיה"ק ת"ו

בס"ד ה' לס' אם בחקותי תלכו ל"ח למב"י תשמ"ו

בן יכבד אב ה"ה הרה"ג החו"ב מוה"ר חיים בנימין גולדברג שליט"א אחרי
שהו"ל ביחד עם אחיו הדגולים הי"ו את הספר פני ברוך על ה' בקור חולים וה
שמחות אשר ערך אביהם המנוח הרב הגאון מוה"ר ברוך פנחס גולדברג זצ"ל
מיקירי קרתא קדישא הדין עם הערות והארות טובות בקראו שמם בפני החיים ובנו
הנ"ל הביא לפני כעת קונטרסים חשובים בביררורי כמה הלכות בענינים אלו הסובבים
על הל' שמחות והפציר בי לעיין בהם וראיתי מסדר דברים כהלכתן מפי סופרים
וספרים שו"ת השייכים להלכות אלו את הכל עשה יפה בעתו בסידור הגון וראוי וגם
אני מסרתי לו איזהו ענינים, ובודאי שכל מעיין בספרו זה יברך בקול תודה להמחבר
אשר טוב בעמיו עשה להראות בכל הלכה מקורן של דברים ולפעלא טבא כזאת
אמרינן יישר חילו לאוריתא לזכות את הרבים וזכות הרבים תלוי בו והנני בזה לברכו
אשר חפץ ד' בידו יצליח יראה טוב בעמלו ויזכה להפיצם בישראל כעתירת מוקירו
ומכבדו כערכו הרם.

הכו"ח פעיה"ק ירושלים תובב"א לכבוד התוה"ק הוגי' ולומדי' ומצפה לישועה
בכב"י,

אברהם דוד הורוויץ

שמואל הלוי ואזנר
רב אב״ד ור״מ
זכרון־מאיר, בני ברק

ב״ה יום ד׳ פ׳ ויק״פ תשמ״ה לפ״ק

הן הובא לפני ספר פני ברוך – והוא אוסף ליקוט נהדר בחכמה ודעת מכב׳ ההגה״צ ר׳ ברוך גולדבערג־יאדלר זצ״ל מירושלים עיה״ק תוב״ב, על עניני בקור חולים, והוא מביא כל ההלכות לפונדק אחד, ומזהיר ע״פ חז״ל הקדושים על חומר המצוה, שהי׳ גבר חולה מכאוב הרבה משנותיו והרגיש בחיות מצוה זו, והיות שהוא ספר הלכה, ולי לא הי׳ פנאי לעבור עליו, הריני סומך על גאון מירושלים מפורסם שליט״א שעבר עליו ושבח בכפילא, ויש בו משום זכוי הרבים.
ע״ז בעה״ח, מצפה לרחמי ה׳,

שמואל הלוי ואזנר
רב אב״ד ור״מ זכרון מאיר בני ברק

הרב אליעזר יהודה וולדינברג
חבר בית הדין הרבני הגדול
בעהמ״ס שו״ת ציץ אליעזר, הלכות מדינה, שביתת הים, ר״ר א׳י וד״א
רח׳ מזור 8, ירושלים, ישראל

ב״ה, ירושלם יום כ״ד לחדש סיון שנת תשמ״ו

חזיתי איש מהיר במלאכתו לפני מלכי רבנן יתייצב ה״ה האברך המופלג הרה״ג המצוין חו״ב מוה״ר חיים בנימין בהרב הגרב״פ גולדברג שליט״א ותנא ואייתי ומתניתא בידיה, ראבוה ודיליה, גליונות דפוס מספר פני ברוך ח״ב על ה׳ שמחות. ובעיניי בו אחת הנה ואחת הנה נוכחתי לדעת כי חלק זה כאחיו הקודם מסודר הנהו בטוב טעם ודעת. דבר דבור על אופניו, והגדיל לעשות בתוספות והערות מרובות על העיקר בהערות והארות מלוא חפניים המאירות עינים בקיבוץ וריבוץ ובבירור וליבון ההלכות ע״י גדול כח הבן האברך היקר הנ״ז.
בטוחני כי כל אשר יעיין בהם בטוב העיון ימצא בהספר חפץ רב, כי מעמיקים בפתרון בעיות עמומות הדורשות לא פעם פתרון מיידי וימצאו בספר יקר זה, המלא על כל גדותיו בבקיאות וחריפות והבנה רבה.
אמינא לפעלא טבא אייישר, וברכתי להרה״ג היקר נ״י כי חפץ ד׳ בידו יצליח להפיץ מעיינותיו חוצה להגדלת התורה והאדרתה...

באעה״ח יום הנ״ל
אליעזר יהודא וולדינברג

◄§ Preface

Sometimes there is an important need for a book that deals meticulously with a topic that most people shun — until knowledge of its details becomes an urgent, though unpleasant, necessity. With *Mourning in Halachah,* it is our privilege to publish such a book.

The laws of mourning, from the days and weeks leading up to the tragedy to its immediate and longer-term aftermath, apply to everyone at some point. Although the basic laws are codified, there are many, many customs and interpretations that vary from community to community. Add to this the unavoidable situation that, when tragedy strikes, there are any number of halachic problems, many unexpected, that demand immediate answers. Often qualified rabbinic authorities are unavailable, and even when they are, families are reluctant to call them over and over again as new questions arise. Needless to say, most families discover that some of the solutions they reached under emotional stress and pressure of time were not correct.

To anyone who has gone through bereavement, this scenario is unpleasantly familiar. Also familiar is the refrain:

> If only there would be a well-documented book that deals with all these matters comprehensively and authoritatively, one that deals with virtually all conceivable circumstances and cites the practices of various communities!

Such a book, entitled *P'nei Baruch,* appeared in Israel in 1986. Its author, Rabbi Chaim Binyamin Goldberg, the *Rosh Kollel* of Nitra, had gained the guidance and approbation of many of the foremost halachic authorities of the generation. *P'nei Baruch* is a voluminous work that begins with the time of death. It continues a posthumously published book by the author's father, Rabbi Baruch Pinchas Goldberg ל״צז, that discussed the laws applicable from the onset of an illness until the time of bereavement. In Israel and the Diaspora, the two volumes of *P'nei Baruch* were regarded as a breakthrough, the last word in these always relevant laws, the source book that the worlds of the rabbinate and laity had been awaiting.

Rabbi Goldberg permitted the Mesorah Heritage Foundation to translate and perfect both his and his father's works in one comprehensive volume. No effort was spared to make the combined English volume as complete, accurate, and useful as possible. To assure this, several steps were undertaken: Rabbi David Cohen, the outstanding halachic authority, reviewed the Hebrew work. The translation was done by Rabbi Shlomo Fox-Ashrei, whose work is known and respected by ArtScroll readers. His translation, in turn, was reviewed by Rabbi Reuven Katz, under the coordination of Shmuel Blitz, in Jerusalem.

The completed manuscript was meticulously edited by Rabbi Meir Zlotowitz, who clarified and augmented countless points, and added information that applies to communities of the Diaspora, all of which were reviewed and approved by the author and such other halachic authorities as Harav David Feinstein and Harav Hillel David. Rabbi Zlotowitz prepared an exhaustively comprehensive index, so that the reader can find answers to questions as soon as they arise. Only someone who has had to find instant responses can appreciate how important this is.

In addition to the laws, an appendix to this work includes the appropriate prayers for such moments as the final confessions, prayers for the burial, visits to graves of loved ones, Mishnah study, and *Tehillim*.

We are confident that this work will be an indispensable reference for multitudes at the very moment when such guidance is most needed — indeed, that it will be the definitive work on the subject for many years. We are grateful that we have had the opportunity to bring it to the public.

⋙ Acknowledgments

We are deeply grateful to the families that dedicated this book. May the comfort it brings to others bring merit to the souls of the departed and to the lives of their heirs. They are DR. ROBERT AND BARBARA BLASHKA; MICHAEL AND JOAN PENN; and JUDAH AND BAILA SEPTIMUS.

We acknowledge those who have worked conscientiously and skillfully to make this volume a thing of esthetic beauty. It is another gem in the crown of the acknowledged genius of Judaica graphics REB SHEA BRANDER, and his colleague REB ELI KROEN. The often demanding typographical work was done by MRS. ESTIE DICKER, MRS. ZISSI LANDAU, EPHRAIM ROSENSTOCK, YEHUDA GORDON, BASSIE GOLDSTEIN, and NICHIE FENDRICH. Proofreading was done by MRS. JUDI DICK, who made valuable comments, and MRS. FAIGIE WEINBAUM.

Finally, we are grateful to the supporters of the Foundation who make it possible for us to engage highly qualified scholars and writers to present the riches of our heritage to the English-speaking public.

Mesorah Heritage Foundation

Elul 5751 — 1991

MOURNING
IN
HALACHAH

The meaning of the numbers and symbols in the footnotes is as follows:

"§36" refers to chapter [*siman*] 36.
"36:3" refers to chapter [*siman*] 36, paragraph [*s'if*] 3.
"36:§§3" refers to chapter [*siman*] 36, sub-paragraph [*s'if katan*] 3.

CHAPTER ONE

Visiting the Sick*

R' Yitzchak son of R' Yehudah said: One should always pray
for mercy that he not become ill; for should he fall ill,
[the Heavenly Court] tells him: "Produce a source of merit,
and you will be spared."[1]

Once a person becomes ill, it is a *mitzvah* to visit him; for we
find that the Holy One, Blessed is He, visited the sick.
Thus R' Chamma son of R' Chanina stated: With regard to
what is written: *'You shall follow* HASHEM *your God'*
[*Deut.* 13:5] — is it possible for a person to 'follow'
the Divine Presence? Has it not been written,
'Hashem your God is a consuming fire' (ibid. 4:24)?

But [what it means is:] Follow the traits (*middos*) of the
Holy One, Blessed is He. . . . [He] visits the sick,
as it is written: *'Hashem appeared to him* [Abraham,
who was ill following his circumcision] *at Elonei Mamre'*
(Genesis 18:1). So must you visit the sick.[2]

◄§ The Obligation and the Reward

1. All *halachic* authorities agree that it is a *mitzvah* to visit the sick. According to
Halachos Gedolos (Behag),[3] this is a Scriptural commandment, and according
to *Rambam*,[4] it is Rabbinic. The Torah states: *'You shall make known to them the*

---

* Chapters 1-5 of this book are adapted from the work entitled *P'nei Baruch: Bikur Cholim
Kehilchaso* (5745/1985), by the author's revered father, Harav Hagaon, R' Baruch Pinchas
Goldberg, זצ״ל.

1. *Shabbos* 32a.
2. *Sotah* 14a.
3. Positive commandment §36. A number of other *Rishonim* rule similarly: See *S'dei Chemed*
   (*Klallim*, *ma'areches habeis* §116).
4. *Hilchos Avel* (14:1). This is also the ruling of *Meiri* (*Nedarim* 39b). See also *Maharatz Chayus*
   (*Nedarim* 39b), who explains *Rambam*'s ruling that the *mitzvah* of visiting the sick is a "*halachah*
   given to Moshe Rabbeinu at Sinai."

way they are to go' (Exodus 18:20), on which the Sages commented: "This refers to visiting the sick."[5]

2. Visiting the sick is one of the *mitzvos* for whose performance a person 'enjoys the fruit' in this world, while the 'principal' awaits him in the World to Come. (See footnote about taking payment for visiting the sick.)[6]

3. The reward in this world for visiting the sick is that *'Hashem will protect him'* — from the Evil Inclination (*Yetzer Hara*); *'and keep him alive'* — by sparing him from suffering. *'He will be fortunate on earth,'* meaning all will honor him; *'and He will not deliver him to the will of his enemies' (Psalms* 41:3). This means that Hashem will provide him friends like those of Na'aman, who healed his leprosy (*II Kings* 5:13), and not like the friends of Rechavam, who caused his kingdom to be divided (*I Kings* 12).

In the World to Come, he will be spared from the punishment of Gehinnom, as it is said *'Fortunate is the one who contemplates intelligently with the needy. . .'* — one who is thoughtful about the sick, to visit them and ascertain their needs; *'. . .on the day of disaster, Hashem will deliver him'* (ibid. v. 2). The Sages tell us that *'the needy'* means the sick, and *'disasters'* means Gehinnom.[7]

4. One does not recite a blessing for performing the *mitzvah* of visiting the sick.[8]

---

5. *Bava Metzia* 30b.

6. The reward of this *mitzvah* is mentioned in *Shabbos* 127a.

The question of accepting payment for visiting the sick is discussed in *Nedarim* 39a, where the Talmud states that one is forbidden to accept payment. *Tosafos* there explains: "This is a *mitzvah*, and should be performed for free." *Rosh* there gives an alternative explanation: that by accepting payment one would appear to be slighting the *mitzvah*.

The Talmud there continues: "When does this [prohibition against accepting payment] apply? When one stands [throughout the visit]. But if one sits, it is permissible to accept payment." *Ran* there explains that to perform the *mitzvah*, it would be enough to stand [i.e., to conduct a briefer visit]. Hence if one sits down [thus visiting for a longer time and doing more than the basic *mitzvah* requires], one may accept payment. However, *Shitah Mekubetzes* there states that in some communities the custom is not to permit taking payment even if one sits. This same source quotes R' Eliyahu Mizrachi as stating: "Some rule that if visiting the sick means losing work time, one is exempt from the *mitzvah*. This is evident from the fact that [the Sages] permitted taking payment if one sits because a great amount of work time is lost when the visitor sits." [See also below, end of footnote 69.]

7. *Nedarim* (40a); *Aruch HaShulchan* (335:2). And see *Keren Orah* (on *Nedarim* 40a), who explains that the reward in this world for performing this *mitzvah* is measure for measure: One is protected from the *Yetzer Hara*, because one helped the sick person do *teshuvah* (repent); one is spared from suffering, because one saw to the needs of the patient and eased his suffering; one is honored, because one disregarded one's own honor, following the dictum that "even a great man is obligated to visit an unimportant person or a child" (below, par. 12); one is rewarded with good friends, because the primary way of performing this *mitzvah* is with friends and contemporaries, to whom one thus demonstrates closeness.

8. A number of explanations have been given:
  (a) This is a *mitzvah* which could be [unexpectedly] canceled; for example, if the patient indicates he does not desire the visit (Responsa of *Rashba*, part I:§18). [Thus, one could be in the position of reciting the blessing and then being unable to perform the *mitzvah*.]
  (b) One does not recite a blessing over a *mitzvah* involving someone else's pain or misfortune, since this would give the impression of giving thanks for the misfortune. The *mitzvah* of

❧ Time for Visiting and Frequency

5. There is no limit on the *mitzvah* of visiting the sick; one may perform it many times a day. The more one does it, the more praiseworthy he is, as long as he does not overburden the patient.[9]

6. The proper etiquette is that the patient's close relatives and friends — those who are accustomed to visit him even when he is well — should visit him as soon as they learn of the illness.[10] More distant friends and relatives should wait until he has been sick for three days.[11] But if the illness is sudden and severe, even the more distant friends and relatives should visit immediately.[12]

7. One should not visit during the "first three hours" — meaning, the first quarter — of the day.[13] The reason is that during the first quarter of the day the suffering of the illness lightens. Therefore the visitor might not be sufficiently motivated to pray for mercy on behalf of the sick person.

Nor should one visit during the last quarter of the day, for the suffering of the illness is especially severe then, and the visitor might despair of praying for mercy.[14]

---

circumcision is different. We recite a blessing over it, because the essence of the *mitzvah* is connected with pain, but it is not a pain of sorrow or misfortune.

(c) We recite a blessing only for *mitzvos* which, like *tzitzis* and *tefillin*, are performed at prescribed times. When the time of obligation arrives, one needs to recite a blessing to express one's love of the *mitzvah*. But regarding those *mitzvos* which are continual obligations, and from which one is never exempt — for example, the *mitzvah* of believing in Hashem. . .and visiting the sick. . . — it is not appropriate to recite a blessing over them, since one is constantly obligated by them. Hence, there is no particular moment at which it is especially fitting to express one's love of the *mitzvah* (*Or Zarua*, part I *Hilchos Birkas HaMotzi* §140).

(d) We only recite a blessing over *mitzvos* which are not performed at all by the other nations; but for *mitzvos* which the other nations also sometimes perform, we do not recite a blessing (Responsa *Binyamin Zev* I:§169).

9. *Nedarim* (39b); *Rambam* (*Hilchos Avel* 14:4); *Shulchan Aruch* (*Yoreh De'ah* 335:2).

10. *Shulchan Aruch* (*Yoreh De'ah* 335:1).

11. Ibid. *Bach* explains that if more distant friends and relatives were to visit during the first three days, this could impair the person's good fortune (*mazal*) by imposing the label of "sick" upon him. But with people who often visit him even when he is well, this problem does not exist. *Levush* (par. 1) writes: "Close friends [follow the same *halachah*] as near relatives, because the patient derives satisfaction from anyone who is familiar and on good terms with him, or is his friend, and [such visits] lighten his illness."

12. *Shulchan Aruch* (*Yoreh De'ah* 335:1). The reason is that if the illness is sudden and severe, the person in any case is labeled as "sick" (see previous footnote), and therefore even the more distant friends and relatives should visit immediately (*Bach*).

13. It must be that the reference is to "variable hours" (*sha'os z'manios*) [see 13:12]. Otherwise, on a day which lasted only six [regular] hours [360 minutes; this could occur in far northern or southern latitudes], the *mitzvah* of visiting the sick could not be performed at all (*Ahavas Chessed*, by the author of *Chafetz Chaim* III:2).

14. *Shulchan Aruch* (*Yoreh De'ah* 335:4). However, *Rambam* (*Hilchos Avel* 14:5) and *Semag* (*Mitzvos Aseh DeRabbanan* §2) give a different reason for not visiting during the first or last three hours: During these times, people are attending to the sick person's needs (cleaning the room or feeding him)

◄§ On the Sabbath

8. One may visit the sick even on the Sabbath,[15] but one does not tell the patient "May you have a complete recovery" (*refu'ah shleimah*) as one would do on a weekday. Instead, one says: 'שַׁבָּת הִיא מִלִּזְעוֹק וּרְפוּאָה קְרוֹבָה לָבֹא,' 'The Sabbath prohibits us from crying out; but may recovery come speedily'.[16]

One who is especially sensitive and will be distressed by the sick person's suffering should not visit him on the Sabbath.[17]

On the Sabbath, the congregation may pray for the patient whose life is in danger that day. Likewise, during the public Torah-reading on the Sabbath it is permissible to recite a prayer (*mi shebei'rach*) for such a person.[18]

However, the custom nowadays is to recite the *mi shebeirach* prayer even for a

---

and sometimes he feels uncomfortable if visitors are standing around him during such activities.

See *Aruch HaShulchan* (*Yoreh De'ah* 335:8), who states that the Talmud, in mentioning these hours, was not laying down a prohibition, but simply offering sound advice, and this is why in our day it is not customary to be particular about this.

Birkei Yosef §2 writes that, according to the reason given by *Rambam*, one should not visit during the first or last three hours, even in cases where there is no change in the severity of the illness during those hours (for example, in a case of a light illness or indisposition); for, in any case, these are times when people are attending to the sick person's needs. He continues: "It would seem that people rely on the explanation given by *Rambam*, and that is why, nowadays, people in our region are not particular about [avoiding these hours]. Since the reason is that during these hours people are attending to the patient's needs, there is no need for concern about this [in our time], since they have another room [in which to conduct the visit], or else no one minds if these things are done in the presence of [the visitor]."

See also responsa *Salmas Chaim*, by the *gaon*, R' Yosef Chaim Sonnenfeld, *zatzal* (part IV:§4). He was asked why the hospitals are not particular about this matter, and fix visiting hours just during the last three hours of the day — which is apparently contrary to the Talmud. He replied: "In the judgment of the doctors, the times [which the Talmud mentions as] most fit for visiting are needed for the doctors' treatments; and the visit of the doctor is more urgent [than that of friends and relatives]. Afterwards, it is time for the patients to eat. Thus, the only time available [for other people's visiting] is that time [the last three hours of the day]. As for the statement of the Talmud, it refers to a situation where one visits the patient in his home, not to a situation in which [adherence to the Talmud's rule about visiting] would be to the patient's detriment."

15. *Shulchan Aruch* (*Orach Chaim* §287). *Sha'arei Teshuvah* cites the *Mussar* Masters that if a person can visit during the week, it is not proper to do so on the Sabbath. Instead, one should go during the week to visit poor people who are ill, so that he can see their suffering and their need and be as merciful as he can afford — and this is the *mitzvah* of visiting the sick. However, if a person is too busy during the week, or even if he has visited during the week and is now visiting a sick friend who will derive satisfaction from the visit — and especially if the visit is for the benefit of the patient, to advise him how to deal with his illness as well as to encourage him — undoubtedly this is a great *mitzvah* (*Be'ur Halachah* §287).

16. If Yom Kippur occurs on the Sabbath, one need not say "The day of rest prevents us from crying out. . ." since it is Yom Kippur, the Day of Judgment, when we cry out and plead throughout the whole day (*Mateh Efrayim* 621:1).

R' Yosef Karo in *Shulchan Aruch* gives a slightly longer version to be said on the Sabbath: "The Sabbath prohibits us from crying out; but may recovery come speedily. Many are His mercies; and rest on your Sabbath in peace."

17. *Sha'arei Teshuvah* §287.

18. *Rama* (*Orach Chaim* 288:10).

sick person whose life is not in imminent danger, but in such a case, the text of the *mi shebei'rach* includes the phrase: "The Sabbath prohibits us from crying out; but may recovery come speedily."[18a]

For a woman in difficult labor, or who is within the first seven days after childbirth, all authorities agree that one may recite a prayer (*mi shebeirach*) for healing on the Sabbath.

◄§ Precedence

9. If a rich and poor person are both sick, and many people are visiting the rich man to honor him — one should give priority to visiting the poor man, even if the rich man is a Torah scholar. As it is written, *'Fortunate is the one who contemplates the needy. . . on the day of disaster Hashem will deliver him on his sickbed'* (Psalms 41:2-4).

If both a Torah scholar [who is not poor] and a poor man [who is not a Torah scholar] need visitors, the honor of the Torah takes precedence, and one should visit the Torah scholar.[19]

10. The *mitzvah* of consoling mourners takes precedence over that of visiting the sick, because consoling mourners is an act of kindness to both the living and the dead.[20] Only if one cannot perform both *mitzvos* must one give priority to consoling mourners. However, if it is possible to perform both *mitzvos*, one should first visit the sick, in order to help them by doing such chores as sweeping and mopping the floor, for one who performs such service for the sick is considered as if he had saved his life.[21]

11. It is extremely important to see a patient who has no visitors; for his psychological state is depressed when he is alone, and he is in danger of despair, God forbid. By conversing with him, one calms him and eases his suffering.[22]

18a. *Mishnah Berurah* 288:§28. [See ArtScroll Ashkenaz Siddur p. 442.]

19. *Sefer Chassidim* (§361). See also *Nedarim* 40a: "Rav said: 'Whoever visits the sick is rescued from the judgment of Gehinnom, as it is said: *'Fortunate is the one who deals intelligently with the needy; on the day of evil, Hashem will rescue him'* (Psalms 41:1). 'The needy' means the sick, and 'evil' means Gehinnom."

Leshon Chachamim writes that it is conceivable to exempt a person from visiting a sick person of high income or social status. . .if one does not regularly visit him when he is well; for it may be assumed that such a visit does not raise the sick person's spirits. This would seem to be the basis for the fact that people are lenient about visiting sick people whom they do not usually visit when they are well.

See *Chafetz Chaim, Ahavas Chessed* (III:3), who writes at length about how important a *mitzvah* it is to visit a sick person who is poor.

20. *Rambam* (Hilchos Avel 14: 7); *Rama* (335:10). The gaon, R' Moshe Feinstein, zatzal, (Igros Moshe, Orach Chaim IV:40:§11) explains that *Rambam's* ruling regarding the priority of consoling mourners over visiting the sick applies only in cases where the life-threatening needs of the patient are being provided; in cases where the life of the patient is in jeopardy, then visiting him and caring for his needs certainly takes priority, for saving a life overrides all other *mitzvos*.

21. *Bach* §335 and *Shach* (ibid. §§1).

22. *Vayakhel Moshe* in the name of *Sefer Chareidim*. It is especially important to visit a patient who is alone and childless, or who lives too far from his family for them to be with him constantly. It is

12. The *mitzvah* of visiting the sick is not dependent on the status or age of the visitor and patient; even a great man is obligated to visit an unimportant person.[23]

13. Although such visits are included in the general *mitzvah* of doing kindness to others (*gemilus chassadim*), we are commanded specifically to visit the sick. Thus, even though a visitor who is the patient's "contemporary" (*ben gilo*)[24] takes upon himself one-sixtieth of his illness;[25] nevertheless, he has a *mitzvah* to visit.[26]

◆§ Intestinal Disorder

14. One should not visit someone who suffers from an intestinal disorder, since the patient might need to rush to the bathroom and would be embarrassed to do so.[27] One should not visit someone who is suffering from pain in his eyes or head, since conversation is harmful to him.[28] In such cases, one stays outside of the patient's room and inquires about his condition: whether his room needs cleaning or if he requires anything; he hears about his discomfort, and prays for him.[29]

◆§ Contagious Disease

15. One should not visit someone sick with leprosy (*tzaraas*).[30] Regarding a person sick with some other contagious disease, there are differing opinions among the *Poskim*, and it is difficult to determine the *halachah*.[31] The prevailing

---

doubly important to visit a patient who has no relatives, or whose relatives are estranged from him, and who lies alone at home, writhing in pain. In such a case, the primary *mitzvah* is to ascertain whether he lacks something necessary for his recovery or to arrange a doctor for him. In such cases, one should also attend to cleaning the house and bringing food. Regarding such a situation, R' Akiva said (*Nedarim* 40a): "Not to visit the sick is tantamount to killing; and whoever visits him causes him to live."

23. *Nedarim* 39b; *Rambam* (*Hilchos Avel* 14:4); *Shulchan Aruch* (*Yoreh De'ah* 335:2). See also the lengthy discussions of this point in *Igros Moshe* (I:§222) and *Minchas Yitzchak* (II:§84).

24. The commentators offer various definitions of "contemporary" (*ben gilo*): ". . .one who was born at the same time, so that they both have the same *mazal*" (*Rashi* on *Nedarim* 27b, cited by *Prishah* on *Yoreh De'ah* §335:§§6); ". . .a young man like him; or an old man [visiting] an old man" (*Rashi* on *Nedarim* 39b); ". . .someone with his same nature and habits" (*Shitah Mekubetzes*, in the name of *Ritz* on *Nedarim* 39b).

25. Each one takes one-sixtieth of what remained after the previous visitor (*Prishah* on *Yoreh De'ah* §335 *os* 7, based on *Nedarim* 39b). [This is based on the halachic principle of *batel b'shishim*, that the taste of an ingredient which is only one-sixtieth of the volume of the total mixture is considered to be so insignificant as to be null and void.]

26. *Bava Metzia* 30b; *Tur*, *Yoreh De'ah* §335.

27. *Nedarim* 41a, and *Ran* and *Meiri* there; *Tur* and *Shulchan Aruch* (*Yoreh De'ah* 335:8).

28. *Nedarim* 41a. The version cited by *Rambam* (*Hilchos Avel* 14:5) and *Meiri* (on *Nedarim* 41a) is slightly different. Instead of "conversation is detrimental for him," they have: "the visit is detrimental for him."

29. *Tur* and *Shulchan Aruch* (*Yoreh De'ah* 335:8).

30. *Knesses HaGedolah*, cited by *S'dei Chemed* (*Klallim*, *ma'areches habeis* §116).

31. See *S'dei Chemed* (loc. cit.). Responsa *Rama* (end of §19) states: "Regarding the law of visiting the sick, we find no distinction between infectious and non-infectious diseases." This ruling is cited by *Da'as Torah* (335:5), and by *Pischei Teshuvah* (§175). See also a lengthy discussion of this matter in *Nishmas Kol Chai*, by the *gaon* R' Chaim Falaghi (*Choshen Mishpat* II:§49).

custom is not to visit.[32]

◆§ *Kohen* Visiting a Hospital

16. If there are compelling circumstances, a *kohen* may visit a patient in a hospital. However, he should try to determine that there is no Jewish deceased in the hospital.[33] In the event the circumstances are not compelling, one should consult a halachic authority.

◆§ Visiting an Enemy

17. One should not visit an enemy.[34] However, each case is to be judged individually, depending on the degree of enmity, and on the personalities involved.[35] On the other hand, if one sends a message that he would like to visit, and the sick person agrees, not only is one permitted to visit, but this even contributes to making peace.[36]

◆§ Visiting a Non-Jew

18. One should visit non-Jewish sick; for this is an aspect of *darkei shalom*, maintaining good relations with the non-Jewish community.[37]

◆§ Women's Obligation

19. Women are also obligated by the *mitzvah* of visiting the sick.[38]

Regarding whether a man should visit a woman, or vice versa, see footnote.[39]

---

32. *Kemach Soless* writes in the name of *Shulchan Gevoha*: "No one can be expected to endanger his life for the sake of fulfilling this *mitzvah*. And this in fact is the custom — that no one visits plague victims except the designated, fully paid staff appointed for the purpose." This ruling is cited by *S'dei Chemed* (*Klallim*, *ma'areches habeis* §116).

33. Responsa *Teshuras Shai* (*mahadura kamma* §559). See also responsa *Igros Moshe* (II:§166), and Responsa *Tzitz Eliezer* (XVI:§33). Regarding permission for a doctor who is a *kohen* to attend to the medical needs of a patient in his final moments, see *Pischei Teshuvah* (*Yoreh De'ah* §370), and below, 3:3.

34. Responsa of *Maharil* (§197) offers proof that if the patient is not one of those whom it is a *mitzvah* to hate, but the enmity simply results from the dominance of one's Evil Inclination (*Yetzer Hara*), one should visit the person, and it is more of a *mitzvah* to visit *him* than to visit a *friend* who is sick. However, *Darkei Moshe* (§335) refutes this ruling and concludes that one should not visit in such a case, since the sick person might think the visitor is happy over his misfortune, in which instance the visit would cause him suffering. Therefore, it is preferable not to visit and thus to avoid the risk. The latter is the ruling given by *Rama* in 335:2.

35. *Shach* (335:§§2) quoting *Bach*. *Hagahos Yad Shaul*, by the *gaon* R' Shaul Nathanson (on §335), writes that one should make sure the patient does not draw the conclusion that he is near death, since his erstwhile enemy has come to visit him.

36. *Aruch HaShulchan* (335:6).

37. *Gittin* 61; *Shulchan Aruch* 335:9. And it is written: '*Hashem is good to all, and His mercies are upon all His creatures*' (*Psalms* 145:9).

38. This is because this *mitzvah* applies day and night, as is explained by *Ridbaz* in his commentary on the Jerusalem Talmud (*Trumos* 11:5), in the name of *Mahar'af*, who gives this as the meaning of the *baraisa*'s statement that the *mitzvah* of visiting the sick "has no limit."

39. *Aruch HaShulchan* (335:11) writes that a man may visit a woman, or a woman visit a man, on condition that they are not secluded together. The same ruling is given by *Zekan Aharon* (part

ﻪ§ The Essence of the *Mitzvah*

20. The·essence of the *mitzvah* of visiting the sick involves the following aspects:

(a) Praying for him.[40]

(b) Cleaning and mopping his room, or making sure that his relatives do so; or seeing to any other material needs of the patient.[41]

(c) Speaking to him in an understanding manner, to encourage, strengthen, and calm him;[42] sitting with him or watching him if he so requests.[43]

As *Shelah HaKadosh* writes: "The *mitzvah* of visiting the sick involves the body and soul of the patient: the body, in that one takes care of him and sees to his material needs; and the soul, in that one prays for him."

21. *Orchos Chaim* writes: "My son, be careful to visit the sick, for the visitor eases his illness. Try to help him return to his Creator [i.e., repent of his sins; but see below, par. 24], and pray for him. Then depart, and do not allow your presence to be a burden on him for his illness is enough of a burden. When you go in to see the patient, be happy and cheerful. Converse joyfully, for his eyes and heart depend upon those who come to visit him."[44]

22. If one visits the sick without benefiting him, and does not pray for him, one has not fulfilled the *mitzvah* of visiting the sick.[45]

II:§76) — that it is certainly also a *mitzvah* for a man to visit a woman, or a woman to visit a man; and all the more so, for a woman to visit a woman.

However, responsa *Vaya'an Avraham* (*Yoreh De'ah* §25) writes that there certainly is no obligation for a woman to visit a man; and, on the contrary, she should avoid doing so, unless he is one of the relatives with whom she is allowed to be secluded; and the same applies with regard to a man's visiting a woman. Responsa *Tzitz Eliezer* (part V, in *Kuntres Ramas Rachel* §16) writes at length on this subject, and concludes that a woman should not visit a man, nor a man visit a woman.

40. *Rambam* (*Hilchos Avel* 14:6); *Shulchan Aruch* (*Yoreh De'ah* §335).

41. *Shulchan Aruch* (*loc. cit.*); and *Prishah* (§335).

42. *Beis Yosef* (§335), citing *Ramban* in his *Toras Ha'Adam, Sha'ar HaMichush*.

43. *Brachos* 54b; *Magen Avraham* (*Orach Chaim* 239:7).

44. In general, one must be careful not to put any strain on the patient, for some sick people make an effort to receive and converse with visitors, and this may harm the patient. In such circumstances, it may be preferable not to enter his room, except to attend to his needs. If one visits to cheer him up, one should not stay long, but just wish him *refu'ah shleimah*, a complete recovery, and then pray for him and leave. Likewise, one must take care not to burden the sick person with questions, especially out of mere curiosity; for example: "What does the doctor say? How are the pains? What medicines are you taking?" etc. Also, one should not depress him by saying he looks bad. Conversely, there are times when saying that he looks good is precisely what puts a strain on him. In all these matters, one must be extremely careful to use good judgment.

45. *Rama* 335:4.

◄§ Conduct of the Visitor

23. The *Zohar* (*Parashas Pinchas*) states that if the patient is an ordinary man (*adam beinoni*), the visitor should not sit at the foot of the bed, for this is the place of the Angel of Death. It also implies (ibid.) that one should not sit at the head of the bed at all, even if one is not sitting higher than the sick person. On the other hand, if the sick person is completely righteous (*tzaddik gamur*), one should sit nowhere except at the foot of the bed, for the Divine Presence (*Shechinah*) surrounds him on all sides except for his feet.[46]

24. One should not mention nor speak to the patient about any specific sin of his. Instead, one should speak in general about the importance of doing *teshuvah* (repenting). One must be especially careful not to mention the sins of a woman who is having difficulty giving birth. (Perhaps for this reason it is customary not to converse while a woman is giving birth.)[47]

25. It is very important to speak to the patient and explain to him in a positive way the value of repentant self-examination (*cheshbon hanefesh*), and remind him that he should pray for himself, as King Hezekiah prayed to the Holy One, Blessed is He, truly and wholeheartedly,[48] and Hashem heard and accepted his prayer, and he was healed.[49]

◄§ Final Instructions

26. It is desirable to explain to the patient that illness in this world is a kindness which the Holy One, Blessed is He, bestowed for mankind. The Patriarch Jacob, may peace be upon him, prayed and requested[50] that people should become sick. . .so that they could give their final commands to their family,[51] and so that their children would have time to come, each one from his place, and be with their father. . .[52] *Pirkei DeRabbi Eliezer HaGadol*[53] states that our father

---

46. *Aruch HaShulchan* (335:7). And see *Beis Hillel* (§ 335), who discusses this matter at length.

47. In the case of a woman having difficulty giving birth, some have the custom of having her husband deliver a synagogue candle to her, and they try to have the woman herself light the candle, so that she will earn the merit of lighting [the Sabbath and *Yom Tov*] candles (*Ma'avar Yabok* 1:4).

48. *II Kings*, ch. 20. But if the visitor cannot explain these things in a sensitive, considerate manner, it is better not to mention the subject at all; for it could, God forbid, have a strongly adverse effect; and all the more so, if the patient is not in good condition.

49. If the patient wishes to pray for mercy in a brief form, he should do so at the end of the *Shemoneh Esrei* prayer, when bowing after taking three steps back. He should concentrate fully, without hurrying, and say three times: אֵל נָא רְפָא נָא לִי, "Please, God, heal me now." This is a tradition received by R' Nassan Meir from a great scholar from Spain.

After the congregation responded 'Amen' to a *mi shebeirach* blessing for a sick person or a woman who had given birth, R' Ezkin would recite this brief prayer one time.

50. *Bava Metzia* 87a.

51. *Rashi* there, s.v. *ba'ei rachmei*.

52. *Rashi* on *Sanhedrin* 107b, s.v. *ba'ei rachmei*.

53. Chapt. 52.

Jacob, may peace be upon him, said: "Master of all the worlds, do not take my soul from me until I command my sons and household. . ." and his prayer was answered. *Radal* there explains that Jacob prayed that this would be the way from then on. . .and when Jacob's prayer was accepted, this matter became part of the natural order forever after.

Furthermore, it is desirable to speak with the patient about the need for giving instructions and putting his affairs in order; [for example,] if he owes money, or if others owe him; if he has money or property deposited with others, or if he is holding deposits for others.

27. Likewise, it is desirable to speak with him in a positive way regarding how he wishes his property to be disposed, and what he wishes to command regarding other personal and family matters.[54] And it is very important to speak with him and explain to him the great spiritual benefit that a person receives when he merits to give *tzedakah* (charity) before parting from his belongings.[55] One should endeavor to see that the sick person wills a portion of his property, or a sum of money, to *tzedakah* and matters of public need.[56]

One must be extremely careful when speaking to the sick person about these matters, to make sure that one's words do not cause him suffering and, God forbid, worsen his condition.

❧ Informing the Patient of a Relative's Death

28. If a sick person's relative dies, he should not be informed, because this could destabilize him psychologically.[57] Nor should one perform *kri'ah* on the sick

---

54. *Sifsei Tzeddek* (chapt. 8) states: "When a person is sick, he should expeditiously put his affairs in order and prepare his will, as the Prophet Isaiah told King Hezekiah: '*Command your household*' (*II Kings* 20:1). Also, efforts should be made that the will is properly witnessed."

55. See *Kesubos* 67b, which relates that Mar Ukva, before departing from this world, said: "Bring me my charity accounts. . ." [He examined them and declared:] "My supplies are scant, and the road is long." [*Rashi*: "I have prepared scant provisions for the long journey on which I am setting out."] He then gave half his property [to charity]. See also *Rama* (*Yoreh De'ah* 249:1), who rules that [even though one is usually not permitted to give more than one-fifth of his possessions to charity], on departing from the world one is permitted to give as much as he wishes. But see *Gesher HaChaim* (1:6), who writes: ". . .the most correct ruling, in my humble opinion, is that one is permitted to give others up to, but not including, half [of one's possessions]."

56. *Har Eivel* (*Dinei Gosess*) writes: "I shall say one small thing, but in so doing I will accomplish a great deal: A person should command before his death that some of his estate be given for the public need; for [the Talmud states that] most people are guilty of taking money that does not belong to them (*gezel*). . .and *Shulchan Aruch* (*Choshen Mishpat* §366) rules: 'If one stole, and does not know from whom he stole, he should give [that amount] for public needs,' and it may be that one has the sin of theft on his hands, without knowing to whom to return the money in order to receive atonement."

See also *Gesher HaChaim*, who states: "Since many people stumble, God forbid, in [taking] other people's money, and there is no one to return it to; or the money of a group, or of the public, in which case returning it is impossible; therefore one should command that part of his money be given for the public need (i.e., he should donate the estimated amount whose legitimacy is in doubt)."

57. *Yoreh De'ah* §337. See also *Beis Hillel* there, who states that even if the deceased is the patient's parent, for whom he should recite *Kaddish*, and is capable of so doing, he should nevertheless not be informed, because this could destabilize him psychologically.

person's garment for him [as would normally be required of a person whose close family member dies; see below, chapt. 6].[58] One should not cry for, nor eulogize the deceased in the presence of a sick person, because this could be emotionally shattering for him.[59] If someone comes to comfort the sick person on the assumption that he is mourning, we prevent the would-be comforter from doing so.[60]

If the patient's friend dies, one must be extremely careful not to tell him — especially if the friend suffered from the same illness.[61]

29. Even if the sick person finds out that his own close family member has died, one should not cry for, nor eulogize the deceased in the presence of the sick person, and one should prevent would-be comforters.[62] From this it may be inferred that it is forbidden to cause the sick person sorrow. On the contrary, people should make efforts to make him joyful to the utmost of their ability.[63]

◄§ Writing a Last Will and Testament

30. When a patient asks his visitor to write down some statements which constitute a kind of last will and testament, the visitor should not try to avoid this. Quite the opposite: He is obligated to fulfill the wish of the sick person — especially if refusal could have an adverse effect on his illness.

◄§ Words Uttered in Pain

31. Even if a sick person, due to his pain and suffering, blasphemes, God forbid, it is proper for the visitor to overlook it and not even to admonish the sick person about it; for a person is not to blame for words uttered in pain.[64]

---

58. Even if the patient learns of the death, one should not tell him to perform *kri'ah* on his garment, since this might increase his anxiety (*Bach*, in the name of *Ran*, as cited by *Shach Yoreh De'ah* 337:§§1).

59. Moreover, even if the deceased is not a relative of the patient, one should not cry for, nor eulogize him in front of the patient, because this too could be emotionally shattering; that is, on seeing that the other person has died, and that people are crying over him and eulogizing him, the sick person might be broken by fear that he, too, might die (*Shach, Yoreh De'ah* 337:§§2 citing *Bach*).

60. The comforter's visit could remind the sick person of his relative's death, and arouse his fear that too might die (ibid.).

61. This could cause him very great suffering, and arouse his fear that he himself might die.
    If the patient already became aware of his friend's death, and there is risk that the news might have an adverse effect on him and endanger his life, it stands to reason that one is permitted to lie and tell him that the information is not true.

62. See *Shach* (*Yoreh De'ah* 337:§§2), who writes: "It would be a valid interpretation to say that the statement, 'one should not cry for, nor eulogize the deceased' also refers to a situation in which the death of his family member has become known to [the sick person]. In this case, too, one should prevent anyone from consoling him."

63. *Aruch HaShulchan* 337:2.

64. See *Avos DeRabbi Nassan* (§41): "It once happened that R' Shimon ben Yochai was visiting the sick, and he met a man who was swollen and suffering from intestinal disease, uttering blasphemies against the Holy One, Blessed is He. R' Shimon told him: 'Empty one! You should be praying for mercy; instead you blaspheme!' The sick man replied: 'May the Holy One, Blessed is He, remove [the illness] from me and put it on you.' R' Shimon said: 'The Holy One, Blessed is He, has justly given me what

⋄ Endangering a Sick Person

32. If a sick person asks his son to give him food or drink which would endanger his life, the son is forbidden to fulfill the request.[65] Some rule that even if it would not endanger his life, but would damage his health, the son is forbidden to fulfill the request.[66] This applies even if the father says that if the son does not give him what he wants, he will not forgive him. The same applies, all the more so, if the sick person puts the request to someone other than his son. In that case, [all authorities concur that] the request should not be fulfilled even if the food or drink would not endanger his life, but would damage his health.

⋄ Visiting in a Group

33. *She'iltos DeRav Achai* (*she'ilta* 93) states that someone visiting a sick person should not go alone, but only accompanied by others.[67]

⋄ Entering Suddenly

34. One should not enter the patient's room suddenly, lest one come upon him in an undignified situation.[68]

⋄ Visiting in Person

35. The *mitzvah* of visiting the sick cannot be fulfilled completely over the telephone, by letter, or by sending one's representative. Only by going in person can one perform the essential aspects of this *mitzvah*, as listed above, par. 20. Nevertheless, if it is impossible to go in person, one should do as much

---

I deserve, for I neglected Torah study and occupied myself with useless things.' " *Hagahos Yavetz* explains that a person is not to blame for words uttered in pain, as we learn from the case of Job. Therefore, when R' Shimon rebuked this ignorant man who was writhing in pain, his words were indeed "useless things."

65. *Sefer Chassidim* §234.

66. *Bris Olam* states, in the name of *Mahari* Molco, that the obligation to go against the wishes of the patient applies only if his request could endanger his life; if there is no danger to his life, but only to his health, one must obey, if the patient is one's parent. But *Mekor Chaim* cites *Yad Shaul* (240:§§11), who interprets the words of [*Sefer Chassidim*] contrary to *Mahari* Molco.

67. *Emek She'eilah* wonders why the *Poskim* do not cite this ruling of *She'iltos*. See *Tzafnas Paane'ach* who mentions the ruling of *She'iltos* to explain the verse (*Genesis* 48:1): 'He [Joseph] took his two sons with him' [to visit Jacob when he fell ill]. However, *Gilyon HaShas*, by the *gaon* R' Y. Engel, writes: "It seems that (*She'iltos*) did not intend to prohibit going alone to visit the sick, but only to require a visitor to influence as many others as possible to go with him, for the more people who visit, the more the illness is relieved, since each visitor takes away one-sixtieth of the disease" [see above, par. 13].

68. *Midrash HaChefetz* (manuscript), cited by *Torah Shleimah* on *Genesis* 48:2.

as possible, even by telephone, letter, or representative, to help the sick person materially, to pray for him, and to encourage him. This, too, is a *mitzvah* to one's credit.[69]

---

69. With regard to whether one can perform the *mitzvah* over the telephone, *Igros Moshe* (I:§223)
     rules that if one can do so only by phoning and thereby demonstrating concern for the patient's plight, and praying for him, he discharges thereby the *mitzvah* of visiting the sick. However, he does not fulfill the obligation completely, since he has omitted some of the essential aspects cited by *Shulchan Aruch* in the name of *Ramban* [as listed above, par. 20]. Therefore, if one can visit in person, it is certainly preferable to do so.

See also responsa *Minchas Yitzchak* (II:§84), who writes: "The initial visit must be made in person for the telephone is impersonal, and sometimes one's words are burdensome to [the patient]. Only after one has seen the patient once, does he become familiar with his plight. Then, each subsequent time one inquires by telephone about his situation, he fulfills an aspect of this *mitzvah* — the aspect expressed by the Sages when they said that the commandment to visit the sick may be performed 'even a hundred times a day.' "

Can one fulfill his obligation by paying someone to visit the sick on his behalf? Even though the hired visitor would seem to be fulfilling *his* personal *mitzvah* to visit rather than that of his employer, nevertheless, if it is impossible for one to go in person, one fulfills the *mitzvah* by paying someone else to go. By spending money for the sake of the patient, one has performed an aspect of the *mitzvah* of visiting the sick. See *Igros Moshe* (*Yoreh De'ah* :§223). For more on this topic, see Responsa *Chelkas Yaakov* (II:§128); responsa *Be'er Moshe* (I:§114); responsa of *Mahari Shteif* (§294); and responsa *Tzitz Eliezer* (V:§8).

CHAPTER TWO

Viduy / Confession

◦§ The Merit of Confessing

1. Even though we take every precaution not to cause the sick person distress, nevertheless the Sages [1] have commanded us that if we see he is near death, we tell him to recite the confession (*viduy*). . . .for this is a major principle, and is of great merit to the soul, to bring him to the life of the World to Come.[2] One can explain to the sick person that reciting the *viduy* is a powerful aid (*segulah*) for rapid and complete recovery. *Ramban*, *Tur*, and *Shulchan Aruch*[3] state that one should tell him: "Most of those who confessed did not die, and many who did not confess died. Many who are walking the streets recite the confession, and in reward for confessing, you will live. Whoever confesses has a portion in the World to Come." One concludes by wishing him *refu'ah shleimah*, a complete recovery.[4]

2. Only if he is near death do we tell the sick person to recite the *viduy*; if he is not near death, we do not do so, because it might be emotionally shattering for him.[5] But some rule that even if he is not near death, we tell him to recite *viduy*.[6]

Shach concludes: "It seems that we tell him to recite the *viduy* only if he is near death; otherwise, he might think his life is in danger, and his emotional strength might be broken. Alternatively, if the patient is not near death, we do not tell him to confess, because there is still time; but when he is near death, he must be told to recite *viduy* lest he die suddenly without confessing."[7]

Indeed, it is proper for a person to form the habit of reciting *viduy* whenever he

---

1. *Shabbos* 32.
2. *Shulchan Aruch* (*Yoreh De'ah* 338:1). And see *Aruch HaShulchan* (338:1), who comments: "Nevertheless, we are obligated to do everything in our power to soothe him."
3. *Yoreh De'ah* §338.
4. See *Gesher HaChaim*, in the name of *Divrei Yosef Avraham*, who cites his teacher, the pious *Mahari Kohen*, as relating that he would often visit the sick, encourage them to accept upon themselves the Thirteen Principles of Faith, and to recite the *Shema*. . .and all those patients recovered.
5. *Bach* §338.
6. *Prishah* §338.
7. "But if the visitor knows how to deal with it sensitively and effectively, it is good to encourage the sick person to recite *viduy* before his condition becomes extreme" (*Gesher HaChaim*).
   Shelah (in *Tractate Pesachim*, part II) has a section on the *mitzvah* of visiting the sick, and in it he includes this matter of encouraging the patient to recite *viduy*. See *Ramas Rachel* §27.

becomes even slightly ill; for if his condition worsens, God forbid, he might be unable to avail himself of the special power (*segulah*) of confession, which also aids recovery.[8]

3. When a person who is ill prays, it is very effective. Therefore the sick person himself should try to pray from the depths of his heart. Even in the most extreme situation, he should not give up praying for mercy.[9] He should base his prayers on the merit of others, and not on his own.[10] He should also accustom himself to recite, with concentration, the *Pitum HaKetores* [Compounding of the Incense].[10a] [He should preface it with the appropriate Torah passages, as it is arranged in the prayerbook, i.e. the three verses beginning with] וַיֹּאמֶר ה' אֶל מֹשֶׁה, *And Hashem said to Moses. . . (Exodus 30:34-36)* [followed by the two verses ending with] לִפְנֵי ה', . . .לְדֹרֹתֵיכֶם *. . .before Hashem, throughout your generations* (ibid. v. 7-8).[11] If he has sufficient time and mental clarity, it is good for him to recite some or all of the following Psalms: 16, 23, 25, 51, 91, 102, 103, 121, 139, 142 — or some of these. If he wishes to add more Psalms, he may add the following: 20, 22, 24, 30, 31, 42, 43, 61, 67, 84, 116, 123, 130, 143, 150.[12] And it is a major principle that he should confess, and accept the illness and the suffering as atonement for his sins.[13]

4. If the sick person is a Torah scholar, and the recitation of the prayers would not put a strain on him, it is important that he recite the prayers, Psalms, and the *viduy* for a critically ill person, as recorded in *Ma'avar Yabok* (cited in the *Appendix*) or the *viduy* of Rabbeinu Nissim or of *Ramban*.[14] Before reciting the *viduy*, the sick person should give money directly to a poor person. He should give at least twenty-six *prutos* [coins of the value of the smallest monetary unit].[15] If no

---

8. *Gesher HaChaim* §1.

9. In *Berachos* (10a) we find that when the Prophet Isaiah informed the sick King Hezekiah of the divine decree that he must die from his illness (*II Kings* 20), the king replied: "I have a tradition handed down from the house of my grandfather [i.e., King David, who had seen the angel with drawn sword over Jerusalem, but did not give up praying for mercy — *II Samuel* 24] that 'even if a sharp sword is poised over a person's neck, he should not give up praying for mercy.' " See also *Ran* (on *Nedarim* 40a, s.v. *ve'chol she'ein*) and *Maharsha* there, as well as the lengthy discussion of [*Maharsha*'s comment] in responsa *Chikkekei Lev* (Falaghi), *Yoreh De'ah* part I:§50.

10. *Berachos* 10b.

10a. ArtScroll Ashkenaz *Siddur* p. 38.

11. *Ma'avar Yabok, Sifsei Tzedek* (chapt. 20). "And this will be beneficial to him in relieving the illness."

12. *Gesher HaChaim* §1.

13. *Ma'avar Yabok* (*ma'avar* 1:20): "It was said to R' Yosef Karo *zatzal*, that when suffering comes upon a person and he accepts it patiently and with good spirit, the resulting merit is so great that it equals the merit of performing a *mitzvah*" (ibid.).

14. *Ma'avar Yabok* (*ma'avar* II:7), cited in *Appendix*.

15. This is the numerical value of the name of Hashem: י-ה-ו-ה; or he should give 91 *prutos*, corresponding to the total numerical value of the Names י-ה-ו-ה and א-ד-נ-י ; or 112 *prutos*, corresponding to the total numerical value of the Names י-ה-ו-ה, א-ד-נ-י, and א-ה-י-ה.

poor person is present, he can give the money to someone who will accept it on behalf of the poor. The sick person should then recite the *viduy*. [For an extensive version of a *Prayer for Recovery* by R' Saadiah *Gaon*, and an associated declaration (*Mesiras Moda'ah*), see *Appendix*.][16]

◆§ The Short Version of *Viduy*

5. If it is difficult[17] for the sick person to recite such a lengthy confession [as referred to above], he should recite the following short version:[18]

מוֹדֶה אֲנִי לְפָנֶיךָ, ה' אֱלֹהַי, וֵאלֹהֵי אֲבוֹתַי, שֶׁרְפוּאָתִי וּמִיתָתִי בְּיָדֶךָ. יְהִי רָצוֹן מִלְּפָנֶיךָ שֶׁתִּרְפָּאֵנִי רְפוּאָה שְׁלֵמָה; וְאִם אָמוּת תְּהֵא מִיתָתִי כַּפָּרָה עַל כָּל חֲטָאִים, וַעֲוֹנוֹת, וּפְשָׁעִים, שֶׁחָטָאתִי, וְשֶׁעָוִיתִי, וְשֶׁפָּשַׁעְתִּי לְפָנֶיךָ. וְתֵן חֶלְקִי בְּגַן עֵדֶן, וְזַכֵּנִי לָעוֹלָם הַבָּא הַצָּפוּן לַצַּדִּיקִים.

'I acknowledge before You, Hashem, my God and God of my fathers, that my recovery or death is in Your hands. May it be Your will that You heal me completely; but if I die, may my death be atonement for all the mistakes, sins, and rebellions I have erred, sinned, and rebelled before You. May my portion be in Gan Eden, and may You allow me to be in the World to Come, which lies in store for the righteous."[19]

◆§ Dispensing of Charity and Confessing

6. If the patient requests help in reciting the required prayer,[20] it is good to endeavor that he personally give to a deserving poor person, or into a charity box, the sum of 26, or 91, or 112 *prutos*, as mentioned above, par. 4.[21] He should repent completely of all his sins, wash his hands, put on a *tallis*, if he is able to do so, and say:

ה' אֱלֹהִים אֱמֶת וְתוֹרָתוֹ אֱמֶת, וּמֹשֶׁה נְבִיאוֹ אֱמֶת, וּבָרוּךְ שֵׁם כְּבוֹד מַלְכוּתוֹ לְעוֹלָם וָעֶד.

---

16. *Ma'avar Yabok* (*ma'avar* I:10). See *Appendix* for the text of these prayers and for a preliminary *Prayer for Recovery* composed by R' Saadiah *Gaon*, and for the text of the *Mesiras Moda'ah*.

17. When one encourages the sick person to recite *viduy* (confession), it is well to remember that the sick person's primary halachic obligation is to preserve his life and health. In dealing with the *viduy*, one must be careful not to weaken him.

18. *Tur* and *Shulchan Aruch* (*Yoreh De'ah* §338), in the name of *Ramban*. They had a received tradition from pious, spiritually accomplished men that this is the essential content of the *viduy* (confession) to be recited by a critically ill person.

19. It is good to add afterwards: אֵל נָא רְפָא נָא לִי, 'Please, God, heal me now.' He should also state: אֲנִי מַאֲמִין בֶּאֱמוּנָה שְׁלֵמָה בַּה׳ אֱלֹהִים אֱמֶת וּשְׁמוֹ אֱמֶת וּבִשְׁלֹשׁ־עֶשְׂרֵה הָעִקָּרִים, 'I believe, with perfect faith, in Hashem, Who is the true God; and His Name is true. And I believe in the Thirteen Principles of Faith.'

"Obviously, if [the sick person] wishes to add more to his confession —even the *viduy* of Yom Kippur — he is permitted to do so" (*Aruch HaShulchan* §338).

20. And if his condition permits the effort.

21. Whoever adds more, they add more life to him from heaven. He should intend the *tzedakah* as an atonement for his soul, in accord with what is found in the writings of the Sage in *Rakanati*.

'Hashem, God, is true, His Torah is true, and his prophet Moses is true. Blessed is the Name of His glorious kingdom for all eternity.'

He should then recite *Ashrei* [i.e., Psalms 84:5, 144:15, Psalm 145, and 115:18], followed by Psalm 86 תְּפִלָּה לְדָוִד, Psalm 4 בְּקָרְאִי עֲנֵנִי... לַמְנַצֵּחַ, and Psalm 121 אֶשָּׂא עֵינַי. Then he should recite the following confession:[22]

מוֹדֶה אֲנִי לְפָנֶיךָ ה' אֱלֹהַי וֵאלֹהֵי אֲבוֹתַי, אֱלֹהֵי אַבְרָהָם יִצְחָק וְיַעֲקֹב, אֱלֹהֵי הָאֱלֹהִים וַאֲדוֹנֵי אֲדוֹנִים, בַּשָּׁמַיִם מִמַּעַל וְעַל הָאָרֶץ מִתָּחַת אֵין עוֹד, עוֹשֶׂה שָׁמַיִם וָאָרֶץ, עוֹשֶׂה חֶסֶד מִשְׁפָּט וּצְדָקָה בָּאָרֶץ, הָיָה וְהוֶֹה וְיִהְיֶה, מְחַיֶּה אֶת הַכֹּל, שֶׁרְפוּאָתִי בְיָדְךָ וּמִיתָתִי בְּיָדֶךָ. יְהִי רָצוֹן מִלְּפָנֶיךָ, ה' אֱלֹהַי וֵאלֹהֵי אֲבוֹתַי, שֶׁתִּרְפָּאֵנִי רְפוּאָה שְׁלֵמָה, כִּי אַתָּה אֵל רוֹפֵא רַחֲמָן, וְאִם בַּר מִינָן אֲמוּת תְּהֵא מִיתָתִי כַּפָּרָה עַל כָּל חַטֹּאותַי, וַעֲוֹנוֹתַי, וּפִשְׁעַי, שֶׁחָטָאתִי, וְשֶׁעָוִיתִי, וְשֶׁפָּשַׁעְתִּי, לְפָנֶיךָ, וְתֵן חֶלְקִי בְּתוֹרָתֶךָ וּבְגַן עֵדֶן. וְזַכֵּנִי לָעוֹלָם הַבָּא הַצָּפוּן לַצַּדִּיקִים. וַאֲנִי מוֹדֶה וּמַאֲמִין כִּי אַתָּה נִמְצָא מְצִיאוּת גְּמוּרָה, וְאַתָּה אֶחָד וְלֹא כְאֶחָדִים, וְרֹאשׁ לְכָל הַנִּמְצָאִים, וְאֵינְךָ גוּף וְלֹא כֹחַ בְּגוּף וְלֹא יַשִּׂיגוּךָ מַשִּׂיגֵי הַגּוּף וּמִקְרָיו, וְאֵין בְּךָ דָּבָר מִתְאֲרֵי הַגּוּפִים, וְאַתָּה קַדְמוֹן לְכָל הַנִּמְצָאִים, וְאַתָּה רָאוּי לְהָעֲבֵד וּלְהָרִים, וְאַתָּה הַנּוֹתֵן נְבוּאָה בְּפִי כָל הַנְּבִיאִים וּנְבוּאַת מֹשֶׁה עַבְדְּךָ נְבִיאֶךָ לְמַעְלָה מִכָּל הַנְּבִיאִים. וְאַתָּה נָתַתָּ לָנוּ עַל יָדוֹ מִן הַשָּׁמַיִם תּוֹרָה שְׁלֵמָה וּמְשִׁיבַת נָפֶשׁ, וְהִיא זֹאת הַתּוֹרָה הַקְּדוֹשָׁה הַמְצוּיָה בֵּינֵינוּ, וְהִגִּיעָה אֵלָיו מִפִּי הַגְּבוּרָה, וְלֹא תִהְיֶה זֹאת הַתּוֹרָה נֶעְדֶּרֶת וְלֹא נְסוּחָה, וְאַתָּה יוֹדֵעַ מַחְשְׁבוֹת בְּנֵי אָדָם וְלֹא תִתְרַשֵּׁל בָּהֶם, וְדַרְכְּךָ לִגְמוֹל טוֹב לַצַּדִּיקִים וּלְהַעֲנִישׁ לָרְשָׁעִים וְתָבִיא מְשִׁיחֵנוּ הָאָהוּב וּתְחַיֶּה מֵתֵינוּ, יִהְיוּ לְרָצוֹן אִמְרֵי פִי וְהֶגְיוֹן לִבִּי לְפָנֶיךָ ה' צוּרִי וְגוֹאֲלִי.

"I acknowledge before You, Hashem, my God and God of my fathers, God of Abraham, Isaac and Jacob, God of gods and Lord of lords — in the heavens above and on the earth below there is no other — Who makes the heavens and the earth, does kindness, judgment and righteousness on earth; Who was, is and will be; Who gives life to all, for my recovery is in Your hands and my death is in Your hands. May it be Your will, Hashem, my God and God of my fathers, to heal me completely, for You are God, the Merciful Healer; but if — may it be far from us — I die, may my death be an atonement for all the mistakes, sins, and rebellions I have erred, sinned and rebelled before You, and may my portion be in Your Torah and in Gan Eden, and allow me to take part in the World to Come, which lies in store for the righteous.

---

22. The wording of this *viduy* (confession) was received as a tradition from pious, spiritually accomplished men (*Sifsei Tzedek* chapters 9-10, in the name of *Ramban*). See *Sheivet Yehudah*, citing Rabbeinu Yerucham, *zal* (28:1). He adds that the sick person should make a will, and ask forgiveness of anyone from whom he is obligated to do so.

"I acknowledge and believe that You exist and are the Absolute
Existence; that You are One, and not like individual beings; and are the
Source of all existing beings; that You are not a physical being nor a
physical force; and are not subject to physical events and forces; nor can
You be described in physical terms; that Your existence precedes all
existing things; that You are to be worshiped and exalted; that You are
the One Who puts prophecy in the mouth of all the prophets; and that
the prophecy of Your servant and prophet, Moses, is above all the
prophets; that through him, You gave us from heaven the perfect,
soul-reviving Torah; that this is the holy Torah that is found among us;
that it reached [Moses] from the mouth of the Almighty; that this Torah is
eternal and unalterable; that You know the thoughts of all human beings
and overlook nothing; that it is Your way to pay goodly reward to the
righteous and punish the wicked; and that You will bring our beloved
Mashiach and resurrect our dead.

"May the words of my mouth and the thoughts of my heart find favor
in front of You, my Rock and Redeemer."[23]

7. If it is difficult for the patient to speak, he should just say:

אִם בַּר מִינָן אָמוּת תְּהֵא מִיתָתִי כַּפָּרָה עַל כָּל חֲטָאַי

'If, God forbid, I die, may my death be an atonement for all my sins.'

If it is hard for him to confess by speaking, he should confess in his heart.[24]

◆§ The Final Moments

8. When the [final] moment is pressing, he should raise his fingers upwards and
say:

רִבּוֹנוֹ שֶׁל עוֹלָם, הֲרֵינִי מְקַבֵּל עָלַי הַמִּיתָה בְּפֹעַל מַמָּשׁ, בְּשִׂמְחָה, וּבְלֵב שָׁלֵם,
לְקַיֵּם מִצְוַת עֲשֵׂה כּוֹלֶלֶת כָּל הַמִּצְוֹת וְתִקּוּן כָּל הַלָּאוִין, שֶׁכֻּלָּן נִתְקִין לַעֲשֵׂה,
לְהַעֲבִיר מַחֲשֶׁבֶת יֵצֶר הָרַע אֲשֶׁר חָפֵץ לְהַדִּיחַ נִשְׁמָתִי מֵעֲבוֹדַת הַקֹּדֶשׁ, וְהִנְנִי
מוֹסֵר גּוּפִי וְנַפְשִׁי וְרוּחִי וְנִשְׁמָתִי עַל יִחוּד שְׁמוֹ הַגָּדוֹל, וְזַכֵּנִי לְיַחֵד שֵׁם קָדְשֶׁךְ
בְּאַהֲבָה רַבָּה וְחִבָּה יְתֵרָה לְסַלְּקָא יְקָרָא לְעֵלָּא, לַאֲתַר דְּשַׁקְיָא עֲמִיקָא דְּבֵירָא
נָגִיד וְנָפִיק, וּתְהִי מְסִירַת נַפְשִׁי בְּסוֹד מֵי נִקְבָּא, לְיַחֲדָא קֻדְשָׁא בְּרִיךְ הוּא
וּשְׁכִינְתֵּיהּ בִּרְחִימוּ וּדְחִילוּ שְׁלִים וּלְבָתַר לְאַמְשָׁכָא מֵעֵלָּא לְתַתָּא מֵהַהוּא
שַׁקְיָא דְּנַחֲלָא לְכָל דַּרְגָּא וְדַרְגָּא עַד דַּרְגָּא בַּתְרָאָה, וּלְקַשְּׁרָא קִשְׁרָא דְּכֹלָּא,
כְּמוֹ שֶׁנֶּאֱמַר כִּי שֵׁם ה' אֶקְרָא הָבוּ גֹדֶל לֵאלֹהֵינוּ, וִיהִי רָצוֹן מִלְּפָנֶיךָ שֶׁתְּהֵא
שָׁלוֹם מְנוּחָתִי

---

23. If, God forbid, time is pressing him very much, he should raise his ten fingers upwards and say: רִבּוֹנוֹ שֶׁל עוֹלָם יְהִי רָצוֹן מִלְּפָנֶיךָ שֶׁיִּהְיֶה שָׁלוֹם מְנוּחָתִי, "Master of the universe, may it be Your will that I rest in peace." (*Ma'avar Yabok*, *ma'avar* 1:9).

24. *Tur* and *Shulchan Aruch* (*Yoreh De'ah* §338).

"Master of the universe, I hereby accept my actual death joyfully and wholeheartedly, to fulfill the positive commandment that includes all the mitzvos and rectifies all [violations of] the negative commandments, since all of them can be corrected by the performance of [this] positive commandment, in order to remove the thought of the Evil Inclination (Yetzer Hara), which desires to entice my soul away from the holy service. And so I hereby transmit my body, life, soul, and spirit for the unification of [Hashem's] great Name. May I merit to unify Your holy Name with great love and exceeding devotion. . . to unify the Holy One, Blessed is He, with perfect love and fear. . . as it is said [Deut. 32:3]: 'When I call the Name of Hashem, attribute greatness to our God.' May it be Your will that my rest be peaceful."

Then he should concentrate on the Name, may it be exalted, and on the giving of the Torah at Mt. Sinai, and recite:

שְׁמַע יִשְׂרָאֵל ה' אֱלֹהֵינוּ ה' אֶחָד

'Hear, O Israel: Hashem is our God, Hashem, the One and Only'

and

בָּרוּךְ שֵׁם כְּבוֹד מַלְכוּתוֹ לְעוֹלָם וָעֶד

'Blessed is the Name of His glorious kingdom for all eternity.'[25]

Then he should recite *Aleinu*, 'It is our duty to praise. . .', followed by אֱמֶת וְיַצִּיב, 'True and certain, established and enduring. . .' (the blessing following the recitation of the *Shema* in the Morning Service), until the words עֶזְרַת אֲבוֹתֵינוּ, *'The Helper of our forefathers.'*[26]

9. It is very important for the sick person to recite the following *mishnah* before his soul departs:[27]

לְשֵׁם שִׁשָּׁה דְבָרִים הַזֶּבַח נִזְבָּח: לְשֵׁם זֶבַח לְשֵׁם זוֹבֵחַ, לְשֵׁם הַשֵּׁם, לְשֵׁם אִשִּׁים, לְשֵׁם רֵיחַ, לְשֵׁם נִיחוֹחַ; וְהַחַטָּאת וְהָאָשָׁם לְשֵׁם חֵטְא. אָמַר רַבִּי יוֹסֵי: אַף מִי שֶׁלֹּא הָיָה בְלִבּוֹ לְשֵׁם אֶחָד מִכָּל אֵלּוּ כָּשֵׁר,שֶׁהוּא תְנַאי בֵּית דִּין, שֶׁאֵין הַמַּחֲשָׁבָה הוֹלֶכֶת אֶלָּא אַחַר הָעוֹבֵד.

'A sacrifice is slaughtered for the sake of six things: for the designation of the sacrifice; for the name of [the] offerer; for the Name of HASHEM; for

---

25. If the sick person wishes, and is able to recite additional prayers, the one helping him confess should have him recite the *viduy* which begins אָשַׁמְנוּ בָּגַדְנוּ גָּזַלְנוּ, *'We have become guilty, we have betrayed, we have robbed. . .'* If possible, he should help him recite *Ashamnu* as it is recorded in *Chayei Adam* (§143).

26. *Chochmas Adam* 151:12.

27. *Sheivet Yehudah* (*Yoreh De'ah* §339) states: "I found it written that this *mishnah* is especially suited for recital before praying, and in particular, by a sick person before his soul departs."

the sake of the fires; for the sake of aroma; for the sake of pleasing; and the chatas and asham offerings for the purpose of [the] sin. Said R' Yose: Even if one did not have any of these [purposes] in mind it is valid, for it is an enactment of the Court, because the intent is determined solely by the one who performs the service.'[28]

⋞ Asking Forgiveness

10. One also tells the patient that he should ask forgiveness from anyone he has sinned against, whether financially or verbally.[29]

11. Before the sick person recites *viduy* all women, children, and people lacking Torah education (*amei ha'aretz*) are taken out of the room, since they might cry and shatter the emotional composure of the sick person.[30] Among Sefardim, the custom is to gather ten men for the recitation of *viduy* (see below, 3:15).[31]

---

28. *Zevachim* (4:6).
29. *Chochmas Adam* (151:11).
30. *Shulchan Aruch* (338:1); *Chochmas Adam* (§151). If relatives are present who cannot control their emotions, it is desirable that they too should go out, as is mentioned below, 3:16.
31. See *Appendix* for the version of *viduy* cited in *Beis Oved*.

CHAPTER THREE

Gosess: On the Threshold of Death

✑ The State

1. A person in his last hours of life, i.e., in the final process of dying, is termed a
gosess. The halachic powers of the *gosess* are equal in every way to those of a
living person.[1] He can issue a divorce, transfer his property to others,[2] and so on.
However, this applies only if we are with him [and thus see that he is alive].[3]
However, if someone is told,[4] "We saw your son (or brother) three days ago,[5] and
he was a *gosess*," it is to be assumed that he died, and the family members are
required to mourn for him.[6]

✑ Desecration of the Sabbath

2. It is a *mitzvah* to desecrate the Sabbath if this is necessary to save the life of a
gosess.[7] This applies not only if he is dying of an illness, but even of
man-inflicted wounds,[8] and not only if the *gosess* is an ordinary person, but even if
he is the kind of person who is not obligated to perform *mitzvos*, i.e., a deaf-mute,
mentally incompetent or minor.[9]

---

1. *Tur, Yoreh De'ah* §339.
2. *Ran* (*Mo'ed Katan, Perek Elu Megalchin*). See also *Gilyon Maharsha* on *Shulchan Aruch* (§339),
   who states that according to one opinion cited in *Hagahos Shulchan Aruch* (*Even HaEzer* 121:6),
   a *gosess* has the halachic powers of a living person only if he can still speak. If he can no longer speak,
   he is considered as if dead as regards his ability to grant a divorce, give property, and so on (but see
   below, end of footnote 11).
3. See *Tur* (*Yoreh De'ah* §339), citing R' Meir of Rotenburg. And see *Rosh* and *Mordechai* (*Perek Elu
   Megalchin*). He cites proof from *Gittin* 28, where the Talmud puts forth the presumption that "the
   majority of *gosessim* die."
4. This applies only if the person is told about his son or brother by several people. A single witness
   is not believed, not even for the purpose of observing mourning. (*Prishah, Yoreh De'ah* §339).
5. The period of being a *gosess* normally lasts three days (ibid.).
6. *Tur* (*Yoreh De'ah* §339).
7. *Tosafos* (*Niddah* 44b s.v. *ihu*) states that even though "the majority of *gosessim* die," one should
   desecrate the Sabbath in order to save his life. As the *Gemara* states in *Yoma*: "In matters of saving
   life we do not go by the majority."
8. Although there are halachic differences between a *gosess* as a result of natural causes and one as
   a result of man-inflicted wounds, these differences do not apply to the *mitzvah* of desecrating the
   Sabbath to save the life of a *gosess*, no matter what the cause (ibid.).
9. See *Be'ur Halachah* (§329), who explains that the obligation to desecrate the Sabbath in order to
   save a person's life does not at all depend on that person's ability or inability to perform *mitzvos*.

The *mitzvah* of desecrating the Sabbath to save the life of a *gosess* applies even if the only goal is to slightly prolong life;[10] for example, if the doctor states that certain medicines will prolong the patient's life for one minute.[11] And it applies even if the *gosess* has already been in the process of dying for the preceeding three days or longer.[12]

If one desecrated the Sabbath in an attempt to save the life of a *gosess*, and the *gosess* died despite one's efforts, one does not need atonement.[13]

৺ A *Kohen* and a *Gosess*

3. A *kohen* is forbidden to enter a house in which there is a *gosess*.[14] However, if a *kohen* is unknowingly sleeping in a house where there is a *gosess*, one is not required to awaken the *kohen* and inform him.[15]

A doctor who is a *kohen* is permitted to enter a house in which there is a *gosess* in order to examine or treat him. One authority permits this even if another doctor is available who is not a *kohen*.[16] On the other hand, a doctor who is a *kohen* is not

---

10. *Shulchan Aruch* (*Orach Chaim* 329:2). And see *Be'ur Halachah* there, who cites *Meiri* (Tractate *Yoma*): "[The *mitzvah* of saving his life applies] even if it is clear that he cannot live even another hour; for during the time [that his life is prolonged] he will repent and confess."

11. See *Shulchan Aruch* (*Orach Chaim* 329:4). And see responsa *Beis Yaakov* (§59), who rules that it is forbidden to use medical means to prevent the departure of the soul; but *Shevus Yaakov* (III:§13) refutes his proofs and rules to the contrary.

See also *Be'ur Halachah* (§329), who points out that a person found with his skull fatally fractured (*merutzatz*) is also a *gosess* and is even more certain to die than an ordinary *gosess*, and yet it is a *mitzvah* to desecrate the Sabbath in order to prolong his life even for a short time. This is also stated by *Isur V'Heter* citing *Semag* and *Semak*: "If the victim is found alive, even though his brain is smashed and he cannot live more than a short time, one must [desecrate the Sabbath in order to] dig him out from under the pile of fallen rocks to prolong his life even a short time."

Gilyon Maharsha (*Yoreh De'ah* §339) states that the *mitzvah* of prolonging the life of the *gosess* applies even if he cannot speak. True, some rule that he is considered as dead regarding his ability to grant a divorce, disperse property, and so on; but it is nevertheless a *mitzvah* to desecrate the Sabbath in order to prolong his life even for a short time.

12. See *Kaf HaChaim* (§329 *os* 13), who cites this *halachah* in the name of *Tosefes Shabbos* (and see above, footnote 5).

13. See *Kaf HaChaim* (loc. cit., *os* 25), who cites R' Yehudah Eyash, *zal*, in *Lechem Yehudah* as ruling that no atonement is necessary, neither for an individual nor for a community [that desecrated the Sabbath in order to save a life], and nothing should be done to seek atonement. See also *Kaf HaChaim* §334 (*os* 129), who writes that if people extinguished a fire on the Sabbath to save a life, and they wish to repent for the desecration of the Sabbath, they should not be permitted to repent, since this might make them hesitate to desecrate the Sabbath under similar circumstances in the future (*Or Zarua*). And in *os* 133, he takes issue with *Chavos Yair* (§236), who permits an individual (but not a community), who desecrated the Sabbath under these circumstances, to seek atonement.

14. *Tur* (*Yoreh De'ah* §370).

15. See *Shach* (§370). Similarly, if the *kohen* was sleeping without his clothes on, he is permitted to delay long enough to get dressed before leaving the building (ibid.).

16. *Nachalas Tzvi* (*Yoreh De'ah* §370). *Pischei Teshuvah*, citing responsa *Chasam Sofer* §338, permits a doctor who is a *kohen* to treat a *gosess* if there is no other doctor available. However, he is reluctant to permit this if there is another doctor available.

permitted to enter just in order to confirm death.[17] However, if no other doctor is available, and it is impossible to bury the deceased without a doctor's certification of death, one is permitted to summon a doctor who is a *kohen*.[18]

4. A *kohen* must be careful not to touch a *gosess*, even a non-Jew.[19]

◄§ Hastening the Death of a Gosess

5. If a person, even an elderly person, is a *gosess* due to natural causes,[20] anyone who kills him is committing murder and is liable to the death penalty.[21] Therefore, one is not allowed to do anything which would hasten his death: It is forbidden to close his eyes as his soul departs;[22] to bind up his cheeks;[23] to wash or oil his body;[24] or to remove his pillow.[25] Whoever touches the *gosess* [for these or similar purposes] is shedding blood.[26]

Likewise, if someone remains a *gosess* for a long time, it is forbidden to do anything which would cause him to die more quickly; for example, to place the synagogue keys under his head to help his soul separate from his body. On the other hand, one is permitted to remove something which is preventing the departure of the soul, as long as one can do so without moving any part of the *gosess*' body.[27] [For example, if a certain nearby sound is hampering the soul's departure, one may stop the sound.]

One should not prepare the needs of burial, nor eulogize the person, before his

---

17. See *Pischei Teshuvah*, who cites *Chasam Sofer* as writing: "Far, far be it even to think about this; there is no way at all to permit it. Moreover, one is forbidden to request [the *kohen* who is a doctor to come and perform this service]; to make such a request would be aiding and abetting a transgressor."

18. In such a case, the situation of the deceased is comparable to a *meis mitzvah*, a body which has no one to bury it (ibid.).

19. See *Tosafos* (*Nazir* 4b, s.v. *dilma gosessim*): ". . . a *nazir* is forbidden to touch a *gosess*." And the topic there is a non-Jewish *gosess*.

20. Sanhedrin 78: "All agree that if one kills a person who is a *gosess* due to illness (*gosess bidei shamayim*), one is liable to the death penalty."

21. *Rambam* (*Hilchos Rotze'ach* 2:7). On the other hand, if a person is a *gosess*, not due to illness, but due to man-inflicted wounds, one who kills him is not liable to the death penalty in a human court.

22. *Rambam* (*Hilchos Avel* 4:5). And in Tractate *Semachos* we find: "Whoever touches [the *gosess*] is shedding blood. To what may this be compared? To a sputtering candle. If someone touches it, it immediately goes out."

23. The purpose of binding up the cheeks is to prevent the mouth from opening (*Shach*, *Yoreh De'ah*, §339:§§2). This is done after death, if necessary (see below, par. 31).

24. "This [washing or oiling the body] is a custom performed with every deceased, to remove any dirt from his flesh" (ibid. §§ 3).

25. This is forbidden because it moves him from his place and [thereby] hastens his death (*Drishah*, *Yoreh De'ah* §339).

26. *Rambam* (*Hilchos Avel* 4:5). However, if the house catches fire, one should not leave the *gosess* in the house. (*Beis Lechem Yehudah* and *Chiddushei R' Akiva Eiger*, *Yoreh De'ah* §339, citing *Sefer Chassidim*).

27. *Rama* (339:1).

soul departs. Some rule that one also may not dig a grave for him until after he dies, even if the grave is not being dug in the vicinity of the *gosess*. [28]

6. One should not give a *gosess* anything to eat, because he cannot swallow. However, one may put water into his mouth. [29]

7. If the sick person is soiled, one must clean him before he becomes a *gosess*.

Once he does become a *gosess*, it is normally impossible to clean him since (as mentioned above, par. 5) one is forbidden to move any part of his body; instead, one covers the soiled place so that it cannot be seen. If there is an odor, anyone saying a prayer, blessing, or words of Torah must go far enough away that he cannot smell the odor. [30]

⋖§ The Moments Before Death

8. Some righteous, spiritually accomplished people, when they sense that they are near death, wash their hands and recite Psalm 29: מִזְמוֹר לְדָוִד, הָבוּ לַה׳ בְּנֵי אֵלִים, 'A psalm of David: Render unto Hashem you sons of the powerful'; [31] for R' Chiya bar Gamda said, quoting R' Yossi ben Shaul: "At the moment when a *tzaddik* departs this world, the Ministering Angels announce before the Holy One, Blessed is He: 'Master of the universe, the *tzaddik* (they specify his name) is coming!' The Holy One, Blessed is He, replies: 'Let the *tzaddikim* assemble and go forth to greet him.' Then they say to the *tzaddik*: 'May he come in peace; they will rest on their beds' (יָבוֹא בְשָׁלוֹם יָנוּחוּ עַל מִשְׁכְּבוֹתָם)." [32]

R' Elazar said: 'When a *tzaddik* departs this world, three groups of Ministering Angels go forth to greet him. One group says: בֹּא בְשָׁלוֹם, 'May he come in peace.' Another group declares: הָלֵךְ נְכֹחוֹ, 'May he go forward.' And a third group declares: יָבוֹא בְשָׁלוֹם יָנוּחוּ עַל מִשְׁכְּבוֹתָם, 'He comes in peace; they will rest on their beds' [Isaiah 57:2]. [33]

Not only does the death of the *tzaddikim* take place by means of the Glory. . .but praises are recited in his presence: יָבֹא שָׁלוֹם יָבֹא שָׁלוֹם, 'He comes in peace, he comes in peace!' [34]

---

28. *Shulchan Aruch* and *Rama* (339:1).

29. *Sefer Chassidim* (§234). And see the commentaries of *Mekor Chessed* and *Bris Olam* there.

30. *Gesher HaChaim* (2:2:8).

31. *Sefer Chassidim* (§560). See *Ma'avar Yabok* (I:22).
    I have heard that the *Chasam Sofer*, in his last moments, asked for something to drink, even though drinking was already difficult for him. He recited the blessing, שֶׁהַכֹּל נִהְיֶה בִּדְבָרוֹ, '. . .*through Whose word everything came to be.'* It is likely that his holy intention was to justify the Divine judgment by indicating that everything, including his own departure from the world, comes about through Hashem's word. I have also heard of other righteous men of spiritual accomplishment who did the same: In their last moments, they asked for something to drink and recited *She'hakol*.

32. *Kesubos* 104a.

33. Ibid.

34. *Tur* (*Yoreh De'ah* §403). And see *Rama* there, who states that three groups of angels greet him with *shalom* (peace). *Be'er HaGolah* explains why there are three groups: The Torah and the deeds of the righteous involve three aspects — good thoughts, speech, and actions (as explained by

9. Many have the custom to recite *Nishmas Kol Chai* ("The soul of every living being shall bless Your Name. . ."), through וּבְקֶרֶב קְדוֹשִׁים תִּתְקַדָּשׁ, '. . .*and amid the holy shall You be sanctified.* '[35]

Some have the custom to recite *Elokai neshamah* ('My God, the soul You placed within me is pure. . .'[35a] omitting the closing benediction ('Blessed are You. . .'). Or they also recite the second blessing of the *Shemoneh Esrei* Prayer אַתָּה גִבּוֹר, 'You are eternally mighty. . .' through וְנֶאֱמָן אַתָּה לְהַחֲיוֹת מֵתִים, '. . .*And You are faithful to resuscitate the dead,* ' omitting the closing benediction.[36]

If the mind of one about to die is clear enough, and if he is sufficiently learned, he should speak words of Torah, for this is what the Sages did with R' Eliezer the Great.[37]

10. When the sick person senses that his time has come, it is proper for him to recite, if possible, the following:

מִי אֵל כָּמוֹךָ נֹשֵׂא עָוֹן וְעֹבֵר עַל פֶּשַׁע לִשְׁאֵרִית נַחֲלָתוֹ, לֹא הֶחֱזִיק לָעַד אַפּוֹ כִּי חָפֵץ חֶסֶד הוּא יָשׁוּב יְרַחֲמֵנוּ יִכְבֹּשׁ עֲוֹנֹתֵינוּ וְתַשְׁלִיךְ בִּמְצֻלוֹת יָם כָּל חַטֹּאתָם.

'*Who, O God, is like You, Who pardons iniquity and overlooks transgression for the remnant of His heritage? Who has not retained His wrath eternally, for He desires kindness! He will again be merciful to us; He will suppress our iniquities. And cast into the depths of the sea all their sins.* '

בְּיָדְךָ אַפְקִיד רוּחִי פָּדִיתָה אוֹתִי ה' אֵל אֱמֶת.

'*Into Your hand I commit my spirit. You have redeemed me, Hashem, true God.* '

יְבָרֶכְךָ ה' וְיִשְׁמְרֶךָ, יָאֵר ה' פָּנָיו אֵלֶיךָ וִיחֻנֶּךָּ, יִשָּׂא ה' פָּנָיו אֵלֶיךָ וְיָשֵׂם לְךָ שָׁלוֹם.

'*May Hashem bless you and safeguard you. May Hashem illuminate His countenance for you and be gracious to you. May Hashem turn His countenance to you and establish peace for you.* '

Ramban, *Parashas Vayera*). Just as the good deeds of the righteous are triple-faceted, so is the reward paid to them.

Sefer Chassidim states: "R' Yehudah, the son of R' Simon, the son of R' Yeshayah said: the Holy One, Blessed is He, greets [the righteous] in person, as it were, with *shalom*, as it is said (*Psalms* 149:5): *The righteous rejoice with glory, they sing out upon their beds.* And there they praise the Holy One, Blessed is He. That is why they wash their hands [before dying]. 'Just as he comes, so does he go' (*Ecclesiastes* 5:15). When he was born they washed him, and when he dies they wash him."

34a. ArtScroll Ashkenaz *Siddur* p. 400.

35. See *Gesher HaChaim* (2:1).
     I have witnessed men of spiritual accomplishment, in our time, who were in a hospital; when they began to feel not well they asked that someone recite *Nishmas Kol Chai* with them.

35a. ArtScroll ibid. p. 19.

36. *Gesher HaChaim* loc. cit.

37. *Ma'avar Yabok* (1:24).

לִישׁוּעָתְךָ קִוִּיתִי ה׳.

'For Your salvation do I hope, Hashem'

ה׳ אֵל אֱמֶת. מֹשֶׁה אֱמֶת וְתוֹרָתוֹ אֱמֶת.

'Hashem is the true God. Moshe is true and his Torah is true.'

שְׁמַע יִשְׂרָאֵל, ה׳ אֱלֹהֵינוּ, ה׳ אֶחָד. בָּרוּךְ שֵׁם כְּבוֹד מַלְכוּתוֹ לְעוֹלָם וָעֶד.

'Hear, O Israel, Hashem is our God, Hashem, the One and Only. Blessed is the Name of His glorious kingdom for all eternity.'[38]

11. We find in *Haggadah DeRabbi Chaninah* (*Parashas Va'eschanan*): When Moshe Rabbeinu, may peace be upon him, was told that his death was but a moment away, he declared: בָּרוּךְ שְׁמוֹ חַי וְקַיָּם לְעוֹלָם וָעֶד, *'Blessed is His Name, He Who lives and exists for all eternity.'*[39]

◈§ Etiquette for Visitors

12. When a person is about to die, one is not allowed to leave him, so that he will not be alone when his soul departs.[40] It is a *mitzvah* to stand next to a person when the soul departs, as it is said (*Psalms 49:10-11*), *He will live eternally; he will not see the pit, for he saw the wise die.*[41]

13. If someone is sitting near a sick person who is about to die, and no one else is present who knows about dying — how to watch the *goses* and ascertain the moment of death, how to close his eyes, and do other necessary things — and the time for prayer arrives, he should not leave him to pray.[42] [See above, par. 5.] It is very important that ten men should stand around the dying person.[43] However, they should not stand at the foot of the bed in which the *goses* is lying. (See also above, 1:23.)[44]

---

38. *Gesher HaChaim* (2:1).

39. *Gesher HaChaim* (2:1): "If a person is able to recite (or think about) these words in his last moments, it is of great merit for him."

40. *Shulchan Aruch* (*Yoreh De'ah* 339:4). See *Shach* there. And *Be'er HaGolah* there, citing *Kol Bo*, explains that the soul becomes desolate if the dying person is alone when it leaves the body.

41. *Rama* (*Yoreh De'ah* 339:4), citing *Hagahos Alfasi* on *Perek Elu Megalchin*.

42. *Sefer Chassidim* (§742), cited by *Chiddushei R' Akiva Eiger* in his *Gilyon* on *Shulchan Aruch* (§339). See also *Ma'avar Yabok* (*Sifsei Tzeddek* ch. 24), who cites *Ba'al Halachos* as stating: "When a person is about to die, one is not allowed to leave him. . .lest his limbs stiffen and he become exposed to disrespect, as we have learned: 'There are four who need to be guarded. . .' But if many people are with him, this weakens the power of the harmful spiritual entities (*mezikim*). . .In this way, those who stay with him do a service to his body and give satisfaction to his soul. The proof is found in *Chagigah* 5, in the story of R' Yaakov of Kfar Chitaya."

43. See *Ma'avar Yabok* (3:3): The kabbalistic sources write in *Parashas Vayechi* (p. 248) that when the soul of a Torah scholar departs. . .if there are ten men present, all of whom are occupied with holy words and with the songs of David, then the *Shechinah* (Divine Presence), which loves the songs of the Psalms, comes to the head of the [dying person's] bed . . . See also *Gesher HaChaim* (ch. 2).

44. See *Ma'avar Yabok* (*Sifsei Rannenus* §6): "I have found a certain amount of support for the Jewish custom not to stand at the foot of the bed in which the *goses* is lying, because the Angel of

14. It is very important to be careful that none of the *gosess'* limbs extends out of the bed.[45] It is good to ascertain this before the sick person becomes a *gosess*. If one of his limbs is found to be extending out of the bed after he becomes a *gosess*, it is forbidden to move him (see above, par. 5). Instead, one should place chairs up against the sides of the bed [to support the limb].[46]

15. In Sefardic communities, when a person is in his final hours, some endeavor to perform a release of vows and curses.[47] They begin as follows:

בִּרְשׁוּת בֵּית דִּין שֶׁל מַעְלָה וּבִרְשׁוּת בֵּית דִּין שֶׁל מַטָּה וּבִרְשׁוּת תּוֹרָתֵנוּ הַקְּדוֹשָׁה
הֲרֵי אֲנַחְנוּ מַתִּירִין הַנְּדָרִים הַשְּׁבוּעוֹת הַקְּלָלוֹת וְהַחֲרָמוֹת שֶׁעָשָׂה אוֹ קַלֵּל אוֹ
קִלְּלוּ אֶת פְּלוֹנִי בֶּן פְּלוֹנִית.

'With the permission of the heavenly court and with the permission of the earthly court, and with the permission of our holy Torah, we hereby annul the vows, oaths, curses, and bans which (here they say the name of the dying person and his mother, e.g., *Ploni ben Plonis*) pronounced, or any curses which others pronounced upon him.'

16. It is of great significance that a person's children and relatives be present when his soul departs.[48] However, they must try to refrain from crying.[49] *Sefer*

Death is standing opposite him with sword in hand, as the Sages have stated. One should not go close to him nor push against his place."

45. See *Be'er Heitev* (§339), citing *Rakanati* on *Parashas Vayechi*. He writes that those present must take care that none of the person's limbs extends out of the bed. He warns very emphatically against being negligent on this point. See also *Ma'avar Yabok* (*Sifsei Rannenus*, chapt. 6) who writes that the kabbalists state that one must be careful that at the moment of death, no part of [the dying person's] limbs are out of the bed . . . Moreover, those present are duty-bound to be alert about this, making sure that none of his limbs extends out of the bed. He discusses the matter at length.

46. *Gesher HaChaim* (2:2:9).

47. I have observed that among the Ashkenazic community, too, an effort is made to annul curses for a sick person. In addition, they bring a *minyan* of ten *kohanim* to recite the Priestly Blessing (*Birkas Kohanim*) for him. And see *Ma'avar Yabok* (*Sifsei Tzeddek* chapt. 3), who writes that if the sick person has made any vows, one should be careful to have them annulled; and those present at the bedside should warn the sick person about this, for it is said that the ability to annul vows was not given to the Ministering Angels.

48. See *Ma'avar Yabok* (5:27), who states: "Undoubtedly the deceased receives pleasure from the presence of his living family at the time when his soul departs, as he took pleasure in his family and friends [during his lifetime]. . .as is mentioned in the *Zohar*, *Parashas Vayechi*, on the verse (*Genesis* 46:4), *And Joseph will put his hand on your eyes*. This [being present at his parent's death] undoubtedly is a benefit which the son does for his father, because the son serves as a chariot for the father, just as we find that the Twelve Tribes constituted a chariot for Jacob; and the same relationship exists between a Torah teacher and his students. . .From this we learn that if the son is present at the time of his father's death, this will be a kindness of the father towards the son and the son towards the father." *Ma'avar Yabok* further discusses this topic at length. He also discusses the Torah's account of how Abraham, Isaac, and Jacob were all buried by their sons. "It seems that it is a great satisfaction for the father when his sons occupy themselves with his burial. This certainly is also of great merit and benefit to the son, both during his lifetime and after his death. It is not for nought that Jewish custom places great insistence on this point. . ."

49. See *Ma'avar Yabok* (*ma'amar* 2:15): "I have seen some whose custom is that when the time of death draws near, any crying relative is taken out of the immediate presence of [the dying person],

Chassidim cautions that those present should not cry out when the soul leaves the body; otherwise, it might return to the body and undergo severe suffering. (*See* also above, 2:11.)[50]

17. It is proper that women should not be in the room at the time of death, especially if they are in the status of *niddah*. It is desirable also that men who are scrupulous to immerse in a *mikveh* [i.e., after marital relations or seminal emission] should do so before entering the dying person's room.[51]

18. Those standing by the bed should turn their thoughts to repentance, contemplating the unworthiness of man, and Hashem's mercy in caring about him. This also adds merit to the dying person.[52]

One must be extremely careful not to engage in idle talk in his presence.[53]

19. Those standing by the bed should be careful not to mention the name of any wicked person, especially if that person is the brother or other relative of the sick person.[54]

20. Those standing by the bed during the sick person's last moments should recite Psalms 121, 130, and 91. Afterwards they should recite *Yigdal*, 'May the Living God be magnified. . .', *Adon Olam*, 'Master of the universe, Who ruled before any form was created. . .'[54a], *Ana Be'ko'ach*, 'We beg You! With the strength of Your right hand's greatness. . .',[54b] and the second paragraph of *Aleinu*, beginning with עַל כֵּן נְקַוֶּה לְךָ , '*Therefore we put our hope in You*. . .'[55]

21. At the moment of death, those present should recite:

שְׁמַע יִשְׂרָאֵל ה' אֱלֹהֵינוּ ה' אֶחָד [One time:]

'*Hear, O Israel, Hashem is our God, Hashem, the One and Only.*'

בָּרוּךְ שֵׁם כְּבוֹד מַלְכוּתוֹ לְעוֹלָם וָעֶד.

[Three times, in a whisper:] '*Blessed is the Name of His glorious kingdom for all eternity.*'

---

and also out of the room. They explain that those who cry cause him suffering. It seems to me that there is support for this custom in *Midrash HaNe'elam* (p. 98), which relates how R' Eliezer the Great told his son he could see he would soon leave the world, and then instructed him: 'Go tell your mother that she should go out. . .' "

50. See *Sefer Chassidim* (§234).
51. *Gesher HaChaim* (2:2:6).
52. Ibid. (2:2:7).
53. See *Ma'avar Yabok* (*Sifsei Rannenus* §4).
54. See *Ma'avar Yabok* (5:24), who cites *Ramban* (end of *Parashas Vayechi*) as stating that it would seem that one should not mention the name of any wicked person near the time of death, especially if the wicked person is the brother or other relative of the sick person.
54a. ArtScroll Ashkenaz *Siddur* p. 12.
54b. Ibid. p. 314.
55. Ibid. p. 160; *Gesher HaChaim* (2:3).

ה' הוּא הָאֱלֹהִים,

[Seven times:] *'Hashem is God.'*

ה' מֶלֶךְ ה' מָלָךְ ה' יִמְלֹךְ לְעוֹלָם וָעֶד.

[One time:] *'Hashem rules, Hashem ruled, Hashem will rule for all eternity.'*[56]

22. If those present finish reciting שְׁמַע יִשְׂרָאֵל, *'Hear, O Israel. . .'* and the subsequent passages mentioned in the previous section, and they see that the dying person has begun to breathe again, they should repeat: עַל כֵּן נְקַוֶּה לְּךָ, *'Therefore we put our hope in You. . .'* (see above, end of par. 20), drawing out the recitation so that it takes some time. Or they should begin from the preceding passage, *Ana Be'ko'ach*.

When they again see the dying person's last breaths approaching, they should recite the end of *Aleinu*: וְהָיָה ה' לְמֶלֶךְ עַל כָּל הָאָרֶץ בַּיּוֹם הַהוּא יִהְיֶה ה' אֶחָד, *'Hashem will be King over all the world — on that day Hashem will be One and His Name will be One'*, and then: וּבְתוֹרָתְךָ כָּתוּב לֵאמֹר שְׁמַע יִשְׂרָאֵל ה' אֱלֹהֵינוּ ה' אֶחָד, *'And in Your Torah it is written: Hear, O Israel, Hashem is our God, Hashem, the One and Only'*, followed again by (three times, in a whisper:) בָּרוּךְ שֵׁם כְּבוֹד מַלְכוּתוֹ לְעוֹלָם וָעֶד, *'Blessed is the Name of His glorious kingdom for all eternity'*; and (seven times:) ה' הוּא הָאֱלֹהִים, *'Hashem is God.,*

If the dying person resumes breathing yet a third time, those present, upon subsequently seeing that the soul is again about to depart, should recite the following verses from the *Mussaf* service of Rosh Hashanah:

וְעַל יְדֵי עֲבָדֶיךָ הַנְּבִיאִים כָּתוּב לֵאמֹר: כֹּה אָמַר ה', מֶלֶךְ יִשְׂרָאֵל וְגֹאֲלוֹ, ה' צְבָאוֹת, אֲנִי רִאשׁוֹן וַאֲנִי אַחֲרוֹן, וּמִבַּלְעָדַי אֵין אֱלֹהִים, וְנֶאֱמַר וְעָלוּ מוֹשִׁיעִים בְּהַר צִיּוֹן לִשְׁפֹּט אֶת הַר עֵשָׂו וְהָיְתָה לַה' הַמְּלוּכָה, וְנֶאֱמַר וְהָיָה ה' לְמֶלֶךְ עַל כָּל הָאָרֶץ בַּיּוֹם הַהוּא יִהְיֶה ה' אֶחָד וּשְׁמוֹ אֶחָד, וּבְתוֹרָתְךָ כָּתוּב לֵאמֹר: שְׁמַע יִשְׂרָאֵל ה' אֱלֹהֵינוּ ה' אֶחָד. בָּרוּךְ שֵׁם כְּבוֹד מַלְכוּתוֹ לְעוֹלָם וָעֶד. ה' הוּא הָאֱלֹהִים, ה' מֶלֶךְ ה' מָלָךְ ה' יִמְלֹךְ לְעוֹלָם וָעֶד.

And by means of Your servants, the prophets, it is written: 'Thus said Hashem, the King and Redeemer of Israel, Hashem of hosts: 'I am first and I am last, and besides Me there is no God.' And it is said: 'The saviors will ascend Mount Zion to judge Esau's mountain, and the kingdom will be Hashem's.' And it is said: 'Hashem will be King over all the world — on that

---

56. Ibid. They should be careful that the recitation of שְׁמַע יִשְׂרָאֵל ה' אֱלֹהֵינוּ ה' אֶחָד, *'Hear, O Israel, Hashem is our God, Hashem, the One and Only,'* should take place exactly at the moment when the soul departs.

Some have the custom to say, in addition, the following:

אֵין כֵּאלֹקֵינוּ, *'There is none like our God. . .'* ArtScroll Ashkenaz Siddur [p. 476];

פִּטּוּם הַקְּטֹרֶת, *'The incense mixture. . .'* [ibid. p. 36]

עָלֵינוּ לְשַׁבֵּחַ, *'It is our duty to praise. . .'*. [ibid. p. 158]

day Hashem will be One and His Name will be One.' And in Your Torah it is written: 'Hear, O Israel, Hashem is our God, Hashem, the One and Only. Blessed is the Name of His glorious kingdom for all eternity. Hashem is God. Hashem rules, Hashem ruled, Hashem will rule for all eternity. [57]

ᵈ§ On the Sabbath

23. If the death is occuring on the Sabbath, a time when prayers are kept to a minimum, those standing at the bedside should nevertheless recite the following:
Psalm 92: מִזְמוֹר שִׁיר לְיוֹם הַשַּׁבָּת, *'A psalm, a song for the Sabbath day. . .'*
Psalms 121, 130, and 91.
Ana Be'ko'ach, 'We beg You! With the strength of Your right hand's greatness. . .'
The second paragraph of *Aleinu*, beginning with עַל כֵּן נְקַוֶּה לְּךָ, *'Therefore we put our hope in You. . ."*

שְׁמַע יִשְׂרָאֵל ה' אֱלֹהֵינוּ ה' אֶחָד, *'Hear, O Israel, Hashem is our God, Hashem, the One and Only.'*[58]

ᵈ§ Kindling a Light

24. It is a Jewish custom to kindle a light during the weedays by the *gosess*.[59]
However the light should not be placed right beside his bed, but in the vicinity of the head of the bed.[60]

ᵈ§ After the Soul Departs

25. In many communities, the custom is to open the windows the moment the soul departs.[61]

26. Immediately after death, the body should not be moved, in case the *gosess* only lost consciousness. Those present should wait a short time.[62] The custom is to put a light feather near his nostrils. If it does not flutter, this is a sign that he is dead.[63] Then the eyes of the deceased are gently closed, and he is covered with a white cloth.[64]

---

57. *Gesher HaChaim* (2:3:2).

58. Ibid.

59. See *Ma'avar Yabok* (*Sefas Emes* §15): "The Jewish custom is to kindle lights by the *gosess*. The reason is known. The Sages tell us that a light drives away harmful spiritual forces (*mazikim*), even at night, the time of their predominance . . ." He also discusses other lofty matters there.

60. *Gesher HaChaim* (2:3:2).

61. *Ma'avar Yabok*. "Some suggest that the purpose of opening windows is to make way for the [departing] soul, so that it can retreat to its desired destination, similar to what we find [in *Daniel* 6:11], that in the room where he prayed he had open windows. Another reason is that opening the windows drives away the [harmful] spirits."

62. *Chochmas Adam* (151:18).

63. Ibid. *Kitzur Shulchan Aruch* (194:5).

64. *Gesher HaChaim* (§3). See *Ma'avar Yabok* (*Sifsei Rannenus* §9): "They cover the face of the deceased, so that the accusers (*mekatregin*) should not increase his suffering by gazing upon his face and forehead, where a person's sins are engraved. Moreover, it is forbidden to look at the

27. After the soul has departed, those present should say:

ה׳ נָתַן וה׳ לָקַח, יְהִי שֵׁם ה׳ מְבֹרָךְ.

"Hashem gave, Hashem took. Blessed be the Name of Hashem from now to all eternity"

הַצּוּר תָּמִים פָּעֳלוֹ כִּי כָל דְּרָכָיו מִשְׁפָּט, אֵל אֱמוּנָה וְאֵין עָוֶל צַדִּיק וְיָשָׁר הוּא

"The Rock! — perfect is His work, for all His paths are justice; God of faith without iniquity, righteous and fair is He."

◆§ Kri'ah

28. According to the basic *halachah*, all present at the departure of the soul must rend their garment [i.e., perform *kri'ah*.][65] However, this is not the current practice.

All present recite the following blessing (omitting the name of Hashem and His kingship):

בָּרוּךְ דַּיַּן הָאֱמֶת , *'Blessed is the true Judge.'*[66]

Those who were not present recite the same blessing (with the same omissions) upon hearing of the death.[67]

◆§ Lowering the Deceased

29. In Jerusalem, the custom is to leave the deceased on his bed for half an hour,[68] and then lower him to the floor in the following manner:

30. He is completely undressed and covered with a white sheet. Then he is lowered to the floor, modestly and respectfully as if he were still alive, so that his body remains covered. He is laid on the floor opposite the door leading out of the room, with his feet towards the door.

In *Eretz Yisrael* the custom is that his back should touch the floor directly, without the intervention of the sheet;[69] but that his entire body should be covered by the

---

face of the deceased, lest one lose respect for him. In addition to these reasons, there is the statement of the *Gemara* (*Horayos* 13b) that looking at the face of the dead causes one to forget one's learning."

65. See below, 6:2, and note 26 there, where it is explained that the current practice is to delay *k'riah* until the funeral.

66. *Bach*, in his commentary on *Tur* (*Orach Chaim* §223), writes: "The prevalent custom is to recite בָּרוּךְ דַּיַּן הָאֱמֶת, 'Blessed is the true Judge,' omitting the Name of Hashem and His Kingship [אַתָּה ה׳ אֱלֹהֵינוּ מֶלֶךְ הָעוֹלָם]. But, in my humble opinion, this is not correct" [i.e., one should mention Hashem's Name and Kingship]. See also other commentators on §223, including *Taz*, *Magen Avraham*, *Mishnah Berurah*, et al.

67. *Gesher HaChaim* (3:1:3).

68. Responsa *Yismach Lev* (*Yoreh De'ah* §9). However, *Gesher HaChaim* (3:2:1) writes that the custom in Jerusalem is to leave the deceased on his bed for twenty minutes.

69. *Gesher HaChaim* (3:2:1). See *Drishah* and *Shach* (§339), who likewise rule that nothing should be placed under the back of the deceased. They explain that intervening substances would

white sheet, from face to feet. A stone should be placed like a pillow under the head, so that it slightly raises the head. These customs — of not allowing anything to intervene between the bare back of the deceased and the floor, and putting a stone under his head — apply in *Eretz Yisrael*, due to the sanctity of the ground, and in accord with the verse (*Psalms* 102:15): '*Your servants love the stones [of Zion].*'

In the Diaspora, the custom is to spread some straw on the floor and cover the straw diagonally with a sheet, and to place a pillow under his head.[70]

31. Those who lower the deceased onto the floor ask his pardon, addressing him by his and his father's name (e.g., *Ploni ben Ploni*). They meticulously straighten his body, arms, and legs. If his mouth is open, they close it. If it is not possible to close it, they bind the jaws so that the mouth will not be open; otherwise, air could enter and the body might swell.[71] The feet are kept together by tying the two big toes.[72]

When they lower him onto the floor, they recite:

בֵּית יַעֲקֹב לְכוּ וְנֵלְכָה בְּאוֹר ה'. אֶל הָאֱלֹהִים ה', דִּבֶּר וַיִּקְרָא אֶרֶץ מִמִּזְרַח שֶׁמֶשׁ עַד מְבֹאוֹ. יָבֹא שָׁלוֹם יָנוּחוּ עַל מִשְׁכְּבוֹתָם הוֹלֵךְ נְכֹחוֹ, כִּי עָפָר אַתָּה וְאֶל עָפָר תָּשׁוּב.

'*House of Jacob, go and let us go in the light of Hashem*' (*Isaiah* 2:5). '*God of gods is Hashem. He spoke and called forth the earth, from the rising of the sun unto its setting*' (*Psalms* 50:1). '*He shall come in peace; they will rest on their beds; he goes straight forward in righteousness*' (*Isaiah* 57:2). '*For you are dust, and to dust you shall return*" (*Genesis* 3:19).

They should say this three times.[73]

After they have placed him on the floor, they recite *Psalm* 23:

מִזְמוֹר לְדָוִד, יהוה רֹעִי, לֹא אֶחְסָר. בִּנְאוֹת דֶּשֶׁא יַרְבִּיצֵנִי, עַל מֵי מְנֻחוֹת יְנַהֲלֵנִי. נַפְשִׁי יְשׁוֹבֵב, יַנְחֵנִי בְמַעְגְּלֵי צֶדֶק לְמַעַן שְׁמוֹ. גַּם כִּי אֵלֵךְ בְּגֵיא צַלְמָוֶת, לֹא אִירָא

---

generate heat and thus hasten decomposition. According to this explanation, the custom should be observed even in the Diaspora.

70. See *Ma'avar Yabok* (*Sifsei Rannenus* §9), who explains why the deceased is placed on the floor:

The ground is not susceptible to the *tum'ah* (ritual impurity) of the deceased, nor does it transmit the *tum'ah* to someone who touches the adjacent ground [unlike a bed or other object or piece of furniture, which would cause *tumah* to anyone who touched it], as is explained in Tractate *Niddah*, based on the verse (*Isaiah* 3:26), '*Clean, she shall sit on the ground.*'

Furthermore, everything desires to return to its source, and there it finds its rest. The supernal parts — the *nefesh*, *ruach*, and *neshamah*, various aspects of the soul — yearn to ascend, while the lower parts — the limbs and organs of the body — yearn to descend, for the body is dust, and to dust it shall return (*Genesis* 3:19).

He further explains: "When they place him on the floor, they customarily cover him with a sheet, to protect him from the forces of harsh judgment (*din*). . .and from certain evil spritual forces which only act upon things which are visible to the eye."

71. See *Shabbos* 151.

72. *Zivula Basraisa*.

73. *Ma'avar Yabok* (*Sifsei Rannenus* ch. 9). There he explains the intentions (*kavanos*) to be contemplated in mind while reciting these verses.

רָע כִּי אַתָּה עִמָּדִי; שִׁבְטְךָ וּמִשְׁעַנְתֶּךָ הֵמָּה יְנַחֲמֻנִי. תַּעֲרֹךְ לְפָנַי שֻׁלְחָן נֶגֶד צֹרְרָי; דִּשַּׁנְתָּ בַשֶּׁמֶן רֹאשִׁי, כּוֹסִי רְוָיָה. אַךְ טוֹב וָחֶסֶד יִרְדְּפוּנִי כָּל יְמֵי חַיָּי, וְשַׁבְתִּי בְּבֵית יהוה לְאֹרֶךְ יָמִים.

'A psalm by David. HASHEM is my shepherd, I shall not lack. In lush meadows He lays me down, beside tranquil waters He leads me. He restores my soul. He leads me on paths of justice for His Name's sake. Through I walk in the valley overshadowed by death, I will fear no evil, for You are with me. Your rod and Your staff, they comfort me. You prepare a table before me in view of my tormentors. You anointed my head with oil, my cup overflows. May only goodness and kindness pursue me all the days of my life, and I shall dwell in the House of HASHEM for long days,'

followed by *Psalms* 91:11,

כִּי מַלְאָכָיו יְצַוֶּה לָּךְ, לִשְׁמָרְךָ בְּכָל דְּרָכֶיךָ.

'He will command His angels for you, to protect you in all your ways.'[74]

◆§ Kindling a Light

32. The custom is to kindle a light near the head of the deceased, or to surround him with lights.[75] Some have the custom to surround the deceased with twenty-six lights.[76]

33. The custom is to remove all the clothes of the deceased, even if the death occurs on the Sabbath.[77] This applies in both summer and winter [even though the purpose of removing the clothes is to prevent the body from decaying, and decay is less likely in winter].[78] If there is no way to undress him except by tearing his clothes, and there is danger that the body might become odorous [if the clothes are not removed], one is permitted to ask a non-Jew to tear them, but a Jew may not tear them.[79]

34. On the Sabbath, too, the deceased is lowered to the floor; but since it is not permitted to carry a dead person on the Sabbath, one must first take a

---

74. *Ma'avar Yabok* (loc. cit.). One should recite these verses with great concentration, especially the verse, *'He will command His angels for you, to protect you in all your ways'*. This verse is extremely effective, as is explained at length there (ibid. *ma'amar* 2).

75. See *Ma'avar Yabok* (*Sefas Emes* §15). He explains that the custom is to light *avukos* (multiple candles, e.g., several candles fused into one, or braided together) for the deceased, because this displays respect and affords protection. . . "and through this and other things done for the deceased, one arouses mercy for him. . ."

76. This number corresponds to the total numerical value of the letters of Hashem's Name (see *Gesher HaChaim* 3:2:2).

77. *Gesher HaChaim* (3:2:3).

78. *Gesher HaChaim* (loc. cit.). He states that removing the clothes on the Sabbath is permitted because this is an indirect way of carrying them (*tiltul min hatzad*), and the clothes are not *muktzah*. For a lengthy discussion of the problem, see *Gesher HaChaim* there.

79. *Gesher HaChaim* (loc. cit.), citing *Lev Chaim*.

non-*muktzah* object, permitted for carrying, such as a loaf of bread, and place it on the deceased, or next to him on the sheet that covers him.[80] This makes it permissible to carry the loaf and the deceased together. The same procedure is followed in cases where it is permitted to remove him from the domain.[81]

If the deceased is still dressed in the clothes that will later be removed from him [and are thus not considered *muktzah*], some rule that there is no need at all for the loaf or similar object.[82]

35. On the Sabbath, it is permitted to bind the jaws in order to prevent the mouth from opening further, but not in order to close it further. Likewise, one may not close the eyes of the deceased on the Sabbath, since this is in the category of moving one of his limbs, which is forbidden on the Sabbath.[83]

36. Some rule that on *Yom Tov* even a Jew is permitted to kindle lights[84] — in order to place them near the deceased.[85] This is permitted because it is for the honor of the deceased.[86] If any oil or candles remain afterwards, one is permitted to use them for other purposes.[87]

37. The custom is to cover the mirrors in the house. Some also have the custom of covering pictures of people.[88]

38. The custom of the women is that they go in first to lament over the deceased.[89]

But the correct practice is that women who are in the status of *niddah* should be careful not to touch the deceased. It is also desirable that the men who handle the deceased should not be in need of a *mikveh* (see above, par. 17).[90]

---

80. *Shulchan Aruch* (*Orach Chaim*, beginning of §311).
81. See *Shulchan Aruch* (311:2).
   Mishnah Berurah there (§§7) notes a lenient opinion [mentioned by *Rama*] that even if the body has has not yet become foul-smelling but seems to be approaching that stage, it may be moved to a *karmelis*, i.e., a domain to which one may carry by Biblical law but not by Rabbinic law. He states that, according to this lenient opinion, the deceased may be removed even if it would otherwise be possible for the family to go somewhere else. [The reason is that if the body becomes odorous, this is demeaning for the deceased and the family.] See also 11:1.
82. *Shulchan Aruch* (311:4). And see *Beis Yosef*, who asks why the clothing should not be considered subordinate (*batel*) and integral to the body, and therefore forbidden for carrying just like the body. *Magen Avraham* offers an answer: that the clothes are not *batel* since those caring for the deceased intend to remove them. But see *Be'ur Halachah* there, who points out a difficulty with *Magen Avraham*'s answer.
83. *Shulchan Aruch* (311:7).
84. The light must be kindled by means of a light which was already burning.
85. However, it is forbidden to heat a candle in order to stick it to the floor or the candelabrum. This is a precautionary ordinance to prevent the forbidden labor called *memare'ach* (spreading a substance onto a surface) (*Mishnah Berurah* 514:§§18).
86. See *Gesher HaChaim* (17:1:2) for a lengthy discussion of this topic.
87. *Chazon Ish* (*Yoreh De'ah* 209:2).
88. See below, 16:4.
89. See *Ma'avar Yabok* (*Sifsei Rannenus* chapt. 10).
90. *Gesher HaChaim* (3:2:5).

◄§ Watching Over the Deceased

39. Someone must watch over the deceased.[91] This is necessary even on the Sabbath.[92] Even a *kohen*, if he is a mourner for this deceased and is one of those responsible for arranging the burial, is permitted to be in the room with the deceased in order to watch over him.[93] And some rule that even on the Sabbath the *kohen* who is a mourner is permitted to become *tamei* in order to watch over the deceased.[94]

40. Those watching over the deceased, even if they are not his relatives, should not greet anyone, nor answer anyone's greeting. [95]

If only one person is watching over the deceased, he is exempt from reciting the *Shema*, praying, putting on *tefillin*, and all other positive commandments.[96] He is not allowed to be strict with himself and perform *mitzvos*.[97]

If two people are watching over the deceased together, they should take turns: One remains on duty while the other recites the *Shema*, [prays, or puts on *tefillin*] and vice versa.[98] And in fact, the proper way is for two people to watch over the deceased.[99] The one doing the *mitzvah* must go out of the room where the deceased is.

41. Those watching over the deceased should be extremely careful not to indulge in idle talk in his presence — and, all the more so, not to utter any type of forbidden speech [such as gossip or *lashon hara*]. On the contrary, they should speak of holy matters, or recite Psalms and prayers.[100]

---

91. This *halachah* is explained in *Shulchan Aruch* (*Yoreh De'ah* §341 and §403).

92. *Rama* (*Yoreh De'ah* 373:5).

93. *Shulchan Aruch* (373:5).

94. *Rama* (loc. cit.). *Nekudos HaKesef* there writes: "The *halachah* to be followed is. . .that the *kohen* is permitted to become *tamei* [for his family member] even if this is not necessary [for the needs of the deceased]; and likewise on the Sabbath [the *kohen*] is permitted to watch over [the deceased], so that he will not be left in neglect. And this [lenient ruling] is the prevalent custom."

95. *Sefer Chassidim* (§741).

96. *Shulchan Aruch* (*Orach Chaim* 71:3 and §38). He is exempt from *mitzvos* because he is occupied with a *mitzvah*, namely, guarding the deceased (*Mishnah Berurah* there).

97. *Mishnah Berurah* (71:§§12): ". . .even if he is sitting farther than four cubits from the deceased" (*Magen Giborim*). [Cf. *Igros Moshe, Yoreh De'ah* §225.]

98. *Shulchan Aruch* (71:4).

99. *Kaf HaChaim* (71:24). This is so that neither one will miss out on the *mitzvos* of reciting the *Shema* and praying.

100. Besides the fact that in general it is forbidden to engage in idle talk — and, all the more so, forbidden speech — one must be even more scrupulous about these things in the presence of the deceased. See also *Ma'avar Yabok* (*Sifsei Rannenus* chapt. 9), who writes: "We have cautioned those who watch over the deceased to be careful not to engage in *lashon hara*, arguing, or fighting. . .and they should keep conversation to the minimum, for 'the more one talks, the more one sins' — especially in such a situation [i.e., in the presence of the deceased]. And it would be even better if they would pray for the deceased, with the Psalms of David, in particular the ones indicated above."

CHAPTER FOUR

Pouring Out the Water

◄§ The Custom

1. It is customary that people pour out all the water that is in the house where the deceased is lying.[1] This applies to any water that has been placed in vessels. The same is done in the 'neighboring houses.'[2]

How is the term 'neighboring houses' defined? In Jerusalem and Hebron —may they be built and established speedily in our days — the custom is to pour out water of the two domiciles (houses or apartments) to the right and two to the left of the dwelling where the deceased is lying.[3] The water is also poured out on the two floors above and the two floors below the domicile where the deceased is lying.[4] In regard to this custom all domiciles belonging to the same person are counted as one.[5]

2. If the death occurred on the Sabbath, the water is not poured out on that day,[6] and one may be lenient and not pour out the water on *motza'ei Shabbos*.[7]

---

1. See *Shulchan Aruch* (*Yoreh De'ah* 339:5) where two main reasons are offered: (1) The mystical connotation is expressed as follows: The Angel of Death whets his knife on water, and a drop of the blood of death falls in (*Taz* and *Shach*); (2) Pouring out the water is a way of informing people that someone has died, so that the neighbors can come and perform acts of kindness for him [e.g., accompany him to burial]. This avoids a direct verbal announcement, which would be undesirable (*Kol Bo* and *Shach* there). [See below, note 11.]

2. See *Taz* (§339), who writes: "The number meant by the expression 'neighboring houses' is not defined here, but *Tosafos* on *Kesubos* 28 (s.v. *ve'im*) writes that it refers to 'three houses,' as we find at the end of the first chapter of *Avodah Zarah* (p. 21)."

Nekudos HaKesef writes: "However, it could be said that the term as used here means actual neighbors; and this is the custom" [i.e., that besides the house where the deceased is lying, only the actual neighbors pour out the water]. See also *Pischei Teshuvah* (§339), citing *Chamudei Daniel* (§26): "It would seem that 'three houses' means two houses plus the house where the deceased is lying." See also *Gilyon Maharsha* (§339), who writes that 'neighboring houses' means 'two houses on every side of the house of the deceased.'

3. This means that the water is poured out in a total of five houses — unless the number is higher because there are apartments above or below that containing the deceased (*Birkei Yosef* and *Beis David* §161).

4. Ibid.

5. *Birkei Yosef*. For example, if the deceased is on the fourth floor, and there are three more floors above, the water is poured out on the second, third, [fourth,] fifth and sixth floors.

6. Responsa *Shemesh Tzedakah* (*Yoreh De'ah* §36).

7. *Gesher HaChaim* (3:3:6).

Likewise, if the death occurred on the first day of *Yom Tov*, one should be lenient and not pour out the water.[8] On the other hand, if the death occurred on the Diaspora's second day of *Yom Tov* the custom of many is to pour out the water.[9]

3. If the house where the deceased is lying is separated from adjacent houses by a main road or even a path that people use, one need not pour out the water in the houses on the other side of the street.[10]

4. Even in our time, when water is poured down a drain in the house instead of being thrown out, one pours out the water.[11]

The *gaon* R' Shmuel Salant, Rav of Jerusalem, is quoted as ruling that if the water was not poured out before the deceased was removed from the house, there is no obligation to do so afterwards.[12]

5. If the water had already been poured out in the house where the death took place, and then the deceased was brought to a second house, the water need not be poured out there.[13]

If the death occurred in a hospital, where the water is not poured out, and from there the deceased was brought to his own home, some rule that its water should be poured out,[14] but one authority is lenient in this circumstance.[15]

6. If the deceased did not die of illness, but was murdered or died of suffocation [some are of the opinion that that the Angel of Death is not involved in such a death and therefore the water need not be poured out. Nevertheless], the water in

---

8. *Mishmeres Shalom (Hilchos Aveilus)*. But he writes: "I have found that *Pri Megaddim (Mishbetzos Zahav*, *Orach Chaim* §455:3) writes that on every *Yom Tov* except Pesach, the water should be poured out." See also *Gesher HaChaim* (3:3:7).

9. *Mishmeres Shalom* (loc. cit.).

10. See responsa *Chessed LeAvraham* (Tumim, *Yoreh De'ah* §106), who states that if there is a public thoroughfare — even a path that people walk on — between the house of the deceased and the nearby houses, they are not called 'neighboring houses.' The same ruling is given by *Chaim BeYad* (§113). The *Gaon* of Brizhan rules even more leniently, that if there is even a private path between the house of the deceased and the nearby houses, the water need not be poured out. (*Kol Bo Al Aveilus*).

11. Even though the neighbors do not see the water being poured out, and hence it cannot serve as a way of informing people that someone has died, nevertheless one should be strict [and pour out the water]. See *Gesher HaChaim* (3:3:3, note 5), who writes: "Perhaps [the death] will become known because those who poured out the water will need water and come to ask their neighbors for it. Or, even if they have tap water they can use, they will tell their neighbors that they poured out all the water they had in their household vessels."

12. *Gesher HaChaim* (loc. cit.).

13. *Chavalim Bin'imim* II:§70.

14. *Kerem Shlomo*.

15. See *Atzmos Yosef*, who rules leniently on this question.

the house where the death occurred should be poured out, [but not that of the neighboring houses].[16] But if he was killed somewhere else and brought to a house, one should be lenient and not pour out the water.[17] All the same, it is best to wait [and not drink or draw more water] until the deceased has been removed from the house.[18]

7. The custom is to pour out the water even in the case of an infant that died within thirty days of birth,[19] if it was born alive.

Also in the case of a non-Jewish deceased, it is well to be strict and pour out the water.[20]

8. Regarding water that is still connected to the main water line, strictly speaking some should be poured out; however, the custom is not to do so.[21] Likewise, the custom is not to pour out water from roof cisterns.[22] Water in a closed bottle need not be poured out.[23]

9. If the water which should have been poured out was used to make dough or to cook, a number of *Poskim* rule that it is forbidden to eat the bread or cooked

---

16. See *Toras Chaim* (on *Sanhedrin* 112), who writes that even in the case of a death not due to illness, regardless of whether [the killer is] man or beast, the Angel of Death has a part in it, and the completion of death comes about by means of the angel.

The *Gaon* of Brizhan states that there is a difference between someone killed by man and someone killed by a wild animal. The latter is in the same category as illness, i.e., "death at the hands of heaven (*biydei shamayim*)," in contrast to death by human hands.

See also *Yoseif Da'as* (§339) who introduces an original ruling: that if someone is killed, or if a fetus is [killed when] taken from the womb by chemicals and instruments, the Angel of Death is not involved. But in §339 he writes that even in the case of someone killed by man, the Angel of Death has a part in the completion of death.

17. Even if one died of illness elsewhere and was then brought to the house, there are conflicting opinions as to whether the water need be poured out, as we saw in the previous paragraph. Moreover, many *Acharonim* maintain that if the person was killed by man, the water need not be poured out. Therefore one should be lenient in the case of one killed by man elsewhere and subsequently brought to the house.

18. *Gesher HaChaim* (3:3:5).

19. *Pischei Teshuvah* (*Yoreh De'ah* §339:5).

20. Ibid.

21. *Metzudas Tzion* on *Kitzur Shulchan Aruch*.

22. *Gesher HaChaim* (3:3:8).

23. ". . .Because it is closed" (*Gesher HaChaim*, 3:3:11), citing *Acharonim*. And see *Sha'arim Metzuyanim BeHalachah*, who states that in the following cases the water need not be poured out:

   (a) If the water has been changed by cooking, or adding minerals, or mixing with other substances.

   (b) If it has a special name, involving an added word, such as "soda-water," "mineral-water," etc.

(c)   If pouring out the water would involve financial loss.

Therefore, there is no need to pour out soda-water, seltzer-water, and the like. This ruling is based upon responsa *Beis Yitzchak* (*Yoreh De'ah* II:107); responsa *Even Yekarah* (*mahadura tinyana* §34), and responsa *Maharsham* (III:§375).

food.[24] However, some rule leniently if not eating it would entail a loss.[24a]

Regarding hot or boiled water, one should be strict and pour it out.[25]

10. Water drawn specially for the purpose of baking *matzos* for the *mitzvah* of the *Pesach Seder* — known as *mayim she'lanu* — should not be poured out.[26] Likewise, after the fact (*bediavad*), one should not pour out water which was boiled for the Sabbath, *Yom Tov*, or some other *mitzvah*.[27]

If one is about to drink water, and has already recited the blessing before drinking, and then learns about the presence of a deceased person, one should drink some water [so that the blessing will not be in vain], and pour out the rest.[28]

11. If the water in a container has turned to ice, it need not be discarded.[29]

Regarding water in a *beth midrash* (house of study or synagogue), one should be lenient and not pour it out.[30]

However, such a place is counted as one of the two houses on either side of the house where the deceased is lying (see above, par. 1).[31]

12. Some write that the water in the vicinity of the deceased is forbidden only for drinking, but is permitted for washing one's face, hands, and feet, or for laundering clothes.[32] And [although one should not use the water to wash hands for eating bread], if one did so, the washing is valid.[33]

---

24. *Pischei Teshuvah* (§339), citing responsa *Beis Yehudah* (part I *Yoreh De'ah* §46), and *Beis David* §161.

24a. *Beis Yisrael* §151.

25. *Gesher HaChaim* (3:3:10).

26. *Rama* (*Orach Chaim* 455:1).

27. See *Pischei Teshuvah* (*Yoreh De'ah* §339), who writes that after the fact (*bediavad*) the water should not be forbidden, since "one who is performing a *mitzvah* will not experience any evil," as is stated in *Shulchan Aruch* (*Orach Chaim* §455). He adds: "I have heard that a number of great rabbis have ruled this way" [i.e., have permitted such water *bediavad*].

28. *Sefer Chassidim* (§851).

29. *Pischei Teshuvah* (§339), citing *Chamudei Daniel*. This applies if the water was already frozen at the time of death; but if it froze afterwards, it should be poured out.

30. *Hadras Kodesh* §78.

31. *Kol Bo Al Aveilus* (2:5), citing *Be'er Moshe* by the *Gaon* Yerushalmski.

32. *Pischei Teshuvah* (*Yoreh De'ah* §339), citing *Adnei Paz* (§26).

33. *Hagahos Yad Shaul* (*Yoreh De'ah* §339); responsa *Sheim Aryeh, Yoreh De'ah* §8.

CHAPTER FIVE

Aninus: The Period
Between Death and Interment

◄§ The State of *Aninus*

1. Generally, the state known as *aninus* is the period from the moment of death,[1]
and the person in this state is an *onen* [plural: *onenim*]. The relatives of the
deceased who become *onenim* are those who are required to mourn. These are:
(a) father; (b) mother; (c) brother; (d) sister; (e) son; (f) daughter; (g) husband;
(h) wife. "Brother" and "sister" include a half-brother or half-sister on the side of
either one's father or one's mother.[2]

[As will be explained below, an *onen* is exempt from performing *mitzvos* and is
forbidden to eat meat and drink wine.]

◄§ For One's Main Torah Teacher

2. If one's main Torah teacher (*rabbo muvhak*) dies, and is lying unburied [in the
city where one lives], one is forbidden to eat meat or drink wine on a weekday,
until the deceased is buried.[3]

◄§ Scriptural and Rabbinic *Aninus*

3. If the deceased is not buried on the day he dies — and even if he remains
unburied for a number of days — the family members are not *onenim* on the
Scriptural (*deOraysa*) level during those days [see below, paragraph 4], except

---

1. *Shulchan Aruch* (*Yoreh De'ah* §341:1).

2. If the death was suicide, some rule that, just as the laws of mourning do not apply, so too the laws
of *aninus* do not apply. Although the next-of-kin of the suicide are required to bury him, they remain
obligated to perform *mitzvos*, and are permitted to eat meat and drink wine.

   Others rule that the laws of *aninus* apply in the case of suicide, as for any other death. Therefore the
family members are exempted, according to the basic *halachah*, from reciting the *Shema* and from the
other *mitzvos*. However, if they wish to be strict with themselves [and perform *mitzvos*], they may do
so (*S'dei Chemed Aveilus* §5).

   This *halachah* applies only if it is known with complete clarity that the death was suicide, and that the
deceased did not have an opportunity to regret his action before he died.

   The laws regarding mourning practices for a suicide are very complex. A halachic authority should be
consulted.

3. *Shulchan Aruch* (*Yoreh De'ah* §242:27); *Rama* (*Yoreh De'ah* §341:1); *Taz* (ad loc. §§10).

for the day of death. However, they are *onenim* on the Rabbinic (*deRabbanan*) level,[4] as long as they need to occupy themselves with the burial.[4a]

4. On the Scriptural level, the only restrictions imposed on the *onen* are that he is forbidden to eat *ma'aser sheni* (a tithe brought to Jerusalem in the Temple eras and eaten there), *bikkurim* (first fruits), and *kodashim* (sacrificial food).

However, on the Rabbinic level there are a number of other restrictions. These are detailed in the following paragraphs.

⇜ Meals During *Aninus* / Sitting on a Chair

5. The *onen* — this also applies to everyone, even non-mourners — is forbidden to eat in the presence of the deceased. If one wants to eat, he should do so in a different room. If he does not have another room, he should eat in someone else's house. If no other house is available, he should make a partition (*mechitzah*) between himself and the deceased. The partition *mechitzah* must be at least ten handbreadths (*tefachim*) in height. (Ten *tefachim* is about 38 inches.) It may even be made of cloth, if it is firm enough not to be moved by an ordinary wind. If making a partition is also impossible, he may turn his face away from the deceased and eat.[5]

The *onen* may not eat as if at a regular meal, sitting at a table.[6]

The Jerusalem Talmud states that he should neither eat nor drink his fill.[7]

He may not eat meat nor drink wine.[8]

He may not sit [on a chair or bed] or sleep on a bed, even if it is overturned. Instead, he must sit and sleep on the floor.[9] However, many follow the prevalent custom to be lenient about this[10] [i.e., they permit sitting on a chair or bed and sleeping on a bed].

---

4. *Zevachim* (99b and 100b).

4a. See *Shulchan Aruch* (§341:1).

5. Ibid. (§341:1). The prohibition against eating in the presence of the deceased includes all eating, since the Sages, in instituting this law, did not want to leave room for various interpretations of what is prohibited or permitted. "Even tasting fruit is included [in the prohibition], and even drinking water is forbidden, since drinking is included in the prohibition of eating" (*Sheivet Yehudah*).

6. *Shulchan Aruch* (§341:1), and *Shach* (§§6).

7. Jerusalem Talmud (*Berachos* 3:1); Tractate *Semachos* (ch. 10). And see *Divrei Chamudos* on *Rosh* (*Berachos* loc. cit.). He quotes *Beis Yosef* as stating that the *Poskim* do not cite this [ruling of the Jerusalem Talmud] because it is not mentioned in the *baraisa* in our [the Babylonian] Talmud. The implication is that it is not the accepted *halachah*. But *Gesher HaChaim* (18:2:3) writes: "Although the *Rishonim* do not cite the prohibition against eating one's fill, the *Acharonim* do cite it."

8. *Shulchan Aruch* (§341:1). Regarding a dish cooked with meat, but not containing meat, see *Sdei Chemed* (*Aveilus* §22).

9. *Shulchan Aruch* (§341:5).

10. *Gesher HaChaim* (18:2:2) writes: "I do not know why the prevalent custom is to permit sitting on a chair before the burial, and also sleeping on a bed, in cases where the burial was not performed on [the first] night [after the death]." To explain this permissive custom, he writes: "[It may be] because in our day it is not the custom to sleep on the floor, since the custom of overturning the bed (*kefiyas*

⚬§ Netilas Yadayim, Zimun, Minyan

6. Some rule that the *onen* must ritually wash his hands (perform *netilas yadayim*) before eating [bread], but should not recite the accompanying blessing.[11] Likewise, he should not recite the blessing over bread, nor the Grace After Meals, nor any other blessings. However, [when he has finished eating] he should wash his fingers (*mayim acharonim*).[11a]

After using the bathroom he should wash his hands, but not recite the blessing *Asher Yatzar* (". . .Who fashioned man with wisdom").[12] If he did violate the *halachah* by reciting a blessing, one should not answer *Amen*.[12a]

The *onen* is not included in the quorum of three or more who recite *zimun* (the introductory blessing before *Birkas HaMazon*). Nor should he respond Amen when others recite *Birkas HaMazon*.[13]

He is not counted among the ten men needed for a *minyan* (the minimum quorum required for public prayer).[14]

⚬§ Shema, Tefillin, Positive and Negative Commandments

7. The *onen* is exempt from: reciting the *Shema*; praying; putting on *tefillin*; and from all the [other positive] *mitzvos* of the Torah;[15] but he must observe the negative commandments, both Scriptural and Rabbinic.[16] However, before going to sleep the night before the burial, he must recite the *Shema*, as well as

---

hamitah; see chapt. 22) is no longer practiced, for the reason mentioned in *Shulchan Aruch* (§387:2). Another explanation may be the 'weakness of the generation,' as explained by the *Acharonim* in *Orach Chaim* (§555), in connection with [the prohibition against sleeping on a bed on] Tishah B'Av. Therefore we are lenient also about sitting on a chair or bench, since the prohibition about sitting is derived from that about sleeping, and the *Rishonim* imply that the *halachah* is identical for both [sitting and sleeping]."

11. *Pischei Teshuvah* (ad loc. §§4).

11a. Ibid.

12. *Aruch HaShulchan* (341:10).

12a. This point is added by the *gaon* R' Shlomo Zalman Auerbach, *shlita*, based on *Tosafos* (*Mo'ed Katan* 23b s.v. *ve'ein*).

13. *Shulchan Aruch* (§341:1).

14. *Gilyon Maharsha* (§341). *Mishnah Berurah* (55:§§24) writes: "The *onen* is not counted in a *minyan*. This refers to any *onen* who is obligated to mourn for the deceased, even if he is not responsible for arranging the burial. (For example, if the *onen* is not an heir of the deceased [he is not responsible for arranging the burial, but still cannot be counted in a *minyan*].) If the *onen* is in the same city as the deceased, he is not counted in a *minyan*, even if he has others who will arrange the burial. This applies as long as the deceased has not been given over to the *chevra kadisha*, as is explained below §71 [see below, our par. 53]. However, if the deceased is in a different city from the family member, and the family member was informed of the death before the burial, and someone in the city of the deceased is taking responsibility for burial. . . the family member is also counted in a *minyan*."

15. *Shulchan Aruch* (341:1).

16. *Pischei Teshuvah* (341:7), citing responsa *Chacham Tzvi*; *Birkei Yosef* (341:8). See also *Chiddushim U'Viurim*, by R' Zalman Margolios (§6), who writes that the *onen* is exempt from the positive commandments, but is obligated by the negative commandments, even Rabbinic ones, just like anyone else.

the blessing before sleep (*Hamapil*, ". . .Who casts the bonds of sleep upon my eyes").[17]

8. Some authorities say that the *onen* is exempt from performing *mitzvos* because [he is busy with the burial, and]: "One who is busy with a *mitzvah* is exempt from other *mitzvos*." Therefore, if he wishes to be strict with himself and perform *mitzvos*, he may do so.

Others maintain that the exemption is for the honor of the deceased, or because there otherwise would be no one to care for the deceased. Therefore, even if the *onen* wishes to be strict with himself and perform *mitzvos*, he may not do so.

The *halachah*, as determined by *Shulchan Aruch* (*Yoreh De'ah* 341:1), is that the *onen* is not permitted to be strict with himself. That is, he is not permitted to perform *mitzvos*.

◄§ Psalms, *Kaddish,* Eulogies, and *Yahrzeit*

9. People are permitted to recite *Tehillim* [Psalms] in the presence of the deceased.[18] And some rule that the *onen*, too, is permitted to do so, if he is not the only one caring for the deceased.[19]

The custom is that the *onen* recites *Kaddish* during the funeral.[20] He also is permitted to eulogize the deceased.[20a]

On the Sabbath and *Yom Tov*, the *onen* is permitted to go to the synagogue and recite *Kaddish*, especially if he is in mourning [for a previous death], or has a *yahrzeit*.[21]

---

17. This point is added by the *gaon* R' Shlomo Zalman Auerbach, *shlita*, who notes that, regarding these recitations, the reasons for exempting the *onen* from *mitzvos* are not as applicable.

18. This is permitted because it is for the honor of the deceased. See *Ma'avar Yabok*, who writes of the great benefit for the deceased from the recitation of Psalms in his presence. He states that, even though at the grave one is forbidden to wear *tefillin* or study Torah, nevertheless one is permitted to recite Psalms there.

It is true that *Kovetz Torani* (1967 p. 24) cites the *Chazon Ish* as ruling strictly and forbidding the recitation of Psalms in the presence of the deceased. However, see *Chazon LaMo'ed* (§2 note 7), who cites *Pe'er HaDor* (V:121) as relating that [when the *Chazon Ish* died] "his students and relatives stood around the burning candles, weeping and reciting Psalms."

See also *Mishmeres Shalom*, who states that the last will and testament of the author of *Knesses Yechezkel* instructed that until the burial three people should watch over him, reciting Psalms and *Shir Shel Pega'im*. *Chazon LaMo'ed* adds: ". . .and this is what I have seen done by great Torah personalities; they recited Psalms near the deceased."

See also *Aruch HaShulchan*, who states that some have the custom that people other than the *onen* recite Psalms, and the *onen* recites *Kaddish*. *Aruch HaShulchan* concludes that "this is not correct." However, it could be he was referring only to the *onen*'s reciting *Kaddish*.

19. *Mordechai*, citing *Raavi*. The same ruling is cited by *Chochmas Adam* (153:1).

20. *Beis Oved*, citing *Birkei Yosef*. This custom is also mentioned by *Gesher HaChaim* (18:2:3) and by *Sdei Chemed* (*Aninus* §26).

20a. *Sdei Chemed* (loc. cit. §29).

21. *Mishnah Berurah* (71:§§7). For more on this topic, see below, 44:10.

◆§ The Blessing at the Cemetery

10. When the *onen* goes to the cemetery, he should not recite the blessing אֲשֶׁר יָצַר
אֶתְכֶם בַּדִּין, ". . .Who fashioned you with justice. . ." even if he has not seen a
cemetery during the past thirty days. Even after the grave is filled with earth, when
the status of *aninus* ceases, he should not recite this blessing.[22] (And see below,
10:14.)

◆§ Informed of Death While Praying

11. If one had begun to recite the *Shema*, *Shemoneh Esrei* prayer, or *Birkas Ha-
Mazon*, and while still reciting it he was informed that a family member died
and he is therefore an *onen*, he should finish the blessing he had begun, and then
stop.[23]

If he had not yet begun the *Shemoneh Esrei* prayer — even if he is between the
recitation of the *Shema* and the *Shemoneh Esrei* — he should stop.[24]

However, if someone else is caring for the deceased, it is preferable (*lechatchilah*)
not to inform him until after the prayer service.[25]

◆§ Missed Prayers

12. As explained above (par. 7), an *onen* is exempt from prayer. Under certain
circumstances, when *aninus* ceases he may be permitted to make up for a
missed prayer. For details, see below (13:13, 15, and 16).

13. For the law regarding the recitation of the *Shema* on the day when *aninus*
ceases, see below (13:13, and footnote 24 there).

14. For the laws regarding putting on *tefillin* after *aninus* ceases, see below
(13:2-8).

For the laws regarding the recitation of the Morning Blessings (*Birkos
HaShachar*) after *aninus* ceases, see below (13:12).

◆§ Permitted and Prohibited Activities

15. Until the burial, the *onen* is permitted to wear shoes.[26]

He is permitted to leave his home in order to care for the needs of the
deceased.

However, he is forbidden to have marital relations, to bathe,[26a] to put lotions and

---

22. *Kaf HaChaim* (224:§§37), citing *Eshel Avraham*.

23. *Sha'arei Teshuvah* (71:§§6).

24. See *Gesher HaChaim* (18:2:6).

25. *Pischei Teshuvah* (71:§§8), citing *Chamudei Daniel*.

26. *Shulchan Aruch* (341:5).

26a. Responsa *Pri HaSadeh* (II:2:§104) writes that in some places the custom is that when a holy
       person dies, those who will carry the bier immerse in a *mikveh* beforehand. In this case, he states,
    the *onen* also is permitted to immerse in a cold *mikveh* [but not in a hot one]. And see the *Biurim* of R'
    Zalman Margolios (§19), who writes: "In any case, if one's family member died of that disease [the

oils on himself, to take part in joyful occasions (*simchah*), to exchange greetings with others, to have a haircut or shave,[27] and to study Torah.[28]

If an individual needs a halachic ruling, and the *onen* is the only authority available, he is permitted to issue a halachic ruling.[28a]

16. The *onen* is forbidden to work,[29] or engage in business. He is not permitted to keep his store open, even if he has a partner.[30] However, some rule that if he has a partner he may keep the store open by withdrawing from the partnership and relinquishing his share of the profits.[31]

◄§ *Aninus* on the Sabbath and Festivals

17. If the death occurs on the Sabbath, the status of *aninus* does not take effect.

Therefore, one is permitted to eat as at a regular meal, sitting at a table, and to eat meat and drink wine.[32] One should eat in another room from that where the

---

reference is to a contagious disease], one should go to the bathhouse and wash one's entire body. Afterwards, due to the contagion, one should definitely not put on any of the clothes he wore before the bath. He should put on other clothes instead."

27. *Rama* (§341:5).

28. *Chiddushei R' Akiva Eiger* (341:1).

28a. *Rama (Yoreh De'ah* 384:1) writes that a mourner may answer a question in the field of *issur ve'heter* for an individual questioner, if a rabbi is needed and he is the only one available. The same applies to an *onen*. And see *Aruch HaShulchan* there, par. 6, who cites this ruling of *Rama* and adds [in reference to mourning]: "However, it would seem that he should not preside over a divorce or a financial case, unless this is unavoidable, as when damage would result if he does not attend to the matter. In that case, he is obligated to attend to it. The decision [whether to give the requested ruling] depends on his evaluation of the particular situation."

29. *Rama* (341:5).

30. See responsa *Chasam Sofer (Yoreh De'ah* §324), cited by *Pischei Teshuvah* (380:§§4).

31. For a detailed discussion of this matter, see below, 18:28.

32. *Brachos* 18a; *Shulchan Aruch (Yoreh De'ah* 341:1). *Rama* there writes that the *onen* may do these things "if he wishes." The same ruling is given by Rabbeinu Yonah on *Berachos* there. He writes: "[The Talmud] does not say that he is *obligated* to eat meat and drink wine. Since his intention is for the *mitzvah* of having pleasure on the Sabbath, if he wishes, he may eat [meat and drink wine], but if he does not wish to, he need not. . .for [in general] a person is not obligated to eat meat and drink wine on the Sabbath. . .Now, you might ask: 'On a weekday, why is [the *onen*] forbidden [to eat meat and drink wine]? After all, following the interment, when the primary obligation of mourning takes effect and wearing shoes is forbidden, [eating meat and drinking wine] is permitted!' The answer is that prior to the interment, the *onen* is forbidden [to eat meat and drink wine], so that he should not be drawn after his pleasures and become negligent in arranging for burial. By the same token, wearing shoes is not forbidden [before the burial], for if he had to go barefoot, he could not properly arrange for the burial."

See also *Shach* (341:1:§§7), who quotes Rabbeinu Yonah's statement: "A person is not obligated to eat meat and drink wine on the Sabbath; these things are optional [even when one is not an *onen*]." *Shach* comments: "This implies that [the *onen*] is obligated to recite blessings and prayers on the Sabbath and *Yom Tov*. [Rabbeinu Yonah stated that the *onen* may do as he wishes regarding meat and wine on the Sabbath because, in general, these things are optional on the Sabbath. This implies that he may not do as he wishes regarding other things which, in general, are not optional on the Sabbath, e.g., blessings and prayers.] And this would also seem to be the ruling of R' Hai."

Chiddushei R' Akiva Eiger (341:1) writes: "See responsa *Veshav HaKohen* (§92), who concludes

deceased lies. If he does not have another room, he should eat in someone else's house. If no other house is available, he may turn his face away from the deceased and eat.[32a]

On the Sabbath and Festivals, an *onen* is obligated to recite the usual blessings of the meal, including *zimun*, and is obligated to pray.[33] He is permitted to go to the synagogue.[34] He must perform all the *mitzvos* of the Torah; however he is bound by the inconspicuous, private restrictions *(devarim shebetzin'a)*. For the definition of "inconspicuous restructions," see below, end of paragraph 55.[35]

18. Under the following *combination of circumstances*, the status of *aninus* does not yet take effect:[35a]

   (a) The death occurred on Friday, *and*

   (b) burial will not be performed before the Sabbath; *and*

   (c) on Friday one does not intend to occupy oneself at all with matters pertaining to the needs or honor of the deceased in preparation for the burial which will take place after the Sabbath.[36]

Accordingly, since *aninus* does not yet take effect, the bereaved should recite *Minchah* on Friday. *Aninus* will begin at the conclusion of the Sabbath.

However, some rule that the laws of *aninus* do apply until the Sabbath. Therefore, one is exempt from reciting *Minchah* on Friday.[37]

Even though *aninus* does not apply on the Sabbath, one is forbidden to study Torah. [Hence] he is not permitted to be called up to the Torah-reading.[38]

---

that [the permission to abstain from meat and wine] applies only on the Sabbath; but on *Yom Tov* [the *onen*] is obligated to eat meat, or at least drink wine, even on the night of the first day of *Yom Tov*." On the other hand, "It seems that the ruling to be followed is that [the *onen*] is obligated to eat meat and drink wine on the Sabbath, for one may not be lenient about the *mitzvah* of *oneg Shabbos* (making the Sabbath pleasurable) or *simchas Yom Tov* (making *Yom Tov* joyful)"(*Sheivet Yehudah*).

32a. *Sheivet Yehudah*. He does not have the option of making a partition, as in par. 5, because a partition that is needed to permit some type of activity may not be made on the Sabbath.

33. *Shach* (341:§§7).

34. *Rama* (341:5).

35. *Shulchan Aruch* (341:5).

35a. This is the ruling of responsa *Yad Eliahu* (§16). He reasons that the exemption from *mitzvos* is so that the *onen* can arrange for the burial. Hence in a situation like this, where the onset of the Sabbath is so close that one cannot occupy oneself with arranging for burial, one remains obligated by all the *mitzvos*.

See also the following: *Sha'arei Teshuvah* (*Shulchan Aruch*, *Orach Chaim* 71:§§6); *Pischei Teshuvah* (*Yoreh De'ah* 341:§§22); *Chiddushim U'Viurim*, by R' Zalman Margolios (§16); *Yoseif Da'as* (§341); and *Gesher HaChaim* (18:1:10).

36. This point is added by the *gaon* R' Shlomo Zalman Auerbach, *shlita*.

37. *Pischei Teshuvah* (ad loc. §§22).

38. *Chiddushei R' Akiva Eiger* (§341) cites *Tiferes LeMoshe*, who states that according to the *Poskim* referred to as "*yesh omrim*" ["some maintain"] by *Rama* (341:5), [the *onen*] is forbidden to study Torah. *Simchas HaNefesh* likewise rules that [the *onen*] should not be called up to the Torah-reading, and is forbidden to study Torah.

However, he is permitted to review the weekly Torah portion twice in Hebrew and once in the Aramaic translation [as explained in *Shulchan Aruch Orach Chaim* §285].[39]

A *kohen* is forbidden to recite the Priestly Blessing even on the Sabbath or *Yom Tov*.[40] Some rule that even if he is asked to recite the Priestly Blessing, he should not do so.[41]

19. If the *onen* is the only one in the congregation capable of leading the prayer-services, he may do so on the Sabbath, and may thereby fulfill the prayer obligation of the others. But if someone else can lead the services, the *onen* should not do so.[42]

Likewise, on the Sabbath, if the *onen* is the one best qualified to perform the Torah-reading, he may do so.[43]

If one is accustomed to recite Psalms every Sabbath, some rule that he may do so when he is an *onen*.[44]

20. The *onen* is permitted to cry on the Sabbath or *Yom Tov*, if he cannot overcome his feelings of grief.[45]

21. If one already is an *onen* when the Sabbath begins, the prevalent custom is that one should not don freshly laundered outer garments on the Sabbath.[46]

22. If, during the Sabbath, it is necessary to occupy oneself with the needs of the deceased — for example, to arrange for a burial place, or to speak with the members of the *chevra kaddisha* (burial society) — then all the restrictions of *aninus* apply, even on the Sabbath, from the time when one begins to occupy himself with these matters.[47]

---

39. This is similar to the permission granted during the first seven days of mourning (see *Yoreh De'ah* §400).
40. *Magen Avraham* (*Orach Chaim* 128:§§6).
41. *Mishnah Berurah* (128:§§158). He states that "some rule" this way.
42. *Shiurei Knesses HaGedolah* (§341); *Aruch HaShulchan* (§341:16).
43. *Kerem Shlomo* (§341), citing *Beis Lechem Yehudah*.
44. *Mishmeres Shalom* (*os aleph* §29).
45. *Rama* (*Orach Chaim* 288:2) writes: "If one takes pleasure in crying, because it relieves the anguish from his heart, he is permitted to cry on the Sabbath." However, *Taz* there quotes an *aggadah* that the students of R' Akiva found him crying on the Sabbath, and he explained to them: "It gives me pleasure. . ." *Taz* comments: "It seems to me that his eyes streamed tears because of his great closeness to the Holy One, Blessed is He; for we likewise find in *Zohar Chadash* (beginning of chapter 1) that he wept profusely while reciting *Shir HaShirim*, because he understood what lofty matters it touched upon. Similarly, it is common that when a person prays with great concentration, he cries. But the explanation given by *Rama* — that one is permitted to cry in order to relieve one's pain — is surprising; for, if so, anyone who feels sorrow could cry, God forbid, on the Sabbath." However, *Elyah Rabbah* and *Tosefos Shabbos* agree with *Rama's* ruling that crying is permitted, since it gives a person relief.
    See also *Sdei Chemed* (*Aninus* §24).
46. *Birkei Yosef* (341:§§14).
47. *Shulchan Aruch* (*Yoreh De'ah* §341:1 and *Orach Chaim* §71:2).

23. If one does not need to go to the *techum* [Sabbath boundary] to be ready to attend to the needs of the deceased when darkness falls, or to otherwise occupy himself on the Sabbath with the needs of the deceased, he is obligated by all the *mitzvos* of the Torah, even close to evening.[48]

Some rule that if he is not occupied with the needs of the deceased, he should recite the evening *Shema*, without the accompanying blessings, before sundown (*sh'ki'ah*).[49]

⊰§ *Havdalah*

24. At the conclusion of the Sabbath, an *onen* should not recite *Maariv*, and he is permitted to eat without reciting *Havdalah*.[49a]

After the interment, he should recite *Havdalah*,[50] omitting the joyful introductory verses, and beginning with the blessing over wine. The custom is that [at the conclusion of the Sabbath], he also recites the blessings over fragrant spices[51] (in addition to the blessing over "the lights of the fire").

If he did not recite *Havdalah* at the conclusion of the Sabbath, he may perform it until sundown on Tuesday.[52] But, in that case, he should not recite the blessings over fragrant spices and "the lights of the fire."[53]

If he did not recite *Havdalah* at the conclusion of a Festival, he has only until the end of the next day to do so. [For example, if the Festival ended on Sunday night,

---

48. *Shulchan Aruch (Orach Chaim* 71:2).

49. *Taz (Orach Chaim* 71:§§4), and *Mishnah Berurah* there (ad loc. §§10).

49a. See *Teshuvah U'Fesakim* of *Maharam* of Rotenburg (§188), who writes: "If one's family member dies on the Sabbath, and will not be buried until the next day, one should not recite *Havdalah* at the conclusion of the Sabbath. And it seems to me that he is permitted to eat without performing *Havdalah*, for we find in *Berachos* 17b: '[The *onen*] is exempt from all the *mitzvos* of the Torah,' and we find in *Talmud Yerushalmi, Berachos* 2:9: 'Anyone who is exempt from something, yet still does it, is called a *hediot* (ignorant).' However, on Sunday, after the deceased is buried, one is forbidden to eat until he recites *Havdalah*." (This responsum discusses this topic at length.) See also *Shulchan Aruch* (*Yoreh De'ah* 341:2) et al.

50. *Shulchan Aruch (Yoreh De'ah* 341:2).

51. This point is added by the *gaon* R' Shlomo Zalman Auerbach, *shlita*.

52. *Mishnah Berurah* (71:§§10).

53. *Shulchan Aruch (Orach Chaim* 299:6) writes: "However, the blessings over fragrant spices and the lights of the fire are recited only at the conclusion of the Sabbath." *Mishnah Berurah* explains that the blessing over the lights of the fire is recited at the conclusion of the Sabbath because that is when these lights were created. The blessing over fragrant spices is recited in order to revive our soul, which is pained by the departure of the additional soul (*neshamah yeseirah*) which we receive on the Sabbath. Both these reasons apply only on the evening following the Sabbath, not afterwards. And see *Ma'adnei Yom Tov*, who gives another explanation: Even at the conclusion of the Sabbath, if one does not have fragrant spices or fire, one need not exert oneself to procure them in order to recite these blessings, as *Rosh* (*Berachos* 8:3) writes, explaining that the blessing over the lights of the fire is "only a reminder" (*zecher be'alma*) [and therefore we are lenient about it]. For the same reason, we are lenient and do not require these two blessings once *motza'ei Shabbos* has passed.

he has only until sundown on Monday.] After that, he cannot make up for the missed *Havdalah*.[54]

25. If, at the conclusion of the Sabbath, the *onen* heard someone recite *Havdalah*,
the law is as follows: If that person intended thereby to fulfill the obligation of the *onen*, and the *onen* also intended that his obligation should be fulfilled through that person's recitation — the *onen* need not recite *Havdalah* again after the burial.[55]

Likewise, if the *onen* mistakenly performed *Havdalah* himself at the conclusion of the Sabbath prior to the burial, he need not recite *Havdalah* again after the burial.[56]

⋙ Death on *Yom Tov*

26. Under the following *combination of circumstances*, the status of *aninus* does not yet take effect:[57] (See also above, par. 17.)

(a) The death occurred on the first day of *Yom Tov*, or the day before *Yom Tov*; *and*

(b) it was not possible to perform burial before *Yom Tov*; *and*

(c) non-Jews do not want to perform the burial on *Yom Tov*; *or*

(d) the family does not want to have non-Jews perform the burial on *Yom Tov*.

Since the status of *aninus* does not yet take effect, one may eat meat and drink wine.[57a]

However, if the death occurred on the Diaspora's second day of *Yom Tov*, and it is possible for the family to perform burial, *aninus* does take effect, even if the family does not want to perform burial that day.[58]

If, due to circumstances beyond their control, they are unable to perform burial, *aninus* does not take effect.[59]

In those communities, where the custom is not to perform burials even on the Diaspora's second day of *Yom Tov*, *aninus* does not take effect.[59a]

---

54. *Mishnah Berurah* (299:§§16), citing R' Akiva Eiger.

55. *Beis David* (§164).

56. *Pischei Teshuvah (Orach Chaim* 299:§§19).

57. *Shulchan Aruch (Orach Chaim* 548:5).

57a. See *Shulchan Aruch (Yoreh De'ah* 341:1). And see *Chiddushei R' Akiva Eiger* there, who cites responsa *Veshav HaKohen* as ruling that the *onenim* are [not only permitted, but] obligated to eat meat, or at least drink wine, even on the night of the first day of *Yom Tov* [see above, note 32].

58. Ibid. (*Yoreh De'ah* 341:1). *Magen Avraham (Aruch Chaim* 548:§§8). *Mishnah Berurah* (71:§§11) writes that on the eve of *Yom Tov*, or even the eve of the second day of *Yom Tov*, most *Poskim* agree that he should make *Kiddush* and pray. The laws of *aninus* do not apply to him. This is due to the fact that it is not the practice to bury at night. The only restriction of *aninus* in this case is that one should not learn Torah because it causes joy.

59. *Mishnah Berurah* (548:§§20).

59a. *Igros Moshe, Yoreh De'ah* part III:§161.

27. In some communities, the custom is that when death occurs, community officials meet to determine the place of burial. If death occurs during the time of the Morning Prayers (*Shacharis* and *Mussaf*) on *Yom Tov*, such a meeting may be impossible to convene until after the prayer. In this case, the family member does not become an *onen* [during the time of prayer], and is obligated to pray *Shacharis* and *Mussaf*.[60]

Nevertheless, if one is occupied even during this time with things pertaining to the honor of the deceased — such as informing relatives and friends, or planning the funeral and burial — he is considered an *onen*.[61]

✑ *Eruv Tavshilin*

28. If one is an *onen* on the day before *Yom Tov*, and the day after *Yom Tov* is the Sabbath [thus requiring that an *eruv tavshilin*[61a] be made on the day before *Yom Tov*], the family member should set aside the food of the *eruv tavshilin*, but should not recite the accompanying blessing. However, he should recite the declaration ("Through this *eruv* may we be permitted to bake, cook. . .").[62]

If it is possible to have someone else make the *eruv tavshilin* on his behalf, this is preferable.

If he waits until just before *Yom Tov* begins, and the burial will not take place that night, he can even recite the blessing over making the *eruv tavshilin*.[63]

✑ *Chol HaMo'ed*

29. If the death occurs during *Chol HaMo'ed*, the laws of *aninus* apply.[64]

Likewise, one should not put on *tefillin*, even if the custom in his community is that one who is not an *onen* puts on *tefillin* during *Chol HaMo'ed*.[65] Moreover, he cannot be counted in a *minyan* until the burial is completed.[66]

✑ Rosh Hashanah

30. If the death occurs on or before the first day of Rosh Hashanah, the same *halachah* applies as for *Yom Tov* (see above, par. 26): That is, if one wants to

---

60. *Chochmas Adam* (153:6) and *Mishnah Berurah* (71:§§11). The reason is that in this case the family member is considered like one who, due to circumstances beyond his control, is unable to make arrangements for the burial. And see *Kol Bo Al Aveilus* (2:10), who states that even though the family member theoretically could attend to other aspects of the burial, it is possible in this case to also take into consideration the opinion of *Maharil*, that there is no *aninus* on *Yom Tov*. He adds: "[Nevertheless,] it seems to me that if [the family member] is actually occupied with other aspects of the burial, he is exempt from praying, like one who is waiting at the Sabbath boundary" (see above, par. 23).

61. This point is added by the *gaon* R' Shlomo Zalman Auerbach, *shlita*.

61a. See ArtScroll Ashkenaz *Siddur* p. 654.

62. Ibid. The reason is that some *Poskim* rule that the *eruv* is not valid without this declaration.

63. Ibid.

64. *Shulchan Aruch* (*Orach Chaim* 548:5).

65. *Chiddushim U'Viurim*, by the *gaon* R' Zalman Margolios §9.

66. *Sha'arei Teshuvah* (*Orach Chaim* 548:§§4), citing *Shevus Yaakov*.

have non-Jews perform the burial that day, the status of *aninus* takes effect, and one is exempt from hearing the *shofar* and from the other *mitzvos*.[67]

If one has completed all the preparations for burial and has given over the deceased to the *chevra kaddisha*, the *aninus* ceases, even if the *chevra kaddisha* has not yet removed the deceased from the home. Once the *aninus* ceases, one is obligated by the *mitzvah* of *shofar*, as well as the other *mitzvos*.[68] (Regarding whether the *aninus* ceases if the family members plan to accompany the deceased to the cemetery, see below, par. 53.)

If one heard the *shofar* blown while he was an *onen*, he should hear it again after the *aninus* ceases, but should not recite the accompanying blessings.[69]

If one does not want to have non-Jews perform the burial that day, *aninus* does not take effect, and one is obligated by all the *mitzvos* of the Torah.[70]

On the second day of Rosh Hashanah, if it is possible to perform the burial, *aninus* does take effect, even if one does not want to perform burial that day.

If, due to circumstances beyond one's control, he is unable to perform the burial, *aninus* does not take effect.

In those communities where the custom is not to perform burials even on the second day of Rosh Hashanah, the laws of *aninus* do not take effect.[71]

◆§ Yom Kippur

31. If the death occurs on Yom Kippur, *aninus* does not take effect. One is obligated to perform all the *mitzvos*.[72]

◆§ Succos

32. The *onen* is exempt from the *mitzvah* of the *succah*. He is therefore permitted to eat and sleep outside the *succah*.[73] If he does eat in the *succah*, he does so without reciting any blessings.

On the first night of the Festival, if the burial is not planned for that night, he is obligated by the *mitzvah* of dwelling in the *succah*, as well as all other *mitzvos*. The same applies for the daytime of the first day of *Yom Tov* if burial is not planned for then. Regarding the Diaspora's second day of *Yom Tov*, see above, par. 26. However, it is desirable that someone else should recite *Kiddush* and the blessing ["...and commanded us to dwell in the *succah*"], and the *onen* should fulfill the *mitzvah* of these blessings through the other person's recitation. If there is no one else to do so, the *onen* himself may recite these blessings.[74]

---

67. *Mateh Efrayim* (596:7).
68. Ibid. 596:11.
69. *Divrei Malkiel* (§22); *Sdei Chemed* (*Pe'as HaSadeh*, *Aninus*).
70. This is like the *halachah* mentioned above, par. 26.
71. This is like the *halachah* mentioned above, end of par. 26.
72. *Shulchan Aruch* (*Orach Chaim* 526:3) states that on the Sabbath or Yom Kippur one may not engage in caring for the needs of the deceased.
73. *Mishnah Berurah* (640:§§31), citing *Bikurei Yaakov*. And see *Sha'ar HaTziyun* there §§48.
74. *Gesher HaChaim* (18:2:11).

◄ᔄ Chanukah

33. The *onen* should not kindle the Chanukah lights himself. Instead, his wife or someone else should light on his behalf. The one who lights should recite the accompanying blessings.[75] As to whether the *onen* is permitted to respond *Amen*, there are differing opinions among the halachic authorities.[76] If there is no one to light for him, he should light for himself, but without reciting the blessings.[77]

◄ᔄ Purim

34. On Purim, the *onen* is permitted to eat meat and drink wine.[78] Some rule that he is also allowed to recite blessings for eating and drinking at the Purim feast.[79]

The permission to eat meat and drink wine applies only during Purim day, not Purim night.[80]

For those living in "unwalled cities," the permission does not apply on the fifteenth of Adar. For those living in "walled cities," the permission does not apply on the fourteenth of Adar.[81]

35. On Purim night, if the burial is not planned for that night, the *onen* should hear someone else read the *Megillah* (Scroll of Esther) [but should not read it himself].[82] Some rule that if there is no one else available to perform the *Megillah*-reading, the *onen* is permitted to do so. But in that case, someone else should recite the accompanying blessings.[83] [If the burial is planned for Purim night, he need not hear the *Megillah*-reading until after the burial.]

---

75. *Elyah Rabbah* (*Orach Chaim* 670:3).

76. *Mishnah Berurah* (670:§§12).

77. *Pri Megaddim* (*Orach Chaim* §670 in *Mishbetzos Zahav* §§5) writes: "It would seem that if his wife is not with him and he is alone, he should kindle the lights for the sake of publicizing the miracle (*pirsumei nissa*), but without reciting a blessing." This ruling is cited by *Mishnah Berurah* there.

78. *Shulchan Aruch* (*Orach Chaim* §696:7).

79. *Chochmas Adam* (*Kuntres Matzeivas Moshe* §1).

80. *Mishnah Berurah* (696:§§24).

81. *Sha'ar HaTziyun* (696:§§28).

82. *Rama* (*Orach Chaim* 696:7) writes: "All the more so, he is obligated by the *mitzvos* of the *Megillah*-reading, prayer, and the recitation of the *Shema*." However, *Kaf HaChaim* (696:§§46) writes: "Some authorities express reservations about *Rama*'s ruling that the *onen* is obligated to hear the *Megillah*-reading at night; for there is even a dispute [among the *Poskim*] as to whether the *onen* is obligated by the *mitzvos* on the night of the Diaspora's second day of *Yom Tov*, as we have written above 548:§§23. All the more so, [there is doubt] regarding Purim night, since the main *mitzvah* of rejoicing on Purim is only in the daytime. Therefore *Derech HaChaim* (§1) writes that on Purim, on the night of the fourteenth [of Adar], the *onen* should go to the synagogue to hear someone else read the *Megillah*" [but should not read it himself]. The same ruling — that the *onen* should hear someone else read the *Megillah* — is given by *Kitzur Shulchan Aruch* (141:21) and *Mishnah Berurah* (696:§§25).

83. *Gesher HaChaim* (18:12:15). But *Kol Bo Al Aveilus* (2:2:18) writes: "On Purim night, the *onen* should go to the synagogue and pray, and he is obligated by the *mitzvah* of the *Megillah*-reading — that is, he should hear [the *Megillah* read] by someone else [but he should not read it himself]; and,

36. Some rule that on Purim night the *onen* is obligated to recite the *Shema* and to pray.[84]

If it is possible to perform the burial during the day, it should be performed before the *Megillah*-reading.[85]

If the *onen* heard the reading in public before the burial, he should hear it again, after the burial, without reciting the blessings.[86]

Some rule that the *onen* should not put on *tefillin* during the entire day of Purim, even after the burial.[87]

◆§ Pesach and the *Omer*-count

37. On the eve of the fourteenth of Nissan, the *onen* is exempt from searching his home for *chametz*. Instead, he should ask someone else to perform the search for him, and that person should recite the blessing (". . .and commanded us concerning the removal of *chametz*"). However, the *onen* himself should recite the nullification (*bitul*) of *chametz*.[88] If there is no one else to perform the search for *chametz*, the *onen* may do so himself, but without reciting the blessing.[89]

38. On Pesach night, if the burial is planned for that night, the *onen* is exempt from all the *mitzvos* of the *Seder*.

If the burial is not planned for that night, the *onen* is obligated to eat *matzah* and *marror* and to drink the Four Cups. However, he should hear someone else recite *Kiddush*; the blessings over *matzah*, *marror*, and the Four Cups; the *Haggadah*; and the blessing at the end of the *Haggadah*. The other person should have in mind to fulfill the *mitzvah* of these recitations on behalf of the *onen*.[90]

---

all the more so, he should not be the one who performs the public *Megillah*-reading to fulfill the obligation of the congregation."

84. *Rama* (*Orach Chaim* 696:7). See *Magen Avraham* there.

85. *Rama* (loc. cit.).

86. *Magen Avraham* (696:§§16).

87. Ibid.

88. [See ArtScroll Ashkenaz *Siddur* p 654.] *Chiddushim U'Viurim*, by the *gaon* R' Zalman Margolios §8. He writes there, in his *Biurim*: "As regards nullifying *chametz* in his usual manner, as he does every year before Pesach, obviously this is permitted, since it involves no effort at all on his part." See also *Gesher HaChaim* (18:2:13), who writes: "And the following [morning], when it is time to nullify [*chametz* again], even if he is still in *aninus* he should nullify the *chametz*."

Pri Megaddim, in his General Introduction to *Orach Chaim* (part II: 8:28), states that the *onen* is not obligated by the prohibition against having *chametz* in one's possession on the day before Pesach after midday, nor is he obligated by this prohibition during *Chol HaMo'ed*. However, this ruling has been challenged by *Sheivet Yehudah*, and by *Orchos Chaim* (§431) et al.

89. *Da'as Torah* (*Orach Chaim* §431).

90. See *Drishah*, *Taz*, and *Shach* on *Yoreh De'ah* §341. *Magen Avraham* (*Orach Chaim* 548:§§8) states that also on the night of the Diaspora's second day of *Yom Tov*, the *onen* is obligated by all the *mitzvos* [if the burial is not planned for that night], and this ruling is cited by *Mishnah Berurah* (§548, §§19). But see also *Chiddushim U'Viurim*, by the *gaon* R' Zalman Margolios (§22), who writes: "On the first night of *Yom Tov*, one should not observe *aninus* at all. And the same applies even on the

If it is impossible to hear someone else recite them, the *onen* himself should recite *Kiddush*, the blessings, and the *Haggadah*.[91]

39. Since he can recite *Kiddush*, in the case just mentioned, when no one is able to recite *Kiddush* for him, he is also obligated to recite the *Shema*, the Evening Prayer, Grace After Meals, and the like. However, he should not perform the *mitzvah* of *heseibah* (leaning on the left side).[92] He also should be strict and not eat meat nor drink wine, except for the wine of *Kiddush* and the Four Cups if burial will take place on *Yom Tov*.[93]

40. If one becomes an onen during the *Omer*-count, and therefore did not count at night, he should count the next day, after the burial, without reciting the accompanying blessing. [For example, if death occurred on Monday, and burial on Tuesday, he would miss counting on Monday night. Therefore he should count on Tuesday during the daytime after the burial, but without reciting the blessing.] Then, during the remaining days of the *Omer*-count, he should continue counting with the blessing.[94]

If he knows that the burial will not take place that day [in our example, Tuesday], as in a case where the cemetery is far away, he should count that night [in our example, Monday night] without reciting the blessing. [The same applies every night until the burial.] Then, [after the burial], for the remaining days of the *Omer*-count, he can count with the blessing.[95]

If he missed the count altogether that entire day [in our example, if he did not count until Tuesday night], he should count the remaining days, but without reciting the blessing.

Diaspora's second night of *Yom Tov*, in communities where the custom is that even on the Diaspora's second day of *Yom Tov* the burial may be performed only by non-Jews."

91. Regarding *Kiddush*, see *Magen Avraham* (loc. cit.). Regarding the recitation of the *Haggadah*, see *Pri Megaddim* (*Mishbetzos Zahav* §480).

92. *Gesher HaChaim* (18:2:12).

93. Ibid.

94. *Chiddushim U'Viurim*, by the *gaon* R' Zalman Margolios §31. *Be'ur Halachah* (§489), in the name of *Nehar Shalom*, explains that this is not similar to the *halachah* regarding prayer, where the *onen* need not make up for the missed prayer (see below, 13:16). There, during the time of obligation for that particular prayer, the *onen* was exempt from all *mitzvos*. Here (regarding the *Omer*-count), some *Poskim* rule that the obligation lasts throughout the entire twenty-four-hour day. According to them, the time of obligation for counting the *Omer* will still be in effect after the interment. Therefore one should count it. However, some *Poskim* disagree that the obligation lasts throughout the whole twenty-four-hour day. According to them, the obligation is only at night. Therefore, in consideration of their opinion, one does not recite the blessing.

95. See *Pischei Teshuvah* (*Yoreh De'ah* 341:6). He cites responsa *Noda BiYehudah* (*mahadura tinyana* §67), who discusses the case where the person will remain an *onen* until the following night [i.e., he will remain an *onen* for at least a night and the whole following day]. Hence, if he does not count at night or sometime during the following day], he will not be able to recite the blessing during the remainder of the *Omer*-count [since he will have missed an entire day of the count]. *Noda BiYehudah* rules that in such a case he should count at night without reciting the blessing. Then he will be able to recite the blessing during the remaining days.

◅§ Rosh Chodesh

41. Some rule that if the death occurred on Rosh Chodesh, one should recite the
Mussaf (Additional) Prayer after the burial, even if the burial took place after
midday (*chatzos hayom*).[96]

◅§ Tishah B'Av

42. On Tishah B'Av, until after the burial, the *onen* must stay in his home. He
should not recite *Kinos* (the special lamentations for this fast-day).[97] He is
required to fast.[98]

After the burial, during the day, some rule that he is permitted to go and sit in the
synagogue [for the Tishah B'Av services].[99]

◅§ Slaughtering, Circumcision, and *Pidyon HaBen*

43. Some rule that the *onen* is permitted to ritually slaughter animals, but without
reciting the accompanying blessing.[100] Others rule that this is permitted only
under pressing circumstances.[101]

44. If the *onen* is a *mohel*, but another *mohel* is available, the *onen* should not
perform a *bris milah* (circumcision).

If no other *mohel* is available, the *onen* should make an effort to perform the
burial before the circumcision.[102]

If it is impossible to complete the burial that day, he should transfer the deceased
to the *chevra kadisha* (burial society), and then perform the circumcision. If this,
too, is impossible, the *onen* should perform the circumcision, but the father or
sandak should recite the accompanying blessings.[103]

---

96. See below, 13:17.

97. *Mishnah Berurah* (559:§§24).

98. The fast is required, because it is a negative commandment mentioned in the Prophets (*divrei
kabbalah*).

99. *Elyah Rabbah* (*Orach Chaim* 559:§§18) cites *Mahar'ak* as ruling that during the day on Tishah
B'Av, the *onen* remains in the synagogue until the recitation of *Kinos* is completed. *Elyah Rabbah*
adds: "It seems to me that this is applicable only after the burial; and this is what I instructed [in an actual
case]." And see *Mishnah Berurah* (§559 §§24) and *Sha'ar HaTziyun* there (§§22), which states that
this ruling is only in accord with those who rule leniently regarding a mourner [allowing him to go to the
synagogue on Tishah B'Av] during the first three days of mourning. According to this lenient opinion,
the leniency to enter the synagogue and remain there until *Kinos* are completed applies even to the
person whose deceased has been buried that same day. However, there are those who rule stringently
regarding a mourner, forbidding him to go to the synagogue on Tishah B'Av during the first three days
of mourning. They would certainly rule that on the day of burial, which is the first day of mourning and
is called "a bitter day," he certainly is forbidden to enter the synagogue.

100. The *gaon* R' Akiva Eiger, *Kesavim* (responsum §12).

101. *Hagahos Yad Shaul* (*Yoreh De'ah* §341).

102. Responsa *Chasam Sofer*, *Choshen Mishpat* §39.

103. Responsa *Yehudah Ya'aleh* (§356).

45. If the *onen*'s son is to be circumcised that day, the *onen* should make an effort to perform the burial before the circumcision.[104]

If this is impossible, the circumcision should be performed in the morning, with the *sandak* reciting the accompanying blessings.[105] This applies even if the circumcision is not on the eighth day from birth,[106] or if the *onen* is both the *mohel* and the father of the baby.[107]

If the burial took place in the morning, the circumcision should be performed immediately after the burial. The *shivah* begins after the circumcision.[108]

46. If the person designated as *sandak* becomes an *onen*, he may serve as *sandak* if the burial is completed before the circumcision; or at least if the body has been transferred to the *chevra kaddisha* before the circumcision. But if the body has not been transferred to the *chevra kadisha*, the *onen* is not permitted to serve as *sandak*, even if others are willing to care for the needs of the deceased. This applies, all the more so, if the *aninus* is for one's parent. However [even in the latter case], if there is no one else available who is fit to serve as *sandak*, the *onen* may do so.[109]

47. One authority writes that if a father becomes an *onen* on the day of his son's *pidyon haben* (Redemption of the Firstborn), he should make an effort to perform the burial first, and then the *pidyon haben*. But if it is impossible to perform the burial that day, the *pidyon haben* should be postponed until after the burial.[110]

48. If the *pidyon haben* is on the thirty-first day from birth, the officiating *kohen* should not be an *onen*, unless no other *kohen* is available. In that case, the *onen* may serve as officiating *kohen*, but should not recite the blessing over the wine.[111]

◄§ Who Is Subject to the Laws of *Aninus*?

49. The laws of *aninus* apply to both men and women. In the words of *Rosh*:
"Whoever is subject to the laws of mourning is also subject to the laws of *aninus*."[112]

---

104. *Taz* (*Yoreh De'ah* 341:§§30).
105. Ibid.
106. *Pischei Teshuvah* (*Yoreh De'ah* 341:§§20).
107. Responsa *Chasam Sofer* (*Choshen Mishpat* §39).
108. *Kol Bo Al Aveilus*, citing *Sha'arei De'ah* (§341).
109. *Chiddushim U'Viurim*, by the gaon R' Zalman Margolios §11.
110. *Gesher HaChaim* (18:2:18).
111. Responsa *Yehudah Ya'aleh* (*Yoreh De'ah* §356).
112. According to responsa *Yavetz* (part I:§65), since a wife is financially subordinate to her husband, the responsibility for arranging the burial does not fall upon her, but upon the people of the town. Since she is not occupied with arranging the burial, the status of *aninus* would not apply to her. However, most of the *Poskim* rule that the reason for exempting the *onen* from all *mitzvos* is in order to show respect for the deceased. Therefore, a woman is also subject to the laws of *aninus*. See *Gesher HaChaim* (18:3:1) and *Kol Bo Al Aveilus* (2:1:3).

50. A boy under the age of thirteen and a girl under the age of twelve are not subject to the laws of *aninus*, even if they have reached the age when they should be trained in the *mitzvos* (*gil chinuch*).[113] Therefore they are even permitted to eat meat and drink wine.[114] Moreover, an adult *onen* is allowed to feed them meat and wine.[115]

If they come of age during the period of the *aninus*, they are subject to all the laws of *aninus*.[116]

51. For an aborted fetus or stillbirth, *aninus* does not apply.

If one's child died within thirty days of birth, *aninus* does not apply.[117] Nevertheless, one should be strict and not eat meat nor drink wine until after the burial.[118]

52. If a father had commanded that only one of his sons should arrange his burial, and the other sons should not occupy themselves with the burial at all, nevertheless the obligation of *aninus* applies to all the sons, and they are exempt from all the *mitzvos* of the Torah.[119]

◦§ When Does *Aninus* Cease?

53. According to the basic *halachah*, once the *onenim* have completed all the arrangements for burial and have given over the deceased to the *chevra kaddisha*, *aninus* ceases, even if the deceased is still in the home. Even so, the laws

---

113. They are not subject to the laws of *aninus*, because they are not subject to the laws of mourning.

See *Kol Bo Al Aveilus* (2:3:19), who refers to the statement of *Magen Avraham* (343:§§8) that only the father is obligated to train the children in *mitzvos*. According to this, says *Kol Bo Al Aveilus*, the concept of *chinuch* (training) could not arise in connection with *aninus*. For if the father dies, the mother is not obligated to train the children. And if the mother dies, the father is an *onen* and therefore is forbidden to fulfill the *mitzvos*, including the *mitzvah* of training. But it would seem that [despite the reasoning of *Kol Bo Al Aveilus*] the concept of *chinuch* could arise in connection with *aninus*, namely, if the mother died after being divorced from the father. In that case, the father would not be an *onen*.

114. *Sdei Chemed* (*Aninus* §14).

115. Ibid. §13.

116. *Kol Bo Al Aveilus* (loc. cit.).

117. *Yerushalmi* (*Yevamos*, *Perek Nosin*, *halachah* 7); and see the commentaries of *Pnei Moshe* and *Korban HaEidah* there.

118. *Chiddushei R' Akiva Eiger* (§341); and *Pischei Teshuvah* (ad loc. §§1). These authorities both cite *Tiferes LeMoshe*, who writes that further study is needed to determine the *halachah* regarding a child that died within thirty days of birth. In such a case, and in the case of an aborted fetus or a child born in the *eighth month of pregnancy*, the laws of mourning do not apply. Nevertheless, it might be that [the parents or other family members] are forbidden to eat meat or drink wine until burial is completed, since they must make arrangements for burial. *Tiferes LeMoshe* concludes: "It would seem that in the case of a child that died within thirty days of birth, one should be strict [and refrain from meat and wine], since the majority of such children are viable. [And if one should ask: If the majority are viable, why don't the laws of mourning apply? The answer is:] Nevertheless, regarding mourning we are lenient" [and assume that the child was not viable, unless there is positive proof to the contrary (see below, 15:7)].

119. *Sdei Chemed* (*Aninus* §25).

of the seven days of mourning (shivah) do not apply [until the grave is filled with earth].[120]

Once aninus ceases, one is permitted to eat meat and drink wine, and is obligated to perform all the mitzvos.[121]

However, if the family members plan to accompany the deceased to burial, giving him over to the chevra kaddisha does not end the aninus. In that case, aninus ends only when the grave is filled with earth.[122] Nevertheless, once the deceased has been given over to the chevra kaddisha, the onenim are permitted to be strict with themselves if they wish, i.e., to recite the Shema and pray.[123]

⋖§ If the *Onen* Is in a Different City

54. Under the following *combination of circumstances*, some rule that the laws of aninus do not apply:

(a) The family member is not in the same city as the deceased; *and*

(b) he does not plan to go there to attend the burial; *and*

(c) there is someone with the deceased to care for the burial and the other needs of the deceased.

Since, in this *combination of circumstances,* the laws of aninus do not apply, the family member is permitted to eat meat and drink wine. He is obligated by all the mitzvos of the Torah, except for wearing *tefillin* on the first day (see below, 13:2-11).[123a]

---

120. *Shulchan Aruch (Yoreh De'ah* 341:3), *Shach* (ad loc. §§13).

121. *Shulchan Aruch* (loc. cit.) and *Dagul MeiRevavah* (ad loc.).

122. *Pischei Teshuvah* (341:§§21), citing *Noda BiYehudah*.

123. See *Gesher HaChaim* (18:2:21).

123a. See *Tosafos* (on *Brachos* 18a s.v. *ve'eino*), who writes: "It occurred that the sister of Rabbeinu
    Tam died on the Sabbath, and after the Sabbath he was informed, while in a different city [from
where she died]. He ate meat and drank wine, and said that since she had a husband who was obligated
to see to her burial, he (Rabbeinu Tam) was not forbidden to eat meat and drink wine. Possibly, even
if he had been in the same city [where she died], Rabbeinu Tam would have been lenient [permitting
himself to eat meat and drink wine], for the same reason" [i.e., that her husband was responsible for her
burial].
    However, *Rosh* there (§3) objects: "If so, no one except sons would ever observe aninus — neither
the father [of the deceased] nor his brother. But the wording of the *Gemara* implies the contrary: that
whoever is obligated to mourn is also obligated to observe aninus." The same ruling is given by *Tur*
(*Yoreh De'ah* §341), who defines onenim] as "all family members who [are required to] mourn." See
Beis Yosef there. This is also the ruling of *Shulchan Aruch* there (par. 1).
    However, *Bach* there writes: "To explain the opinion of Rabbeinu Tam, I suggest that had he been
in the same city with her, he would have been forbidden to eat meat and drink wine, since the obligation
of arranging the burial applies to all [the family members]. . .but since [Rabbeinu Tam] was in a different
city, and her husband was with her, under that circumstance [Rabbeinu Tam] was not obligated to
arrange the burial, since her husband was there to care for her."
    See also *Shach* there (§§5), who writes: "However, *Bach* rules like Rabbeinu Tam — that the laws
of aninus do not apply to family members who are in a different city, unless the deceased has no family
in his own city who are obligated to arrange his burial and to mourn for him."
    However, *Kaf HaChaim* (*Orach Chaim* 71:§§2) writes [that the laws of aninus apply] "even if [the

In this case, the family member immediately begins *shivah*, even if the burial will not take place until the next day [or later].

Others rule that he does not begin *shivah* until the time of burial.[124]

If he travels to the city where the deceased is, he becomes subject to the laws of *aninus* as soon as he reaches that city, even if others — and not he— are caring for the needs of the deceased and he is not doing so.[125]

◂§ Interment in a Different City; Beginning of *Shivah*

55. If the death occurred in the city where the family members are located, but they are taking the deceased to a different city for burial, the *halachah* depends on how far away the place of burial is. If it is nearby, the family members are *onenim* from the time of death until the grave is filled with earth. But if it is far away — for example, two days' journey — *aninus* does not begin until they arrive with the deceased at the city of burial.[126]

If the deceased is taken to a distant city for burial, and a family member does not go along with him, but only accompanies him to the edge of the city in which the death occurred or to the airport, then his *aninus* ceases, and *shivah* begins, as soon as the deceased is taken out of the city and the family member takes leave and returns home. (See below, 12:6.)

The count of the first seven days of mourning sometimes depends upon the location of the leading member of the bereaved family (*gedol habayis*). [For the explanation of this law, see below, 12:7.] If the *gedol habayis* accompanies the deceased to the distant place of burial, and will stay there during the *shivah*, then even those who remained at home do not begin the *shivah* until the completion of the burial.[127] In this case, during the days before the burial [once the deceased is taken out of the city,] those who remained at home are subject neither to the laws of *aninus* nor to the laws of mourning (*aveilus*). Therefore they are permitted to eat meat and drink wine, and are obligated by all the *mitzvos* of the Torah. However, they are subject to the inconspicuous restrictions (*devarim shebetzin'a*). Therefore

---

family member] is in a different city, provided he was informed before the burial. . . and this is the ruling to be followed, in accord with [*Shulchan Aruch*], contrary to the ruling of *Bach*, who permits [eating meat and drinking wine if the family member is in a different city from the deceased]. The same [prohibitive] ruling is given by *Ma'amar Mordechai* (§1); see also his refutation of *Bach* and *Pri Chadash*." This [prohibitive] ruling is also given by *Shulchan Aruch HaRav* (*Orach Chaim* 71:1) and *Aruch HaShulchan* (341:12).

On the other hand, the following authorities adopt the ruling of *Bach* in accord with Rabbeinu Tam, namely, that the laws of *aninus* do not apply to a family member in a different city from the deceased: *Pri Chadash* (*Orach Chaim* §71); *She'eilas Yavetz* (part II: §125); and *Kitzur Shulchan Aruch* (196:4). *Chochmas Adam* (153:2) cites the two conflicting opinions and concludes that *Shach* (§§5) follows the lenient ruling. And this is also the ruling adopted by *Gesher HaChaim* (18:1:5-6).

124. For a detailed discussion of when mourning begins, see below, 12:11.

125. *Pri Chadash* (*Orach Chaim* §71).

126. *Rama* (*Yoreh De'ah* 348:3).

127. See below 12:7,8.

they are forbidden to sit on a chair or bed, or sleep on a bed,[128] and also are forbidden to have marital relations, to bathe, to put oils or lotions on themselves, to attend celebrations, and to exchange greetings (see below, chapters 19, 20, 21 and 25).[129]

56. If the death occurred in another city, but the deceased is being brought for burial to the city where the family member is located, and will arrive in a few days, the family member is not an *onen* prior to the arrival of the deceased. Therefore he is permitted to eat meat and drink wine, and is obligated by all the *mitzvos* of the Torah. However, he is subject to the inconspicuous restrictions (*devarim shebetzin'a*) mentioned at the end of the previous paragraph. But during any period of time that he is actually preoccupied with arranging the funeral and burial, he is exempt from other *mitzvos*.

Once the body arrives at the family member's city, the family member becomes an *onen* until the grave is filled with earth.[130]

◆§ Government-Mandated Waiting Period

57. In a situation where the government prevents people from interring until after a certain number of days elapse, some rule that the family members are considered *onenim* during those days.

Others rule that during the period between death and interment they are obligated by all the *mitzvos* of the Torah.[131] However, they are subject to

---

128. See above, par. 5, where we note that many have the custom to be lenient on this point.

129. *Derech HaChaim*. He states that these prohibitions apply in every case where, following the death, there is an interim during which one is subject neither to the laws of *aninus* nor to the laws of mourning.

130. I heard this ruling from major contemporary *Poskim*.

131. There are many different rulings on this subject. I shall summarize some of them:

    (a) *Noda BiYehudah* (*Yoreh De'ah* §211, cited by *Pischei Teshuvah* 341:§§22) rules that the laws of *aninus* apply during the days when burial is governmentally forbidden. The same ruling is given by the *gaon* R' Yaakov of Lisa in his prayerbook (s.v. *onen* §11). He states that if the deceased is in the hands of the family, and has not been seized by the government, the laws of *aninus* apply, even though the government does not permit burial [for a certain number of days].

    (b) *Tiferes Yisrael* (*Berachos* 3:2) writes: "It seems to me that in this country, where the law of the land forbids burial within three days of death, [the family members] are obligated by all the *mitzvos* of the Torah during the days between death and burial — especially when there are other people who are attending to the needs of the burial; for some rule that in this case [i.e., when others are attending to the burial], the family member is permitted to be strict with himself [and perform *mitzvos*] if he wishes." The same ruling is given by R' M. Bennet in his commentary on *Mordechai*. He considers it obvious that in such a case [i.e., when the government forbids burial for a certain number of days] we rule leniently, that is, we do not apply the laws of *aninus*. [This is a leniency in that the family members may eat meat and drink wine, and are exempt from the other restrictions mentioned above, paragraphs 4 and 5.] This [that *aninus* does not apply in such a case] is also the ruling of R' M. Teitelbaum in his *Hagahos* on *Yoreh De'ah*. He further states that the family members are required to put on *tefillin*.

the inconspicuous restrictions (*devarim shebetzin'a*; see end of par. 55).[132]

◄§ Missing Bodies

58. If a person was killed in a distant land, or in combat [and the body has not been returned], or was dragged off by a wild animal, or drowned in a river, and the like, the family members are subject neither to the laws of *aninus* nor to the laws of mourning (*aveilus*) as long as they have not given up hope of finding and burying the body. This applies even if some of the limbs are found, as long as the head and most of the body have not been found, and they have not given up hope of finding them.

On the day they give up hope of finding and burying the body, they are required to tear their garment (perform *kri'ah*; see below, chapt. 6), and to begin observing *shivah* and *shloshim*. This applies even if they do not give up hope until more than thirty days after the death.

If the body is found after they had given up hope, the same *halachos* apply as for reinterment (*likut atzamos*); i.e., they observe mourning only on the day the body is buried (see below, chapt. 45).[133]

(c) In his responsa *Yehudah Ya'aleh* (*Yoreh De'ah* §370), the *gaon* R' Yehudah Asad writes: "In view of the government regulation that burial may not be performed until two days [after death], what should the *onen* do regarding prayer and blessings? I have already discussed this in another responsum (*Orach Chaim* §14), where I conclude that, as regards *tefillin*, he is subject to circumstances beyond his control, and is forbidden to put them on during the whole time [that he is an *onen*; see below, chapt. 13]. On the other hand, he is obligated to recite the *Shema*, pray, recite blessings, and perform all other *mitzvos*, in accord with the ruling of *Magen Avraham* (*Orach Chaim* §548), that if burial is impossible due to circumstances beyond his control, *aninus* does not apply."

(d) *Chasam Sofer* and *Maharam* Shick (*Yoreh De'ah* §340) discuss a situation where the government forbids burial for forty-eight hours after death. They rule that the family member may not put on *tefillin* [see below, chapt. 13]. On the first day [the day of death], which is not the day of burial, he is permitted to perform all other *mitzvos*; for, they state [the *onen*'s exemption from *mitzvos* is in order to show respect for the deceased; but in the usual case of *aninus*, the exemption lasts only one day]. It is unreasonable to say that refraining from all *mitzvos* for two days is a proper sign of respect for the deceased. [Accordingly, on the day after death, which is the day of burial, the *onen* in such a case is exempt from all *mitzvos*.] And see *Maharam* Shick, *Even HaEzer* §102.

(e) The *gaon* R' Yosef Shaul in *Yosef Da'as* (§341) rules that on the first day, *aninus* applies. However, on the second day, unless it is the day of burial, the family member is obligated to put on *tefillin* and perform all other *mitzvos*, since he has already shown respect for the deceased by not performing *mitzvos* on the first day. R' Yosef Shaul adds that the requirement to perform *mitzvos* on the second day is especially logical if other people are seeing to the needs of the deceased. [See also the *gaon* R' Shlomo Kluger, in *Tuv Ta'am VeDa'as* (part III:§201).]

132. These are the same inconspicuous restrictions mentioned in the previous two paragraphs.

133. *Chazon Ish* (*Yoreh De'ah* §213a) mentions that there is a dispute between *Rosh* and *Maharam* of Rotenburg regarding reinterment (*likut atzamos*). [*Maharam* of Rotenburg rules that *aninus* applies, while *Rosh* rules that there is no *aninus* in the case of reinterment.] In our case, however, states *Chazon Ish*, it is logical to assume that *Rosh* would agree that *aninus* applies; for, regarding this deceased, there had never yet been a period of *aninus*, and he had never yet been buried. "And, just

✺ Accompanying Family Member

59. If a family member is accompanying the deceased on a ship, airplane, or auto,
he is subject to all the laws of *aninus* and is therefore exempt from all the
mitzvos of the Torah. This applies even if there are others who are watching over
the deceased.[134]

However, one authority states that this *halachah* requires study: It may be that it
applies only if the deceased is actually in the presence of the family member.[135]

✺ Death in Prison

60. If a person dies in prison and the authorities will not release the body to the
family for burial until they pay a sum of money, the family members are subject
neither to the laws of *aninus* nor to the laws of mourning (*aveilus*) [until burial
becomes possible].[136] But if the authorities do not permit burial at all, *aninus* is
canceled and the family members are immediately subject to *shivah* and the laws of
mourning.[137]

Similarly, if the family members are in prison and it is impossible for them to
attend to the burial, the laws of *aninus* do not apply to them.[138]

---

because he had not been found until now, does this in any way weaken the obligation to arrange
burial?"

For a detailed discussion of the laws of mourning in a case where the body is not found immediately,
see below, 13:14 and 15.

134. *Chiddushim U'Viurim*, by the *gaon* R' Zalman Margolios §26.

135. The *gaon* R' Shlomo Zalman Auerbach, in his remarks on *P'nei Baruch: Bikur Cholim
Kehilchaso*.

136. The laws of mourning do not apply, because the family has not given up hope of performing
burial (*Shulchan Aruch*, *Yoreh De'ah* 341:4). *Shach* there (§§15) adds that even if the
authorities demand a large sum of money, the laws of mourning do not yet apply. This is because the
matter nevertheless is a financial one, and the authorities may in the end settle for a smaller sum.

137. *Shulchan Aruch* (loc. cit.), and *Shach* (ad loc. §§15).

138. *Shulchan Aruch* (loc. cit.).

CHAPTER SIX

Kri'ah: Rending the Garment

✦§ The Family of the Deceased

1. One must perform *kri'ah* (rend one's garment) upon the death of any of the family members for whom one is obligated to mourn.[1] These are:

(a) father; (b) mother; (c) brother; (d) sister; (e) son; (f) daughter; (g) wife; (h) husband.

"Brother" and "sister" include a half-brother or half-sister on the side of either one's father or one's mother.

The obligation of *kri'ah* is a Rabbinic institution (*deRabbanan*). One who knowingly refuses to perform this *mitzvah* is liable to death at the hands of Heaven.[2]

---

1. *Shulchan Aruch, Yoreh De'ah* 340:1 and 374:4. Regarding the reason for performing *kri'ah*, some write that it is in order to arouse weeping and increase the mourner's grief (*Beis Yehudah, Yoreh De'ah* §26, cited in *Menachem Aveilim os kuf*, §6).

Others write that the purpose is to prevent the mourner from losing his self-control in the face of his great tragedy; for a person becomes overwhelmed when a member of his family dies. The *kri'ah* hence comes to take his mind off the death by diverting his attention to the financial loss involved in tearing his garment (*Menachem Aveilim*, loc. cit., quoting responsa *Halachos Ketanos* §116).

Some also attribute spiritual meanings to the *kri'ah*. One of these is that the body is like a garment for the soul, and death is like tearing the garment (*Gesher HaChaim* 4:1, citing *Zohar, Noach* 66 and *Zohar, Beha'aloscha*).

2. *Mo'ed Katan* 24. "R' Tachlifa bar Avimi quoted Shmuel: A mourner who does not let his hair grow and does not rend his garment is liable to death at the hands of Heaven, as it is said (*Leviticus* 10:6): *'Do not leave your head unshorn, and do not rend your garments that you not die'*. From this it may be inferred that someone else who did not let his hair grow and did not tear his garments would be liable to death." ["Someone else" means someone other than Aaron and his sons; they were not allowed to show signs of mourning because of the special circumstances of the dedication of the Tabernacle.]

Ravad (cited by *Rosh* and *Ramban*) holds that this death penalty is of Scriptural (*d'Oraysa*) standing. However, *Tosafos* (*Mo'ed Katan* 24, s.v. הא אחר) write: "It would seem that [the Talmud's reference to the verse] is only an *asmachta* [allusive support from the verse, but not a legally binding exegesis], since it [this death penalty] is not included in the list of death penalties at the end of Chapter 'HaNisrafin' " (*Sanhedrin* 83a). *Ramban* writes the same in *Toras HaAdam*. He adds: "The death penalty referred to by the Talmud is related to the concept that one who violates the command of the Sages is liable to the death penalty." *Rosh* writes the same on *Mo'ed Katan* 3:3: "The death penalty referred to is a Rabbinic one, as in the statement, 'Wherever the Sages cast their glance [in disapproval, the result is] either death or poverty.' And the source for the concept of a Rabbinic death penalty is found in *Avodah Zarah* 27b, citing *Ecclesiastes* 10:8, 'He who breaches a fence — a snake will bite him.' "

◆§ When the Soul Departs *(Yetzias Neshamah)*

2. Anyone (even not a relative) who is present when the soul departs the body *(yetzias neshamah* ; i.e., the moment of death as halachically defined) is required to perform *kri'ah* .[3] This applies whether the deceased is a man, a woman,[4] or even a child, if the child studied *Chumash* [Pentateuch].[5] It applies even if the deceased was not a meticulously observant person *(adam kasher)*[6] — for example, if he *occasionally* committed a transgression because his urges overcame him *(letei'avon)* ,[7] or *occasionally* omitted doing a *mitzvah* because it was too much trouble. However, if he *regularly* committed one or more transgressions, even if only because his urges overcame him, one who is present at the moment of death does not perform *kri'ah* .[8] And all the more so, *kri'ah* is not required if the person was a *mumar* , one who altogether rejected one or more *mitzvos* .[9]

> **Note:** The term *mumar* refers to a person who denies the existence of God ר"ל, or the validity of a *mitzvah*. Such a person is regarded as equivalent to an idolater, and upon his death one does not carry out the practices of mourning.
>
> In recent generations, however, many authorities have ruled that most

---

3. *Shulchan Aruch* (339:4) writes: "When a person is about to die, one is not allowed to leave him, so that his soul will not depart when he is alone." *Taz* comments (§§3): "Because the soul is desolate at the time when it leaves the body." *Rama* adds: "It is a *mitzvah* to stand next to a person when the soul departs, as it is said *(Psalms 49:10-11)*: 'He will live on forever; he will not see Gehinnom; for he saw the wise dying.' "

4. A *baraisa* cited in *Mo'ed Katan* 25 states: "One who is in the presence of the deceased when the soul departs is obligated to perform *kri'ah* . To what may this be compared? To a Torah scroll which is burned up, for which one is obligated to perform *kri'ah* ." *Rashi* explains: "The Torah is called a light, as it is said *(Proverbs 6:23)*: 'A mitzvah is a candle, and Torah is light'. And the soul is called a candle, as it is written (ibid. 20:27): 'Man's soul is the candle of Hashem' " [see footnote 26 below].
   Beis Yosef (§340) writes: "According to this, it is obvious that for a woman, too, one is obligated to perform *kri'ah* ; for the soul is called a candle equally for man or woman. This also fits what is explained in Chapter "*Rabbi Eliezer*" *(Shabbos* 105): 'You will not find even the most insignificant Jew who does not have Torah and *mitzvos* .' A woman is included in *mitzvos* . And she is included in Torah as well, for she must learn how to perform the *mitzvos* by which she is obligated" *(Shulchan Aruch* 340:5).

5. *Shach* 340:§§7, citing *Bach* .

6. This can be inferred from the *Gemara* (loc. cit.), since for an *adam kasher* one must perform *kri'ah* even if one was not present at the time of death *(yetzias neshamah)* .

7. Even if the transgression is so severe that it would incur death at the hands of the human court, one performs *kri'ah* for the person — as long as he was not a *mumar* , and as long as he did not commit the transgression in deliberate defiance, but only through lack of self-control *(letei'avon)* *(Pischei Teshuvah* §§4, citing *Tiferes LeMoshe)* .

8. *Rama* (340:5), and *Shach* §§8. And see our next footnote.

9. *Rama* loc. cit. *Tur* writes in the name of *Maharam* of Rotenburg that one is obligated to perform *kri'ah* for any Jew, except a *mumar* or one who worships an idol. If a person violates every single *mitzvah* of the Torah for the sake of defiance *(lehach'is)* , he is considered the same as a *mumar* . But if a person occasionally committed a transgression because his urges overcame him *(letei'avon)* , or occasionally omitted doing a *mitzvah* because it was too much trouble, one is still obligated to perform *kri'ah* for him, since he did not deny the Torah nor violate it for the sake of defiance.

non-observant Jews do not fall under this category, even though their beliefs and practices would seem to be those of a *mumar*. In this view, non-observant Jews who were raised in secular society and not taught traditional Jewish practice have the halachic status of *anusim* (people who were coerced to transgress), or *tinokos shenishbu* (children who were taken captive and raised in a non-Jewish atmosphere), who are not considered *mumarim*.

Since this is a complex issue for which there is no general rule, a competent halachic authority should be consulted regarding such matters as they apply to mourning practices.

2a. Even if the dying person turned his face away from the onlooker, the latter must still perform *kri'ah*, since the dying person's body was visible to him. However, if the dying person was in a place where the other person could not see him, *kri'ah* is not required, even if they were in the same house.[10]

If one witnessed the moment of death on the Sabbath, there are two opinions among the *Poskim*:

(a) He must perform *kri'ah* on the termination of the Sabbath, as long as the deceased has not been buried; but if he did not do it before the burial, he is exempt.[11]

(b) He is exempt from *kri'ah* on the termination of the Sabbath.[12]

Some rule that in our time a person who was present at the moment of death does not have to perform *kri'ah*.[13]

⋖§ For a Meticulously Observant Person *(Adam Kasher)*

3. For the death of a meticulously observant person *(adam kasher)*,[14] meaning a person who was not suspected of any transgression, nor of neglecting any *mitzvah*,[15] one is obligated to perform *kri'ah*, even if the deceased was not a great

---

10. *Pischei Teshuvah* §§3, citing *Radbaz*.

11. *Tiferes LeMoshe, Yoreh De'ah* §340, cited by *Pischei Teshuvah* §§3.

12. Responsa *Chasam Sofer, Yoreh De'ah* §323. He writes that this is stated clearly in the Talmud: Since he did not perform *kri'ah* at the appropriate time, he does not perform it at all, unless there is a new cause for grief.

13. The reason is that it is of great benefit for the dying person to have someone standing by him when the soul leaves the body. And if people who were present at that moment were required to tear their garment, people would not want to be presen *(Gesher HaChaim* 4:9). The same reason is given in *Eretz HaChaim*, citing *Shulchan Gavoha*. *Kol Bo Al Aveilus* p. 26, citing *Zachor LeAvraham* 3, *Yoreh De'ah alef* §100. *Mishmeres Shalom, yud*:45. [See note 26 below.]

14. *Pischei Teshuvah* §§6, citing *Tiferes LeMoshe*, states that further study is required concerning the question of a meticulously observant woman *(ishah kesherah)*. Must one likewise perform *kri'ah* for her, since this obligation does not depend upon the deceased's having learned Torah? Or does the deceased have to have been someone who studied Torah, but simply does not have to be a great scholar? In the latter case, a woman would not be included, since women are not commanded about Torah study as a *mitzvah* in itself.

15. *Shulchan Aruch* 340:6. *Beis Yosef* there writes: "*Rosh* states in the name of Rabbeinu Meir: 'I do not know the definition of *adam kasher*. But it seems to me that if he did not have a bad reputation,

Torah scholar, and even if one was not present at the moment of death, as long as one was present during the time between death and burial.[16] Regarding recitation of the blessing, *Dayan HaEmes* (". . .the True Judge"), see note.[17]

Others rule that one is not required to perform *kri'ah* for an *adam kasher* unless one was present at the moment of death. However, one is required to cry for him and grieve over him. This more lenient opinion is the accepted practice.[18]

Torah scholars (*talmidei chachamim*) are exempt from performing *kri'ah* for an *adam kasher*.[19]

◄§ For One's Main Torah Teacher

4. For the death of a Torah sage who was capable of giving halachic rulings in every area of Torah, one is required to perform *kri'ah*.[20] This applies on the day one hears of the death, even if burial already took place, as long as the news is heard within the first thirty days from death. If one did not perform *kri'ah* upon hearing of the death, one must do it when attending the eulogy, if this is within the thirty days. Once the thirty days have passed, one does not perform *kri'ah* for the

---

is not suspected of any transgression, and did not omit doing any *mitzvah*, he is called an *adam kasher* even though he is not a great Torah scholar.' "

Bach there, cited by *Shach* §§11, writes: "According to Rabbeinu Yonah, a man of this sort is not called an *adam kasher*, for whom one must perform *kri'ah* even if one was not present at the time of death. [A person is called an *adam kasher* for the purpose of this *halachah*] only if he follows the practice of the fit (*kesherim*), seeking out *mitzvos* of kindness to others (*gemilas chasadim*). This seems also to be the opinion of *Ramban*, and this is the opinion which should be adopted in practice."

16. *Shulchan Aruch* 350:6.

17. *Magen Avraham, Orach Chaim* 223:§§4, writes that one should recite the blessing *Dayan HaEmes*, and all the more so one should recite it for the death of a Torah scholar (*talmid chacham*), since this is in the category of "bad news." *Bach* writes that the common practice is to recite it without using the Name of Hashem (*Shem U'malchus*) — but that this is not correct.

Mishnah Berurah there, §§8, writes: "In any case, for the death of a *talmid chacham* one certainly must sorrow and grieve. . .and certainly recite the blessing, including the Name of Hashem."

18. *Rama* 340:6. This is the opinion of *Hagahos Maimon*, ch.11, citing *Ravyah*. They state that even for an *adam kasher* one need not perform *kri'ah*, unless one was in his presence at the time of death. *Ran* in Chapter "*Rabbi Eliezer*" (*Shabbos* 105b) writes that regarding people who were not present at the death of an *adam kasher*, it could be said that they are required to perform *kri'ah*, and it could be said that they are not required to perform *kri'ah*, but are simply obligated to weep and grieve.

It is noteworthy that *Beis Yosef* there expresses surprise that the common practice is to rely on the opinion that one need not perform *kri'ah* for an *adam kasher*. It is understandable, he says, why learned men act this way — they are relying on the opinion of *Ramban* (see following footnote). However, ordinary people have nothing on which to rely, except for the doubt expressed by *Ran* and the reasoning of *Ravyah*. Clearly, says *Beis Yosef*, these are not sufficient grounds to abandon a ruling which seemed obvious to so many *Poskim*.

19. The reason is that the requirement to perform *kri'ah* is like that of rising for a person to show respect. And it may be inferred from the first chapter of *Kiddushin* (33b) that a Torah scholar need not rise for someone less learned. *Ramban*, cited by *Beis Yosef* loc. cit.

20. *Baraisa, Mo'ed Katan* 25a: "If a sage (*chacham*) dies, everyone is like his relative. . .everyone performs *kri'ah* for him." *Rosh* there cites the *Yerushalmi*: "Just as one performs *kri'ah* for a *chacham*, so one performs *kri'ah* for a *talmid chacham* (Torah scholar). Who is a *talmid chacham*? One who is capable of giving halachic rulings in every area of Torah."

death of a Torah sage.[21]

Some rule that one does not perform *kri'ah* for every sage, but only for the rabbi who taught one the majority of one's Torah knowledge.[22] The practice is to be lenient and follow this second opinion.[22a]

5. Likewise, one is required to perform *kri'ah* on the day when the bones of a family member are gathered [reinterred], just as one performs *kri'ah* for him if he dies. Details of this *halachah* are explained below, 45:4.

◆§ Time of Performing *Kri'ah* for a Family Member / Current Practice

6. The basic *halachah* is that one must perform *kri'ah* at the moment of death (*yetzias neshamah*), when one recites the passages called *Tzidduk HaDin* [see *Appendix*] and reaches the blessing of *Dayan HaEmes*.[23] And at the latest, the *kri'ah* must be done before burial.[24] The custom in many places is that the mourners recite *Dayan HaEmes* and perform *kri'ah*[25] before the deceased is removed from the house. (Regarding the current practice of performing *kri'ah* at the funeral service just before the deceased is taken out to be buried, see footnote.)[26]

---

21. *Shulchan Aruch* 340:7, and *Shach* §§14, citing *Bach*.

22. See *Shach* §§17, who quotes *Agudah* on the first chapter of *Chullin*: "Nowadays, due to our sins, no one is a *talmid chacham*, for no one knows even Tractate *Kallah*."

22a. *Rama* 340:7 and 8.

23. *Beis Yosef* §340 cites *Kolbo*, who writes: "The custom is that when someone dies, the whole congregation assemble and go to his house. And [there] they recite *Tzidduk HaDin*; and when they *Dayan HaEmes*, the mourner performs *kri'ah*." And this is how *Shulchan Aruch* rules (loc. cit., par. 3).

24. *Rama* 340:1. And see *Shach* §§3: "Above, 340:3, it is explained that when one reaches *Dayan HaEmes*, the mourner performs *kri'ah*." And *Ba'er Heitev* §§2 comments: "This refers to those communities where the custom is to recite *Tzidduk HaDin* at the time of death (*yetzias neshamah*)."

25. *Brikei Yosef* (on *Shulchan Aruch* loc. cit.) writes: "The common practice is to recite the blessing *Dayan HaEmes* for the *kri'ah*, including the Name of Hashem (*Shem U'Malchus*). Clearly, the reason for this is the teaching of the Mishnah: 'For bad news. . .' Moreover, it is taught [in the Mishnah]: 'If someone is told that his father died, he recites *Dayan HaEmes*.' And since [the Sages] instituted this blessing to be recited for a death, they connected this blessing to the *kri'ah*. And this is what is written by *Knesses HaGedolah*, except that he expresses doubt about the matter. But one who studies it will see clearly that there can be no doubt about the matter, and that raised by the *Knesses HaGedolah* is easily reconciled. Moreover, [in this case we should follow the rule:] 'Go out and see what the people do.' "[See *Sheivet Yehudah*, *Yoreh De'ah* §340.]

Gesher HaChaim (4:8) expresses doubt whether a mourner should respond "Amen" when another mourner recites *Dayan HaEmes* — since the mourner is still an *onen* and thus exempt from responding "Amen" to blessings. *Gesher HaChaim* concludes that he should not respond "Amen." But on the question of whether to respond, "Amen, yehei shmei rabba. . ." to the recitation of *Kaddish*, he writes that it is reasonable to conclude that the mourner should respond, since the *Kaddish* relates directly to the deceased, and the response is an integral part of the *Kaddish*.

Shevet Shimon (§376) gives a similar reason to explain why the mourner recites the *Dayan HaEmes* blessing, although he is exempt from the obligation of prayers, blessings, and all commandments not related to the needs of the deceased. He recites *Dayan HaEmes*, however, because it was instituted in honor of the deceased.

26. The *Acharonim* express surprise at this custom, wondering why the *kri'ah* and the recitation of the blessing should be put off until this time. Regarding the current practice of not performing *kri'ah*

✥ The Blessing *Dayan HaEmes*

Before performing the *kri'ah* the following blessing is recited:

בָּרוּךְ אַתָּה ה' אֱלֹהֵינוּ מֶלֶךְ הָעוֹלָם, דַּיַּן הָאֱמֶת.

Blessed are You, Hashem, our God, King of the universe, the true Judge. [26a]

For the text of *Tzidduk HaDin*, see Appendix.

7. The following applies to all family members for whom one is required to mourn, except one's parent:

If one did not perform *kri'ah* at the correct time, he must do it afterwards, anytime within the first seven days from the burial. With regard to reciting the blessing of *Dayan HaEmes*, see note. [27] After the seventh day, one does not perform *kri'ah*.

---

until of the funeral, when the deceased is taken out to be buried, *Gesher HaChaim* (ch. 4, note 1) gives the following explanations:

    (a) It may be that this is because not everyone is expert in the laws of *kri'ah*. Therefore, it is postponed until the time when the deceased is taken out to be buried. Then the members of the *chevra kaddisha* are present. They are expert in the laws and can instruct the mourner how to fulfill them.

    (b) The delay may be so that someone else may begin by cutting the garment a little with a knife, as explained below, par. 9.

    (c) By that time [when the deceased is taken out to be buried], all the mourners have gathered. In the holy city of Jerusalem, the custom is that the children do not accompany their father's body to the cemetery (see below, 9:14). Therefore, the custom was established to perform the *kri'ah* when all the mourners are together.

In addition to these reasons offered by *Gesher HaChaim*, another may be suggested. The *halachah* states that for one's parent, *kri'ah* must be performed in public (*Shulchan Aruch* 340:13; and see below, par. 10). Hence the custom was established to perform *kri'ah* at the time when the public are present.

Chiddushim U'Viurim, *Hilchos Kri'ah* §2, explains that the obligation of *kri'ah* applies when grief is strongest (*sha'as chimum*). Hence, if a person did not perform *kri'ah* at the time of death or upon hearing of the death, he waits until the time when the deceased is taken out to be buried, or a similar time, for then the grief is felt most strongly.

26a. The blessing refers not to *kri'ah*, but to the death, as *Birkei Yosef* (§340) writes: The universal custom is to recite "upon performing *kri'ah*, the blessing '*Dayan HaEmes*,' including the mention of Hashem's Name and Kingship... Since they ordained that the blessing recited for a death, they associated its recital with *kri'ah*." Although *kri'ah* is an independant *mitzvah*, the Sages did not institute a blessing for it because one does not recite a blessing upon an act of destruction (*Shevet Yehudah*, *Yoreh Deah* §340).

27. *Shulchan Aruch* 340:18 writes: "If someone did not have a garment [to tear], if [a garment] becomes available to him within seven days, he tears it; after seven days, he does not tear it."

Shach §§26 explains the phrase "did not have a garment": "For example, if he was ragged (meaning that all his garments were torn), or was wearing borrowed garments (*Ramban*), or if he had only an undergarment, upon which one cannot perform *kri'ah*, as explained below, par. 10, in *Hagah* (*Bach*)."

Chiddushim U'Viurim, *Hilchos Kri'ah* par. 27 writes: "It seems reasonable to rule that part of the seventh day is considered like the entire day [as for the other laws of mourning]. Once the restrictions of *shivah* are removed [i.e., in the morning of the seventh day], one may no longer perform *kri'ah*; for we never find *kri'ah* without the restrictions of *shivah*. Likewise, if burial took place just before a festival, if the mourner did not perform *kri'ah* before the festival, he does not perform it after the festival, even though it is still within seven days. And this is the ruling given by responsa *Chaim BeYad* §119, citing *P'nei Mevin*, §402." He also states that this is the opinion of the author of *Beis Oved*.

If one performs *kri'ah* during *shivah* [i.e., after the burial], should he recite the blessing *Dayan HaEmes* when doing so? On this question, *Sdei Chemed* (*Aveilus* §180) writes in the name of *Yad Ne'eman* (p.

This is true whether one's omission to perform *kri'ah* was unintentional (*shogeig*) or intentional (*meizid*).[28]

However, if the omission was completely unavoidable, for example:

(a) one was dangerously ill, or (b) one's mind was not clear and settled,

then, upon recovery, one is required to perform *kri'ah*, even after the seventh day.[29]

Some rule that the requirement to perform *kri'ah* after the seventh day applies only if one omitted *kri'ah* because of the second reason (b). But if the omission was due to the first reason (a), one is exempt from performing *kri'ah* upon recovery.[30]

We have stated that after seven days from the burial, one does not perform *kri'ah*. Some authorities place a limitation on this rule. They state that it applies only when the person observed the laws of mourning during the first seven days (sat *shivah*), but omitted to perform *kri'ah*. If he did not sit *shivah* at all, and hence must make up the *shivah* during the first thirty days from death, he must perform *kri'ah* when he makes up the *shivah*. However, other authorities disagree.[31] They rule

---

14a) that one should not recite the blessing. "This blessing is not mentioned by the Talmud nor by the major *Poskim*, but is only a custom. Hence it should be limited to being recited at the proper time of *kri'ah*, i.e., at the time of death or when news of the death is heard; but not at any other time." *S'dei Chemed* then comments: "But with all due respect, in my humble opinion I cannot agree. Rather, the simplest assumption is that the entire seven days are to be considered the same as the time of death and burial. . . Later, I saw what the *gaon*, our master, the *Chida* writes in *Shiurei Brachah* 340:7 that if, due to confusion, one forgot to perform *kri'ah* for the deceased, and remembered after three days had passed, one should perform *kri'ah* when one remembers, but should recite the blessing of *Dayan HaEmes* without including the Name of Hashem (*Shem U'malchus*)."

Chaim Sha'al writes the same in the name of *Beis Oved*. And *Gesher HaChaim* (4:26) writes that it is worthwhile to follow the opinion of *Chida* — i.e., if one remembers to perform *kri'ah* within three days of the death, one should recite the full blessing, including the Name of Hashem. But if one remembers after three days, one should not recite it with the Name of Hashem.

28. *Shulchan Aruch* 396:1. The reason is that *kri'ah* is only performed at a time of intense grief (*sha'as chimum*). Once the seven days have passed, it is no longer considered *sha'as chimum*. And the rule is that if one did not perform *kri'ah* during *sha'as chimum*, one does not perform it afterwards.

29. *Shach* 396:§§1, citing *Bach*. *Shach* goes on to write: "This is not comparable to one [who omitted *kri'ah*] by mistake or deliberately. In that case, the moment of intense grief (*sha'as chimum*) passed [without *kri'ah*]; the person was healthy when he heard of the death, and the obligation of *kri'ah* applied to him. [Therefore if he omitted it, he cannot perform it later.] But in this case [cases (a) and (b) in our text], the moment of intense grief occurs only when the person recovers to the point that his mind is clear and settled. It is at that time that the obligation of *kri'ah* applies to him."

30. *Taz*, loc. cit., §§1. "But it is irrelevant to us that he could not perform *kri'ah* due to his dangerous illness; for in the final analysis he was aware of his intense grief (*sha'as chimum*) at that time. Therefore he is exempt from *kri'ah* afterwards."

31. *Chiddushei R' Akiva Eiger* on 396:1, citing *Tiferes LeMoshe*. R' Akiva Eiger concludes: "But from the ruling of *Knesses HaGedolah*, in his responsum in *Ba'ei Chayei* (*Yoreh De'ah* §239), it is clear that he does not agree; rather, in all cases the person does not perform *kri'ah*."

And see *Chiddushim U'Viurim*, loc. cit., who writes: "In the matter of a burial during a festival, when *shivah* is postponed until after the festival: It would seem that here, too, one may perform *kri'ah* [as soon as possible] any time during the seven days, after the festival, if he did not perform it before the festival. This is in accord with the ruling of *Tiferes LeMoshe*. And it is possible that on this point, *Knesses HaGedolah* would not disagree, since the entire period of mourning is legally postponed until after the festival."

And see *Terumas HaDeshen* §288, who writes: "The custom is that for family members other than

that he may not perform *kri'ah* even in this case.

As stated, none of the above applies to mourning for one's parent. For them, one performs *kri'ah* on all one's garments, and there is no time limit.[32]

◂§ How to Perform *Kri'ah*

8. *Kri'ah* must be done in a standing position.[33] One who performed *kri'ah* while sitting did not fulfill the *mitzvah* and must tear again.[34] In such a case, he does not repeat the accompanying blessing in its complete form, with Hashem's Name and Kingship (*shem umalchus*).[35] One must be careful not to lean on anything while performing *kri'ah*, since (as explained in *Orach Chayim* §141) this would be equivalent to sitting.

If one is sick and cannot stand up, he performs *kri'ah* in a sitting or lying position.[36]

9. If possible, it is preferable that the mourner perform *kri'ah* himself, following the rule that "it is more of a *mitzvah* to do it oneself than through an agent." But the usual practice is that someone else begins by cutting the garment a little with a knife, and then the mourner completes the tear.[37]

---

one's parent, one does not perform *kri'ah* during a festival, but only after the festival. And even though we have the rule, 'Any *kri'ah* performed at a time other than that of intense grief (*sha'as chimum*) is not *kri'ah*,' this applies only if the person [mistakenly] thought that he was exempt [from performing *kri'ah*]. But one who knew that he was obligated, but that the *mitzvah* was postponed, certainly should perform *kri'ah* [afterwards]."

See *Chiddushim U'Viurim* on this passage.

32. *Shulchan Aruch* 340:18. *Ramban* writes in *Toras HaAdam*, citing *Halachos Gedolos*: "The reason is that we find the same with regard to mending the tear: One is forever forbidden to mend it. And it is not logical to think that the father would die and the son would never perform *kri'ah* for him."

33. *Shulchan Aruch* 340:1. And in *Mo'ed Katan* 20a the source given is the verse, *And Job stood up and tore his coat (Job 1:20)*, and the verse, *And the king stood up and tore his clothes (II Samuel 13:31)*.

34. *Shulchan Aruch*, loc. cit.

35. *Mishmeres Shalom os kuf*:64. He compares this to the case of one who recited the blessing [*Dayan HaEmes*] at the time of death, and therefore does not recite it again at the time of *kri'ah*. But he also quotes *Zachur LeAvraham*, *Yoreh De'ah*, *Hilchos Avel*, *os Kuf*, s.v. *kri'ah*, who in turn cites *Sheivet Yehudah* as ruling that the mourner must recite *Dayan HaEmes* again [at the time of *kri'ah*].

36. Responsa *Kinyan Torah* part III:§108. He writes that "since there is no way the person can stand up, it is not reasonable to exempt him completely from the *mitzvah* of *kri'ah*. Therefore he should perform it in a sitting [or lying] position." And *Chiddushim Uviurim* writes the same in his *Hilchos Kri'ah*, par. 4, stating: "It is reasonable to rule that [the mourner] is not required to perform *kri'ah* again when he recovers. But the question requires study."

37. See *Pischei Teshuvah* §§1, on *Shulchan Aruch* 340:1: "*Ri* writes that it is good for the *kri'ah* to be done by someone else, since [the mourner] is embarrassed by him, and this involves more intense aggravation, since someone is tearing his garment and he must remain silent and accept upon himself the decree of Hashem, Blessed is He. — *Mahari Molco*, in a responsa manuscript, §88."

See *Chiddushim Uviurim*, by the gaon R' Zalman Margolios (*Hilchos Kri'ah* §2), who quotes these words of *Mahari Molco*. And the same is written in responsa *Halachos Ketanos* §116.

Responsa *Beis Yehudah* (§26) writes: "If it is possible for [the mourner] to make the tear himself, it is better for him to do so, [in accordance with the rule,] 'it is more of a *mitzvah* to do it oneself than through an agent.' Moreover, this resembles those *mitzvos* [such as *tefillin* and the like] which apply to

10. For all family members for whom one is required to mourn, except one's parent, one performs an "inner" *kri'ah*[38] in two senses of the word:

(a) One inserts one's hand underneath the garment and tears it from the inside.

(b) One performs *kri'ah* inside the home, that is, in private rather than in public.

For one's parent, one tears the garment from the outside, and in public.[39]

For all family members for whom one is required to mourn, except one's parent, one has the option of tearing either by hand or with an instrument. For one's parent, one must tear by hand.[40] If it is difficult to begin the tear by hand, one cuts the garment slightly with a knife, and then completes the tear by hand.[40a]

◆§ What Part of the Garment to Tear, and the Size of the Tear

11. Some authorities say that one must tear along the length of the garment. If one tears along the width, he does not fulfill the *mitzvah*, since it looks as if the garment simply got a rip in it, rather than having been deliberately torn.[41]

---

one's body and cannot be performed by means of an agent. . ." He concludes: "The custom is that one of the *chevra kadisha* members begins by cutting the garment a little with a knife at the neck of the garment. Then the mourner grasps the edge of this tear and enlarges the tear in a downward direction. Thus, both requirements are fulfilled: Someone else begins, but the main part of the *mitzvah* is performed by the mourner himself — and this is the correct practice."

38. *Shulchan Aruch* 340:13. And *Tur* writes: "One performs an inner tear if he wishes; but for one's mother or father, one must perform an outer tear." [*Shulchan Aruch* does not disagree with *Tur*; *Tur*'s words are cited here only to show the intent of *Shulchan Aruch*: that for other family members, one has the option of either an "inner" or "outer" tear.]

39. *Shulchan Aruch* loc. cit. And *Or Zarua (Hilchos Aveilus)* comments: "It stands to reason that if one performs *kri'ah* in a way that violates any of these requirements established by the Sages, one has not fulfilled the *mitzvah* of *kri'ah*."

40. *Shulchan Aruch* 340:14. From the passage of *Or Zarua* cited in the previous footnote, one may infer that if this requirement is not fulfilled, one has not fulfilled the *mitzvah* of *kri'ah*. But *Da'as Torah* ad. loc. writes that this is not so. He goes on to say that even according to the opinion of *Or Zarua*, if it is impossible to make the tear without a knife, one is permitted to do it with a knife. He explains that the requirement to tear by hand is simply in order to show respect for one's parent. Thus, if it is impossible to make the tear without a knife, one shows more respect by doing it with a knife than by not doing it at all.

40a. *Aruch HaShulchan* 340:12.

41. *Pischei Teshuvah* 340:§§2.. This *halachah* is also recorded by *Chochmas Adam* 152:2, in the name of *Radbaz*, part III:§560. But see *Da'as Torah*, loc. cit.: "This is not found in *Radbaz* there." And *Chiddushim U'Viurim* loc. cit., §6, writes the same. He writes further: "His words there mainly concern whether to tear the garment in the actual middle, over the center of the body, opposite the navel, or to tear a little to one side or the other. In this connection, he wrote that one should tear in the direction of the heart. . . Moreover, regarding his statement that if one tears along the width, it looks as if the garment simply got a rip in it, rather than having been deliberately torn — this requires study; at first sight, it seems uncommon for a[n accidental] rip to be along the width. It seems to me that it is more common for [such] a rip to be along the length. . ." He concludes: "In any case, we cannot introduce new *halachos* which we have not seen, and since the tears mentioned by the Talmud and *Poskim* are along the length of the garment, one should not tear along the width. But after the fact (*bediavad*), [if one did tear along the width] the matter [whether one fulfilled the *mitzvah*] requires study."

12. For all family members for whom one is required to mourn, except one's parent, the custom is to tear on the right side; for one's parent, on the left.[42] However, if one tore on the other side, one still fulfilled the *mitzvah*.[43]

13. For all family members for whom one is required to mourn, except one's parent, one has the option of leaving the edge of the garment whole and beginning the tear somewhere below the edge. For one's parent, one must include the edge.[44] Some rule that even for the other family members one must tear the edge of the garment. This latter opinion is followed in practice.[45]

14. If one is wearing valued clothes, one is permitted to change into plainer clothes in order to tear them, even if the *kri'ah* is for one's parent.[46]

15. For all family members for whom one is required to mourn, except one's parent, one makes a tear of only one handsbreadth (*tefach*)[46a] in length, and tears only the outermost garment.[47] If one tore an inner garment, some rule that

---

42. See *Taz* §§6: "*Rashal* writes: 'The custom is to tear on the left side for one's father or mother; but for other family members, such as a son or brother, on the right. And this is what I have found, too.' But in *Maharil* it is written that he had his son tear for [the death of] his mother on the right side. And my teacher and father-in-law [*Bach*], *zal*, wrote: 'However, it is reasonable to conclude that since for one's father or mother one must tear the garments until one bares the heart, and the heart is on the left, therefore one should tear on the left in order to bare the heart; and this is the custom followed in the communities, in accord with *Rashal*.'" *Hadras Kodesh*, part II:§41, writes that fathers should also tear for their sons on the left side.

43. *Chochmas Adam* 152:6 writes: "But in any case, this does not prevent fulfillment of the *mitzvah*. This is also the ruling of *S'dei Chemed*, *Aveilus* §173, citing *Tiferes Adam*, *Yoreh De'ah* 64:7, in the name of *Zachur LeAvraham*. And the same ruling is given by *Beis Oved* p. 221, os 45, and *Kesones Yosef*. And the same applies if one tore on the left side for a family member other [than one's father or mother]." *Da'as Torah*, loc. cit., writes the same, adding: "This is proven by what *Taz* and *Bach* wrote in the name of *Maharil*."

44. *Shulchan Aruch* 340:12. The reason is so that the garment will be divided into two parts (*Nimukei Yosef* loc. cit.).

45. *Rama* loc. cit..

46. *Gilyon Maharsha* on 340:9. And in this respect there is no difference between the *halachah* for one's father or mother and that for other family members, *Chikkekei Lev* §51; and *Chaim BeYad* p. 128 §83. The same ruling is given by *Chochmas Adam* 152:6, in the name of responsa *Maharil* §198; and by *Gesher HaChaim* 4:1; and by *Kol Bo Al Aveilus* p. 28.

46a. According to Rav Moshe Feinstein [*Igros Moshe*], a *tefach* is 3.55 inches. According to the *Chazon Ish*, it is 3.8 inches.

47. *Shulchan Aruch* 340:9. In commenting on 340:10, the *Poskim* are divided about the definition of "outermost garment." *Taz* in §§5 writes that the outer garment called *ruk* in German should not be torn, since people do not wear it in the home. And even if someone occasionally wears it in his home, his habit is of no halachic significance, being nullified by the practice of the majority of people. Moreover, he states, one should not be stringent and tear this garment, for this would be the type of stringency that leads to leniency. The reason is that for family members other than a parent, one tears only the outermost garment; and it certainly is not right to attempt to fulfill the *mitzvah* of *kri'ah* by tearing only the *ruk* in place of a garment that is undoubtedly required to be torn.

However, *Masas Binyamin*, cited by *Taz* here, writes that one is definitely required to tear the *ruk*, since it is definitely a garment, and *Shach*, in *Nekudos HaKesef*, agrees with this ruling; as does *Aruch HaShulchan* 340:9. See below, note 53.

one has not fulfilled the *mitzvah*, while others disagree. (For the application of this law to women's garments, see note.)[48] One should not make the tear any longer than a *tefach*.[49]

For one's parent, one tears all garments until baring one's heart, even if one is wearing many clothes[50] [see par. 17 below]. If the person does not tear all his garments, he has not fulfilled the *mitzvah*, and others should insist to him that he do so (*go'arim bo*). As long as he is still wearing the untorn garment, he is required to tear it, even if more than thirty days have passed since the death.[51]

16. The laws of *kri'ah* are the same for both men and women, except that a woman, when performing *kri'ah* for her parent, must first tear the inner garment, then move the garment so that the tear is in the back, and then tear the outer garment.[52]

17. An outer garment, worn only for modesty and dignity, need not be torn. The same applies to a winter overcoat. One also need not tear a garment worn only to absorb perspiration [such as an undershirt].[53] Likewise, one need not tear a

---

48. *Chiddushei R' Akiva Eiger*, on §340, cited by responsa *Toras Chessed* (§55), rules that this does not fulfill the *mitzvah*. But responsa *Parach Mateh Aharon* (part I:§99) writes that it does fulfill the *mitzvah*. The same ruling is given by responsa *Ginas Veradim*, *Yoreh De'ah* 5:8; and by *Gilyon Maharsha* ad loc., in the name of *Knesses HaGedolah*'s commentary on *Tur* §11; and by *Mishmeres Shalom*, os kuf §70, in the name of *Beis Lechem Yehudah*, in the name of *Zachur LeAvraham*, and in the name of *Tal Chaim*; and by *Sha'arei De'ah* §340, in the name of *Shiurei Knesses HaGedolah*.

Zachur LeAvraham writes that women should be permitted, even preferably (*lechatchilah*), to tear an inner garment, as this is more dignified [than tearing an outer garment in the presence of others].

49. The *gaon* R' Zalman Margolios, *Chiddushim U'Viurim*, Hilchos Kri'ah §3.

Chaim Sha'al §23 expresses surprise that this *halachah* is not mentioned by the *Poskim*. And in fact it is explicitly stated by the *Gemara*, *Bava Kamma* 91b: "Rabbi Elazar said: 'I have heard that one who tears too much for the deceased is liable to a lashing due to the prohibition against wanton destruction (*bal tashchis*).'" (*Tosafos'* version of this *Gemara* passage does not mention a lashing, but reads: "...is in violation of the prohibition against *bal tashchis*...")

50. This means the place opposite the biceps muscle of the upper arm (*Yavetz*; and *Kitzur Shulchan Aruch* 195:3). The reason is given by *Ramban* in the name of the *Yerushalmi*: because one can no longer fulfill the *mitzvah* of honoring one's father and mother.

Responsa *Chasam Sofer*, *Yoreh De'ah* §323, writes that even if tearing until reaching the place opposite one's heart would result in a tear less than a *tefach* in length, one must nevertheless tear a full *tefach*, since the requirement of tearing "until the place opposite the heart" is to be applied when it results in stringency, but not when it results in leniency.

51. *Shulchan Aruch* loc. cit. And see *Biur HaGra* §§29, who writes: "...as is the law for one who did not perform *kri'ah* at all; hence the law is that [as long as he is wearing the untorn garment, he is required to tear it, even if more than thirty days have passed]." And see *Da'as Torah*, ad loc., who writes: "It would seem that this applies only if he did not replace this garment with another one, tearing the other one instead. But if he changed garments and tore the other one, he fulfilled the *mitzvah* of tearing all the garments he is wearing, and is not required to tear the original garment."

52. This is for reasons of modesty: so that she will not expose a part of her clothing not usually revealed, thus causing undesirable thoughts on the part of the men present.

53. *Shulchan Aruch* 340:10. The source of this *halachah* is a *baraisa* cited in *Mo'ed Katan* 22b: "...[tearing the garment called] *epikarsion* is not essential." The *Poskim* agree that there is no

prayer shawl (*tallis gadol*). Some rule that one need not tear a *tallis katan* (the four-cornered fringed garment worn all day),[54] but others disagree.[55]

18. The tear must be at the neck of the garment, in the front. If one tears the garment in back, or at the bottom, or at the sides, he has not fulfilled the *mitzvah* and must make another tear, this time at the neck.[56]

This applies to performing *kri'ah* for one of the family members for whom one is required to mourn. As we saw above, however, one is sometimes required to perform *kri'ah* for someone other than a relative, such as a great sage, a meticulously observant person (*adam kasher*), or anyone with whom one was present at the moment of death (*yetzias neshamah*). In all such cases, one tears in the lower part of the garment.[57]

19. When one tears at the neck of the garment, it is not enough to tear the lapel.

The tear must extend into the main body of the garment — especially for one's parent, where the tear should be over the heart.[58]

---

requirement at all to tear it, even if one has the choice of doing so (*lechatchilah*). This is in contrast to the opinion of *Ravad*, who understands that one should tear it if possible (*lechatchilah*), but if one did not tear it, then after the fact (*bediavad*) it is not necessary to do so.

54. Responsa *Meishiv Davar* (part II:9) writes that one is not required to tear the *tallis katan* (and, all the more so, one is not required to tear the *tallis gadol*). The same ruling is quoted by *Ramas Rachel* §37, in the name of *Shevilei David*.

55. See *Ramas Rachel*, loc. cit., who quotes a commentary on the Minor Tractates called *Binyan Yehoshua* (published in 5548/1788): "Even the undergarment called *leibel*, and the *arba kanfos* (*tallis katan*) must be torn. The only garments not requiring *kri'ah* are the long undergarment, worn against the flesh, and the outermost garment, called the *feltz mantel*."

Kerem Shlomo, on *Yoreh De'ah*, cites and agrees with the ruling of *Binyan Yehoshua*. The same ruling is given by *Leshon Chachamim*, *Hilchos Kri'ah*; and by *Ramas Rachel* himself, who concludes that the *tallis katan* is exempt from *kri'ah* only if it is smaller than the size required for the *mitzvah* of *tzitzis*. The same ruling is given by *Da'as Torah* on *Shulchan Aruch* 340:9. He writes: "Even though it is worn only for the sake of the *mitzvah*, nevertheless one of the requirements of that *mitzvah* is that the garment be worn for the benefit of being clothed; otherwise, it does not require *tzitzis*."

And *Chiddushim U'Viurim* §22 writes: "But apparently the *tallis katan* must [be torn], since it is a garment. But I heard that our master, *zal*, (the *Chazon Ish*) was in doubt about the matter. Therefore it requires further study."

56. See responsa *Sheivet HaLevi* (part IV:§156), who states that in a case where one is required to make another tear, one should not recite the blessing, *Dayan HaEmes*, a second time. The blessing was essentially instituted for the hearing of bad news, but the Sages simply stipulated that the proper time to recite it is when performing *kri'ah*. Therefore, the obligation of the blessing was already fulfilled the first time he recited it.

57. *Shulchan Aruch* and *Rama*, loc. cit., par. 2. And see *Chiddushim U'Viurim*, who writes that "the lower part of the garment" means below the navel. But if one tore the inner side of the garment (Yid. *untershelk*, "lining"), it would seem that one did not fulfill the *mitzvah* at all, since this is not the essential part of the garment.

58. My father and teacher, *zatzal*, in his work, *Zichron Eliahu* (manuscript), expresses doubt as to whether the lapel is considered the same as the garment, since in cold weather one raises the lapel and covers oneself with it. Therefore he concludes that for one's father or mother, since one is required to tear in the area of the heart, one certainly must tear part of the garment itself [not just the lapel], so that the tear will be in the area of the heart. For family members other than one's father or mother, one should also be stringent about this whenever possible (*lechatchilah*).

‌ **Changing *Kri'ah* Clothes During *Shivah***

20. For all family members for whom one is required to mourn, except one's
parent, one may, if necessary, remove the garment one tore and replace it with
another; and one is not required to perform *kri'ah* on the garment one has changed
into.[59] However, unless necessary, one should not change out of the garment one
tore.[60] Likewise, one should not replace it before the burial.[61]

For one's parent, one must tear any garment one changes into during *shivah*.[62]
Some authorities write that this applies only if one *changes* the garment for another,
but if one *adds* a garment to keep warm, he need not tear it.[63]

On Friday, one must be careful not to change into Sabbath clothes before the
Sabbath begins. If one did so, one must perform *kri'ah* on the garment one changed
into,[64] but others disagree.[64a]

At night, one may change into pajamas or nightgown, and one need not tear
them, even for one's parent. However, if one puts on a robe, one must tear it.[64b]

The same ruling is given by *Zichron Betzalel*: *Lechatchilah*, one should be stringent on this matter
even for family members other than one's father or mother. Moreover, if one performed *kri'ah* for one's
father or mother in the middle of the lapel, one did not fulfill the *mitzvah* even after the fact (*bediavad*).
If one tore at the edge of the lapel, where it joins the main part of the garment, he concludes that one
fulfilled the *mitzvah*.

Chiddushim U'Viurim §7 writes: "For other family members, it would seem that [tearing the lapel]
fulfills the *mitzvah*; but for one's father or mother, one must question whether this is so, since one is
required to bare the heart."

Responsa *Sheivet HaLevi*, *Yoreh De'ah*, *tinyana*, § 167, writes: "Regarding a woman who performed *kri'ah* for her father on the collar of a wide-collared garment, and the tear did not reach the garment itself, it would seem that she fulfilled the *mitzvah* of *kri'ah*. . .since this is an integral part of the
garment."

59. *Shulchan Aruch* 340:14.

60. *Meiri* to *Mo'ed Katan* (24a), in the name of "some rule." The same ruling is given by *Chikkekei
Yoreh De'ah* §51.

61. *Da'as Torah*, citing *Birkei Yosef* in *Shiurei Brachah*.

62. *Shulchan Aruch* loc. cit. For the garment one changed into, as for the one originally torn, one is
forever forbidden to mend it with a regular, straight mend (*le'achos*; see below, par. 29).

In responsa *Binyan Olam*, *Yoreh De'ah* §62, the author raises the following question: Let us suppose
that a person performed *kri'ah* during *Chol HaMo'ed*, the Intermediate Days of Pesach or Succos. His
seven-day period of mourning (*shivah*) therefore began only after the end of the festival. He changed
his garment during the *shivah*, but by that time more than seven days had already passed since the
burial. Is he required to perform *kri'ah* on the garment he changed into? The author states that he does
not find a discussion of this question in the writings of the *Poskim*, and he concludes that the person
would be required to perform *kri'ah* on the garment he changed into. The same ruling is given by
Chiddushim U'Viurim, *Hilchos Kri'ah*.

63. *Orchos Chaim*, by R' Aharon of Lunille (*Hilchos Avel* §6), writes: "This applies only if he changes
the garment for another; but if he adds garments due to the cold, he does not tear [the added gar-
ments]. And this seems to be the opinion of *Ravad*, as well as the *Shalman*, *zal*, who acted on this assumption at the funeral of his mother." I am surprised not to have found any *Poskim* who cite this ruling.

64. *Orchos Chaim* loc. cit.. For the time when it is permitted to change clothes for the Sabbath, see
below, chapt. 23.

64a. See below, note 68.

64b. Leading contemporary *Poskim* have ruled that one may change into pajamas without
performing *kri'ah* on them, since this is not a garment made for dignity.

On the Sabbath[65] and likewise during *Chol HaMo'ed* (the Intermediate Days of Pesach and Succos),[66] one is required to change clothes, and is not required to tear the clothes one changes into.

Some rule that upon the departure of the Sabbath or *Yom Tov* one must be careful to immediately change out of one's Sabbath or festival clothes; otherwise, one must tear them.[67] But others disagree.[68]

On the seventh day, as soon as the mourners get up from sitting *shivah*, they are permitted to change clothes [without tearing the new clothes].[69]

◆§ *Kri'ah* for Two Family Members

21. If two family members, for whom one is required to mourn, die at the same time, one performs *kri'ah* only once, for both of them together,[70] and also recites only one blessing of *Dayan HaEmes* for both of them together.[71] The same is true even if they did not die at the same time, but news of their death was received simultaneously. The same rules apply if one's parent dies at the same time as one of the other family members.[72]

If one's parent dies at the same time as one of the other family members for whom one is required to mourn, one first performs *kri'ah* for one's parent, tearing all the garments until baring the heart. Then, at a place on the outer garment at least

---

65. *Shulchan Aruch* 400:1. He adds there: "If he does not have another garment to change into, he should move his garment around so that the tear is in the back."

66. This is in order to honor the festival (responsa *Be'er Moshe* part 4).

67. *Chikkekei Lev*, *Yoreh De'ah* §51.

68. The *gaon* R' Shlomo Zalman Auerbach writes in *Minchas Shlomo* §73 that the plain meaning of the *Gemara* and *Poskim* indicates that they do not mention any requirement to change clothes as early as possible at the conclusion of the Sabbath, in order to avoid having to perform *kri'ah* on one's Sabbath clothes. Moreover, one could reason as follows. If one changes clothes on *erev Shabbos* (Friday afternoon), even before accepting the Sabbath, one is not required to perform *kri'ah* again, since it is obvious that one put on the new garment in honor of the Sabbath. In the same way, at the conclusion of the Sabbath, as long as it is obvious that one is still wearing the clothes in honor of the Sabbath, one is likewise exempt [from performing *kri'ah* on them].

69. The reason is that in this matter, as in other *halachos* of mourning, the first part of the seventh day is counted as the whole day (*Mishmeres Shalom*, os kuf §85, in the name of *Zachur LeAvraham*, *Yoreh De'ah*, *Hilchos Avel*, os kuf, who cites a manuscript work, *Kuntres Rav Achai*). And see *Darkei Chaim VeShalom* §981, who writes that the mourners should immediately change their clothes so as not to be wearing torn clothes [when not required to do so].

70. *Shulchan Aruch* 340:23.

71. *Shulchan Aruch Orach Chaim* 222:2 writes: "For bad news (*shmu'os*), one recites: 'Blessed are You, Hashem, our God, King of the universe, the true Judge [*Dayan HaEmes*].' " *Mishnah Berurah* there §§2 comments: "The plural form (*shmu'os*) is used to teach us that if one hears several bad reports at the same time, one recites the blessing only once." And *Sha'ar HaTziyun* there §§2 adds: "It would seem that this applies even if the bad reports are not at the same time. As long as he has not yet recited the blessing for the first report, this is considered as if the bad reports were heard at the same time."

72. *Shulchan Aruch Yoreh De'ah* 340:23.

three fingerbreadths (*etzba'os*) from the first tear, one makes a tear of one handsbreadth (*tefach*) for the other family member.[73]

22. If one performed *kri'ah* for the death of a family member, and then a second family member died, the *halachah* is as follows:

   (a) If the second death occurred during the *shivah* of the first one, one must perform another *kri'ah*. It can be done in one of two ways:
      (i) by extending the original tear another *tefach*, or
      (ii) by making a new tear of one *tefach*, separated from the first tear by a distance of at least three *etzba'os*.
   (b) If the second death occurred after the *shivah* of the first, one simply extends the original tear a slight amount (*kol shehu*).

   If a third family member dies after the *shivah* of the second, one again extends the original tear a slight amount.[74]

   If the second person to die was one's parent, one performs *kri'ah* as in (ii) above, whether it was during or after the first *shivah*. The same applies if the first person who died was one's father, and the second, one's mother, or vice versa.[75]

◆§ Mistaken or Incomplete Information About a Death

23. Following are some laws applying to a situation when information about a death is mistaken or incomplete.

   (a) A person was told that his father died. He performed *kri'ah*. Then he found out that the one who died was his son rather than his father. If the correction came immediately (within *k'dei dibbur*, about one or two seconds), the original *kri'ah* is valid. But if the correction was delayed more than *k'dei dibbur*, the *kri'ah* is invalid.
   (b) A person was told only that one of his family died; he was not told which one, but he thought it was his father, and performed *kri'ah*. Afterwards, he found out that it was his son. Even if the correction was

---

73. Ibid.

74. Ibid. 340:21 and 23. The source is *Mo'ed Katan* 26b. *Rashi* there explains that during the *shivah* for the first death, simply adding to the original tear would not be sufficient because it would appear to be all one tear. But after the seven days, the mourner has already mended the original tear with a crooked mend (see below, par. 29). For the second death, he rips open the stitches of this mend, and extends the tear a slight amount (*kol shehu*). Thus it is noticeable that he is performing *kri'ah* for a second death.

75. *Kitzur Shulchan Aruch* 195:10; *Derech HaChaim, Dinei Kri'ah*. Responsa *Beis Av, Hilchos Teshuvah*, responsum 336, writes that he tried hard to find the source of the ruling given by *Derech HaChaim*. "*Sheivet Shimon* expresses doubt about the case of a person who performed *kri'ah* for his father and then, after *shivah*, his mother died. Does he need to make a new tear for his mother, or is it sufficient to add a slight amount (*kol shehu*) to the original tear? He concludes that if a person originally performed *kri'ah* for his father, and then his mother died within thirty days [of burial], the mourner must add a whole handbreadth (*tefach*) to the original tear; extending it a slight amount is not sufficient. But after thirty days, it is sufficient to extend the original tear a slight amount. However, the matter still requires further study" (*Kol Bo Al Aveilus* p. 32).

delayed more than *k'dei dibbur*, the *kri'ah* is valid.[76] In this case, some rule that it was invalid.[77] However, if the person's intention was simply to perform *kri'ah* for one of his family, without intending any specific member, then all *Poskim* agree that the *kri'ah* is valid.[78]

(c) A person was told that his father had died. He performed *kri'ah* and observed the laws of mourning for less than seven days. Then he was told that his father had not died, so he stopped mourning. Then he was told that his father had actually died at the time of the first announcement. In this case, the original *kri'ah* is valid.

However, if his father had died after the first *kri'ah*, that *kri'ah* is not valid.[78a]

✥ Miscellaneous *Halachos*

24. If one performed *kri'ah* on the Sabbath for one of his family members who died, it is valid, even though it was a desecration of the Sabbath.[79]

25. If one performs *kri'ah* on a stolen garment, the *kri'ah* is invalid. The same applies to a borrowed garment, unless one has permission from the owner to make the tear on it.[80]

---

76. *Shulchan Aruch* 340:24. "*Sheivet Shimon* §340 raises the following question: In accord with the ruling of *Maharshal* [see above, footnote 42], the custom now is to perform *kri'ah* on the left side for one's father or mother, and on the right side for any other family member for whom one is obligated to mourn. If a person thought that his father had died, and performed *kri'ah* on the left side, and then he found out that it was his son who had died, would the *kri'ah* be valid? After all, when he performed *kri'ah*, the fact that he did it on the left side made it obvious that he intended it for his father, just as if he had explicitly said so. Therefore, the *kri'ah* should not be valid for the death of the son. True, the *Rishonim* and *Shulchan Aruch* rule that as long as no one stated explicitly that the *kri'ah* was for the father, it is valid for the son. But it may be that this ruling only applies in their time, when the custom of *Maharshal* to tear on the left side for the father had not yet been widely adopted. In their time, there was no outwardly apparent difference between a *kri'ah* performed for a father or for a son. Hence no one could know for which family member the person intended his *kri'ah*. But in our time, now that the custom of *Maharshal* has been accepted, it could be that the *kri'ah* intended for the father is not valid for the son. The matter requires further study" (*Kol Bo Al Aveilus* p. 31).

77. *Shach* §§37, citing *Bach*.

78. Ibid. And he writes the same in §§38, citing *Darkei Moshe* as stating that in this case the principle of retroactive selection (*breirah*) applies. In other words, once it becomes clear who died, we state retroactively that the *kri'ah* was for him.

78a. *Shulchan Aruch* 340:26, and *Shach* §§39.
    Regarding whether the original seven-day mourning period was valid, see below, chapt. 25.

79. *Shulchan Aruch* 340:28.

80. Ibid. 340:29. And see *Taz* §§16, and *Shach* §§42.
    Regarding a borrowed garment, if one has permission to tear it, one fulfills the *mitzvah* by tearing it, but one must pay the owner for the damage to the garment. When it is returned to the owner, he is permitted to mend it with a straight, regular mend (*le'achos* — see below, par. 29), even if the tear was for the mourner's father or mother (*Shulchan Aruch* loc. cit. 340:34).
    If he does not have permission to tear it, it follows the same *halachah* as for a stolen garment, i.e., the *kri'ah* is not valid; for this is considered borrowing without permission, which is the same as stealing (*Shach* §§50).

26. An infant may be in one of two categories:

(a) We have no absolute proof that the pregnancy was full term. (This is the usual case.)[81]

(b) We have absolute proof that the pregnancy was full term.

If a child in the first category (A) dies within thirty days of birth, or even on the thirtieth day, one does not perform *kri'ah* for it.[82] But if it dies on the thirty-first day, even though thirty full days may not have passed since birth, one performs *kri'ah* on it. [For example, if a child was born in the last hour of 1 Nissan and died in the first hour of 1 Iyar, it did not live thirty full days. Nevertheless, since it died in the thirty-first calendar day of its life, one performs *kri'ah* for it.] Others rule that one does not perform *kriah* unless the infant lived thirty twenty-four-hour days.[83]

27. If a child is capable of understanding that a family member has died and that people tear their clothing as a sign of grief, he is said to be of *gil chinuch*, "educable age."

Upon the death of a family member for whom the child (if he were adult) would be required to mourn, the following *halachos* apply:

For a child who has not yet reached *gil chinuch*, someone makes a small tear in the child's garment for the sake of grief *(agmas nefesh)*.[84]

For a child who has reached *gil chinuch*, someone tears the child's garment to the same extent required of adults — a handsbreadth *(tefach)*.[85] However, some *Poskim* disagree.[86] They require no more than is done for the younger child.

---

81. But if we do have absolute proof that the pregnancy was full term — for example, if the parents did not have marital relations for nine months prior to the birth — one performs *kri'ah* and observes mourning, even if the infant died less than thirty days from birth (*Shach* §§43).

82. The reason is that *kri'ah* is a Rabbinic *mitzvah*; therefore, in cases of doubt, we are lenient. Here, there is doubt as to whether the infant was viable, since we are not sure that the pregnancy was full term. But see the opinion of *Ramban* above, footnote 26.

83. Responsa *Chasam Sofer*, *Yoreh De'ah* §343. The same ruling is given by *Beis Shlomo*, *Yoreh De'ah* II:§219; and by *Minchas Pitim*. And see *Yad Shaul*, who disagrees, stating that thirty full days are required.

See below 15:7, for further details regarding such an infant, in connection with the obligation of mourning. The same details apply with regard to *kri'ah*.

84. *Shulchan Aruch* 340:27. *Drishah* there writes that for a minor who is definitely a child (*katan mamash*), someone should make a small tear in his garment, for the sake of grief.

85. *Chiddushei Rabbi Akiva Eiger*, citing *Drishah*. The same ruling is given by *Bach* there. He states that *Tur* wrote "tear for them" (מקרעין) rather than "they tear" (קורעין) in order to teach that for a child, one need not be careful to tear in accord with the *halachos* of *kri'ah*, since the only purpose of this tear is for the sake of grief. The purpose is not to educate the child in the proper performance of *mitzvos*. However, once the child reaches educable age, one must have him tear in accord with the *halachos* of *kri'ah*.

86. *Chochmas Shlomo*, ad loc. See *S'dei Chemed*, *Aveilus* §178, who writes (citing *Chida* in *Shiurei Brachah*) that where there is no possibility of *agmas nefesh*, one should be lenient [and not have the child perform *kri'ah*], even if he has reached educable age (*gil chinuch*). The same ruling is given by *Mishmeres Shalom os ches* §27, *Yoreh De'ah* §381. He states that, contrary to the opinion of *Ritz Ge'us*, one does not have a child perform *kri'ah* solely for the sake of educating him. The same ruling is given by responsa *Igros Moshe*, *Yoreh De'ah* part 1 §224.

28. Someone who wears a ripped garment in the presence of the deceased, on pretense of having performed *kri'ah* when in fact he had not, is considered to be robbing both the living and the dead.[87]

> Regarding *kri'ah* on *Yom Tov* and *Chol HaMo'ed* see 33:1; on Purim, see 34:23.
>
> See below, 35:3, on the question whether a bride or bridegroom is required to perform *kri'ah*.

◄§ Mending the Tear

29. The following *halachos* apply only to a male mourner.

For all family members for whom one is required to mourn, except one's parent:

One is permitted to mend the tear crookedly (*lishlol*; i.e., baste) after *shivah*. After the first thirty days (*shloshim*), one is permitted to perform a regular, straight mend (*le'achos*).

Some communities have adopted a stricter practice, prohibiting even a crooked mend until after *shloshim*.[88]

As long as a crooked mend is prohibited, one is forbidden even to join the two edges of the tear with a straight pin.[89]

For one's parent:

A crooked mend is permitted only after the *shloshim*,[90] and one who chooses never to mend the tear at all is praiseworthy.[91] A regular mend is forbidden forever.[92]

As mentioned, the above *halachos* apply only to a male mourner. For a woman,

---

87. *Shulchan Aruch* 340:33. The source is a *baraisa* cited in *Mo'ed Katan* 26b. *Rashi* there explains that the *baraisa* is speaking of a garment that had already been ripped before the death occurred. "He is robbing everyone, because he is deceiving everyone, pretending to have torn his garment for the deceased."

In *Maseches Semachos* chapt. 9, we find: "Robbing the dead is [a] greater [sin] than robbing the living; for one who robs the living can ask forgiveness and return what he stole. One who robs the dead cannot ask forgiveness and cannot return what he stole."

88. *Shulchan Aruch* 340:15. And see *Da'as Torah* there, who writes that with regard to this *halachah* we do not apply the rule that "part of the [last] day is counted as a whole day." [If we were to apply that rule, one could mend the tear crookedly on the morning of the seventh day, but since we don't apply the rule, one must wait until the day is over.] The whole reason for adopting that rule with regard to the laws of mourning is because of a more general principle: "in regard to [the *halachos* of] mourning, the *halachah* follows the lenient opinion." But *kri'ah* is a separate category of *halachah*, not identical with "the *halachos* of mourning," and with regard to *kri'ah* we do not apply the principle that "the *halachah* follows the lenient opinion." The same applies to the thirtieth day; there, too, one must wait until the day is over before mending the tear.

89. *Rama* 340:15.

90. *Shulchan Aruch* 340:15.

91. *Ritva* to *Mo'ed Katan* 22b. He writes: "This is stated in the *Yerushalmi*."

92. *Shulchan Aruch* loc.cit.

93. Ibid. And see *Ritva* loc. cit., who writes that a woman may not mend the tear until after the burial — "and this is proven by [what the *Gemara* says] further on." But *Shulchan Aruch*, who writes

due to reasons of modesty, a crooked mend is required immediately, even if the *kri'ah* was for her parent.[93]

30. As explained below, Chapter 27, the occurrence of a Festival interrupts the observance of mourning, both the laws of the *shivah* and those of the *shloshim*. This includes the matter of mending the tear. Therefore, the arrival of the Festival makes it permitted to perform a crooked mend (if the tear was for one's parent) or a regular mend (if the tear was for another family member). The earliest time to do the mend is the day before the Festival, after *Minchah*, the Afternoon Prayer.[94]

31. One authority writes that if a mourner erroneously mends the tear, he must tear the garment again.[95]

32. If a tear is the type forbidden to be mended, one is also forbidden to turn the garment upside down (using what was formerly the bottom of the garment for the neck, and vice versa) and then mend it.[96] Even if one sells the garment, the buyer is forbidden to mend the tear. Therefore one is required to inform the buyer that the tear must not be mended.[97] Even if the seller did not inform him, the buyer

---

simply, "she mends it immediately, for the sake of her dignity," implies that she is permitted to mend it even before the burial.

94. *Rama* 340:15 writes: "it makes no difference [with regard to mending the tear] whether a Festival occurs [during the thirty days] or not."

Chiddushei R' Akiva Eiger writes: "This would seem to be intended literally: that the Festival doesn't count at all [in the count of the seven or thirty days], and one must count an actual thirty days. However, in my humble opinion, a study of *Teshuvos Maimonios* (§17) shows that the days before the Festival count as seven, and the Festival itself — even Shavuos or Rosh Hashanah — counts as another seven days, and then one must complete what is left to make up a total of thirty days. Thus, one day before Rosh Hashanah, combined with Rosh Hashanah itself, counts as fourteen days."

But *Shach* §§25 writes: "However, in our time the custom is to do a straight, regular mend (*le'achos*) whenever the mourning ends. The reason of the *Rama* [for saying that the Festival doesn't count at all] is that he rules, in accord with *Avi HaEzri*, that '[the halachos of] mourning and those of *kri'ah* are two separate categories.' We, however, rule in accord with *Ramban*, that they are separate categories only in the sense that regarding the *halachos* of *kri'ah* we do not apply the principle, 'the *halachah* follows the lenient opinion.' But for all other matters, there is no difference between the *halachos* of mourning and those of *kri'ah*. Thus, when the *Poskim* rule below, §399, that the Festival cancels the seven and the thirty days of mourning, they state this flatly, mentioning no distinction [between mourning and *kri'ah*]. This implies that the cancellation applies in every matter connected with the seven and the thirty days [including mending the tear]."

The same ruling is given by *Aruch HaShulchan* 340:13.

95. Responsa *Tzitz Eliezer* part VII §49, 2:4. He cites this in the name of *Mashcha Derevusa* (in the section containing the *chiddushim* of *Rash* Alfasi), *Yoreh De'ah* §340. And see *Chiddushim U'Viurim*, *Hilchos Kri'ah* §31.

96. The prohibition is only if one mends the tear. However, it is permitted to turn the garment upside down without mending the tear. This is implied by the *Gemara* which states, "if [the garment] becomes full [of tears] on the upper part, one turns it upside down." This is a flat statement, including even the type of garment forbidden to be mended (*Chiddushim U'Viurim* §34).

97. The requirement to inform the buyer is in order to prevent selling on false pretenses — in other words, the buyer must know that the merchandise he is purchasing cannot be mended.

The purpose of informing the buyer cannot be in order to ensure that he will not commit a

is forbidden to mend the tear until he knows for certain that it is the type which may be mended. Likewise, the mourner may not sell the garment to a non-Jew (since the non-Jew might mend the tear).[98]

33. Regarding *kri'ah* for one's parent, some rule that after twelve months of mourning it is permitted to cut out the piece of cloth where the tear is and replace it with other cloth, since this is not called mending the tear.[99] But others disagree.[100]

---

transgression by mending the garment; for even without any information, the buyer is forbidden to mend it until he finds out whether this is allowed (*Shach* §§28).

98. *Shulchan Aruch* 340:19.

99. *Taz* ad loc. §§10. The same ruling is given by *Bach*, and by *Chochmas Adam* §69, and by *Aruch HaShulchan* 340:17. *Maharsham* part 3, §356, writes that he was asked about a person who gave his garment, on which he had performed *kri'ah*, to a tailor. The tailor cut out the place where the tear was, and replaced it with other cloth, in accord with the ruling of *Taz* just cited. *Maharsham* writes that there are some who disagree with this ruling; therefore, the questioner should re-dye the garment. Then it will be considered like a new one. But see responsa *Mahari* Shteif, who expresses surprise at this suggestion, since the usual rule is that a change in the surface appearance of an object does not affect its halachic status (חֲזוּתָא לָאו מִילְתָא). "How, then, can the re-dyed garment take on a new halachic status?"

100. *Pischei Teshuvah* §§9, citing the following authorities: *Birkei Yosef, Beis David, Yoreh De'ah* §162, *Gilyon Maharsha* in the name of *Knesses HaGedolah*.

Responsa *Mahari Shteif*, loc. cit., writes: "It seems that the generally accepted custom is not in accord with *Taz*, since the plain meaning of the *Gemara* proves the contrary to his ruling."

SEVEN: THE KOHEN'S OBLIGATION TO RELATIVES

CHAPTER SEVEN

The *Kohen's* Obligation
to Become *Tamei* for Relatives

৵ The Family Members for Whom a Kohen Is Required
to Become Ritually Contaminated *(Tamei)*

1. Touching, or carrying a dead body, or entering a house where there is a dead
person, causes a *kohen* to become ritually contaminated *(tamei)*. Ordinarily, a
kohen is required to avoid this, as it is written, *'he shall not contaminate himself
[יִטַּמָּא] to a dead person'* (Leviticus 21:1). A *kohen* is also not allowed to be within
four cubits [*amos*; about eight feet] of a dead body. However, if the deceased is one
of certain family members, it is a *mitzvah* for the *kohen* to become *tamei* through
participation in the burial, as it is written, *'. . .except for the relative who is closest to
him'* (ibid. v. 2). If the *kohen* does not want to become *tamei* in such a case, we
compel him to do so.[1]

This *mitzvah* of becoming *tamei* applies whether the deceased is a man or a
woman.[1a]

2. The following are the family members for whom a *kohen* is required to become
tamei:

(a) father
(b) mother[2]
(c) son or daughter[3]

---

1. *Shulchan Aruch* 373:3.

1a. *Shulchan Aruch* loc. cit., in accord with the ruling of *Ramban*, *Ravad*, and *Rosh*, and contrary to
the ruling of *Rambam*.

2. This applies even if she becomes ineligible to marry a *kohen*; for example if, after giving birth to the
kohen in question, she was divorced and then nevertheless married a *kohen*. (*Shulchan Aruch*
373:4, and *Shach* ad loc.).

3. This applies even if they are the offspring of a marriage not permitted to a *kohen* — such as marriage
with a divorcee. However, if they are the offspring of marriage with a non-Jew (*kusis*) or a
non-Jewish female slave (*shifchah*), the *kohen* is not allowed to become *tamei* for them (*Shulchan
Aruch* loc. cit.).

The *kohen's* obligation to become *tamei* for his daughter applies even if she was married (*She'eilas
Yavetz* part II §136).

(d) brother — including half-brother on the father's side, but excluding half-brother on the mother's side

(e) sister, if she never married — including half-sister on the father's side, but excluding half-sister on the mother's side[4]

(f) wife, if she was the kind of woman a *kohen* is permitted to marry.[5] However, the *kohen* is not permitted to become *tamei* for his wife under the following circumstances:

> (i) If the *kohen* was forbidden to marry her (for example, she was a divorcee).
>
> (ii) If they are no longer married.[6]
>
> (iii) If she was his *arusah* [a woman's halachic marital status between the time of formal *kiddushin* and *nesuin*].

ᴥᴅ *Meis Mitzvah*

3. Likewise, it is a *mitzvah* for a *kohen* to become *tamei* in the case of a *meis mitzvah*, a Jewish corpse which will not have proper burial if he, the *kohen*, does not attend to it [see *Deut.* 21:1-9].

The *kohen* is required to become *tamei* only if he finds the head and most of the body of a *meis mitzvah*. But once he has found this much, he must become *tamei* again, if necessary, in order to bury even a single additional limb of the same body.[7]

A corpse is considered a *meis mitzvah* in this connection when it is found on the road, or in a city of non-Jews, there are not enough Jews to bury it, and if the *kohen* cannot summon Jews to attend to its burial from the place where he found the *meis mitzvah*.

In such a case, it is forbidden to leave the body, even to go to the nearest city to bring people to bury it. Instead, the *kohen* must become *tamei* by burying it. But if,

---

4. The obligation to become *tamei* for a brother or sister applies even if they are the offspring of a marriage not permitted to a *kohen*, as in the previous footnote (*Shulchan Aruch* loc. cit.). However, a *kohen* is not allowed to become *tamei* for a sister who is an *arusah* [betrothed; halachically referring to a woman's marital status at the first stage of marriage], even the betrothed of another *kohen*. Nor is he allowed to become *tamei* for a sister if she had been raped or seduced. But he is required to become *tamei* for a sister who was betrothed and then divorced, as well as for a sister who had reached maturity (*bogeres*).

   Regarding a sister who was betrothed on the Rabbinic, but not on the Scriptural level, see *Pischei Teshuvah* §§3.

5. For the exact time when she becomes his wife, see *Even HaEzer* §61, *Beis Shmuel*, beginning of §57; and *Chiddushei Rabbi Akiva Eiger, Yoreh De'ah* §373.

6. This applies, according to *Shach* §§4, "even if he has children from her (*Mordechai*) — and the same ruling is given by the *Acharonim*."

   Regarding the case where the *kohen* had quarreled with his wife and intended to divorce her, and she died during the time of their estrangement, see responsa *Maharash Engel* part VI:§25.

   Regarding whether one is required to mourn for his wife under these circumstances, see below, 14:4.

7. *Shulchan Aruch* 374:1,2. In this respect, the obligation of the *kohen* towards a *meis mitzvah* is even more stringent than towards a member of his family.

in the interim, a sufficient number of people come to carry the bier and to bury the deceased, the *kohen* need not become *tamei* any further.

If there are Jews close enough for the *kohen* to summon without leaving the body, and who, if summoned, will come and perform the burial, this is not the kind of *meis mitzvah* for which a *kohen* is required to become *tamei*. He should summon them, and they should bury the deceased.[8]

What if the Jews he can find in the vicinity will attend to the body only if paid to do so? In such a case, some rule that the *kohen* is not required to spend his own money to avoid becoming *tamei*; he may become *tamei* and bury the deceased, if he chooses. For further details on this situation, see footnote.[9]

If the *kohen* finds a body and doesn't know whether it is Jewish, he should act on the basis of the majority: if the majority of people passing that point are Jewish, he should assume that it is a *meis mitzvah*; otherwise, not.[10]

This rule of following the majority applies whenever no Jewish person had been in a known, fixed position (*kavua*) before the present doubt arose. However, if a Jewish person had been *kavua*, and the *kohen* now is in doubt about whether this is the body of that person, he should not become *tamei* to bury it. For an example, see footnote.[11]

---

8. *Shulchan Aruch* 374:3; *Taz* §§1, citing *Roke'ach*.

9. *Rama*, ad loc.

For the *halachah* in the case where non-Jews are willing to bury the deceased for payment, see *Ikrei HaDat*, *Yoreh De'ah*, §35 os 6. He writes: "*Teshuvah MeAhavah* replied to a disciple-colleague of his, named *Ra'ach*...that not only is it permitted [for the *kohen* to become *tamei*], but it is a *mitzvah* for him to do so; for who ever heard of such a thing: having non-Jews bury a *meis mitzvah*? And he cited a number of great authorities who agreed with this ruling." But *Ikrei HaDat* himself writes: "I, in my ignorance, would hesitate in an actual case like this to permit [the *kohen* to become *tamei*], as is written in *Shuta Deyenuka* §180." And see responsa *Maharatz Chayus*, at the end of §26, who permits the *kohen* to become *tamei* in such a case.

For the *halachah* in the case where non-Jews are willing to bury the deceased without payment, see *Sdei Chemed*, *Aveilus* §112. He cites *Tzemach Tzedek* (Lubavitch) as permitting [the *kohen* to become *tamei* by performing the burial himself]. The same ruling is given by *Gesher HaChaim* 6:7:3. However, responsa *Tuv Ta'am Veda'as*, *mahadura Kama* §289 writes: "I say that this ruling should be forgotten and never mentioned; for even though it is truly not respectful to have non-Jews bury [the *meis mitzvah*], nevertheless, on what basis can we permit [the *kohen* to become *tamei*]? ...Obviously, all this applies only in a case where there are non-Jews who wish to bury the deceased without payment. But if they request payment [the *kohen* is permitted to become *tamei* by performing the burial himself], for after all, even if there are Jews willing to perform the burial, but only on condition that they be paid, this is considered a case of *meis mitzvah* [where the *kohen* is allowed to become *tamei*]." The same ruling is given by *Aruch HaShulchan* 374:3.

10. *Rama* ad loc. there writes that we rule according to whether the majority of people in the area are Jews or non-Jews.

11. Ibid. For example, if it is known that nine non-Jews and one Jew were in that place, and one of them was killed where he was, this is considered *kavua*; we do not go according to the fact that the majority were non-Jews; instead, we consider as if there were equal numbers of Jews and non-Jews, and, as in other cases of doubt about a Scriptural *mitzvah*, we rule stringently — i.e., that it is a *meis mitzvah* whom one is obligated to bury. Nevertheless, since it is a case of doubt, the *kohen* is not permitted to become *tamei* by performing the burial himself.

◄§ Deceased for Whom a *Kohen* Is Forbidden to Become *Tamei*

4. A *kohen* may not become *tamei* for a half-brother or half-sister on his mother's side. He may not become *tamei* even for a sister on his father's side if she is someone's betrothed [see above, par. 2 (iii)], is married, or has been raped or seduced. He also is forbidden to become *tamei* for someone who died at an age of less than thirty days. [12]

He is not permitted to become *tamei* in cases of doubt. The following are two examples of doubt:

> (a) A child had been mixed up with another child at birth and it is not certain whether this is the child of its mother;

> (b) the mother of a child had been divorced and quickly remarried, and it is not certain whether the child came from the first or the second husband. [13] [In both cases, there is doubt whether the child is related to the *kohen*.]

5. If a *kohen's* family member had "departed from the ways of the community" — meaning that he threw off the yoke of *mitzvos* and hence is not included in *Klal Yisrael* (the Jewish People) — the *kohen* is not permitted to become *tamei* for his burial. The same applies if the family member committed suicide. [14] Please note, however, that the practical application of these laws regarding suicides and other special cases are very complex, and a competent halachic authority should be consulted should the question arise.

6. A *kohen* is permitted to become *tamei* only for a deceased whose body is whole.

If even a small part of the body is missing, the *kohen* may not become *tamei*. This applies even if the missing piece is lying next to the deceased, and even if the piece has been sewn back onto the body. [15] Regarding whether the body is

---

12. *Shulchan Aruch* 374:4. And see *Sdei Chemed*, *Aveilus* §107, who cites *Yad Shaul* and responsa *Shaagas Aryeh HeChadashos* as ruling that in a case of doubt as to whether the infant lived until the thirtieth day, the *kohen* is required to become *tamei*.

13. *Shulchan Aruch* 374:8. And see *Chiddushei Rabbi Akiva Eiger*, ad loc., who writes that if the one whose parentage is in doubt is a *kohen*, he is not permitted to become *tamei* for his possible family members; and if they are *kohanim*, they are not permitted to become *tamei* for him. This is stated in the Mishnah, and cited explicitly by *Shulchan Aruch*, *Even HaEzer* (3:9). This is contrary to the ruling of responsa *Beis Yaakov* (§130).

14. *Shulchan Aruch* 373:8. The reason is that the Torah says, '*He shall not contaminate himself to a dead person among his people*' (*Leviticus* 21:1). And the Sages (*Sanhedrin 40a*) derive from the words '*among his people*' that the *kohen* is required to become *tamei* only "when he acts like your people."

15. *Shulchan Aruch* 373:9. And see the commentary of *Radbaz* on *Rambam*, *Hilchos Avel* 2:15, where *Radbaz* writes that even if the disconnected limbs are sewn back onto the body, they are not considered connected, and consequently the body is considered to lack limbs and the *kohen* is not permitted to become *tamei*.

In a case where the body is lacking blood, responsa *Mishneh Halachos* (part III: §121) writes that this is considered as if part of the body is missing [and the *kohen* is not permitted to become *tamei*]. He supports this conclusion by the fact that the body of an executed person (*harug*) is considered incomplete because his blood is lacking. However, responsa *Maharam* Shick, *Yoreh De'ah* §359

considered whole if the blood has been removed, see footnote.[15]

Some rule that this *halachah* applies only if the missing piece of the body was removed at the time of death or afterwards. If a limb had been removed during the person's lifetime, the *kohen* must become *tamei* for him even though the body is not whole.[16]

Some rule that a *kohen* may not become *tamei* for someone who was murdered, rather than having died as a result of an accident or natural causes, because this comes within the category of one whose body is not whole. It is proper to follow this stringency.[17]

A *kohen* may not become *tamei* for the reinterment (*likut atzamos* — see below, chapter 45) of a family member.[18]

◄§ Miscellaneous *Halachos*

7. Some rule that a *kohen* who is a bridegroom is forbidden to become *tamei* for any family member during the seven days of his wedding feasts (*sheva brachos*).[19]

8. Some rule that a *kohen* who is a child, and thus is not obligated by the laws of mourning, is forbidden to become *tamei* for any family member. However, if the child attempts to enter the place where he will become *tamei*, adults are not required to make him stay out, even if he has reached *gil chinuch*, educable age.[20]

---

writes: "In light of what has been said, it would seem that with regard to his father, [the *kohen* is forbidden to become *tamei*] only if the body has changed after death from what it was [during life]. This means there must be a lack which is evident and visible to the eye, as is the law regarding physical defects [which disqualify a *kohen* from performing sacrifices in the Temple]. In that case [when there is such a visible lack], we say that this is not the body of his father as it originally was. But where the body is lacking blood, this is not evident, and it is still called the body of his father as it originally was." The same ruling is given by responsa *Sheivet HaLevi, Yoreh De'ah tinyana,* §161.

For the *halachah* in a case where the body is lacking part or all of some internal organ, see responsa *Igros Moshe* (*Yoreh De'ah* §251), who rules that this is not considered an incomplete body, since the lack is not evident. The same conclusion is implied by the words of *Maharam* Shick cited above. However, *Chazon Ish, Yoreh De'ah* §210:15, writes that study is required on the question of a puncture which does not involve the lack of any flesh, such as a hole in the esophagus or heart. This implies that in his opinion it is obvious that if part of the organ were missing, this would be considered an incomplete body, even though the lack is internal.

Afterwards, I saw that *Sheivet HaLevi*, loc. cit., draws exactly this conclusion from these words of the *Chazon Ish*, ruling that this is considered a lack. The same ruling is given by responsa *Mishneh Halachos* loc. cit.

16. *Rama* 373:9.

17. Ibid. And see *Igros Moshe* loc. cit., who states that if the body is not lacking anything — for example, if the person was killed by poisoning or strangulation — the *kohen* is required to become *tamei*.

18. *Rama* loc. cit., and *Shach* 403:§§1. And see *Kol Bo Al Aveilus* p. 253 par. 10.

19. Responsa *Zekan Aharon* §108, cited by *Ikrei HaDat* §35 *os* 14. But he himself, in *Orach Chaim* §14, questions this ruling. And see *Da'as Torah* ad loc.

20. *Pischei Teshuvah* 373:§§1 cites responsa *Veshav HaKohen* (end of §56), who asks the following question. *Rambam* (*Hilchos Avel* ch. 2) states that the *mitzvah* of a *kohen* to become *tamei* for the members of his family is an aspect of mourning (*aveilus*), and any *kohen* who is not commanded to

9. Some rule that a *kohen* may become *tamei* for the specified family members even when this is not necessary for burial, or in order to bring burial wrappings or a coffin.[21] Therefore even on the Sabbath, though it is impossible to bury the deceased, a *kohen* is permitted to become *tamei* by staying with and watching over the body so that it should not be left in neglect.[22]

However, others rule that the *kohen* is not allowed to become *tamei* except for the needs of burial, or in order to bring burial wrappings or a coffin to the deceased. It is proper to be stringent and follow this second opinion.[23]

Some authorities write that the *kohen* is permitted to be in the same house with the deceased on a weekday (but not on the Sabbath), even though others are attending to the body. This is in case the *kohen* might be needed for some purpose such as readying the coffin.[24]

---

mourn is forbidden to become *tamei*. According to this, is a *kohen* who is not yet *bar mitzvah* permitted to become *tamei* for a family member? After all, he is "not commanded to mourn." The author of *Veshav HaKohen* concludes that the matter requires study.

See *Minchas Chinuch*, mitzvah 264, end of §§1. He concludes that a *kohen* who is not yet *bar mitzvah* is forbidden to become *tamei* for his family members. "But if the child does so of his own accord, his father does not have to remove him [from proximity to the deceased] for the sake of training him (*chinuch*)."

If so, asks *Mishmeres Shalom*, os 20, §5, why should the father remove the child from proximity to the deceased? After all, when he comes of age he will be not only permitted, but commanded, to become *tamei* for a member of his family. And *Gesher HaChaim* (6:10) writes the same.

And see *Chikkekei Lev* (*Yoreh De'ah* §145), who discusses this question and concludes that a *kohen* who is not yet *bar mitzvah* is permitted to become *tamei* for his family members. He reasons by analogy with the *mitzvah* of *tzitzis* as follows: The *mitzvis* of *tzitzis* is a positive commandment. In fulfilling it, one is permitted to violate the negative commandment against *kila'im*, wearing wool and linen together. Nevertheless, for the sake of education the Sages permitted a minor to wear *tzitzis*, even though his parents are ordinarily forbidden to have him wear *kila'im*. The same applies in our topic. The *mitzvah* of a *kohen* to become *tamei* for a family member is a positive commandment. In fulfilling it, one is permitted to violate the negative commandment against becoming *tamei*. Nevertheless, for the sake of education the Sages permitted a minor to become *tamei* for his family members.

21. *Shulchan Aruch* 373:5. And see *Shach* §§5, who states that it is even a *mitzvah* for the *kohen* to become *tamei*. And in *Nekudos HaKesef* he writes: "This is the principal ruling, and is the accepted custom."

22. *Rama* ad loc.

23. Ibid. And see *Kerem Shlomo* (ad loc.), who comments on *Rama*: "From this it would seem that it is forbidden for a *kohen* to close his deceased father's eyes, as non-*kohanim* do for their deceased. . .since this is not considered to be for the needs of burial." But I have heard from *chevra kadisha* members that, contrary to this ruling of *Kerem Shlomo*, the custom is that a *kohen* does close his father's eyes. And see the next footnote.

See also *Chochmas Adam* §160: 5, who writes: "It seems to me that in any case [the *kohen*] is required to become *tamei* for the needs of burial, even if there is a group of men there [who could perform the burial without the *kohen's* help]. The proof is that, [as the Talmud relates,] they forced Yosef the *Kohen* to become *tamei* on the day before Pesach (see *Beis Yosef*) — and undoubtedly [in that instance] there were enough men to perform the burial without him."

24. *Pischei Teshuvah* §§4, citing *Derech HaChaim*. The same ruling is given by *Gesher HaChaim* 6:6.

And see *Kol Bo Al Aveilus* p. 70, citing *Eivel Yachid*, who in turn cites *Maaseh Betzalel* as stating that according to this, it is also permitted for the *kohen* to close his father's eyes, contrary to the ruling of *Kerem Shlomo* cited in the previous footnote.

10. If one of the specified deceased family members (see above, paragraph 2) is in
a house, the *kohen* is permitted to enter the house, thereby becoming *tamei*.
This applies even if there are other dead persons there.[25] Nevertheless, he must
leave the house before his own family member is removed.[26]

11. The *kohen's* permission to become *tamei* lasts only until the grave is filled with
earth.[27] If it is the intention to rebury the deceased, the *kohen* may become
tamei, for the needs of burial, until the second grave is filled with earth.[28]

12. The *kohen* may accompany the deceased relative to the grave if there are no
other graves in the immediate vicinity.[29] If there are other graves there, he must
stay at a distance of four *amos* (about eight feet) from the graves.[30] One authority
writes that even if there are other graves, if there was no space to bury at the edge
of the cemetery, the *kohen* may accompany the deceased to the grave.[31]

---

25. *Ikrei HaDat*, *Yoreh De'ah*, §35:31. The same ruling is given by *Gesher HaChaim* (6:8), and by
Chazon LaMo'ed (8:3). But I have heard that some have the custom of being stringent on this
matter [i.e., their custom is that if any other deceased is in the house, the *kohen* is forbidden to be there,
even though his own deceased family member is also there].

26. *Har Tzvi*, *Yoreh De'ah* §282. And this is an obvious conclusion.

27. *Shulchan Aruch* 373:6. And see *Shach* there, §§11.

28. *Rama* 373:6. And see *Kol Bo Al Aveilus* p. 253, who states that *Rama* is referring to a situation
where the second burial occurs immediately after the first, and the body is still whole. And see the
ruling he cites there in the name of *Machaneh Chaim* part 3, *Yoreh De'ah* §45.

29. This is because he is allowed to become *tamei* until the grave is filled with earth (*stimas hagolel*).
And this is the ruling given by *Gesher HaChaim* loc. cit.

30. This prohibition obviously applies according to the ruling of R' Yosef Karo in 373:7 — that a *kohen*
is forbidden to become *tamei* from another deceased even if his own deceased family member is
present. And the prohibition even applies according to the ruling of *Rama*, who permits a *kohen* to
become *tamei* from another deceased if his own deceased family member is present. The reason why
the prohibition applies even according to *Rama* is that in returning from the burial, the *kohen* will have
to come near other graves, after he has already separated from his own family member and no longer
has permission to become *tamei* from other deceased.
    And see *Shach* §§12, who cites *Bach* as ruling that even on the way to the grave of his own family
member the *kohen* is forbidden to increase his *tumah* by coming near other graves, since it would be
possible to perform the burial at the edge of the cemetery. This seems also to be the opinion of R' Yosef
Karo. The same ruling is given by *Ateres Zahav*, who states, "It is correct to be stringent [i.e., not enter
the cemetery] in accord with this reasoning."
    My father and teacher, *zatzal*, in his work *Zichron Eliahu* (manuscript) mentions the requirement to
stay at least four *amos* from the graves. The reason is obvious: Since the *kohen* is forbidden to become
tamei, the *halachah* for him is the same as for any other *kohen* — he is forbidden to come within four
amos (about eight feet) of a grave, as explained in *Shulchan Aruch* 371:5.

31. Responsa *Igros Moshe* (*Yoreh De'ah* §252) writes that he was asked regarding a *kohen* whom
there was no space to bury at the edge of the cemetery. Were his family members [*kohanim*]
permitted to go [into the cemetery] for his burial? "I replied that it is obvious that they are permitted to
do so, since it was impossible [to bury him at the edge of the cemetery]. Even *Bach*, cited by *Shach*
(373:§§12), who forbids going into the cemetery [for the burial], writes, '. . .since it would be possible
to perform the burial at the edge of the cemetery.' Afterwards, on their return, they will have to pass
near other graves in order to go out, as is the case with one who becomes *tamei* in a cemetery; but they
may not leave by a long path. They are not allowed to wait for the recitation of *Tzidduk HaDin* and
Kaddish, but must leave immediately after the burial. If in the place where they are standing there are

13. If the body of the deceased is stationary, a *kohen* is not permitted to go within four *amos* (about eight feet) of the body. However, while the body is being moved, this distance does not apply. Then any *kohen* (even not a relative) may come near, as long as he keeps a distance of at least four handsbreadths (*tefachim*).[32]

---

no graves and they are more than four *amos* from the graves, they may wait for *Tzidduk HaDin* and *Kaddish*. When they leave they must not stop while passing places where there are graves."

32. See *Shach* 371:§§18, who cites *Roke'ach* §315: ". . .but when the deceased is on the bier on which they take him to burial, and while reciting *Tzidduk HaDin* — when the funeral procession halts, the perimeter of four *amos* does not apply, and [the deceased] is not considered to be in a fixed location (*kevius*)." *Shach* adds: "As for the statement [that the perimeter of four *amos* does not apply] 'when the funeral procession halts,' it would seem that this is all the more true when the procession is in motion."

CHAPTER EIGHT

Hesped: The Eulogy

◦§ The *Mitzvah*

1. Delivering a proper eulogy (*hesped*) is a major *mitzvah*. The *mitzvah* is to raise one's voice,[1] and to speak heartrending words about the deceased in order to arouse the weeping of the audience, and to mention his praises. When one sheds tears over the passing of an upright Jew, the Holy One, Blessed is He, counts the tears and puts them in His treasure house. If one is negligent about the eulogy of an upright Jew, one does not live long, and is worthy of being buried alive.[2]

◦§ Exaggerating Praise

2. It is forbidden to exaggerate excessively in praising the deceased. However, one is permitted to exaggerate slightly,[3] as long as one does not go too far.[4] If the

---

1. We find in the first chapter of *Berachos* (6b): "The merit of a eulogy (*hesped*) lies in the *dilevai* (דְּלָוֵי)." *Rashi* explains: "To raise one's voice in lamentation and anguish, so that the listeners will weep." *Ramban* interprets *dilevai* as meaning: "to raise one's voice in eulogy for the learned and the meticulously observant, as we find [*Shabbos* 153a]: 'Be fervent in my eulogy for I will be present there.'" In the Jerusalem Talmud we read: "[In commanding the prophet Ezekiel *not* to mourn, Hashem told him:] '*Silence your groan*' (*Ezekiel* 24:17) — from this we learn that ordinarily the mourner *should* bewail the deceased."

   Darkei Moshe (§344) cites the Jerusalem Talmud as saying: "The deceased knows and hears his praises as in a dream, and knows everything that is said about him until the grave is filled with earth and he returns to the dust." This is cited by *Taz* (loc. cit. §§1), and the same is found in the Babylonian Talmud, *Shabbos* 152b.

2. These are the words of *Shulchan Aruch* 344:1, and *Shach* §§1. The source is *Shabbos* 105b.

   Rashi comments there: "This is measure for measure: He failed to grieve that the life of the sage was shortened; therefore Heaven is not concerned about his life." *Gilyon Maharsha* writes there: "The eulogy saves the deceased from Gehinnom."

3. *Shulchan Aruch* loc. cit. And *Sheivet Yehudah* (loc. cit.) writes that the term "exaggerate" means that for any given trait which the deceased actually possessed, one may somewhat exaggerate the extent to which he possessed it. However, if he did not possess a certain trait at all, one is forbidden to attribute it to him.

4. *Bach* (loc. cit.) explains that one is forbidden to understate the praise of the deceased. Therefore, the Sages permitted slight exaggeration, for if all exaggeration were forbidden, there would be danger of understating, God forbid. *Taz* (loc. cit.) writes: "This is difficult to understand. What difference is there between lying slightly or lying a lot? But apparently there is a logical reason for this. Anyone who does a *mitzvah*, such as *tzedakah* (charity) and the like, certainly would do slightly more if the need arose. He would not ruin the *mitzvah* just because of the small extra expense. Therefore, it is counted as if he had actually done [a little more], and there is no false testimony about him." *Birkei*

deceased had no good qualities, one should not mention his character. If he was learned or pious, one should mention his scholarship or piety.

If one attributes good qualities to someone who did not possess them at all, or excessively exaggerates the good qualities he had, this causes evil to the speaker and to the deceased.[5]

◆§ Eulogizing Women

3. Just as one should eulogize a man, one should eulogize a woman, in accordance with her qualities. It is proper to deliver her eulogy in the presence of men and sages.

In communities where it is customary to hire *mekonnenos*, women who recite mourning chants, a husband is obligated to hire them for his wife's funeral. If he does not wish to do so, her father may hire them and can legally force the husband to pay.[6] If the woman had no husband, her heirs and family members who are obligated to mourn for her must hire *mekonnenos*.[7]

For a woman of great accomplishments, or the wife of someone great in Torah, the practice in some communities is to deliver eulogies in the streets, just as is done for a man who was great in accomplishments and scholarship.[8]

◆§ Obligation of the Heirs

4. If heirs inherited money from the deceased, but refuse to pay the expenses of the eulogy, the Torah court can force them to pay.[9] The reason is that הֶסְפֵּדָא יְקָרֵי דְּשִׁיכְבָא הוּא, the eulogy is for the honor of the deceased, not of the living.

◆§ Command Not to Eulogize

5. If one commanded his family not to eulogize him, he must be obeyed.[10] However, if he commanded them not to observe the laws of mourning during

---

Yosef writes: "This is not lying, since it may be assumed that people did not know the full extent of his good traits. Undoubtedly part of them did not become known, either because he purposely hid them, or because people did not investigate so thoroughly." *Sheivet Shimon* explains: "Death atones for a man's transgressions. His sins are reduced, but his merits remain intact" (*Kol Bo Al Aveilus* p. 98).

5. *Shulchan Aruch* loc. cit. "For this serves as a reminder of the sins of the deceased, and he is punished for not possessing the good trait which his eulogizers attribute to him. And it goes without saying that the eulogizers are punished for speaking falsehoods and flattering someone who is not a *tzaddik* by saying about him, 'You are a *tzaddik*' " (*Bach* loc. cit.).

6. *Shulchan Aruch* 344:2,3.

7. *Gesher HaChaim* 13:8.

8. Ibid.

9. *Shulchan Aruch* 344:9 (*Taz* §§4; *Shach* §§8).

10. *Shulchan Aruch* loc. cit. §10. And see *Pischei Teshuvah* §§1, who cites responsa *Beis Yaakov* §83, as ruling that if the *gedol hador*, the greatest scholar of the generation, dies, having commanded not to eulogize him, anyone who acts leniently — i.e., disobeys this command — will forfeit nothing thereby. And see responsa *Teshuvah MeAhavah* I:§174.

See also responsa *Minchas Elazar* II: §63. He states that the only prohibition is against an oral eulogy, but writing and publishing a eulogy involves no prohibition.

the *shivah* (first seven days) and *shloshim* (first thirty days), he must not be obeyed.[11]

◦§ Citing Verses

6. It is permitted to quote verses or deliver a Torah discourse in honor of the deceased[12] even while standing within four *amos* (an *amah* is about eight feet) of the body, or while in the cemetery.[13]

◦§ Eulogy in the *Beth Midrash*

7. For a sage (*chacham*) and a major Torah leader (*aluf* and *gaon*), the body is taken into the *beth midrash*. The bier is placed where he used to stand when delivering Torah talks. There the eulogies are delivered. Then he is taken out, and those present continue to deliver eulogies on the way to the cemetery.[14]

For other people, their body should not be taken into the *beth midrash* or synagogue.[15]

◦§ Two Eulogies

8. It is wrong to hold two different eulogies in the same community for the same deceased, unless there are so many people that they can be divided into two groups, and each eulogy will still be properly attended.[16]

It is wrong to hold two different eulogies in one community for two different deceased, unless there are enough speakers to eulogize each one properly.[17]

◦§ Near a Festival

9. For the definition of *Yom Tov* ["Festival"] for purposes of the following laws, see footnote 20.

If someone dies more than thirty days before one of the Festivals, eulogies should not be held for him within thirty days of the Festival.[18]

If a person dies within thirty days of a Festival, it is permitted to eulogize him,

---

11. *Rama* loc. cit., citing *Mahariv* par. 4.
12. "It is certainly forbidden to say things [of this nature in the proximity of a deceased or a grave] for any reason other than to honor the deceased — contrary to those whose intention in eulogizing is to exhibit their own wisdom. That certainly is not for the honor of the deceased, and those who do it are not acting correctly. I have heard many great Torah leaders who expressed dissatisfaction about this" (*Taz* §§5).
13. *Shulchan Aruch* 344:17.
14. *Shulchan Aruch* 344:20.
15. *Chochmas Adam* 155:18.
16. *Shulchan Aruch* 344:14. See *Chochmas Adam* 155:14.
17. *Shulchan Aruch* 344:15. See *Prishah* (loc. cit. §§18), who states that the emphasis here is on cantors and public speakers who tell the praises of the deceased and arouse the public's grief. Thus, even if there is a large public to attend both funerals, but there are not sufficient speakers, it is wrong to hold the two eulogies at the same time.
18. *Shulchan Aruch Yoreh De'ah* 347:1, and *Orach Chaim* 547:3.

even if he died the day before the festival.[19] But at this eulogy one may not include a eulogy for someone who died more than thirty days before the Festival.[20]

If someone died more than thirty days before a Festival, but the mourner did not hear of the death until less than thirty days before the Festival, it is permitted to eulogize the deceased.[21]

At the completion of the year of mourning, it is customary to eulogize the deceased and commemorate his soul. This type of eulogy is not governed by the rules mentioned in this paragraph. It may be held even less than thirty days before a Festival.[22]

⋘ Days When Eulogies Are Forbidden

10. On certain days of the year, it is forbidden to deliver a eulogy. The only exception is for a sage (chacham) whose unburied body is present.[23] These days are:

---

19. This applies even if the eulogizer takes payment, and even if the deceased is an ordinary person, not a Torah scholar (talmid chacham). The reason is that the loss of the mourner is still recent, and since the bitterness of grief is strong, the eulogy will not produce any more grief than already exists (Mishnah Berurah 547:§§5).

20. Once the memory of the deceased is aroused, he is not forgotten for thirty days. Hence, if he were eulogized fewer than thirty days before the Festival, the mourner would come to weep and feel sorrow during the Festival, since he would not yet have forgotten.

The prohibition against eulogy within thirty days before the Festival applies even if the eulogizer does not take payment, but speaks only for the sake of the mitzvah.

For the purposes of this prohibition, it makes no difference whether the eulogizer is himself one of the mourners. Even if one of the mourners is eulogizing another deceased, he is forbidden to include eulogy of the person for whom he is in mourning, since in any case this would add to his feelings of sorrow during the Festival (Mishnah Berurah loc. cit. §§2 and 6).

[For this halachah, Yom Tov, "Festival", means Pesach, Shavuos, and Succos.] There is a question whether Rosh Hashanah and Yom Kippur are also included. Pri Megaddim (loc. cit.) expresses doubt on the matter. Yeshuos Yaakov rules leniently [i.e., he permits eulogy even fewer than thirty days before Rosh Hashanah or Yom Kippur]. See also Toras Adam (loc. cit. §§4), who cites R' Nissim Gaon as permitting eulogies during the month of Elul. The same ruling is given by Pischei Teshuvah §§1, citing Agudas Ezov, who states that Rosh Hashanah and Yom Kippur are not considered "Festivals" with regard to this prohibition.

[The prohibition does not apply to Rabbinic Festivals like Chanukah and Purim.]

21. The reason is that, since the bitterness of grief is still strong, the eulogy cannot be said to produce any more grief than already exists. This is similar to the situation when the death itself occurred within thirty days before the festival, and it is permitted to eulogize (Shulchan Aruch Yoreh De'ah 347:2, and Orach Chaim 547:4; Mishnah Berurah loc. cit. §§17).

22. Yoreh De'ah 347:3; Orach Chaim 547:5. And see Pri Megaddim (loc. cit., in Eshel Avraham, §§2), who writes that the practice of going to the grave and reciting memorial prayers and אֵל מָלֵא רַחֲמִים, 'God, full of mercy,' is considered like a eulogy and is forbidden within thirty days before the festival. Only after the year of mourning is finished is this permitted, for then it signifies the end of mourning [and hence does not increase grief]. However, Sha'ar HaTziyun (loc. cit. §§6) writes "It seems that in this matter, too, the prevalent custom is to be lenient, i.e., to visit the grave at any time, even [during the thirty days] before the Festivals."

23. Shulchan Aruch Yoreh De'ah 401:5. It is further stated there that just as one is permitted to eulogize while the sage is not yet buried, so too one is permitted to eulogize on the day when news of his death is received, even if the news is a shmu'ah rechokah, i.e., even if death occurred more than

- □ Rosh Chodesh;[24]
- □ The entire month of Nissan;
- □ *Pesach Sheni* (the fourteenth of Iyar);
- □ In some communities from Rosh Chodesh Sivan until the day after Shavuos (Some congregants do not resume *tachanun* until 14 Sivan.);
- □ Lag B'Omer;
- □ Chanukah;
- □ Both days of Purim (the fourteenth and fifteenth of Adar or Adar II);
- □ Both days of Purim Katan (the fourteenth and fifteenth of Adar I);
- □ Tu BiShvat;
- □ The fifteenth of Av;
- □ *Isru Chag* (the day after the last *Yom Tov* day of Pesach, Shavuos, or Succos);
- □ The four days between Yom Kippur and Succos. In some communities, through the end of Tishrei;
- □ Friday, after *chatzos* (around noon; exact time varies according to the season);
- □ The day before a Festival, after *chatzos* (around noon; the exact time varies according to the season);
- □ The day before Yom Kippur (even before *chatzos*).

However, on Tishah B'Av it is permitted to eulogize a sage who has just died.[25]

On *Chol HaMo'ed* it is forbidden to eulogize even a sage whose unburied body is present.[26]

On the Sabbath[27] and *Yom Tov*[28] (including the Diaspora's second day of *Yom Tov*), a eulogy may not be delivered. On the Diaspora's second day of *Yom*

---

thirty days before the news was received.

See *Gesher HaChaim* (13:10), who writes that when eulogizing a still unburied sage on Rosh Chodesh, Chanukah, or Purim, the eulogy should be brief. He also states that for the wife of a Torah scholar (*eishes chaver*), the *halachah* is lenient, i.e., while she is not yet buried one may eulogize her even on the days listed in our text.

24. *Shulchan Aruch Orach Chaim* §420. And see responsa *Devar Shmuel* (§69), who permits eulogizing on Rosh Chodesh Av, since "they are days of troubles" (*Kol Bo Al Aveilus* p. 102, note 12).

25. *Mishnah Berurah* 559:§§17. He states that even though Tishah B'Av is called a *mo'ed* (Festival), it is a day established for weeping and eulogy. This implies that one may eulogize even if the deceased has been buried.

26. *Be'ur Halachah* §547, citing "*Poskim.*" And see *Igros Moshe*, *Orach Chaim* I:§165, where the author expresses doubt as to whether the mourner himself may eulogize during *Chol HaMo'ed*.

27. Responsa *Minchas Elazar* part 4 §45. He refutes the arguments of those who permit eulogies on the Sabbath.

28. *Gesher HaChaim*, loc. cit. os 13, writes that the prohibition applies even for the death of a great Torah scholar, and even in order to arouse weeping.

Tov, someone from outside *Eretz Yisrael* is forbidden to take part in a eulogy in *Eretz Yisrael*, even if the eulogy is for a great scholar.[29]

◄§ After Twelve Months

11. After twelve months from the day of burial, no eulogy should be delivered, not even for a Torah sage, and not even on the day that news of his death is received.[30]

◄§ Displays of Grief

12. It is forbidden to pluck out even a single hair in grief for the deceased.[31] It is also forbidden to cut one's flesh in grief.[32] To strike oneself with one's hand, even to the point of bleeding, is permitted. Some rule that it is permitted only for the death of a great man, in grief over the loss of Torah, but simply for a member of one's family, it is forbidden.[33]

29. *Igros Moshe, Orach Chaim* part 3 §77.

30. *Shulchan Aruch* 394:2; *Shach* §§1. And see *Taz* 344:§§5, who writes in the name of *Toras HaAdam* that it is not the custom and is not proper behavior (*derech eretz*) to commemorate the deceased after twelve months, and if news of the death is received after twelve months, there is no obligation of eulogy. Moreover, since the term used is "twelve months" rather than "a year," this implies that in a leap-year [when the year contains thirteen months], one counts only twelve actual months, not the full [thirteen-month] year.

31. *Shulchan Aruch Yoreh De'ah* 180:9.

32. Ibid. 180:6,7. The prohibition applies even when one is not in the presence of the deceased.

33. *Shulchan Aruch* §180; *Shach* §§10.

CHAPTER NINE

Scheduling the Funeral

◄§ Taking the Deceased to Burial

1. The deceased should not be taken for burial[1] in early morning, close to the prescribed time for reciting the *Shema*,[2] unless there is time to complete the funeral procession and burial before the time for reciting the *Shema* arrives.[3]

However, if the funeral commenced just before, or even after, the earliest possible time to recite the *Shema*,[4] then, those carrying the bier should not stop to recite the *Shema*, even if this means that they will miss the latest time for reciting it. But those who are not needed for carrying the bier (see below, 10:11) should stop and recite the *Shema* at the earliest possible time, even though there will still be time to recite it later.[5]

2. If the time for reciting the *Shema* has arrived, whether in the morning or evening, the funeral should not be started until it may be assumed that the majority of the community has finished praying.[6]

3. On the morning of *erev* Pesach, if there is enough time to bury the deceased and still finish eating *chametz* before the hour when eating *chametz* is forbidden, the burial should take place first.[7] However, if time is short, and it is possible that after the burial there will not be enough time for eating *chametz*, it is better to eat first. The *mitzvah* of destroying *chametz* (*biur chametz*) should also be performed on time. Afterwards, the burial should be attended to.[8] But if the funeral has already begun, it should not be interrupted for the eating of *chametz*.[9]

---

1. This applies even for the burial of an important man (*adam chashuv*), because for the purpose of relaxing this prohibition, no one in our time fits the Talmud's category of "important man." (*Mishnah Berurah* 72:§§5).
2. *Shulchan Aruch Yoreh De'ah* 358:2, and *Orach Chaim* 72:2.
3. *Be'ur Halachah* (§72), citing *Talmidei Rabbeinu Yonah* and *Beis Yosef*.
4. *Mishnah Berurah* 72:§§7.
5. *Shulchan Aruch Yoreh De'ah* 358:2; *Mishnah Berurah* 72:§§8.
6. *Mishnah Berurah* loc. cit. §§4,6.
7. The reason is that "it is not right for those involved in the burial to eat before the burial, as explained in §526, *Taz* §§6" (*Mishnah Berurah* 443:§§6).
8. *Mishnah Berurah* loc. cit..
9. *Magen Avraham* loc. cit. 72:§§2. And he adds: "If they will not be able to eat [*chametz*] afterwards, they should eat *matzah ashirah* [e.g. egg *matzah*] or meat and fish."

4. During the eulogies, as long as the body of the deceased is present, those present do not, as a group, interrupt to recite the *Shema* and pray. Instead, people go out[10] individually to do so.[11]

If the body of the deceased is not present, the public sits down to recite the *Shema*. During this time, the family members who are required to mourn (*onenim*) should remain silent [for until the burial, they are exempt from *mitzvos*]. Then the public stands to recite the *Shemoneh Esrei* prayer. While they pray, the family members engage in *Tzidduk HaDin*, justifying the Divine decree upon them. They say: יְהִי רָצוֹן מִלְפָנֶיךָ ה' אֱלוֹהַי שֶׁתִּגְדּוֹר פִּרְצוֹתֵינוּ וּפִרְצוֹת עַמְּךָ בֵּית יִשְׂרָאֵל, "May it be Your will, Hashem my God, to heal our losses and the losses of Your people, the House of Israel."[12]

◆§ *Halanas HaMeis*: **Leaving a Body Unburied Overnight**

5. It is forbidden to leave the deceased unburied overnight. Anyone who does so violates a negative commandment, as it is said (*Deut*. 21:23): *'Do not leave his corpse on the tree overnight, but you shall certainly bury him that day.'*[13]

In the opinion of many authorities, one is obligated to bury one's dead on the day he dies, before sunset; otherwise, one violates a positive commandment (ibid.): *You shall certainly bury it that day.*[14] Some rule that in *Eretz Yisrael* one also violates another negative commandment (ibid.): *'You shall not make your land ritually contaminated (tamei)'.*[15]

The prohibited act of leaving the dead unburied overnight is called *halanah* ("leaving overnight"), or *halanas hameis* ("leaving the dead overnight"). This prohibition applies to those who are obligated to bury the deceased. If close family members (those listed above, 6:1) exist, it applies to them. If they do not exist — or even if they exist, but they do not take the initiative to arrange for burial — the

---

10. They cannot recite the *Shema* here, in the presence of the deceased, for this would violate the prohibition against "ridiculing the helpless" (*lo'eg larash*, performing *mitzvos* in the presence of the deceased) — *Mishnah Berurah* 72:§§9.

   Be'ur Halachah (loc. cit.) writes: "The implication is that even if this means the time for reciting the *Shema* will be missed, one does not recite it. Since they had already begun the *mitzvah* [of eulogy] they are exempt from the other *mitzvah* [reciting the *Shema*]. This is true even though the second *mitzvah* [reciting the *Shema*] is much more weighty. This is proven by what *Magen Avraham* writes in §§4."

11. "But many *Poskim* disagree, ruling that [one need not go out to pray, but only to recite the *Shema*, because] the Sages were lenient about the requirement for prayer while the deceased is still in the presence [of those attending the eulogy]. Since prayer is a Rabbinic *mitzvah*, they exempted them from it under these circumstances. And it would seem that, regarding the speaker who is delivering the eulogy, one certainly should rely on the lenient ruling, and he should not have to interrupt [the eulogy] to pray, since there are some who rule that he is exempt even from reciting the *Shema* in this situation" (*Mishnah Berurah* loc. cit. §§10).

12. *Shulchan Aruch Yoreh De'ah* 344:12.

13. *Shulchan Aruch* 357:1.

14. *Sefer HaChinuch mitzvah* 537. And see *Minchas Chinuch* loc. cit.; *Sefer HaMitzvos mitzvah* 231. And this is the ruling cited by *Mishnah Berurah* 72:§§6.

15. *Ramban*, *Parashas Ki Setzei*.

obligation falls upon the members of the *chevra kadisha* (burial society), who areconsidered emissaries of the public and of the Torah court.[16]

6. Even if a person was completely wicked his whole life, it is forbidden to leave his corpse unburied overnight.[17] For the corpse of a non-Jew, however, some rule that the prohibition does not apply.[18]

The prohibition does not apply to the corpse of an aborted fetus. But some rule that it does apply.[19]

7. For the honor of the deceased, it is permitted to leave the body unburied overnight[20] — for example: to have time to bring burial wrappings (*tachrichim*) or a coffin; to bring *mekonnenos* (see above, 8:3), to allow the family members to arrive; or to inform people of the death.[21]

Once the body has been left overnight one night for the honor of the deceased, the prohibition of *halanas hameis* no longer applies.[21]

If the deceased had commanded his family not to bury him until after two days, some rule that it is permitted to leave him unburied overnight. Others disagree.[22]

In Jerusalem, it is forbidden to leave the body unburied overnight, even for the honor of the deceased.[23]

---

16. *Chochmas Adam, Kuntres Matzeivas Moshe* par. 12.

17. Responsa *Besamim Rosh* §64. He writes that even though the Sages said that the reason for burial is to show respect for our fellow man (*kevod habrios*), nonetheless, the basis of the prohibition against leaving a body unburied overnight is a negative commandment of the Torah. And see *Mishmeres Shalom os lamed* §36, citing responsa *Ri HaLevi*.

18. *Gesher HaChaim* 7:1:10. The reason is that the positive commandment, 'You shall certainly bury. . .' (Deut. 21:23) does not refer to a non-Jew.

19. *Hagahos Maimoni*. This ruling may also be inferred from the words of R' Yosef Karo and *Rama*, *Orach Chaim* 526:10. But see *Magen Avraham* (loc. cit. §§20), who writes that the Talmud in *Niddah* 57 implies that the prohibition against leaving a body unburied overnight applies even to an aborted fetus. And see *Mishmeres Shalom* loc. cit. §32, and *Gesher HaChaim* loc. cit.

20. *Shulchan Aruch* 357:1. And see responsa *Radbaz* part 1 §107, cited in *Pischei Teshuvah* loc. cit. §§2.

21. *Shulchan Aruch* loc. cit.

21a. *Or Same'ach* on *Rambam, Hilchos Sanhedrin* 15:6. The same ruling is given by responsa *Shaagas Aryeh HeChadashos*.

22. See *Sdei Chemed* (*Aveilus* §87), who cites *Ikrei HaDat* (*Orach Chaim* §11:os 13) as stating that there is no prohibition against fulfilling the command of the deceased in this matter; this involves no transgression of *halanas hameis*, and is even more justifiable than leaving the body unburied overnight for the honor of the deceased.

However, *Mishmeres Shalom* (*os tzadi*, §19) cites *Zachur Le'Avraham* (part 3, *os tzadi*, §24), who in turn cites *Yosef Ometz* (§89): "One who fulfills his command does him evil by making his soul *tamei*, God forbid. And there are other reasons, as well. But one who buries him on that day [the same day he died] has done a great *mitzvah*, and the deceased will certainly have spiritual satisfaction (*nachas ruach*), and his soul will bless him." The same ruling is given by responsa *Shevus Yaakov* (part I:§168), who states that the principle, "it is a *mitzvah* to fulfill the commands of the deceased" applies only to the disposition of his property, but not to other matters.

23. *Bava Kamma* 82b: "In Jerusalem. . .the deceased may not be left overnight." And see *Gesher HaChaim* (7:3:3) for the boundaries of "Jerusalem" with respect to this *halachah*.

8. Jews are forbidden to perform a burial on the first day of *Yom Tov* in the Diaspora, but they may arrange for non-Jews to bury the dead. On the Diaspora's second day of *Yom Tov*, Jews may perform the burial themselves. Nevertheless, it is forbidden to leave the body unburied overnight just so that the burial will be performed by Jews rather than by non-Jews.

On the Sabbath and *Yom Tov*, a Jew is forbidden to walk beyond the *techum*, a distance of about two thirds of a mile (two thousand *amos*) from the end of the city. On the Diaspora's second day of *Yom Tov*, this restriction does not apply for those accompanying the dead. Nevertheless, it is forbidden to leave the body unburied overnight just so that the wife and children will be able to walk beyond the *techum* to accompany the deceased to burial.[24]

9. If the head and most of the body of the deceased have not been found, leaving other limbs or bones unburied does not violate the prohibition of *halanas hameis*.[25]

10. For all family members except one's parent, it is praiseworthy to have the funeral and burial as soon as possible.[26] For one's parent, on the other hand, this was originally considered reprehensible, except on Friday or *erev Yom Tov*, or if rain was pouring down on the body.[27] Nowadays, however, the practice is not to make a distinction between other family members and one's father or mother. In all cases, the funeral and burial is performed as soon as possible.[28]

11. A bier is not used to carry the deceased unless the head and most of the body are being taken to burial.[29]

◄§ Two Burials

12. If there are two burials to perform in the same community, the first to die should be the first to receive a funeral, all other things being equal.[30]

If, for the sake of honoring the one who died first, it is desired to leave him unburied overnight (see above, par. 7), the one who died second may be buried first.[31]

---

24. Details of this *halachah* are explained below in chapt. 11.

25. *Gesher HaChaim* 7:1:10. He writes that this is true even according to the *Poskim* who rule that the *mitzvah* of burying the dead applies to disconnected limbs or bones.

26. That is because, for relatives other than a parent, one usually does not mourn or lament them excessively. Therefore, it is a display of honor to them to hasten their interment. This is not so in the case of one's parents where one is required to mourn and express extensive grief. Hastening their interment would therefore be considered reprehensible *(Shach* §§1).

27. *Shulchan Aruch* 357:2. And see previous footnote.

28. *Beis Hillel* loc. cit.

29. *Shulchan Aruch* 353:7.

30. *Shulchan Aruch* §354. And see *Pischei Teshuvah*, loc. cit., §§1.
    If the body of the one who died second is swollen and in danger of splitting, he should be buried first *(Sefer Chassidim* §743).

31. *Shulchan Aruch* loc. cit.. The reason is that in any case the one who died first will not be given a funeral immediately *(Shach* §§1).

As stated, these rules are followed when all other factors are equal. However, if one of the deceased was a Torah sage (*chacham*) and the other a regular Torah scholar (*talmid chacham*), the sage must be buried first. If one was a Torah scholar and the other unlearned (*am ha'aretz*), the Torah scholar must be buried first. If one was a woman and the other a man, the woman must be buried first, because her body is liable to decay more rapidly.[32]

If two or more people were killed, the practice is to conduct a single funeral for all of them, in order to allow for the greatest possible expression of grief and maximum number of eulogies.[33]

◄§ After Purification

13. After the body has been purified and clothed in burial garments, if the funeral is not to begin immediately, the body should not be left where the purification took place. Instead, it should be lain just inside the exit of the building from which it will be taken for burial,[34] or inside the funeral chapel following the custom of the local *chevra kaddisha*.

◄§ Descendants of the Deceased on the Cemetery

14. The practice in Jerusalem is that before the funeral procession of a male, a rabbinic decree (*cherem*) is proclaimed. (Some say that this is an especially severe type of *cherem*, called a "*cherem* of Yehoshua bin Nun.") The decree forbids the descendants of the deceased from accompanying him or following his body to burial. Accordingly, in communities following this custom, none of the sons, daughters or other descendants of the deceased accompany him to burial. However, sons-in-law and daughters-in-law do accompany him.

If a son or other descendant must be present in the cemetery to help with the burial, he goes there before the funeral procession begins, and waits there for the deceased to arrive.

Before the deceased is taken out to begin the funeral procession, the practice in Jerusalem and some other communities is that the sons recite *Kaddish* in the building where he is.[35]

---

32. According to *Prishah*, the reason is that the female body contains menstrual blood. And
   Pischei Teshuvah (loc. cit. §§2) writes: "See *Tashbatz* (part II:§41), who states that it makes no difference in this respect whether the woman was young [i.e., still capable of menstruating] or [in a situation where it is assumed that she did not menstruate, i.e.,] aged, pregnant, or nursing.
   Chiddushei Rabbi Akiva Eiger (loc. cit.) states: "Even if the man died first. . .but I am in doubt about the case of two women, one young and one aged, whether the young one should be buried first even though the aged one died first.
   Da'as Torah (loc. cit.) concludes that in our time a woman takes precedence even over a Torah scholar (*talmid chacham*).
33. *Gesher HaChaim* 14:2:6. "However, their praises should not be said at the same time, unless their praises are identical."
34. *Gesher HaChaim* 12:1:1. The source is *Tzavaas R' Yehudah HeChassid*, cited by the *Siddur* of *Yavetz* et al.
35. *Gesher Hachaim* 12:4:1.

In all these cases, the custom of the local *chevra kaddisha* should be followed.

ᴥ§ Exiting Before the Deceased

15. When the deceased is removed from the building to begin the funeral procession, no one should exit in front of him. But this does not apply to people who must exit first in order to carry the bier.[36]

16. As the deceased is taken out through the door of the building, it is the custom in Jerusalem and some other communities that a clay vessel is broken just outside the threshold. Some have the custom that when the vessel is broken those standing near the door say: "הַפַּח נִשְׁבָּר וַאֲנַחְנוּ נִמְלָטְנוּ, *The snare is broken and we have escaped' (Psalms* 124:7); וְלֹא יְהִי עוֹד שֶׁבֶר בִּגְבוּל יִשְׂרָאֵל, may there be no more breaking within the boundary of Israel."[37]

17. Those who are leaving the procession after having been in the building, with the bier, or within four *amos* [about eight feet] of it, wash their hands. See below, 10:23.

---

36. *Mishmeres Shalom os hei,* §57, in the name of *Mateh Yehudah,* who cites R' Yehudah HeChassid. This *halachah* is cited by *Zachor LeAvraham os kuf.* The source is *Tzavaas R' Yehudah Hechassid* §5, cited by *Roke'ach.* And see *Ba'er Heitev* (358:§§4), who writes: "Those participating in the funeral who need to go first in order to carry [the deceased] are not affected by this restriction." The same applies when there are many people in the house and they need to go out in order that the deceased can be taken out."

37. *Gesher HaChaim* 12:3:1.

CHAPTER TEN

The Funeral

◈§ The *Mitzvah*

1. It is a *mitzvah* to accompany the deceased to burial. This is an aspect of the command, '*You shall love your fellow Jew like yourself*' (*Leviticus* 19:18).[1] It is one of the *mitzvos* for which one receives "interest payments" in this world, while the "permanent fund" of reward awaits him in the world to come.[2]

◈§ The Prohibition Against Exchanging Greetings

2. In a small town, it is forbidden to exchange greetings [שְׁאֵלַת שָׁלוֹם, lit. *inquiry of Shalom*; see below, 21:10] as long as an unburied body is in the town. Likewise, it is forbidden to exchange greetings in a cemetery — even in a large city — as long as an unburied body is in the cemetery. If there is no unburied body in the cemetery, it is permitted to exchange greetings if standing at least four *amos* (about eight feet) from the nearest grave.[3]

Some authorities write that even in a large city it is forbidden to exchange greetings while taking part in the funeral.[4]

◈§ Canceling Torah Study to Accompany the Deceased

3. It is a *mitzvah* and an obligation[5] to cancel Torah study in order to accompany

---

1. *Rambam, Hilchos Avel* 14:1.

2. Mishnah *Pe'ah* 1:1. And see *Berachos* 18a: "If he accompanies [the deceased], what is his reward? R' Asi said: Of him Scripture declares (*Proverbs* 19:17), *He who accompanies Hashem is gracious to the poor.*'" *Rashi* explains: "One who is gracious to the poor is said to accompany the Omnipresent. No one is poorer than the dead, and when one accompanies him it is as if he accompanies the Omnipresent."

3. *Shulchan Aruch* 343:2; *Rama* loc. cit.; *Shach* loc. cit. §§3. And see *Da'as Torah* loc. cit., who cites *Kerem Shlomo*: "A small town is one with a population of less than a hundred." *Aruch HaShulchan* 343:4 writes: "It seems to me that the same applies in a small city when everyone is aware of the death. From this it would appear that when a great man dies, even in a large city, people are not permitted to exchange greetings. . .and it seems to me that in the mourner's home as well people are not permitted to exchange greetings. Since it is a place of sorrow, it is not fitting to exhibit one's good fortune." See also *Even Yaakov* §55. It is reported that *HaGaon* R' Moshe Feinstein, *zatzal* [*Igros Moshe*] would not even extend his hand in greeting while in the home of a mourner.

4. *Gesher HaChaim* 14:16. He cites a number of sources for this claim, but none of them are decisive proof.

5. *Shulchan Aruch* 361:1, and *Shach* §§1, in the name of the *Poskim*.

the deceased.[6] For a Torah scholar (*talmid chacham*) who taught others, this applies even if thousands of people — no matter how many thousands — are already taking part in the funeral. For someone who learned Scripture or Mishnah but did not teach others, it is not necessary, according to the basic halachah, to cancel Torah study if 600,000 people are already taking part in the funeral.[7] For someone who learned neither Scripture nor Mishnah, it is not necessary to cancel Torah study, as long as there are already sufficient people to attend to the burial, and as long as there is a *minyan* (ten adult males), making it possible to recite *Kaddish*.[8] [See the end of this paragraph for the current practice regarding canceling Torah study to attend a funeral.]

In a situation where it is not known if the deceased learned or taught, some rule that Torah study should be canceled for his funeral, since "in our time every Jew studies Scripture and Mishnah."[9] In such a case, however, a rabbi who is teaching students should not cancel his lesson.[10]

Regarding the funeral of a woman, some rule that the *halachah* is the same as for a man who learned Scripture and Mishnah, since women in any case are not commanded to engage in Torah study, and the woman in question performed the *mitzvos* applying to her. Others rule that the *halachah* is the same as for a man who did not learn Scripture or Mishnah. The accepted practice is not to cancel Torah study for the funeral of a woman or child.[11] But some authorities write that Torah study should be canceled for the funeral of an important woman.[11a]

In all cases, no matter whose funeral is taking place, it is forbidden to cancel or

---

6. *Baraisa* cited in *Kesubos* 17a. And see *Tosafos* there, s.v. להוצאת המת: "This does not refer [only] to a *meis mitzvah* [a situation where no one else is available to bury the deceased], but to any deceased."

7. "Just as it was given at Sinai, so is it taken away. Just as the Torah was given at Sinai among six hundred thousand, so is it taken away [from the deceased] among six hundred thousand. When he dies his learning is lost" (*Kesubos* ibid.). Now, *Shulchan Aruch* (loc. cit.) writes that the reference is to someone who learned Scripture *and* Mishnah; and *Shach* (§§2) writes that this implies that the person must have learned both. However from the statement of *Ritva*, cited by *Beis Yosef*, that "There is no Jew who has not studied either Scripture or Mishnah. . ." it may be inferred that either one is sufficient.

8. *Shulchan Aruch* 361:1, and *Shach* §§4. Moreover, one is not required to go and see if anyone is burying the deceased, since it may be assumed that someone is attending to him, and Torah study takes precedence. (*Shulchan Aruch* loc. cit. and *Shach* §§5).

9. *Rama* 360:1. And see *Aruch HaShulchan* 361:2, who writes: "That, of course, was in accordance with the situation in their generations [the generations of R' Yosef Karo and *Rama*]."

10. *Taz* §§1.

11. *Tur* and *Shulchan Aruch* loc. cit..

11a. *Mateh Moshe* writes: "Even according to those who rule that a woman has the same halachic status as someone who learned neither Scripture nor Mishnah, nevertheless the wives of Torah scholars have the halachic status of someone who learned Scripture, since these women look forward day and night to their husbands' coming home from the house of study, and when they arrive, they give them food and drink." *Shulchan Gevoha* (§§8) notes the words of R' Yosef Karo, that the accepted practice is not to interrupt Torah study for a woman or child, and comments: "This is his own opinion, but he cannot testify about the practice in every community, for in our region, if it is an important woman, such as the wife of a Torah scholar (*chaver*) or influential man (*gevir*) — and likewise if it is the

interrupt the Torah study of schoolchildren.[12] However, some rule that their Torah study may be canceled for the funeral of one of the generation's great Torah leaders.[13]

In cases where Torah study is to be canceled, this is only to accompany the deceased as he is taken to burial. Before he is taken out to be buried, Torah study should not be canceled if there is someone to attend to him.[14]

◄§ Current Practice

Some rule that the *mitzvah* of canceling Torah study to accompany the deceased applies only to those who see him being taken to burial.[15] On this basis, the current practice is not to cancel Torah study[16] unless one actually sees the deceased being taken to burial, or unless he was a major Torah scholar.

---

child of a sage or *gevir* — Torah scholars interrupt their study in order to attend the funeral, out of respect for the husband or the father."

12. *Shulchan Aruch* loc. cit., and *Shach* §§6. *Tur* states the reason: "They do not interrupt [their Torah study] even for the building of the Holy Temple."

13. The author of responsa *Silmas Chaim* (*Yoreh De'ah* §418) was asked whether it is correct to interrupt Torah study for the funeral of one of the generation's great Torah leaders. He replies: "Allow Israel [to follow their accepted custom, i.e. to interrupt Torah study in such a case], for it may be assumed that this was instituted by the leaders of the previous generation, for the honor of the Torah. In any case [even when it is not for such a reason, today's schoolchildren] interrupt their study for a number of days [e.g., *bein hazmanim* (intercession or vacation)], even though, strictly according to the *halachah*, one is not allowed to interrupt except in the late afternoon on Friday or *erev Yom Tov*. This being the situation, apparently the Torah leaders saw fit to be lenient [for this type of funeral] as well."

Gesher HaChaim (14:14) writes: "The custom is to be lenient and interrupt Torah study for the funeral of a Torah scholar (*chaver*) or supporter of Torah, because in our time those who support Torah are few — especially those who support children's Torah study. Under these circumstances, such an interruption actually ensures the continuation of Torah study. . . .However, it is proper to take care, as much as possible, not to interrupt the children's studies, except in situations where such an interruption ensures the continuation of Torah study."

14. *Shulchan Aruch* loc. cit.

15. *Emek She'elah*, *Parashas Vayechi* 34:§§2. As proof, he cites a number of places where we find the phrase, "if one sees the deceased and does not accompany him. . ." This opinion of *Emek She'elah* is contrary to that of *Beis Shmuel* in his commentary on *Even HaEzer* 65:§§3.

See also *She'elas David* (in his *chiddushim* on *Yoreh De'ah*), who writes: "A person who is studying Torah is not required to interrupt in order to go out and accompany the deceased, if it is known that there is someone there [with the deceased] to do [what is necessary], even if the public attending the funeral is not as large as befits the deceased. As for the statement that 'one should interrupt Torah study to attend a funeral,' the intention is that if one encounters a funeral, but needs to go to the *beis midrash* to study, one is required to accompany the deceased. The only exception to this rule [that one is not required to interrupt in order to go out and accompany the deceased] is a person [whose death directly affects] the entire public, such as a great rabbi. In such a case, the scholars are required to interrupt their Torah study in order to honor the deceased by attending the funeral."

16. Responsa *Minchas Elazar* (part I:§26) notes the statement of *Rama* that in a situation where it is not known if the deceased learned, some rule that Torah study should be canceled for his funeral, since "in our time every Jew studies Scripture and Mishnah." He comments: "If so, we of the land of Ashkenaz, who follow the rulings of *Rama*, are faced with the following situation. In the large cities, hundreds of thousands of Jews reside, and funerals occur (may it not happen to us!) every day — sometimes quite a few, Hashem save us. If so, it is forbidden for any Torah scholar to study while the funeral is in progress. Everyone is required to go to the funeral, since there are not enough people

◄§ Canceling Work

4. In a city where there is no *chevra kaddisha* (burial society) to attend to the dead, all residents of the city are forbidden to engage in their work whenever there is a dead Jewish person in the city. This applies even before the deceased is taken out to be buried.

If there is a *chevra kaddisha*, the residents are allowed to work until the deceased is taken out to be buried. Then, even if he was a person who did not learn Scripture or Mishnah, the residents must leave their work and accompany him to burial.[17]

◄§ Canceling the Reading of *Megillas Esther* on Purim

5. If the deceased has no one else to bury him (*meis mitzvah*; see above, 2:3), burying him takes precedence over hearing the reading of *Megillas Esther*.

---

attending — for undoubtedly there are not [the required] six hundred thousand. The result, in such large cities, would be that the Torah scholars would literally be unable to study all their lives; and obviously this is not the accepted practice, for if it were, what would become of the Torah?"

The commentary on *Minchas Elazar*, *Kuntres Shayarei Minchah* (part I) cites the words of *Emek She'elah* (just quoted) as a source which may be relied upon to permit [continuing to study Torah even though a funeral is in progress].

Responsa *Silmas Chaim* (*Yoreh De'ah* §420) comments on those words of *Emek She'elah*: "I myself do not have the authority to decide such a dispute. But anyone who relies on the lenient *Poskim* in order not to interrupt Torah study in such a case obviously is not in the slightest danger of sinning thereby."

Responsa *Maharshag* (2:§28) cites his teacher, *Maharam Shick,* as saying that for studying Torah one certainly will have no cause to regret. And see *Even Yaakov* (§21), who cites several other reasons why one should be permitted not to interrupt Torah study.

17. *Shulchan Aruch* 343:1, and 361:2. Only with regard to interrupting Torah study does it make a difference whether or not the deceased learned Scripture or Mishnah, but with regard to interrupting work, it makes no difference at all (*Shulchan Aruch*, loc. cit. 361:2).

Gesher HaChaim (14:8, and note 3 there) writes that if there is a *chevra kaddisha* (burial society), people do not need to leave their work even during the funeral. It would seem that this contradicts what is implied by the words of *Shulchan Aruch*. And see *Gesher HaChaim* (part 2: 10:2), where the author interprets these words of *Shulchan Aruch* as referring to something else. The matter requires further study.

Responsa *Minchas Elazar* (part 1 §26 *hagah*) notes that current practice contradicts this *halachah* and writes that even though, halachically, he does not find any way to permit [continuing one's work and not attending the funeral], "nevertheless one can make excuses for workers and merchants, as does *Taz* in *Hilchos Chol HaMo'ed* (539:1), due to heavy taxation and the great difficulty of earning a living, especially in our day. Moreover, in the large cities, [if they had to attend every funeral,] when would they have time to work? (This is similar to the problem mentioned above in connection with Torah study.) However, one must ask: Is the fact that we find a parallel [with the laws of *Chol HaMo'ed*,] sufficient grounds to give a lenient ruling in practice? Nevertheless, since the lenient custom is already established, one should not protest or reprimand those who follow it, for 'just as it is a *mitzvah* to speak when one will be heard, so is it a *mitzvah* to refrain from speaking when one will not be heard.' Moreover, this *halachah* is impossible to implement in the large cities, both for Torah scholars and for merchants, as mentioned. Therefore, 'leave Israel to follow their customs.' All the same, I in my ignorance have found no halachic permission [for not attending the funeral]."

The same ruling is given by *Mashcha Derevusa*, in the *chiddushim* of R' Shimon Alfasi, zal (*Yoreh De'ah* §361). And see *Ramas Rachel* §50, and *Even Yaakov* §23.

When is this so? If there will be time afterwards to hear the *Megillah*. Otherwise, the *mitzvah* of the *Megillah*-reading should be performed first, and the deceased should be buried at night.[18]

Some rule that a *meis mitzvah* takes precedence even if this means the *Megillah*-reading will be missed altogether.[19]

In a case where there are enough people to bury the deceased, but not enough for a properly attended funeral, some authorities rule that attending the funeral takes precedence over the *Megillah*-reading, as long as there will be time afterwards for the *Megillah*-reading.[20] Others disagree. However, if the deceased was a Torah scholar (*talmid chacham*) who studied Scripture and Mishnah — or, all the more so, one who taught others — all agree that one should attend his funeral before the *Megillah*-reading.

Once the people have begun to take out the deceased for burial, they must not interrupt the funeral, even if it is not a case of *meis mitzvah*, and even if the *Megillah*-reading will be missed altogether.[21]

◄§ Miscellaneous Laws of Accompanying the Deceased

6. If one sees a deceased person being taken for burial and does not accompany him, one violates the prohibition against "ridiculing the helpless" (*lo'eg la'rash*), and is worthy of having a ban (*nidui*) imposed on him. According to *Shulchan Aruch* one must at least accompany the deceased for a distance of four *amos* (about eight feet). Some rule that this law applies if enough people are already accompanying the deceased; but if there are not enough people, one must accompany him all the way to the grave.[22] Others rule that even if there are not enough people already accompanying the deceased, one need walk only four *amos*. When there are enough people, one need not accompany the deceased at all; one need only stand.[23]

Even in a situation where one is not required to accompany the deceased, one

---

18. *Shulchan Aruch* and *Rama*, *Orach Chaim* 687:2.

19. *Mishnah Berurah* loc. cit. §§12, citing a number of *Acharonim*.

20. *Rama* 687:2 and 696:7; *Mishnah Berurah* 667:§§8 and 12.

21. *Mishnah Berurah* loc. cit. §§8.

22. *Pischei Teshuvah Yoreh De'ah* 361:§§2, citing responsa *Yad Eliahu* §24. And see *Charedim* chapt. 6, who writes that the essence of the *mitzvah* is to accompany the deceased until he is buried; but one who does not at least accompany him for a distance of four *amos* [about eight feet] incurs a great punishment.

23. *Emek She'elah*, *she'ilta* 34:2. And see *Even Yaakov* §19.

See also *Orchos Chaim*, by R' Aharon HaKohen of Lunille (*Hilchos Avel* §17), who writes: "Even if one does not accompany the deceased all the way to the cemetery, one receives great reward, as we find in *Pirkei DeRabbi Eliezer*: 'Whence do we learn about doing kindness to mourners? From Jezebel, whose house was near the main street, and whenever a funeral would pass by, she would go out of her house, strike her palms together, wail, and go ten paces [to accompany the deceased]. . .As a reward for this, the dogs [see *II Kings* 9] could not touch her hands, skull, or feet.' "

must stand in his presence.[24]

Even when the deceased is not being taken for burial, but only being moved from one place to another, [those who see him] must accompany him for a distance of four *amos*.[25]

If a coffin is being transferred from place to place, and the skeleton of the deceased is intact, one is required to accompany the coffin just as for burial. Regarding the obligation of accompanying the ashes of the deceased, or his bones which have been gathered up, or the body of an aborted fetus (*nefel*), see footnote.[26]

7. When one stops accompanying the deceased, the custom is to wait until the procession has gone out of sight[27] and then say: לֵךְ בְּשָׁלוֹם וְתָנוּחַ בְּשָׁלוֹם וְתַעֲמוֹד

---

24. *Shulchan Aruch* 361:4. And see *Taz* there, who states that the reason for standing up is to show respect for those performing the funeral, since they are doing an act of kindness. *Tur* writes the same, citing the Jerusalem Talmud.

See *Gesher HaChaim* (14:8), who specifies when one is required to walk four *amos* (about eight feet) with the deceased, and when one is only required to stand up. He also writes that if a person is traveling in a wagon or bus, and a funeral passes by the vehicle, and it is difficult for him to get out of the vehicle and accompany the deceased, it is desirable to go beyond the letter of the law (*lehader*) by standing up in the vehicle. But if the vehicle is not moving, then even according to the letter of the law (*min hadin*) one must rise and remain standing while the funeral procession goes past.

Responsa *Be'er Moshe* (part IV:§98) writes that the requirement (upon seeing the funeral) to accompany the deceased for a distance of four *amos* applies to any deceased, whether or not the required number of people [see above, par. 3] are already accompanying him. And the requirement [just] to stand up applies when the deceased is in a different domain [for example, when the onlooker is in a bus].

25. *Beis Yosef*, citing Rabbeinu Yonah.

26. *Shulchan Aruch* 361:5. And see *Gesher HaChaim* (14:10), who writes: ". . .certainly, one is not required to accompany the ashes of burned martyrs when they are being taken to burial, even though the custom is to bury the ashes." And in §11, *Gesher HaChaim* writes: "It would seem that also in the case of bones gathered up after the flesh is no longer on them, there is no requirement to accompany them, even though the backbone and ribs are intact." In §12, he writes: "Even if there is no *mitzvah* to accompany [disconnected] limbs, when the skeleton is not intact, or bones after the flesh is no longer on them, nevertheless one must stand up for them — either to show respect for those occupied with the *mitzvah* of carrying the remains, or to show respect for the limbs (or bones), which are comparable to fragmentary pages of a Torah scroll." In *os* 13 he writes that there is no *mitzvah* to accompany an aborted fetus (*nefel*), and the *mitzvah* in such a case is only to attend to the burial.

27. See *Sdei Chemed* (*Aveilus* §190), who writes about this: "At present, I do not know the reason. Nor have I seen this custom mentioned in the works of the *Poskim*. Perhaps it is done to show respect for the deceased, as it is mentioned in *Shulchan Aruch* 244:2 with regard to standing up for a Torah scholar until he walks past."

Mishmeres Shalom (*os lamed* §9) writes: "In my humble opinion, this practice is derived from a statement in the *siddur* of R' Yaakov Emden, *zal*, among the laws of *tefillas haderech* (the traveler's prayer) and of accompanying [guests], §§1. He writes that when one is accompanying a friend on his way, and parts from him, one must stand there until the friend goes out of sight. And I have found this in *Chizkuni*, *Parashas Shoftim*. [The Torah discusses the case of a murdered body found outside a city. The elders of the city must perform the *mitzvah* of the beheaded calf (*eglah arufah*), declaring:] '. . .our eyes did not see' (*Deut.* 21:7). *Chizkuni* writes: 'From this we learn that someone who accompanies another person must stand where he is until the other goes out of sight.' This is cited in *Elyah Rabbah*, *Orach Chaim* §106. If this is the *mitzvah* for a live person, all the more so when one accompanies the

לְגוֹרָלְךָ לְקֵץ הַיָּמִים, "Go in peace and rest in peace, and stand up for your destiny at the end of days." If the deceased was a woman, one says the same thing, but in the feminine gender: לְכִי בְשָׁלוֹם וְתָנוּחִי בְּשָׁלוֹם וְתַעַמְדִי לְגוֹרָלֵךְ לְקֵץ הַיָּמִים.[27a]

8. If for some reason one is unable to accompany the deceased, one should at least pray for mercy for him, say two or three chapters of Psalms for him, or give charity on his behalf at the time of his burial.[28]

9. Even if one disliked a person, he may accompany his body to burial,[29] but in this case he should not be among those who carry the bier.[30]

⋖§ Women Accompanying the Deceased

10. Originally, in a community where it was customary for women to walk in front of the bier, they were permitted to do so, and in a community where it was customary for them to walk behind the bier, they were permitted to do so. Now, the custom is that they walk only behind the bier, and this should not be changed.[31] Moreover, great vigilance should be exercised to make sure that they do not walk among the men.[32]

---

deceased, who is going on a long journey. [See responsa *Meshivas Nefesh* §17]. He must certainly stand in this manner, to intimate that (*Deut.* loc. cit.) '*our hands did not shed this blood and our eyes did not see.*'"

And see *Leket Yosher* (*Yoreh De'ah* p. 88), a work which describes the customs practiced by the author of *Trumas HaDeshen*: "I recall that when he accompanied the deceased, he stood until he could no longer see the bier." See also *Gesher HaChaim* 14:18.

27a. See below, footnote 76.

28. *Ma'avar Yabok* in *Sifsei Rannenus* ch. 21.

29. *Shach* 338:§§2, citing *Bach*: "We need not fear that the mourners will feel that [the deceased's former enemy] is happy that he died, since this is the fate of all men." And see *Sefer Chassidim* §537.

30. *Yesodei Semachos* p. 12, citing the *gaon*, R' Moshe Feinstein, *zatzal*.

31. *Shulchan Aruch* 359:1. And *Beis Yosef* cites the *Yerushalmi*: "The Sages taught [in a *baraisa*]: Women go first, since they introduced death into the world [through the sin of Eve in the Garden of Eden]. The one who rules that the men go first, and the women behind them, [rules this way] for the honor of Jewish women, so that [the men] will not be looking at the women."

32. *Gesher HaChaim* 14:15. And in a note there he writes: "The holy *Zohar* warns about this (because it constitutes danger to life): 'At the time of death, [when] they take [the deceased] from his house to the cemetery, the Angel of Death is present among the women, for this is his way ever since the day he persuaded Eve, and through her introduced death. . .and [during the funeral] he has permission to kill. . .'"

And see *Ma'avar Yabok* in *Sifsei Rannenus* ch. 10, who cites the holy *Zohar*, *Parashas Vayakhel*, p. 196: "It warns very emphatically that the women should not be seen among the men when they go to the cemetery, and even more so, on their way back; for the Angel of Death is among them. . .and he said that a number of men leave the world before their time because they are not careful about this."

Mishmeres Shalom (os lamed §4) cites *Shulchan Aruch HaRav* (part 5 *Hilchos Shmiras Guf VeNefesh* §10), who cites *Zohar*, *Parashas Vayakhel*, as stating that if there are fewer than seven women, the problem is not as severe. The same citation of the holy *Zohar* is found in *Sheivet Yehudah* §359, and in *Da'as Torah* loc. cit.

And see *Yad Eliahu* (*Ragoler* 1:68), who writes: "The *Zohar*, *Parashas Vayakhel*, states that it is dangerous to walk among the women during a funeral. In my humble opinion, it may be possible to say

Women should not be allowed to go to the cemetery, neither in front of the bier nor behind it.[33] However, some authorities rule leniently on this point.[33a]

✥ Recitation of the *Shema* by Pallbearers

11. Those carrying the bier, as well as those waiting to replace them,[34] are exempt from the *mitzvah* of reciting the *Shema*. This includes both those at the front of the bier and those at the back of it, as long as they are needed[35] for carrying the bier.[36]

The rest of those accompanying the deceased, not being needed to carry the bier, are obligated by the *mitzvah* of reciting the *Shema*.[37] However, they are exempt from the *mitzvah* of prayer.[38] If they miss one of the three daily prayers because they were accompanying the deceased, they need not make up for the missed prayer by reciting an extra *Shemoneh Esrei* during the next time for prayer.[39]

12. Those accompanying the deceased should recite Psalms — especially Psalm 91, which begins: יֹשֵׁב בְּסֵתֶר, '*He who dwells in the shadow of the Supreme*

---

that this danger does not exist in the case of a martyr, since he did not die from the Angel of Death." He cites proof of this thesis from the case of King David. The same idea is suggested by responsa *Beis Yaakov* §72, cited in *Beis Lechem Yehudah* loc. cit.

33. *Shulchan Aruch* 359:2. There he writes ". . .behind the bier," but *Chiddushei Rabbi Akiva Eiger* (loc. cit.) writes, citing *Tiferes LeMoshe*, that it is also forbidden for women to go in front of the bier. And see *Even Yaakov* §17. See also *Shach* §§2, who writes that if the women do go, they cause harm to the world, God forbid.

33a. Responsa *Beis Yaakov*, cited by *Beis Lechem Yehudah* loc. cit.

34. Even though the last ones have time to recite the *Shema* while the first ones are still carrying the bier, they are all exempt from reciting it, because sometimes the order is changed and their turn comes up unexpectedly. Hence they should not begin reciting the *Shema* (*Mishnah Berurah* 72:§§1).

35. In a city where a specific group of men is designated for carrying the bier, and all the members of the group take turns because they all desire to have a part in the *mitzvah*, all these men are exempt from reciting the *Shema*, since all of them are preoccupied with a *mitzvah* — even those distant from the bier. But in a place where there is no specific group of men designated for this purpose, those close to the bier are exempt from reciting the *Shema*, since the usual practice is to allow them to take part in the *mitzvah* when the ones carrying the bier get tired; but those distant from the bier are obligated to recite the *Shema* (*Mishnah Berurah*, 72:§§2).

36. *Shulchan Aruch Orach Chaim* 72:1, and *Yoreh De'ah* 358:1. *Shach* (loc. cit. §§1) writes: ". . .because a person preoccupied with a *mitzvah* is exempt from other *mitzvos*."

37. *Shulchan Aruch* loc. cit. Even though accompanying the deceased is included in the *mitzvah* of doing kindness to others (*gemilus chassadim*), and this *mitzvah* is of Scriptural status, nevertheless these people are not at all preoccupied with the *mitzvah*. They can stand still and recite the first verse of the *Shema* with intent (*kavanah*), and then recite the remaining verses while they walk (*Mishnah Berurah* loc. cit. §§3).

38. *Shulchan Aruch Orach Chaim* 106:1. The reason is that the *mitzvah* of prayer is of Rabbinic status. Moreover, one must stand still to pray, and those accompanying the deceased cannot stand still for such a long time. By contrast, the requirement to stand still and recite the *Shema* with intent applies mainly to the first verse. It is easy for those taking part in the funeral to stand still and concentrate for just one verse (*Mishnah Berurah* loc. cit. §§3).

39. *Mishnah Berurah* loc. cit. The reason is that at the time when the person would have been required to pray, he was halachically exempt from doing so. This is explained by *Mishnah Berurah* at the end of §93.

One. . .' This psalm, according to the Talmud (*Shevuos* 15b), drives away harmful spiritual influences. When reciting *Psalms* at the funeral, one opens with the blessing of Moses (*Psalms* 90:17), וִיהִי נֹעַם, *'May the pleasantness of Hashem our God be upon us. . .'*[40] At the funeral of a woman, one also recites *Eishes Chayil* (*Proverbs* 31). Among Sefardic Jews, some also recite *Ana Beko'ach* (אָנָּא בְּכֹחַ) and *Mi Kel Kamocha* (מִי אֵל כָּמוֹךָ).[41]

Those not reciting verses or prayers should at least remain silent and serious. People who converse continually about irrelevant matters during the funeral procession are not behaving properly. This does not show respect for the *mitzvah* of accompanying the deceased. Preventing such conversation should be part of the duties of the *chevra kaddisha* officials.[42]

While accompanying the deceased to burial, one should pray that the Holy One, Blessed is He, have mercy on the departed and, by the merit of his ancestors, spare him from punishment. One should give *tzedakah* (charity) on his behalf, saying: "I am giving this *tzedakah* for the benefit of the departed soul: May the Holy One, Blessed is He, save it from all misfortune; and may the soul merit to rise to the level of the *tzaddikim*."[43]

⋖§ Covering the *Tzitzis*

13. Anyone going within four *amos* of a deceased person (an *amah* is about two feet) must cover his *tzitzis*. Not to do so is considered a violation of the prohibition against "ridiculing the helpless" (*lo'eg la'rash*), as if he were taunting the deceased for no longer being capable of performing *mitzvos*. This *halachah* applies even if the deceased was a woman or child, who were not obligated by the *mitzvah* of *tzitzis*.[44]

⋖§ The Blessing, *Asher Yatzar Es'chem*
". . .Who Fashioned You with Justice"

14. Usually, if one has not seen Jewish graves in the past thirty days, upon seeing them one recites the blessing, *Asher Yatzar Eschem BaDin*: "Blessed are You, Hashem, King of the universe, Who fashioned you with justice. . ."

When an *onen* [one whose close family member has died and has not yet been buried; see above, chapter 5] goes to the cemetery, he does not recite the blessing *Asher Yatzar Eschem BaDin*, even if he has not seen a cemetery within the past thirty days. Even after the grave is filled with earth, whereupon he ceases to be an *onen* and resumes his obligation to perform *mitzvos*, he nevertheless does not

---

40. *Gesher HaChaim* 14:17.

41. My father and teacher, *zatzal*, in his work *Zichron Eliahu* (manuscript).

42. *Gesher HaChaim* loc. cit.

43. "It is a great *mitzvah* to pray for the deceased, whether righteous or wicked, that Hashem should ease their sufferings" (*Mishmeres Shalom os lamed* §6, citing *Or Chadash*, who states this in the name of *Birkas Avraham*; *Yad Eliahu* p.195, citing *Emes LeYaakov*).

44. *Shulchan Aruch Orach Chaim* 23:2. And see below, ch. 42.

recite this blessing.[45]

Regarding whether the other people accompanying the deceased should recite this blessing, there are several opinions. One authority writes that they are obligated to recite it.[46] Others rule that they should not recite it, even on the way back from the burial.[47] Another authority writes that after the burial, they are required to recite it.[48]

৺ঙ্গ. The Halts (*Maamados*) in the Funeral Procession

15. Some rule that once the funeral procession brings the deceased into the cemetery, they should halt every four *amos*.[49] Nowadays, too, the custom is to halt two or three times before reciting the passages of consolation called *Tzidduk HaDin* [see *Appendix*]. On the days when it is forbidden to recite *Tzidduk HaDin*, it is not necessary to make these halts.[50] Some rule that the procession should make seven halts.[51] In all cases, the custom of the local *Chevra Kadisha* should be followed.

In Jerusalem, the custom is not to be particular about the number of halts. Instead, whenever the procession passes a synagogue, they halt and recite the *mishnah* (*Avos* 3:1) which begins, "Akavya ben Mehallalel says, 'Look upon three things. . .' " This is followed by two verses from *Tzidduk HaDin*: הַצוּר תָּמִים פָּעֳלוֹ, "*The Rock — perfect is His work. . .*" and גְּדֹל הָעֵצָה וְרַב הָעֲלִילִיָּה, "*Great in wisdom and mighty in deed.*" Then they say *Kaddish*. If they pass a number of synagogues,

---

45. The reason is that he had already seen the graves at the time when he was exempt from reciting the blessing (*Kaf HaChaim* 224:§§37, citing *Eishel Avraham*).

46. Responsa *Kinyan Torah* (part III:27:2) writes: "It seems to me that the custom is to recite the blessing. They should not be exempted on the basis of being preoccupied with the *mitzvah* of accompanying the deceased, since it is possible to fulfill both *mitzvos*, and this does not detract from their performance of the *mitzvah*." And see below, footnote 48.

47. *Eishel Avraham* (loc. cit.) writes that when they come to the cemetery they are exempt from reciting the blessing because they are preoccupied with the *mitzvah* of accompanying the deceased. Afterwards, they are no longer obligated to recite it, since they have already seen [the graves] within the past thirty days [i.e. when they came to the cemetery]. The same ruling is given by *Ketzos HaShulchan* (§46), and by *Badei HaShulchan* (loc. cit. §§18).

48. The *gaon* R' Shlomo Zalman Auerbach, *shlita*, in his remarks on part 1 of the Hebrew edition of this book writes: "In my humble opinion, it seems that even if the *onen* himself is completely exempt from reciting this blessing, nevertheless it seems logical that the others accompanying the deceased are required to recite it after the burial. As long as they have not left the cemetery, it is all considered one act of 'seeing' [the graves]. Moreover, according to the basic *halachah* they — especially those who are not holding the bier — are able to recite the blessing even while they are accompanying the deceased before the burial, by reciting it in such a manner that it does not cause them to halt with the deceased."

49. *Rama* 358:3. *Shach* (§§4) adds, "*Ateres Zekeinim* writes: 'I have heard that the reason for these halts is in order to drive away spirits of impurity (*tumah*) that want to take hold of [the deceased], so that they will not enter into the grave with him. Halting makes [these spirits] go away.' "

50. *Rama* loc. cit. *Shach* (loc. cit.) explains, citing *Ateres Zekeinim*: "On those days, the impure spirits are not so prevalent."

51. *Ma'avar Yabok* 43:17.

they halt in front of each. If they don't pass any synagogues, they halt once or twice before reaching the cemetery.[52]

~§ Gravediggers Exempt from *Shema*

16. One who is digging a grave for a deceased is exempt from the *mitzvah* of reciting the *Shema* even while he is taking a short rest.[53] If two or more are digging the grave, all those needed to dig the grave at the same time are exempt from the *mitzvah* of saying the *Shema*. If there are those who are not needed to dig at the same time, they should leave and say the *Shema* and pray while the others dig; then they should change places.[54]

With regard to circling the grave (*hakafos*) and the manner of burial, the *chevra kadisha* of each city and congregation follows its particular custom.

~§ Burial Customs

17. While the deceased is being put into the grave, some have the custom that all the members of the *chevra kadisha*, as well as all others present, recite *Psalm* 91: יֹשֵׁב בְּסֵתֶר עֶלְיוֹן, *"He who dwells in the shadow of the Supreme One. . ."* in its entirety. Then they recite אֵל מֶלֶךְ יוֹשֵׁב עַל כִּסֵּא רַחֲמִים, *"God, the King, sitting on the throne of mercy. . ."* and ה' ה', *The Thirteen Attributes*, timing the recitation so that they say the Thirteen Attributes as they lay the deceased on his resting place.[55] There are many customs, and the *chevra kadisha* of each city and congregation follows its particular custom.

On Friday, the day before a *Yom Tov*, on *Rosh Chodesh*, and during *Chol HaMo'ed* (the Intermediate Days of Pesach or Succos), when it is forbidden to recite *Tzidduk HaDin* or to perform the circlings (*hakafos*), the Thirteen Attributes also are not recited. The Thirteen Attributes are not recited at the burial of a woman.[56]

During the burial, all present recite aloud, three times: וְהוּא רַחוּם יְכַפֵּר עָוֹן, 'He is merciful, atoning for sin' (Psalms 78:38), followed by: וְסָר עֲוֹנֶךְ וְחַטָּאתְךָ תְּכֻפָּר, 'Your transgression will depart and your sin will be atoned' (Isaiah 6:7). This recitation is an act of great kindness to the deceased.[57]

The practice is that each of those present puts some earth on the grave.[58] Care is taken that the shovel or other digging tool used for this purpose is not passed from

---

52. *Gesher HaChaim* 14:3:1.

53. Even when he rests, he is considered to be occupied with the *mitzvah*, since this restores his strength so that he can continue digging (*Shulchan Aruch Orach Chaim* 71:5; *Mishnah Berurah* loc. cit. §§13; and *Shulchan Aruch Yoreh De'ah* 361:1).

54. *Shulchan Aruch Orach Chaim*, 71:6.

55. *Gesher HaChaim* 15:2:1.

56. Ibid. 15:2:2.

57. My father and teacher, *zatzal*, in his work, *Zichron Eliahu* (manuscript), citing *Ma'avar Yabok* 45 ch. 18.

58. *Ma'avar Yabok* loc. cit.

hand to hand. Instead, one man puts it down and the next picks it up.[59]

◆§ Tzidduk HaDin

18. After the grave is filled with earth, *Tzidduk HaDin* (passages of consolation and acceptance of the Divine decree) is recited. [For the text and translation, see Appendix.][59a]

[In this moving prayer, the mourners declare their acceptance of the Divine judgment and also plead with God to be merciful upon the living. The word צוּר has the dual connotation of *Rock*, in the sense that God is impregnable and unchanging, and *Molder* (from צָיָר, *One Who fashions*), in the sense that He is the Creator Who molds people and events to suit His purposes. In this prayer as in many others, both connotations are equally appropriate.

[His work is תָּמִים, *perfect*, meaning that the totality of His deeds forms a harmonious whole. Man's intelligence is incapable of comprehending how all the pieces of God's puzzle fit together, but we have faith that this is so.]

18a. On the days when *Tachanun* is not recited, the same applies to *Tzidduk HaDin*.[60] Likewise, one does not recite *Tzidduk HaDin* after *chatzos* on Friday or the day before *Yom Tov*.[61] (*Chatzos* is usually about noon; the exact time varies with the season.) However, on the day before Rosh Chodesh or the day before Chanukah, it may be recited even after *chatzos*.[62] (In Jerusalem, the custom is not to recite it after *chatzos* on the day before Rosh Chodesh.)[63]

On the day before Tishah B'Av, *Tzidduk HaDin* is recited, even after *chatzos*.[64]

Tzidduk HaDin is not recited at night,[65] but is recited at dusk (*bein hashmashos*).[66]

---

59. *Chochmas Adam* 158:30, citing *Ma'aneh Lashon*; *Beis Lechem Yehudah* §376.

59a. *Shulchan Aruch* 339:3 cites *Kol Bo* (*Hilchos Aveilus*), who rules that *Tzidduk HaDin* should be recited at the time of death (*yetzias neshamah*). However, *Roke'ach* (*Hilchos Aveilus*) writes: "Strictly according to *halachah*, *Tzidduk HaDin* should be recited at the time of *yetzias neshamah* [i.e., the moment of death]. But now the custom is to recite it at the cemetery, for the honor of the deceased." The same ruling is given by *Tur* §376, where he states that it is recited at the cemetery after the burial. And see *Drishah* there, §§4.

60. *Rama* 401:6.

61. *Rama* loc. cit., and *Shach* 401:§§3. And *Chazon LaMo'ed* (chapt. 10, note 9) writes, citing *Zibula Basraisa* (p. 20) that on Friday or the day before *Yom Tov*, *Tziduk HaDin* should not be recited after the fifth hour. [The fifth hour is about one hour before *chatzos*.] He explains that this is related to the *halachah* of *Tosefes Shabbos*.

62. *Shach* loc. cit. §§3, citing *Ateres Zekeinim*. *Chok Yaakov* (*Orach Chaim* §429) likewise writes that the custom in Prague was to permit reciting *Tzidduk HaDin* on the day before Rosh Chodesh, after *chatzos*, since the [special prayers for the fast of] *Yom Kippur Katan* are recited then. The same ruling is given by *Mishnah Berurah* 429:§§7.

63. *Gesher HaChaim* 16:6:2.

64. This is true even though Tishah B'Av is called a *mo'ed* (festival) (*Pischei Teshuvah* 401:§§1, citing responsa *Givas Shaul* §71).

65. *Rama* 401:6. The same ruling is given by *Shach* 376:§§3. The reason is that *Midas HaDin*, the quality of strict judgment, prevails at night (*Yosef Da'as* §376).

66. *Chazon LaMo'ed*, in the notes at the end of the book.

Sefardic Jews recite *Tzidduk HaDin* on any day, even on the Diaspora's second day of *Yom Tov* and during *Chol HaMo'ed*. On the first day of *Yom
Tov*, since it is forbidden to bury the dead (except through the agency of
non-Jews), Sefardic Jews do not recite *Tzidduk HaDin*.[67] They also do not recite it
at night.[68]

19. *Tzidduk HaDin* is not recited for the burial of an aborted fetus (*nefel*), nor for
the burial of limbs, nor for the burial of the ashes of someone whose body was
completely burned, even if he was martyred.[69]

The practice is to recite *Tzidduk HaDin* for a child that lived more than thirty
days[70] (see above, 6:26), and for a woman.[71]

◄§ The Great *Kaddish* (*Kaddish HaGadol*)

20. *Tzidduk HaDin* is followed by recitation of the special version of *Kaddish*
which contains the additional words beginning, בְּעָלְמָא דִּי הוּא עָתִיד לְאִתְחַדָּתָא,
"...in the world which will be renewed." [For text and translation, see
Appendix.][72] If a mourner is present at the cemetery, he recites this *Kaddish*.
Otherwise, someone else recites it.[73] The practice is to recite it even at graveside.[74]

On the days when *Tzidduk HaDin* is not recited, the same applies to *Kaddish
HaGadol*. On those days, *Tzidduk HaDin* is replaced by *Psalms* 16, and *Kaddish
HaGadol* is replaced by the regular mourner's *Kaddish*.[75]

21. On departing from the deceased after the burial, one says: לֵךְ בְּשָׁלוֹם וְתָנוּחַ
בְּשָׁלוֹם וְתַעֲמוֹד לְגוֹרָלֶךְ לְקֵץ הַיָּמִים, "Go in peace and rest in peace, and stand up
for your destiny at the end of days."[76] If the deceased was a woman, one says the

---

67. *Shulchan Aruch* 401:6.

68. *Sdei Chemed*, *Aveilus* §212.

69. *Gesher HaChaim* 16:6:2.

70. *Shulchan Aruch* 344:4. *Rama* there disagrees and writes that the custom is not to recite *Tzidduk
HaDin* for an infant less than twelve months old, this being the minimal age for which a bier is
used to carry the deceased. However, *Shach* (loc.cit. §§3) writes that the custom is to recite it even for
a younger infant, and *Gesher HaChaim* (loc. cit.) also writes that this is the custom.

71. *Gesher HaChaim* loc. cit.

72. *Shulchan Aruch* 376:4.

73. *Gesher HaChaim* loc. cit.

74. *Shulchan Aruch* (loc. cit.) writes: "They go a little distance from the cemetery and say *Kaddish*."
Shach there (§§3) writes, citing *Ateres Zekeinim*, that one must be at a distance of at least four
amos (about eight feet) from the nearest grave to recite *Kaddish*. But *Gesher HaChaim* (loc. cit.)
writes: "However, our custom follows *Ma'avar Yabok* (42:29), to recite prayers and *Kaddish* even at
graveside, since these, too, are recited for the deceased and hence may be said even in the presence
of the deceased before he is buried."

75. *Gesher HaChaim* loc. cit.

76. *Chochmas Adam*, *Matzevas Moshe* par. 14. He cites *Ma'avar Yabok*: "The blessing of those who
accompany [the deceased] remains with him as an excellent source of protection even after he is
buried. This *mitzvah* is for the benefit and protection of the deceased. Accompanying the deceased,
with all the attendant practices, is true kindness, for in this way the soul of the deceased is strengthened
in the bond of life." He also mentions other customs connected with the funeral.

same thing, but in the feminine gender: לְכִי בְשָׁלוֹם וְתָנוּחִי בְשָׁלוֹם וְתַעֲמְדִי לְגוֹרָלֵךְ לְקֵץ הַיָּמִים.

The Hebrew letters of the word for bier (מִיטָה, *mitah*, i.e. the funeral cot) have the same numerical total (*gematria*) as those of *din* (דִין, "strict justice"). Therefore, some have the custom that after the deceased has been placed in the grave, the bier is overturned three times, to symbolize that the Divine Attribute of Strict Justice will be turned into that of mercy, and mourning will be turned into dancing, as reflected in *Psalms 30*: '*You have turned my mourning into dancing.*'[77]

Commencement of the Mourning (*Aveilus*) Period

◄§ The *Shurah*: Row of Comforters

22. Immediately after interment, i.e., when the grave is filled with earth [see 12:1], the state of *aninus* ends, and the period of formal mourning (*aveilus*) commences. The seven days (*shivah*) and thirty days (*shloshim*) are counted from then. Following the recitation of *Kaddish*, those present move away at least four *amos* (about eight feet) from the nearest grave and form a *shurah*: two parallel rows of comforters facing each other. The *shurah* must consist of at least ten men.[78]

The mourners remove their shoes and walk between the two rows of comforters.[79] The comforters say: הַמָּקוֹם יְנַחֵם אוֹתָךְ [אֶתְכֶם] בְּתוֹךְ שְׁאָר אֲבֵלֵי צִיּוֹן (וִירוּשָׁלָיִם), '*May Hashem console you among the other mourners of Zion and Jerusalem.*'

In some communities a *shurah* is not formed to comfort a woman or a minor, while in others it is the practice to form a *shurah* even in these cases.

A *shurah* is formed even if the deceased was a child, as long as it lived more than thirty days.[80]

Afterwards, the mourners put a bit of earth inside their regular shoes, put them

---

77. *Chochmas Adam* 158:31.

78. Mishnah *Megillah* 23b. And see *Rashi* there. Likewise we find in *Sanhedrin* (19a): "The *shurah* must consist of at least ten."

79. *Shulchan Aruch* (375:1) writes: "The mourner does not remove his shoes until he arrives home (*Ramban*). But now the custom is to remove the shoes after the grave is filled with earth." *Shulchan Aruch* rules the same in 376:1.

80. See *Gesher HaChaim* loc. cit. There he also explains why the custom (followed in Jerusalem) is not to form a *shurah* to comfort a woman. (It has its basis in whether or not women mourners go to the cemetery.) However, this custom of a *shurah* for women varies—especially outside of *Eretz Yisrael*—according to the practice of the *chevra kaddisha* of each city and congregation. In some communities, the practice is for women comforters to form a separate *shurah* for the women mourners; other communities allow the women mourners to pass through, or alongside, the regular *shurah*, while others prohibit it entirely.

on, and wear them until they arrive home. But if they are being driven home, [or are wearing non-leather shoes which are permissible during the *shivah* (see below 20:1)] they are not permitted to wear their regular shoes.[81]

◄§ Practices When Leaving the Cemetery

23. As the participants leave the cemetery, they pluck up some blades of grass or other herbage, along with some earth, and throw these behind them, saying (*Psalms* 72:16): וְיָצִיצוּ מֵעִיר כְּעֵשֶׂב הָאָרֶץ, '*May they blossom forth from the city like the grass of the earth*'; and (*Psalms* 103:14): זָכוּר כִּי עָפָר אֲנָחְנוּ, '*remember that we are but dust.*'[82]

Then they wash their hands with water. Some have the custom of saying, while washing hands, כַּפֵּר לְעַמְּךָ יִשְׂרָאֵל, '*Atone for Your people Israel*' (*Deut.* 21:8).

Some have the custom of washing their face as well.

After washing hands, the participants recite (*Isaiah* 25:8): בִּלַע הַמָּוֶת לָנֶצַח וּמָחָה ה׳ אֱלֹהִים דִּמְעָה מֵעַל כָּל פָּנִים וְחֶרְפַּת עַמּוֹ יָסִיר מֵעַל כָּל הָאָרֶץ כִּי ה׳ דִּבֵּר, '*May He swallow up death forever, and may Hashem, God, wipe away tears from upon every face and remove the scorn of His people from the entire world; for Hashem has spoken.*'[83]

After washing hands, one should not dry them.[84] In cold weather, one may be lenient and dry them.[84a] However, some rule that [even in summer] there is no

---

81. *Rama* 382:5 writes: "Some rule that if the deceased is his parent, the mourner must go without shoes from the cemetery to his home; but I have not seen this custom observed." And see *Shach* (loc. cit. §§3), who writes: "The reason [why this custom was not observed] is the wickedness of non-Jews [i.e. it would provoke harassment], as is mentioned in *Kol Bo*. . .However, where there is no problem of the wickedness of non-Jews, the shoes should be removed immediately at the cemetery." But *Mishnah Berurah* (loc. cit. §§32) cites *Magen Avraham* as stating that the reason for not observing this custom is that "it is extremely difficult to walk a long distance without shoes. . .and according to this, if [the mourner] is riding in a wagon or on an animal, he must remove his shoes even when going a long distance."

82. *Shulchan Aruch* 376:4. And *Shach* (§§4) writes: "This is also an allusion to the resurrection of the dead, who will come back to life from their earth, as it is said (*Psalms* 72:16): '*They will sprout forth from the city like the herbs of the earth*.'" And in §§5 he writes: "They pick up some earth. . .to indicate that this *tumah* (ritual impurity) can only be purified by means of three things such as the following: water, the ashes of the Red Heifer, and hyssop (*Ramban*)." According to *Kol Bo*: "They uproot some herbage with the attached earth and cast it on their heads as an expression of grief, as it is said (*Job* 2:12): '*They threw earth upon their heads heavenward.*'

Sheivet Yehudah (loc. cit.) writes: "I have found it written: 'As for the reason why they throw the blades of grass behind them rather than in front of them, I have seen in the Midrash that the soul accompanies the body as far as the grave, and it is not allowed to return until the public grants permission. When they throw [the grass] behind them, this is the taking leave, indicating: 'Go to your rest.' " According to this explanation, when one visits the cemetery at a time other than the burial, one need not perform this custom of tearing up herbage and earth.

83. *Shulchan Aruch* 376:4, and *Beis Lechem Yehudah* loc. cit.

84. In this way one shows that one is not removing one's attention from the mourning, and is not casting aside [thoughts about] the day of death (*Ma'avar Yabok* 43:9).

84a. *Kaf HaChaim* 4:8.

objection to drying them.[85]

When washing hands, one should not take the vessel directly from the hand of the one preceding him.[86]

The custom is that each person, after washing hands, pours out any remaining water from the vessel.[87]

Those who accompanied the deceased but did not enter the cemetery should also wash their hands if they came within four *amos* (about eight feet) of the bier.[88] Others wash their hands even if they did not come within four *amos* of the bier.[88a]

Some rule that in washing hands one must wash each hand three times.[89] According to some, it is not necessary to use a vessel.[89a]

24. Some have the custom when leaving the cemetery to sit down seven times, because spirits accompany him out, and each time one sits down, they flee from him. "But in our region, the practice is to sit down only three times"[90] after washing hands. Each time one sits, one recites: וִיהִי נֹעַם..., '*May the pleasantness of Hashem our God be upon us. . .*' (Psalms 90:17) followed by ... יֹשֵׁב בְּסֵתֶר עֶלְיוֹן, '*He who dwells in the shadow of the Supreme One. . .*' (ibid. 91:1).

If the burial occurred on *Yom Tov*, one is permitted to sit down in this manner just as on an ordinary day. Likewise, if the burial occurred just before *Shabbos*, one may sit down in this manner.[90a]

(One authority writes that nowadays most people do not follow this custom; instead, in *Eretz Yisrael,* only the family of the deceased perform these sittings.)[91]

---

85. *Ikrei HaDat* 35:9, citing "some rule."

86. *Chochmas Adam* 158:30, citing *Ma'aneh Lashon*.

87. *Ma'avar Yabok* 42:35. And *Nachamu Ami* writes: "Apparently this is the reason why one overturns the vessel after washing hands — in order to empty it of all the water."

88. *Aruch HaShulchan Orach Chaim* 4:21. The same ruling is given by *Nachamu Ami*, citing *Pnei Moshe*: that if one did not come within four *amos* of the bier, one need not wash hands. *Pri Megadim* in *Eshel Avraham* (§4) writes: "It seems to me that those who did not come within four *amos*, do not have to wash."

88a. This ruling is given by *Imrei Yosher* in the name of the *Chazon Ish*.

89. *Shulchan Aruch Orach Chaim* §4, and *Mishnah Berurah* 4:§§39.

89a. *Elyah Rabbah* loc. cit.

90. *Rama* 376:4. And *Taz* there (§§3) cites *Maharshal*, who received a tradition from his grandfather that one should recite seven times the verses beginning, וִיהִי נֹעַם, *May the pleasantness of Hashem our God be upon us* (Psalms 90:17) through, כִּי מַלְאָכָיו יְצַוֶּה לָּךְ, *For He will command His angels about you, to protect you in all your ways* (ibid. 91:11). The first time, one concludes with the first word of this latter verse, כִּי, *for;* the second time, one concludes with its second word (מַלְאָכָיו), and so on. This involves a kabbalistic secret. *Taz* cites *Levush* as writing that he, too, observed this custom. And *Shach* (§§6) writes, citing *Maharshal*, that one should sit down seven times while reciting the verses in this manner.

90a. *Rama* 376:4.

91. *Gesher HaChaim* loc. cit.

✺ Entering a House Before Washing Hands

25. The practice is to be careful not to enter someone else's house before washing hands and sitting down three times — and "the customs of our ancestors are Torah."[92] Some are also careful not to enter their own house before washing hands.[93]

✺ Leaving by a Different Route

26. Some have the custom of leaving the funeral by a different route, if possible, from that by which they came.[94]

✺ Accompanying the Mourners Home

27. The practice is to accompany the mourners from the cemetery back to their home.[95]

---

92. *Rama* loc. cit.

93. *Kaf HaChaim* (4:80) cites *Yafeh LaLeiv*: "Our custom is to be careful not to enter even one's own house before washing. . ." The same may be inferred from *Levush* and *Shiurei Knesses HaGedolah*, who state simply that one should not enter a house before washing — thus implying even one's own house.

94. *Ta'amei HaMinhagim* (§834) — in order to avoid meeting women who are taking part in the funeral [see above, par. 10]. *Gesher HaChaim* (14:20) writes the same in the name of *Zichron Shai*.

95. *Rosh*, *Mo'ed Katan*, Chapter *Elu Megalchin* §86. The same ruling is given by *Beis Yosef* §378, citing *Mordechai*.

CHAPTER ELEVEN

Funerals on *Yom Tov* and *Chol HaMo'ed*

ᴥᔑ The First Day of *Yom Tov,* and the Diaspora's Second Day

1. A Jew may not attend to the deceased on the first day of *Yom Tov*.[1] This applies even if the deceased will become odorous if not attended to,[2] and even if it is impossible to arrange for non-Jews to bury him. One authority writes that it is permitted to light candles from an already burning candle in order to place them around the deceased.[2a]

However, the *halachah* about moving the body is the same as on the Sabbath: As explained below, par. 4, it is only permitted if one first places a loaf of bread or other non-*muktzah* item on the body and then moves both the body and the loaf or non-*muktzah* item together.[3]

It is permitted to ask non-Jews to attend to and bury the body on *Yom Tov* — even if death occurred on *Yom Tov* itself and delaying burial until the next day will not mean that the body will become odorous.[4] If *Yom Tov* is on Friday, and the

---

1. The reason is that the *mitzvah* of burying the dead does not take precedence over *Yom Tov*, which is both a positive and negative commandment. *Shulchan Aruch Orach Chaim* 526:1, and *Mishnah Berurah* 526:§§1.

2. The body could be in danger of becoming odorous if, for example, death had occurred the day before *Yom Tov*, or if the weather was hot.
    "Even if the first day of *Yom Tov* is followed immediately by the Sabbath, meaning that it will be impossible to perform burial until the day after the Sabbath. . .in this case, too, Jews are forbidden to perform burial" (*Mishnah Berurah* loc. cit. §§2).

2a. *Gesher HaChaim* 17:1:2. The candles may be lit in this manner from an already burning flame, even by a Jew. The *halachah* is that if a candle is not needed for purposes of *Yom Tov*, or for one's physical needs, one is forbidden, by Rabbinic decree (*deRabbanan*), to light it even from an already burning flame on *Yom Tov*. An exception is made in the present case, however, in order to give respect to the deceased, for on the Scriptural (*deOraysa*) level, lighting a candle from an already burning flame is permitted, due to the principle that "since lighting is permitted for the needs of *Yom Tov*, it is permitted [even when not required for the needs of *Yom Tov*]."

3. *Beis Yosef*, citing *Kol Bo*; *Levush* §2; *Chochmas Adam* 170:1.

4. The Rabbinic prohibition against asking a non-Jew to perform labor for us on *Yom Tov* does not apply to the labor of burying a deceased Jew. The Sages made an exception in order to give respect to the deceased. Even in a case where there is no danger of the body's becoming odorous, it is considered more respectful to the deceased not to leave him unburied overnight; for delaying burial is

cemetery is more than a day's journey away, the non-Jews will not be able to get there until after the Sabbath. In that case, it is forbidden to have them start the journey. Rather, one must have non-Jews bury the deceased in the city where he died, and then after the Sabbath remove him from the temporary grave and take him to the cemetery. Or one could leave the deceased in the coffin and have non-Jews seal the coffin so that the odor cannot escape. Then, after the Sabbath, one could remove the body and bury it.[5]

The prohibition against having a Jew attend to the deceased on *Yom Tov* applies only to digging the grave,[6] or making the coffin or burial wrappings (*tachrichim*).[7] However, it is permitted to have a Jew dress the body, heat water in order to purify the body,[8] or place the deceased in the grave.[9] Some rule that these things, too, are forbidden for a Jew to do.[10] If someone follows the lenient opinion, one should not protest against his action.[11]

2. If someone dies on the first day of *Yom Tov*, it is forbidden to leave the body unburied overnight solely in order that he should be buried by Jews[12] rather than by non-Jews. This applies even if the deceased was a Torah scholar, even though it would befit his honor more to be buried by Jews. However, some rule that if the deceased was a great man (*adam gadol*), it is permissible to leave him unburied overnight in order that he should be buried by Jews.[12a]

Likewise, it is forbidden to leave the deceased unburied overnight solely in order that his wife and children should be able to accompany him beyond the *techum*, the

---

not the preferable practice. Moreover, delaying burial adds to the suffering of the family (*Beis Yosef*, citing a number of *Poskim*). *Be'ur Halachah* (loc. cit.) cites *Rashal* as ruling that in those places where there is no established custom of burying on *Yom Tov* by non-Jews, one should be strict, and delay burial until after the first day of *Yom Tov* if possible. But *Be'ur Halachah* concludes that one need not take this ruling of *Rashal* into account, even in a place where there is no established custom.

5. *Mishnah Berurah* loc. cit. §§3.

6. The reason is that digging the grave and making the coffin or burial wrappings are types of labor which are forbidden on the Scriptural (*deOraysa*) level.

7. "If it is possible to acquire ready-made burial wrappings, since they are the right size for the deceased, certainly one may not have them made [on *Yom Tov*], even by non-Jews" (*Mishnah Berurah* loc. cit. §§7).

8. These things (dressing the body, heating water to purify the body, and placing the deceased in the grave) are permitted because they are not Scripturally prohibited forms of labor (*Mishnah Berurah* loc. cit. §§9). But in purifying the body, one must take care not to perform the Scripturally prohibited labor of squeezing (*sechitah*) water from cloth and the like (*Rama* 526:1).

9. "However, covering the body with earth afterwards is forbidden according to all opinions, and may only be done by means of non-Jews, since filling a hole is like [the Scripturally forbidden labor of] *boneh*, building" (*Mishnah Berurah* §§11).

10. Those forbidding these things include a number of *Rishonim*. This is also the ruling of *Radbaz* in a responsum, and of *Gra* (*Mishnah Berurah* loc. cit. §§12).

11. *Mishnah Berurah* loc. cit. — ". . .because there are a number of authorites who [rule permissively on this issue]."

12. *Shulchan Aruch Orach Chaim* 526:2; *Mishnah Berurah* loc. cit. §§16.

12a. *Gesher HaChaim* loc. cit.

boundary which extends to a radius of about two-thirds of a mile (2,000 *amos*) from the last house of the city, beyond which one normally is forbidden to walk on *Yom Tov*.

One authority has written that if the person died on the first day of *Yom Tov* and was left unburied until the second day, it is forbidden to have Jews bury him. But another authority disagrees.[12b]

3. On the Diaspora's second day of *Yom Tov* — or even on the second day of Rosh Hashanah in *Eretz Yisrael* and the Diaspora[13] — Jews may perform the burial.

In communities where the practice is to put myrtle sprigs on the bier, it is permitted to cut the sprigs from a plant that is growing in the ground.[14] Likewise, it is permitted to cut cloth and sew it to make burial wrappings (*tachrichim*) if none are available;[15] to make the coffin;[16] to dig the grave;[17] to heat water for purifying the body, and to cut its hair.

If there is no Jewish cemetery in the city, it is permitted to take the deceased to another city that has a Jewish cemetery, even if this means going beyond the *techum* (see previous paragraph).[18] If there is a Jewish cemetery in the city where he died, but he had commanded that he be buried alongside his ancestors, in a different cemetery, this is not sufficient reason to desecrate *Yom Tov*, and it is forbidden to take him there. But since it is a *mitzvah* to fulfill the wishes of the deceased, it is permitted to leave him unburied overnight (see above, 9:7), in order to bury him alongside his ancestors after *Yom Tov*. But if it is likely that the body

---

12b. *Mishnah Berurah* loc. cit. §§16, and *Be'ur Halachah* there.

13. *Shulchan Aruch Orach Chaim* 526:4. And *Kaf HaChaim* (loc.cit.) explains why *Shulchan Aruch* found it necessary to add "or even on the second day of Rosh Hashanah": "One might have thought that since [the two days of Rosh Hashanah] are considered like one long day [for purposes of certain *halachos*], a Jew would be forbidden to perform the burial [on the second day, just as on the first]. Hence, [*Shulchan Aruch*] tells us that this is permitted."

14. *Shulchan Aruch* loc. cit. — ". . .even though this is not an essential need of burial, but is simply to give respect" (*Mishnah Berurah* loc. cit. §§18).

15. This applies even though it would be possible to wrap the body in cloth without sewing it. Nevertheless, if one can acquire burial wrappings ready-made to the right size, one should not make new ones. If they are soiled, it is permitted to launder them (*Mishnah Berurah* loc. cit. §§19).

16. If boards [of the needed size] are not available, it is permitted to saw them on [the Diaspora's second day of] *Yom Tov* (ibid. §§20).

17. Some write that, all the same, the desecration of *Yom Tov* should be kept to a minimum. Therefore they write that in a place where a certain group normally dig the grave, sew the wrappings, and attend to the deceased, others who do not belong to this group are not permitted to perform the burial. (The exception is late Friday afternoon, when it is praiseworthy for anyone to help as quickly as possible, so that no one will desecrate the Sabbath. However, a number of later authorities (*Acharonim*) are lenient in this matter [i.e. they make no distinction at any time between the usual burial staff and anyone else]. They reason that, with regard to burying the dead, the Sages made the Diaspora's second day of *Yom Tov* like an ordinary weekday [but see below, footnote 22] (*Mishnah Berurah* §§21).

18. *Shulchan Aruch* loc. cit.

awould become odorous due to the delay, he should be buried on the second *Yom Tov* day in the city where he is.[19]

If the cemetery is far away, it is permitted to hire a boat, wagon, or car[20] to take the deceased there.[21] But see below, paragraph 6.

It is permitted to perform the burial in the usual manner, and to mark the site by making a mound of earth.[21a]

With specific regard to burying the dead, the Sages made the second day of *Yom Tov* exactly the same as an ordinary workday; therefore, the permission for Jews to do various kinds of work for the purpose of burial applies even if it would be possible to have non-Jews do it. This is the opinion of *Shulchan Aruch*.[22] However, *Rama* rules that if non-Jews are readily available,[23] they (the non-Jews) should be given the work of digging the grave and making the burial wrappings and the coffin. The remaining work,[24] even filling the grave with earth, can be done by Jews.[24a] And if it is impossible to have the burial performed by non-Jews, everything can be done by Jews. The *Rama*'s ruling is the one followed in Ashkenazic communities.

Some rule that in our time, when conducting a funeral can cause desecration and disrespect of *Yom Tov*, funerals should not be held on the Diaspora's second day of *Yom Tov*, even though this may sometimes entail leaving the deceased unburied for three days.[25]

4. The permission to do these types of work on the second day of *Yom Tov* applies only when the intention is to perform the burial that day. Other-

---

19. *Mishnah Berurah* loc. cit. §§22.

20. *Gesher HaChaim* 17:2:4. "The driver should be a non-Jew. But if this is impossible, a Jew may drive them."

21. *Shulchan Aruch* loc. cit. And *Mishnah Berurah* (loc. cit. §§23) writes: "And it is permitted to carry [the deceased] on an animal belonging to a Jew."

21a. *Igros Moshe*, *Yoreh De'ah* III:154b.

22. *Shulchan Aruch* loc. cit. All the same, it is not entirely like an ordinary weekday. Anything forbidden during *Chol HaMo'ed* is, all the more so, forbidden on the Diaspora's second day of *Yom Tov* [even to those involved in burying the dead]. This includes quarrying stones for the grave, etc. (*Mishnah Berurah* loc. cit. §§24).

23. However, if one would have to wait many hours for non-Jews to come, and this would result in unbefitting conditions for the body — for example, it might swell up in the meantime — one need not wait, but may have Jews attend to the burial (ibid. §§25).

24. "Nevertheless, the *Acharonim* write that it is permitted to use a cloth in the process of purifying the body, as on an ordinary weekday; the danger that one might perform *sechitah*, the forbidden labor of squeezing water from the cloth, is not considered sufficient grounds to forbid using a cloth. [Those purifying the body] should simply be careful not to squeeze the cloth. And it seems to me that they should make sure that the cloths used are clean; otherwise, soaking them constitutes [the forbidden labor of] laundering" (ibid. §§26).

24a. It is even permitted to follow the usual custom of piling up dirt into a small mound on top of the grave, since this is considered the final part of burial (ibid. §§27).

25. *Igros Moshe*, *Orach Chaim* III:§76. The *gaon*, R' Shlomo Zalman Auerbach, cited in *Yom Tov Sheini Kehilchaso* 1:37, writes that in those places where burial on the second day of *Yom Tov* will definitely cause desecration and disrespect of *Yom Tov*, it is preferable not to bury on the second day of *Yom Tov*.

wise,[26] it is forbidden — even to ask non-Jews — to do any kind of work not normally permitted on *Yom Tov*.[26a]

The body of a deceased person is *muktzah* and may not be moved on the Sabbath or *Yom Tov*. If it is necessary to move the body in a case when it will not be buried on *Yom Tov*, one must first place a non-*muktzah* object such as a loaf of bread on the body or on the bed alongside the body, and then move the body together with the non-*muktzah* object.[26a] In places where there is no *eruv* to permit carrying in the street on *Yom Tov* and the Sabbath, it is forbidden to take the body from the house to the street and vice versa — even into an adjacent alleyway (*karmelis*).[27] Likewise, it is forbidden to move the body a distance of more than four *amos* (about eight feet) in the street.

5. On the first day of *Yom Tov*, family members and others may accompany the deceased only within the *techum*, the boundary which extends to a radius of about two-thirds of a mile (2,000 *amos*) from the last house of the city, beyond which one normally is forbidden to walk on the Sabbath or *Yom Tov*.[28] But on the second day of *Yom Tov*, it is permitted to accompany the deceased, even if this involves going many miles (even more than three *parsaos*) beyond the *techum*.[29] A visitor to *Eretz Yisrael*, observing the Diaspora's second day of *Yom Tov*, may take part in a funeral.[30]

It is permitted for those who accompanied the deceased to return home that same day after the funeral.[30a]

---

26. An example of a situation where the intention is not to perform the burial on *Yom Tov* would be
    if, for the honor of the deceased [see above, 9:7], he is to be left unburied overnight. "The same would apply if death occurred in the late afternoon at the end of *Yom Tov*, and there is not enough time to perform the burial on *Yom Tov*" (*Mishnah Berurah* loc. cit. §§29).
    And see *Be'ur Halachah* (loc. cit.), who writes that leaving the body unburied overnight in order that the burial can be performed by Jews after *Yom Tov* is forbidden, "since this is not considered to be in the category of 'to give respect to the deceased' (*Elyah Rabbah*). Nevertheless, if the deceased was a Torah scholar (*talmid chacham*), the matter requires further study [i.e., in that case it might be permitted to postpone the burial for this reason]. This is not comparable to the cases concerning which R' Yosef Karo prohibited in 526:2 (regarding the first day of *Yom Tov*), because his reasons there are those explained in *Mishnah Berurah*, and those reasons do not apply in this case."
26a. *Shulchan Aruch* §311; see *Magen Avraham* §§1; *Pri Megaddim*.
27. *Mishnah Berurah* 526:§§30. It is also forbidden to remove the body from the house for the sake
    of the living — for example, so that *Kohanim* will be able to enter the house; or to relieve the mental anguish of those in the house.
28. According to all opinions, the prohibition against going outside the city is of only Rabbinic status
    until one reaches a distance of three *parsaos*. Nevertheless, the Sages did not consider the purpose of accompanying the deceased to be sufficient grounds for permitting more than 2,000 *amos* (ibid. §§33).
29. This applies even to those who are not needed to perform the burial, but are accompanying the
    deceased solely in order to give honor to him. Nevertheless, they are permitted to go even more than three *parsaos*, since for purposes of burial, the Sages made the Diaspora's second day of *Yom Tov* like an ordinary day.
30. *Igros Moshe*, *Orach Chaim* III:77.
30a. *Mishnah Berurah* 526:§§35.

Those who accompanied the deceased are also permitted to bring back any burial tools which they carried with them beyond the *techum*.[31]

6. Those accompanying the deceased, including the mourning family members, are forbidden to ride an animal or get on a boat, even on the second day of *Yom Tov*, and even within the *techum*.[32]

If there is no alternative, the burial workers who are indispensable for burying the deceased[33] may ride an animal outside the city. But within the city, this is forbidden.[34] These same individuals may likewise ride in a car, if it is driven by a non-Jew. If no non-Jewish driver is available, it is permitted to use a Jewish driver.[35]

7. If the person died in the evening on the second day of *Yom Tov*, and is to be buried by Jews,[36] the participants rise early and perform the burial before the morning prayers.[37] But if he died in the daytime — or even if he died in the evening but is to be buried by non-Jews — the burial should take place after the morning *Yom Tov*-meal.[38] However, some rule that the burial should take place before the morning meal.

8. If the residents of a city hear of a Jewish person who has died in a city four or five days' journey away, and is lying unburied with no Jew to attend to him, they may set out on the second day of *Yom Tov* in order to bury him as soon as possible, even though they will not be able to reach the deceased until after the festival.[39]

9. One who performs a service on the second day of *Yom Tov* in connection with the burial — for example, digging the grave, or selling the cloth for the burial wrappings (*tachrichim*) — is permitted to receive payment after *Yom Tov* for his services. However, this is on condition that on the *Yom Tov*-day itself he does not mention the amount he is charging, and only presents the bill after *Yom Tov*.[40]

---

31. Ibid. §§36.

32. *Shulchan Aruch* 526:7, and *Mishnah Berurah* loc. cit. §§37. In §§38, *Mishnah Berurah* writes: "It is implied that [riding an animal or getting on a boat] is forbidden even if it is impossible to go on foot in that place, with the result that people will not be able to accompany the deceased."

33. See *Be'ur Halachah* loc. cit. The same ruling — that this permission applies only where it is very difficult to walk — is given by *Nehar Shalom*, and by *Shulchan Aruch HaRav*.

34. *Shulchan Aruch* loc. cit. And *Mishnah Berurah* (§§39) explains: "However, they may not ride within the city, because if they did so, the non-Jews would think they were violating *Yom Tov*."

35. *Gesher HaChaim* 17:2:4.

36. According to the ruling of R' Yosef Karo, the deceased will be buried by Jews even if non-Jews are readily available to perform the burial; according to *Rama*, only if it is not possible to have non-Jews perform it. [See above, par. 3.]

37. *Shulchan Aruch* 526:12.

38. Ibid.

39. Ibid. 526:8.

40. Ibid. 526:5; *Mishnah Berurah* loc.cit. §§32.

If the gravedigger refuses to work unless his wages are explicitly stated, or unless he is given cash on *Yom Tov*, although he is acting sinfully, the family members of the deceased may pay him.[41]

10. An aborted fetus (*nefel*) has the same halachic status on *Yom Tov* as a stone, and one is forbidden even to move it. One is forbidden to have it buried, even by non-Jews on the second day of *Yom Tov*.[42]

An infant that dies within its first thirty days of life is assumed to have been viable if it had fully formed hair and fingernails. Hence, it has the same halachic status as a deceased adult: It can be buried on the first day of *Yom Tov* by non-Jews, and on the second day of *Yom Tov* by Jews. Since most women give birth to viable infants, this *halachah* applies even if there is no absolute proof that the infant in question was born after a full nine-month pregnancy.[43]

However, some rule that since the infant in question died, it cannot be judged on the basis of "most women give birth to viable infants." Therefore its halachic status is stricter, and it can be buried only by non-Jews, even on the second day of *Yom Tov*.[44]

If the infant did not have fully formed hair and fingernails, even if it died on the thirtieth day of its life, it is not assumed to have been viable, and is considered the same as an aborted fetus (*nefel*). Nevertheless, one is permitted to have non-Jews bury it on the second day of *Yom Tov*, since there is doubt as to whether it was viable.[45]

If it is the type of infant whose foreskin should be removed after death,[45a] this may not be done on *Yom Tov*, not even the second day of *Yom Tov*.[46] But some rule that one should wait to bury the infant until after *Yom Tov*, so that the foreskin can be removed before burial.[47]

As stated, the above applies to an infant that died within its first thirty days of life. If it lived more than thirty days, but had not been circumcised, due to sickness or the like, it may be buried on *Yom Tov*, and the foreskin may also be removed then.[48]

---

41. *Mishnah Berurah* loc. cit. The reason is that, for purposes of burial, the Sages made the Diaspora's second day of *Yom Tov* like an ordinary day.

42. Ibid. §§44. And see *Chochmas Adam* 170:7.

43. *Shulchan Aruch* 526:9; *Mishnah Berurah* §§46-47. We attribute the infant's death to some cause [other than being non-viable].

44. *Mishnah Berurah* loc. cit.

45. Ibid. §§45-47.

45a. As explained in *Yoreh De'ah* 263:5, if an infant dies before it is eight days old, it is circumcised at its grave with a stone or a reed. A blessing is not recited over this circumcision. However, a name is given the infant as a memorial, so that Heaven should have mercy on him.

46. *Shulchan Aruch* 526:10. *Mishnah Berurah* (loc. cit.) explains that this is not considered an essential need of burial.

47. *Rama* loc. cit.; *Mishnah Berurah* loc. cit. §§49.

48. *Mishnah Berurah* loc. cit.

◈§ The Sabbath and Yom Kippur

11. On the Sabbath or Yom Kippur, it is forbidden to do any of the work involved in attending to the deceased, nor can one even have non-Jews do it.[49] Even if a grave had already been dug the previous day, one is forbidden to have non-Jews remove the deceased and place him in the grave.[50]

◈§ *Chol HaMo'ed*

12. All the work necessary for burial may be done on *Chol HaMo'ed*. This includes sewing burial wrappings (*tachrichim*), even if the sewing is the type requiring a professional. If someone is making the coffin, this should be done in the courtyard of the same building where the deceased is, so that it will be clear that it is being done for him. If boards for the coffin are not on hand, it is permitted to bring wood and saw it to the needed dimensions, but this should be done unobtrusively, inside the house.[51] If it cannot be done unobtrusively, it may even be done in public.[52]

If the deceased was a well-known personality, the work can even be done in the marketplace.

Where the Jewish community is small, and everyone knows when someone has died, the *halachah* is the same as for a well-known personality.[53]

The *halachos* of *kri'ah* (tearing the garment) on *Yom Tov* or *Chol HaMo'ed* are presented below, 33:1,5.

---

49. The reason is for the honor of the deceased — that people should not say that his death caused desecration of the Sabbath (*Kaf HaChaim os* 28, citing *Beis Yosef* and *Magen Avraham*).

50. *Mishnah Berurah* loc. cit. §§17.

51. *Shulchan Aruch Orach Chaim* 547:10.

52. *Mishnah Berurah* loc. cit. §§20. The permission to saw the boards "in public" means in public view of other Jews. One is forbidden to do it in public view of non-Jews, even if doing it unobtrusively is impossible [*Magen Avraham*]. But *Elyah Rabbah* is lenient, permitting it to be done even in public view of non-Jews if doing it unobtrusively is impossible.

53. *Shulchan Aruch* loc. cit.

CHAPTER TWELVE

When Does Mourning Begin?

ᴥᵌ **Filling the Grave With Earth (*Stimas HaGolel*) /
Beginning of *Shivah* and *Shloshim***

1. As soon as the deceased is buried and the grave is filled with earth,[1] *aninus* ends
and mourning (*aveilus*) begins.[2] The seven days (*shivah*) and thirty days
(*shloshim*) are counted from then.

If a person thought the grave had been filled with earth, and began mourning,
and then found out that the grave actually had not been filled at that time, he must
begin the mourning period again.[3]

If he began mourning before sundown, without having been informed that the
grave had been filled with earth, and then found out that at the time he began
mourning the grave had already been filled, the short time that he mourned before
sundown counts as a full first day of mourning.[4]

---

1. See *Da'as Torah*, who writes that the wording of *Shulchan Aruch* implies that the moment referred
    to is when the grave is filled according to the customary procedure, and no more earth need
be added.

2. *Shulchan Aruch* 375:1. For the *halachos* of removing the shoes after the burial, see above, 10:22.

3. *Rama* 375:1.
    If burial occurred just before the Sabbath began, and the mourners went immediately to the
synagogue, so that they did not begin sitting low at all [before the Sabbath], that Friday is nevertheless
counted as the first of the seven days (*shivah*) (*Gilyon Maharsha* ad loc. citing responsa *Beis Yosef*
§93; see par. 10 below). [This is unlike the case of burial immediately prior to a Festival which cancels
the *shivah* only if the mourner observed an act of mourning — even for a short time — before the
Festival. See below, 32:2 (*Da'as Kedoshim*).]
    See responsa *Tuv Ta'am Vada'as* (§215), who states that if burial took place on Friday after the
mourner had already accepted the Sabbath upon himself, nevertheless that Friday counts as the first
of the seven days. True, this author reasons, if he had already recited *Maariv*, that day [i.e., Friday]
would not count. But, unlike reciting *Maariv*, accepting the Sabbath is no indication that the person
considers it nighttime already. Instead, it is a way of extending the Sabbath to include the last part of
the previous day. But this extension of the Sabbath (*Tosefes Shabbos*) is still considered daytime.

4. *Pischei Teshuvah* loc. cit. §§1, citing *Derech HaChaim*. He writes that this can be proven from
    what *Rama* wrote in 375:1: "If a person thought the grave had been filled with earth, and began
mourning, and then found out that the grave actually had not been filled at that time, he must begin
the mourning period again." This implies that if he found out that he had been correct in observing
mourning, it counts.

◄§ Reinterment

2. The effect of reinterment upon the mourning period depends upon the intention at the time of the original burial:[5]

(a) If the deceased was buried with the intention of reinterring him at some unspecified future opportunity, mourning begins immediately with burial in the first grave. If he is later reinterred within seven days of the first burial, the mourning period starts anew. However, if the reinterment takes place more than seven days after the first burial, the essential mourning period is considered to have passed, and no second mourning period is begun;

(b) If the original intention was to reinter the deceased within seven days, mourning begins only with the second burial;[6]

(c) If the intention at the time of the original burial was not to reinter the deceased, the mourning period is counted solely from that original burial, even if he was later reinterred within seven days.

◄§ A City Under Siege

3. If, because a city was under siege, a deceased was placed in a coffin which is then sealed and put in a different house from where he died, the counting of the seven days begins immediately — even if the intention is to bury him in a cemetery after the siege is lifted. The sealing of the coffin is considered like burial, and mourning begins immediately.[7]

◄§ If the Body Was Consumed by Fire

4. If the body was consumed by fire, mourning begins from the time that it was consumed, not from the time when the ashes were buried. The counting of the seven days also begins from that time.[8]

◄§ If the Mourner Does Not Accompany the Deceased to the Cemetery

5. If the mourner does not accompany the deceased to the cemetery, and the cemetery is near the city, mourning begins from the time when the mourner

---

5. *Shulchan Aruch* 375:3.

6. Responsa *Betzel HaChachmah* 2:64 writes that if the original intention was to reinter the deceased within seven days, but mourning was begun immediately, and then the reinterment in fact took place after more than seven days, it is not necessary to observe mourning a second time.

He writes further that if the burial took place on the day before *Yom Tov* with the intention of reinterring the deceased after *Yom Tov*, mourning should be begun immediately, before *Yom Tov*, and then the festival cancels the first seven days of mourning (*shivah*).

7. *Shulchan Aruch* 375:4.

8. Responsa *Chelkas Yaakov* 1:32. He explains that there is no *obligation* to bury ashes of the deceased, even though it is certainly correct and meritorious to bury them in a cemetery. The same ruling is given by *Gesher HaChaim* 16:8:5.

is informed that the deceased has been buried,[9] or from the estimated time of burial.[10]

6. If the deceased is sent to another city or country for burial, and those remaining behind do not know when burial will take place,[11] they begin mourning, and commence *shivah*, from the time when they take leave, and cease accompanying the deceased. [*See* footnote 11 and above, 5:55.]

Those who accompany the deceased to the cemetery begin mourning, and commence *shivah*, from the time of burial.[12]

---

9. *Shach* 375:§§1.

10. Responsa *Tuv Ta'am Vada'as* (*mahadura* 3, part II:215) writes that being informed burial took place is not the only way the obligation of mourning begins. It also begins if there is a reasonable estimate that by this time burial must have taken place.

11. *Shulchan Aruch* 375:2.

Aruch HaShulchan (375:8) writes: "These words would seem to imply that they begin counting immediately [from the time when they take leave] only if they do not know when he is buried. And in fact one of the great *Poskim* writes explicitly that since they do not know when the grave will be filled with earth, their taking leave is, for them, equivalent to filling the grave with earth (*Bach*). However, the words of *Tur* imply differently. . .and also from the words of [*Beis Yosef*] one may infer that [their ignorance of the time of burial] is not an essential requirement [for being allowed to start counting the seven days immediately upon taking leave]. Otherwise, why would [*Beis Yosef*] distinguish between whether the deceased is buried here or in another city? Instead, he would simply have distinguished between whether the mourners do or do not know the time of burial, even if it takes place in another city. Therefore [the phrase, 'and those remaining behind do not know when burial will take place'] is not meant to imply the converse. Rather, [R' Yosef Karo] simply described the typical case, which is that when the deceased is buried in a different city the time of burial is unknown. But this [ignorance of the time of burial] is not an essential requirement [for beginning the mourning immediately]. Therefore it seems in my humble opinion that the *halachah* is as I have written. Moreover, it may be that even *Bach* did not intend to imply that it is an essential requirement. But this requires further study."

Igros Moshe (*Yoreh De'ah* part I §253, and part II §170) writes: "Regarding the deceased who are taken to *Eretz Yisrael* for burial while the children remain at home: It is obvious that they become obligated to observe their mourning immediately when the airplane leaves with the deceased, for this must certainly be considered for them as 'taking leave [from accompanying the deceased].'

Igros Moshe continues: "One should not draw any inference from the words of R' Yosef Karo (375:2): '. . .and those remaining behind do not know when burial will take place. . .' which would seem to imply that if they *do* know when burial will take place, they should not begin observing the laws of mourning until after the burial. (Of course when the deceased is taken to *Eretz Yisrael*, those remaining behind do know the exact time when burial will take place, and they are even informed by telegraph or telephone.) For if burial were the essential factor for beginning mourning even when burial takes place in a different city, the following objection would be raised: [In the case when those remaining behind do not know the time of burial,] why should they begin mourning from when they turn back from accompanying the deceased? Instead, they should begin from the earliest possible time when burial might take place. Thus, if the city of burial was one or two days' journey from the mourners' city, they should not begin mourning for one or two days, since before that it would be impossible for burial to have taken place, and at the time when they turned back from accompanying the deceased, burial certainly could not have taken place. Therefore, we are forced to say that the basis for beginning the observance of mourning is not burial. But when burial takes place nearby, so that it is possible to know when it occurred, the mourners' minds are on the deceased as if he still lay unburied in front of them."

12. *Shulchan Aruch* 375:2.

◄§ When the Leader of the Household (*Gedol HaBayis*) Accompanies the Deceased to Another City or Country

7. The leading member of the mourning family is called *gedol habayis*, the leader of the household. For the definition of this term, see par. 8 below and pars. 16-19.

If the leader of the household accompanies the deceased to burial in another city or country, the *halachah* depends on the scheduled time of burial.

> (a) If the burial is scheduled to take place within three days of their departure,[13] even the family members who remain behind begin mourning, and begin counting the seven days, from the time of burial.[14]

> (b) If burial is scheduled to take place after three days, those who remain behind begin mourning and counting from the time when they turn back from accompanying the deceased.

When does this apply? When the leader of the household remains in the city of burial for the whole first seven days of mourning. But if he returns to the city where the other mourners are, his mourning period also begins from the

---

13. *Shach* §§3, citing *Ravan*.

14. *Shulchan Aruch* loc. cit. The reason is that all the mourners follow the count of the leader of the household (*gedol habayis*), since he is the main member of the family.

If the leader of the household remains in the home city, *Shach* writes in §§2: "Those who go with the deceased to a different city for the burial begin counting [their days of mourning] from the time of burial. The reason is that the rule about other mourners following the count of the leader of the household is applied only when it results in stringency [but not when it would result in lenience — i.e., in this case those who go with the deceased to burial could end their count sooner]. The same idea is espoused by *Tosafos*, *Mo'ed Katan* 22a, s.v. מהדריתו. *Tur*, however, writes that all the mourners follow the count of the leader of the household. If he remains in the home city, even those who accompany the deceased to another city begin their count from when the deceased leaves the home city. It seems," *Shach* continues, "that this is also the opinion of *Ramban* and *Rosh*. . .However, according to the version of the Jerusalem Talmud cited by *Beis Yosef*, the opinion of *Tosafos* is proven to be the halachically correct one. And it seems to me that this version [of the Jerusalem Talmud] is the most accurate one. . .and it seems to me that this is also the opinion of *Avi Ha'Ezri*, cited by *Mordechai*. . ."

As stated, if the leader of the household accompanies the deceased to a different city for burial, the *halachah* is that even those remaining in the home city begin their count from the time of burial. In that case, a number of days may pass between the time the deceased leaves the home city and the time of burial. *Derech HaChaim* writes that during these intervening days the family members are considered neither as *onenim* (family members whose deceased is waiting to be buried) nor as mourners. Hence, they are permitted to eat meat and drink wine, and they are obligated by all the commandments. Their halachic status is equivalent to a case mentioned by *Shulchan Aruch* 341:3, where the family members no longer bear responsibility for burial, yet the deceased is not yet buried. Family members with this status are, nevertheless, forbidden to sit on a bed [i.e. they must sit on the floor or on something low], and must also observe the prohibitions against marital relations, bathing, anointing themselves with oil or lotion, taking part in joyous occasions, and asking about the welfare of others [see below, Chapters 16, 17, 18, 22]. This, adds *Derech HaChaim*, is the *halachah* for any situation in which a family member is not required to observe mourning between the time of death and the time when he begins to observe the *halachos* of *shivah*.

time when they turned back from accompanying the deceased. This is true even if the leader of the household returns only on the seventh day of mourning.[15]

8. The leader of the household *(gedol habayis)* is the person upon whom the entire household depends, and whose opinion they tend to follow. It makes no difference whether he is a brother of the deceased, a son, or even a son who is not yet of bar-mitzvah age. However, one authority rules that he must be at least thirteen years old.[16] To identify the leader of the household in questionable situations, a competent halachic authority should be consulted.

✑ Delayed Burial

9. If the deceased was sent to another city for burial, and the family members remaining behind began mourning, as they should, upon turning back from accompanying the deceased,[17] but then a delay occurred and the deceased remained unburied for a long time, they need not interrupt their period of mourning. Nor are they required to mourn again after the burial finally takes place. The reason is that they began their mourning in accordance with the *halachah*.[18]

✑ Burial Just Before Sundown

10. If burial took place in late afternoon, the family members should ideally *(l'chatchilah)* accept the state of mourning upon themselves[19] before sundown *(sh'ki'ah)*. This ensures that the period between burial and sundown will be counted as the first day of mourning.

If burial took place after sundown, one should be lenient and count the last minutes of that day as a whole day of mourning, as long as burial took place within thirteen minutes after sundown.[20]

This applies only if the mourner had not recited *Ma'ariv* — even if the

---

15. *Shach* loc. cit. §§12, cited by *Chiddushei R' Akiva Eiger* 375:2.

16. *Shulchan Aruch* loc. cit.

17. This refers to the case where the leader of the household did not accompany the deceased to the other city *(Shach* §§10).

18. *Rama* 375:7.

19. They do so by sitting on the floor or performing some other act of mourning. If they did not accept the state of mourning upon themselves before sundown, nonetheless, if the burial ended before sundown, it is counted as the first day. See footnote 3.

20. *Gesher HaChaim* 19:4:1. The same ruling is given by *Ketzos HaShulchan*. And see *Sdei Chemed*, *Aveilus* §15.

I have heard in the name of great contemporary *Poskim* that the time limit is thirteen minutes after *sh'ki'ah* (sundown), contrary to the figure given by *Gesher HaChaim*, loc. cit.

All this refers to *Eretz Yisrael*, where the opinion of the *Gra* about the definition of *sh'ki'ah* is primarily followed, even though some also follow the opinion of Rabbeinu Tam wherever this results in stringency.

In the Diaspora, those who follow the opinion of Rabbeinu Tam when it results in stringency should not go beyond the thirteen-minute time limit mentioned in the text. However, those who follow the opinion of Rabbeinu Tam even when it results in leniency could be lenient here, too, until the hour defined by Rabbeinu Tam as nightfall *(tzeis hakochavim)*.

congregation had already recited it. [21] But if the mourner had already recited *Maariv* — even if he had recited it before sundown — the day of the late-afternoon burial cannot be counted, and he must count the next day as the first day of mourning.[22]

◀§ If Mourner Will Not Travel to the City of Burial

11. If a person received news that a family member died in another city but will not be buried for another day or two, and the one who received the news is not going to travel to the city of burial, some rule that the laws of mourning do not apply to him until the burial takes place.[23] Others rule that they apply to him as soon as he receives the news.[24]

◀§ If the Deceased Cannot Be Buried

12. The *halachah* in this section concerns someone executed by hostile government authorities, who do not permit burial. After a time, the relatives of the deceased give up hope of getting the government's permission for burial, but only subsequently do they also give up hope of stealing the body and giving it proper burial.

From the time they gave up hope of government permission, the laws of mourning apply and the count of *shivah* begins, even though they may not yet have given up hope of stealing and burying the body.[25] It makes no difference whether they gave up hope within or after thirty days from the death.[26]

13. If someone was informed that non-Jews killed a member of his family in another city, and he began immediately to mourn for him, and then later found out that the deceased could not yet be buried — the mourning period which he already observed is not counted. He must begin mourning again, counting the seven days from the time when the deceased is buried, or from the time when hope

---

21. *Shach* 375:§§14.

22. *Shulchan Aruch* 375:11.

23. *Netziv*, in his *Meshiv Davar* part 1:72. And *Sheivet Sofer* (§106) writes that during the time before burial such a person would also not be subject to the laws of an *onen* (a family member whose deceased is not yet buried); nevertheless, he does not begin observing the laws of mourning until the burial. The same ruling is given by *Gesher HaChaim* (19:4:10). And see *Sdei Chemed*, *Pe'as HaSadeh*, *Aveilus* §14.

In his written comments on part 1 of the Hebrew edition of *P'nei Baruch*, the *gaon* R' Shlomo Zalman Auerbach, *shlita*, cites the *gaon*, author of *Tiferes LeMoshe*, as agreeing with the ruling of *Meshiv Davar*.

24. The *gaon* R' Rafael Shapira, *zatzal* (son-in-law of *Netziv*), in responsa *Maharsham*. The same ruling is given by responsa *Chelkas Yaakov* part 1 §188; and by responsa *Igros Moshe*, *Yoreh De'ah* part 1 §253; and by *Chazon LaMo'ed* 2:33. The latter, in a note there, writes that the *gaon* R' Tzvi Pesach Frank agreed with this ruling. The same ruling was given by the *gaon*, R' Yosef Eliahu Henkin, *zatzal*. The *gaon* R' Shlomo Zalman Auerbach, *shlita*, in his comments on part 1 of *P'nei Baruch*, questions this ruling.

25. *Shulchan Aruch* 375:5.

26. *Shach* (375:§§6) writes that this is the agreed opinion of the *Poskim*.

of burying him is given up.[27]

14. When a person drowns, the *halachah* distinguishes between "finite" and "infinite" bodies of water (*mayim sheyesh lahem sof* and *mayim she'ein lahem sof*). "Finite" water means all the four banks of the body of water can be seen at one time. "Infinite" water refers to a large body of water where the four sides of the body of water cannot be seen at one time. In either case, if the victim was someone's husband, she is forbidden to remarry until there is adequate evidence of his death.

This section concerns someone who drowned in "finite" water, or who is said to have been killed by bandits or wild animals. Definite proof of his death is found, on the basis of which his wife is given permission to remarry.[28]

The mourning period begins from the time when hope of finding the body is given up.

Even if some of his limbs are found and positively identified by means of distinguishing physical marks and the like, the period of mourning does not begin until the head and most of the body are found, or until hope of finding the body is given up.

If the body is found after the family have finished observing *shivah*, they need not mourn again. Instead, they observe the same *halachah* when someone's remains are reinterred (*likut atzamos*; see below, chapter 45). That is, the family members tear their garments[29] and observe mourning for the remainder of that day.[30] This applies only if they heard about the finding of the body on the day it was found. But if they heard about it the next day, they are not required to mourn.[31]

15. If someone drowned in "infinite" water (see previous section), or it is said that he was killed by bandits or wild animals, but his wife has not yet been given permission to remarry [i.e., and has the status of an *agunah*], the family do not mourn for him.[32] Likewise, the sons do not say *Kaddish* for him.[33] However, the

---

27. *Shulchan Aruch* 375:6.

28. *Shach* loc. cit. §§7. The *halachah* in the case where his wife has not yet been given permission to remarry is explained in the next section.

29. *Taz* (loc. cit. §§2) writes that *kri'ah* is required. The same ruling is given by *Chochmas Adam* 162:10.

30. *Shulchan Aruch* 375:7.

31. *Shulchan Aruch* (loc. cit.) writes: "If they are present when [the body] is found, they observe the laws of mourning for him that day. . .but if they are not present, but heard after the day passed, they are not required to observe the laws of mourning." But see *Shach* (§§9), who writes that the *Shulchan Aruch* was simply speaking in terms of the usual circumstances. Ordinarily, if they were not present, they didn't hear that day. "But certainly even if they were not present but did hear the same day, they must observe the laws of mourning that whole day, as is written below, 403:5."

32. *Beis Yosef*, citing *Sefer Haltur*, who in turn cites *Rif* as stating that in this circumstance the person is still given the halachic presumption of being alive. This ruling is cited by *Shach* §§7. The same ruling is given by *Rama* in *Even HaEzer* 17:5.

33. *Pischei Teshuvah* loc. cit. §§3, citing responsa *Chinuch Beis Yehudah* §91; *Sha'ar Efrayim sha'ar* 10:26. The same ruling is given by responsa *Avodas HaGershuni* §18.

sons of the reputed deceased are allowed to name their sons after him.[33a] If the reputed deceased is a woman, some authorities permit the sons to say *Kaddish* for her.[33b]

If the person who is believed to have drowned had no wife, so that there is no danger of halachic complications, some rule that the family must mourn for him; but others disagree.[34]

⮷ One Who Arrives During *Shivah*

16. This section concerns someone whose family member died in another city. He did not hear of the death until coming to the place where the other family members are already observing mourning, that is, to the same city where the deceased died or was buried.[35]

If, at the time of burial, the newcomer had been in a nearby place, no more than a day's journey away [by any means of transportation],[35a] he joins the count of the other mourners and observes mourning only for the same number of days as they do.

Even if the newcomer arrives only on the seventh day of mourning, he joins the count of the other mourners, as long as they have not yet stood up from sitting *shivah*. This applies even if they have already made preparatory motions to stand up, but consoling visitors are still present. Even in this case, his count is the same as theirs; he sits with them for a few minutes, and then stands up (concludes the seven days of mourning) along with them.

When does this apply? When the leader of the household [*gedol habayis*] is among the mourners. Then the newcomer joins in his count. If the leader of the household is not among the mourners, then the newcomer counts his seven days independently of the others,[36] from the time he is initially informed of the death.

33a. See *Mishmeres Shalom (os alef* §85), who writes in the name of *Darkei Moshe* that, all the same, [the family members] can name their newborn son after the reputed deceased.

33b. Responsa *Duda'ei HaSadeh* §70.

34. The dispute is cited in *Chiddushei R' Akiva Eiger, Yoreh De'ah* §345. He quotes *Ezras Nashim Even HaEzer* §17 §§62), who sees the wording of *Beis Yosef* as implying that in such a case mourning is forbidden. *Ezras Nashim* cites *Shai LaMorah* (§16) as giving the same ruling. However, the author of *Ezras Nashim* himself rules that mourning is permitted. Responsa *Shevus Yaakov* (part 1 §103) also rules that mourning is permitted.

35. *Shulchan Aruch* 375:8. The same ruling is given by *Shach* (loc. cit. §§11), citing *Hagahos Asheri*, who bases his ruling on *Or Zarua*, and is cited in turn by *Beis Yosef* and *Darkei Moshe*. However, *Meiri* in his commentary on *Mo'ed Katan* disagrees with this opinion of *Or Zarua* and rules that even if the newcomer joins the other family members in a city other than where the deceased died, he joins their count. Responsa *Tzitz Eliezer* (11:§72) writes that in this case, if there is pressing need, the newcomer may be permitted to join the count of the other mourners. The same ruling is cited by *Chazon LaMo'ed* (ch. 12, note 13), who states that "some are lenient on this issue."

35a. *Kol Bo Aveilus* (p. 331); responsa *Chelkas Yaakov* (3:§67).

36. *Shulchan Aruch* loc. cit.

It should be noted that *Tiferes Shmuel (Mo'ed Katan* 3:12) writes: "In our time we do not follow this practice, because there are many distinctions among different circumstances, and also we do not

One authority has written that if there is no leader of the household in the family, the newcomer joins the the count observed by the majority of the mourners whom he finds sitting shivah .[37]

If the leader of the household himself is the newcomer, arriving from a nearby place (within one day's journey) during the first seven days of mourning, most of the authorities rule that he does not join the count of the others, but must begin his own independent count[38] from the time he hears of the death.

Some rule that the above laws concerning a newcomer apply even if he had heard of the death while he was still in his original place,[39] but had not begun to mourn.[40] However, if he had heard of the death and had already begun to mourn, he does not join the count of the other mourners, but continues his independent count.[41]

17. The law that a newcomer joins the count of the leader of the mourning household applies only if he comes to where the leader of the household is mourning. If the leader of the household comes to him and informs him of the death, he does not join the count of the leader of the household.[42]

∽§ Belated News

18. The preceding halachos (paragraphs 16-17) result from the rule that all members of the mourning family follow the count of the leader of the mourning household. This rule, however, is applied only when it results in leniency for the other family members. If it were to result in stringency, it would not be applied.

For example, the halachah is that a person observes shivah only if he heard of the death within thirty days of the death (shmu'ah krovah). However, if he heard of the death after thirty days (shmu'ah rechokah), he observes mourning for only

---

know how to define the concept, 'the visits of consoling visitors have ended' (עָמְדוּ מְנַחֲמִים), especially in our time when there are fewer consoling visitors than in the past. Thus, in Ashkenaz [i.e., Germany] and Poland, it is not the custom to follow this halachah . Instead, without exceptions [the newcomer] counts his seven days independently of the others. And this is the correct ruling."

37. Gesher HaChaim 19:5:9. And see Even Yaakov (42:4), who supports his ruling with a citation from responsa Ri Migash §91.

38. Shach (loc. cit. §§12 and 13) writes that leader of the household must begin his own independent count. The same ruling is given by the following authorities: Chochmas Adam 162:14; Lechem HaPanim kuntres acharon to 375:8; Beis Lechem Yehudah §§11; Dinei Aveilus §§7; Aruch HaShulchan 375:18; responsa Divrei Malkiel 2:96; Mishmeres Shalom os gimel; Gesher HaChaim 19:5:10.

39. Mishmeres Shalom os gimmel §5. The same conclusion is reached by Sdei Chemed, Aveilus §72. And the same ruling is given by Kol Bo Al Aveilus p. 330, citing responsa Duda'ei HaSadeh §18 and Zachur LeAvraham part 3, Yoreh De'ah os 3. The same ruling is given by Gesher HaChaim 19:5:3, and Chazon LaMo'ed 12:10.

40. See Mishmeres Shalom loc. cit. citing responsa Harei Besamim (tinyana), beginning of §251.

41. Shulchan Aruch 375:9.

42. The reason is that the one who comes is considered secondary to the one who is there, not the reverse (Bach, in the name of Rashba, cited by Chiddushei R' Akiva Eiger loc. cit.).

a short time on the day he hears the news. Moreover, if he hears during the Sabbath which was the thirtieth day (a *shmu'ah krovah*), he need not observe *shivah*, since at the termination of the Sabbath it is already past the thirty-day limit and the news has become a *shmu'ah rechokah*.

Now, let us assume that the leader of the household had heard of the death on a Friday, which happened to be the twenty-ninth day from the burial, thereby obligating him to observe seven days of mourning. And let us assume further that another family member did not hear of the death until the Sabbath.

If we were to follow the rule that the other family members follow the count of the leader of the household, this would result in a stringency for the one who did not hear until the Sabbath: He would have to observe seven days, like the leader of the household. So in this case, the rule is not applied.[43] The leader of the household observes seven days, while the one who heard on the Sabbath observes only a small part of one day.

◄§ Bereaved Bridegroom Joining the Leader of the Household

19. If a member of a bridegroom's family dies during the days of the wedding
  feasts (*sheva brachos*), the bridegroom postpones observing *shivah* until after the period of the *sheva brachos* has passed. If he then goes to the house where the mourners are sitting *shivah*, some rule that he does not join the count of the leader of the household, and must begin his own count of seven days.[44] Others disagree.[45] They rule that he joins the count of the leader of the household.

Regarding a family member who follows the count of the leader of the household, the question whether he should put on *tefillin* on his first day of mourning is explained in chapter 13.

---

43. *Mishmeres Shalom* (loc. cit. §9), citing *Tal Chaim* (*Mo'ed Katan* 22b). The same ruling is given by *Kol Bo Al Aveilus* p. 329, citing *Pachad Yitzchak*.

44. *Sdei Chemed* (*Aveilus* §75), citing *Misgeres HaShulchan* (375:9), who in turn cites *Beis David* (§177). The same ruling is given by *Chaim BeYad* §500. Likewise, *Zachur LeAvraham* an *Rov Dagan* (p. 174) write that the bridegroom does not join the count of the leader of the household. The same ruling is given by *Chazon LaMo'ed* 12:12, in the name of responsa *Har Tzvi*, *Yoreh De'ah* §265; and by *Yad Shaul* and *Beis Shlomo* 2:221; and responsa *Tuv Ta'am Vada'as mahadura* 3:2:§238.

45. *Sdei Chemed* (loc. cit.) states: "Indeed, *Mishnas R' Eliezer* (2: §35) writes that the rabbis of his generation were lenient in practice, contrary to the ruling of *Beis David*. And see *Yismach Leiv* §15 [and] *Zochreinu LeChaim* I p. 18:4."

And in §216 he writes in the name of *Mishnas R' Eliezer* (loc. cit.) that he testified that the rabbis of his city, generation after generation, had ruled this way in practice, permitting the bridegroom to join the count of the leader of the household. He agrees with them and gives reasons for their ruling.

Sdei Chemed concludes there: "It would seem that since [the rule is that] we follow the lenient opinion in [disputed issues regarding] the *halachos* of mourning, we can rely, in this matter, on the opinion of the aforementioned holy rabbis — that [the bridegroom] should join the count of the leader of the household."

Yismach Leiv (loc. cit.) states that the custom in the city of Constantinople is that the bridegroom

◄§ Double Bereavement

20. If two family members die on the same day, the mourners observe only a single seven-day period of mourning for both.[46]

If a person is observing seven days of mourning for a member of his family, and a second member of the family dies, the mourner observes seven days of mourning for the second deceased, and this also fulfills the seven-day period for the first.[47]

For example, a person observed three days of mourning for a member of his family. Then a second member of the family died, and was buried on the third day of mourning for the first deceased. The mourner now observes seven more days of mourning, with the third day of the original mourning period counting as the first day of the new one. At the end of these last seven days, he need observe no further mourning. Altogether, he observed *shivah* for nine days.

---

joins the count of the leader of the household.

    See also *Kol Bo Al Aveilus* p. 68 and the note there. The same ruling is given by *Gesher HaChaim* 19:7:4; and by *Yikrei DeChayei* 5:6.

46. Responsa of *Rashba* §207, cited by *Beis Yosef*.

47. *Shulchan Aruch* 375:10.

CHAPTER THIRTEEN

The First Day of Mourning

1. We have learned in the previous chapter [paragraphs 5-6] that the mourning period begins when the burial has been completed, or when the mourner takes leave of a body being taken elsewhere for burial. This marks the formal end of the *aninus* period. The mourner now resumes the obligation to perform *mitzvos* .

The remainder of this day counts as the 'first day of mourning' (even though it is less than a full day).[1] The laws of this first day are, in most respects, the same as those that apply to the other seven days of mourning, with the exception of *tefillin* .

◆§ *Tefillin* on the "First Day"

2. The mourner is forbidden to don *tefillin* on the first day of mourning.[2] If he mistakenly put them on, he must remove them.[3]

On the second day, it is proper not to put them on until sunrise (*neitz hachamah*).[4]

---

1. If the first day of mourning coincides with the day of death and burial [for example, if death and burial both occurred on Wednesday during the daytime, so that the remainder of Wednesday is the first day], some rule that the obligations of mourning on this day have Scriptural (*deOraysa*) status [*Shulchan Aruch, Yoreh De'ah* §398:1; this is the opinion of the *Geonim*, also adopted by *Rif*, *Rambam*, *Ramban*, and *Rashba*]. Others hold that they have Rabbinic (*deRabbanan*) status [this is the opinion of *Tosafos* and *Rosh*; it is also the ruling of *Rama, Orach Chaim* 548:3; and R' Yosef Caro, *Yoreh De'ah* 329:13].

2. *Shulchan Aruch, Orach Chaim* 38:4 and *Yoreh De'ah* 388:1. In *Mo'ed Katan* 15a, the *halachah* is derived from the fact that when *forbidding* the Prophet Ezekiel to mourn, God told him (*Ezekiel* 24:17): '*Don* פְּאֵרְךָ, *your majesty* ,' which in the tradition of the Sages refers to *tefillin* . That Ezekiel was specifically commanded to don *tefillin* while being forbidden to mourn implies that in mourning one does not wear *tefillin* .

3. *Kaf HaChaim* 38:§§17, citing "the *Poskim* ."

4. *Shulchan Aruch Orach Chaim* (38:5) implies that it is permissible to don *tefillin* on the second day, even before sunrise [*neitz hachamah*] (*Mishnah Berurah* ad loc.). This is also the ruling of *Shach* in *Yoreh De'ah* 388:§§1, citing *Bach*. However, *Shulchan Aruch* in *Yoreh De'ah* (loc. cit.) writes that donning *tefillin* is permitted only after sunrise of the second day. *Mishnah Berurah* (loc. cit. §§19) writes: "Therefore it is proper to wait until after sunrise to don them."

Gesher HaChaim (18:4:9) writes: "If one finds it necessary to pray before *neitz*, or if waiting means that he will have to pray without a *minyan*, we are lenient, and permit him to don *tefillin* even before *neitz hachamah*, even on the day after the death, and all the more so on the day after the news reached him [if this was later than the day after the death]." The reason is that, according to many *Acharonim*, *Shulchan Aruch* was simply applying an extra stringency, *chumra be'alma* (in order to take into account the opinion of *Rosh*), when he wrote that one should wait until after *neitz hachamah*.

If, on the second day, someone who has not previously consoled him (*panim chadashos*) visits him, he should not put on *tefillin* until that person leaves. If he had already put on *tefillin* before that new comforter arrived, he does not have to take them off.[5]

However, some rule that if such a visitor arrives during the time for reciting the *Shema* and prayer, the mourner need not miss the *mitzvah* of putting on *tefillin* just for the sake of the new comforter.[5a]

3. If death occurred in the daytime and burial took place that night or the next day, the mourner may not put on *tefillin* during the day of the burial.[6] (For example, if death occurred on Tuesday during the day, and burial took place on Tuesday night, or Wednesday during the daytime, the mourner may not put on *tefillin* on Wednesday.) However, some rule to the contrary, that he *must* put on *tefillin* that day, after the burial.[7] And some do put on *tefillin*, but only in private and without reciting the blessing.[8]

4. If death and burial occurred on *Yom Tov*, or on the second day of *Yom Tov* of the Diaspora, or on *Chol HaMo'ed*, the mourner may put on *tefillin* on *Isru Chag*, the day after the last *Yom Tov* day of the festival.[9]

For those whose custom is to put on *tefillin* during *Chol HaMo'ed*, some rule that one must put them on, even on the day when death and burial took place. Others disagree.[9a]

---

5. *Mishnah Berurah* 38:§§20, citing *Magen Avraham* and *Pri Megadim*.

5a. *Kaf HaChaim* 38:§§22.

6. *Mishnah Berurah* 38:§§16. The same ruling is given by *Sha'arei Teshuvah* (ad loc. §§2). And *Kol Bo Al Aveilus* (p. 274) states that most of the great *Acharonim* agree with this, and it is the most widely adopted custom (*minhag ha'olam*). See also *Mishmeres Shalom os tes* §56.

7. *Ba'er Heitev* 38:§§4, citing the ruling of *Maharitatz*. And see *Minchas Elazar* (II:§4), who explains and justifies the ruling of *Maharitatz*. See also *Minhagei Eretz Yisrael* (*Hilchos Aveilus* §23).

8. *Chayei Adam* (14:19) writes: "It seems to me that if it is not the day of the death, he should put on *tefillin* without reciting the blessing."

In the opinion of R' Shlomo Zalman Auerbach, *shlita*: "It is proper to mention what many books (including *Orchos Chaim HeChadash* §38, citing "*Rabbanei HaSefaradim*") state: that the custom of Jerusalem is to take into account the opinion of *Maharitatz*: namely, if the burial was not on the same day as the death, one must put on *tefillin* after the burial. Even though we do not follow this opinion, many God-fearing people nevertheless are careful to put on *tefillin* in private, on condition, without saying the blessing, because of the doubt as to whether one is obligated to do so. ["On condition" means that before putting them on, one states: "If I am obligated to put on *tefillin*, may this be the *mitzvah*; if I am not obligated, may this not be for the sake of a *mitzvah*."] However, if the death occurred on the Sabbath, *Maharsham* writes in *Da'as Torah* that according to all opinions one should not put on *tefillin* on the day of the burial." (According to R' Auerbach's reasoning, in this case too one should put on *tefillin* in private, as mentioned above.)

9. *Mishnah Berurah* 38:§§16. This applies even though *Isru Chag* in this case is the first day of mourning [when one usually does not put on *tefillin*]. See also *Mishmeres Shalom os tav* §47.

9a. *Magen Avraham* (548:§§4) writes that one must wear them. However, *Sha'arei Teshuvah* (ad loc. §§4) cites responsa *Shevus Yaakov* (part 2 §25) as forbidding one to wear them. Likewise, *Pri Megaddim* (cited by *Mishnah Berurah* 38:§§16) raises objections to the ruling of *Magen Avraham* and writes that if one does don them, one should be careful not to recite the blessing for doing so.

5. If news of the death arrives within thirty days of the death (*shmu'ah krovah*), the *halachah* treats the day of hearing the news as if it were the day of burial.[9b] Therefore, even if the news arrives at night, the mourner may not put on *tefillin* during the day. (For example, if the news arrives on Wednesday during the day, or even on Tuesday night, he may not put on *tefillin* on Wednesday.) Even if the news arrives after he has already put on *tefillin* and begun to pray, he must remove them.[10] However, if news of the death arrives after thirty days (*shmu'ah rechokah*), the laws of mourning apply for only one hour. Therefore the mourner may put on *tefillin*. And of course, if he had already put them on before the news arrived, he need not take them off.[11]

6. The twilight period between sundown (*sh'ki'ah*) and nightfall (*tzeis hakochavim*) is called *bein hashmashos*. If burial occurs during this period, the mourner may put on *tefillin* the next day, but without reciting the *brachah*.[12]

Some people recite *Maariv* before sundown. If burial occurs during the daytime, but after the mourner has recited *Maariv*, he may put on *tefillin* the next day, but without reciting the accompanying blessing.[13]

In either of the two cases mentioned in this section, when putting on *tefillin* one should make the following condition: If I am allowed to perform the *mitzvah* of *tefillin* today, I intend this act of putting them on for the sake of the *mitzvah*. If I am forbidden to perform the *mitzvah* of *tefillin* today, I intend that this act of putting them on is not for the sake of the *mitzvah*.

◆§ A Bereaved Bridegroom

7. During the first seven days after his wedding (the days of the *sheva brachos* feasts), a bridegroom is exempt from the laws of mourning. If a family member dies during these seven days, some rule that the bridegroom must put on *tefillin*.[14]

If the death occurred on the seventh day of the *sheva brachos*, the bridegroom should put on *tefillin* without reciting the accompanying blessing.[14a]

◆§ A New Arrival

8. In 12:16, we discussed the case of one who arrived from a nearby town and found the other mourners (including the *gedol habayis*, the leader of the

---

9b. In this case, the *halachah* depends on the disagreement mentioned above, par. 3.

10. *Mishnah Berurah* 38:§§16. See also *Kol Bo Al Aveilus* (p. 275), who states in the name of *She'eris Yaakov* that if a person hears a *shmu'ah krovah* on the Sabbath, on Sunday he should don *tefillin* (and recite the accompanying blessing) since the bitterness already passed on the Sabbath.

11. *Mishnah Berurah* loc. cit. And see below chapt. 31 par. 21.

12. See *Mishmeres Shalom* (os tav §50), who expresses doubt about this case, and concludes that one should put on *tefillin* without reciting the blessing.

13. *Pischei Teshuvah* 388:§§2.

14. *Gesher HaChaim* 18:4:12.

14a. *Da'as Kedoshim* (342:§§4) writes that if the death occurred on the seventh day of the *sheva brachos*, the bridegroom should not recite the blessing when putting on *tefillin*, since it may be that the days of rejoicing after the wedding need not be seven whole days — that is, it may be enough to rejoice for only part of the seventh day.

mourning household) already having begun *shivah*. In that case, the new arrival counts his seven days from when the others began theirs. However, on the day of his arrival he may not put on *tefillin*.[15] (This is in accord with the opinion mentioned above, par. 3, that one does not put on *tefillin* on the day of burial.) If he arrived on the seventh day (in which case he observes mourning for only a short time that same day), he should put on *tefillin* after he concludes this mourning observance (i.e., gets up from sitting *shivah*).[16]

◆§ One Who Did Not Observe *Shivah*

9. If one either intentionally or unintentionally failed to observe mourning, he must make up the seven days of *shivah* observance during the first thirty days [from the death of the deceased]. In that case, he must put on *tefillin* even on the day when he begins the seven days.[17]

◆§ *Tefillin* During the Remaining Days of *Shivah*

10. During the remaining days of mourning (excluding the first day), the mourner puts on *tefillin*. When doing so, he should settle his mind in order to concentrate properly on the *tefillin*. He should constantly keep in mind that he is wearing them. During times of eulogy and weeping, he should not wear them.[18]

◆§ Rabbeinu Tam *Tefillin*

11. Some rule that one should not put on Rabbeinu Tam *tefillin* throughout the seven days of mourning.[19] Others permit putting them on.[20]

◆§ Making up for Missed Blessings and Prayers

11a. Prior to the interment (or taking leave of the body), the mourner was classified an *onen*, and was exempt from *mitzvos*. Consequently, he did not recite blessings or prayers, as explained above [chapt. 5].

After the burial (or leave-taking), he is no longer an *onen*, and is thus again

---

15. *Da'as Torah* 378:8.

16. Ibid.

17. *Kol Bo Al Aveilus* p. 275, citing *Kuntras Evel Yachid* (by *Maharash Kluger*). The same ruling is given by *Mishmeres Shalom os tav* §48.

18. *Shulchan Aruch* 388:2.

19. *Chiddushei HaGraz Margolios* (*Aveilus* §3, and notes there). The same is written in the name of the *Ari, zal*. But *Birkei Yosef* (§38) writes that since the matter is disputed, it is better not to do it (*shev ve'al taaseh adif*). See also *Shalmei Tzibbur*, who seems to have the same view. And see *Mishmeres Shalom os tav* §45.

20. See *Chiddushei HaGraz Margolios* (loc. cit.), who states: "*Birkei Yosef* writes that the kabbalist *Maharash* donned *tefillin* of Rabbeinu Tam throughout the seven days of mourning. And he said that this was the correct practice according to *Kabbalah* as well." The same is written in *Sha'arei Teshuvah* 555:§§1. And see *Vayitzbor Yosef* (§2), who discusses the issue at length, citing great authorities who wrote that one should don them. Nevertheless, he was "afraid to render a decision against the great Torah authorities who ruled that one should don them." *Os Chaim VeShalom* (§38) writes that he saw his holy forefathers, of blessed memory, don *tefillin* of Rabbeinu Tam during their days of mourning, but only in private.

obligated to perform *mitzvos* (with the exception of *tefillin* on the first day; see above, par. 2).

12. If a person was an *onen* in the morning until the end of the "fourth hour" of the day, and hence did not recite the Morning Blessings (*Birchos HaShachar*), he should not recite them afterwards. The reason is that during the essential time for these blessings, he was exempt.[21]

However, this does not apply to the blessings for Torah-study (*Birchos HaTorah*),[21a] and the blessings, שֶׁלֹּא עָשַׂנִי גּוֹי, ". . .Who did not make me a non-Jew," שֶׁלֹּא עָשַׂנִי עָבֶד, ". . .Who did not make me a slave," and שֶׁלֹּא עָשַׂנִי אִשָּׁה, ". . .Who did not make me a woman." These should be recited as long as it is still day.[22]

> Note: For many halachic purposes, the daytime is divided into twelve equal parts, called "variable hours" (*sha'os zemanios*). The length of each such "hour" varies from day to day and from place to place. In summer, each "hour" is longer than sixty minutes, and in winter, shorter than sixty minutes. Ordinarily, recitation of the *Shema* should be completed before the end of the "third hour," ($1/4$ of the daylight period) and the *Shemoneh Esrei* prayer, before the end of the "fourth hour" ($1/3$ the daylight period). For the exact times on any given day, a calendar should be consulted.

13. If a person was an *onen* in the morning until the end of the "third hour," and hence did not recite the *Shema*, he should recite it, with its blessings, after the burial. He may do so until the end of the "fourth hour."[23] If he did not recite it until after the end of the "fourth hour," he should still recite it — but without its blessings — as long as it is still day.

Some rule that he may recite the *Shema* with its blessings until *chatzos hayom*[24] (the end of the "sixth hour," which is usually within half an hour before or after noon).

Until the end of the day, one is obligated to commemorate the Exodus by reciting *Parashas Tzitzis* (the third paragraph of the *Shema*), or other verses which mention the Exodus.[24a]

---

21. *Mishnah Berurah* 71:§§4.
21a. ArtScroll Ashkenaz *Siddur* p. 16.
21b. Ibid. p. 18.
22. *Mishnah Berurah* 71:§§4.
23. *Shulchan Aruch Orach Chaim* 58:6.
24. Ibid. See also *Mishnah Berurah* (ad loc. 58:§§27). He interprets *Shulchan Aruch* as meaning that it is proper to recite the *Shema* even after the end of the fourth hour, in order to accept upon oneself the yoke of the Kingdom of Heaven; but one is not *obligated* to recite it, since one is not thereby fulfilling the positive commandment of reciting the *Shema*. See also *Be'ur Halachah* (ad loc.), which cites *Mishkenos Yaakov* (§77). He rules that after the fact (*bediavad*), one may still recite the blessings of the *Shema* until *chatzos hayom*, just as with the *Shemoneh Esrei* prayer. *Be'ur Halachah* writes: "Conceivably, one may rely on this ruling in a case where it was impossible for him to recite the blessings of the *Shema* before the end of the fourth hour; for I have found that *Maharil* (*Hilchos Tefillah*) writes, in the name of *Maharash*, that in a case where the delay was unavoidable, the custom is to be lenient, so that the person should not lose the *mitzvah* of reciting the blessings."
24a. *Mishnah Berurah* loc. cit.

Similarly, if he missed reciting the *Shemoneh Esrei* prayer during the designated time, he may recite it until *chatzos hayom*. After that, he may not recite the *Shemoneh Esrei* prayer of the morning.[25]

Regarding the question of making up for a missed prayer by reciting the next prayer twice, see below, par. 16.

14. If a person was an *onen* in the morning until almost the end of the "third hour," if he was to recite the prayer-service in the usual order he would possibly miss the time for the *Shema*. In that case, he should first recite the *Shema* without its blessings. Then he should recite the prayer-service in the usual order, including the *Shema* with its blessings.[26]

15. If a person was an *onen* in the morning until almost the end of the "fourth hour," it could be that by reciting the prayer-service in the usual order he would miss the time for the *Shemoneh Esrei* prayer. In that case, he should skip the introductory psalms (*Pesukei DeZimrah*), in the manner explained in *Shulchan Aruch Orach Chaim* §52,[26a] in connection with one who arrives late to the synagogue. However, he should not skip any of the *Shema* and its blessings, even if this means that he will have to pray *Shemoneh Esrei* after the end of the "fourth hour."[27]

16. Ordinarily, a person is required to recite the *Shemoneh Esrei* prayer three times a day — evening (*Maariv*), morning (*Shacharis*), and afternoon (*Minchah*). If he missed one of these times, he can make it up by reciting it the next time. For example, if he missed the *Shemoneh Esrei* of the morning, he recites the *Shemoneh Esrei* of the afternoon twice, first for the afternoon, and then again to make up for the morning.

At the beginning of each part of the day, a person becomes obligated to recite the *Shemoneh Esrei* of that part. With the light of daybreak (*he'ir kol pnei hamizrach*)

---

25. *Shulchan Aruch Orach Chaim* 89:1, and *Rama* there. *Mishnah Berurah* (89:§§7) writes: "The words of [*Rama*] imply that even immediately after *chatzos* one is forbidden to recite the Morning Prayer (*Shacharis*)...but some are lenient [allowing one to recite *Shacharis*] during the half-hour after *chatzos*. In practice, one may infer from *Pri Megaddim* and *Derech HaChaim* that one should not budge from the ruling of [*Rama*]. This is also implied by *Be'ur HaGra*. He states that in fact the time for the Afternoon Prayer (*Minchah*) has already arrived at the beginning of the seventh hour [i.e., exactly *chatzos hayom*]. But in order to prevent error, the Sages forbade one to recite *Minchah* until a half-hour after *chatzos*. Therefore, if by mistake or through unavoidable circumstances one did not recite *Shacharis* before *chatzos*, one should wait until a half-hour after *chatzos* (i.e., until the time for *Minchah* arrives); then he should recite *Minchah*, and afterwards recite [the *Shemoneh Esrei* prayer] a second time in order to make up for the missed *Shacharis*. One should not do the reverse [i.e., first make up for the *Shacharis*, and then recite *Minchah*]...However, after the fact (*bediavad*), if one recited *Shacharis* during the half-hour after *chatzos*, one fulfilled the obligation, and need not recite it a second time (*Derech HaChaim*; and see there for further details).

26. *Mishnah Berurah* 71:§§90.

26a. See ArtScroll *Siddur; Laws* §30: "Instructions for Latecomers."

27. *Mishnah Berurah* loc. cit. in the name of *Derech HaChaim*.

he becomes obligated to recite the *Shemoneh Esrei* of the morning; after midday (*chatzos hayom*), he becomes obligated to pray the *Shemoneh Esrei* of the afternoon; and similarly for the Evening Prayer.

An *onen* is exempt from prayer. Hence, if a person was already an *onen* at the beginning of one of the three parts of the day, and remained an *onen* throughout that part, he is exempt from reciting the *Shemoneh Esrei* of that part.

However, if the person was not an *onen* when one of the parts began, he becomes obligated to pray the *Shemoneh Esrei* of that part, and he remains obligated, even if he afterwards becomes an *onen*.

These principles are exemplified in the following *halachos*:

(a) A person became an *onen* before it was permissible to recite the Evening Prayer. If the burial took place in the morning and was completed before the end of the time for *Shacharis*, the person should recite *Shacharis* after the burial. However, he should not recite a second *Shemoneh Esrei* to make up for the missed *Maariv*.[28]

(b) If, in the above case, burial was not completed until after midday, the person should recite only *Minchah*, and does not have to recite a second *Shemoneh Esrei* to make up for the missed *Shacharis*.[29]

(c) A person became an *onen* after the beginning of the time for *Maariv*. Burial took place in the morning. After the burial, the person must recite *Shemoneh Esrei* twice: first for *Shacharis*, and then a second time, to make up for the missed *Maariv*.

(d) A person became an *onen* in the morning, after daybreak [when it was permissible to recite *Shacharis*]. Burial took place after midday. He must recite *Shemoneh Esrei* twice: first for *Minchah*, and then a second time, to make up for the missed *Shacharis*.[30]

◆§ *Mussaf* on *Rosh Chodesh*

17. If death occurred on *Rosh Chodesh*, and burial was completed after the "seventh hour" (see above, note to par. 12), the mourner should recite the

---

28. *Shulchan Aruch Yoreh De'ah* 341:2. The reason is that at night he was exempt from praying.

29. The reason is that during the time for *Shacharis*, he was exempt from praying.

30. *Dagul Meirevavah*, ad loc. The same ruling is given by *Mishnah Berurah* 71:§§4. *Mishnah Berurah* also writes there: "It may be that in this case one is also obligated to recite the Morning Blessings (*Birchos HaShachar*), if he did not recite them upon rising in the morning. The reason is that during the time for reciting them, he was obligated to do so [i.e., he was not yet an *onen*]." And see *Be'ur Halachah* §52.

But see *Graz Margolios* (*Aninus* §29), who writes that the mourner is not required to make up for the missed prayer even if the death occurred after he had already become obligated to pray. In his *Bi'urim* there he writes: "See *Birkei Yosef* and *Shalmei Tzibbur*, who cite *Beis David* as ruling that even in this case it is not considered that he had already become obligated to pray, since [before the death] there was still time for him to recite the prayer in question. The essential moment of obligation is at the end of the time; and by then, he was exempt because he was an *onen*. Therefore he does not have to make up for the missed prayer." He writes that this is the ruling adopted in practice by the authors of *Pri Chadash* and *Magen Avraham*.

Additional (*Mussaf*) Prayer. The reason is that this prayer, if not recited at its proper time, may be recited at any time of day.[31]

⊷ Grace After Meals

18. The obligation to recite Grace after Meals (*Bircas HaMazon*) lasts until the meal is digested (see *Shulchan Aruch Orach Chaim* 184:5). If a person ate a meal while he was an *onen*, and burial was completed before enough time passed for the meal to be digested, some rule that he must recite *Bircas HaMazon*.

⊷ Asher Yatzar

There is no time limit for the blessing אֲשֶׁר יָצַר, ". . .Who made man wisely,"[31a] which is recited after relieving oneself. If a person relieved himself while he was an *onen*, some rule that he must recite *Asher Yatzar* after burial is completed, even if he relieved himself early in the day and the burial was late in the day. However, if he needs to use the bathroom again after the burial, he need recite *Asher Yatzar* only once, and it applies to both times.[32]

⊷ Other *Mitzvos*

19. Once burial is completed, the mourner is obligated to put on the prayer shawl (*tallis gadol*), even on the first day of mourning.[33] Likewise, he is obligated by all other *mitzvos* — except for *tefillin* on the first day of mourning— as explained at the beginning of this chapter.

---

31. *Graz Margolios* (*Aninus* §30). He states there that according to responsa *Birkas Yaakov* (part 2 §188), he should not recite *Mussaf*, since the essential time for this prayer is only until the seventh hour; one is forbidden to recite *Mussaf* later than this, and one who does so is termed "negligent" (*poshe'a*). But *Birkei Yosef* rules to the contrary [i.e., that after the fact (*bediavad*), one should pray *Mussaf* even after the seventh hour].

31a. ArtScroll Ashkenaz *Siddur* p. 14.

32. *Be'ur Halachah* §71, in the name of *Derech HaChaim*. The same ruling is given by *Chochmas Adam* §153; and by *Kisvei HaRav HaGadol Maharar Daniel, zatzal*; but he writes that it is best to eat a small additional amount before reciting *Bircas HaMazon*.

However, *Aruch HaShulchan* (341:17) writes: "Certain great authorities have written that the *onen*, after the burial, is required to recite *Bircas HaMazon*, as long as his meal is not yet digested; and that the same applies to the blessing *Asher Yatzar*. But in my humble opinion, this does not seem correct. Since at the time when he was eating or relieving himself he was exempt from reciting blessings, he does not become obligated afterwards. And this seems to me the *halachah* which should be followed in practice."

33. *Darkei Moshe* 388:§§1, in the name of *Mordechai*.

CHAPTER FOURTEEN

Se'udas Havra'ah
The Mourner's Meal of Condolence

✑ The *Mitzvah*

1. The first meal eaten by the mourner after the burial [or after receiving news of a "recent death" (*sh'muah k'rovah*)] is called the *se'udas havra'ah* (meal of condolence, lit. "meal of recovery"). At this meal, he is forbidden to eat his own food.[1] For his second meal, however, he is permitted to eat his own food, even if it is still the first day of mourning.[2]

It is a *mitzvah* for the neighbors to feed him their food, so that he need not eat of his own.[3] But if they do not send him the meal of condolence, or if he lives in a place where there are no other Jews, he need not afflict himself for this *mitzvah*, and may eat his own food.[4]

---

1. *Mo'ed Katan* 27b. *Ateres Zekeinim* (§378) cites *Rabbeinu Yerucham's* reason for this law: In his grief over the passing of his dear one, the mourner does not want to eat, for he wishes that he, too, were dead. Therefore, Hashem commands others to bring him their food and see to it that he eats. Since such bitter feelings are most pronounced at the time of the first meal after the funeral, friends and neighbors should provide at least that meal; afterwards — even on the first day — the mourners may eat their own food.

As his own explanation, *Ateres Zekeinim* suggests that the *mitzvah* of providing the first meal is part of the general process of consolation, for it shows the mourner that we are concerned for his welfare and do not reject him to fend for himself.

Sheivet Yehudah (§378) takes a different tack in explaining the meal. If the mourner were left to himself, he might seek to drown his grief in food and drink on this bitter day, and might even become intoxicated, all of which would dishonor the deceased. If others feed him, however, self-respect would force him to eat and drink moderately. *Sheivet Yehudah* suggests that if the mourner wishes to fast, therefore, on that day, he is permitted to do so.

2. *Shulchan Aruch* 378:1. However, *Chiddushei R' Akiva Eiger* (loc. cit.) cites *Roke'ach* as following the ruling of *Tosafos* (*Mo'ed Katan* 27b) that the mourner is forbidden to eat his own food the entire first day of mourning. *Bi'ur HaGra* also cites the ruling of *Tosafos*. The same ruling is given by *Tanya Rabbasi* (§68), citing the *chaver*, R' Tzidkiah ben R' Avraham HaRofeh, *zal*. This is found in his work, *Shibolei HaLeket, Hilchos Semachos*, at the beginning of §23. And the same ruling is given by *Ravan* at the end of *Mo'ed Katan*.

3. *Rosh* cites the Jerusalem Talmud [*Mo'ed Katan* 3:5]: 'A curse will come upon the neighbors [of a mourner] if they put him in the situation of having to eat his own food' (*Beis Yosef*).

4. *Taz* 378:§§1. He writes that this is why *Tur* and *Shulchan Aruch* wrote: "It is a *mitzvah* for the

✎§ The Meal

2. The custom is to include (round) cakes and boiled eggs in the meal of condolence. The mourner should not peel the eggs himself, so as not to appear ravenous.[5]

3. Some rule that the prohibition against eating his own food applies only to bread, but not to eating pastries or fruit, and not to drinking.[6] Others forbid even drinking.[7] Still others permit drinking, but forbid eating fruit or cooked dishes.[8]

✎§ *Havdalah*

3a. At the conclusion of the Sabbath, the mourner is permitted to make *Havdalah* (the ceremony for the conclusion of the Sabbath) over a cup of his own wine, even before the meal of condolence.[9]

✎§ Women Mourners

4. A man is not permitted to bring the meal of condolence to a woman mourner. Instead, a woman should do so.[10] Some write that if the mourning woman's husband, brothers, or grown sons are also mourners, men can bring them the meal of condolence even though it is also for her.[11] Some rule that women are not permitted to bring the meal of condolence to men, but others permit this.[12]

4a. A married woman is not permitted to eat her husband's food for the meal of condolence.[13]

✎§ Employees / Poor Persons

5. If someone employs a scribe or other employee, providing his meals as part of his salary, and the employee becomes a mourner, he cannot eat his employer's

---

seems to be superfluous. But the intent is that the main *mitzvah* is upon the neighbors, who should not cause the mourner to have to eat his own food; for if they do not send him the meal, he will be permitted to eat his own food, since he is forced to do so.

5. *Shulchan Aruch* 378:9, and *Chiddushei R' Akiva Eiger* loc. cit.

6. *Chochmas Shlomo* loc. cit. And *Aruch HaShulchan* (378:2) writes: "However, he may eat a cooked dish of his own food."

7. *Kitzur Shulchan Aruch* (196:10 *hagah*) writes: "However, I saw in *Leshon Chachamim*, citing *Yoseif Ometz* and *Binyan Yehoshua*, that the mourner is forbidden even to drink his own coffee or tea. And this seems reasonable, since [whenever] eating [is forbidden, it] always includes drinking."

8. Responsa *Divrei Malkiel* part II:§97. The same ruling is given by *Gesher HaChaim* 20:2. This is also the conclusion reached by responsa *Yabia Omer* part II, *Yoreh De'ah* §25. And see *Even Yaakov* §51.

9. This applies even according to those who hold the strict opinion, that ordinarily even drinking his own drinks is forbidden. They make an exception for the wine of *Havdalah*, since it is a *mitzvah* obligation (*Kitzur Shulchan Aruch* loc. cit. The same ruling is given by *Gesher HaChaim* loc. cit).

10. *Shulchan Aruch* 378:2. The reason is to prevent causing improper acts.

11. *Aruch HaShulchan* 378:2.

12. *Gesher HaChaim* loc. cit.

13. *Shulchan Aruch* loc. cit. Since the husband is obligated to provide his wife with food, when she eats his food it is as if she is eating her own.

food for the meal of condolence. However, if someone is supporting a poor person or orphan, or is giving unconditional support to his own son or daughter, and the person supported becomes a mourner, he can eat the food of the one supporting him for the meal of condolence.[14]

⋖§ Exchanging Meals

5a. One mourner can give the meal of condolence to another mourner, even if they are mourning for the same deceased, and the second can then give the meal of condolence to the first, as long as neither one stipulated that he was giving the meal in order to receive one in return.[15]

⋖§ Miscellaneous Laws

5b. Some rule that a son supported by his father can give the meal of condolence to his father.[16]

6. If the mourner does not wish to eat on the first day of mourning, he is not required to.[17] In that case, he may eat his own food on the second day, even if it is his first meal since he became a mourner.

Likewise, if he was not given the meal of condolence because the funeral did not end until late afternoon, he is permitted to eat his own food that night, and need not be given a meal of condolence.[18] However, if the burial took place at night, the mourner must be given the meal of condolence that night or the next day.[19]

If the mourner has already eaten his own food for the first meal after the burial, there is no longer any obligation to feed him a meal of condolence.[19a]

7. On Friday or the day before *Yom Tov*, a mourner should not be given the meal of condolence after the "ninth [variable] hour" of the day, so that he will have appetite for the Sabbath or *Yom Tov* meal.[20] Thus, if he did not eat before that time, he is forbidden to eat until nighttime.[21]

---

14. *Shulchan Aruch* loc. cit.

15. *Shulchan Aruch* 378:1. And *Shach* (§§2) writes: "This means [that they can give each other the *se'udas havra'ah*] even though both of them are mourners." See also *Prishah* loc. cit. §3.

16. *Menachem Aveilim os* 5, citing *Mishnas R' Eliezer*. As support, he points to the passage which describes Jacob as preparing the *se'udas havra'ah* for his father, Isaac, upon the death of Abraham (see *Genesis* 25:29, and *Rashi* there v. 30). However, he cites *Ruach Chaim* as expressing doubt about this *halachah*.

17. *Tur*, citing *Ramban*. And the same is implied by *Shulchan Aruch* 378:3. The same ruling is given by *Shach* loc. cit. §§4.

18. *Shulchan Aruch* and *Rama* 378:3.

19. *Pischei Teshuvah* §§2.

19a. Responsa *Noda BiYehudah*, *Yoreh De'ah* §98.

20. *Gesher HaChaim* loc. cit. See there for further details.

21. *Shulchan Aruch* 378:5. And see *Gesher HaChaim* (20:2:11), who explains that the latest time is the "ninth hour" of the day. The same ruling is given by *Sdei Chemed*, *Aveilus* §100.

Note: (To calculate the ninth ["variable"] hour, one divides the time between sunrise — *neitz* — and sunset — *sh'k'iah* — by twelve. This gives the length of one "hour." One then calculates the end of nine such hours. For example, if sunrise is at 5:00 a.m. and sunset at 7:00 p.m., each "variable hour" consists of 70 minutes. Nine such hours equals 630 minutes, or ten and one-half regular — 60-minute — hours. Adding ten and one-half hours to 5:00 a.m. yields 3:30 p.m. After this hour, the meal of condolence could not be eaten. According to some *Poskim*, instead of calculating from *neitz* until *sh'ki'ah*, one calculates from dawn — *alos hashachar* — until nightfall — *tzeis hakochavim*.)

8. If news of the death of a family member is heard on the Sabbath, and the burial had taken place no more than thirty days previously [*shmu'ah krovah*—briefly delayed news], some rule that the mourner must be given a meal of condolence on the Sabbath;[22] but other authorities disagree.[23]

If the burial had taken place more than thirty days before the news was heard [*shmu'ah rechokah*—extensively delayed news), no meal of condolence is required, even on a weekday.[24]

9. For the death of an infant, a meal of condolence is given only if the infant was at least thirty days old, or if there is absolute evidence that the pregnancy was nine months or more.[25]

10. If the deceased committed suicide, the mourners are not given a meal of condolence. However, some authorities disagree with this ruling.[26]

◆§ Grace After Meals

11. Whenever three or more men have a meal together, in which they ate bread, the Grace After Meals (*Bircas HaMazon*) is preceded by the recitation of a formal "invitation" called *zimun*. *Zimun* has a special form if the number of men eating together was ten or more. At a meal of condolence, the mourner cannot be included in a *zimun* of ten. However, he is included in a *zimun* of three.[27] See 16:13.

---

22. *Beis Yosef* §393; also cited by *Darkei Moshe* 378:§§3. The same ruling is given by *Chochmas Adam* 163:15.

23. This is implied by *Shulchan Aruch* 393:11. And see *Shach* loc. cit. §§11, and *Ba'er Heitev* §§6. The same ruling is given by *Gesher HaChaim* loc. cit.

24. *Shulchan Aruch* 393:12. See above, 3:26 as to what is considered thirty days.

25. *Shulchan Aruch* 393:6.

26. However, *Sdei Chemed* (*Aveilus* §103) writes: "It is stated in the name of Rabbeinu Yonah that if the deceased committed suicide, the mourners are not given a meal of condolence, and the same ruling is given by *Moharim* and *Moharin*. And this is the opinion which should be followed (*Tzapichis BiDevash* §69)." And see *Chaim BeYad* §140.

27. *Shulchan Aruch* 379:5, and *Dagul Meirevavah* loc. cit.

✺ Consecutive Mourning Periods

12. If a second family member dies while the mourner is still sitting *shivah* for the first, the neighbors must give him a meal of condolence for the second deceased, even though he has already eaten a meal of condolence for the first one.[28]

> The *halachos* of the meal of condolence during *Chol HaMo'ed*, on the day before Pesach, and on Chanukah and Purim are explained below, chapters 30 and 31.

---

28. *Aruch HaShulchan* loc. cit. §§6.

CHAPTER FIFTEEN

For Whom Does One Mourn?

1. A person is obligated to mourn for any of the family members mentioned in
Parashas Emor (Leviticus 21:1-3) for whom a *Kohen* is obligated to become
ritually contaminated (*tamei*). These are:

> father
> mother
> son
> daughter
> brother or half-brother (paternal)
> unmarried sister or half-sister (paternal)
> wife
> husband

To these were added:

> half-brother (maternal)
> married sister or half-sister (maternal or paternal)
> unmarried half-sister (maternal).[1]

Thus, in effect, one mourns for any brother or sister, whether full or half-sibling,
married or unmarried.

2. One mourns for a wife only if she was married to him by Torah law, and only if
the marriage did not constitute a violation of Torah law. One does not mourn for
an *arusah* (a marital status common in Talmudic times), nor for a wife whom the
Torah forbade one to marry (*pesulah*; for example, if a *Kohen* married a divorcee).
However, one does mourn for a son, daughter, brother or sister born from marriage
with a *pesulah*. (Thus, if a *Kohen* married a divorcee and they had a son, the
Kohen could mourn for his son but not for his wife.) If someone married a non-Jew
(*kusis*) or a non-Jewish slavewoman owned by a Jew (*shifchah*), he would not
mourn for this wife; nor for a son, daughter, sister or brother resulting from such a
marriage.[2]

3. If a man's married brother dies childless, the Torah commands the surviving
brother (*yavam*) to marry the widow. This type of marriage is called *yibum*

---

1. *Shulchan Aruch* §374:4.
2. Ibid.

(levirate marriage). If the brother does not want to marry the widow, she cannot marry anyone else until he releases her through the ceremony of *chalitzah*. (In our time, *chalitzah*, rather than *yibum*, is performed.) From the time of her husband's death until *yibum* or *chalitzah* is performed, the widow's legal bond to the surviving brother gives her the status of *shomeres yibum*, which means "waiting for *yibum*."

Some rule that one mourns for one's *shomeres yibum*, and she mourns for her *yavam*. But others disagree.[3]

4. If one was in disharmony with his wife and intended to divorce her, but before he did so she died, some rule that he is not obligated to mourn for her. But others disagree.[4]

If a man gave his wife a conditional divorce which would take effect (retroactively) only if he were to die, and then he died, she does not mourn for him. If she wishes to be stringent with herself by crying for him and accompanying his body at the funeral, she is not prohibited from doing so.[5] But she is not allowed to wear black for him. All the more so, she is not allowed to observe the seven- and the thirty-day mourning periods, to perform *kri'ah* (tearing the garment), and the like.[6]

↜ Persons for Whom One Does Not Mourn

5. If a non-Jew and his sons, or a non-Jew and his mother convert, they do not mourn for each other.[7]

6. One does not mourn for a person who "departed from the ways of the community" (*porshim mi'darkei tzibbur*). This refers to one who rejected the yoke of the *mitzvos* and hence is not considered part of *Klal Yisrael*, the Jewish People.

One also does not mourn for a *mumar*, one who "converted" to another religion, nor for a *moser*, one who informed on his fellow-Jews to hostile authorities.[8]

If a person regularly transgressed the Torah, even if this was due to urges that overcame him (*le'tei'avon*), one does not mourn for him, unless he confessed

---

3. *Chiddushei R' Akiva Eiger* (loc. cit.) writes: "The obvious conclusion is that [the *yavam*] mourns for his *shomeres yibum*, since[, if he is a *kohen*,] he is required to become *tamei* for her, as is mentioned above [§373:4]." The same ruling is given by responsa *Masas Moshe* §27. However, see *Shiurei Knesses HaGedolah* 374:§§1.

   Pischei Teshuvah loc. cit. §§2 cites responsa *Parach Mateh Aharon* (part II:§100) as ruling that if one's *shomeres yibum* dies, he is not required to mourn for her. The same ruling is given by responsa *Nechpah BeChesef* (*Yoreh De'ah* §1).

   And see *Kol Bo Al Aveilus* (p. 301), who writes: "The majority of the *Poskim* have decided that [the *yavam*] is not required to mourn [for his *shomeres yibum*]."

4. *Chiddushei R' Akiva Eiger* (loc. cit.); *Yeshuos Yaakov*, *Even HaEzer* 4:§§8.

5. *Rama*, *Even HaEzer* §145:9.

6. *Pischei Teshuvah* loc. cit. §§7, citing responsa *Teshuvah MeAhavah* part III, end of §412.

7. *Shulchan Aruch* and *Rama*, *Yoreh De'ah* 374:5.

8. *Shulchan Aruch Yoreh De'ah* 345:5.

before he died.[9] [See 6:2 above.]

For a *mumar* who was killed by non-Jews, some rule that one mourns; but others disagree.[10]

7. For an infant which died within thirty calendar days of birth (including the thirtieth day), one does not mourn,[11] even if its hair and fingernails were fully formed. This applies when there is no absolute proof that the pregnancy was a full nine months. If there is such proof — for example, if the parents had relations nine months prior to the birth and then abstained for at least three months — one does mourn. For such an infant, born alive after a full nine-month pregnancy,[12] one mourns even if it died on the day of birth.[13]

For an infant which died on the thirty-first day of life or thereafter, one mourns,[14] unless it is known that the pregnancy was eight months[15] (not seven or nine).

If an infant living in an incubator dies at the age of more than thirty days, the family members are required to mourn.[16] However, if he was born ill, a halachic authority must be consulted about whether to mourn.

If an infant died on its thirty-first calendar day of life, and yet did not live a full thirty days (for example, if it was born in the last hour of 1 Nissan and died in the first hour of 1 Iyar), some rule that one mourns.[17] Others rule that one does not mourn unless the infant lived thirty full twenty-four-hour days.[18]

---

9. *Rama*, *Yoreh De'ah* 340:5, and *Shach* loc. cit. §§8. The same ruling is given by *Chochmas Adam* 156:3. And see responsa *Sheivet HaLevi* (§213), who writes that if the deceased was married to a non-Jew, one does not mourn for him unless it is clearly known that he repented.

10. *Rama* loc. cit. He writes there that the correct ruling is that one does not mourn for him. The same ruling is given by *Ateres Zekeinim*.

11. *Shulchan Aruch* §374:8.

12. See *Pischei Teshuvah* loc. cit. §§9, citing *Me'il Tzedakah* §5. See also *Da'as Torah* loc. cit.

13. *Shulchan Aruch* loc. cit.

14. See *Tiferes LeMoshe*, who rules that this applies only if its hair and fingernails were fully formed. And see *Da'as Torah* (loc. cit.), who cites evidence that according to *Or Zarua* it applies even if the hair and fingernails were not fully formed.

15. *Shulchan Aruch* loc. cit. This applies even if its hair and fingernails were fully formed (*Levushei Mordechai tlisai*; *Orach Chaim* §14). However, *Be'er Moshe* (part 1 §64) writes that one is obligated to mourn even if it is known that the pregnancy was eight months.

16. *Da'as Sofer*, *Yoreh De'ah* §114. For more on this topic, see *Kol Bo Al Aveilus* p. 305 note 6.

17. *Pischei Teshuvah* loc. cit. §§8, citing responsa *Chasam Sofer*, *Yoreh De'ah* §343. The same ruling is given by *Beis Shlomo*, *Yoreh De'ah* part 2 §219.
   Responsa *Oneg Yom Tov* (*Yoreh De'ah* §103) writes that if the infant lived 29 days, 12 hours, and 793 *chalakim* (44 minutes), one is obligated to mourn. The same ruling is given by *Erech Shai*, *Yoreh De'ah* 374:8.

18. *Hagahos Yad Shaul* loc. cit. He writes: "Even though *Chasam Sofer* rules otherwise, I have written what seems correct in my humble opinion." The same ruling is given by responsa *Sho'el U'Meishiv mahadura tinyanya* part 3 §18; and by responsa *Rav Pe'alim* part 1 §51. He states that this ruling should be followed in practice, since "the *halachah* goes according to the more lenient opinion in [a disagreement about the *halachos* of] mourning."

8. If twins are born and one of them dies within thirty days, some rule that one does not mourn, even though the other twin lived more than thirty days.[19]

9. If a woman was divorced, remarried within three months, and gave birth seven months after the wedding, it may not be clear whether the child was conceived from the first husband after a nine-month pregnancy, or from the second husband after a seven-month pregnancy. In such a case, both men are required to mourn for the child if it dies.[20]

10. If a person wishes to be stringent with himself and mourn for someone for whom he is not required to mourn, others should not try to prevent him from doing so. The same applies if he wishes to wear black clothing for a relative for whom he is not required to mourn.[21]

The permission to mourn in such a case applies only in matters — such as not wearing shoes and the like — where no *mitzvah* is contradicted. However, one is not permitted to refrain from Torah study [since it is a *mitzvah*].[21a]

One is not permitted to observe an additional seven days of mourning in the manner of the first seven days, for this would be like adding to the *mitzvos* of the Torah.[21b]

◆§ Those Who Mourn With the Mourner / Limited Mourning

11. The original *halachah* as stated in the Talmud is: כָּל הַמִּתְאַבֵּל עָלָיו מִתְאַבֵּל עִמּוֹ, "Whomever one mourns for, one mourns with." In other words, if one has a family member for whom one would be required to mourn if he died, and that family member becomes a mourner, one is obligated to mourn with him. [An example of this would be the death of one's grandparent, in which case one's parent is a mourner.] In our day, however, this is not practiced.[22] Moreover, anyone who wishes to be stringent with himself in this matter "is only acting foolishly."[23]

---

19. *Shulchan Aruch* loc. cit. 374:9; *Taz* loc. cit. §§4; *Shach* loc. cit. §§9.

20. *Rama* 374:8.

21. *Rama* 374:6.

21a. *Chiddushei R' Akiva Eiger* loc. cit. And *Pischei Teshuvah* (loc. cit. §§7) writes, citing responsa *Besamim Rosh* (§123), that in any case it is not fitting in such a case to observe all the laws of the seven days; and anyone who does so is a "commoner" (*hedyot*).

21b. *Gilyon Maharsha* beginning of §380, citing *Knesses HaGedolah*.

22. *Rama* 374:6. He explains that this *halachah* originally existed in order to show respect for the mourner; and now the universal custom is for the mourner to waive his right to this sign of respect. *Aruch HaShulchan* (loc. cit.) discusses the case of a mourner who states that he does not waive his right, and wants his family member to mourn with him when in his presence, as originally stipulated by the *Gemara*. He does not have the power to demand this, states *Aruch HaShulchan*, since the practice has already been annulled. However, *Da'as Kedoshim* (loc. cit.) rules stringently if the mourner does not waive his right. [That is, he rules that the other family member is obligated to mourn with him when in his presence.] If there is doubt as to whether the mourner waives his right, one may be lenient [and not mourn with him].

23. By acting this way he does not give the impression of showing respect for the mourners, but of mocking them (*Rama* loc. cit. in the name of *Hagahos Maimonios*).

Nonetheless, this *halachah* still leaves its traces with regard to those family members with whom one has such a close blood-relationship that one could not serve as witness in a court case involving them.[24] If such a family member becomes a mourner, one also adopts certain practices of mourning from after the burial until the conclusion of the Sabbath after the burial.[25] One bathes only in lukewarm water, but not hot.[26] One refrains from attending group meals, even a *mitzvah* meal such as that for a *bris milah* (circumcision).[27] In communities where the custom is that the mourner does not change clothes for the Sabbath, one refrains from changing one of his garments for the Sabbath.[28] Some rule that one is permitted to wash one's hair in hot water on Friday (i.e. the eve of the Sabbath) if one is accustomed to do so on that day every week.[28a] If the seventh day of mourning falls on the Sabbath, one is permitted to bathe on Friday.[28b]

◄§ For In-Laws or Step-Parents

12. This limited type of mourning described in the preceding paragraph should be observed for one's father-in-law or mother-in-law, even though they are related to one only by marriage. The same applies to one's stepmother if one's father is living.[29]

---

24. Those related only by marriage are not included — for example, if the deceased is one's daughter-in-law, sister-in-law, son-in-law, or brother-in-law, this *halachah* would not apply (*Shach* loc. cit. §§6). For the list of the relatives for whom one may not serve as witness, see *Shulchan Aruch Choshen Mishpat* §33.

25. This applies whether there are few or many days until the termination of the Sabbath (*Shach* loc. cit. §§7). And *Erech Shai* (*Yoreh De'ah* §374) writes that "the mourning practices of those who 'mourn with the mourner' apply only after the burial, not before."

    The *gaon* R' Avraham Yaakov Zelznick, *shlita*, told me that he asked the *gaon* R' Tzvi Pesach Frank, *zatzal*, and the *gaon* R' Eliahu Ram, *zatzal*, about two cases of this type of mourning. They answered him that the custom is not to observe it. However, he could not tell from their answer whether they were referring to the custom only in Jerusalem, or everywhere.

26. See *Shevus Yaakov* (part 3 §98), who states: "In any case, if one's hair is long, one may have it cut on the day before the Sabbath even if it is the first Sabbath after the burial. This is contrary to the opinion of *Lechem HaPanim*, who rules stringently, requiring one to refrain from having a haircut and the like. But, argues *Shevus Yaakov*, we have no source to rely on except *Rama*'s statement that 'one practices partial mourning during the first week, that is, one bathes only in lukewarm water, but not hot. . .' Hence we may not generalize beyond the details of this statement. Let us not add to it. . ."

27. *Shach* 374:§§7, citing *Bach*. And *Lechem HaPanim* (loc. cit.) writes that the prohibition against taking part in a group meal includes even serving as a waiter.

    See also *Da'as Kedoshim* (loc. cit. §§2), who writes: "Since this [the practice of partially mourning with the mourner until the conclusion of the Sabbath] is only a custom, one need not extend the prohibition to an informal meal. As long as the participants do not wash hands for bread, it is not considered a meal in this regard."

28. *Rama* 374:6; see *Shach* loc. cit. §§7.

28a. *Da'as Kedoshim*, who draws an analogy with *Shabbos Chazon*, the Sabbath before Tishah B'Av, when the same principle is applied.

28b. *Hagahos Kesav Sofer*, who writes that the *halachah* in this situation is not more stringent than during the *shloshim* (the time between the seventh and thirtieth day of mourning).

29. *Pischei Teshuvah* loc. cit. §§3, citing responsa *Teshuvah MeAhavah* part 1 §175.

13. Some rule that this type of mourning is observed only while one is in the place where the actual mourners are sitting *shivah*, but not when one is elsewhere. Others disagree.[30]

14. This type of mourning is observed only during the first week after the death — or during the first week after hearing of the death, if the news arrived within thirty days of the death (*shmu'ah krovah*). If the news arrived more than thirty days after the death (*shmu'ah rechokah*), this type of mourning is not observed at all.[31]

15. If the death occurred during the week of Pesach or Succos, this type of mourning is observed when the festival ends, until after the first Sabbath.[32]

---

30. *Pischei Teshuvah* loc. cit. §§4.
31. *Rama* 374:6.
32. *Pischei Teshuvah* 399:§§4, citing responsa *Shivas Tzion* §59.

CHAPTER SIXTEEN

Laws and Customs
in the House of Mourning

❧ Kindling a Light

1. It is customary to kindle a light for the benefit of the departed soul. It is kindled in the house — and preferably in the room[1] — where he died. If a light cannot be lit where he died (for example, if he died in a hospital), the custom is to kindle it in the house where he lived. If this, too, is impossible, it is kindled where the mourners are sitting *shivah*.[2]

2. The most preferable light is an olive-oil lamp.[3] If this is not available, one may light a candle or a kerosene lamp. If the only thing available is an electric light, one lights that.[4]

---

1. The *Acharonim* state that this helps and honors the soul of the deceased. In *Kesubos* 103a we find that R' Yehudah *HaNasi* commanded that after his death: "The light should be burning in its [accustomed] place." *Hagahos Yavetz* (ad loc.) writes: "Perhaps this is a homiletic support for [this] custom."

   Shibolei HaLeket (*Hilchos Semachos* end of §21) writes: "In our place, the custom is to kindle a light on the floor every night throughout *shivah* in the place where the body of the deceased was washed, in order to console the soul, which returns and mourns for [the deceased] throughout the seven days." The same custom is mentioned by *Tanya Rabbasi* (*Hilchos Avel* §67). See also *Mishmeres Shalom* (os nun §29), who writes: "In our time, the custom is to put [the light] on the table or the window near the place where he died."

   See also *Gesher HaChaim* (20:1:1): "It is preferable that the light be in the room of the deceased."

2. *Gesher HaChaim* loc. cit. The same ruling is given by *Kenaf Renannah* (*Yoreh De'ah* §37).

   Kol Bo Al Aveilus (p. 262) cites *Kerem Shlomo* (§399): "(a) [The light] should only [be kindled] immediately after the death, that is, during *shivah*. (b) [It should be kindled] only in the house where he died, not elsewhere. (c) If the mourner heard of the death more than seven days after it occurred, he does not kindle a light, even if he is conducting his mourning in the house where the deceased died — and all the more so, if he hears the news [and conducts his mourning] in a different city."

   Responsa *Divrei Sofrim* (§146) states: "Even if oil [for the light] is expensive, one should not be lenient, but should light in the place where the deceased died. But in the home of the mourner, in a place other than where the deceased died, one may be lenient [and omit lighting], since there is no basis [for lighting there]. But perhaps people follow this practice so that they will not forget the deceased, and will fulfill the laws of mourning."

3. See *Pischei Teshuvah* (*Even HaEzer* 102:§§1), who cites responsa *Chasam Sofer* §42 as stating that the custom is to keep an oil lamp burning all seven days. And *Gesher HaChaim* (loc. cit.) writes: "It is preferable to light with olive oil, as alluded to in *Tikkunim* §19 beginning of chapt. 1."

4. *Gesher HaChaim* loc. cit. And see below, chapt. 44 note 31, with regard to using an electric light for commemoration of the *yahrzeit* (anniversary of the death).

3. The light should be kept burning during the entire seven days of *shivah*, including the Sabbath.[5] It is kindled from the time of death and kept burning until the end of *shivah* even during days when no one is mourning — for example, if death occurred just before a Festival, so that the Festival terminates the mourning;[6] or if death occurred during the Festival, so that the beginning of mourning is postponed until after the Festival (see chapt. 32).[7]

Concerning kindling this light on *Yom Tov*, see below, 33:22, and note there.

◄§ Covering the Mirrors

4. It is customary to cover the mirrors in the mourner's home.[8] Some also cover any pictures of people.[9]

In rooms not used by the mourner, the mirrors need not be covered.[9a] On the Sabbath, too, they need not be covered. However, if people pray in the room the mirrors should be covered even on the Sabbath.[9b]

◄§ Housework

5. It is permitted to sweep the house and mop the floors in the mourner's home, and also to wash dishes.

One should not bring in fragrant spices, nor burn incense.[10] However, for the *Havdalah* ceremony at the termination of the Sabbath one may recite the blessing over fragrant spices as usual.[11]

For further laws concerning the mourner performing housework, see below, 18:15.

◄§ Taking Things from the Mourner's Home

6. Some authorities write that one should not take anything from the home of the mourner during the entire *shivah*, because the house is under an unfavorable

---

5. *Gesher HaChaim* loc. cit. §2.

6. *Mishnah Berurah* 548:§§3. He states that the Festival does not annul practices observed to honor the deceased (*kevod hameis*).

7. *Gesher HaChaim* loc. cit. *Tzavaas R' Naftali Katz, zatzal*, states that a continual light (*ner tamid*) should be lit in the house of the deceased throughout *shloshim*, and in the synagogue until after the first *yahrzeit*.

8. *Kol Bo Al Aveilus* (p. 262) cites several reasons: (a) Mirrors cause joy, and the mourner is forbidden to rejoice. (b) People pray in the mourner's house, and as explained in *Ba'er Heitev* (§90), one is forbidden to pray in front of a mirror. (c) *Chasam Sofer* is quoted as saying that the basis of this custom is a passage in the Jerusalem Talmud (*Mo'ed Katan* 3:5), which states that the reason why the Talmud requires the mourner to overturn his bed is to repress the impetus to marital relations. It is true that in our time we do not follow the practice of overturning beds (see below, 22:2). Nevertheless, mirrors also constitute such an impetus (see *Exodus* 38:8, with *Rashi*). Moreover, people see their faces in them. Therefore one overturns the mirrors (*Ginzei Yosef* §148).

9. My father and teacher, *zatzal*, in his work *Zichron Eliahu* (manuscript).

9a. Major contemporary authorities.

9b. *Shmiras Shabbos Kehilchasah* 65:8 with footnote.

10. *Shulchan Aruch* 378:7.

11. Responsa *Maharam Shick* §363.

spiritual influence (*ruach ra'ah*). Some rule that one need be careful about this only if the death occurred in that house.[12] Other authorities write that the custom of not taking things from the mourner's house has no halachic basis.[13]

◄§ Saying "*Shalom*"

7. Some write that people should not say "*Shalom*" to each other in the mourner's home.[14]

◄§ Rising for a Torah Sage

8. The mourner is not required to rise from his seat in respect for a visiting Torah Sage, not even for the *nasi*, the leader of the entire Jewish people.[15] If he does rise, the visitor should not tell him, "Sit," because this may imply, "Sit in your mourning."[16] However, the mourner is required to rise for a Torah Scroll.[16a]

◄§ Excessive Conversation/Talking on the Telephone

9. The mourner should not converse excessively, because this gives the impression that he has forgotten his grief.[17]

The mourner is permitted to talk on the telephone for his and also his household's physical necessities. He may also speak on the phone with those who call to comfort him. However, he is forbidden to conduct ordinary conversations on the

---

12. *Chiddushei R' Akiva Eiger* §376, and *Beis Lechem Yehudah* ad loc. And see *Even Yaakov* (44:3), who writes: "It would seem reasonable to say, accordingly, that all this applies only when the death occurred in the house where the mourners are sitting [*shivah*]; but if it occurred elsewhere, the concept of *ruach hatum'ah* (spirit of contamination) in their house is not relevant at all." He cites support for this argument from *Misgeres HaShulchan* (*Yoreh De'ah*), who writes that one need only be careful not to take things from the room where the death occurred, but one may take from the rest of the house.

13. *Yoseif Ometz* (by R' Yosef Yuzpa Han, a contemporary of *Shelah*), in the section called *Dinei Hanhagas HaShivah*, writes: "I have received a tradition from my teacher, the *gaon Maharar Segal*, *zal*, that there is no basis in the world for the custom not to take anything from the home of the mourner during *shloshim*. He said that this error derives from something the *Poskim* write: that if one lends another a garment to wear to the home of the mourner, one is not permitted to take it back from him until the end of *shivah*." His ruling is also cited by *Noheg Katzon Yosef*.

14. *Aruch HaShulchan* 385:4. See *Even Yaakov* (§55), who cites support for this ruling from *Shibolei HaLeket*, *Hilchos Semachos* §22.
It is reported that HaGaon Rav Moshe Feinstein *zatzal* [*Igros Moshe*] would not even extend his hand in greeting in a mourner's home.

15. *Rama* 376:1.

16. *Shulchan Aruch* 376:2. And see *Da'as Torah* (ad loc.), who writes: "However, one is permitted to use some other expression such as, 'Don't trouble yourselves to stand up." He cites *Nimukei Yosef* (p.27) as giving this ruling.

16a. *Shiurei Berachah* 376:§§4.

17. *Shibolei HaLeket* (*Hilchos Semachos* §10) writes: "We read in the first chapter of *Berachos*: 'The reward at the home of the mourner is for silence.' This means that he [the mourner] is forbidden to indulge in much conversation, for if he talks excessively, it gives the impression that he has forgotten his sorrow, and he does not appear like a mourner. We find [a source in the Torah for the concept of] reward for silence on the part of the mourner, in the case of Aaron [see *Leviticus*, chapt. 10]. . ."

phone, and all the more so, he is forbidden to call people — even his own children — to ask about their welfare.[17a]

◦§ Meals

10. Once the deceased is buried, the mourner is permitted to eat meat. He may also drink a little wine during the meal, to help digest his food, but he should not drink wine as a beverage.[18]

11. When the mourner is eating with others, and one person recites the blessing over bread for all present and cuts the loaf for them, he should put the mourner's slice of bread directly into the mourner's hand.[19] On the Sabbath, however, the mourner should cut his own bread. The reason is that on the Sabbath he is not permitted to publicize the fact that he is in mourning. If someone were to cut bread for him and put it directly into his hand, this would be like publicizing his mourning.[20]

12. The custom is that a cup from which the mourner drank should not be used by anyone else until it is rinsed. But on the Sabbath one need not be particular about this.[21]

◦§ *Zimun* and *Bircas HaMazon* / Grace After Meals

13. In general, when three or more adult males eat bread together, *Bircas HaMazon*, the Grace After Meals, is preceded by the recitation of an introductory formal "invitation" called *zimun*. Some authorities rule that it is preferable (*lechatchilah*) for a mourner to refrain from eating in a group of three or more, so that it will not be necessary to recite the *zimun*.[22] However, other *Poskim*

17a. *Igros Moshe Orach Chaim* IV:§40:11. See 17:12; note 25.

18. *Shulchan Aruch* §378:8. See *Da'as Torah* (ad loc.), who cites *Hagahos Maimonios* (*Hilchos Avel* end of ch. 7) as stating that the mourner is *required* to eat meat and drink wine. However, *Da'as Torah* cites *Darkei Moshe* as ruling otherwise.

19. *Shulchan Aruch Orach Chaim* 167:18 — *Zion stretches forth her hands* (*Lamentations* 1:17): This [description of the bereaved stretching forth her hand] alludes to the *halachah* that when one is in mourning, we put directly into his hand his slice of bread over which the blessing was recited [unlike the case of non-mourners where we do not hand the slice directly to the recipients, but place it on the table for them to pick up] (*Beis Yosef* and *Abudraham*, citing *Rambam*, *Hilchos Brachos* 7:5, and *Teshuvos HaRashba*).

20. *Mishnah Berurah Orach Chaim* §§89.

21. *Shibolei HaLeket*, *Hilchos Semachos* §23. He writes there: "And on the Sabbath they are not careful to refrain from drinking from the cup the mourner drank from, because this is something they are careful about during the week; [therefore, being careful about it on the Sabbath too would be like mourning conspicuously (*befarhesia*), which is forbidden on the Sabbath]."

22. *Responsa HaElef Lecha Shlomoh* (§318) writes: "Certainly it is preferable (*lechatchilah*) to refrain from eating in a group of three or more, so that it will not be necessary to recite *zimun*. However, if they have already eaten together, the mourning should not annul the *zimun*." The same ruling is given by *Hagahos Chochmas Shlomoh* (ad loc.), who states that eating in a group of three or more is forbidden just as on the eve of Tishah B'Av. He says that in his work, *Kinas Sofrim*, he refutes all apparent evidence to the contrary.

are more lenient and permit mourners to eat in such a way as to require *zimun*.[23]

14. Some use the following special wording when reciting the *zimun* in the home of a mourner: נְבָרֵךְ מְנַחֵם אֲבֵלִים שֶׁאָכַלְנוּ מִשֶּׁלּוֹ, 'Let us bless the One Who comforts mourners, [and] of Whose we have eaten.'[24]

15. When reciting Grace After Meals in the mourner's home, a special passage is added. The fourth blessing is revised to read as follows:[25]

בָּרוּךְ אַתָּה ה' אֱלֹהֵינוּ מֶלֶךְ הָעוֹלָם, הָאֵל, אָבִינוּ מַלְכֵּנוּ, אַדִּירֵנוּ, בּוֹרְאֵנוּ, גּוֹאֲלֵנוּ, יוֹצְרֵנוּ, קְדוֹשֵׁנוּ, קְדוֹשׁ יַעֲקֹב, רוֹעֵנוּ רוֹעֵה יִשְׂרָאֵל, הַמֶּלֶךְ הַטּוֹב וְהַמֵּטִיב לַכֹּל, שֶׁבְּכָל יוֹם וָיוֹם הוּא הֵטִיב, הוּא מֵטִיב, הוּא יֵיטִיב לָנוּ. הַמֶּלֶךְ הַחַי, הַטּוֹב וְהַמֵּטִיב, אֵל אֱמֶת, דַּיַּן אֱמֶת, שׁוֹפֵט בְּצֶדֶק, לוֹקֵחַ נְפָשׁוֹת בְּמִשְׁפָּט, וְשַׁלִּיט בְּעוֹלָמוֹ לַעֲשׂוֹת בּוֹ כִּרְצוֹנוֹ. כִּי כָל דְּרָכָיו בְּמִשְׁפָּט, וַאֲנַחְנוּ עַמּוֹ וַעֲבָדָיו. וְעַל הַכֹּל אֲנַחְנוּ חַיָּבִים לְהוֹדוֹת לוֹ וּלְבָרְכוֹ. גּוֹדֵר פְּרָצוֹת יִשְׂרָאֵל, הוּא יִגְדּוֹר אֶת הַפִּרְצָה הַזֹּאת, מֵעָלֵינוּ וּמֵעַל הָאָבֵל הַזֶּה, לְחַיִּים וּלְשָׁלוֹם וְכָל טוֹב וּמִכָּל טוּב לְעוֹלָם אַל יְחַסְּרֵנוּ.

'Blessed are You, Hashem our God, King of the universe, the Almighty, our Father, our King, our Sovereign, our Creator, our Redeemer, our Maker, our Holy One, Holy One of Jacob, our Shepherd, the Shepherd of Israel, the good and beneficent King, for every single day He did good, does good, and will do good to us. He is the living King, Who is good and Who does good for all, God of truth, Judge of truth, Who judges with righteousness, Who takes souls with justice, Who rules His universe to do with it as He wishes, for all His ways are with justice and we are His nation and His servants. For everything we are obliged to thank Him and to bless Him. He Who repairs the breaches of Israel, may He repair this breach from us and from this mourner for life, for peace, and for all good; and of all good things may he never deprive us.'

Some authorities write that in our day the custom is not to recite this special passage.[26]

---

23. See *Kores HaBris* (by R' Eliyahu Posek, *zal*), *Hilchos Milah* §265 in §§66 of the notes entitled *Nachal HaBris*. He argues that there is no objection to the mourners' eating in a group of three or more in such a way that it will be necessary to recite *zimun*. The same ruling is given by the following authorities: responsa *Chemdas Moshe* §19; *China VeChisda* on Tractate *Kesubos* 8; and *Gesher HaChaim* II:§19.

   Even Yaakov (§53) writes: "Therefore, in practice, if the mourners wish to recite *zimun* they have authorities on whom to rely [for permission]."

24. *Shulchan Aruch* 379:3.

25. *Shulchan Aruch* and *Rama* 379:1, and *Shach* ad loc.

26. *Be'er HaGolah* (ad loc.) writes: "I have not observed that the custom is to add [this special passage] to the fourth blessing. In my humble opinion, the reason is that they base themselves on the words of *Tosafos* in *Kesubos* (5b), who prove that this passage (*birkas aveilim*) is only to be recited when ten [or more men eat together]." The same ruling is given by responsa *Maharam* §676; and by *Beis Yosef*, citing *Ramban* and *Rambam*. *Gesher HaChaim* (20:2:13) also writes that in our time the custom is not to add this special passage.

   See also *Kol Bo Al Aveilus*, who cites *Zachur LeAvraham*, *Yoreh De'ah os* 2: "The custom is not to recite any of the passages beginning הָרַחֲמָן, 'the Merciful One,' in the mourner's home."

16. Some add the following special passage in the third blessing as a substitute for "Rebuild Jerusalem" (וּבְנֵה יְרוּשָׁלַיִם) of *Bircas HaMazon*:

נַחֵם ה' אֱלֹהֵינוּ, אֶת אֲבֵלֵי יְרוּשָׁלַיִם, וְאֶת הָאֲבֵלִים הַמִּתְאַבְּלִים בָּאֵבֶל הַזֶּה. נַחֲמֵם
מֵאֶבְלָם וְשַׂמְּחֵם מִיגוֹנָם, כָּאָמוּר: כְּאִישׁ אֲשֶׁר אִמּוֹ תְּנַחֲמֶנּוּ, כֵּן אָנֹכִי אֲנֶחֶמְכֶם
וּבִירוּשָׁלַיִם תְּנֻחָמוּ. בָּרוּךְ אַתָּה, ה', מְנַחֵם צִיּוֹן בְּבִנְיַן יְרוּשָׁלָיִם. אָמֵן.

"O comfort, Hashem our God, the mourners of Jerusalem and those who mourn this sad event. Console them from their mourning and gladden them from their grief, as it is said (Yeshayahu 66:13), 'Like a man whose mother consoles him, so I will console you, and in Jerusalem you will be consoled.' Blessed are You, Hashem, Comforter of Zion through the rebuilding of Jerusalem." "Amen". [27]

Some authorities write that in our day the custom is not to recite this special passage. [28]

17. As mentioned above (paragraph 11), on the Sabbath one is not permitted to publicize the fact that he is in mourning. Thus on the Sabbath, if a mourner recites Grace After Meals by himself, or together with other mourners, he adds the same special passages as during the week. This is not considered publicizing his mourning. But if non-mourners are eating with him, all special passages of mourning are omitted. Since non-mourners are present, it would be considered publicizing his mourning. [29]

Prayers in the House of Mourning

18. It is a *mitzvah* to hold daily services [for all three daily prayers — Morning (*Shacharis*), Afternoon (*Minchah*), and Evening (*Maariv*)] with at least ten men (a *minyan*) in the place where the deceased died. This applies even if no mourner is present, for it gives satisfaction to the soul of the departed. [30] It is especially important to pray there if the deceased did not leave family to mourn for

---

27. *Shulchan Aruch* 379:2 and *Shach* ad loc.

28. *Gesher HaChaim* loc. cit.

29. *Shulchan Aruch* 379:4 and *Shach* §§5.

30. *Rama* 384:3. See *Chiddushei R' Akiva Eiger* ad loc.; he cites *Chiddushei HaGershuni*, who writes in the name of *Kol Bo* that: "prayer services are not conducted in his house if the deceased was less than a year old."

Da'as Torah (ad loc.) writes in the name of *Ramban* that the mourners must conduct their mourning in the place where the deceased died, because the [departed] soul mourns there, and is consoled only by prayer.

Gesher HaChaim (20:3:3) writes: "As for those whose custom is to pray in the home of the mourner even [if the deceased was] less than a year old — this is for the sake of the mourners, who do not go to the synagogue. However, if the deceased was more than a year old, they pray [in the mourner's home] for the sake of the deceased. They also recite *Kaddish*, study Torah and recite memorial prayers, even if the deceased was not yet old enough to be held accountable for his sins [i.e., *bar mitzvah*]."

him.[31] The custom is to pray in the mourner's home even if the death did not occur there.[32]

19. The mourner is included in the minyan of ten, even on the first day of mourning.[33] The custom is that someone mourning for his parent leads the prayer-service even if there is someone else who could serve as leader.[34] But someone mourning for a family member other than a parent serves as leader only if no other leader is available.[35]

In Talmudic times, some or all members of the congregation fulfilled their obligation of prayer by listening to the leader. Nowadays, everyone recites the prayer himself, so the prayer of the leader does not serve to fulfill the prayer-obligation of the congregation. Some rule that, this being the case, any mourner may serve as leader.[35a]

One praying in the mourner's home should not raise his voice.[35b]

✎ Tachanun

20. Tachanun is not recited in the mourner's home throughout shivah,[36] even if no mourner is present.[37] Moreover, when those who prayed there go home,

---

31. In Rama §376:3 we find: "It is written in Maharil: 'The custom is to pray in the presence of a minyan during the entire seven days, in the place where the deceased died.' This refers to a case where the deceased did not leave any known next-of-kin to mourn for him. But if anyone is mourning for him anywhere, this is not necessary." This contradicts the words of Rama (§384) referred to in the previous footnote. The Acharonim discuss this problem in their commentaries on 384:3.

32. Gesher HaChaim loc. cit. And see responsa Duda'ei HaSadeh (§47); he writes that even if this means there will be no minyan in the synagogue for a few days, the ten should pray in the home of the mourner. And see Gesher HaChaim (loc. cit.), who writes that even if it is impossible to pray in the place where the death occurred, it is worthwhile to make an effort, as far as possible, to pray at least the first prayer [after burial] in that place, as is written in Beis Yosef end of §393.

33. Rama 384:3 and Chiddushei R' Akiva Eiger ad loc.

34. Beis Hillel ad loc. The reason is that the mourner's leading the prayer services is even more effective for the benefit of the soul of the deceased than the recitation of Kaddish.

However, Ikrei HaDat (Orach Chaim 3:9) cites responsa Mekom Shmuel (§78) as contradicting Beis Hillel by ruling that even someone mourning for his parent should not serve as chazzan during shivah, if there is someone else capable of being chazzan.

35. This is the implication of Shulchan Aruch 384:3. But Nachamu Ami (18:12) writes: "Likewise, if he is saying Kaddish for a family member other than his father or mother, the mourner should serve as chazzan, since [serving as chazzan in] prayer is [even] more effective [for the aid of the departed soul] than [reciting] Kaddish."

35a. Responsa Maharam Shick §370, citing Chasam Sofer.

35b. Leket Yosher, citing Or Zarua.

36. Shulchan Aruch Orach Chaim 131:4. And Mishnah Berurah (ad loc. §§20) adds: "This refers to the entire seven days. The reason is that the mourner is under the influence of Midas HaDin, the Divine Attribute of Strict Justice; therefore he must be careful not to do anything that would strengthen this Attribute of Justice. This is similar to the reason why Tachanun is not recited at night (Levush)."

And see Derech HaChaim (Dinei Nefillas Apayim), who states that the omission of Tachanun in the mourner's home applies even if the mourner is a child. He also writes there that even in the Minchah (Afternoon) Prayer of the seventh day, Tachanun should not be recited.

37. See Mishnah Berurah (loc. cit.), who cites Elyah Rabbah as expressing doubt about this question. However, Sha'arei Teshuvah (ad loc. §§10) cites Pri HaAdamah: "Ri states that the custom in

they do not have to recite *Tachanun* in their own homes to make up for what they omitted. However, on Monday or Thursday the passages recited on those two days, beginning וְהוּא רַחוּם, "He, the Merciful One," should be recited by the others when they return home. Some authorities are lenient and do not require this either.[38]

If the mourner prays in the synagogue or in someone else's home, the rest of the congregation recites *Tachanun*, but the mourner does not.[39]

21. The passages beginning, אֵל אֶרֶךְ אַפַּיִם, "O God, slow to anger," and לַמְנַצֵּחַ, "For the Conductor," are not recited in the mourner's home.[40] Some authorities rule that the same applies to the verse beginning וַאֲנִי זֹאת בְּרִיתִי, "And as for Me, this is My covenant with them. . .". However, all authorities agree that the mourner himself should not say it.[41]

22. During the Ten Days of Repentance, *Avinu Malkeinu* is recited in the mourner's home.[42] *Selichos* (prayers for forgiveness) are recited there in shortened form: from the beginning of *Selichos* until (and including) the passage beginning, זְכוֹר רַחֲמֶיךָ, "Remember Your mercies. . ."; after that, skipping to the three verses beginning, שְׁמַע קוֹלֵנוּ, "Hear our voice. . ."; and stopping at the end of those three verses.[43]

Jerusalem is to omit *Tachanun* in the house of the deceased, even if there is no mourner there." The same ruling is given by *Gesher HaChaim* loc. cit.

38. *Mishnah Berurah* loc. cit.

39. *Mishnah Berurah* loc. cit.

   If people have come to the synagogue to comfort the mourner, *Nachamu Ami* (chapt. 18) writes, in the name of *Shenos Chaim* (§8) that *Tachanun* should be omitted. In the same place he quotes the gaon R' Shlomo Zalman Auerbach, *shlita*, as ruling that if the mourner himself serves as leader of the prayer-services, *Tachanun* should be omitted.

40. *Pri Megaddim* §131 in *Mishbetzos Zahav* par. 115. The same ruling is given by *Gesher HaChaim* loc. cit.

41. *Tur* (*Hilchos Tishah B'Av* §559) writes that this verse should not be omitted in the home of the mourner. [The reason for presuming that it might be omitted is that it refers to Torah-study, and Torah-study is forbidden to the mourner. But] even though the mourner cannot study Torah, the comforters can. Therefore the verse should be included. The same ruling is given by *Roke'ach* §312; *Magen Avraham* 131:§§10; and *Elyah Rabbah* 559:§§9. However, *Abudraham* and *Kol Bo* write that the verse should be omitted, and the same ruling is given by *Derech HaChaim*; by *Ma'avar Yabok*; and by *Gesher HaChaim* loc. cit.

   See also responsa *Maharil Diskin* (*Kuntres Acharon*), who writes that it does not seem that the verse should be omitted. He explains that even if a child is in mourning, he is not permitted to stop studying Torah; and this particular verse alludes to the Torah-study of children. This is in contrast to Tishah B'Av, when schoolchildren cease their Torah-study.

42. *Elyah Rabbah* §131. The same ruling is given by *Yavetz*. And see *Nachamu Ami* (chapt. 18 note 35), who infers from *Elyah Rabbah* that *Avinu Malkeinu* is recited in the mourner's home only during the Ten Days of Repentance, but not on other days.

43. See *Pri Megaddim* §684, at the end of *Eshel Avraham*. He states that those praying in the home of the mourner — including the mourner himself — are permitted to recite *Selichos*; and the same applies to the [*selichos* recited during the] fasts known as *Shovavim* [days designated for fasting during the weeks of *parshios Shemos* through *Tetzaveh*]. And see *Gesher HaChaim* (loc. cit.), who states that the *selichos* are shortened in the manner indicated in our text.

Some authorities permit the mourner to recite the service of *Yom Kippur Katan*, which is recited on the day before Rosh Chodesh. Others forbid this.[43a]

◄§ *Tiskabel* in *Kaddish*

23. The *Tiskabel* passage included in the main *Kaddish* of the prayer service — תִּתְקַבֵּל צְלוֹתְהוֹן וּבָעוּתְהוֹן דְּכָל בֵּית יִשְׂרָאֵל קֳדָם אֲבוּהוֹן דִּי בִשְׁמַיָּא, וְאִמְרוּ אָמֵן — "May the prayers and supplications of the entire Family of Israel be accepted before their Father who is in Heaven; now respond: *Amen*" is recited when praying in the mourner's home. Although some rule that if the mourner serves as *chazzan* he does not include this passage,[44] nevertheless, the prevalent custom is to include it.[44a]

◄§ The Public Torah-Reading

24. It is permitted to bring a Torah Scroll to the mourner's home for the public Torah-reading.[45] The custom is to be sure to read from it there at least three times.[46]

The mourner cannot be called up to the Torah-reading, even if he is the only *kohen* present.[47] However, he can be the one honored to take the Torah Scroll out of, and return it to, the Ark (*hotza'ah ve'hachnasah*). He may also be selected to

---

43a. Responsa *Yehudah Ya'aleh* (§353) writes that the mourner is permitted to recite it, but omitting the *viduim* (confessions). However *Yoseif Da'as* (§376) writes: "On the day before Rosh Chodesh I was in mourning. My usual practice is to recite the *selichos* designated for *Yom Kipppur Katan*. In this circumstance I did not recite them, because this is not such an essential part of the day's service, since many do not recite it, and it is not part of the prayer-service."

44. *Teshuvos R' Akiva Eiger* (*tinyana* §24) cites *Sefer HaChaim* as writing that *Tiskabel* is not recited.
    R' Akiva Eiger disputes this, calling it "an erroneous ruling." *Teshuvos Maharam Shick* (*Yoreh De'ah* §370) attempts to defend their custom. *Yoseif Da'as* (§376) writes that if the mourner serves as leader of the prayer-services, he should not include *Tiskabel*. *Gesher HaChaim* states the same as his own opinion, but concludes: "However, in our time the custom is that even the mourner recites *Tiskabel*."

44a. The *gaon* R' Moshe Feinstein, *zatzal*, in the Torah journal *LeTorah V'Hora'ah*, vol. X, Shavuos 5744. He writes: "Even the mourner himself must recite *tiskabel*. This is not a matter requiring any research at all, for in our countries, in Europe, there was never even a doubt regarding this; it was never even something one asked about . . ."

45. *Kol Bo Al Aveilus* p. 277. And see *Even Yaakov* §54, who writes that even if most or all of the *minyan* are mourners, they are permitted to take out the Torah Scroll for the public reading. He explains that [even though the mourner is forbidden to study Torah,] he is required to hear the Torah-reading, since it is included in the prescribed prayer-service of that day.

46. *Aruch HaShulchan* (135:32) writes: "The custom is to be careful to read from it [at least] three times, since this gives it an established status (*kevius*) [in the new location], and there is no disrespect in moving it from the synagogue. But [if it is read from] less than three times, this is considered moving it for temporary needs, which is disrespectful." The same ruling is given by responsa *Toras Chaim* end of §135. And see responsa *Kinyan Torah* (IV:§18), who writes that in the case of a mourner, three times are not necessary. But see *LeTorah V'Hora'ah* (loc. cit.), where the *gaon* R' Moshe Feinstein, *zatzal*, writes that it is preferable, if at all possible, that the Torah should be read from at least three times, by either arranging for a *minyan* for *Minchah* on Sabbath afternoon, or, if this is not possible, by arranging for an additional *minyan* after *shivah*. .

47. *Shulchan Aruch Yoreh De'ah* 384:2, and see *Shach* loc. cit. §§3.

raise up the Torah Scroll at the end of the reading, or to roll it closed, tie and cover it (*hagbahah u'gelilah*).[48] If he is chosen to raise up the Torah Scroll at the end of the reading, he is permitted to sit on a chair to hold the Scroll.[49]

The mourner is obligated to rise in the presence of a Torah Scroll.[50]

The passages beginning, יְהִי רָצוֹן מִלִּפְנֵי אָבִינוּ שֶׁבַּשָּׁמַיִם, "May it be the will of our Father Who is in heaven. . .,"ordinarily recited after the Torah-reading, are also recited in the mourner's home.[51]

◈§ Priestly Blessing by *Chazzan*

25. Ordinarily, the leader of the prayer-service recites the words of the Priestly Blessing in a passage beginning, אֱלֹהֵינוּ וֵאלֹהֵי אֲבוֹתֵינוּ, "Our God and the God of our forefathers. . ." Some rule that this passage should not be recited in the mourner's home, and others rule that it should be recited.[52] On the Sabbath, however, it should be recited.[53]

---

48. *Taz* loc. cit. §§1.

49. *Drishah* (loc. cit.) writes: ". . .and he [the mourner who performed *hagbahah*] should remain seated until after the *chazzan* stands."

50. *Shiurei Berachah* 376:§§4.

51. *Da'as Kedoshim* loc. cit. 30:16:6.

52. *Elyah Rabbah* (559:§§13) cites *Shiurei Knesses HaGedolah* as ruling that in the *Amidah*, the Priestly Blessing אֱלֹהֵינוּ וֵאלֹהֵי אֲבוֹתֵינוּ, "Our God and God of our forefathers. . .,' is not recited in the home of the mourner, when the mourner is praying there; the reason is that the mourner himself, if he is a *kohen*, does not confer the Priestly Blessing.

But *Dagul MeiRevavah* (§127) questions this ruling. He points out that, according to *Rama*, the mourner does not confer the Priestly Blessing during the entire twelve months of mourning. If the ruling cited by *Elyah Rabbah* were correct, this would mean that during the entire twelve months אֱלֹהֵינוּ וֵאלֹהֵי אֲבוֹתֵינוּ, "Our God and God of our forefathers. . ." could not be recited in his home. Moreover, when he served as leader of the prayer-service in the synagogue, he would not be able to recite it. "Therefore," writes *Dagul MeiRevavah*, "It seems to me that, contrary to the ruling of *Shiurei Knesses HaGedolah*, ["Our God. . ."] is recited in the home of the mourner. What difference does it make that the mourner himself, if he is a *kohen*, does not give the Priestly Blessing? After all, the *halachah* is that if he does go up to give the blessing, he is not made to go back down, but is permitted to give it. And even if he has not yet gone up to give it, but has only been requested to do so, he is obligated to go up and give the blessing; and if he does not, he violates a positive commandment, as explained by *Magen Avraham* there. Therefore, the requirement to recite אֱלֹהֵינוּ וֵאלֹהֵי אֲבוֹתֵינוּ in the mourner's home is no less stringent than during the *Minchah* service of Yom Kippur; there, too, it is recited even though the *kohanim* are not permitted to confer their blessing. There, too, the reason is that if the *kohanim* do go up to recite the blessing, they are not made to go back down, but are permitted to recite it."

Chayei Adam (27:25) adopts the ruling of *Dagul MeiRevavah*, as does *Teshuvah MeAhavah* I:§50. Likewise, *Sha'arei Teshuvah* (§122) states that the custom followed in Jerusalem is to recite אֱלֹהֵינוּ וֵאלֹהֵי אֲבוֹתֵינוּ, "Our God and God of our forefathers. . ." in the mourner's home.

However, *Chiddushei R' Akiva Eiger* (§131) writes that it should not be recited there, since the mourning period is analogous to Tishah B'Av, and on Tishah B'Av it is not recited.

[The generally accepted practice in most Diaspora communities is not to recite the Priestly Blessings in the home of the mourner on weekdays during *shivah*. However, on the Sabbath, it is recited.]

53. *Yoseif Da'as* §376. The reason is that omitting "אֱלֹהֵינוּ וֵאלֹהֵי אֲבוֹתֵינוּ" would be like mourning conspicuously on the Sabbath.

⋘ Hallel

26. On Rosh Chodesh, Hallel is not recited in the mourner's home.[54] Some rule that the others praying there are not required to recite it even when they return to their homes.[55] The custom, however, is that the others praying there go elsewhere and recite Hallel, then return to the mourner's home and finish the prayer-service.[56] Alternatively, the mourner goes elsewhere while the others recite Hallel. But if the deceased was over six years old, and died in the home where they are praying, Hallel is not recited there.[57]

27. Hallel is recited in the mourner's home under the following circumstances:

    (a) When Rosh Chodesh falls on the Sabbath.

    (b) On *Chol HaMo'ed*, if death occurred on the Festival or during the Festival week.[58]

Some rule that under these circumstances, the mourner also recites Hallel.[59]

If the mourner prays in the synagogue, some rule that he recites Hallel even when Rosh Chodesh falls on an ordinary weekday.[60]

28. On the seventh day of mourning, after the mourner has already concluded sitting *shivah*, some rule that he is not permitted to recite Hallel.[61] Others

---

54. *Mishnah Berurah* 131:§§20. Two reasons are given: (1) Passages designated especially for joyous occasions should not be recited in the mourner's home; (2) in the presence of the deceased, one is careful not to do things which would seem to flaunt one's ability to perform *mitzvos*. Otherwise, one violates the prohibition called *lo'eg larash* ("ridiculing the helpless"). Hallel contains the verse: *The dead cannot praise God, nor can any who descend into silence.* Since the soul of the deceased mourns in the home of the mourner, reciting this verse would be like a violation of *lo'eg larash*.

55. *Mishnah Berurah* loc. cit. But *Shulchan Aruch HaRav* (§131) writes that the others praying there are required to recite it when they return to their homes. *Gesher HaChaim* writes: "If they wish to recite it afterwards in their home, there are authorities on whom they can rely [to do so]."

56. The *gaon* R' Zalman Margolios (*Aveilus* §1 and *Biurim*) writes: "However, if there is a clean room in the mourner's home, the congregation should go there and recite Hallel." The same ruling is given by *Gesher HaChaim* loc. cit.

57. Responsa *Noda BiYehudah tinyana Yoreh De'ah* §215. And responsa *Pri HaSadeh* (II:§104) concludes: "On Rosh Chodesh the obligation to recite Hallel is not so great. Therefore, in a house where the deceased died, even if no mourners are present, Hallel should not be recited, because of *lo'eg larash* [see above, footnote 54]. This is especially true since there is the possibility of reciting it in a different house." The same ruling is given by *Erech Shai*, *Orach Chaim* §422. When the Rebbe of Sanz, author of *Divrei Chaim*, was a mourner, he left his room [when the congregation praying there reached Hallel] on Rosh Chodesh, and the congregation recited Hallel. The same practice was followed by the *gaon* R' Y. Sh. Nathanson (*Nimukei Orach Chaim* §131).

　　Gesher HaChaim writes that if the deceased was under six years old, Hallel may be recited in the mourner's home, even if that is where the deceased died.

58. *Mishnah Berurah* §131. The reason is that at these times mourning is not observed.

59. *Mishmeres Shalom os hei* §37, citing *Sefer HaChaim*, *Orach Chaim* §526.

60. The *gaon* R' Zalman Margolios (*Aveilus* §8); and *Zachur LeAvraham*, *Yoreh De'ah*, *Hilchos Avel* §5.

61. *Yoseif Da'as* (*Yoreh De'ah* §376) writes that he should not recite it. "True, the usual rule is that the first part of the seventh day is counted as if it were a whole day [with the result that the laws of

permit it.[62]

The laws regarding whether a mourner may recite Hallel during Chanukah are presented below, chapt. 34.

◄§ Special Psalms

29. The custom is to recite Psalm 49, לַמְנַצֵּחַ לִבְנֵי קֹרַח, *For the Conductor, by the Sons of Korach*, after *Shacharis* and *Maariv*; and, according to some, after *Minchah*.[63] On the days when *Tachanun* is not recited, and also at the termination of the Sabbath, Psalm 16, מִכְתָּם לְדָוִד, *A Michtam by David*, is recited instead of Psalm 49. But on the Sabbath and *Chol HaMo'ed*, the special Psalm is omitted altogether.[64]

The question whether the mourner is permitted to recite the passages about the sacrificial services (*korbanos*) and the incense offering (*ketores*) is discussed below, chapter 21.

The laws regarding prayer in the mourner's home on the Sabbath is presented below, chapter 28.

◄§ Miscellaneous Blessings

30. The mourner should not recite the blessing over the new moon (*Kiddush Levanah*) during the *shivah* if he will have time to do so afterwards.[65] If the last day for reciting *Kiddush Levanah* will already have passed by the time his *shivah* is finished, he is permitted to go outside and recite it before then.[66] But he should not

---

mourning only apply at the beginning of the seventh day]. However, the soul of the deceased mourns [in the mourner's home] throughout the whole seventh day, and therefore the prohibition of *lo'eg larash* [see above, footnote 54] applies. Nonetheless, I permitted that the mourner could go out to a different place, and they [the congregation] could recite Hallel."

62. *Pischei Teshuvah* (376:§§2) writes: "The writings of the great *rav*, Maharar Daniel, zatzal, state: 'If the mourner's seventh day falls on Rosh Chodesh, he should recite Hallel after leaving the synagogue, for then he is no longer a mourner.' " The same ruling is given by *Kol Bo Al Aveilus* p. 283, citing *She'elas Shalom tinyana* §208: "The mourner should recite Hallel after the comforters have left his house, since the soul [of the deceased] is no longer mourning."

Da'as Kedoshim writes that those who wish to comfort the mourner on the seventh day should do so before [the morning] prayer-service, and then the mourner, too, can recite Hallel.

Responsa *Tzur Yaakov* (130:3) writes that the mourner is forbidden to go to pray early in order to end his period of mourning — and afterwards recite Hallel and be called up to the Torah. He cites responsa *Givas Shaul* (§70), who comments on the statement of *Rama*, which mentions [that the *shivah* ends] "after leaving the synagogue in a place where consolers do not come on the seventh day." He explains that this [does not refer exclusively to the specific synagogue where the mourner prayed,but] includes all the town's synagogues. [In other words, the mourner is considered to be in a period of mourning until the *Shacharis* services in his community have concluded.]

63. *Be'er HaGolah* §393.

64. *Gesher HaChaim* and *Chazon LaMo'ed*.

65. This is the ruling of *Be'ur Halachah* §426 — contrary to *Magen Avraham*, who writes that if the mourning is to end on the tenth of the month, the mourner should recite *Kiddush Levanah* [during *shivah*].

66. *Mishnah Berurah* loc. cit. §§11. And *Sha'ar HaTziyun* loc. cit. §§11 cites *Elyah Rabbah* as ruling that the mourner should recite *Kiddush Levanah* in his home if possible.

Chazon LaMo'ed (§16 note 24) cites *Teshuvah MeAhavah* as ruling that if the mourner can recite

say the customary *"Shalom Aleichem"* passage, since a mourner is forbidden to exchange greetings.[67] A mourner reciting *Kiddush Levanah* during *shivah* says only the blessing and omits the Psalms and other additions. Some permit the mourner to say, *"Shalom aleichem."* A person who is reciting *Kiddush Levanah* should not say, *"Shalom aleichem,"* to a mourner (during the twelve months after the death of a father or mother or thirty days after the death of other relatives).[67a]

31. The mourner is permitted to recite the following blessings:
> (a) *Bircas HaChamah* (for the beginning of the 28-year solar cycle).[68]
> (b) *HaGomel* (for escape from danger).[69]
> (c) *Shehecheyanu* (for joyous occasions such as the arrival of a Festival or eating a fruit that has been out of season).[70]
> (d) *HaTov VeHaMeitiv* (for the occurrence of good fortune which benefits both oneself and others).[71]

32. In the mourner's home one should not engage in *halachic* or *aggadic* discussions, but should sit silently.[72]

◦§ Mishnah Study

33. For the benefit of the soul of the deceased, it is customary to study *mishnayos* in the mourner's home throughout the *shivah*. One chooses chapters whose initial letters spell the name of the deceased.[73] Afterwards, one learns the four

---

Kiddush Levanah without going out of his house, then under all circumstances [regardless when *shivah* ends] he may recite it as early as possible [even during *shivah*].

67. *Kol Bo Al Aveilus* (p. 290) cites *Beis David* (Bistritch) §393 who writes: "If it is impossible to recite *Kiddush Levanah* in his home, the mourner should not recite it with a group of people. Rather, he should recite it by himself after the hour when most people are no longer out in the streets. Moreover, he should not say, 'Shalom aleichem,' since a mourner is forbidden to exchange greetings."
  The same ruling is cited by *Nachamu Ami* (ch. 15), in the name of *Divrei Nechemiah* §333.

67a. *Shmiras Shabbos Kehilchasah* §65 note 163, citing the gaon R' Shlomo Zalman Auerbach, *shlita*.

68. *Kol Bo Al Aveilus* p. 290, citing *Likutei Sofer* p. 29.

69. *Sdei Chemed* (*Aveilus* §52), in the name of *Yafeh LaLeiv* (part I 219:5), who cites responsa *Moharaf* part III 449:4.

70. See *Magen Avraham* (551:§§42), who writes: "We do not find that the mourner is forbidden to recite *Shehecheyanu*." The same ruling is given by *Mishnah Berurah* §§98. But *Yad Efrayim* writes that the mourner should recite *Shehecheyanu* only if not doing so would mean losing the opportunity altogether. But if he will be able to recite it after the seven days of mourning, he should not recite it during them.

71. *Kol Bo Al Aveilus* p. 281, citing *HaLeket* part II §175.

72. *Shulchan Aruch* 378:7. And *Ma'avar Yabok* (*Imrei No'am* ch. 37) writes: "It is not sufficient for the mourner to remain at home, mourning in total silence. He should refrain only from conversation and ordinary *halachos*. But it is his duty to recite many Psalms, memorial prayers, supplications, and to weep over his deceased — especially during [the first three days of mourning, which are called] the three days of weeping."

73. *Gesher HaChaim* 20:4:1. He writes there that if those particular chapters which spell the name of the deceased are not available, others may be studied, for all *mishnayos* have special power to benefit the soul of the deceased. [The Hebrew letters of the word *Mishnah* are the same as those of the word *neshamah*, soul.]

mishnayos (Mikvaos 7:4-7) whose initial letters spell the word neshamah (נְשָׁמָה, "soul"). This is followed by the prayer beginning, אָנָא, "Please. . ."[73a]. The mourner concludes by reciting Kaddish DeRabbanan, the Rabbis' Kaddish.[74]

The custom is not to study mishnayos in the mourner's home on the Sabbath or after the time of Minchah on Friday.[75]

73a. ArtScroll Ashkenaz Siddur pp. 802-808.

74. Gesher HaChaim loc. cit.

75. Gesher HaChaim loc. cit. §3.

CHAPTER SEVENTEEN

Consoling Mourners

✑ The *Mitzvah*

1. To console mourners is a major precept. Some consider this *mitzvah* to be Scripturally ordained (*deOraysa*).[1]

We find that the Holy One, Blessed is He, comforted mourners, as it is written (*Genesis* 25:11), '*After the death of Abraham, God blessed Isaac*.' The *Talmud* (*Sotah* 14a) interprets this to mean that God Himself, as it were, comforted the bereaved Isaac. Likewise, we find that God consoled Jacob in his bereavement, as *Rashi* explains on the verse (ibid. 35:9), '*. . . and He blessed him*.'

2. It is not enough merely to console the mourner; one must also say good things to him until one makes him happy, and his face becomes cheerful.[2]

✑ The Manner of Consolation

3. The comforters are not permitted to begin speaking until the mourner speaks first.[3] However, even if the mourner does not speak, one is permitted to say the customary condolence blessing: הַמָּקוֹם יְנַחֵם אֶתְכֶם . . . , "May Hashem console

---

1. See *Rabbeinu Yonah* on the *mishnah* in *Berachos* (17b): "When they have buried the deceased and gone back. . ." He writes: ". . .[the *mitzvah* of] comforting mourners is Scripturally mandated (*deOraysa*), because it is included in doing kindness to others (*gemilus chassadim*); and *gemilus chassadim* is Scripturally mandated, as the Sages proclaim (*Bava Kamma* 99a): '*And you shall make them know the way*' (*Exodus* 18:20) — this refers to *gemilus chassadim*.'" However, *Rambam* (*Hilchos Avel* 14:1) writes that the *mitzvah* is Rabbinically mandated (*deRabbanan*).
2. *Shelah* 144a. And *Ma'avar Yabok* (*Imrei No'am*, chapt. 35) writes: "It is obligatory upon the comforters in the home of the mourner to pray for mercy for the deceased; for the ordinary conversation customarily conducted there is only a burden, not a comfort."
   Responsa *Sheivet HaLevi* (*Yoreh De'ah* §213) writes that the *Zohar* (*Parashas Korach*) implies that before a person goes in to console the mourner, he should carefully consider what he will say and how he will comfort him.
   Prishah (393:3) comments on the words of *Tur*, who wrote there: "They sit for a period of time." He points out that *Tur* did not write, "They sit and speak words of consolation," but only afterwards wrote: "They say: 'May He Who dwells in this home comfort you.'" From this *Prishah* infers a certain amount of support for the current custom of comforting mourners, whereby, usually, the mourner does not open any dialogue at all. People come into his home, sit awhile, and then say: '*May Hashem console you among the other mourners of Zion and Jerusalem*.' One must ask: Is this called comforting mourners? But, *Prishah* concludes, from the words of *Tur* one may draw some evidence that simply entering the home and sitting there to show respect to the mourner is called comforting him.
3. *Shulchan Aruch* 376:1.

you. . ." (see paragraph 5).[4]

4. Once the mourner nods his head in a manner indicating that he has dismissed the comforters, they are not permitted to remain sitting with him.[5]

5. Upon entering or leaving the mourner's home, the visitor should not extend greetings to him, because such greeting are not appropriate to one who is grieving.[6] When the visitor gets up to leave, he should say:

הַמָּקוֹם יְנַחֵם אֶתְכֶם בְּתוֹךְ שְׁאָר אֲבֵלֵי צִיּוֹן וִירוּשָׁלָיִם,

"May Hashem console you among the other mourners of Zion and Jerusalem."[7]

The mourners should reply, *"Amen."*[8]

One should not say things as, "I haven't received all the punishment I deserve," because one should not imply to the Accuser that further punishment is in order. Similarly, one should not tell the mourner, "What can you do? There's no way to change things," because this is an insult [to Heaven], implying that if it were possible, one would change things. Instead, one should lovingly accept the decree of Hashem, Blessed is He.[8a]

◄§ The Time for Comforting

6. Some have the custom not pay a condolence call until after the third day of mourning,[9] but others rule that one may perform the *mitzvah* even during the first three days.[10] In any case, if it is difficult to go after the third day, one may do so during the first three days.[11] It is also permitted to comfort mourners at

---

4. *Nachamu Ami* chapt. 21, in the name of the *gaon*, R' Shlomo Zalman Auerbach, *shlita*.
5. *Shulchan Aruch* loc. cit.
6. *Shulchan Aruch* 385:1.
7. *Prishah* 393:3 (cited above, footnote 2).
8. *Nachamu Ami*, in the name of the *gaon*, R' Shlomo Zalman Auerbach, *shlita*.
8a. *Rama* 376:2.
9. See *Gesher HaChaim* (20:5:5), who explains that the first three days are for weeping (*Mo'ed Katan* 27), and during that time the grief is most intense.
   Da'as Torah (§376) writes: "It was pointed out to me that *Midrash Tanchuma* (*Parashas Miketz*) implies that during the first three days one does not accept consolation."
   Mishmeres Shalom (os nun §12) cites responsa *Tuv Ta'am* (*mahadura* 3, part 2, end of §10): "The custom is not to comfort the mourner until the third day, for that is when the 'three days of weeping' end; and part of the [last] day is counted as a whole day." See also *Da'as U'Mezimah*, who writes: "This custom has its source in the words of *Midrash Rabbah* (*Vayikra*): 'For the first three days, grief is at its strongest, since the facial features [of the deceased] are still recognizable.' According to *Yedei Moshe*, this means that during this time it is as if the deceased is still alive; therefore the mourner does not accept consolation."
10. *Da'as Torah* (loc. cit.) writes: "However, in my humble opinion, the Gemara in *Mo'ed Katan* (21a), with *Rashi* and *Rosh* there, proves [that the mourner may be comforted during the first three days]. . ." *Kol Bo Al Aveilus* (p. 297) writes: "There is explicit evidence in *Kesubos* (8b) that one is permitted [to comfort the mourner during the first three days]; and likewise I have heard from a number of great scholars that they deliberately go to comfort the mourner during the first three days, since there are not many other comforters then."
11. *Gesher HaChaim* loc. cit.

night.[12]

7. The *mitzvah* of consoling a mourner takes precedence over that of visiting the sick, if it is impossible to do both.[13] This is because comforting the mourner is an act of kindness to both the living and the dead.[14]

‌⋇ Consoling an Enemy

8. One should not attempt to console a mourner who is one's enemy, because the mourner would think that the comforter is happy about his misfortune, and this would only cause him anguish. However, this depends on the individual case — on the severity of the enmity and the character of the adversaries.[15]

‌⋇ On the Sabbath

9. The custom in most Ashkenazic congregations is that on Friday eve, before the congregation recites מִזְמוֹר שִׁיר לְיוֹם הַשַּׁבָּת, *"A psalm, a song for the Sabbath day,"* the mourner enters the synagogue, and the *shamash* announces, "Come forth towards the mourner." Then the congregation consoles him. [See also 28:5].[16] If the death occurred during a Festival, see below, 33:19.

10. One may console mourners on the Sabbath, but it is better (*lechatchilah*) to perform the *mitzvah* only on an ordinary weekday.[17] If one does comfort a mourner on the Sabbath, one should not do so in the same manner as on the weekday.[18] Instead, one should say:

שַׁבָּת הִיא מִלְּנַחֵם וּנְחָמָה קְרוּבָה לָבוֹא,

"The Sabbath is not a time to console, but consolation will swiftly come."[19]

Some rule leniently, permitting one to say the traditional consolation blessing: הַמָּקוֹם יְנַחֵם אֶתְכֶם . . . , "May Hashem comfort you. . ."[20]

---

12. *Kol Bo Al Aveilus* (loc. cit.) states that the custom in a number of communities is not to go to comfort mourners at night. "But the truth is that we find in *Job* 2:13 that [Job's] comforters sat with him 'seven days and seven nights;' and a number of *halachos* are derived from the Book of *Job*. Therefore it would seem that the custom of not comforting mourners at night has no basis (*Ginzei Yosef* 74)." The same ruling is given by *Gesher HaChaim*.

13. See above, 1:10, where this *halachah* of precedence is discussed.

14. *Rambam, Hilchos Avel* 14:7. The same ruling is given by *Rama* 335:10, in the name of *Kol Bo*.

15. *Rama* 335:2, and *Shach* ad loc. §§2.

16. *Be'er HaGolah* §393.

17. *Shulchan Aruch Orach Chaim* 287:1. "The *Gemara* says, 'Only with difficulty did they permit comforting mourners on the Sabbath.' Therefore, it is not proper to do as some people do, not going to comfort the mourner during the week, but only on the Sabbath." (*Mishnah Berurah* 287:§§1)

18. The reason is that this would cause them pain and arouse weeping; and it is forbidden to do that on the Sabbath (*Mishnah Berurah* ad loc. §§2).

19. *Mishnah Berurah* loc. cit. §§3, citing "*Taz* and other *Acharonim*." The same ruling is given by *Maharshal*.

20. *Tur* (*Yoreh De'ah* §393) writes that one is permitted to say, הַמָּקוֹם יְנַחֶמְךָ, "May Hashem comfort you." *Drishah* (ad loc.) explains the reason. Likewise, *Mishnah Berurah* (ad loc.) cites *Magen Avraham*, who states in the name of *Drishah* that some rule leniently.

One also may comfort mourners on *Yom Tov* or *Chol HaMo'ed*.[21] For details on this subject, see below, chapt. 33.

⋅§ Condolence Calls to Women

11. The custom is that men also console women who are in mourning. If the mourners are all women, men go there accompanied by other men; or, if the men pray at the house of the women who are in mourning, they console them in public, after the prayer-service.[22]

⋅§ Comforting Mourners by Telephone

12. One authority rules that one should not comfort mourners by telephone. This is because the *mitzvah* is an act of kindness not only to the mourner, but also to the deceased, whose soul grieves at the house of the mourner.[23] Therefore, if it is possible to go to the mourner's home, one cannot fulfill the *mitzvah* by telephone. However, if it is impossible to go there, one is obligated to do as much as possible, and should comfort the mourner by telephone.[24] The mourner is permitted to speak on the telephone for such a purpose;[25] however, such calls should be kept brief.

However, *Kaf HaChaim* (287:4) writes: "*Shiyurei Knesses HaGedolah* (§20) states that the custom now is that when visiting the sick on the Sabbath one says, שַׁבָּת הִיא מִלִּזְעוֹק וּרְפוּאָה קְרוֹבָה לָבוֹא, 'The Sabbath is not a time for crying out, but healing will swiftly come,' and no more. But in comforting mourners one says שַׁבְּתוּ בְשָׁלוֹם, 'May you have a peaceful Sabbath' and no more. Likewise, *Mateh Yehudah* (§1) writes: 'In some communities the custom is not to recite any consolations on the Sabbath; they just enter and sit a little while, and nothing else.' And this is a good custom."

Kol Bo Al Aveilus (p. 298) cites *Nimukei Orach Chaim*: "The generation is a worthy one, and today people refrain from comforting mourners on the Sabbath and Festivals, for this involves many pitfalls." The same ruling is given by *Gesher HaChaim*, who states that in our time the custom is not to comfort mourners on the Sabbath and *Yom Tov*.

21. "If they permitted on the Sabbath, all the more so during *Chol HaMo'ed*" — *Kaf HaChaim* 287:§§3.

22. *Gesher HaChaim* 20:5:1. He asks: If men are permitted to comfort women in mourning, why is there a custom not to form the *shurah* (two parallel lines of comforters) for a woman mourner following the interment (see above, 10:22)? The answer he gives is that in general the custom is to be careful not to allow women to accompany the deceased to the cemetery. Therefore, even if they do go there, the custom is not to comfort them there. The same ruling is given by responsa *Chelkas Yaakov* part 3 §38. [However, see above 10:22, that many communities — especially outside of *Eretz Yisrael* — do have the custom to form a *shurah* and comfort women mourners on the cemetery, and the custom varies according to the *chevra kaddisha* of each city and congregation.]

23. Responsa *Minchas David* §72,73. [See *Shabbos* 152b: "A certain man died in the neighborhood of R' Yehudah. As there were no mourners to be comforted, R' Yehudah assembled ten men every day and they sat in his place. After seven days, the deceased appeared to R' Yehudah in a dream and said to him, 'May your mind be at rest, for you have set my mind at rest.' "]

24. Responsa *Igros Moshe*, *Orach Chaim* part IV:§40:11: ". . . for one should not say, 'Since I cannot *personally* visit the mourner, there is no obligation upon me of any kind.' "

25. *Igros Moshe* ibid. He rules that a mourner is allowed to speak on the telephone regarding any matters that it is otherwise permitted for him to speak about, for example necessary household requirements that are his responsibility, such as arranging for a *minyan*. Similarly he may receive a telephone call of consolation. However, he may not use the telephone for mundane matters, or to inquire about the welfare of others—even of his children.

◦§ Consoling a Mourner After *Shivah*

13. If one did not comfort a mourner during his *shivah*, one may still do so until the thirtieth day of mourning. After the thirtieth day, one does not recite the usual consolation formula, but simply tells him, תִּתְנַחֵם, "May you be comforted."

The above applies to someone who is mourning for a family member other than his father or mother. If he is in mourning for his father or mother, one may comfort him in the usual manner within the first twelve months. After the twelve months, however, one simply tells him, תִּתְנַחֵם, "May you be comforted."[26]

---

26. *Shulchan Aruch* §385:2.

CHAPTER EIGHTEEN

The Prohibition Against Work

✑ Work by the Mourner

1. The mourner is forbidden to work for the entire first seven days of mourning.

During the first three days,[1] he is forbidden to work even if he is a poor person whose income is from charity.[2] After the first three days, if he is poor and does not have enough to eat,[3] he is permitted to work in an inconspicuous manner in his home. However, the Sages proclaimed that a curse will come upon the neighbors if they leave the mourner in circumstances whereby he is forced to work after the first three days.[4]

2. Some rule that these must be three full days, and that for this *halachah* we do not apply the rule that מִקְצָת הַיּוֹם כְּכֻלּוֹ, "part of the [last] day counts as a whole day."[5] Others rule that for this *halachah*, too, part of the last day counts as a whole day.[6]

3. The mourner is forbidden to write personal letters or other things which are not necessary. However, he is permitted to write down his daily financial transactions and calculations of expenses, since not doing so [might result in his forgetting and thereby] would cause him a loss (*davar ha'aveid*).[7]

---

1. "Talmud *Yerushalmi* explains the reason why the *halachah* is more strict for the first three days than for the remaining ones: For three days, the soul flutters over the body, believing that it will return to it. When it sees that the facial features [of the deceased] have changed, it leaves the vicinity of the body and goes away. And Rabbeinu Yerucham gives another reason, citing *Ravad*: The Sages said (*Mo'ed Katan* 27a) that the first three days are for weeping; and if the mourner works, he will be negligent about weeping" (*Beis Yosef* §380).

2. *Bach*, *Yoreh De'ah* §380.

3. *Shulchan Aruch* 380:2.

4. Ibid.

5. R' Akiva Eiger loc. cit., citing *Chochmas Adam, Kuntres Matzeivas Moshe* §4. The same ruling is given by *Be'ur HaGra* 386:6; and by *S'dei Chemed, Ma'areches Aveilus* §38, citing *Kevod Yom Tov*. Moreover, he saw the rabbis of his generation ruling this way in practice. *Moharit* (loc. cit.) writes that, in his opinion, they must be three full days.

6. *Rama* 393:1 and *Da'as Torah* loc. cit. And see *Zachur LeAvraham* (*Hilchos Avel* §40), who cites *Ginas Veradim* as ruling, likewise, that even on the third day, part of the day is counted as a whole day. See also *Eshkol* (*Hilchos Mo'ed Katan Ve'Aveilus* §48), who rules explicitly that in the matter of work, part of the third day is counted as a whole day. The same ruling is given by *S'dei Chemed* (loc. cit.) in the name of *Yad HaMelech* (*Hilchos Avel* 5:7), and by *Gesher HaChaim* 21:1:7.

7. *Rama* 380:2. He maintains that in cases that it is permitted to write on *Chol HaMo'ed*, as defined in *Shulchan Aruch Orach Chaim* §545, it is similarly permitted for the mourner to write during *shivah*. See also *Aruch HaShulchan*, *Yoreh De'ah* 380:10.

4. Just as he is forbidden to work, so is he forbidden to engage in business; for example, buying and selling merchandise.[8]

5. The mourner is forbidden to work even if this will result in financial loss (*davar ha'aveid*).[9] If not working will result in financial loss, the mourner should have someone else do the work for him. If there is no one to do it for him, the *halachah* is explained below, par. 6.

According to *halachah*, when a man's wife works, the money she earns belongs to him. The same applies to earnings of his children — even grown children — whom he is supporting. Therefore, the same prohibition against work that applies to him applies also to his wife,[10] his sons and daughters (even adult ones) whom he is supporting,[11] and his male or female slaves.[12]

Some rule that if he relinquishes his right to the earnings of his wife or children during his period of mourning, they are permitted to work in an inconspicuous manner.[12a]

✤ The Work of Others

6. The ruling of *Shulchan Aruch* is as follows:

The mourner is forbidden to have others, even non-Jews, do work for him — unless this would result in financial loss (*davar ha'aveid*). In that case, he is permitted to have others do work for him — even the kind of work which is forbidden during *Chol HaMo'ed* because of the strenuous effort involved, and even if it is skilled work (*ma'aseh oman*).[13]

Rama adds: "Some rule that if it is impossible to have the work done by others, and if not doing it will result in financial loss,[14] the mourner is permitted to do it himself, even if it involves effort and is the kind of work which requires professional skill.[15]

---

8. *Shulchan Aruch* 380:3.

9. Ibid. 380:4.

10. *Shulchan Aruch* (loc. cit.) does not mention his wife. However, *Da'as Kedoshim* (loc. cit.) writes that the prohibition also applies to his wife, because according to *halachah*, whatever his wife earns belongs to him; therefore when she works, it is as if she is acting as his agent to perform his work.

11. *Shach* 380:§§3, citing *Tur* and *Ateres Zekeinim*. What he means is that the prohibition applies even to adult sons and daughters whom he is supporting, and all the more so to young children (not yet *bar mitzvah*) whom he is supporting. But if he is not supporting them, even young children may work, since in that case their earnings belong to them, as is explained by *Shulchan Aruch* in *Choshen Mishpat* 74:2.

12. *Shulchan Aruch* loc. cit.

12a. *Da'as Kedoshim* loc. cit. (with regard to the wife). And *Chazon LaMo'ed* 17 (note 14) writes: "It would seem that the same applies to his sons and daughters — i.e., he may also relinquish his right to their earnings."

13. *Shulchan Aruch* 380:5. The reason is explained by *Shach* (380:§§4, citing *Tur*): Work involving strenuous effort is forbidden during *Chol HaMo'ed* because it would detract from the honor of the Festival. But when a mourner has others perform work for him, there is no objection to their exerting strenuous effort.

14. See *Chiddushei R' Akiva Eiger* loc. cit.

15. *Shach* 380:§§5.

And after the first three days, one should be lenient [i.e., follow the ruling just cited]. Even during the first three days, one should be lenient if a large loss is involved. However, he should do the work inconspicuously."[16]

If it is the kind of work which cannot be done inconspicuously, some rule that it may be done publicly; but others forbid this. Still others rule that it may be done publicly, but only after the first three days.[17]

However, under certain arrangements described below (par. 19-23), it may be permitted for people to perform work that will benefit the mourner.

☙ Doing Business to Prevent Loss

7. In order to prevent a loss,[18] the mourner is permitted to have others sell merchandise for him.

For this purpose, "loss" (*davar ha'aveid*) means that already existing capital will be lost. The permission applies even if there is only doubt as to whether a loss will be incurred.[19] If there will be no loss of existing capital, but selling now will mean a higher profit than selling later,[20] this is not within the category of *davar ha'aveid*, and the mourner is forbidden to sell, or even to have others sell for him.

If caravans or ships arrive, or if they are about to depart, and the merchants in them are selling at low prices or buying at high prices, the mourner is permitted to have people buy or sell for him. This applies even if he does not want the merchandise for his personal use, but only to do business and make a profit.[21]

☙ Loans

8. If non-Jews are accustomed to borrow from him at interest, the mourner is permitted to have people lend to them, since not doing so would cause a loss (*davar ha'aveid*).[22] One authority rules that it is likewise permitted to have people sell merchandise to those who are accustomed to buy from him.[22a]

☙ Collecting Debts

9. If someone owes the mourner money, and the debtor is available now but will not be available after *shivah*, the mourner may send someone to collect the debt.[23] The same applies if, for some other reason, the mourner will incur a loss if

---

16. Ibid. §§6.

17. See *Mishmeres Shalom os kof* §19; and *Sdei Chemed, Aveilus os* 211.

18. *Shulchan Aruch* 380:6. And see *Pischei Teshuvah*, loc. cit., §§2.

19. *Shulchan Aruch* loc. cit. And see *Be'ur Halachah* §539 s.v. *yafsid*.

20. This applies even if he believes that by selling now he will make a large profit; because forgoing profit is not considered "loss" [הַעֲבָרַת רֶיוַח לֹא מִקְרֵי פְּסֵידָא] (*Mishnah Berurah* 539:§§15).

21. *Shulchan Aruch* 380:6. The reason is that this is an unusual occurrence (*Shach* §§7).

22. Ibid. 380:7. The reason is that if he does not lend to them, they will go to someone else, who will accustom them to do business with him; thus a loss is involved (*Shach* §§8).

22a. *Chochmas Adam* 164:5.

23. *Shulchan Aruch* 380:8. And *Shach* (loc. cit. §§9) explains that this is in the category of "loss" (*davar ha'aveid*).

he does not collect the debt now.[24]

◌§ Lawsuits

10. During *shivah*, the mourner is forbidden to take someone to court. If delaying
the lawsuit would mean loss (*davar ha'aveid*) — for example, if the person
he wants to sue is about to leave the country, or if the witnesses are ill and he is afraid
they might die — he should appoint an agent to conduct the lawsuit for him.[25]

◌§ *Chol HaMo'ed*

11. During *Chol HaMo'ed*, the Intermediate Days of Pesach and Succos, Jews are
forbidden to work. Certain types of work, however, are permitted because
> (a) not doing them would involve loss (*davar ha'aveid*); or
> (b) they are essential for the needs of the festival week.

All types of work which are permitted during *Chol HaMo'ed* due to reason (b), but
not due to reason (a), are forbidden for the mourner to do or even to have others
do for him.[26]

◌§ A Doctor

12. A doctor who is in mourning may go to attend a patient, even if there is
another doctor attending to that patient.[27]

The mourner is permitted to have his blood let.[28]

◌§ A Scribe

13. A scribe [*sofer*] who is in mourning is permitted to write a *get* [bill of divorce]
if there is apprehension that otherwise the woman might become an *agunah*,
i.e., unable to remarry for lack of a proper divorce.[29]

◌§ A *Shochet*

14. Some rule that if a city's ritual slaughterer [*shochet*] is in mourning, and there
is no one else who can slaughter, he is permitted to slaughter on his premises.
If this is impossible, he may go to another's premises to slaughter, but only at night.
If it is impossible to go at night, he may go even during the day. This applies even

---

24. *Mishnah Berurah* 539:§§3. And see *Chochmas Adam* (loc. cit. par. 6), who writes: "I wrote
there, in the name of *Taz*, that in our day it is permitted to collect debts during *Chol HaMo'ed*,
because all debts are considered to involve risk. According to that, the same would apply to the
mourner. Thus it seems to me that under all circumstances [the mourner] is permitted [to collect
debts]."

25. *Shulchan Aruch* 380:9.

26. Ibid. 380:10.

27. The reason is that not everyone is capable of curing the specific patient (*Sdei Chemed*, *Aveilus*
§44, citing responsa *Chayei Adam* §86). The same ruling is given by *Pischei Teshuvah* 380:§§1,
citing *Chamudei Daniel*; and by *Mishmeres Shalom os dalet* §13.

28. *Taz* §§1. According to contemporary *Poskim*, this applies also to general medical procedures.

29. Responsa *HaElef Lecha Shlomo* §311.

if he receives a weekly salary from the congregation for slaughtering. However, he may not take payment for each fowl or animal that he slaughters, unless he is poor and does not have enough to eat. In that case, after the first three days of mourning he is permitted to take payment for each fowl or animal.[30]

Others rule that he is forbidden to slaughter anything except what he himself wishes to eat.[31]

❧ Housework

15. Housework, such as baking and cooking, washing dishes, sweeping floors, and making beds, is not included in the work forbidden to a mourner. Therefore, he may do as much housework as he needs. However, he is forbidden to do unnecessary housework.[32]

Some write that a woman who is in mourning and who has guests may bake and cook not only for her own family, but for the guests, too, since they are considered like members of her household, even if she receives payment for this.[33]

A housemaid who is in mourning may do all necessary housework, even if she receives payment for her work. However, she is forbidden to do work that is not needed for the house, in order to earn money. She is certainly forbidden to work for profit outside the house.[33a]

❧ The Hired Worker

16. A mourner who is a hired worker is forbidden to work for his employer during *shivah*. However, he is permitted to send someone to work instead of him.[34]

Some authorities are strict in this matter (they do not permit sending a substitute), unless loss (*davar ha'aveid*) would result.[35]

17. If people had given the mourner work to do (such as making a piece of furniture for them, or repairing an appliance), he is forbidden to work on it,[36] even if he could do it inconspicuously.[37] This applies whether, as an inde-

---

30. *Chochmas Adam* 164:12. The same ruling is given by *Kuntres Matzeivas Moshe* §7. And see *Kol Bo Al Aveilus* (p. 290), who writes that the *gaon*, R' Shlomo Kluger, agreed with this ruling.
31. *Gilyon Maharsha* on 380:16.
32. *Shulchan Aruch* and *Rama* 380:22. Regarding mopping the floor, see below, chapt. 36.
33. *Aruch HaShulchan* 380:32. See responsa *Zera Emes* part 2 §150.
33a. *Shulchan Aruch* loc. cit.
34. This is analogous to the sharecropper (*aris*) mentioned by *Shulchan Aruch* (380:12), since the substitute is not considered to be doing the mourner's work, but his employer's (*Shach* 380:§§13).
35. *Shach* loc. cit. §§17 and §§19. See *Da'as Torah* (loc. cit.) who cites *Sefer Yehoshua, Pesakim U'Kesavim* (§20), as concluding that both R' Yosef Caro and *Rama* are referring to a case of *davar ha'aveid*.
36. *Shulchan Aruch* 380:17.
37. *Shulchan Aruch* (loc. cit.) writes: ". . .even [if the work involves] something not connected to the land, as with weaving." And *Shach* (loc. cit. §§18) explains that the advantage of such work is that it can be done in an inconspicuous manner. Even so, it is forbidden. All the more so, the mourner is

pendent contractor, he is paid a fixed sum for the total job (*kablanus*), or whether he receives payment for his time, such as a fixed amount per week.[38] If not working on it would cause a loss (*davar ha'aveid*), he may have someone do it for him.[39]

◄§ Accepting Work for After *Shivah*

18. The mourner is permitted to accept work during *shivah* in order to work on it after *shivah*. However, he should not weigh or measure things as he normally would.[40]

◄§ Employing Others

19. A mourner's employees may not work for him during *shivah*. However, if they are legally independent, as noted above, they are permitted to work. One such arrangement is that of a *kablan*, or independent contractor, who receives a fixed sum for his finished work, but he makes his own hours and conditions and is not under the direct control and supervision of the mourner. Common examples of *kablanus* are laundry sent to a cleaner, or furniture ordered from a carpenter. A *kablan* may perform the mourner's work under the following conditions:

    (a) The work is not recognizable as belonging to the mourner.

    (b) The person works on his own premises, but not on the premises of the mourner.[41]

If it is recognizable that the work is being done on behalf of the mourner — for example, if men are building a house for him — they are forbidden to work on it. This applies even if they are wage-earners, but are paid a fixed sum for finishing the work (*kablanus*), and even if the building is outside the city.[42]

20. People may work a field owned by a mourner under any of the following circumstances:

    (a) Sharecropper (*arisus*): a person who works the land in return for a percentage of the crop.

    (b) Tenant farmer (*chakirus*): a person who works the owner's land and keeps the crop for himself, paying the owner a fixed amount of the field's produce, no matter what the size of the crop.

    (c) Contractor (*kablanus*): a person who is paid a fixed sum to work the land for the owner. Since the contractor's payment is not dependent on the amount of time he worked or the size of the crop, he is considered to be independent rather than an employee of the mourner.[43]

---

forbidden to do work involving something connected to the land (such as plowing or reaping), which must be done out in the open where all can see.

38. *Shulchan Aruch* loc. cit.

39. *Rama* loc. cit.

40. *Rama* 380:17, citing *Mordechai*.

41. *Shulchan Aruch* and *Rama* 380:18. And see *Sdei Chemed*, *Aveilus* §32.

42. *Shulchan Aruch* loc. cit. 380:19, and *Shach* loc. cit. §§21.

43. *Shach* §§12.

These types of workers are permitted to work the field even if their contract had expired before the owner became a mourner, but they go on working the field as usual on the assumption that the contractual arrangement will continue.[44]

21. If people have an arrangement to use the mourner's property [the examples of property given in *Shulchan Aruch* are a donkey or a ship], they may go on using it if the following conditions are fulfilled:

    (a) The arrangement began before the owner became a mourner.

    (b) The time of the arrangement has not expired.

However, if the time of the arrangement has expired — and all the more so if the arrangement began after the owner became a mourner — the mourner's property may not be used.

This applies whether payment is monetary (*sechirus*) or in kind (*chakirus*).[45]

22. If the arrangement is that the people use the mourner's property to produce income, in return for a percentage of the income, some rule that they may continue using it. Others rule that they may not.[46]

23. If someone had contracted to plow or sow the owner's field for a lump sum, some rule that he may continue plowing or sowing during the owner's seven days of mourning.[47] Others forbid this.[48]

◄§ Partners

24. If people are partners in a business or a store, and one of them becomes a mourner, they must close the business or store during the seven days of mourning.[49]

The partners who are not in mourning are forbidden to work in the store or the business,[49a] even if the mourner will not receive a share of the profits for those

---

44. *Shulchan Aruch* 380:11. See *Aruch HaShulchan* 380:19.

45. *Shulchan Aruch* 380:14.

46. Ibid. 380:15. *Shach* (loc. cit. §§16) explains why, according to some, the use of property such as a donkey or ship is prohibited, even though the use of land under the same type of arrangement is permitted. The reason is that with land this is a common arrangement, but not with a donkey or ship. Therefore, people seeing someone working the owner's land will realize that this is the arrangement. But if they see someone working with his donkey or ship, they might suspect him of employing hired workers during his period of mourning.

47. *Shulchan Aruch* 380:20. According to *Be'ur HaGra* (loc. cit. §§26), this is analogous to the case of the contractor mentioned by *Shulchan Aruch* 380:11 (see above, par. 20).

48. *Shulchan Aruch* 380:20. *Aruch HaShulchan* (380:24) explains the difference between contracting to produce the crop (see above, par. 20) and contracting just to plow or sow. When someone contracts to produce the crop, people regard the land as if it belongs to the contractor during the period of the contract. Therefore all authorities permit him to go on working when the owner is a mourner. But when someone contracts for only a specific task such as plowing or sowing, the land does not appear to become his. Therefore some *Poskim* forbid him to go on working when the owner is a mourner.

49. See par. 28 below.

49a. *Shulchan Aruch* 380:21. And *Aruch HaShulchan* (380:27) writes: "It would seem that this prohibition applies even if it will result in a loss (*davar ha'aveid*)."

days.[50] However, the non-mourning partners are permitted to conduct the business of the partnership in an inconspicuous manner in their homes.[51]

If the mourner is a prominent person, and the business is referred to by his name, it will be known that he has a part in it even if the other partners conduct business in an inconspicuous manner in their own home. In such a case, the other partners are forbidden to conduct the business of the partnership even in their own homes.[52]

Some authorities are lenient, permitting the non-mourning partners to work, even on the premises of the business, after the first three days of mourning.[53] The generally accepted custom is to follow this leniency.[54]

The above applies only if the partnership includes both the premises and the merchandise. However, if they are simply partners in owning or renting the premises, but each conducts business with his own separate merchandise, the prohibitions regarding partnership and mourning do not apply. In that case, if one of the partners becomes a mourner, the others are permitted to continue dealing in their own merchandise.[55] Some authorities are lenient and rule that in this case, if necessary, even the mourner may hire someone to stay in the store and sell his merchandise for him.[56]

25. Some rule that if the partners operate separate stores, each one working in his own store, but they are partners in the combined profits, each of the non-mourning partners may open his store, even on the first day of mourning.[57]

26. If Partner X does not know of the death of his family member, Partner Y is permitted to open the store, even if he knows that Partner X's family member died.[58]

Likewise, the members of Partner X's household may open his store, and they are not required to inform him of the death.[59]

---

50. *Gesher HaChaim* 21:2:7. The same ruling is implied by the *Poskim* cited below.

51. *Shulchan Aruch* 380:21. See *Shach* §§23. See also *Pischei Teshuvah* loc. cit. §§5; and ibid. §§6, citing responsa *Ranach* part 2 §93.

52. *Shulchan Aruch* 380:21.

53. *Chiddushei R' Akiva Eiger* loc. cit. citing *Maharshal*.

54. *Chochmas Adam* 164:16, and *Matzeivas Moshe*.

55. *Aruch HaShulchan* 380:29, cited by *Gesher HaChaim* loc. cit.

56. *Aruch HaShulchan* loc. cit. cited by *Gesher HaChaim* 21:2:9.

57. *Moram* of Trani, quoted by *Beis Lechem Yehudah* (loc. cit.). He cites *Shiurei Knesses HaGedolah* as ruling that the partner may open his store only after the third day. However, *Ikrei HaDat* (36:30) writes that "in the laws of mourning, the *halachah* follows the lenient opinion," and the non-mourning partner may open his store [even on the first day]. The same ruling is given by *Gesher HaChaim* loc. cit.

58. *Birkei Yosef* loc. cit., citing *Zekan Aharon* §61, and *Devar Moshe*, *Yoreh De'ah* §71. And *Kol Bo Al Aveilus* (p. 322) writes the same, citing *Beis Meir* (*Yoreh De'ah*, §380). The same ruling is given by *Sdei Chemed* (*Aveilus* 7); by *Aruch HaShulchan*; and by *Gesher HaChaim* (loc. cit.), who cites *Ikrei HaDat*, adding: "There is much evidence for this."

59. *Aruch HaShulchan* 380:29, citing *Radbaz*. The same ruling is cited by *Sdei Chemed* (loc. cit.), citing *Kerem Shlomo*, end of §402. *Beis Meir* (loc. cit.) writes the same, as does *Chiddushei R' Akiva Eiger* loc. cit.

If the people of the town know of the death, but do not realize that Partner X has not been informed, the members of Partner X's household should preferably close the store, in order to avoid giving a false impression (*mar'is ayin*). Otherwise, people might think that Partner X opened his store while he was in mourning.[60]

27. If one member of a partnership dies, and the deceased partner's heirs are *not* mourners [because they are not among the immediate family members who are required to mourn, as listed above, 6:1], the surviving partners are permitted to open the store or business, even on the first day of mourning.[61]

If, however, in the above case where one of the partners dies and the deceased partner's heirs are mourners, some authorities rule that the same *halachos* apply as in the case of partners, one of whom is in mourning (see par. 26, above). Thus, the surviving partners are forbidden to open their store, at least during the first three days of mourning.[62] But other authorities permit the surviving partners to open their store even on the first day of mourning. They reason that when the partner died, the partnership was annulled.[63]

28. In practice, some communities have adopted the following custom. If a member of a partnership becomes a mourner, he removes himself from the partnership before the burial.[64] This is accomplished by a transaction known as *kinyan sudar* (confirmed by exchanging a handkerchief or other item),[65] in the presence of a representative of the Beth Din, or in the presence of the city fathers. This makes it public that the mourning partner has no share in the profits during his *shivah*. Then the non-mourning partners may open the store, since there is no further risk of giving a false impression (*mar'is ayin*).[66]

◄§ Renting Out Facilities

29. The town baker [and similar kinds of businessmen], to whom most of the town's residents pay a fee for the use of his oven, may permit someone to conduct his business after the first three days of mourning. However, he may not make a profit, but is permitted only to recoup the cost of the firewood and his

---

60. *Gesher HaChaim* writes this in the name of *Ach LeTzarah*, who in turn cites *Machaneh Chaim* (part 3 *Yoreh De'ah* §55), adding: "This is logical."

61. *Gesher HaChaim*, loc. cit.

62. *Sdei Chemed*, *Aveilus* §36.

63. *Kol Bo Al Aveilus* p. 324, citing *Tel Talpios Marsach* p. 92. And see *Gesher HaChaim* loc. cit. *os* 13.

64. See *Gilyon Maharsha* loc. cit. citing *Shev Yaakov*. See also responsa *Chasam Sofer* §325 cited in *Pischei Teshuvah,* loc. cit. §§20.

65. *Sdei Chemed*, *Aveilus* §6, in the name of *Kerem Shlomo*, who cites *Teshuvah MeAhavah* and *Leshon Chachamim*. But *Shevus Yaakov* states that a purely oral agreement is sufficient, without any confirmatory act such as passing a handkerchief.

66. See *Da'as Torah* (loc. cit.), who writes: "In my humble opinion, to avoid the danger of giving a false impression (*mar'is ayin*), a notice should be put on the entrance of the store, informing the public that the store does not belong to the mourner."

expenses for the use of the oven.

If he is a poor man, the *halachah* is lenient and permits him to operate the business in any manner [even for profit] after the first three days of mourning.[67] One authority writes that for a poor man, the *halachah* is lenient even during the first three days.[68]

◄§ Employing Workers

30. Some write that if a businessman employs workers, and must pay their salary even if they do not work, they may work for him on his premises even during the first three days of his mourning. The reason is that this is very clearly an instance where not working would result in loss (*davar ha'aveid*; see above, par.6).[69]

◄§ If the Mourner Works When Not Permitted

31. If a mourner, during *shivah*, performs work which is forbidden to him, he is placed under a ban [*nidui*],[70] and it is forbidden to go to console him.[71]

---

67. *Mishmeres Shalom os mem* §46, citing *Zachur LeAvraham* (*Yoreh De'ah, Hilchos Avel* §40).

68. *Mishmeres Shalom* (loc. cit.) writes: "According to what was explained above, *os dalet* §§1, one may rule leniently for a poor man even during the first three days."

69. *Aruch HaShulchan* 380:6. And see ibid. 380:22, cited by *Gesher HaChaim* loc. cit. §3.

70. *Taz* 380:§§1, citing *Kol Bo*. The same ruling is given by *Birkei Yosef* §§2, citing *Rash*, the son of *Rashbatz*, responsum 214.

71. *Shibolei HaLeket, Hilchos Semachos* §35. The same ruling is given by *Tanya Rabbasi* §65.

CHAPTER NINETEEN

Bathing and the Use of Lotions

The *halachos* set forth in paragraphs 1-7 apply to the first seven days of mourning, the *shivah* period. Unless otherwise stated, they also apply until the thirtieth day (*shloshim*). For leniencies and other laws which take effect at the end of the first seven days, see below, paragraphs 8-16.

◆§ Bathing

1. The prohibition against bathing depends upon whether one bathes the entire body or only part of it, and also upon the temperature of the water. Showering is included in this prohibition.

Washing the entire body, even in cold water, is forbidden.[1] But washing face, hands and feet is only forbidden if the water is hot or lukewarm.[2] Washing them in cold water is permitted.

According to the basic *halachah*, the prohibition against bathing applies only during *shivah*. However, the custom is to refrain during the first thirty days. For differences in the *halachah* which take effect at the end of the first seven days, see below, paragraphs 8-16.[3]

2. If one becomes dirty with mud or excrement, one may wash oneself in the usual manner.[4] Likewise, one who has head lice is permitted to wash his hair with hot water.

---

1. *Shulchan Aruch* 381:1.

   Beis Yosef (§381) writes: "At the beginning of *Perek Elu Megalchin* (*Mo'ed Katan* 15b) we find: The mourner is forbidden to bathe, for it is written (*II Samuel* 14:2): '*Joab sent to Teko'ah. . .and said to [the wise woman], "Please mourn. . .and do not anoint yourself with oil . . ."* ' 'Bathing' is included in the category of anointing oneself with oil.' " *Beis Yosef* explains the Talmud: "Since we never find a case where anointing with oil is forbidden but washing is permitted [,we may conclude that if applying oil is forbidden, bathing is also]. At the end of the first chapter of *Taanis* (13b) we find: 'The halachic conclusion is that the mourner is forbidden to wash the entire body, whether in hot water or cold, for the entire seven days. But washing face, hands and feet is forbidden in hot water; permitted in cold.' "

2. *Pischei Teshuvah* 381:§§1, citing *Tiferes LeMoshe*.

3. *Rama* 381:1. He adds: "One should not depart from this, for it is an ancient custom, established by men of exceptional piety (*vasikin*)."

4. *Shulchan Aruch* 381:1. See *Aruch HaShulchan* 381:1: If one became soiled with mud, excrement, or other dirty substance, one washes in the usual manner [to remove the dirt] without compunction, for it would be permissible even on Yom Kippur in such a case. The Sages prohibited only bathing for pleasure, not in cases of distress.

An inordinately delicate person (*istanis*) who is accustomed to bathe frequently, and who will experience severe discomfort and feel ill if he refrains during this period, is permitted to bathe in his usual manner.[5] However, if the necessity is not too pressing, one should be strict on the first day of mourning and refrain.[6]

The mourner is permitted to brush his teeth during *shivah*.[6a]

3. A woman who is in mourning and has just given birth within the past thirty days may bathe if necessary.[7] Likewise, a sick person may bathe, even in hot water, if the doctor so orders. This applies even if the sickness is not life threatening.[8]

In these two instances also — the sick person and the woman who has just given birth — the mourner should be strict on the first day of mourning, if the necessity of bathing is not too strong.[9]

4. If a person is in mourning two consecutive times, he is permitted to wash his entire body in cold water after *shivah* of the first mourning.[10] After the *shloshim* of the first mourning, he is permitted to wash his entire body even in hot water.[11]

5. If a woman mourner is a *niddah* and the time for her immersion in the *mikveh* falls during *shivah*, she may not immerse in the *mikveh*.[12]

She may wash herself, even with hot water, in order to put on white underclothes for the counting of the seven clean days. But she should wash only the halachically required parts of the body.[13]

If her time of immersion falls on the conclusion of the Sabbath, and the Sabbath

---

5. Ibid. 381:3.

6. *Shach* writes in 381:§§2 that this (i.e., being stringent about bathing on the first day of mourning) is the *halachah* for a woman mourner who has just given birth. It would apply, all the more so, even to the inordinately delicate.

6a. Major contemporary *Poskim* rule this way, since the purpose of brushing teeth is to remove dirt.

7. *Shulchan Aruch* 381:3.

8. *Aruch HaShulchan* 381:5. The same ruling is given by *Gesher HaChaim* 21:3:1.

9. *Shach* 381:§§2, citing "the *Acharonim*."

10. *Shulchan Aruch* (381:4) writes that in this case the mourner "is permitted to wash his entire body in cold water." He does not state to which time period this applies. However, he obviously meant *after* the *shivah* period for the first deceased, since *before* that time the same law applies as for any other mourner. And this is in fact the ruling given by *Aruch HaShulchan* 381:7.

11. *Aruch HaShulchan* 381:7.

12. *Shulchan Aruch* 391:5. Despite the importance of not delaying immersion in its proper time, that factor is not relevant here since she is forbidden to have marital relations. Consequently, there is no reason to permit immersion during *shivah*. See also *Tur* and *Beis Yosef* loc. cit.

13. *Rama* (loc. cit.) writes: "All the more so, she may not wash herself in order to put on white underclothes [*levanim*; worn during the counting of the seven 'clean' days]." However, *Taz* (loc. cit. §§2) and *Shach* (loc. cit. §§3) cite responsa *Masas Binyamin* (§5) as disagreeing, and permitting a woman to wash for this purpose even during *shivah*. *Taz* and *Shach* agree with the permissive ruling of *Masas Binyamin*. *Taz* adds: "One who is 'strict' in this matter, and postpones the wearing of white underclothes, is simply acting incorrectly."

is the seventh day of mourning [the last day of *shivah*], some rule that she is permitted to wash her hair on Friday.[14]

◆§ The Use of Lotions (*Sichah*)

6. It is forbidden for the mourner to rub even the smallest amount of oil or any similar substance on his body for pleasure; but he is permitted to rub himself with these things for the sake of removing dirt — and all the more so, for the sake of healing; for example, if he has sores on his scalp, and the like.[15]

The prohibition includes rubbing oneself with oil or soap — and all the more so, with fragrant lotions [for example, colognes]. Likewise, it is forbidden to rub these or similar substances on the hair. The prohibition applies to both men and women.[16] However, the mourner may use deodorants.[16a]

7. During the first thirty days of mourning, a woman is forbidden to use eye-shadow and face-powder on her face or other parts of the body. But a married woman is permitted to use these cosmetics after *shivah*, so that she should not become unattractive to her husband.

The following applies — even during *shivah* — to a bride during the first thirty days after her wedding, and also to a grown girl for whom a match is being sought:

(a) She may use eye-shadow and face-powder.

(b) She may wear jewelry.

(c) She may not bathe.[17]

A girl who is not yet *bas mitzvah* (i.e., is under twelve years old) may bathe. However, a girl in the category called *na'arah* (halachically defined as between twelve and twelve-and-a-half years old, but in this context, a girl past *bas mitzvah*) is forbidden to bathe.[17a]

> For the *halachos* of bathing on the day before a festival or the day before Yom Kippur, see below, chapter 32.

---

14. *Aruch HaShulchan* 381:8, citing *Pri Megaddim*. The same ruling is given by *Gesher HaChaim*, citing *Pri Megaddim*. *Beis Lechem Yehudah* also cites *Pri Megaddim* as ruling this way. But he disagrees, forbidding her to wash her hair on Friday.

15. *Shulchan Aruch* 381:2.

16. *Aruch HaShulchan* 381:6. He is cited by *Gesher HaChaim* loc. cit.

16a. This is the common practice, and also follows the ruling of the *gaon*, R' Moshe Feinstein, *zatzal*, since the suppression of body odor is not considered a "pleasure" from which a mourner must refrain.

17. *Shulchan Aruch* 381:6. Our statement that a grown girl (*bogeres*) for whom a match is being sought may use eye-shadow and face-powder and wear jewelry, even during *shivah*, is also the ruling given by *Aruch HaShulchan* 381: 9. It may in fact be inferred from the words of *Shulchan Aruch*: "...but she may not bathe" — for, according to R' Yosef Karo, the prohibition against bathing applies only during *shivah*.

See also responsa *Tzitz Eliezer* (XI:§73), who writes that the permission mentioned here is only for a *besulah*, a girl or woman who has never been married. It does not extend to a widow or divorcee, even if she is seeking to remarry.

17a. *Shulchan Aruch* 381:6, and *Aruch HaShulchan* 381:9.

During *Shloshim*

The term *shloshim* literally means "thirty." However, with regard to the *halachos* of the following paragraphs, it means the period from the seventh to the thirtieth day. Laws applying only to the first seven days (*shivah*), or applying uniformly throughout the first thirty days, were set forth above, paragraphs 1-7.

The rule is that "part of the [last] day is counted as the whole day." Hence, the seventh day is halachically divided into two parts. During the early morning, the laws of *shivah* still apply. Then the mourners "get up from sitting *shivah*," and for the rest of the day the laws of *shloshim* are in effect. The thirtieth day is similarly divided.

8. Some rule that during the *shloshim* period one is forbidden to wash his body in its entirety, even in cold water.[18] Others permit washing the entire body in cold water.[19] With hot water one is forbidden even to wash one's hair.[20] However, some authorities are lenient and permit washing one's hair in hot water on Friday, in honor of the Sabbath.[21]

---

18. See *Shach* (loc. cit. §§1), who writes: "Certainly there is no prohibition whatever against washing in cold water." *Chiddushei R' Akiva Eiger* (loc. cit.) comments on this: "It seems to me that his intention is. . .to washing face, hands and feet [but not the whole body]." Afterwards, he cites *Elyah Rabbah*, who understands *Shach* to permit washing the whole body in cold water. R' Akiva Eiger concludes: "In my humble opinion, truth will show its way, and the intent of *Shach* is as I have written."

  Dagul MeiRevavah (loc. cit.) likewise writes: "But according to our [Ashkenazic] custom, washing one's whole body, even in cold water, is forbidden during the entire *shloshim*." The same ruling is given by *Da'as Torah* loc. cit. He gives proofs for this opinion. The same ruling is also given by *Hagahos Yad Shaul*.

  See also *Birkei Yosef* (loc. cit.), who states: "*Shach* writes that bathing in cold water is permissible. But his position is not irrefutable, as will be seen from studying the words of *Darkei Moshe*." The same ruling is given by *Orach Mishor*, in *Beis HaRo'eh*, and by responsa *Megiddos* (by the author of *Pri Megaddim*) §50.

19. In the first edition of *Dagul MeiRevavah*, he writes that in cold water one may even wash the entire body — the opposite of his ruling quoted in the previous footnote. The same ruling is given by *Sha'arei Teshuvah* (§548, §§13), who states: "The custom is to be lenient about immersing in cold water, in accord with the opinion of *Shach*." The same ruling is given by *Aruch HaShulchan* (loc. cit. 381:3).

  Chazon LaMo'ed writes that this is also the opinion of *Yavetz* and *Derech HaChaim*. And *Pischei Teshuvah* (loc. cit. §§2) cites responsa *Teshuos Chein* (§31), who writes on this question at length, concluding that a God-fearing person should take a cautious position and forbid himself to wash his entire body even in cold water; but to others, one should rule leniently [permitting them to wash the entire body in cold water]. And even to others, one should rule leniently only with regard to Friday, when bathing may be considered to some extent for the needs of a *mitzvah*. But one should forbid bathing for pleasure in a river [or at the beach].

  Gesher HaChaim (22:1:7) writes: "Bathing in order to strengthen one's body when in weak condition, or in order to remove sweat, is permitted even in hot water (*Acharonim*)." See also *Da'as Torah*, who states that *Hagahos R' Baruch Frankel* cites *Tiferes LeMoshe* as ruling leniently.

20. *Rama* 381:6.

21. See *Da'as Torah*, who cites the ruling of *Rama* (551:16), stating that if one *regularly* washes his hair in hot water on Friday, he may do so on the Friday before *Shabbos Chazon* (the Sabbath prior to Tishah B'Av). *Da'as Torah* concludes: "In any case, on Friday, for the honor of the Sabbath, [the

9. If a man has a regular practice of immersing in a *mikveh* under the following three circumstances, some authorities permit him to do so during the *shloshim*:

(a) Before prayer.[22]

(b) If one is a *baal keri* [i.e., has had relations or a seminal emission]. (In this case, one may go to the *mikveh* in an inconspicuous manner.)[23]

(c) On Friday.[24]

10. The *mohel*, the *sandak*, and the father of the boy are permitted to bathe, even in hot water, on the night before a *bris milah* (circumcision) during *shloshim*.[25]

11. One authority permits a married woman to bathe in hot water during *shloshim*, if refraining from bathing causes her much distress, or if other circumstances necessitate bathing.[26]

12. Some authorities write that during the *Sefiras HaOmer* period, a mourner, during his *shloshim*, is permitted to bathe, even in hot water.[27] Others

---

mourner] is certainly permitted [to wash his hair in hot water]."

22. *Hagahos Yad Shaul* (loc. cit.) writes: "However, if one [normally] goes to the *mikveh* every day, one may [go during the *shloshim*]. The prohibition is only because of a preventive decree (*gezeirah*) regarding haircutting. [Strictly according to the law, bathing is permitted during the *shloshim*, while having a haircut is forbidden. But people usually had a haircut when they went to the bathhouse. Therefore the *gezeirah* forbids bathing, lest one forget and have a haircut.] Hence, if one is not going to the *mikveh* for the sake of bathing, but for the sake of [preparing for] prayer, one can be lenient." The same ruling is given by *Aruch HaShulchan* (551:35), permitting immersion in the *mikveh* on the day before Tishah B'Av.

23. See the *Siddur* of R' Yaakov Emden (*Dinei Ba'al Keri* §7 and §§13), where the author writes: "When one is in mourning, he is permitted to go to the *mikveh* in an inconspicuous manner if he is a *baal keri* (has had marital relations or a seminal emission) — but only if he always goes to the *mikveh* when he is a *baal keri*." The same ruling is given by *Da'as Torah*, and by *Gesher HaChaim* (22:1:7).

24. *Da'as Torah* §381. *Mishnah Berurah* §551 permits immersing in cold water on the Friday before *Shabbos Chazon* (the Sabbath before Tishah B'Av).

25. *Beis Yosef* (§391), citing *HaParness*. The same ruling is given by *Maharil*, *Hilchos Milah*.

26. *Chochmas Adam* 165:1.

27. The following is related in *Toldos Yitzchak*, a contemporary biography of R' Yitzchak Elchanan, head of the *Beth Din* of Kovno. It was written by his secretary, R' Yaakov HaLevi Lifshitz:
One day in 5636 (1876), a guest was sitting with our Teacher, when a man came and asked:
"Rabbi, I am a mourner. Am I permitted to go to the bathhouse?"
Without hesitation, he answered him: "You are permitted."
The questioner was not satisfied with this instant response, and spoke again: "Rabbi, I am in mourning for my father."
"Permitted; you are permitted," *Rabbeinu* answered him, using a double expression of permission. But this still did not settle the mind of the questioner, who asked a third time:
"Only to sweat, or even to wash in hot water?"
Rabbeinu answered him with a friendly smile, but also with surprise: "I just told you that you are permitted, and I said it without adding any details or qualifications. If so, go without delay, before I change my mind!"
After the man left, *Rabbeinu* looked at the guest, noticing his amazement, and guessing his thoughts: How and why could he rule leniently, contrary to the ruling of *Rama*, who cites an enactment of the early Rabbis? He said jokingly: "My guest will go on his way and tell people that the

disagree.[28]

13. In the event that *Chol HaMo'ed* occurs during the *shloshim* (for example, if *Yom Tov* cancels *shivah* — see below, chapt. 32), the mourner is permitted to wash on *Chol HaMo'ed*, even in hot water.[29]

14. A man who becomes a bridegroom during his *shloshim* is permitted to bathe even in hot water.[30]

---

head of the *Beth Din* of Kovno gives hasty, mistaken rulings."

The guest also responded in jest:

"Certainly I will."

"If so," *Rabbeinu* answered, "let me ask you: Does Your Honor know *Rashal's* reason for forbidding bathing?"

The guest replied: "Because of the prohibition against having a haircut; for the usual way is to have a haircut in the bathhouse."

"In that case," continued *Rabbeinu*, "why are we allowed to bathe during *Chol HaMo'ed*? That is also a period when we are forbidden to have a haircut! I know that this is the problem posed by *Taz* in 381:§§1. And the answer is given there, too: Since *everyone* is forbidden to have a haircut then, we do not worry that one might forget." Then *Rabbeinu* continued with a charming smile: "Why should [my questioner] forget? Today is one of the days of *Sefiras HaOmer*. The custom is to forbid having a haircut. I urged my questioner to go immediately, because I noticed that he felt himself strong in Torah, and wanted to argue against my ruling. He wanted to object that the prohibition against having a haircut during *Chol HaMo'ed* is a basic law, while during the *Sefiras HaOmer* period it is only a custom. I did not want to enter into a detailed discussion with him, so I did not point out to him that the prohibition against bathing in hot water after *shivah* is also not the basic law, but a custom."

This ruling is also cited by *Atzei Broshim* (*Yoreh De'ah* §62) and by *Beis Levi* (II:§2).

It would seem, according to this, that it would also be permissible to bathe during the days from the seventeenth of Tammuz through Rosh Chodesh Av, since *Rama* (551:4) rules that the custom then is to be strict and not have a haircut. The matter requires further study.

See also *Pischei Teshuvah* loc. cit. §§2. He notes the ruling of *Taz* that it is permitted to bathe during *Chol HaMo'ed*, and comments: "According to this, it is possible [to draw a conclusion concerning the laws of mourning]. We know, from §399, that if the festival of Pesach or Succos occurs during *shivah*, the laws of the *shloshim* are not canceled. Nonetheless, perhaps the mourner is permitted to bathe during *Chol HaMo'ed*. The *gezeirah* concerning a haircut would not be relevant, since in any case during *Chol HaMo'ed* everyone is forbidden to have a haircut. However, based on this reasoning I do not understand the ruling of *Rashal*. When someone is mourning for his parent, taking a haircut is forbidden even after the *shloshim*, until friends object to one's long hair (see 390:4). Why, then, did *Rashal* not forbid bathing until such time as a haircut is permitted?"

28. *Tuv Ta'am Vada'as* (III:§228). He gives many arguments against the reasoning cited in the previous footnote, and concludes: "Therefore, [bathing] is forbidden [to the mourner] during the *Sefiras HaOmer* period as well; and that is clear and obvious."

29. See the citation from *Pischei Teshuvah* above footnote 27. *Mishnah Berurah* (548:§§41) writes: "Certainly one may rely on the lenient opinion. . .for the honor of the Festival."

30. See *Chiddushei R' Akiva Eiger* (§390), who cites *Elyah Rabbah* as even permitting the bridegroom to have a haircut, although the prohibition against having a haircut during the *shloshim* is a basic law. Moreover, states R' Akiva Eiger, although *Pri Megaddim* raises doubt about the permissibility of a haircut, even he would permit bathing, since the prohibition against bathing during the *shloshim* is not a basic law, but simply a custom. And one who studies the words of *Pri Megaddim* will find that this is implied.

The same ruling is given by responsa *Chasam Sofer*, *Yoreh De'ah* §348.

15. If the thirtieth day of mourning falls on the Sabbath, the mourner is permitted to bath, even in hot water, on Friday.[31]

16. Some write that the mourner is permitted during the *shloshim* to go to a bathhouse in order to sweat [but not bathe].[32] Others forbid this.[33]

---

31. *Rama* 400:2. He explains: "According to the basic law, [bathing] is permitted after *shivah*, but there is simply a custom to be strict throughout the *shloshim*. Hence, in a case like this, bathing is permitted in honor of the Sabbath."

32. See *Mishmeres Shalom os zayin* §10. He cites *Yad Shaul* as permitting the mourner after the first seven days to go to the bathhouse in order to sweat — contrary to the ruling of *Atzei Levonah*.

    See also responsa *Beis Shlomoh* (*Orach Chaim* §105), who states that the custom has already been established to be lenient on this question. He goes on to say that he heard from the *gaon*, author of *Neta Sha'ashu'im*, that, even so, the mourner should not rinse off his body with cold water during the sweating. However, he notes that the general custom is to be lenient about this, too.

    Sdei Chemed (*Aveilus* §24) cites the responsa of *Rama* (*Orach Chaim* §42) as also writing that the custom is to permit the mourner [during the *shloshim*] to go to the bathhouse in order to sweat.

    Responsa *Amudei Eish* (19:13) gives proofs that the Rabbis never decreed against going to the bathhouse in order to sweat after *shivah*. He states that this is the correct ruling to give, and writes that the same ruling is given by *Korban Todah* p. 45b.

    The same ruling is also given by *Aruch HaShulchan* 381:4.

33. See *Atzei Levonah* (*Yoreh De'ah* §381), who writes that even after *shivah*, the mourner is forbidden to go to the bathhouse in order to sweat, even if he doesn't bathe in hot water.

    See also *Erech Shai* (*Yoreh De'ah* §381), who offers proof that sweating is forbidden because it is like bathing in hot water. He is also cited by *Mishmeres Shalom* loc. cit.

CHAPTER TWENTY

Wearing Shoes; Marital Relations

✑ Wearing Shoes

1. During *shivah*, the mourner is forbidden to wear shoes; this prohibition takes effect immediately following interment.[1] The prohibition applies only to shoes made of leather or other animal skin,[1a] including even the skin of fish or birds.[2] But he is permitted to wear footwear made of cloth, reeds, hair, or wood, since the halachic definition of "shoes" includes only those made of animal skin.[3]

The prohibition applies also to footwear made of some permissible material, but covered with leather or other animal skin on top.[4]

The mourner is permitted to stand on leather pillows or cushions, but if he is stringent and refrains from this, a blessing will come upon him.[5]

Some rule stringently, forbidding shoes made of wood, even not covered with leather. Some also forbid shoes made of cloth [such as tennis shoes], and also shoes made of rubber. Thus, for those who are able to do so, it is proper to be stringent and wear only socks.[6]

Regarding a type of wooden sandal (Yid. *galetches*) that includes a leather strap, some rule leniently, since the only purpose of the strap is to hold the sandal on the foot.[7]

---

1. *Shulchan Aruch* 375:1; 376:4.

1a. *Shulchan Aruch* 382:1. *Beis Yosef* identifies the source as *Mo'ed Katan* 15b: "The mourner is forbidden to wear shoes, since the Merciful One told Ezekiel [when commanding him *not* to mourn]: '. . .and you shall put your shoe on your foot' (*Ezekiel* 24:17). From this we may infer that anyone else [in mourning] is forbidden to do so."

2. *Kaf HaChaim* 554:77, citing *Eshel Avraham* (ad loc.); *Ikrei HaDat* 28:1.

3. *Shulchan Aruch* 382:1. He writes the same in *Orach Chaim* 554:16, regarding Tishah B'Av. *Mishnah Berurah* there (554:§§30) comments: "Even though it protects the foot, and also is made exactly in the form of a shoe, it is permitted; for it is only called a shoe [for the purposes of this *halachah*] if it is made of leather."

4. *Shulchan Aruch* loc. cit. regarding a wooden shoe covered with leather. And *Mishnah Berurah* (ad loc. 554:§§31) adds: "The same applies if [the shoe] is made of cloth covered with leather on top, or if the soles are of leather. [All these are] forbidden."

5. *Rama. Orach Chaim* 614:2, regarding Yom Kippur.

6. *Mishnah Berurah* 614:§§5, regarding Yom Kippur. The same ruling is given by *Kaf HaChaim* 554:§§70, regarding Tishah B'Av. Likewise, *Sha'ar Teshuvah* (*Hilchos Tishah B'Av* 554:§§11) writes: "If one is strict [in this matter], a blessing will come upon him."

7. *Kaf HaChaim* 554:§§75, citing *Maharikash* in *Erech Lechem* (§614). *Zachur LeAvraham* §9; *Pri Chadash* (ad loc.); and by *Beis Yosef*, who writes that one should permit this type of footwear in

2. A woman who has given birth is permitted to wear leather shoes within thirty days from the birth, since she is especially susceptible to cold.[8] For the same reason, a sick person, or a person with a foot injury, is permitted to wear leather shoes.[9]

3. Where there is danger from scorpions, any mourner is permitted to wear leather shoes.[10]

Likewise, if one must appear before a high government official or the like, and going without shoes would be offensive, one is permitted to wear them. Nonetheless, in such a case one should put some earth in one's shoes.[11]

4. If one must walk to a distant place, and it would be difficult to do so without shoes, he may wear them.[12] But in such a case it is good to put earth in one's shoes.[13]

5. The mourner must recite the blessing, שֶׁעָשָׂה לִי כָּל צָרְכִּי "... Who provided me with all my needs,"[13a] even when he is not wearing shoes.[14]

---

accord with the ruling of *Maharikash* and *Pri Chadash*. This is also the opinion of *Yafeh LaLeiv* (II:6), who disputes the arguments of *Shem Chadash* p. 36c. The permissive ruling is also cited by *Gesher HaChaim* 21:4:1.

8. *Shulchan Aruch* 382:2. However, I heard from the *gaon* R' Shlomo Zalman Auerbach, *shlita*, that this applies only if she would be harmed even if she wore rubber footwear. If rubber shoes would adequately protect her from harm, she is not permitted to wear leather shoes.

9. *Shach* ad loc. §§1; in accord with the *halachah* found in *Orach Chaim* 614:3.

10. *Shulchan Aruch* 382:3. The leniency likewise applies in any situation where it is not adequate to wear rubber shoes and the like.

11. *Taz* §§1. He writes: "The same applies in a situation of danger. In any situation where he must wear shoes, he should do so."

12. *Shulchan Aruch* 382:4. The reference is to a distant place, involving much effort to go there barefoot. But if he is going to a field just outside the town, he is forbidden to wear shoes; and the same applies if he is going to the cemetery just outside the town, unless there is mud or dung along the way, or he must walk among non-Jews. Accordingly, if he is riding in a wagon or the like, he must remove his shoes even for a long journey (*Mishnah Berurah* 554:§§33).

   Shulchan Aruch (loc. cit.) writes: "There is an authority who says that if the majority of the city are non-Jews, one need not remove his shoes until he reaches the Jewish quarter, because the non-Jews would ridicule us." But *Chochmas Adam* (Hilchos Tishah B'Av) writes: "One need not protest against [those who follow this ruling], for there are great authorities who permit [wearing shoes in such a situation]. Nonetheless, it is not reasonable; for what does it matter if they ridicule us? They ridicule us in any event!" His opinion is cited by *Mishnah Berurah* loc. cit. §§36.

13. *Mishnah Berurah* loc. cit. §§33.

13a. ArtScroll Ashkenaz *Siddur* pp. 20-21.

14. *Mishnah Berurah* 554:§§31, regarding Tishah B'Av.

   Kaf HaChaim (554:§§78) writes, citing *Baal Haltur*: "There are those who rule that one does not recite this blessing on Yom Kippur and Tishah B'Av, since it is forbidden to wear shoes on these days. It would seem reasonable, however, that one may recite the blessing just as on any other morning, since his shoes are always available to him if needed — for example, in case of danger from scorpions." But in 46:§§17, he writes: "One should not recite this blessing on Tishah B'Av or Yom Kippur, even if one puts on cloth shoes. But a mourner should recite it, even if he is going barefoot." This is the ruling cited in his name by *Gesher HaChaim* loc. cit. §4.

◄§ Marital Relations

6. During *shivah*, the mourner is forbidden to have marital relations.[15] One should also be stringent and refrain from hugging and kissing.[16] One should not sleep in the same bed with his wife.[17]

7. Other types of interaction (for example, handing things to each other) are permitted.[18] The wife is even permitted to fill her husband's cup, make his bed, and wash his face, hands, and feet[19] [in situations where he is permitted to wash; see previous chapter]. All this applies whether the one in mourning is the husband or the wife. She is also permitted to eat with him from the same plate.[20]

> The prohibition against marital relations on the night and the morning of the seventh day of mourning will be presented below, 29:5.

---

15. *Shulchan Aruch* 383:1. *Beis Yosef* (ad loc.) identifies the source in *Mo'ed Katan* 15b. There the Talmud cites *II Samuel* 12:24: '*And David comforted Bathsheba his wife* [i.e., following her period of mourning], *and he came unto her.*' From this the Talmud deduces that until her mourning period was concluded, they were forbidden to have marital relations.

16. *Rama* 383:1, citing Rabbeinu Yerucham. *Chiddushei R' Akiva Eiger* (ad loc.) writes: "I saw in print, in the name of the *gaon* R' Zalman of Vilna, that this is explicit in *Targum Koheles* on the verse (*Eccles.* 3:5), '*There is a time to embrace, and a time to refrain from embracing.*' This is rendered: '. . .a time suitable to embrace one's wife, and a time suitable to refrain from embracing one's wife, i.e., during the seven days of mourning.' "

17. See *Shulchan Aruch* 383:1 and *Shach* §§2.

18. *Shulchan Aruch* loc. cit.

19. Ibid.

20. Ibid.

CHAPTER TWENTY-ONE

Torah-Study
and Exchanging Greetings

1. During *shivah*, the mourner is forbidden to study Torah,[1] even on the Sabbath.[2]
Likewise, he is forbidden to read *Tanach* (the twenty-four books of the Bible),
Mishnah, *halachos*, or *aggados* (the non-halachic parts of the Oral Torah).[3] The
prohibition includes even silent reading (*hirhur*).[4]

⋖§ The Book of *Job;* Studying Laws of Mourning

2. It is permitted to read the Book of *Job*, *Kinos* (*Lamentations*), and the references
to disaster in the Book of *Jeremiah*.[5] However, one must skip any passages of
consolation.[6] It is forbidden to study about disasters which befell the idol worshipers.[7]

It is also permitted to study the *halachos* of mourning, and chapter *Elu Megalchin*
in Tractate *Mo'ed Katan*.[8] However, one may only study the plain meaning; one

---

1. The Babylonian Talmud (*Mo'ed Katan* 15a) states: "The mourner is forbidden to study Torah,
since the Merciful One said to Ezekiel (*Ezek.* 24:17): '*Sigh in silence.*'"
   The Jerusalem Talmud derives this *halachah* from a verse about Job, '*And no one spoke a word to
him*' (*Job* 2:13).
   Shach (384:§§1) writes that the source is the same for the prohibition against Torah-study on Tishah
B'Av (*Orach Chaim* 554:1): *The commands of Hashem are just, rejoicing the heart* (*Psalms* 19:9) [and
during periods when one must refrain from joy, one should not study Torah which contains Hashem's
commands].

2. Practices of mourning which are inconspicuous are permitted even on the Sabbath; and refraining
from Torah-study is inconspicuous (*Shulchan Aruch Yoreh De'ah* 400:1).

3. Ibid. 384:1.

4. *Shulchan Aruch Orach Chaim* 554:3. Usually, *hirhur* (silent reading, or having words in mind) is
not considered halachically equivalent to speech. Here, however, the *halachah* is different, since
the basic reason for the prohibition is in order to refrain from joy; and silently thinking words of Torah
also gives joy (*Mishnah Berurah* 554:§§5).

5. *Shulchan Aruch Yoreh De'ah* 384:4. And *Sheivet Yehudah* (ad loc.) comments: "It would seem
that the intent of *Shulchan Aruch* is to say that Torah-study in these areas is permitted, but optional.
If he does not wish to study, he is not required to study anything, not even [things permitted to him,
such as] the accounts of disaster."

6. *Shulchan Aruch Orach Chaim* 554:2.

7. *Mishnah Berurah* 554:§§2.

8. *Shulchan Aruch Yoreh De'ah* 384:4; and *Orach Chaim* 554:3 (regarding Tishah B'Av). Even
though this chapter discusses other matters, such as the *halachos* of a person who is placed under
a ban [*cherem*], one is permitted to study it (*Mishnah Berurah* ad loc. §§4).

may not engage in deep analysis of the subject (*pilpul*), not even silently.[9]

The mourner may only study these permitted things by himself, but not with others. Others may sit in the mourner's presence and discuss and debate the *halachos* of mourning, and if they make a mistake the mourner may quietly point it out. But he may not ask them questions.[10]

∽§ Works of *Mussar*

3. The mourner is permitted to study works which inspire reverent fear of God and religious self-examination. These arouse a person to return to our Father Who is in heaven. This is especially appropriate during a period of mourning, when one is confronted with the Divine Attribute of Strict Justice (*Midas HaDin*). Repentance (*teshuvah*) is powerful, for it brings healing to the mourner and to the whole world, '*for My wrath will go back from him*' (*Hoshea* 14:5) and he '*shall grieve no more*' (*Jeremiah* 31:11).[11]

∽§ Secular Reading

4. It is forbidden to read science books, novels, and the like; it is certainly forbidden to read newspapers, journals, magazines [and the like]; for these would distract one from one's mourning. These are certainly forbidden if they give one pleasure.[12]

∽§ *Tehillim* (Psalms)

5. Some rule that the mourner is forbidden to recite *Tehillim* [Psalms], since this is within the category of Torah-study.[13] Others permit him to recite them if he customarily does so every day,[14] and especially if he recites them in the manner of prayer and arousal to repentance.[15]

∽§ *Korbanos* / Offerings

6. The mourner is permitted to recite the following passages (found in the prayerbook before the morning prayers):

---

9. This is the ruling given by *Taz Orach Chaim* 554:§§2.

10. *Shulchan Aruch Yoreh De'ah* 384:4.

11. This whole paragraph is quoted from *Sdei Chemed* (*Aveilus* §25), and cited in turn by *Mishmeres Shalom os lamed* §21. The same ruling is given by *Gesher HaChaim* 21:5:1.
    See also *Meiri* (on *Mo'ed Katan* 21), who writes: ". . .but it is not forbidden to study books which arouse a person's heart to repentance; rather, it is *desirable* to [study them]."

12. *Aruch HaShulchan* 384:15. The same ruling is given by *Chazon LaMo'ed* 17:1, in the name of *Menachem Aveilim*, who cites *Chiddushei HaRan*, *Mo'ed Katan* p. 11.

13. *Gesher HaChaim* (21:5:1), in the name of *Zichron Shai* (p. 32), *Mahari'a* (*Yoreh De'ah* §368). The same ruling is given (regarding the afternoon of Tishah B'Av) by *Hagahos HaLevush* (§554), citing the custom in the city of Pozen.

14. *Mishmeres Shalom os tav* §2. And *Leket Yosher* (*Hilchos Semachos*) writes: "A person may recite his accustomed daily portion of Psalms, even during his period of mourning."

15. *Gesher HaChaim* loc. cit. just as *Magen Avraham* (*Orach Chaim* §554 §§6) permits on the afternoon of Tishah B'Av.

(a) The Continual Offering (*Parashas HaTamid*)[15a]
(b) The Mishnah chapter *Eizeihu Mekoman*[15b]
(c) Baraisa of R' Yishmael.[16]

However, he may not recite the accompanying request ("*Yehi ratzon. . .*"), "May it be Your will as if I had offered the sacrifice. . ."[17]

He is forbidden to recite the following passages, even if he customarily recites them every day:

(a) The Offerings (*Korbanos*) — except for the Continual Offering (*Tamid*)[18]
(b) The Incense Mixture (*Pitum HaKetores*)[19]
(c) *Ma'amados*.[20]
(d) The book, *Chok LeYisrael*.[21]

15a. ArtScroll Ashkenaz *Siddur* p. 32.

15b. Ibid. p. 42.

16. Ibid. p. 48. *Shulchan Aruch Orach Chaim* 554:4 writes (regarding Tishah B'Av): "One is permitted to recite the entire order of the day [describing the order of services in the Holy Temple], and the *parashah* of the offerings (*korbanos*), and the Mishnah chapter *Eizeihu Mekoman*, and Baraisa of R' Yishmael." But *Mishnah Berurah* (554:§§7) writes: "The *parashah* of the offerings mentioned here refers the Continual Offering (*Tamid*), but not the order of *korbanos* mentioned in 554:1 (i.e., the passages about the laver (*kiyor*) and the taking of the ashes (*trumas hadeshen*)." In 51:§§1, *Mishnah Berurah* writes: "In some communities, chapter *Eizeihu Mekoman* is not recited in the mourner's home, since he is forbidden to study Torah. But this is not correct; for (similar to the ruling in 554:4) everything included in the daily prayer service is permitted to the mourner, even though he is forbidden to study Torah."

17. *Pischei Teshuvah* 384:§§2. The same ruling is given by *Kitzur Shulchan Aruch* 210:4. The reason is that a mourner does not send offerings to the Temple.

18. [ArtScroll Ashkenaz *Siddur* pp. 30-52.] *Mishnah Berurah* 1:§§17.

19. [ArtScroll Ashkenaz *Siddur* p. 36.] *Pischei Teshuvah* (loc. cit.) writes: "See responsa *Zichron Yitzchak* (§6), who writes that during *shivah*, the mourner does not recite *Pitum HaKetores* and the order of the *korbanos* mentioned in *Orach Chaim* §1. This is derived from the *halachah* for Tishah B'Av, as set forth in 559:§§4 (see *Magen Avraham* 50:§§1). See also *Chomas Yerushalayim* (§54), who states that the same ruling is mentioned by *Tabash*, that during *shivah*, the mourner does not recite the passage of the *korbanos*, since a mourner cannot send offerings to the Temple. However, *Chomas Yerushalayim* criticizes this ruling; his own opinion tends towards *permitting* the mourner to recite it. He states that even immediately after the burial, when mourning is a Torah commandment, one could permit this, as long as the mourner does not add the accompanying request (*Yehi ratzon. . .*)."

   Pischei Teshuvah adds: "It requires further study to understand why [*Chomas Yerushalayim*] does not mention the reason of *Zichron Yitzchak* [for forbidding the mourner to recite the passage of the *korbanos*]."

   The same ruling [forbidding the recitation of *Pitum HaKetores* and the order of the *korbanos*] is given by *Gesher HaChaim* 21:5:3.

20. See *Sha'arei Teshuvah* (554:§§4), who cites *Birkei Yosef* as ruling (regarding Tishah B'Av): "It is forbidden to study the Order of the *Ma'amados*, even if one is accustomed to read them every day — contrary to some, who err and read the *Ma'amados* even on the day of Tishah B'Av." And the same prohibition applies to the mourner (*Gesher HaChaim* loc. cit.).

21. *Menachem Aveilim* (p. 80); *Zachur LeAvraham* and *Kaf HaChaim* 554:§§19, citing the *Acharonim*. But *Gesher HaChaim* (loc. cit.) writes: "Nevertheless, it would seem that if one is

❧ Teaching Torah

7. A mourner who is a halachic authority is permitted to render halachic rulings if a ruling is needed and no one else is available to render it.[22]

8. A teacher of Torah is permitted to teach after the first three days of mourning in cases of public need, where there is no available substitute.[23] Some rule that he may teach even on the first day of mourning.[24]

9. Children under the age of *bar mitzvah* are not required to observe mourning.

Therefore, if their parent is in mourning, they should not be kept from attending their Torah school.[25]

With regard to the mourner's being called up to the Torah-reading during the prayer-service, see the following chapters of this book:

During the weekday: 16:24
On the Sabbath: 28:24
On Tishah B'Av: 34:32.

Sh'ilas shalom / Inquiring About Another's Welfare

10. The mourner is forbidden to inquire about another's welfare [*sh'ilas shalom*; lit. inquiry of *shalom*].[26]

During *shivah*, a mourner should be strict even about expressions which are not actually inquiries of *shalom* — for example, "Good morning" and the like.[27]

---

accustomed to read the daily portion of *Chok LeYisrael*, and will feel bad about omitting it, one should not object if he reads it."

22. *Rama* 384:1.

23. *Shulchan Aruch* 384:1.

24. See *Yoseif Da'as* (ad loc.), who, commenting on *Taz*, says that one could infer from the *Gemara* that the Torah teacher is permitted to teach even on the first day. This is also implied by *Shach*, since he mentions no time limit on the permission.

25. *Shulchan Aruch* 384:5 and *Shach* §§5.

26. In *Mo'ed Katan* 15a, the Talmud derives this from the fact that the Merciful One told Ezekiel: '*Sigh in silence*' (*Ezekiel* 24:17). *Rashi* explains: "That is to say, in this respect you should observe mourning: you should be silent and not inquire about another's welfare."

27. *Rama* (385:1) writes: "Some are lenient in our time regarding inquiring about the welfare of a mourner after *shloshim*. There can be no reason for this, unless they say that the expressions used in our time are not the same as what the Talmud calls שְׁאֵלַת שָׁלוֹם, 'inquiry of *shalom*.'" And *Shach* (ad loc. §§3) writes: "In truth, this reason is not correct, for if that were the case, one could be lenient even within the *shloshim*; and we do not find any *Posek* who [is lenient about this during the *shloshim*]."

Magen Avraham (554:§§21) also objects to *Rama's* suggestion; for *Tur* (ad loc.) quotes the Jerusalem Talmud as stating explicitly that the expression referred to is "*shalom aleichem*." Moreover, the Talmud often uses a measure of time called "long enough for a student to say to his teacher, '*shalom aleicha, Rebbe.*'" Hence, says, *Magen Avraham*, one cannot be lenient.

Ba'er Heitev (385:§§2) writes: "Nevertheless, one may suggest that [the explanation for the leniency

However, nodding the head (in greeting) is permitted even during *shivah*.[27a]

⊷§ When Does this Prohibition Apply?

During the first three days of mourning, the mourner is forbidden to ask about anyone's welfare. If others, who do not know that he is a mourner, ask about his welfare, he should not answer, except to inform them that he is a mourner.

From the third to the seventh day, he is forbidden to ask about others' welfare. If others, who do not know that he is a mourner, inquire about his welfare, he is permitted to answer them.[28]

If the one who asks about his welfare knows that he is a mourner, and knows that it is forbidden to ask about his welfare, the mourner should not answer him.[28a]

From the seventh until the thirtieth day, he is permitted to ask about others' welfare, since they are in a state of well-being; and, all the more so, he is permitted to answer them [if, being unaware that he is a mourner, they ask him]. But others are forbidden to ask about his welfare.

After *shloshim*, others may ask about his welfare just like anyone else. However, if the mourning is for his parent, he is permitted, after *shivah*, to inquire about another's welfare. But others are forbidden to ask about his welfare until the end of the first twelve months.[29]

The mourner is permitted to ask about another's welfare, even if it is likely that

---

is that] nowadays, people simply say, 'Good morning,' and this is permitted, since it is not actually an 'inquiry of *shalom*,' as is stated in *Beis Yosef Orach Chaim* §89, and also cited by *Shulchan Aruch* there."

It would seem, according to this interpretation of *Rama*, that it is possible to be lenient only after *shloshim*. And in fact this is how *Elyah Rabbah* (554:20) explains *Rama*'s intent. He concludes: "It seems to me that on Tishah B'Av, all [types of greetings] are forbidden, for there is no more reason to be lenient there than in the case of a mourner during the *shloshim*, when all [types of greetings] are forbidden." The same ruling is given by *Pri Megaddim* (§554, in *Eshel Avraham*, §§21). This is also the ruling of *Mishnah Berurah* (ad loc. §§41).

However, *Leket Yosher* (p. 110) writes: "I have cited *Mahari Obernick*,)who recorded the words of *Maharar Pinchas*, who in turn heard from the *Gaon* (the author of *Trumas HaDeshen*), of blessed memory, that the prohibition against an inquiry of *shalom* applies only if one uses the expression, '*shalom aleichem*.' But 'Good Shabbos' and 'Good Yom Tov' are not classified as 'inquiries of *shalom*.' " And this is the ruling given by *Kol Bo Al Aveilus* part II p. 104, and by responsa *Be'er Moshe* (R' Moshe Stern, *shlita*) part IV:§106. But he adds that in practice it is better not to use *any* expression of greeting (during *shivah*); instead, one should enter silently, and on leaving should use the formula of consolation [i.e., "*HaMakom yenachem . . .*"; see above, 11:4].

27a. See *Ritva*, *Mo'ed Katan* 27b. See also responsa *Silmas Chaim* (§422), who writes that even according to the basic law, it is forbidden to nod in greeting to the mourner. In light of *Ritva*'s ruling, that of *Silmas Chaim* requires further study.

28. *Shulchan Aruch Yoreh De'ah* 385:§§1.

28a. *Da'as Torah* ad loc.

29. *Shulchan Aruch* loc. cit.

this will cause the other to ask about his welfare.[29a]

11. When a group comes to comfort him, he is permitted to tell them, "Go to your homes in peace," for the prohibition is relaxed in order to give honor to the public.[30]

Some authorities state that the present-day manner of asking about others' welfare is not the same "inquiry of *shalom*" as in Talmudic times. Therefore, they rule leniently and permit others to ask about the welfare of someone who is in mourning for his parent, after the end of the *shloshim* (the first thirty days of mourning).[31]

⋙ On the Sabbath

12. Conspicuous mourning is forbidden on the Sabbath. If the mourner were to refrain from inquiring about others' welfare, this would be conspicuous mourning. Therefore, he is permitted to inquire.[32]

Regarding whether one is permitted to inquire about the mourner's welfare on the Sabbath, there are various customs. In some communities, the custom is to inquire about his welfare even during *shivah*. In other communities, the custom is not to inquire.[33]

⋙ Sending Gifts

13. It is forbidden to send a gift to a mourner during the first thirty days of mourning. If his mourning is for his parent, this is forbidden during the first twelve months. In communities where the custom is not to inquire about the mourner's welfare on the Sabbath, sending gifts is also forbidden even on the Sabbath. But in communities where the custom is to ask about the mourner's welfare on the Sabbath, sending gifts is also permitted then.[34]

> The laws regarding sending *mishlo'ach manos* on Purim are presented below, 34:26.

29a. Responsa *Tzitz Eliezer* part 8, 33:3.

30. *Rama* 381:1. *Gesher HaChaim* (21:7:3) writes that this applies even during the first three days of mourning.

31. *Rama* loc. cit. And see above, footnote 27.

32. *Shulchan Aruch* 381:3, citing *Rambam*. *Gesher HaChaim* (loc. cit.) writes: ". . .and the other is permitted to respond in kind."

33. *Shulchan Aruch* 381:3. And *Gesher HaChaim* (21:7:4) writes: "Most people follow the strict custom in this matter during the mourner's first thirty days. And in order to avoid publicizing the mourning on the Sabbath, they avoid meeting the mourner on the Sabbath. If one is mourning for his parent, the custom after the first thirty days (i.e., during the remainder of the twelve months of mourning) is to ask about the mourner's welfare and tell him, '*Shabbat shalom.*' This is all the more permissible if some other expression is used [e.g., '*Good Shabbos*'], as is customary among us Ashkenazim."

34. *Rama* 381:3. The reason is that sending gifts is considered in the same category as asking about another's welfare.

ᴥ§ Blessing Others

14. The mourner is permitted to bless another person with other types of blessings, such as long life, health, *mazal tov*, and the like. It is likewise permitted for others to bless the mourner.[35] They are also permitted to shake hands when blessing each other.[36]

---

35. *Gesher HaChaim* loc. cit. The same ruling is given by *Silmas Chaim* §425.

36. Responsa *Har Tzvi* (§290) writes: "It would seem that the practice of wishing the mourners long life, and shaking their hand, is not included in the prohibition against asking about their welfare. It is simply part of the blessings which the comforter expresses to the mourner."

CHAPTER TWENTY-TWO

Atifas HaRosh: Wrapping the Head
Kefias HaMitah: Overturning the Bed
Sitting on a Low Chair

৵ Wrapping the Head

1. The mourner is required to "wrap the head" (*atifas harosh*),[1] i.e., cover his head
with a cloak or scarf and draw part of it over his mouth and nostrils.[2] This requirement applies throughout the day, if no comforters are present. But when comforters
come to him, he should remove his head-wrapping as a sign of respect to them.[3]

In our regions wrapping the head is not practiced. This has become the accepted
ruling, and "one should not be strict and adopt a practice not followed by our
fathers."[4] Nevertheless, some rule that the mourner should perform a slight act of
"wrapping" — namely, to lower the hat in front of the eyes during the entire *shivah*.[5]

৵ Overturning the Bed

2. The mourner is required to overturn his bed.[6] When sleeping or eating,* he
should sit [or recline] on the overturned bed.

---

* The *Gemara* refers to eating, because in Talmudic times the custom was to recline on a kind of "bed"
or couch when dining.

---

1. In *Mo'ed Katan* 15a we find: "The mourner is obliged regarding wrapping the head (*atifas harosh*),
for the Merciful One told Ezekiel [when commanding him *not* to mourn]: '. . .and you shall not veil
yourself to the lips' (*Ezekiel* 24:17). From this we may infer that anyone else [in mourning] is required
to do so."

2. The Talmud (loc. cit. p.24a) says: "Any *atifah* (wrapping the head) that is not like the *atifah* of
the Ishmaelites is not *atifah*. R' Nachman [when in mourning] covered [his face] to the lip." In
Shulchan Aruch, this *halachah* is found in *Yoreh De'ah* §386:1.

3. *Shulchan Aruch* 386:1.

4. *Rama* 386:1. And *Shach* (§§1) explains why wrapping the head is not practiced: "It leads to great
ridicule by the non-Jews, servants, and maidservants among us."

5. *Shach* 386:§§1. The same ruling is given by *Taz*, citing *Bach*.
    Aruch HaShulchan loc. cit. writes that "it is proper for the mourner not to remove his hat from his
head during the whole seven days, and to sit in this manner [i.e., with his hat on], if this is possible for
him." However, *Chochmas Adam* and *Gesher HaChaim* do not mention this form of wrapping.

6. The Talmud states in *Mo'ed Katan* 15a: "The mourner is required to overturn his bed, as Bar Kapara
taught: [The Holy One, Blessed is He, said:] 'I have set the likeness of My image on them, but because
of their sins I overturned it: Overturn your beds.' "

In our time, however, overturning the bed is not practiced. This is for two reasons:

(a) Non-Jews might think it is a form of sorcery.

(b) Our beds are not made like those of Talmudic times, and overturning them would not be a conspicuous sign.[7]

Some have the custom of overturning the pillows and cushions.[8] But one authority writes that this custom does not apply to modern-day pillows and cushions.[8a]

Some rule that one should overturn the bed of the deceased.[9] In our day, however, this is not practiced. Instead, the bed of the deceased is covered, and for the entire *shivah* it is not adorned with pillows and cushions. It is left unadorned as a sign that this was the place of the deceased.[9a]

◆§ Sitting on a Low Chair

3. According to the basic *halachah*, the mourner is forbidden to sit on a bench or chair, or on pillows and cushions. Instead, he must sit on the floor. If he is ill or elderly, and sitting on the floor would cause him suffering, he is permitted to put a small pillow under him.[10]

He is not required to sit throughout the day; he may stand or walk. However, when comforters are with him, he must sit on the floor.[10a] The comforters are permitted to sit on a bench or chair.[11]

The prevalent custom in our time is to be lenient and sit on a low chair, or on a pillow or the like.[12]

Some are particular that the height of the chair should not be more than a handbreadth (*tefach*).[13] Others are not particular about this,[14] only requiring that it

---

7. *Shulchan Aruch* 387:1 and 2.

8. *Chiddushei R' Akiva Eiger* loc. cit. citing *Beis Yosef*, who cites Rabbeinu Yerucham.

   Beis Hillel (loc. cit.) states: "*Ribash* writes that this is the custom in his land: to overturn the pillows and cushions." The same ruling is given by *Darkei Moshe* loc. cit. §§3.

8a. *Da'as Torah* loc. cit.

9. *Ma'avar Yabok* p. 179.

9a. *Mishmeres Shalom* os chaf §18.

10. *Shach* 387:§§1. See note 12, below.

10a. Ibid.

11. Ibid. citing *Drishah*.

12. *Aruch HaShulchan* §387. The same ruling is given by *Gesher HaChaim* 20:5:11. *Aruch HaShulchan* explains: Support for this may be found in *Yerushalmi Berachos* chapt. 3, where the reason for overturning the bed is derived from *Job* 2:13, *'They sat with him upon the ground seven days'*. The Hebrew word for *on the ground* [לָאָרֶץ] literally means *toward* the ground, i.e., close to the ground; it is accordingly inferred that a mourner may sit on a low chair. . . . Also, one who is ill, or a pregnant woman, may sit on an ordinary chair.

13. *Gesher HaChaim* loc. cit. based on responsa *Adnei Sadeh* (regarding Tishah B'Av). The same ruling is given by *Kaf HaChaim* 552:§§40. He states that a wooden board less than a *tefach* in height is not a proper seat; hence, sitting on it is considered the same as sitting on the floor.

14. *Gesher HaChaim* loc. cit.

be no higher than three handbreadths.[15]

4. According to the basic *halachah*, the mourner is not permitted to sleep on a bed, but only on the floor.[16] But the prevalent custom is to follow those who rule leniently on this matter.[17]

---

15. *Ta'amei HaMinhagim* §864. *Da'as Torah* (§386) cites authorities who require a height of less than a *tefach*, and others who state that anything less than three *tefachim* is sufficiently low.

16. *Taz* 387:§§1, citing *Rashal*. The same ruling is given by *Shach* §§1; by *She'elas Yavetz* part 1 §91; and by *Hagahos Nachal Eshkol* part II end of 10:2.

17. *Pischei Teshuvah* §387 loc. cit. citing responsa *Panim Me'iros* part II §119. He is also cited by *Gilyon Maharsha*.

See also: *Da'as Torah* (loc. cit.), citing *Shevus Yaakov* part I §90; *Chiddushei R' Akiva Eiger* loc. cit.; and *Ba'er Heitev* loc.cit.

See also *Mishmeres Shalom os chaf* §17. He cites *Birkei Yosef* (beginning of 387:§§1), who in turn cites responsa *Panim Me'iros*, who defends today's custom, writing: "One who is lenient in this matter will forfeit nothing — especially in these generations, when the average person is of weak constitution." He is quoted by *Zachur LeAvraham* (*Yoreh De'ah Hilchos Avel* §10 s.v. *yeshivah*).

See also *Ikrei HaDat* (*Yoreh De'ah* 36:26), who states: "The majority of people are considered 'ill' with regard to this matter."

Responsa *Divrei Malkiel* (part 2 §92) writes: "With regard to sleeping, most people rely on what *Sdei Chemed* wrote in §387" [i.e., on the lenient opinion]. The same ruling is given by *Gesher HaChaim* (loc. cit.), who states: "The custom is to be lenient [and sleep] on a bed." The same ruling is given by *Chazon LaMo'ed* 13:7.

CHAPTER TWENTY-THREE

Laundering and Ironing

During *Shivah*

◄§ The Prohibition

1. Throughout *shivah*, the mourner is forbidden to wash or iron his clothing.[1] The prohibition includes even laundering without soap or detergent, and even if the intent is to wear the clothing only after *shivah*.[2] Likewise, it is forbidden for others to wash or iron his clothing.[3] If one had taken his clothing to the laundry before he became a mourner, the laundry is permitted to launder them in the usual way.[4]

◄§ Wearing Laundered Clothes

2. Just as it is forbidden to launder, so too is it forbidden to wear newly laundered clothing, even if they had been laundered before he became a mourner,[5] and even if someone else puts them on first.[6] The same applies to clothing cleaned chemically, without water (dry-cleaning).[6a]

It goes without saying that the mourner is forbidden to wear new clothing.

---

1. *Shulchan Aruch Yoreh De'ah* 389:1. *Levush* (loc. cit.) writes that this *halachah* is derived from the verse: 'Joab sent to Teko'ah, and took from there a wise woman, and said to her, "Please mourn, and please wear the clothes of mourning . . ." ' (*II Samuel* 14:2). 'The clothes of mourning' is understood to mean clothes that are not washed or ironed.

2. *Shulchan Aruch* 389:4.
   Shach (§§7) explains that the mourner is forbidden to work [see above, ch. 18]. This is why he may not wash or iron clothes, even if he will not wear them during his period of mourning.

3. *Shulchan Aruch* 389:4. The reason is that this is like other types of work which the mourner is forbidden to have others do for him [see above, ch. 18].

4. Ibid. This follows the *halachah* for other types of work. If the work is not something like construction or agriculture (where everyone would know whose building or field is being worked on), and if the worker is working on his own premises and on his own time, for a set fee (*kablanus*), the work is permitted [see above, ch. 18].

5. Ibid. *sif* 1.

6. *Sdei Chemed* (*Aveilus* §40) states that the permission to put on newly laundered clothes, by having someone else wear them first, applies only after *shivah*.
   See also *Ikrei HaDat* (36:60), who cites *Zera Emes* as ruling that, in case of great need, it is possible to permit the mourner to wear newly laundered clothes if someone else first wears them for at least half a day.

6a. *Igros Moshe Orach Chaim* part III:§79.

Likewise, it is forbidden to launder blankets, sheets and pillowcases, or to use newly laundered ones.

The same prohibition applies to towels, napkins, and handkerchiefs.[7]

3. If one has to observe two consecutive *shivah* periods, he is permitted to wash his clothing — only in water, without laundering agents — at the end of the first seven-day period.[8] The same applies if his seven-day mourning period is followed immediately by the week of Tishah B'Av.[8a]

4. If his clothing are soiled by sweat and the like, or infested with lice, the mourner is permitted to change clothing; for the prohibition only applies to changing clothing for pleasure. Likewise, he is permitted to wash them in water, without soap or detergent, in order to remove the dirt.[9] One authority writes that if he changes or launders clothing, he should have someone else put them on first.[10]

⊷ Children's Clothes

5. Other people are permitted to wash the clothing of a child whose family member has died.[11]

⊷ Members of the Mourner's Household

6. A mourner's children, and other members of the mourner's household — even those who are supported by him — are permitted to launder their clothing or wear newly laundered clothing (unless they themselves are in mourning).[12]

⊷ Woman Who Is a *Niddah*

7. A woman mourner who is a *niddah* is permitted to wear a clean garment in order to count the Seven Clean Days. Likewise, she is permitted to put a clean sheet on her bed.[13]

---

7. *Shulchan Aruch* 389:1.

8. Ibid.

8a. *Shulchan Aruch Orach Chaim* 551:15.

9. *Pischei Teshuvah* 389:§§2.

10. *Sdei Chemed Aveilus* §40.

11. *Shulchan Aruch* 389:2. The term we use here, "other people," reflects the ruling of *Beis Hillel* (loc. cit.). He states that only other adults, who are not in mourning, may give the children a haircut or wash their clothes. The same ruling is given by *Chazon LaMo'ed*.

12. *Tiferes Adam* (§22), cited by *Sdei Chemed* (*Aveilus* §39), writes: "Anyone whose earnings would belong to the mourner is forbidden to work. However, this applies only to working for pay. They are allowed to work for other people without payment. True, one could argue that the mourner is responsible to provide all their needs. Therefore, when they do their own laundry it is as if they are working for him. Nevertheless, it seems logical to permit [them to do their own or each other's] laundry. And it seems to me that this is the accepted custom: to permit laundering the clothes of all members of the household, except for the mourners."

This ruling is also cited by *Gesher HaChaim*, *Chazon LaMo'ed*, and *Da'as Torah*.

13. *Taz* and *Shach* (§381) write that she may dress and make her bed just as she usually does for the purpose of confirming menstrual purity [i.e., wear clean white clothes and put a clean white sheet on her bed]. However, *Taz* there cites responsa *Masas Binyamin* (§5) as ruling that she should wear a clean garment, but not a white one.

Regarding the question of donning newly laundered clothing for the honor of the Sabbath, see below, chapter 28.

During *Shloshim*

The term *shloshim* here refers to the period from the end of *shivah* (the first seven days) until the thirtieth day of mourning. (Since the *shivah* ends on the morning of the seventh day, the *shloshim* includes the remainder of the seventh day.)

◦ Wearing Laundered Clothing

8. After *shivah*, the mourner is permitted to iron and launder his own clothing in order to wear them after the *shloshim*. Likewise, he may iron and launder for others.[14] However, during the *shloshim* he is not permitted to wear newly laundered or ironed clothing, except under the conditions set forth below, paragraph 9.

Some authorities permit him to launder clothing during the *shloshim* in order to have someone else put them on first, and then wear them himself. Others forbid this.[15]

9. After *shivah* the mourner is permitted to wear clothing which were laundered (by someone else) in water without soap or detergent.[16]

If the clothes were laundered with soap or other laundering agents, the custom is

---

14. *Shulchan Aruch* 389:7.

15. See *Da'as Torah* (loc. cit.), who cites *Hagahos Imrei Baruch*: "There is a custom to have someone else wear the clothes first. According to that custom, one could argue that it is permissible for the mourner to launder the clothes [i.e., have someone else wear them,] and then wear them himself. However, this hypothesis is refuted by the wording of *Rama* in *Orach Chaim* 548:10, where he writes that there is no way to permit the mourner to launder his clothes just before a Festival — even though in the discussion there, the mourner is regarded as if he had completed *shivah*. But according to our hypothesis, it should have been possible to permit him to wash his clothes on the eve of the Festival, by having someone else wear them before he (the mourner) puts them on."

About this, *Da'as Torah* comments: "It is not necessarily [a valid refutation]; for it may be that *Rama* was referring to a situation where there is no one else to wear them first, and the mourner would be the first to put them on."

Now, *Kerem Shlomo* cites *Lechem HaPanim* as ruling that instead of having someone else wear them first, one may simply put the clothes on the floor [thus removing their status of "newly laundered"; and see below, footnote 18]. This could be done even in a situation where there is no one else to wear them first. If so, the refutation suggested by *Imrei Baruch* remains valid.

Moreover, *Kerem Shlomo* himself writes that "the generally accepted custom is not to permit [the mourner] to launder clothes in order to wear them [before the end of the *shloshim*]."

Erech Shai (*Yoreh De'ah* §389) writes: "On the eve of a Festival, [the mourner] is forbidden to launder clothes in order to have someone else put them on first and then wear them himself. However, during the *shloshim* [i.e., after *shivah*] this is permitted."

See also *Da'as Kedoshim* loc. cit. §§3.

16. *Shach* loc. cit. §§2, citing *Tosafos*. *Bach* writes: "According to this, if the clothes were laundered only in water, there is no need to have someone else put them on first. And, obviously, this is permitted immediately after *shivah*."

to forbid wearing them throughout the *shloshim*. However, if someone else first puts them on for a short time, the mourner is permitted to wear them.[17] In this manner, he may even wear clothing which have been laundered with laundering agents, and ironed.[18]

10. One authority writes that a newly laundered garment whose purpose is to absorb perspiration, such as an undershirt, may be worn without having someone else put it on first.[19]

◄§ New Clothes

11. The mourner is forbidden to wear new clothing during the *shloshim*.[20] If the mourning is for one's parent, the custom is not to wear new clothing during the first twelve months.[21] If it is necessary[22] to wear new clothing, it is permitted, if someone else first wears them for two or three days.[23]

It is permitted to buy a used garment or to have it remade to fit the mourner. However, if the garment is so important that the mourner would feel great joy at acquiring it, it is forbidden.[23a]

Some rule that if the new clothing are the kind whose purpose is to absorb perspiration, rather than to dignify the wearer, they may be worn, after the *shloshim*, even without having someone else put them on first.[24]

The mourner is permitted to buy new shoes during the twelve months of mourning, after the *shloshim*. It is not necessary to have someone else wear them first, since shoes are not classified as a "garment."

---

17. *Rama* 389:1. He writes there that this custom is the correct practice, "and this is the custom in our region after *shivah*; and if someone else wears [the clothes] for an hour, that is sufficient." *Shach* (loc. cit. §§4) comments: "The intent is a short time, not a full hour. This may also be inferred from the writings of the *Poskim*, and is the accepted custom — contrary to the ruling of *Ateres Zekeinim*, who states 'for an hour or two.' But perhaps he also did not intend this literally."

18. *Shach* 389:§§3. The same ruling is given by *Bach*. And *Kerem Shlomoh* (loc. cit.) cites *Lechem HaPanim* as ruling that it is also possible to just put the clothes on the floor for a short time, or to slightly rumple the creases.

19. *Aruch HaShulchan* 389:6.

20. *Shulchan Aruch* 389:5 and *Rama* 389:3.

21. *Rama* 389:3. *Rama* writes that it is forbidden "to make" new clothes, not "to wear" them. *Hagahos Chochmas Shlomoh* comments that the intent is to make them in order to wear them, and offers a number of proofs for this interpretation. However, *Da'as Kedoshim* (§§7) writes that simply making new clothes is forbidden, just as wearing new clothes is forbidden.

22. *Da'as Kedoshim* (loc. cit. §§3) writes that "necessary" here means "extremely necessary."

23. *Be'er HaGolah* (389:§§17) writes: "*Kol Bo* states, in the name of R' Moshe, that in a case where it is forbidden to wear new clothes, one can have someone else wear them first for two or three days, and then the mourner is permitted to wear them. But in my humble opinion it seems that this applies only in case of necessity."

23a. The *gaon* R' Moshe Feinstein, *zatzal*, in *Kuntres Am HaTorah mahadura* 2, *choveres* 12 §18.

24. The *gaon* R' Shlomo Zalman Auerbach, *shlita*, and the *gaon* R' Eliezer Yehudah Waldenberg, *shlita*, in their responsa printed at the end of the Hebrew edition, present work, under the title *Ohel Channah*. And I heard the same ruling from the *gaon* R' Yisrael Yaakov Fisher, *shlita*.

He is also permitted to wear new eyeglasses even if he already has a pair — since changing eyeglasses is a medical need.[24a]

The mourner should not wear Sabbath clothes on a weekday during *shloshim*. If the mourning is for one's parent, this applies throughout the Twelve Months.[24b]

◦§ New Household Items

12. After *shloshim*, one is permitted to buy new utensils and furniture; and it is not necessary to have someone else use them first.[25] After *shivah*, one is permitted to have his house painted.[26]

24a. Major contemporary *Poskim*.

24b. *Rama (Yoreh De'ah* 389:3; 391:3).

25. This is the ruling given by *Yikrei DeChayei* 19:29.

26. This is the ruling I have heard from contemporary *Poskim*.

CHAPTER TWENTY-FOUR

Cutting Hair or Nails

◆§ Haircut

1. The mourner is forbidden to take a haircut or shave during the entire first thirty days of mourning (*shloshim*).[1]

If one is mourning for his father or mother, the prohibition applies "until his friends reprimand him [for his unkempt appearance]." The definition of this time-limit will be discussed below, paragraphs 19-22.[2]

The prohibition applies to the hair of the head and the beard, and even to unseen areas.[3]

Regarding the mustache and the hair at the sides of the mouth,[4] if it interferes with eating, there are three opinions:

  (a) It may be cut only after *shivah*.[5]

  (b) It may be cut only after *shloshim*.[6]

---

1. In *Mo'ed Katan* 14b, the prohibition against cutting hair is derived from the Torah passage about the death of Aaron's two sons. In commanding Aaron and his two remaining sons *not* to mourn, Moses told them, '*Do not let your hair grow long*' (*Lev.* 10:6). From this the Talmud infers that mourners are otherwise forbidden to have their hair cut.

   The fact that the prohibition lasts for thirty days is derived (*Mo'ed Katan* 19b) from a *gezeirah shavah*, a parallelism of phrasing. The verse just quoted uses a word (תִּפְרָעוּ) based on the root פרע, referring to long hair. A verse regarding the vow of the nazirite uses a word (פֶּרַע) derived from the same root: ". . .growing his hair long" (*Numbers* 6:5). From this the Talmud learns that just as the standard length of time for the nazirite to maintain his vow and refrain from cutting his hair is thirty days, so too the prohibition against the mourner's cutting his hair is thirty days. "And how do we know," asks the Talmud, "that the time-limit for the nazirite is thirty days? R' Masnah said: Unless he specifies otherwise, the nazirite's vow lasts for thirty days. Why? Because the Torah states, '*He shall be holy*' (ibid.), and the numerical equivalent of the letters of יִהְיֶה, *shall be*, is 30."

2. *Shulchan Aruch Yoreh De'ah* 390:§§4. The source is a *baraisa* in *Mo'ed Katan* 22b.

   See also *Sheivet HaLevi* (§213), who deals with the case of a man whose father had died. The mother was ill, and learning of her husband's death would endanger her life. Therefore the son was permitted to take a haircut after *shivah*.

3. *Shulchan Aruch* 390:1.

4. The term cited by *Shulchan Aruch* is, "the hair of the lip and at the sides." *Beis Yosef*, citing *Ramban*, defines this as "the part extending from corner to corner [of the mouth], i.e., that [hair] which is above the mouth along the whole length of the mouth's opening. 'At the sides' means the hair at either side of the mouth's opening. And whatever [hair] interferes with eating is permitted [to cut]."

5. This is the opinion of *Ritz Ge'us* and *Halachos Gedolos*, as well as *Tosafos*, and is the ruling given by *Shulchan Aruch* 390:1.

6. This is the opinion of *Rambam* and *Ravad*. *Beis Yosef* writes: "As for the *halachah*, since both *Rambam* and *Ravad* agree, we follow their opinion." Thus *Be'er HaGolah* (loc. cit. §5) and *Shach*

(c) It may be cut even during *shivah* .[7]

2. If someone in the midst of taking a haircut is informed of the death of a family member for whom he is obligated to mourn, he is permitted to finish the haircut, for the sake of human dignity (*kevod habrios*).

Even if the barber is informed that his (the barber's) family member has died, he is permitted to finish giving the haircut, if there is no other barber in town.[8]

Some authorities permit finishing the haircut even if the barber did not yet begin cutting hair, but only placed the apron over the customer's knees.[9]

3. If someone needs to observe two consecutive *shivah* periods, he may cut his hair after the first *shivah* period, provided it is after the *shloshim* of the first mourning period. He may do so only in private, and may only reduce the length of his hair with a razor, but not have a regular haircut with scissors.[10]

◄§ Combing the Hair

4. The mourner is permitted to comb his hair even during *shivah* .[11] However, some authorities permit only a woman mourner to comb her hair.[12]

◄§ Cutting Nails

5. The mourner is forbidden to cut his nails with an instrument (scissors, knife, etc.) during the entire *shloshim* . This includes fingernails and toenails.[13]

(390:§§1) both find it "surprising that *Shulchan Aruch* (390:1) follows the ruling of *Ritz Ge'us* (cited by *Tur*), while *Beis Yosef* writes that the *halachah* follows *Ravad* and *Rambam*, who rule that this hair may not be cut during the entire *shloshim*, regardless whether it interferes with eating."

7. This is the opinion of *Ramban*. And *Be'ur HaGra* (390:§§2) rules accordingly, writing: "However, the opinion of *Ramban* is the one which should be followed, as is proven by [a passage in] the Jerusalem Talmud; and this is also the opinion of *Tur*." *Mishnah Berurah* (*Sha'ar HaTziyun* 551:§§90) cites this ruling of *Be'ur HaGra*, stating: "One should not be strict about cutting the moustache if it interferes with eating with regard to our topic [the week in which Tishah B'Av falls], since in any case *Gra* rules there that the principal opinion is that of *Ramban*, that even during *shivah* it is permitted [to cut hair which interferes with eating]."

8. *Shulchan Aruch* 390:2, and *Taz* loc. cit. §§1.

9. *Shulchan Aruch* (loc. cit.) writes: "If he sat down to take a haircut. . .he may finish." *Chiddushei R' Akiva Eiger* (loc. cit.) writes: "From the Jerusalem Talmud (*Shabbos* chapt. 1) one may infer that the same rule applies here as in the Mishnah there, which states: 'One may not sit down at the barber just before *Minchah*.' And about this it is stated: 'When is he considered to have begun the haircut? When he places the haircutting apron over his knees.' "

However, *Aruch HaShulchan* writes that this inference of R' Akiva Eiger "requires further study."

10. *Shulchan Aruch* 390:3, and *Rama* loc. cit.

11. *Shulchan Aruch* 390:6. According to *Taz* (§§2) and *Shach* (§§3), *Shulchan Aruch* means that even a man is permitted to comb his hair. The same interpretation of *Shulchan Aruch* is given by *Ateres Zekeinim* and *Bach*.

12. *Shach* (loc. cit.) writes: "However, *Hagahas Sefer Mitzvos Katan*, citing *Or Zarua*, permits only a woman [to comb her hair], but not a man [to comb his]; and this is cited by *Bach*." And *Gesher HaChaim* (21:11:11) writes: "If a man is used to combing his hair, and it is difficult for him not to do so, he is permitted. This is the *halachah* to be followed in practice (see *Shulchan Aruch* 390:6, and *Bach*, *Shach*, and *Aruch HaShulchan*)."

13. *Shulchan Aruch* 390:7.

In the Talmud (*Mo'ed Katan* 18a) we find: "R' Anan bar Tachlifa said: 'It was explained to me

After *shloshim*, cutting nails is permitted,[14] even if the mourning is for one's parent.[15] But some rule more strictly with regard to mourning for one's parent.[16]

Paring fingernails with one's hands or teeth is permitted even during the *shivah*.[17] It is also permitted to cut a little with a knife, and then remove the remainder with one's hands or teeth.[18]

6. If a woman's day for going to the *mikveh* occurs during her *shloshim*, and if she cannot properly cut her nails with her hands or teeth, she is permitted to have a non-Jewish woman cut them with a knife or scissors.[19] Some authorities also permit having a Jewish woman cut them.[20] If it is impossible to have another woman cut them, some rule that she may cut them herself.[21]

7. A *mohel* who needs to cut his nails for the purpose of performing a circumcision may do so, even with scissors,[22] if no other *mohel* is available. But if another

---

from [the yeshivah] of Shmuel. . .that this applies equally to [the nails of] the hand and the foot.'" And this is cited by *Be'er HaGolah* §15.

14. See *Ben Ish Chai*, *Shanah* 1, *Parashas Devarim* §13. He states that once the thirty days of mourning are completed, even if they end on Tishah B'Av, the mourner should cut his nails, as protection against harmful spiritual forces (*chitzonim*). See *Kol Bo Al Aveilus* (p. 355), who cites *Tuv Ta'am Vada'as* (part III:§220) as stating that one who is inordinately delicate (*istanis*), whose habit is to cut his nails twice a week, should have a non-Jew cut them; and if this is impossible, he may have another Jew cut them.

15. *Chiddushei R' Akiva Eiger* loc. cit. in the name of *Halachos Ketanos*, who writes: "It is possible that [the stringency of waiting until one's friends] reprimand him [see below, par. 19] applies only to hair, which is constantly visible; but it is not usual for people to stare at their friend's hands, since this is unpleasant." The same ruling is cited by *Da'as Torah* (loc. cit.) in the name of *Shiurei Brachah* (§399), who states that cutting one's nails does not depend on one's friends' reprimanding (see *Shayarei Shirayim* par. 4).

16. *Da'as Torah* (loc. cit.) cites responsa *Leshon Zahav* (§4), as ruling that one who is mourning for his father or mother is forbidden to cut his nails even at the end of *shloshim*, but must wait "until his friends reprimand him," as is the case with haircutting; even if a festival occurs in the meantime, it does not annul this waiting period.

17. *Shulchan Aruch* 390:7.

18. Responsa *Shevus Yaakov* part III:§100. He is cited by *Da'as Torah* (loc. cit.), and also by a number of *Acharonim*.

19. *Shulchan Aruch* 390:7.

20. *Rama* loc. cit.

21. *Chochmas Adam* (165:30) writes: "If it is impossible to have someone else do it, it seems to me that she may cut them herself; for some rule that a married woman is permitted to launder clothes and have her hair cut — see *Beis Yosef* §381 regarding the use of makeup, and §390."

See *Da'as Torah*, who states that *Ikrei HaDat* (36:55) cites *Chaim Sha'al* (part 1 §2) as ruling likewise that if having someone else cut her nails is very painful for her, she is permitted to cut them herself for the purpose of immersing in the *mikveh*. He also states there, in the name of *Yad Eliahu*, that even during *shivah* she is permitted to cut her nails, even by herself, if she does it in other than the usual manner.

See also *Zachur Le'Avraham* (III:§490), who cites this ruling of *Chaim Sha'al*. Moreover, he writes that the custom is in accord with the ruling of *Taz*: that she herself may cut her nails, whether during *Chol HaMo'ed* or during mourning.

22. See *Rama* (393:3), who writes that he is permitted to prepare his fingernails for the purpose of the circumcision.

mohel is available, the one in mourning is forbidden[23] to cut his nails during his entire *shloshim*.[24] However, some rule that he may cut them after *shivah*.[25]

8. Some rule that on the day before Pesach the mourner is permitted to have someone cut his nails, in case there might be *chametz* caught under them.[26] Likewise, if he has been hired to knead *matzah* for Pesach, he is permitted to have someone cut his nails.[27]

Special Cases

◆§ Child's Haircut

9. It is permitted to cut the hair of a child (not yet *bar-* or *bas mitzvah*) whose family member has died.[28]

◆§ Married Woman

10. Some rule that a married woman is permitted to remove hair after *shivah*. But others forbid this, and the latter opinion should be followed. Nevertheless,

---

23. *Rama* 393:3.

24. *Chiddushei R' Akiva Eiger* loc. cit. The same ruling is given by *Elyah Rabbah Orach Chaim* 551:§§28.

25. See *Kol Bo Al Aveilus* p. 355, who writes that in our time, when the *mohel* charges a fee, he may be permitted to cut his nails if he needs to perform a circumcision for his livelihood.

See also *Pri Megaddim* (§551 in *Mishbetzos Zahav* par. 13), who cites *Elyah Rabbah* (see previous footnote) and concludes: "It could be argued that the prohibition instituted by the Sages was only against cutting the nails for pleasure or beauty. But for the purpose of performing a circumcision, cutting nails is prohibited during *shivah* only if another *mohel* is available; and even then it does not come within the general prohibition against cutting nails, but is forbidden because in any case it gives him a certain amount of joy."

26. *Sdei Chemed* (*Aveilus* §64) writes: "On the day before Pesach, I permitted a mourner to have someone cut his nails, in case there might be *chametz* absorbed within them. For even if he generally eats with a fork, it could happen that he had eaten something with his hands. This permission may be derived from responsa *Yad Eliahu* §96. And see *Ikrei HaDat* (§36 os 55)."

(This opinion requires study. Why should he be permitted to cut his nails in the usual manner? After all, for the needs of Pesach he could achieve the same result by cutting them in other than the usual manner, with his hands or teeth.)

Moreover, it must be that this permission is intended only for someone in mourning for his father or mother, in which case some rule that cutting nails is forbidden even after *shloshim* (see above, footnote 16). If the mourning is for someone other than one's father or mother, this permission is not needed, since in any case the Festival annuls the mourning of the first thirty days.

27. *Sdei Chemed* (loc. cit.) citing *Chaim BeYad* (§195 os 76 and §11) writes: "I examined that source, and its topic is the *halachah* of a woman whose day of immersion in the *mikveh* occurs during her *shloshim*. The question discussed is whether she must have another woman cut her nails, or can cut them herself. Apparently, [*Chaim BeYad*] wishes to draw an inference from that discussion to our topic. This would seem to be a great leniency — but who can question the words of the king?"

28. *Beis Hillel* §389:2. The same ruling is given by *Mishmeres Shalom* (os gimmel §34), citing *Beis Yosef* (§389). *Tiferes LeMoshe* (loc. cit.) adds: "In fact this ruling is also given by *Mordechai* on *Mo'ed Katan*, end of §875 . . . but obviously this applies only if the one giving the haircut is not himself in [the first seven days of] mourning. (This is stated explicitly in *Gilyon HaShas* there.) Otherwise, he could not give the haircut, since a mourner is forbidden to work."

some permit her to cut hair in areas where women usually do so, such as excessive hair at the temples, and the like.[29]

◆§ Appearing Before Government Officials

11. If a mourner needs to appear before a high government official to represent the needs of his community, some rule that he may take a haircut (and shave) after *shivah*, even if the mourning is for his father or mother.[30]

◆§ A Bridegroom

12. The *Poskim* write that if a man is getting married during his *shloshim*, he may take a haircut, shave, and cut his nails on the wedding day. This applies even if the mourning is for his father or mother.[31]

◆§ For a Circumcision

13. For a circumcision, even the *sandak*, *mohel*, and father of the baby are forbidden to take a haircut or shave if they are in their *shloshim*.[32] However,

---

29. *Shulchan Aruch* (390:5) writes: "A woman is permitted to remove hair after the first seven days of mourning." This follows the opinion of *Rif* and *Rambam*. *Darkei Moshe* (loc. cit. sif 5) writes: "Even though the *halachah* follows the lenient opinion in the laws of mourning, nevertheless, since the majority disagree — i.e., *Rashi*, *Tosafos*, *Ramban*, and *Rosh* — the *halachah* follows the majority. This is all the more true since *Ramban* and *Rosh*, who [have the advantage that they] came later [and summarized the work of the earlier authorities], both find difficulties in the reasoning of *Rif*, and write that *Rashi*'s opinion is the principal one. Hence, as mentioned, it should be followed in practice." Likewise, *Shulchan Aruch* writes: "Some rule that a woman, too, is forbidden [to cut her hair]; and this is the principal ruling." See also *Chochmas Adam* 165:28.

30. This is the ruling given by *Kol Bo Al Aveilus*, p. 353, citing *Pachad Yitzchak* (s.v. *Karov LeMalchus*). The same ruling is given by *Gesher HaChaim* (21:11:5), citing *Ikrei HaDat* — "even though some *Acharonim* rule strictly on this; see §390."

31. *Elyah Rabbah* 132:4, cited by *Chiddushei R' Akiva Eiger* §390. The same ruling is given by *Chasam Sofer Yoreh De'ah* responsum 348.

Pri Megaddim (§132 in *Mishbetzos Zahav* par. 2) writes: "Nevertheless, this *halachah* requires further study, since his personal festival [i.e., his wedding] is [only classified as a "festival"] on the Rabbinic level. And since he had already become subject to the laws of mourning previously, who is to say that his personal festival. . .takes precedence over the prohibition against taking a haircut during *shloshim*, which is explained in *Yoreh De'ah* §390 as a law of the Talmud? How can his personal festival come and annul it?. . .However, after *shloshim* [for his parent] it might be argued that his personal festival [takes precedence]. . .See *Levush* (*Yoreh De'ah* §390), who states that in this situation the requirement of 'until his friends reprimand him' is fulfilled. But, as regards during the thirty days, the *halachah* requires further study."

See also *Pachad Yitzchak* (part 1 p. 9), cited in *Kol Bo Al Aveilus*, (p. 353), for an extensive discussion of whether the wedding cancels the first thirty days of mourning. He cites arguments on both sides.

And see *Shemesh Tzedakah* (*Orach Chaim* §17 p. 29), who (in explaining why the wedding does not cancel the first thirty days of mourning) states that the wedding is not the same as a festival; for during a festival the mourner is still forbidden certain things — such as laundering or taking a haircut — while during the [seven] days of his wedding, he altogether ceases to mourn.

32. Responsa *Noda BiYehudah tinyana Yoreh De'ah* §213, cited by *Pischei Teshuvah* 390:§§1.

There it is explained that even the father of the baby is not allowed to take a haircut. Likewise, *Elyah Rabbah* (551:10) prohibits a haircut even to the father of the baby, since "regarding things

some rule that the father of the baby may take a haircut and shave.[33]

◄§ On Friday Before *Shloshim*

14. If the thirtieth day of mourning falls on the Sabbath, the mourner is forbidden to take a haircut or shave on Friday.[34] As regards cutting nails, some authorities forbid, and others permit.[35]

◄§ On the Thirtieth Day

15. On the thirtieth day, part of the day is counted as all of it. Therefore, the mourner is allowed to take a haircut and shave that day after sunrise (*neitz hachamah*), but not before. This applies if the mourning is for a family member other than one's father or mother.[36] (For the *halachah* regarding mourning for one's father or mother, see below, paragraphs 19-22.)

---

prohibited by the law of the Talmud, one cannot be lenient." Similarly, responsa *Chasam Sofer* (*Orach Chaim* §158) prohibits even the father of the baby to take a haircut, and his ruling is cited by *Sha'ar HaTziun* §551 §§4.

See also *Chiddushei R' Akiva Eiger* §393; *Be'er HaGolah* and *Pischei Teshuvah* there, §§4. All these authorites forbid the *mohel* to take a haircut.

33. See *Shevus Yaakov* part III:§94.

34. The Jerusalem Talmud (*Mo'ed Katan* ch. 3 *halachah* 5) states: "One might assume that even if his thirtieth day of mourning falls on the Sabbath, he could take a haircut on Friday." But it concludes that he may *not* take a haircut; and this ruling is cited by *Tosafos* (*Mo'ed Katan* 19b s.v. *halachah*). Thus *Dagul MeiRevavah* (§400) is surprised at *Maharil*, who writes in *Hilchos Lag B'Omer* that if the mourner's thirtieth day falls on the Sabbath, he may take a haircut on Friday.

Kol Bo Al Aveilus (p. 353 note 8) cites *Chaim Sha'al* (part II:§23), who in turn cites *Kerem Shlomo* as permitting this. However, *Chaim Sha'al* himself forbids it.

See also *Har Avel* (p. 25) and *Pachad Yitzchak* (s.v. *avel asur begilu'ach*), who raises a stormy protest against those who permit it.

And see *Sdei Chemed*, who concludes that, in a community where there is no custom to the contrary, one may be lenient about this. He, too, makes no mention of the Jerusalem Talmud cited above.

The prohibitive ruling is also given by *Gesher HaChaim* (21:11:7), who comments at the end: "However, the *Acharonim* write that in case of pressing need, one may be lenient — unless the mourning is for one's father or mother."

35. Responsa *Panim Me'iros* (part 2 §149) writes that it is forbidden. But *Gesher HaChaim* (21:11:9) writes in the name of *Misgeres HaShulchan* that it is permitted. He also quotes this source as stating that if the mourner's nails are long, he may cut them even for the honor of the Sabbath; and all this applies even if the mourning is for one's parent.

Likewise, responsa *Zera Emes* (§390) writes that the mourner is permitted to cut his nails on Friday if the thirtieth day of mourning falls on the Sabbath.

36. *Shulchan Aruch* (§390:4) writes: "For all the deceased, [i.e., except for his parent, the mourner] may take a haircut after *shloshim*." However, the word "after" is not to be taken literally, for even on the thirtieth day this is permitted, as explained in 395:1, which states that part of the thirtieth day is counted as all of it, and the prohibitions of *shloshim* are annulled after sunrise (*neitz hachamah*). See also *Shach* (loc. cit. §§1).

And see *Kol Bo Al Aveilus* (p. 351), who writes: "However, on the night [of the thirtieth day] he certainly is not permitted to take a haircut; for the [whole, 24-hour] day is made of day and night, 'evening and morning, one day' [Genesis 1:5]. Thus, granted that part of the night passed, nevertheless none of the day passed at all (*Yoseif Da'as* §395)."

Regarding taking a haircut and shave on the day before a festival during *shloshim*, see below, chapter 32.

⋖§ Between the Seventeenth of Tammuz and Tishah B'Av [The "Three Weeks"]

16. If *shloshim* ends between the seventeenth of Tammuz and Rosh Chodesh Av, the mourner is permitted to take a haircut and shave then.[37]

If it ends after Rosh Chodesh Av, some authorities forbid a haircut or shave,[38] and others permit it. In case of hardship, one may be lenient [and take a haircut and shave].[39]

If it ends during the week in which Tishah B'Av falls, and the length of his hair makes him uncomfortable, the mourner may shorten his hair with a razor, but not with scissors.[40]

⋖§ During the *Omer*-Count

17. If *shloshim* ends between Rosh Chodesh Iyar and Lag B'Omer, the mourner is permitted to take a haircut and shave; but [since the custom of not having haircuts or shaving during the *Omer*-count is of the nature of a vow], it is preferable to first perform an annulment of the vow.[41] However, some authorities disagree and altogether forbid the mourner to take a haircut or shave in this situation.[42]

⋖§ First Haircut Celebration [*Upsheren; Chalakah*]

18. Some people have the custom of making a celebration when a boy has his first haircut, since this initiates him into the *mitzvah* of not removing the entire sideburns (*pe'os*). One is forbidden to make such a celebration during one's period of mourning.[43]

---

37. *Elyah Rabbah* 551:§§15.

38. *Elyah Rabbah*, loc. cit. citing *Roke'ach* (§318) and *Tanya* (§59). This ruling of *Elyah Rabbah* is cited by *Mishnah Berurah* loc. cit. 551:§§86. In *Sha'ar HaTziyun* there (§§93), the same ruling is cited in the name of *Derech HaChaim*, *Chayei Adam*, and R' Baruch Frankel in his *Hagahos*.

39. *Taz* loc. cit. citing *Bach*. And *Sha'ar HaTziyun* (loc. cit.) states that *Dagul MeiRevavah* cites this ruling of *Taz* as the correct *halachah*: "It is possible that in case of pressing need (*mekom hadechak*) one could be lenient, since in any case [the prohibition against taking a haircut or shave from Rosh Chodesh Av until the week in which Tishah B'Av falls] is only a custom."

40. *Shulchan Aruch Orach Chaim* 551:15. He may shorten his hair with a razor, because this method is not for the sake of beauty (*Mishnah Berurah* loc. cit. §§86). [The reference is to shortening hair with a razor but not shaving with a razor which is never permitted.]

41. *Sha'arei Teshuvah* 493:§§7, in the name of *Zera Emes*. The same ruling is given by *Sha'arim Metzuyanim BeHalachah* 120:§§11.

42. *Beis David* §277. The same ruling is given by responsa *Devar Moshe* part 1 §32 (cited by *Birkei Yosef* 493:§§3); and by *Ikrei HaDat* (21:1), in *Pischei Teshuvah* (493:§§2).

43. *Mishmeres Shalom os gimmel* §34. He does not indicate whether he means to prohibit this only during *shivah*, or during the entire thirty days.

If the Mourning Is for One's Parent

৵ "Until His Friends Reprimand Him"

19. If one is mourning for one's parent, he is forbidden to cut his hair even after *shloshim*, until his friends reprimand him for his unkempt appearance.[44]

Once his friends reprimand him, he may cut his hair, even if they do so on thethirtieth day itself.[45] However, if they reprimand him before the thirtieth day, he still may not take a haircut,[46] even if a festival occurs during the thirty days.[47] [See par. 21 below.]

The term, "his friends reprimand him" (*ga'aru bo chaveirav*), means that people [even non-Jews] tell him his hair is long.[47a] However, a mourner may not make a remark to friends about his long hair in order to cause them to reprimand him.[47b]

৵ Excessively Long Hair: The Time-limit for "Reprimanding"

20. When the mourner's hair is so long that one would expect his friends to reprimand him, he is permitted to take a haircut or shave even if they do not actually reprimand him.[48]

When would one expect his friends to reprimand him? Halachic authorities disagree on this time-limit, but the custom is to define the time-limit for a haircut as at the end of three months.[49]

Some rule that the three months are counted from his last haircut, even if three

---

44. *Shulchan Aruch Yoreh De'ah* 390:4.

45. *Chiddushei R' Akiva Eiger* loc. cit. citing *Elyah Zuta*. The same ruling is given by *Birkei Yosef* loc. cit. in the name of "several *Poskim*."

   Sdei Chemed (*Aveilus os* 19) states that the authorites are divided on this question. But he concludes that the consensus of the *poskim* is that the mourner may take a haircut on the thirtieth day if his friends reprimand him for his long hair.

46. See *Beis Yosef* (loc. cit.). He writes that if the mourner's friends reprimand him during *shloshim*, this has no effect. The *halachah* of someone mourning for his parent is certainly no more lenient than in the case of mourning for other family members; and in the latter case, the mourner may not take a haircut during the entire thirty days.

47. See *Rama* 390:4. He writes: "If a Festival occurs before his friends reprimand him, it has no effect [in canceling the prohibition against taking a haircut]." And *Pischei Teshuvah* (loc. cit. §§20) writes: "It would seem that the same applies to the combination of his friends' reprimand *and* a Festival, if the Festival occurs during the *shloshim*. This is clarified above, 389:5, with regard to ironing."

47a. See *Beis Yosef* (§390), who cites the Jerusalem Talmud: "What is 'reprimanding'? It is when they tell him, 'Go away from us.' " But see *Mishmeres Shalom os gimmel*, §47, who writes: "In our present version of the Jerusalem Talmud we do not find these words, and it is sufficient if they tell him his hair is long.' "

47b. See the responsa of *Maharshag* (§214), who writes that even the reprimands of [non-Jewish] high government officials are effective [in permitting the mourner to have his hair cut]. He goes on to state that the mourner is forbidden to tell his friends that his hair is long in order to have them reprimand him. "It would seem that all he can do is to uncover his head so that they will see that his hair is long."

48. *Birkei Yosef* loc. cit.

49. *Rama* 390:4.

months of mourning have not yet passed.[50] Others are strict, and count the three
months from the beginning of his mourning. If a festival occurs during this time, or
if the need for a haircut is urgent, one may be lenient and count from the last
haircut.[51]

Some rule that the time-limit is twice the person's customary amount of time
between haircuts. Thus, if he customarily has a haircut once a month, the time-limit
would be two months.[51a]

In some communities, the custom is that a person in mourning for his father or
mother does not take a haircut or shave during the entire twelve months of
mourning, except in case of need — for example, if his hair is so long that it
distresses him; or if he must go among non-Jews who would be disgusted by his
unkempt appearance.[52]

After the three-month time-limit has passed, the mourner is permitted to take
a haircut as often as he chooses. He does not have to wait another three
months for the next haircut.[53] This lenient custom is the prevalent one. However,
some rule strictly [and require that after each haircut the mourner must again wait

---

50. *Maharam Shick* (*Yoreh De'ah* §371) writes: "The time-limit the *halachah* gives us for
    'reprimanding' — three months — is to be calculated from the previous haircut, not from the
beginning of the mourning." He says that this may be deduced from the words of *Noda BiYehudah*
(*mahadura kamma Orach Chaim* §14), who writes that the reason for the three-month limit is that after
this time the long hair becomes disgusting and repulsive to people. "If so," reasons *Maharam Shick*,
"the implication for our question is that once the mourner's hair has reached three months' growth,
what does it matter whether three months have passed since the death? When all is said and done, his
hair is repulsive to all who see him. *Noda BiYehudah* in the same responsum writes that in those
countries where the custom of Jewish men is to shave, the stubble of a beard becomes repulsive after
two or three weeks; 'the short hairs sprouting on the person's face appear to the beholder likethorns
. . .' According to this, the same should apply to haircutting [i.e., the time-limit depends on how long
it takes for the hair to appear repulsive]."
    The same ruling is given by *Gesher HaChaim* 21:11:3.
51. *Maharam Shick* (loc. cit.) writes: "But in truth, the *Poskim* mention 'three months' without stating
    that it is to be counted from the previous haircut. This would imply [that in fact it is counted from
the beginning of the mourning]. Perhaps, in order to make the time-limit uniform, they instituted that
everyone should wait three months from the beginning of the mourning. In that case, my opinion is
annulled, unless there are other, independent reasons to permit [cutting the hair]; for example, if a
festival occurs after the first thirty days of mourning, or if the need for a haircut is urgent. In such a case,
it seems in my humble opinion that the custom is not [to be strict, but to count from the previous
haircut]."
    See also *Da'as Torah*, who states that for an important person who will look repulsive if his hair grows
long, one may be lenient [and permit him to cut his hair] after two months, and perhaps even after the
first thirty days of mourning.
51a. *Igros Moshe Yoreh De'ah*, part III, §156.
52. *Rama* loc. cit. citing *Or Zarua*.
53. *Chiddushei R' Akiva Eiger*, loc. cit. He deduces this from the words of *Darkei Moshe*, who cites
    Or Zarua. The same ruling is given by *Pischei Teshuvah* loc. cit. §§4, in the name of responsa
Adnei Paz §8. He interprets *Rama* as meaning that after the time-limit of "reprimanding him" has
passed (three months), the mourner may take a haircut whenever he wishes, in accord with his habit
before he became a mourner.

until his friends reprimand him for his long hair, or until three months have passed[54].

◄§ Shaving

21. For those who shave, the time-limit after which one would expect his friends to reprimand him for his unshaven beard is thirty days.[55] After that time, the mourner is permitted to shave. Regarding from when to count the thirty days, see above, par. 20.

◄§ During *Chol HaMo'ed*

22. If the time when his friends reprimand him (or when they would be expected to reprimand him) is during *Chol HaMo'ed*, the mourner is forbidden to take a haircut or shave during *Chol HaMo'ed*.[56]

---

54. *Siddur Derech HaChaim* states that whenever the mourner wishes to take a haircut, he must again have his friends' reprimands. Similarly, *Hagahos Yad Shaul* writes that after the mourner has his hair cut, he must again wait three months. The same ruling is given by *Igros Moshe* (*Yoreh De'ah* part 3 §156), who writes that it is proper to be strict on this matter; but that in a case of necessity, one need not be strict. He also writes that it "requires further study" to find a justification for the permission to take haircuts at will after the first instance of "reprimand."

55. *Pischei Teshuvah* loc. cit. §§4, citing *Noda BiYehudah mahadura kamma Orach Chaim* §14. The same ruling is given by responsa *Maharam Shick Yoreh De'ah* §371, cited above, footnote 50.

56. *Noda BiYehudah* loc. cit.
        See also *Ba'er Heitev* (*Orach Chaim* 548:§§11), who cites *Halachos Ketanos* (part 1: §285) as ruling that in this circumstance a haircut is permitted. But see *Sha'arei Teshuvah* (loc. cit. §§11), who cites many authorities as disagreeing with this ruling of *Halachos Ketanos*.

CHAPTER TWENTY-FIVE

Joy and Celebration

During *Shivah*

1. The mourner is forbidden to do things which produce or express joy.[1]

Therefore, he should not take a child onto his lap during the entire *shivah*, lest he [the mourner] become playful.[2]

He is forbidden to engage in much talk, frivolity or laughter, as it is written (*Ezekiel* 24:17), '*Sigh in silence*.'[3]

✑ Joyous Verses Preceding *Havdalah*

2. During *shivah* the mourner is forbidden to recite the joyous verses which usually precede *Havdalah* at the conclusion of the Sabbath.[4]

✑ The *Bris Milah* [Circumcision] of a Mourner's Son

3. Some have the custom that, on the night before a *bris,* they conduct a festive meal for their relatives and friends. If the *bris* of a mourner's son occurs during the mourner's *shivah*, one should not conduct this meal. Instead, he should arrange for a *minyan* of ten men to recite the customary verses.[5]

The father, while in *shivah*, is permitted to wear Sabbath clothes at the *bris*. Some rule that he is also permitted to wear shoes; but others disagree.[6]

---

1. *Levush* (*Yoreh De'ah* 391:1) writes: "It is self-evident that since he is called a 'mourner' (*avel*), he is forbidden joy and celebration for the entire first thirty days, for joy is the opposite of mourning, and that would be combining two opposites in one subject. . .Moreover, this [prohibition] is also included in [the Divine command to Ezekiel when he was in mourning]: '*Sigh in silence*' (*Ezekiel* 24:17)."

2. *Shulchan Aruch Yoreh De'ah* 391:1.

3. *Rambam* (*Hilchos Avel* 5:20) writes: "If the mourner is forbidden to ask about the welfare of others, all the more so is he forbidden to talk much or indulge in laughter, as it is said (*Ezekiel* 24:17), '*Sigh in silence*.' "

4. [ArtScroll *Siddur* p. 618.] *Pis'chei Teshuvah* loc. cit. §§1 citing responsa *Har HaKarmel* §20.

5. *Zachur LeAvraham* (*Dinei Avel*), cited in *Da'as Torah* §393, and in *Kol Bo Al Aveilus* p. 293.

6. *Zachur LeAvraham* (part 1 and part 3 *Dinei Avel* §1), cited in *Da'as Torah* (loc. cit.). The same ruling is given by *Gesher HaChaim* (28:8:8); and by *Pachad Yitzchak* in the name of *Halachos Ketanos* (part 1 responsum 289).

However, *Elyah Rabbah* (132:2) cites *Agudah* (end of *Mo'ed Katan*) as ruling that the mourner must go without shoes to the synagogue. The same ruling is given by responsa *Shevus Yaakov* (part 1 §86), and by *Be'ur Halachah* (§559), in the name of *Bigdei Yesha*, with regard to Tishah B'Av. He

Likewise, he is permitted to wear newly laundered clothes, if he has someone else put them on first.[7]

He may go to the synagogue to pray, and may remain there until after the *bris*.[8]

Some rule that he is permitted to be called up to the Torah-reading on the day of the *bris*. However, it is preferable that he go out momentarily so as not to be called up to the Torah-reading.[9]

After the *bris*, he must resume all the restrictions of mourning.[10]

Even if the *bris* is not performed on the eighth day after the birth, the father is obligated to have his son circumcised as soon as possible; he is forbidden to purposely postpone the *bris* until after the first three days of mourning.[11]

4. In some communities, it is customary to bring the baby to his *bris* to the accompaniment of musical instruments. If the father is in mourning, this is forbidden during *shivah*.[12] [See below, par. 32.]

5. The father of the baby is permitted to conduct the festive meal of the *bris* in his own home during his period of mourning. He may also eat at this meal, but he should not sit at the table.[13]

---

states that the mourner is forbidden to wear shoes to the *bris*, since the prohibition against wearing shoes is a law of the Talmud.

7. *Sdei Chemed, Aveilus* §40.

8. The *gaon* R' Zalman Margolios, *Hilchos Aveilus* §11.

9. *Pachad Yitzchak* (part 1 p. 5b), citing *Halachos Ketanos* (loc. cit.). The same ruling is given by *Leket HaKemach* (§289). However, he mentions that *Maharshal* disagrees, forbidding the mourner to be called up to the Torah-reading, even if the *bris* is on the Sabbath. The same prohibitive ruling is cited by *Kol Bo Al Aveilus* (p. 293).

Gesher HaChaim (21:8:8) permits the mourner to be called up to the Torah-reading, but adds: "However, since the *bris* is a personal festival, this is comparable to the *halachah* regarding the mourner on a festival. Then, even on Simchas Torah, he can go out momentarily so as not to be in the synagogue during the Torah-reading. Similarly, [in the case of a *bris*] the mourner can go out momentarily so as not to be called up to the Torah-reading. However, if he did not go out, and is present in the synagogue, he is permitted to be called up to the Torah-reading, since [the *bris*] is his personal festival."

10. The *gaon* R' Zalman Margolios (loc. cit.). The same ruling is given by *Elyah Rabbah* (§132 *sif* 2).
   He states there that a certain halachic authority erred and ruled that no mourning was to be observed that day.

11. The *gaon* R' Zalman Margolios loc. cit. par. 12.

12. *Da'as Torah* (§391), citing *Zachur LeAvraham*. The same ruling is given by *Sdei Chemed* (*Aveilus* §50), citing *Ma'aseh Avraham* (*Yoreh De'ah* §48). This ruling is also cited by *Gesher HaChaim* (loc. cit.).

13. *Drishah* (394:6) cites *Maharshal*, who in turn cites *Roke'ach*: "If a man is in mourning, and during the first thirty days a son is born to him, he should not make a celebration and feast on the day of the *bris milah*." *Shach* (loc. cit. §§2) quotes this, and concludes: "It seems to me that this is not the custom." [In other words, the father *should* make a celebration.]

Hagahos Yad Shaul comments: "I am surprised [at the ruling of *Roke'ach*]; for [the Sages] said: 'When a boy is born, the whole family is healed.' All the more so, if a boy is born to him, why should he not rejoice and make a feast; and this rejoicing is obligatory, as is derived from the verse (*Genesis* 21:8), 'Abraham made a great feast on the day Isaac was weaned' [which according to *Tosafos, Shabbos* 130a, refers to the feast Abraham made at Isaac's circumcision]. *Shach* wrote, 'this [the

✌ The *Sandak*

6. During *shivah*, a mourner is permitted to be the *sandak* (the one who holds the baby on his lap at the time of circumcision). After the first three days of mourning, he is even permitted to go to the synagogue for the purpose of being *sandak*.[14] However, he may not wear Sabbath clothes or put on shoes.[15]

Some rule that it is preferable (*lechatchilah*) not to offer the role of *sandak* to a mourner; but if someone offers, the mourner is permitted to accept.[16] Others rule that there is no objection to choosing a mourner to be *sandak*.[17]

✌ The *Kvatter*

7. The one who carries the baby into the room for the *bris* is called the *kvatter*. A man or woman in mourning is not allowed to leave his or her home to be the

---

prohibitive ruling of *Roke'ach*] is not the custom.' And in my humble opinion, it is forbidden to follow this custom [of *Roke'ach*]."

Sdei Chemed (*Aveilus* §50) cites *Chikrei Lev* and *Pe'as Yam* as ruling that the mourner is permitted to make the circumcision feast in his home, even during *shivah*. The same ruling is given by *Yavetz* in his *Migdal Oz* (*nachal* 13:6). He states that a mourner connected with the *bris* is permitted to eat at the same time as [the other guests] if the meal is in his own home, even within *shivah*; but that he should not sit at the table.

The lenient ruling is also given by *Gesher HaChaim*, in the name of *Zera Emes* (*Yoreh De'ah* §158), *Zachur LeAvraham* (*Avel* §1), et al.

14. *Rama* (393:3) writes: "If the mourner is a *mohel* or *baal bris*, after the first three days of mourning, he should pray at home; then, when they bring the baby to be circumcised, the mourner should go to the synagogue." *Shach* (loc. cit. §§4) explains: " '*Baal bris*' means the *sandak*. Therefore, during the first three days he may not leave his home. But obviously, according to all opinions, the *father* of the baby may leave his home even during the first three days of mourning."

15. *Birkei Yosef* 391:1.

16. See *Birkei Yosef* (loc. cit.). See also *Hagahos Yad Shaul* (§393), who writes: "Thus, it seems to me that if the honor [of being *sandak*] is offered to the mourner, he should accept it; but it is not fitting to honor him [with being *sandak*]." He writes the same in his *Yoseif Da'as* (loc. cit.).

See also *Os Shalom* (265:27), by the *gaon* of Munkatch, who writes at length on this, concluding that it "would require further study" to permit the mourner to sit on a chair for the purpose [of being *sandak*].

17. *Birkei Yosef* (loc. cit.) writes: "*Maharam Mintz* (§86) states in the name of *Or Zarua* that the mourner is permitted [to be *sandak*] even during *shivah*. This also seems to be the opinion of *Beis David* (§191)."

See also *Mishmeres Shalom* (*os samech* §30), who writes: "I have seen in *HaParness* (§238), in the name of *Roke'ach*, that the mourner is permitted to be *baal bris* [*sandak*] on any day [of his mourning]. The same ruling is given by *Rikanti* (§591, citing *Avi HaEzri* and *Beis David*), and by *Or Zarua* (§440; and see *Or Zarua* also in *Hilchos Milah* 107:§§4); and this is the *halachah*."

Sdei Chemed (*Aveilus* §48) cites the ruling of *Hagahos Yad Shaul* (quoted in our previous footnote) and comments: "His words present difficulty, for they imply that there might be reason to prohibit the *mohel*, too, from performing the *bris* when in mourning. He ultimately permits the *mohel* to do so, since 'not everyone knows how to perform circumcisions.' But the reasoning is questionable, for it is clear from the words of *Rama* that, after the first three days of mourning, a mourner may perform a circumcision even if another *mohel* is available [see par. 8 in text]. And even during the first three days, it seems that the only prohibition is against the mourner's leaving his home [to perform the circumcision; but he is permitted to perform it in his own home]. . ." Further, *Sdei Chemed* writes that the permissive ruling is also given by *Zachur LeAvraham* (s.v. *sandak*), *Misgeres HaShulchan*, *Pachad Yitzchak*, and *Ikrei HaDat*.

kvatter, since this role at the *bris* is not a *mitzvah*. But if the *bris* is performed in the mourner's home, the mourner may be permitted to be *kvatter*.[18]

⌁ The *Mohel*

8. If the mourner is a *mohel*, he is permitted, after the first three days of mourning, to go to the synagogue to perform the *bris*. But he is forbidden to wear Sabbath clothes.[18a]

During the first three days of mourning, he may not go to the synagogue unless there is no other *mohel* in town. In that case, he may go even on his first day of mourning.

Some rule leniently, permitting him to go even during the first three days of mourning, even if there is another *mohel* in town.[19]

If the *bris* is performed in the *mohel*'s home, then according to all authorities he may act as *mohel*, even during the first three days of mourning.[20]

⌁ The Redemption of a Firstborn (*Pidyon HaBen*)

9. [On the thirtieth day after the birth of a firstborn boy, it is a *mitzvah* to perform a *pidyon haben* — see *Shulchan Aruch Yoreh De'ah* §305.]

Even if the father and mother are in mourning, they are permitted to wear Sabbath clothes at the *pidyon haben*.[21]

Some rule that they are also permitted to wear shoes; but others forbid this.[22]

They are permitted to take part in the festive meal of the *pidyon haben*, if it is conducted in their home.[23]

If the *kohen* is a mourner, and there is no other *kohen* in town, he is permitted to leave his home to go to the *pidyon haben*, even on the first day of mourning. But if there are other *kohanim* in town, he may leave his home only after three days of mourning.[24]

---

18. *Sdei Chemed* (loc. cit.), in the name of *Ba'ei Chayei* (*Yoreh De'ah* §242); and *Mishmeres Shalom* (loc. cit.), citing *Ikrei HaDat* (*Yoreh De'ah* 36:8, in the name of *Ba'ei Chayei*). See also *Birkei Yosef* (*Yoreh De'ah* §393, in *Shiurei Berachah* §§2). He cites this ruling in the name of *Knesses HaGedolah* (*Yoreh De'ah* §242).

18a. *Birkei Yosef* 391:1.

19. *Rama* 393:3, and *Shach* 393:§§5.

20. This may be inferred from *Shach* (loc. cit. §§5), who implies that the whole prohibition is only because the mourner is forbidden to leave his home [see note 17 above].
    This permission is also the ruling of *Sdei Chemed* loc. cit.

21. *Shevus Yaakov* (part 2 §102), cited in *Mishmeres Shalom* os pe §1.

22. The discussion cited above (footnote 6) applies here as well.

23. *Rama* 391:2. The discussion cited above (footnote 13) applies here as well.

24. See *Chiddushei R' Akiva Eiger* (§393). He writes, citing the author of *Knesses HaGedolah* (in his work, *Ba'ei Chayei*), that the same *halachah* applies to the *kohen* as to a *mohel*. Thus, for those authorities who rule leniently in the case of a *mohel*, permitting him to perform the circumcision even within the first three days of mourning, the same would apply to a *kohen* in the case of *pidyon haben*.

◈ Attending a Wedding

10. Some rule that even during *shivah*, parents may attend their child's wedding, but during the meal they should not be seated in the usual 'honorable and prominent manner" [see footnote].

Other relatives of the bridegroom or bride are forbidden to attend the wedding if they are in mourning.[25]

During *Shloshim* and the Twelve Months

◈ Attending a Festive Meal

11. One who is mourning for any family member except his father or mother may not attend a festive meal until after *shloshim*. If he is mourning for his father or

---

25. *Igros Moshe* (*Yoreh De'ah* part II:§169) writes that the parents may go to the wedding during *shivah*, but other relatives are forbidden to attend. His source is *Knesses HaGedolah*, cited by *Gilyon Maharsha* §391 and §392. He writes, "A father may attend his daughter's wedding . . ." To explain this ruling, *Igros Moshe* draws an analogy with the prohibition against working, where an exemption is made in the case of financial loss [*davar ha'aveid*; see above, chapter 18]. The reason is obvious: "It is extremely painful for a father not to be able to attend his child's wedding. Such pain is stronger than financial loss; for we see that a father spends a great deal on all kinds of expenses in order to attend his child's wedding. Hence, there could be no greater *davar ha'aveid* than [not being able to attend the wedding] — and in the case of *davar ha'aveid*, the prohibition is waived even during *shivah*. However, other mourners, such as the brother or sister [of the bridegroom or bride], if unable to attend the wedding, do not have as much pain [as the father]; therefore, one should not permit them [to attend]. . . ."

Igros Moshe mentions that *Maharsha* (§391) cites *Ra'nach* as permitting a mother to attend her son's wedding only because the son was unwilling to get married unless his mother could attend as a *shoshvinis* ['*unterfierer*']. *Igros Moshe* states: "It may be that [*Ra'nach*] disagrees [with *Knesses HaGedolah*], for *Knesses HaGedolah* implies that the parent's attendance is in any case permitted, even if his or her pain would not cause the wedding to be canceled. In practice, we should apply the rule that in matters of mourning, we follow the more lenient ruling [i.e., to allow the parent to attend even if the wedding would otherwise not be canceled]. Likewise, it is obvious that the mother, too, should be permitted to attend her child's wedding even if she is in mourning. . ."

Igros Moshe (*Orach Chaim* part IV:§40,16) elaborates further on this and rules that since the loss felt by a parent who cannot attend the wedding of a child "is incalculable, and goes beyond money, a parent who is mourning may attend the wedding of a child even within the first three days of *shivah*. . . . As for *Maharsha's* stipulation: . . .'however, they [the mourning parents] should not eat there,' it is obvious that the intent is not to prohibit him from deriving benefit from the meal for there is no reason for such a prohibition. Rather, it is clear that the intent is that the mourner should not participate in the meal in an honorable and prominent manner, as is the custom for the parents of the bride and groom who are seated at the head table where they are served. Instead, they should be seated with the other guests. Perhaps it is correct to be stringent and not be seated at a specific place for the meal; rather, they should eat each course at a different table. The primary consideration is that it should not be in an honorable and prominent manner." [See also below, footnote 38.]

However, *Kol Bo Al Aveilus* (p. 272) writes: "I was chosen to officiate at a wedding, and the brother of the bridegroom's mother died. It was difficult to postpone the wedding . . . The mother longed to see her son under the *chupah*. Likewise the maternal grandmother, who was in mourning for her son, wanted to see her grandson on his day of joy. A few days of their mourning had already passed, and I permitted, after the first three days of mourning, that they should come to the wedding — but only at night, [and] at a time when there was no music or dancing; and they were not allowed to eat or drink there; and they returned home immediately after the seven blessings [recited under the *chupah*]."

See also responsa *Kinyan Torah* IV:§121.

mother, he must wait until after twelve months. Even in a leap-year (of thirteen months), the time-limit is only twelve months.[26]

12. A "friendly exchange of meals" (*simchas merei'us*) is when one friend invites the other to a festive meal, and then the other reciprocates the next day.

If a person is invited to such a meal, and thus becomes obligated to reciprocate the next day, but in the meantime becomes a mourner [for any family member except a parent], he is permitted to reciprocate the meal immediately after *shivah*. However, if he is not obligated to reciprocate, he may not attend such a meal until after *shloshim*.

If the mourning is for his father or mother, he may not attend such a meal for the entire twelve months of mourning, even if he had become obligated to reciprocate.[27]

13. The custom, as noted above, is that one who is mourning for any family member except for a parent may not attend any festive meal until after *shloshim*. If he is mourning for his parent, he must wait until after twelve months before attending such a meal. (However, as will be seen in the following paragraphs, there are exceptions to this rule.)

The previous paragraph applies to a meal outside the mourner's home.[28] If it is in his own home, the *halachah* is more lenient, permitting him to attend even the meal of a circumcision — and all the more so, other meals, which are less joyful celebrations. Some permit this even during *shivah*; but others forbid it.[29]

In the case of a wedding feast, one should be strict, and not attend even if it is held in his home.[30]

(For more on the topic of the wedding feast, see below, par. 17.)

---

26. *Shulchan Aruch* 391:2. And see *Taz* (loc. cit. §§1), who writes: "I am surprised that there are people who observe some mourning also in the thirteenth month [of a leap-year]. What is their source for this? In truth it is groundless. And [*Bach*] writes the same."

27. *Shulchan Aruch* 391:2. *Shach* §§1 states: "But it seems to me that the custom of *simchas merei'us* is no longer practiced."

28. *Rama* 391:2.

29. *Rama* (loc. cit.) writes that this is permitted "even during *shivah*." The same ruling is given by *Chazon LaMo'ed*, citing *Da'as Kedoshim*.

   Migdal Oz (nachal 13 os 6) writes that a mourner connected with the *bris* is permitted to eat at the same time as [the other guests] if the meal is in his own home, even within *shivah*; but he should not sit at the table.

   However, *Gesher HaChaim* (21:8:6) writes that this is not the custom; the *Acharonim*, he states, have ruled that only the father of the baby is permitted to eat at the meal, on condition that it takes place in his home. But under that condition, he may take part even within *shivah*.

   And see *She'elas Yavetz* (part 2 §181), who writes: "In any case, it seems obvious to me that if the mourning is for one's married sister, no one prohibits attending any meal which does not involve rejoicing (*simchah*), even on a weekday, and even outside the mourner's home. And the permission is all the more obvious if the meal is also a *mitzvah*, such as a *bris milah* or *pidyon haben*."

30. *Rama* 391:2. I have heard from major contemporary *Poskim* that the custom is to be lenient [and permit the mourner to take part] even in a *sheva brachos* feast, if it is in the mourner's home [, but not in a wedding feast].

14. [On a weekday,] the *sandak* and the *mohel* are permitted to wear Sabbath clothes until after the *bris*,[31] if their *shloshim* have passed.

Some rule that they may eat at the festive meal of the *bris*, even if it is not in their home. This applies after *shivah* for any family member except their parent. If the mourning is for their parent, it applies after *shloshim*.[31a]

⋄ Taking Part in Meals on the Sabbath / *Non-Simchah* and *Simchah*

15. Some rule that the mourner may take part in certain types of Sabbath meals which are not defined as *simchah* (joyous celebrations). This applies after *shloshim* for one's parent; and in the case of mourning for other family members, after *shivah*. It includes a *shalom zachar* (on Friday night, in honor of the birth of a boy); the meal of a *bris*; a *kiddush* in honor of the birth of a girl; and the like.[32] However, others disagree.[32a]

---

31. *Rama* loc. cit.

31a. *Rama* (loc. cit.) writes: "The mourner is permitted to go to the *bris milah* and to eat there, if he is after *shloshim*, even if the circumcision is not in his home."

Taz (loc. cit. §§3) comments: "This is surprising to me, for a responsum of *Maharil* (§116) implies that this is permitted after *shivah*; and this ruling is cited by *Beis Yosef*. Afterwards, I saw that [*Rama* in his earlier work,] *Darkei Moshe*, on the strength of his own reasoning, concludes that the prohibition [against going to the meal] lasts until after *shloshim*. Now, it is obvious that he was speaking about [someone mourning for] his father or mother; for if the mourning were for some other family member, it goes without saying that one is permitted [to go to a meal] after *shloshim*. And it cannot be that the intention [of *Darkei Moshe*] was to indicate that this is prohibited during *shloshim* [in the case of mourning for someone other than one's parent]; for, if so, he would have said, 'it is forbidden for the entire *shloshim*.' It must be, therefore, that he was speaking of mourning for one's parent after *shivah* had passed [and indicating that, even so, one may not take part in the meal until after *shloshim*]. This ruling is surprising, for *Rosh* (*Perek Elu Megalchin*) writes explicitly that during *shloshim*, the halachah [in this respect] is the same whether one is mourning for some other family member, or for one's parents. Nevertheless, one should not contradict the ruling of *Rama* by being lenient during *shloshim*, in the case of mourning for one's parent."

Nekudos HaKesef (loc. cit.) writes that *Maharil* did not permit [participating in a meal] during *shloshim*, in the case of mourning for one's parent.

See also *Da'as Torah* (loc. cit.), who cites responsa *Pnei Yehoshua* (part II:§38) as permitting the *mohel* or the *baal bris* [*sandak*] to go to the festive meal of the *bris milah* even within *shloshim* [but after *shivah*], in the case of mourning for a family member other than one's parent. The same ruling is given by *Beis Lechem Yehudah* (loc. cit.); but he adds that this applies only to the *mohel* and *sandak*, but not to those performing other honored functions at a *bris milah*. This is also the conclusion of *Gesher HaChaim* (loc. cit.).

32. *Chiddushei HaGaon R' Zalman Margolios* (*Aveilus* §23) in the name of *She'elas Yavetz*. He writes: "Even though, on a weekday, the custom is that the mourner may not go to any festive meal at all, nonetheless on the Sabbath he is permitted." This ruling is cited by *Kol Bo Al Aveilus* (p. 361), and also by *Gesher HaChaim* (21:8:12). *Gesher HaChaim* also writes that, in the case of mourning for one's parent, the permission applies only after *shloshim*.

32a. *Pischei Teshuvah* (391:§§2) writes: "See *She'elas Yavetz* (part II:§179-185), who rules on numerous details of this question; but, in my opinion, his conclusions are not indisputable, so I am not citing them." And in §§4, *Pischei Teshuvah* writes: "See responsa *Adnei Paz* (end of §10), who rules that 'if one forgot on Friday night and took part in the meal [*shalom zachar*] for the birth of a son, he is permitted to go to the meal of the circumcision the next day (the Sabbath); for if he were not to go, this would be publicizing his mourning.' But this ruling is not clear." The implication is that, if one did

The mourner is permitted to eat the regular Sabbath meal at a friend's house, or to eat with a group of friends at the Third Meal (Se'udah Shlishis). Even if this meal continues into the night following the Sabbath, this is permitted.[33]

16. For a meal of *simchah* [joy], such as a wedding celebration, the mourner is forbidden to take part even on the Sabbath. However, in the case of relatives whose absence from the meal would be conspicuously noticed — for example, the bridegroom's/bride's brothers or sisters, or their nephews and nieces — one may be lenient and permit them to attend the meal if invited. If they were not to go, this would be like conspicuous mourning, which is forbidden on the Sabbath.[34]

⋖§ Assisting with the Meal at a Wedding

17. Some rule that the mourner is permitted to assist with serving a festive meal — even at a wedding. If he is mourning for a family member other than his parent, this applies after *shivah*. If he is mourning for his parent, it applies after *shloshim*. However, he must eat by himself, not at the table with the other guests. The permission also depends on where the mourner assists. For details on this aspect, see note.[35]

---

not forget, one is forbidden to go to the meal. And this prohibitive ruling is given by responsa *Yad HaLevi* (*Yoreh De'ah* §230 os 2). Likewise, responsa *Igros Moshe* (*Yoreh De'ah* part III:§161) states that the mourner is only permitted to go to [the *shalom zachar*] of a relative or close friend, since staying away would be considered publicizing his mourning on the Sabbath; but if the one holding the meal is not a relative or close friend, the mourner is forbidden to go.

33. *Chiddushei HaGaon R' Zalman Margolios* loc. cit.

34. *She'elas Yavetz* part II:§180.

35. See *Rama* (391:3), who writes: "Some rule that the mourner is permitted to eat with those that serve at a wedding feast or a circumcision, on condition that the feast is not in a place of celebration, such as a different house; but others forbid this [even under that condition] and the custom follows this second opinion. However, if he wishes, the mourner may assist with the meal there, and then, in his own home, eat food sent to him from the wedding."

Aruch HaShulchan (391:13) comments: "It seems to me that the permission to assist with the meal refers only to work in the kitchen where the cooks are, and in the place where the food is prepared for serving, but not to hand the food to the guests; for [directly serving the food to the guests], too, is part of the rejoicing. But the prevalent custom is to be lenient in this matter."

Likewise, *Da'as Torah* (loc. cit.) writes in the name of *Beis Meir* that the mourner may only assist in a place other than where the rejoicing is. He goes on to quote *Rama*'s statement that "the custom follows [the strict] opinion. However, if he wishes, the mourner may assist with the meal there. . ." He interprets the word "there" as meaning, "in a place other than where the rejoicing is." For, "if the intention were that the mourner could even serve food where the rejoicing is, this would be no better than someone who goes to listen to the blessings, which *Rama* testifies is prohibited, citing 'the custom of Ashkenaz.' As *Bach* points out, this is also why [*Rama*] cited only the opinion that the permission applies even within *shloshim*, without mentioning any dissenting opinion."

Nachamu Ami cites the *gaon* R' Shlomo Zalman Auerbach, *shlita*, as ruling that "to serve at the wedding means to serve like waiters do, not like the hosts who honor their guests by bringing them a cup of wine, and the like." And I heard the same from the *gaon* R' Elyashiv, *shlita* — that the mourner must serve all the time, and it is not sufficient for him to serve a little at the beginning of the meal. The same ruling is given by *Kol Bo Al Aveilus* (p. 359 note 27), citing *Naharei Afarsemon* (*Yoreh De'ah* §54), who states that the intent is that the mourner should serve in the kitchen, but not in the banquet hall.

In practice, the custom is that only the relatives of the bridegroom and bride take advantage of this permission.[36]

If the mourner is the brother/sister of the bridegroom/bride, some rule leniently and permit attending the wedding even during the *shloshim* for a parent, on condition that the mourner serve as a waiter and eat by himself.[37]

◆§ Eating at a Child's Wedding

If the mourner is the father/mother of the bridegroom/bride (for whom the wedding is considered a personal festival), and if the parent's absence from the wedding meal would cause pain to the bridegroom/bride, some authorities are lenient and permit the parent to eat at the wedding meal even without serving as a waiter.[38] [See also above, par. 10 regarding a parent attending the wedding of a child during *shivah*.] And if the custom at weddings is that the father sits at the table with the bridegroom, the mourner is permitted to sit there, even though the Grace after Meals includes the special passage for a wedding, שֶׁהַשִּׂמְחָה בִּמְעוֹנוֹ, '. . .in Whose abode is this celebration.' However, it is preferable that the mourner should not be the one to lead the blessing, but only respond with the other participants.[39]

◆§ The Officiating Rabbi

18. A rabbi or other Torah scholar is permitted to serve as the officiating rabbi (*mesader kiddushin*) at a wedding, even during the *shloshim* but after the

---

36. *Gesher HaChaim* 21:8:11.

37. Ibid. and *Chazon LaMo'ed* 17:16:5.

38. *Aruch HaShulchan* (391:10) writes: "In my humble opinion, in case of necessity one should rely on the lenient opinions, since הֲהֲלָכָה כְּדִבְרֵי הַמֵּיקֵל בְּאָבֵל, 'the *halachah* follows the lenient opinion in the laws of mourning.' Thus, at a celebration of his sons or grandchildren, [the mourner] is certainly permitted [to take part in the meal]."

Igros Moshe (*Yoreh De'ah* part II §171) writes: "With regard to eating, *Gilyon Maharsha* states, '. . .on condition that he should not eat at the wedding feast.' However, it would seem that the prohibition is only against eating like an invited guest at the meal. But if he eats as the waiters do, the prohibition does not apply, since this kind of eating is not classified as rejoicing. Hence it is preferable that he should not eat in one fixed place, but should eat one food here, another there, so that it will be obvious that this is merely an ordinary [i.e., non-festive] type of eating. The reason for prohibiting eating is not that eating *per se* constitutes rejoicing . . . rather, the celebration of the wedding is prohibited, and eating is included in the general prohibition of rejoicing. But since the mourner [who is a parent of the bridegroom or bride] is permitted to be present from the standpoint of the wedding, how could eating be prohibited? One must say, then, that the prohibition against eating is simply a reminder, so that he will not forget that he is in mourning. Hence, the prohibition is only against eating like an invited guest, but not against ordinary eating like that of the waiters." [See also *Igros Moshe* cited above, note 25.]

A similar ruling is given by *Gesher HaChaim* loc. cit. who states that one should permit [the parents] to eat at the wedding feast, even if they do not assist with the meal. Likewise *Zera Emes* (part 3 §170) permits this, "since it is no less permissible than the case of someone who is marrying off an orphan boy or girl, in accord with the opinion of *Ravad*."

39. *Igros Moshe* loc. cit.

Responsa *Sheivet HaLevi* (*Yoreh De'ah* §213) writes that in a case where one is permitted to go to the wedding, one is also permitted to hear the music played there, for, as *Magen Avraham* states (§338, citing *Maharil*), "there is no *chupah* without music."

shivah of mourning for his father or mother.[40] If this is necessary for his livelihood, some even permit him to sit at the meal,[41] but he should not eat there.[42]

ᦥ *Shoshvin*

19. The mourner is permitted to serve as *shoshvin* (those who accompany the bridegroom or bride to the *chupah*; Yiddish: *unterfierer*) for the bridegroom or bride. If the mourning is for a family member other than father or mother, this is permitted after *shivah*. If the mourning is for one's father or mother, it is permitted after *shloshim*.[43]

Some rule that a relative of the bridegroom or bride may serve as *shoshvin* after *shivah*, even if the mourning is for his father or mother.[44] In performing this function, the mourner is permitted to wear Sabbath clothes,[45] but not to eat at the wedding meal.[46] Some authorities also permit the mourner to eat at the meal, after first serving as a waiter for a short time.[47]

---

40. See *Darkei Moshe* (loc. cit. §§2). He permits the mourner to serve as the officiating rabbi (*mesader kiddushin*). He states that this is the ruling given by *Maharam*, cited in *Mordechai* (*Mo'ed Katan* §891). He also wrote this opinion to the *gaon* R' Meir Padua, who agreed. The same ruling is given by responsa *Maharam Mintz* (§86), cited by *Chiddushei R' Akiva Eiger* loc. cit.

41. Responsa *Tuv Ta'am Vada'as* III:§241.

42. *Dudaei HaSadeh* (§62), cited in *Kol Bo Al Aveilus* p. 359. He also cites him as ruling that a Torah scholar who customarily speaks at weddings is permitted to go to the wedding and speak there, even if he is not the officiating rabbi; for if people are permitted to attend the wedding on the basis of giving ordinary assistance with the meal, delivering a Torah discourse is no less justification.

 Kol Bo Al Aveilus also mentions that, according to some authorities, a mourner assisting with the meal may be present only in the kitchen, but not in the dining hall. According to this opinion, he writes, further study would be required to determine if the mourner is allowed to go to deliver a Torah discourse. But *Dudaei HaSadeh* permits this if the scholar is also a relative of the bridegroom or bride, since there are authorities who in any case permit a relative to attend, even without delivering a Torah discourse.

 A cantor (*chazzan*) or a caterer (*shamash*) are also permitted to go to the wedding to perform their function, even within *shloshim*, since this is comparable to conducting business [,which is permitted after *shivah*].

43. *Rama* 391:3. *Shach* (§§5) cites the ruling of *Rama* that this permission applies "only after *shloshim*." However, he mentions that *Bach* rules more leniently [i.e., permitting after *shivah*]. *Taz* (loc. cit. §§4) also cites *Bach*, who draws an inference from the case of mourning for one's parent. In that case, the mourner may serve as *shoshvin* after *shloshim*. If so, reasons *Bach*, in the case of mourning for a family member other than one's parent, one may certainly serve as *shoshvin* after *shivah*. "There is more reason to permit, *within* thirty days, in the case of another family member, than to permit, *after* thirty days, in the case of one's parent." We have already noted above that the ruling of the *Acharonim* follows that of *Bach*. This is also the ruling given by *Pischei Teshuvah* (loc. cit. §§7) in the name of *Noda BiYehudah*.

44. The *gaon* R' Zalman Margolios, *Aveilus* §22. He also writes that the permission may even be extended to a mourner who is not a relative, if it would be difficult to find someone else to serve as *shoshvin*." The same ruling is given by *Gesher HaChaim* (loc. cit. §4). And see *Pischei Teshuvah* loc. cit.

45. *Rama* loc. cit. And see *Shach* loc. cit. §§4.

46. *Taz* 391:§§4.

47. *Beis Lechem Yehudah* loc. cit. He is also cited by *Chiddushei R' Akiva Eiger* loc. cit. The same ruling is given by *Pischei Teshuvah* (loc. cit.), citing responsa *Panim Me'iros* (part 3, end of §37). However, *Sha'arei Teshuvah* (551:§§3), after citing the ruling of *Panim Me'iros*, writes: "In our

In the case where parents during mourning are *shoshvin* at the marriage of their children, see above, note 25.

⋅⋅⋅ If the Mourner's Presence Is Crucial

20. If the gathering is purely for the sake of a *mitzvah* — for example, if someone, for the sake of Heaven, is marrying off a bridegroom and bride who are orphans — and if the mourner's absence would mean that the wedding would not take place, a mourner for his father or mother is permitted to take part after *shloshim*.[48]

Some rule that this applies not only if the match would be canceled altogether, but even if the mourner's absence would cause pain to the bridegroom and bride.[49]

If the mourning is for a family member other than one's parent, some authorities permit the mourner to take part in such a wedding after *shivah*.[50] And if the mourner's absence would mean canceling the match altogether, some authorities permit even someone mourning for his father or mother to take part after *shivah*.[51]

⋅⋅⋅ Tenth Man at a *Sheva Brachos*

21. If the mourner is needed as the tenth man to complete a *minyan* for one of the seven wedding feasts (*sheva brachos*), he may eat at the meal.[52]

At a *sheva brachos* feast, there is a requirement that one of the participants should be *panim chadashos* (lit., "a new face"), i.e., someone who was not at the wedding or the subsequent feasts. If the mourner is needed to fulfill this requirement, he is permitted to eat at the meal.[53] Others prohibit the mourner to

---

lands, the custom is to be strict, in accord with the ruling of *Taz*. However, if [the mourners] are relatives [of the bridegroom or bride], they assist with the meal, like the hosts, and then eat with them. Nevertheless, it is not proper for [the mourners] to be there when the musicians play their instruments; and this applies all the more so to someone mourning for his parent, or to a woman mourning for her husband. Even though she assists with the meal, she should refrain from hearing the singing."

48. *Rama* 391:2. The reason is explained by *Even Yaakov* (56:5) in the name of *Yoseif Da'as*: The observance of mourning for one's parent, after *shloshim*, is only for the sake of honoring them. Therefore, we can be certain that if something is done for the sake of Heaven, one's parent would relinquish their honor for the sake of the *mitzvah* — and, on the contrary, doing such a great *mitzvah* is in itself the best way of honoring them.

49. *Aruch HaShulchan* 391:5.

50. We have already mentioned, above, the disagreement between *Shach* and *Bach* on this issue. *Shach* prohibits, even in the case of mourning for a family member other than one's parent, until after *shloshim*. *Bach* permits, in that case, after *shivah*. The *Acharonim* agree with *Bach*.

51. *Aruch HaShulchan* 391:6.

52. *Hagahos Asheri*, citing *Or Zarua*, and cited by *Chiddushei R' Akiva Eiger* loc. cit. In fact, *Or Zarua* does not clarify whether the leniency applies even within *shloshim*. *Gesher HaChaim* (loc. cit.) wrote that it does, but he did not give his source. Perhaps, since *Or Zarua* did not mention any distinction between before or after the thirtieth day, *Gesher HaChaim* inferred that the permission applies even before.

53. Apparently, in the case of the "tenth man," the permission is granted because otherwise, without a *minyan* of ten men, it is impossible to recite the seven wedding blessings. If so, the same applies when there are already ten men, but there is no "new face." In that case, too, it is impossible to recite

participate even if he is needed for *panim chadashos*.[53a]

✎§ Attending a Wedding Ceremony [*Chupah*]

22. Some rule that a mourner may go in to where a wedding ceremony [*chupah*]
    is taking place, in order to hear the wedding benedictions, as long as he does
not go in while the guests are eating.

Others forbid this, ruling that the mourner must stand outside to hear the bene-
dictions.[54] But he should not go into the wedding hall at all during the time of dancing
and celebration. "And this is the custom followed in Ashkenaz and these lands."[54]

The above applies when both the *chupah* and the celebration take place in the
same hall. If the *chupah* takes place elsewhere — for example, in the synagogue —
and the wedding blessings are recited there, but no celebrating takes place there at
all, the mourner is permitted to take part. This applies immediately after *shivah*.
However, others rule that it applies only after *shloshim*, and this latter opinion is the
one followed in practice.[54a]

In some communities, a stricter custom prevails. Until the end of the twelve
months of mourning, the mourner may hear the blessings of the *chupah* only by
standing outside the synagogue.[55]

✎§ Attending a Circumcision, *Pidyon HaBen*, *Bar Mitzvah*, or Engagement Celebration [*Tena'im*]

23. After *shivah*, until the end of *shloshim*, the mourner is permitted to attend a
    circumcision, *pidyon haben*, *bar mitzvah*, or engagement (*tena'im*), but may
not partake of the meal.[56] If refreshments (pastries and the like) are served, he may
partake of them. But if there is dancing and music, the mourner should not attend.
The same applies to all the types of celebrations discussed below.[57]

✎§ Attending a *Siyum*

24. After *shloshim*, some authorities permit the mourner to take part in the festive
    meal for completing the study of a tractate (*siyum*).[58] Others rule that he may

---

the seven blessings. Thus, if the mourner can fulfill the need for a "new face," he is permitted to take
part. And R' Shlomo Zalman Auerbach, *shlita*, wrote to me that this is correct.

53a. Major contemporary *Poskim*.

54. *Shulchan Aruch* 391:8.

54a. *Rama* 391:3. He adds [referring to the stricter opinion], "This seems correct to me."
     Gesher HaChaim (loc. cit.) writes: "The custom is to be strict within *shloshim*, but after that to
permit [taking part, even] in the case of mourning for one's parent."

55. *Rama* loc. cit., in the name of *Hagahos Maharil*.

56. *Gesher HaChaim* loc. cit. 8:5. The same ruling is given by *Chazon LaMo'ed* 17:16:12.

57. The *gaon* R' Shlomo Zalman Auerbach, *shlita*, in *Kuntres Ohel Channah* at the end of this book.

58. See *Shach* 246:§§27, citing *Maharam Mintz*. The permissive ruling is also cited by *Kol Bo Al
     Aveilus* (p. 360), in the name of *Shibolei HaLeket* (*Hilchos Semachos*); *Pri Megaddim* (*Orach
Chaim* §444, in *Mishbetzos Zahav* §§9); and *Mishmeres Shalom os samech* §24, citing *Tanya Rabbasi*.

take part only if he himself also completed the tractate.[59] But *Rama* states that the mourner should not eat at any festive meal whatsoever outside his home, during the entire twelve months of mourning; and some rule that this prohibition includes a *siyum*.[60]

◈ Charitable Dinners

24a. There is an opinion that after *shloshim* a mourner may accept the honorarium of being the guest of honor at a dinner where there is no music[60a], and that after *shloshim* a mourner may attend a dinner for a charity if there is a possibility that his donation will be greater if he attends the affair.[60b]

◈ *Bar Mitzvah* Meal

25. Some rule that, after *shloshim*, the mourner is permitted to take part in the festive meal for a *bar mitzvah*.[61] Others forbid this.[62] The custom is to follow the latter ruling.[63]

---

59. *Beis Lechem Yehudah* loc. cit. This ruling may also be inferred from the words of *Chiddushei R' Akiva Eiger* (loc. cit.) and *Dagul MeiRevavah* (loc. cit.). Referring to the custom cited by *Rama* that "the mourner should not eat at any festive meal whatsoever outside his home, during the entire twelve months of mourning," they cite the ruling of *Maharam Mintz* that the mourner is permitted to take part in a *siyum*. This implies that, even according to the custom cited by *Rama*, participation in the *siyum* is permitted. And I have heard from major contemporary *Poskim* that current practice follows this interpretation.

60. See *Chochmas Adam* (166:2), who writes: "Regarding the meal of a *siyum*, see *Shach* (246:§§27), who states that, after *shloshim*, one is permitted to eat at such a meal. But this requires further study in light of our custom, as recorded by *Rama*, that one should not eat at any *mitzvah* meal. And *Derech HaChaim* writes the same. Moreover, *Tuv Ta'am Vada'as* (part 3 §86) mentions that *Maharam Mintz* permitted [taking part in a *siyum*], but states that this was only according to the opinion first quoted by *Rama*, namely, that the mourner may attend any meal (for example, a *bris milah*) which does not involve celebration. That permission would also include [a *siyum*]. But according to what *Rama* afterwards cites — the custom of prohibiting all festive meals — [the *siyum*], too, would be prohibited."

60a. *Yesodei Semachos* p. 112, citing *HaGaon Rav Moshe Feinstein zatzal*, who explains that because the mourning practices of the Twelve Months are a display of parental honor, one can assume that parents would forgo the honor due them when their child is being honored.

60b. *Yesodei Semachos* ibid., citing *HaRav Feinstein, zatzal*, who explains that the Sages were lenient in cases of financial loss even within *shloshim*, nevertheless in the case of such a dinner it is best to wait until after *shloshim*.

61. *Dagul MeiRevavah* loc. cit. And the same may be inferred from the words of *Beis Lechem Yehudah* loc. cit.

Gilyon Maharsha (loc. cit.) also states that the mourner may attend a *bar mitzvah* meal. However, he does not connect this with *Rama*'s citation of the strict custom. Hence, one cannot draw any conclusion about the position of *Maharsha*. Possibly, according to that custom, he would prohibit attending.

Gesher HaChaim (loc. cit. §6) writes that even according to the strict custom cited by *Rama*, the mourner may attend a *bar mitzvah* meal.

62. Those who permit the mourner to take part in a *bar mitzvah* meal base their ruling on the grounds that it is comparable to a *siyum*. Hence, those authorities cited above (footnote 60), who forbid taking part in a *siyum*, also forbid the *bar mitzvah* meal. And in fact, *Tuv Ta'am Vada'as* writes explicitly that the mourner may not attend a *bar mitzvah* meal.

63. This is what I have heard from major contemporary *Poskim*.

◀§ *Bar Mitzvah* of a Child

26. If a mourner during his *shloshim* is making a *bar mitzvah* celebration for his
son, some rule that he may take part in the meal. However, he should not sit
with the guests at the table, but should stand and serve them.

He may also wear his outer Sabbath garment.

If the *bar mitzvah* boy is a mourner, he is permitted after *shivah* to wear Sabbath
clothes at the *bar mitzvah* meal.[64]

◀§ Engagement Celebration [*Tena'im*]

27. After *shloshim*, some permit the mourner to take part in a celebration of the
signing of an engagement contract,[65] while others forbid this.[66]

◀§ *Chasan Torah* / *Chasan Bereishis*

28. On Simchas Torah, the man called up for the last Torah-reading in the Book of
Deuteronomy is called the *Chasan Torah* ["bridegroom of the Torah"], and the
one called up for the first Torah-reading in Genesis is called the *Chasan Bereishis*
["bridegroom of Genesis"]. On one of the subsequent Sabbaths, they customarily
hold a festive meal for the congregation. The mourner, after *shloshim*, is permitted
to eat at this meal.[67]

As to whether he may take part in the festive meal for the inauguration of a new
Torah Scroll (*hachnasas Sefer Torah*), see footnote.[67a]

---

64. *Kol Bo Al Aveilus* p. 360, citing responsa *Ribad* (*Yoreh De'ah* §22). The same ruling is given by
Zera Emes §168.

65. *Beis Lechem Yehudah* (§391) cites *Magen Avraham* (444:§§9) as stating that this is a *mitzvah*
meal (*se'udas mitzvah*). The implication is that he permits the mourner to attend. Similarly, *Gilyon
Maharsha* (loc. cit.) states that this is a *mitzvah* meal.

66. *Mishmeres Shalom* (os samech §31) writes, in the name of *Atzmos Yosef*, that it is forbidden. He
concludes: "In any case, as is stated by responsa *Chavos Ya'ir* (end of §70), this is not a *mitzvah*
meal."

67. *Bikurei Yaakov* (669:§§7) comments on the statement of *Shulchan Aruch* there: "The custom is
that the one who completes the final passage [of Deuteronomy] and the one who begins Genesis pledge contributions, and invite the rest of the congregation to a feast." "It seems to me,"
writes *Bikurei Yaakov*, "that a mourner, after *shloshim*, may also eat at this feast; for responsa
Maharam Mintz (cited by *Shach Yoreh De'ah* §246) permits the mourner, after *shloshim*, to eat at the
meal of a *siyum*. True, *Bach* forbids this. However, *Beis Lechem Yehudah* has already pointed out that
the prohibition applies only when the mourner did not learn the tractate, and wants to celebrate with
[those who learned it]. But in our case, every Jew has completed the Torah, and has a part in the
celebration of the *mitzvah*." This ruling is cited by *Mishnah Berurah* (loc. cit. §§8). Regarding the
Chasan Bereishis, one must say, similarly, that every Jew has a part in the *mitzvah* of beginning the
Torah.

67a. It would seem that the same *halachah* applies as for the *siyum* (see above, par. 24). There, the
Acharonim have concluded that if the mourner did not take part in the learning, he should
not take part in the meal. In our case, the meal is in honor of finishing the *mitzvah* of writing the
Torah-scroll. Thus, the mourner should be permitted to take part in the meal only if he took part in
[e.g., contributed money for] the writing. And this is what I have heard from major contemporary
Poskim.

◆§ *Chanukah* Meal

29. After *shloshim*, some rule that the mourner is permitted to take part in a festive meal of Chanukah.[68] Others forbid this.[69]

◆§ House Dedication (*Chanukas HaBayis*)

30. After *shloshim*, some rule that the mourner is permitted to take part in the festive meal for the dedication of a new house (*chanukas habayis*), on condition that the house is in *Eretz Yisrael*, and the celebration includes a Torah discourse. Others rule that he is permitted to take part in such a meal even in the Diaspora.[70] Some forbid the mourner to take part in this type of festive meal.[71]

◆§ Playing a Musical Instrument or Listening to Music

31. During the entire twelve months of mourning, the mourner is forbidden to listen to a musical performance, even if it is not at a celebration. All the more so, he is forbidden to play a musical instrument.[72] However, if he must play a musical instrument for his livelihood, he is permitted to do so.[73]

32. Some rule that in a community where the custom is to play musical instruments on the night before a *bris milah*, and on the day of the *bris milah*, this is permitted even if the father or mother of the baby is in mourning, as long as *shivah* has passed.[74]

---

68. *Gilyon Maharsha* (loc. cit.) writes that, in relation to the laws of mourning, this is considered a *mitzvah* meal. The same ruling is given by *Gesher HaChaim* (loc. cit. os 6). I heard that this is also the ruling of the author of *Minchas Yitzchak*, *zatzal*.

69. Responsa *Igros Moshe* (loc. cit. part 3 §161). He adds: "[The mourner] also should not go to the festive meals given by the Chassidic Rebbes during Chanukah."

70. *Beis Lechem Yehudah* (loc. cit.) and *Gilyon Maharsha* (loc. cit.) state that this is a *mitzvah* meal. And see *Kol Bo Al Aveilus* (p. 361) citing *Devar Moshe* (§88).

71. *Igros Moshe* (loc. cit.). The reason is that not everyone has the custom of holding such a meal.

72. Responsa *Maharam Shick*, *Yoreh De'ah* §368. And see *Sdei Chemed* (*Pe'as HaSadeh*, *Aveilus* §13). Likewise *Gesher HaChaim* (21:8:3) rules that "he should not go to a place where there is a band simply for a friendly get-together [and this applies even according to the *Poskim* who rule that where there is no *mitzvah* it is not considered actual rejoicing]." The prohibitive ruling is also given by *Kol Bo Al Aveilus* p. 361.

73. *Mishmeres Shalom* (os chaf §19) writes: "See *Tosefes Merubah* who writes that during the year of mourning for one's parent, if the mourner is a musician, he is permitted to play music at weddings. And see *Pri Megaddim* (*Orach Chaim, Eshel Avraham* 551:§§10). In discussing the period of general mourning before Tishah B'Av (*bein hametzarim*), he rules that a Jew who makes his living as a musician, performing for non-Jews at banquets, may do so to the extent needed for his livelihood.
    Gesher HaChaim cites *Zachur LeAvraham* (*Avel* §1), who states in the name of *Zekan Aharon* (§218) that a musician, after his *shloshim*, is permitted to perform on Purim, since he does so for the sake of his income, not for the sake of rejoicing.

74. *Ikrei HaDat* (*Yoreh De'ah* 36:§§24) citing *Chaim Sha'al* (part 1 §81): "And I saw that *Zekan Aharon* goes even further, permitting the mourner to play music for others." This is cited by *Mishmeres Shalom* (os mem §23), and by *Da'as Torah* loc. cit.
    Sdei Chemed (*Aveilus* §50) cites *Ma'aseh Avraham* (*Yoreh De'ah* §48) as stating that in his community the prevalent custom is for the mourner to hold a meal with rejoicing, songs, and praises, and to play musical instruments for the *bris milah*, just as someone not in mourning would do. He writes that this is permitted after *shivah*.

CHAPTER TWENTY-SIX

Leaving the Home During Shivah

◆§ The Prohibition

1. A mourner may not step out the door of his home [i.e., where *shivah* is being observed] during the entire *shivah*,[1] even for something involving a *mitzvah*, such as hearing the blessings under the *chupah* at a wedding, or the blessings of a circumcision.[2]

During the first three days of mourning, he does not go to the home of another mourner to comfort him, nor to the cemetery for the funeral of someone else's deceased.

However, after the first three days of mourning, if the funeral procession is in his neighborhood, he accompanies the deceased to the cemetery. But he sits with the mourners, not with the comforters (*Shulchan Aruch*).

Part of the third day is counted as the whole day [that is, the above restrictions apply only until the morning of the third day] (*Rama*).

Rama adds: "I have not seen this custom followed in our time; for, during the entire *shivah*, he goes neither to the cemetery nor to the house of another mourner. Perhaps [the *Shulchan Aruch's* statement, 'he accompanies the deceased to the cemetery,'] means, not that he *must* do so, but that he is *permitted* to do so. And since, in our time, mourners are not consoled as they were in Talmudic times, inaction is preferable to action."[3]

◆§ Leaving to Attend a Funeral

Nevertheless, if during the *shivah* there occurs the death of another relative for whom the mourner is obligated to mourn[4] — or even in the case of the death of

---

1. *Shulchan Aruch Yoreh De'ah* 393:2. *Terumas HaDeshen* (§290) gives the reason: ". . .so that he will not forget his mourning by going among people. But when he remains isolated in his house, and no one is with him except his own household, his mourning is visible and obvious."

2. Ibid. Even though the mourner is obligated by all the *mitzvos*, this refers only to the negative *mitzvos*, and to those positive *mitzvos* which involve one's own body, and which he is *personally* obligated to perform, such as *tzitzis* and *tefillin*, or circumcising one's son. But for an act of kindness, such as attending a wedding or a *bris milah* in order to hear the blessings, he should not leave his home (Responsa of *Rosh*; *Shach* ad loc. §§3).

3. *Aruch HaShulchan* (393:8) interprets *Rama* to mean that, "in early times there were fit arrangements for comforting mourners, unlike our time when, due to our sins, the comforter simply sits for a while and then leaves, and we do not have designated places for the mourners and designated places for the comforters, as they did in early times."

4. *Ba'er Heitev* ad loc. §§1; and responsa *Chasam Sofer*, *Yoreh De'ah* §325, cited by *Pischei Teshuvah* (ad loc. §§1) and by *Gilyon Maharsha*.

someone who is not related to the mourner, but who lacks sufficient people for the funeral and burial — the mourner should go out and accompany him, even on the first day of mourning, and even in another neighborhood.[5]

Some also rule that the mourner is permitted, after the first three days of mourning, to go to the funeral of a relative [for whom he is not obligated to mourn], or that of a great man, if the funeral procession is in his neighborhood or passes through it. But he should not walk with the others attending the funeral. Instead, he should stay at a distance from them. He should only follow the funeral for a distance of four *amos* (about eight feet).[6]

During *shivah*, he should not attend the dedication of a monument (*hakamas matzeivah*; i.e., 'unveiling'), even for his parent.[6a]

◄§ Leaving To Fulfill A *Mitzvah*

2. If it is necessary for the mourner to fulfill a *mitzvah* that he is personally obligated to perform — for example, to acquire *tefillin* or *tzitzis*, or to circumcise his son, and the like — he is permitted, and indeed required, to leave his home, even during the first three days of mourning.[7]

◄§ Joining Other Mourners

3. The authorities rule that the mourner is permitted to travel to the city where the deceased died, in order to conduct his mourning with the other mourners.[8]

◄§ Leaving at Night

4. If necessary, the mourner is permitted to go out at night, after most people are no longer on the streets.[9] Likewise, if it is difficult for him to sleep in the house where *shivah* is being observed, he may go home at night to sleep.[10]

---

5. *Shulchan Aruch* loc. cit.

6. *Gesher HaChaim* 21:13:4.

6a. The *gaon* R' Moshe Feinstein *zatzal*, in *Kuntres Am HaTorah mahadura* 2 *choveres* 12:3.

7. *Gesher HaChaim* loc. cit. based on responsa of *Rosh*, cited by *Shach* 393:§§1. (We have already cited from this responsum of *Rosh* above, footnote 2.)

8. *Sha'arei De'ah* (*Yoreh De'ah* §393) cites responsa *Beis Yehudah*, who asked his teacher the following question: "If a person is out of town, and he hears of the demise of a relative for whom he is obligated to mourn, is he permitted to return to his city and mourn with his family?" His teacher answered: "Even though the *halachah* is that the mourner may not leave his home. . .this means that he may not go somewhere else, so that his attention will not be diverted from the mourning. But [if he wishes to go] to the place where the deceased lived, then on the contrary, in that place, in the presence of his relatives, mourning and weeping will be awakened." He goes on to state that a certain Torah sage followed this ruling in practice.

Sha'arei De'ah comments: "I am somewhat doubtful about this ruling, since in any case, while traveling, the mourner will have his attention diverted from the mourning."

Kerem Shlomo (ad loc.) and *Da'as Torah* (ad loc.) cite the lenient ruling of *Beis Yehudah*.

9. *Rama* (393:2), citing *Trumas HaDeshen* (§290). This responsum of *Trumas HaDeshen* is also cited in summary form by *Beis Yosef*.

10. *Chochmas Adam* 165:11. And see *Igros Moshe* (*Yoreh De'ah* II:§172), who writes that this leniency applies only in case of need, but it may be that the definition of "need" is an individual

In circumstances where the mourner is permitted to go out at night, he should not do so with a group of people.[11] However, it is preferable that he not go alone, because a mourner needs to be safeguarded.[12] [Thus, he should go with only one or two other people.]

5. In case of great need, or of financial loss (*davar ha'aveid*), and the mourner cannot go out at night, he may go out even during the daytime.[13]

6. If a person's brother or sister dies, and then his father approaches their home, unaware of the death, some rule that the son is permitted to go out to greet him, so that he will not become aware of the death.[14] But others disagree.[15]

◄§ Leaving to Attend Services

7. If it is impossible to arrange for a *minyan* of ten men to pray in the mourner's home, some permit the mourner to go to the synagogue in order to pray with a *minyan* and say *Kaddish* for his parent.[16]

In all cases where the mourner is permitted to leave his home during *shivah*, and has no choice but to wear shoes, he must put some earth in them.[17]

---

matter. Some people cannot sleep in an unfamiliar place, and this, too, he writes, may perhaps be defined as "need."

11. *Trumas HaDeshen* loc. cit.

12. *Brachos* 54b, quoted by *Magen Avraham Orach Chaim* 239:§§7.

    (*Trumas HaDeshen* loc. cit. states that when the mourner goes home at night to sleep, he does not go with groups of people, but "alone, or one or two men go with him." In light of our Talmudic passage, the word "alone" requires a certain amount of clarification.)

13. *Rama* 393:2. *Gesher HaChaim* (loc. cit. §2) writes: "If he must unavoidably go out in the daytime, he should wrap himself (i.e., be as inconspicuous as possible), so that people will not meet him."

14. *Pischei Teshuvah* ad loc. §§7, citing *Shevus Yaakov* (II:§99). *Pischei Teshuvah* writes: "See responsa *Shevus Yaakov* there; his words imply that the permission applies only in the case of his father's arrival, because of the obligation to honor one's father; but if his brother arrives, he is forbidden [to go out to greet him]". *Pischei Teshuvah* is also cited by *Gilyon Maharsha* (ad loc.) and by *Pachad Yitzchak*.

15. *Beis Lechem Yehudah* (ad loc.), after quoting *Pischei Teshuvah*, comments: "It would seem that this is forbidden."

16. *Shulchan Aruch* (393:3) writes: "The mourner does not go out during the week to the synagogue, but on the Sabbath he goes out. But our custom is that on every day when there is a Torah-reading, he goes out to the synagogue."

    Rama comments: "In these lands, the custom is that he goes out only on the Sabbath."

    Pischei Teshuvah (ad loc. §§2) cites *Chochmas Adam* (*Kuntres Matzeivas Moshe* §8): "This [statement of *Rama*] is based on what is written in §376, that it is a *mitzvah* to pray in the mourner's home. Hence, there [normally] are ten men there. But in a case where it is impossible to gather ten men, and for that reason [the mourner] would miss saying *Kaddish*, *Kedushah*, and *Borchu*, he is permitted to go [to the synagogue]."

    See also *Igros Moshe* (*Yoreh De'ah* part III: §158). He permits the mourner to go to the synagogue when he has *yahrzeit*, even according to those who rule that he may not go in order to recite *Kaddish*.

17. *Taz* 382:§§1.

8. On the Sabbath, he is permitted to go to the synagogue and the house of study.[18]

9. On Tishah B'Av, he should go to the synagogue for the service, both at night and during the day, remaining until the recitation of *kinos* is completed.[19] Some rule that if he is in the first three days of mourning, he may go only for the daytime, but not the nighttime, service.[20]

10. On the day before Pesach, firstborn sons are required to fast. Some have the custom that if firstborns are present at a *mitzvah* meal, such as a *siyum* (festive meal at the completion of a tractate), they need not subsequently fast.

If the mourner is a firstborn, one authority states that he is forbidden to go to the synagogue on the day before Pesach in order to hear a *siyum* and break his fast.[21] Others rule more leniently on this question, permitting the mourner to go to the synagogue to hear the *siyum* after *chatzos* (about noon),[22] or even to hear it in the morning if it is held in the mourner's home.[23]

11. The mourner should not leave his home to recite *Selichos* in the synagogue, except on the day before Rosh Hashanah, when many *Selichos* are recited.[24]

The question whether the *mohel*, the father of the baby, and the *sandak* (the one who holds the baby on his lap during circumcision) may leave their home during *shivah* to take part in a circumcision is discussed above, chapter 25.

The question whether a *shochet* (slaughterer) or a doctor may leave his home to perform his work is discussed above, Chapter 18.

---

18. *Shulchan Aruch* 393:3.

19. *Shulchan Aruch* (*Orach Chaim* 559:6) writes: "If [on Tishah B'Av] there is a mourner in the city, he should attend the synagogue service at night and during the day, until they complete the *Kinos* [lamentations]." *Mishnah Berurah* (ad loc. §§24) explains: "This applies even during the first three days of mourning. Even though the mourner usually is forbidden to go out during the first three days, even to the home of another mourner, in this case [i.e., on Tishah B'Av], since all Jews are mourners, the *halachah* is more lenient."

20. *Mishnah Berurah* (loc. cit.) writes: "Some are strict regarding the first three days of mourning, and the *gaon* R' Shlomo Kluger takes both sides of the disagreement into account by ruling that at night, when there are few *Kinos*, the mourner should not go. But in the day, when there are many *Kinos* and it would distress him not to go, he is permitted. And after the first three days of mourning, he may go to the synagogue even at night."

21. *Hagahos Yad Shaul* 393:3.

22. *Mishmeres Shalom os samech* §23.

23. *Chazon LaMo'ed* ch. 13, citing *Yoseif Da'as* §399.

24. *Rama* 581:1. Details of this *halachah* are presented below, 34:2.

CHAPTER 27

Changing One's Place
in the Synagogue

✧ The Basic *Halachah*

1. "In the second week [of mourning], the mourner leaves his home, but does not
sit in his regular place [in the synagogue]. In the third week, he sits in his regular
place, but does not speak. If he prefers, in the third week he may continue not to
sit in his regular place, in which case he is permitted to speak. In the fourth week,
he [sits in his regular place and speaks], like anyone else. This applies even if three
full weeks have not yet passed. For example, if the death occurred in the middle of
the week, then as soon as that week is over, and two more weeks have passed, this
is considered the fourth week."[1]

"In our time, the custom is not to sit in one's regular place for the entire *shloshim*
— and in the case of mourning for one's parent, for the entire twelve months. This
custom has no fundamental basis. Nevertheless, one should not change it, for every
community follows its own custom."[2]

---

1. *Shulchan Aruch* 393:2, based on a *baraisa* in *Mo'ed Katan* 23a.

2. *Rama* ad loc.

  Chochmas Shlomo gives the following explanation of the requirement to change one's place: "It
would seem that any change from one's normal way of life is a form of exile (*galus*). It seems, therefore,
that changing one's seat in the synagogue is also meant as a substitute for exile. The reason some form
of exile is appropriate is because a mourner is required to imagine that his own sins may have
contributed to the death of the deceased [since his own merits were insufficient to prevent the
deceased's death]. Nevertheless, even if this contributed to the death, he did not do so intentionally, for
he did not intend to kill the deceased; hence he is like one who kills accidentally (*shogeg*); for this, exile
is sufficient atonement. Thus, by changing his place in the synagogue, the mourner undergoes a form
of exile, and gains atonement for his sins. May it be the will of [the Holy One, Blessed is He,] that all
our sins be forgiven."

  In a similar vein, responsa *Shem MiShimon* (*Yoreh De'ah* §32) notes that besides being a
manifestation of mourning, the requirement to change one's seat may be attributed to the concept that
the mourner has become subject to the Divine Attribute of Strict Justice [and a change of place affords
a measure of protection against further suffering]. A similar idea is found in *Taanis* (24b), where Rava
incurred Divine displeasure by praying for — and receiving — an obvious miracle. His father appeared
to him in a dream and told him to change his place.

◄§ At Home

At home, he need not change the place where he sits.[3] And [both in the synagogue and at home], he need not change the place where he stands.[4]

◄§ Direction and Distance of Change

2. When he leaves his regular seat in the synagogue, some rule that he must move to a seat at least four *amos* (about seven feet) away, since everywhere within a radius of four *amos* is considered the same "place."[5] But others rule that any change from his normally assigned seat is sufficient — even moving to the next seat.[6]

He must move to a seat farther from, not closer to, the Holy Ark.[7] But if he already sits at the western edge of the synagogue [i.e., the row farthest from the Ark], he may move either to the north or to the south [i.e., he may move sideways in either direction].[8]

◄§ On the Sabbath

3. "Some have the custom, when in mourning, not to change their seat in the synagogue on the Sabbath. [They sit in some other seat during the week, but in their regular seat on the Sabbath.] They are to be commended."[9]

---

3. *Chochmas Adam* 167:2. However, *Gilyon Maharsha* (ad loc.) writes that at home, too, he must change the place where he sits.

4. Responsa *Tzitz Eliezer* VII:§49. He draws this inference from the words of responsa *Maharam Shick* §369. However, responsa *Lev Avraham* (§97) disagrees, ruling that he must also change the place where he stands.

5. *Pischei Teshuvah* 392:§§7, citing *Chamudei Daniel* (manuscript). Similarly, regarding the requirement to have a permanent place to pray, *Magen Avraham* (90:§§34) states that everywhere within a radius of four *amos* is considered the same place. The same ruling is given by *Kitzur Shulchan Aruch* 211:15.

6. Responsa *Maharam Shick*, *Yoreh De'ah* §369. He states: "I saw that *Leshon Chachamim* cites *Noheg Katzon Yosef* as relating that in the community of Frankfurt am Main the custom is that the mourner simply changes places with the person standing next to him."

7. *Leshon Chachamim*. And *Maharam Shick* (loc. cit.) comments: "This is because the closer a place is to the Holy Ark, the more prominent it is. And it would seem that the mourner should not change to a prominent place."

Responsa *HaElef Lecha Shlomo* (§315) writes: "In the matter of (the mourner's) changing his place: If he moves from the middle row eastward [i.e., closer to the Holy Ark], this is not considered changing his place. . .The rule is as follows: Any change which is not usually made except in case of mourning, and which is made purely because of the mourning, is considered changing one's place. But the kind of change which people normally make, even when not in mourning, is not considered changing one's place. And a change to a more prominent place can be made even by someone who is not in mourning. . ."

8. *Gesher HaChaim* 22:3.

9. *Shulchan Aruch* loc. cit. par. 4.

Sdei Chemed (*Aveilus* §209) cites *Chida* as stating (in his *Birkei Yosef* ad loc.) that the custom of the *Arizal* was not to change his place on the Sabbath. "Thus, someone who is well-known for his piety, and will not be suspected of merely trying to appear pious, may follow the custom of the *Ari*, even if that is not the custom in his community. Each case must be judged in accordance with the particular place and time."

Rama comments: "But some rule that [the mourner] *should* change his seat even on the Sabbath. This is the prevalent custom, and one should not depart from it."[10]

Some interpret that, even according to *Rama*, the requirement to change one's seat on the Sabbath applies only if one arrives at the synagogue before the Sabbath begins. Since he had already begun sitting in the unaccustomed seat in the afternoon, he is permitted to continue sitting there on the Sabbath. However, if he arrives at the synagogue after the congregation recited *Borchu* ("Bless Hashem, the Blessed One"), he must sit in his regular seat. Otherwise, he would be initiating conspicuous mourning on the Sabbath.[11]

Others disagree with this interpretation. They understand *Rama* to rule that the mourner may change his seat even if he arrives after *Borchu*.[11a]

◄§ The Rabbi of the Community

4. The rabbi of the community is not required to change his seat on the Sabbath.[12]

Some rule that even during the week he is not required to change his seat. Nevertheless, he should change it slightly. Otherwise, ignorant people, not knowing that that *halachah* is different for the rabbi, might follow his example.[13]

◄§ Permanent Seats

Some people rule that in a synagogue where permanent seats are assigned, the mourner need not change his seat on the Sabbath.[13a]

---

10. *Rama* loc. cit. and *Shach* §§7. The same ruling is given by *Be'ur HaGra* (ad loc.); responsa of *Radbaz* (§662); and *Igros Moshe* (*Yoreh De'ah* §257).

11. *Taz*, *Orach Chaim*, beginning of §526. He is cited by *Chiddushei R' Akiva Eiger*, *Yoreh De'ah* §393. The same ruling is given in responsa *Panim Me'iros* (II:§124).

11a. However, *Pri Megaddim* (ad loc.) writes: "*Elyah Rabbah* (§548) states: 'Since the change of place is a practice observed throughout *shloshim*, it is not considered conspicuous mourning on the Sabbath.' " The same may be inferred from *Shach*, who offers other reasons why the change of place is not to be considered conspicuous mourning on the Sabbath; and according to his reasons, the *Rama*'s permission to change one's place on the Sabbath would apply even if one arrives after the congregation has recited *Borchu*.

12. *Ikrei HaDat* (*Yoreh De'ah* §36:58) writes in the name of *Ne'eman Shmuel* (§35) that "Those rabbis who, when in mourning, do not change their place on the Sabbath, are to be commended." And see *Gilyon Maharsha*, who writes (commenting on *Shach* §§7): "I relied on this and was lenient during my period of mourning for my father and master, the light of Israel, זצללה"ה, and did not change my place on the Sabbath; for certainly it is not usual for the rabbi of the community to change his place; hence, [if the rabbi does so,] it constitutes conspicuous mourning. Nevertheless, on the second Sabbath after the death, when the requirement to change one's place is a basic law, I did not go to the synagogue."

Chazon LaMo'ed (§17 note 58) writes: "*Hagahas Kesav Sofer* states that this [that the rabbi does not change his place] was the custom of *Chasam Sofer*."

13. Responsa *Maharam Shick* §369.

13a. *Even Yaakov* (58:3) writes: "According to this [explanation of *Maharsha*, quoted above, footnote 12], there is room to be lenient not only with the rabbi of the community, but with anyone who establishes a permanent, unvarying place where he prays [*makom kavu'a*], and all the members of the congregation know that he never sits anywhere else; for we may apply the same reasoning here [as *Maharsha* applied in the case of the rabbi]. . .Likewise, further study is required concerning the

◦§ If Death Occurs During a Festival

5. If death occurs during a Festival [Pesach, Shavuos, Succos, Rosh Hashanah, or Yom Kippur], the mourner should not change his seat during the
Festival.[14]

◦§ Tishah B'Av

6. On Tishah B'Av, the mourner need not change his place.[15]

◦§ Returning to the Regular Seat After Shloshim

7. If the mourning is for a family member other than one's parent, and the
thirtieth day of mourning falls on the Sabbath, the mourner may return to his
regular seat at the evening service of the Sabbath.[16]

---

question of a synagogue where the seats are sold, everyone's place is written down, and it is not usual
to change one's seat."

14. *Gilyon Maharsha* ad loc., citing responsa *Maharam MiLublin*.

15. *Chazon LaMo'ed* 17:15:7, citing *Maharil*.

16. *Rama* 400:2. Since the requirement to change one's place is not a basic law on the Sabbath, but
only a custom, one should be lenient in this case, for the honor of the Sabbath.

See also responsa *Megiddos* (by the author of *Pri Megaddim*), who writes: "In the matter of changing
one's place during the twelve months of mourning [for one's parent]: On the eve of the *yahrzeit*, the
mourner may resume sitting in his regular place. For example, if the *yahrzeit* falls on Rosh Chodesh
Tammuz, he may return to his place at the Evening Prayer after *Yom Kippur Katan* [i.e., on the eve of
Rosh Chodesh], because the day of the *yahrzeit* is the day *after* the end of the Twelve Months. This may
be inferred also from *Ba'er Heitev* (*Yoreh De'ah* §395)." However, in §89 he writes: "I did not want to
return to my regular place on the day of the *yahrzeit*, because in the eyes of the public this is an
innovation."

CHAPTER TWENTY-EIGHT

Sabbath During *Shivah*

1. Unlike a Festival, the Sabbath does not terminate mourning (since there could never be a consecutive seven-day mourning period unless it included the Sabbath). Moreover, the Sabbath is counted as one of the first seven days of mourning, since some aspects of the mourning laws are observed on it.[1]

2. Conspicuous mourning practices [אֲבֵלוּת שֶׁבְּפַרְהֶסְיָא] are not observed on the Sabbath, but the inconspicuous, private ones [אֲבֵלוּת שֶׁבְּצִינְעָא] are. (The inconspicuous practices are detailed below, beginning with par. 18.)[2]

Some rule that those mourning practices observed throughout the entire *shloshim* are observed on the Sabbath as well, even if conspicuous.[3] But others disagree.[4]

---

1. This is quoted from *Tur* §400.

2. *Tur* and *Shulchan Aruch* §400.

3. This is the ruling of *Shach* ad loc. §§2. He gives the same ruling in 393:§§7, citing *Mahariv*, who writes that wrapping the head (*atifas harosh*; see above, chapt. 22) is permitted on the Sabbath, since this is practiced even after *shivah*. *Mahariv* explains that the only conspicuous practices forbidden on the Sabbath are those applying solely during the *shivah* period. His ruling is also cited by *Darkei Moshe* ad loc. §§1. The same ruling is given by *Yoseif Da'as* (§389), regarding the wearing of Sabbath clothes.

4. *Gilyon Maharsha* (§393). He permits the community rabbi not to change his seat in the synagogue on the Sabbath, even though the requirement to change one's seat applies during the entire *shloshim* (see *Shach* ad loc. §§7). This is also the opinion of all those *Poskim* (cited above, chapt. 27) who agree with *Maharsha* that the rabbi should not change his seat on the Sabbath.

This is also the ruling of the *gaon* R' Zalman Margolios, citing *Yavetz* (*Aveilus* §23). He permits the mourner to attend a wedding celebration on the Sabbath if his absence would be a conspicuous act of mourning; and the permission applies even though the prohibition against attending celebrations applies during the entire *shloshim*.

Yavetz (loc. cit. §26) also cites responsa *P'nei Yehoshua* as permitting the mourner to wear newly laundered clothes on the Sabbath if there is no one to put them on before the mourner does. The reason is that wearing unlaundered clothes would constitute conspicuous mourning; and this permission applies even though the prohibition against wearing newly laundered clothes applies during the entire *shloshim*. The same opinion is held by all the *Poskim* cited below, footnote 9, who permit the mourner to wear Sabbath clothes because wearing ordinary clothes would constitute conspicuous mourning; and they rule leniently on this matter even though the prohibition against wearing Sabbath clothes applies after *shivah*. (In fact, it was this leniency which prompted the contrary ruling of *Yoseif Da'as* §389, cited in our previous footnote. He argues that wearing ordinary clothes would not constitute conspicuous mourning, since wearing Sabbath clothes, like wearing newly laundered clothes, is forbidden during the entire *shloshim*; and *Rama* 399:3 also writes that the mourner is forbidden to wear Sabbath clothes during the first four weeks of mourning.) [See par. 4 in text.]

◄§ The Time to Suspend Conspicuous Mourning on Friday

3. Some rule that all the laws of mourning are observed on Friday until dark.[5]

Others are more lenient, permitting the mourner to sit on a regular chair from the time of *Minchah Ketanah*[6] [approximately two and a half hours before sunset (*sh'ki'ah*)]. Still others take an intermediate position, being lenient only from *Plag HaMinchah*[7] [approximately an hour and a quarter before sunset]. They are also lenient about wearing shoes from this time on.[8]

◄§ Sabbath Clothes

4. The custom is to be lenient and permit the mourner to wear Sabbath clothes.

However, some communities have the custom that the mourner does not wear Sabbath clothes the first thirty days. Nonetheless, he should not wear the clothes that he tore.[9] The mourner may wear newly laundered undergarments (those garments whose purpose it is to absorb perspiration). However, it is preferable that someone else don them on before the mourner does.[10] It is also permitted to spread

---

5. *Elyah Rabbah* 132:§§4 cited by *Mishnah Berurah* ad loc. §§39. The same ruling is cited by *Pischei Teshuvah* §400, in the name of *Givas Shaul* §72.

   See also responsa *Shivas Tzion* §60. And see responsa *HaElef Lecha Shlomo* (§318), who writes: "People commonly make the mistake of belittling the mourning after midday (*chatzos hayom*) on Friday; but the truth is that all the laws of mourning — including sitting on the floor [i.e., low] — all apply until candle-lighting." See also *Bechor Shor* (§47), who maintains that the practice of being lenient about mourning on Friday is a custom of "uninformed ignorance."

6. *Sdei Chemed* (*Aveilus*, os 61) cites this ruling in the name of *Chaim BeYad* 125:70.

   Aruch HaShulchan (387:3) writes: "On Friday, a few hours before night, [the mourners] get up from the floor; and a little before candle-lighting, they put on their shoes." And in 400:5 he writes: "It has already been explained that from the time of *Minchah Ketanah* [i.e., the last two-and-a-half hours of the day], the signs of mourning are removed."

   Responsa *Tzitz Eliezer* (part VII 49:11) concludes that on Friday, after midday — or at least from *Plag HaMinchah* [the last hour-and-a-quarter of the day] — the mourner may get up and go to his home in preparation for the Sabbath. And, all the more so, if he goes by a route where there are not many people out on the street.

   Yesodei Semachos p. 83 cites the gaon R' Moshe Feinstein, zatzal, that a mourner who is sitting shivah away from his family may return home for the Sabbath even if the necessity of traveling will require him to arise from shivah early Friday morning.

7. *Gesher HaChaim* 21:12:3; also cited by *Chazon LaMo'ed* 17:5:3.

8. *Aruch HaShulchan* (387:5) writes: "But one should not put on shoes until shortly before the Sabbath — i.e., *Plag HaMinchah*, an hour and a quarter before night."

9. *Rama* (389:3) writes: "Some rule that it is forbidden to wear Sabbath clothes during the first four weeks [of mourning]." The same prohibitive ruling is given by responsa of *Ribash* §67. However, see *Radbaz* (II:§693), who rules that the mourner *should* wear Sabbath clothes, since otherwise it would constitute conspicuous mourning on the Sabbath. He rules that the same applies [for the public in general] on *Shabbos Chazon*, the Sabbath preceding Tishah B'Av.

   Permission for the mourner to wear Sabbath clothes is also given by *Birkei Yosef* (§400), who states: "I have also seen this written by *Mahari* Zain in responsa *Sha'arei Yeshu'ah*, *Yoreh De'ah* sha'ar 10 §4, citing *Radbaz*." *Ma'asah Rav* of the Vilna Gaon §193 also permits a mourner to wear Sabbath clothes.

10. See *Aruch HaShulchan* 387:5.

    See also *Da'as Torah*, who cites responsa *Pnei Yehoshua* (II:§39) as ruling that "on the

a newly laundered tablecloth on the table.[11]

❧ Entering the Synagogue

5. The custom in most Ashkenazic congregations is that the mourner enters the synagogue before the congregation recites, מִזְמוֹר שִׁיר לְיוֹם הַשַּׁבָּת, 'A psalm, a song for the Sabbath day,' and the *shamash* announces, "Come forth towards the mourner." Then the congregation greets him with the words, הַמָּקוֹם יְנַחֵם אֶתְכֶם בְּתוֹךְ שְׁאָר אֲבֵלֵי צִיּוֹן וִירוּשָׁלָיִם, "May Hashem comfort you among all the mourners of Zion and Jerusalem." (For more details of this practice, see above, 17:9.)

❧ לְכוּ נְרַנְּנָה, "Come! — Let Us Sing," and *Kabbalas Shabbos* [11a]

6. The mourner does not recite הוֹדוּ, "Give thanks. . ." [in the *Nusach Sefard* version of the Friday afternoon *Minchah* service], nor the portion of *Kabbalas Shabbos* beginning with לְכוּ נְרַנְּנָה, "Come! — let us sing. . ." [Psalm 95]. He begins with מִזְמוֹר שִׁיר לְיוֹם הַשַּׁבָּת, 'A Psalm, a song for the Sabbath day.'[12] However, the congregants praying with him recite all these passages, even if they are praying in the mourner's home.[13]

7. The custom among some *chassidim*, however, is that the mourner does recite הוֹדוּ, "Give thanks. . ." [in the *Minchah* Service], and לְכוּ נְרַנְּנָה, "Come! — let us sing," as well as לְכָה דוֹדִי, "Come my Beloved" [in the *Kabbalas Shabbos*]; and they do not deviate at all from the regular *Kabbalas Shabbos*.[14]

Sabbath the mourner is permitted to wear an undergarment which is not new but is freshly laundered, even during *shivah*. This applies even if he does not have someone wear it first. However, because of the prevalent custom, it is preferable (*lechatchilah*), if possible, to have someone else wear it first. However, if there is no one to do this, the mourner is certainly permitted to wear it — as is the *halachah* regarding Tishah B'Av that falls on the Sabbath. *Siddur Ri, zal,* of Lissa, rules strictly on this matter. But the *gaon Pnei Yehoshua, zal,* is sufficiently authoritative to be relied upon in a matter involving the honor of the Sabbath."

Gilyon Maharsha (§389) cites *Rashal* as stating that on the Sabbath during *shivah*, one who does not don a freshly laundered undergarment is observing "foolish piety" (*chassidus shel shtus*).

Eretz Chaim cites *Shulchan Gevoha* as stating that the custom in the Holy City of Jerusalem is for the mourner to wear Sabbath clothes, even white ones, on the Sabbath.

11. See *Taz* (§389 §§1), who writes in the name of *Rashal*: "See *Orach Chaim* §551, where it is considered obviously permissible, for the honor of the Sabbath, to spread a laundered tablecloth." The same ruling is given by *Kitzur Shulchan Aruch* 211:4.

11a. [See ArtScroll Ashkenaz Siddur p. 308.]

12. Responsa *Teshuras Shai* (II:§171) states that the congregation is not yet considered to have accepted upon themselves the onset of the Sabbath until they recite *Borchu* or מִזְמוֹר שִׁיר לְיוֹם הַשַּׁבָּת, 'A psalm, a song for the Sabbath day.' The same ruling is given by *Gesher HaChaim*, citing the *Acharonim*.

13. *Even Yaakov* §61.

14. *Darkei Chaim VeShalom* §1031. He states that the author of *Minchas Elazar*, when in mourning, did not depart at all from his usual customs of the Sabbath.

Ta'amei HaMinhagim (p. 182) relates that the holy *tzaddik*, R' Tzvi Hirsch of Rimanov, recited *Lechah Dodi*, the song for receiving the Sabbath, during his *shivah*.

◆§ Mishnas *Bameh Madlikin* ("With What Do We Light?")

8. The mourner does not recite Mishnas *BaMeh Madlikin*.[15] However, the congregation praying in the mourner's home recites it,[16] and the mourner recites *Kaddish 'DeRabbanan*, the Rabbis' Kaddish.[17]

◆§ *Shir HaShirim* (Song of Songs)

9. One authority writes that if a person customarily recites *Shir HaShirim* [Song of Songs] between *Kabbalas Shabbos* and *Maariv*, he may do so even when in mourning.[18]

◆§ בְּרָכָה מֵעֵין שֶׁבַע, The Seven-Faceted Blessing

10. The Seven-Faceted Blessing[18a] is not recited in the mourner's home.[19]

◆§ *Shalom Aleichem* ('Peace Upon You')

11. On arriving home after the *Shabbos* evening service, the mourner does not recite the hymn beginning שָׁלוֹם עֲלֵיכֶם, 'Peace upon you, O ministering angels.'[20]

---

15. [ArtScroll Ashkenaz *Siddur* p. 322.] Responsa *Megiddos* (by the author of *Pri Megaddim*) §51.
    This ruling is also given by *Tuv Ta'am VaDa'as* (III:§219), who writes: ". . .the mourner does not recite it, since Torah-study is forbidden to him." The same ruling is given by *Gesher HaChaim*.
    However, responsa of *Maharil Diskin* (*Kuntres Acharon* §199) argues: "According to our custom, whereby we do not recite *Mishnas BaMeh Madlikin* ("With What Do We Light?") until after receiving the Sabbath, it would be illogical [for the mourner to omit this passage] because that would constitute conspicuous mourning on the Sabbath." See also the following footnote.

16. *Beis Yosef* (§393) cites *Kol Bo* as stating that *BaMeh Madlikin* is not recited in the mourner's home. However, responsa of *Maharil Diskin* (loc. cit.) states that the rest of the congregation should recite it, for omitting it would constitute even more conspicuous mourning. He notes the ruling of *Kol Bo*, but explains that this relates only to congregations where the custom is to recite *BaMeh Madlikin* before receiving the Sabbath. But considering our current custom, which is to recite it after receiving the Sabbath [i.e., after *Mizmor Shir*], to omit it is almost tantamount to conspicuous mourning on the Sabbath. (It is also clear that he is not comfortable with the ruling of *Elyah Rabbah*, who states that the Priestly Blessing [*Bircas Kohanim*] should be omitted in the mourner's home during *shivah*, as well as the verses, וַאֲנִי זֹאת בְּרִיתִי, "And as for Me, this is My covenant", and וִיהִי נֹעַם, "May the pleasantness. . .," at the conclusion of the Sabbath. In the opinion of *Maharil Diskin*, all these passages should be recited.)
    The same ruling (that the rest of the congregation praying in the mourner's home recite *Bameh Madlikin*) is given by *Tosefos Shabbos* (*Orach Chaim* §210); and this is also the opinion of *Yad Shaul* (*Yoreh De'ah* §384), and *Chazon LaMo'ed* (16:9), citing *Gur Aryeh Yehudah* (*Orach Chaim* §125).

17. *Even Yaakov* §81. There he refers the reader to his §52, which we cited above, 16:35.

18. *Chazon LaMo'ed* §16 footnote 14. He states that he was told this by the *gaon* R' Yosef Chaim Sonnenfeld in the year 5686 (1926).

18a. ArtScroll Ashkenaz *Siddur* p. 346.

19. *Shulchan Aruch Orach Chaim* 268:10. But *Magen Avraham* (ad loc. §§14) comments that if the local custom is to recite it, one should not protest (*Radbaz* and *Ralbach*).
    Pri Megaddim (ad loc.) writes: "The matter requires some study, regarding whether this does not raise doubt about the risk of a needless blessing (*safek berachah*)." *Mishnah Berurah* (ad loc. §§24) rules that if the prayer-service is in a place permanently used for prayer, the Seven-Faceted Blessing *should* be recited.

20. [ArtScroll Ashkenaz *Siddur* p. 354.] *Teshuras Shai* (§172). The same ruling is given by *Kol Bo Al Aveilus* (p. 81), and *Gesher HaChaim*, who explain that the omission of *Shalom Aleichem* is in

◄§ Blessing the Children

12. In some congregations, it is customary to bless the children on Sabbath Eve. The mourner should not do so during his *shivah*.[21]

◄§ Sabbath Songs (*Zemiros*)

13. The mourner sings *zemiros*, as on any other Sabbath.[22]

◄§ *Bircas HaMazon* (Grace After Meals)

14. Some communities add special passages to Grace After Meals during *shivah*.

On the Sabbath, if the mourner ate alone or with other mourners, he recites these passages, just as on a weekday. But if non-mourners ate with him and are saying Grace with him, he does not recite them.[23] (See above, 16:13-17.)

◄§ Prayer in the Mourner's Home

15. When the Sabbath Morning Service is conducted in the mourner's home, the passage beginning, אַב הָרַחֲמִים, "May the Father of compassion. . . ,"[24] is recited.[24a] At the Afternoon Service, the custom is to omit the verse, וַאֲנִי תְפִלָּתִי, "As for me, may my prayer. . . ".[25]

The passage beginning, צִדְקָתְךָ צֶדֶק, "Your righteousness is an everlasting righteousness. . . ,"[26] is recited as usual.[26a]

---

the category of an inconspicuous, private mourning practice, and therefore it is proper not to recite it.

Megiddos (by the author of *Pri Megaddim*) §51 writes: "It would seem that the mourner should not recite *Shalom Aleichem*, since he is in a state of sorrow; but the matter requires study."

See also responsa *Be'er Moshe* (V:§78), who writes that if others are eating with the mourner, he should recite *Shalom Aleichem*.

21. In *Maharil* (*Hilchos Semachos*) it is written that (when *Maharil's* wife died) he did not bless the children or his other relatives on Friday night during *shivah*.

22. *Kol Bo Al Aveilus* loc. cit. in the name of *Shibolei HaLeket*, *Semachos* §22.

23. *Shulchan Aruch* 379:4. The reason is explained there and in *Shach* ad loc. §§5: If no one eats with him except other mourners, the omission of special passages is considered an inconspicuous, private mourning practice. But if non-mourners eat with him, the omission of these passages is considered a conspicuous display of mourning; and one does not mourn conspicuously on the Sabbath.

24. ArtScroll *Siddur* p. 432.

24a. *Pri Megaddim Orach Chaim* §131 in *Eshel Avraham* §§10.

25. *Kaf HaChaim* (292:§§8) writes: "The custom in Ashblai is not to recite this in the mourner's home (*Rada*, *zal*, *Knesses HaGedolah*, note 9)." His ruling is cited in *Zachur LeAvraham* (*Aveilus os* 5); *Kol Bo Al Aveilus* (p. 281); and *Gesher HaChaim* (20:3:9).

26. ArtScroll ibid. p. 524.

26a. *Pri Megaddim* loc. cit.

Gesher HaChaim (chapt. 20) cites *Kaf HaChaim* (292:§§18) as stating: "Nevertheless, the custom is not to recite it. The omission is not considered conspicuous mourning, since this passage is also omitted when there is a bridegroom in the congregation." *Gesher HaChaim* comments: "May I be pardoned the remark, but this is not valid reasoning."

Kol Bo Al Aveilus (p. 281) cites the following argument in the name of *Yoseif Da'as* §400: "It is true that on occasions [e.g., Rosh Chodesh] when *Tachanun* would not be recited on a weekday, צִדְקָתְךָ, 'Your righteousness. . . ,' is not recited on the Sabbath. But that is because those occasions are joyous ones. In our case, the nature of the occasion is mourning. It is just that *Tachanun* is omitted during the

The mourner does not recite בָּרְכִי נַפְשִׁי, "Bless Hashem, O my soul. . .,"[27] during the winter,[27a] nor *Pirkei Avos* during the summer.[28]

At the end of the prayer service in the mourner's home on the Sabbath, neither Psalm 49 nor Psalm 16 of *Tehillim* is recited.[29]

◄§ The Prohibition Against Leaving the Home on the Sabbath

16. Some rule that the mourner may not leave his home on the Sabbath, except to go to the synagogue.[30]

The requirement for the mourner to change his seat in the synagogue, and the question whether it applies on the Sabbath, is discussed above, 27:3.

◄§ Wrapping the Head / Wearing Shoes / *Kri'ah* Garment

17. As stated above (paragraph 2), the conspicuous mourning practices are not observed on the Sabbath. Therefore, the practice of wrapping the head (see above, chapt. 22) is not observed on the Sabbath. Even the form of this practice which some nowadays observe on the weekday, namely, to lower the hat in front of the eyes, should not be done on the Sabbath; hence, as soon as the mourner accepts the Sabbath, he must return his hat to its normal position.[31]

Likewise, he must wear his shoes on the Sabbath, and must change out of the garment in which he made a tear (*kri'ah*). If he has no other garment to change into, he must turn the garment so that the tear is in the back.[32] But some rule that in our time one is not required to turn the garment in such a case.[33]

Concerning the prohibition against asking about another's welfare, see above, 21:12.

◄§ Inconspicuous Mourning Practices

18. Inconspicuous mourning practices (*devarim shebetzin'a*; literally "private things") are observed even on the Sabbath. Therefore, the mourner is forbidden to have marital relations (see above, chapt. 20), to bathe (chapt. 19), or to study Torah (chapt. 21).[34]

---

weekday because the mourner is subject to the forces of Strict Justice. However, this is no reason to omit צִדְקָתְךָ, 'Your righteousness. . .' "

27. ArtScroll ibid. p. 530.

27a. *Pri Megaddim* §292 in *Mishbetzos Zahav* §§2.

28. Ibid. in the name of *Tosefos Shabbos*. The same ruling is given by responsa *Meggidos* (§51); *Leket Yosher (Hilchos Aveilus)*; *Kerem Shlomo*; et al.

29. *Gesher HaChaim* (20:3:12); *Chazon LaMo'ed* §16.

30. *Zeh HaShulchan* part II *Yoreh De'ah*.

31. *Shulchan Aruch* 400:1; and *Shach* §§2.

32. *Shulchan Aruch* loc. cit.

33. *Shach* §§3. But in light of our currently accepted custom that the mourner changes into Sabbath clothes, these *halachos* are not applicable.

34. *Shulchan Aruch* 400:1.

✺ Reviewing the Weekly Torah Portion

19. Every week, a Jew is required to read the weekly Torah portion twice in the original Hebrew, and once in the Aramaic translation. (See *Shulchan Aruch Orach Chaim* §285.) Even though the mourner is generally forbidden to study Torah, he is permitted this review of the weekly Torah portion. Since it is obligatory, it is considered comparable to reciting the *Shema*, which is permitted.[35]

20. If the seventh day of mourning falls on the Sabbath, the mourner should postpone his review of the weekly Torah portion until after leaving the synagogue in the morning, and then review the weekly portion, if possible, before the morning meal.[36] [See also below, 29:4.]

✺ Torah-Study on the Sabbath

21. Some rule that the mourner is also permitted to study *Rashi*'s commentary on the weekly Torah portion, if this is his regular practice on the Sabbath when he is not in mourning.[37] Others forbid this.[37a] However, it is permitted to study the portion in a vernacular translation such as *Tz'enah Ur'enah*.[38]

22. Some rule that if a person is accustomed to study eighteen chapters of Mishnah each day, he is permitted to do so on the Sabbath during mourning.[39] Likewise, some rule that the mourner is permitted to learn the weekly selection of *Chok LeYisrael*, if he is accustomed to do so.[40] But others disagree.[41]

✺ The Torah-reading in the Synagogue

23. If the mourner is the *baal korei*, the one who regularly reads the Torah in his synagogue, he should not pray there on the first Sabbath of his mourning.[42] If

---

35. Ibid.

36. *Pri Megaddim* (§285 *Eshel Avraham* §§6), cited by *Chiddushei R' Akiva Eiger* §400. He explains: The reason the mourner is permitted to read the portion is because the Sages made it obligatory to keep up with the weekly public reading. In our case, he has the possibility of keeping up with it by reading it after the *Shacharis*. At that time, his *shivah* will already have ended, because part of the seventh day of mourning is counted as the whole day. Since he has the option of reading the portion when his *shivah* has ended, of course he is forbidden to read it before then. Nevertheless, R' Akiva Eiger concludes that "this requires study."

37. *Lechem HaPanim*, cited by *Beis Lechem Yehudah* §400. The same ruling is given by *Aruch HaShulchan* 400:6.

37a. *Beis Lechem Yehudah*; and the *gaon* R' Zalman Margolios (*Aveilus* §18).

See also *Leket Yosher* (*Minhagei Trumas HaDeshen*), who writes of R' Yisrael Isserlein, author of *Terumas HaDeshen*: "[During his *shivah*] he read the weekly portion on the Sabbath, with the *Targum* (Aramaic translation), but not with *Rashi*."

38. *Beis Lechem Yehudah* loc. cit.

39. *Korban Nesanel*, *Mo'ed Katan* 3:§28 *os nun*. The same ruling is given by *Aruch HaShulchan* 400:6.

40. *Aruch HaShulchan* loc. cit.

41. The *gaon*, R' Zalman Margolios (*Aveilus* §18). His reason is that there is no general obligation to study *Chok LeYisrael*.

42. Ibid. §16. See *Kitzur Shulchan Aruch* 219:3.

it is difficult for him to pray in another synagogue, and therefore he prays in his regular synagogue, some rule that he should nevertheless not perform the Torah-reading that Sabbath.[43] According to others, he is permitted to perform it.[44]

◦§ Receiving an *Aliyah*

24. The mourner is forbidden to be given an *aliyah* (be called up to the Torah-reading),[45] even if he customarily receives an *aliyah* every Sabbath.[45a] But if the entire congregation, or the majority, are mourners, they are permitted to receive an *aliyah*.[46]

In the situation where the mourner is forbidden to be given an *aliyah*, if he nonetheless is offered one, he must accept. If he refused, it would be like mourning conspicuously on the Sabbath.[46a]

25. Even at a time when a person would normally be obligated to receive an *aliyah* — for example, when he has a *yahrzeit* or the like — he should not receive an *aliyah*.[47] However, some rule that in such circumstances he is permitted to receive one.[48]

---

43. The *gaon* R' Zalman Margolios (loc. cit.), citing *Shalmei Tzibbur*, who in turn cites *Devar Moshe*.

44. The *gaon* R' Zalman Margolios (loc. cit.). The same ruling is cited by *Chazon LaMo'ed* (17:1:4), in the name of *Yoseif Da'as* (*Yoreh De'ah* §400); *Orach Ne'eman* (141d); and *Zeh HaShulchan* (part 2 p. 111). This ruling is also given by *Kol Bo Al Aveilus* p. 337, citing *Zachur LeAvraham* (*Yoreh De'ah* §300).

45. *Shulchan Aruch* loc. cit.

45a. R' Zalman Margolios (*Aveilus* §14).

46. *Kol Bo Aveilus* p. 338.

46a. *Shulchan Aruch* loc. cit.

47. See *Taz* (ad loc. §§1), citing responsa of *Rashal* (§71), who discusses the case of a man whose son's *bris milah* occurred on the Sabbath during *shivah*. Even though in some communities the custom is that on the day of the son's *bris* the father is obligated to receive an *aliyah*, *Rashal* ruled that the mourning father should not be given an *aliyah*, since forgoing it is not a very conspicuous act of mourning. And see responsa *Nachlas Shivah* §17.

See also *Birkei Yosef* (ad loc.), who states that *Nachlas Shivah* and *Ne'eman Shmuel* agreed with the ruling of *Rashal*.

The *gaon* R' Zalman Margolios (*Aveilus* §15) writes: "It is preferable for the mourner not to come to the synagogue until after the Torah-reading. However, if he did come, and the custom there is that the congregants form rows in honor of the baby's father, and those called to the Torah-reading recite a *Mi Shebeirach* blessing for the father, and he is also called up to the Torah — they should do all these things as usual, so as not to make the mourning conspicuous. However, in cases where the father goes to the synagogue, but the *bris* is not performed there, the congregants going instead to the father's home for the *bris*. . .in such circumstances the father should not receive an *aliyah* even if he is present in the synagogue during the Torah-reading. Since the *bris* is not performed there, forgoing the *aliyah* is not a conspicuous act of mourning. . ."

48. See *Birkei Yosef*, who cites *Pri Chadash* in *Likutei Yoreh De'ah* as disagreeing with *Rashal* (whose prohibitive ruling is noted in our previous footnote; but see also the *gaon* R' Zalman Margolios, *Aveilus* §15, who brings an interpretation of the passage from *Pri Chadash*).

See also *Pischei Teshuvah* (ad loc. §§5), who cites responsa *Eish Das* (§6) as ruling differently from *Rashal*. He writes that if, during the first seven days of mourning, the mourner has an obligation to receive an *aliyah* on the Sabbath — for example, if his wife has given birth, or if he has a *yahrzeit* — he is permitted to receive an *aliyah*, since forgoing it would constitute conspicuous mourning.

26. If the mourner is the only *kohen* in the synagogue, it is preferable for him to step outside before the Torah Scroll is taken out of the Ark. However, if he did not step outside then, he should not do so afterwards. All the more so, no one should tell him to go out. Instead, he must be given the first *aliyah*.[49] Some rule that the same applies, regarding the second *aliyah*, if the mourner is a Levite.[50]

27. If a bridegroom becomes a mourner during the seven days of celebration (*sheva brachos*) following his wedding, he is permitted to receive an *aliyah* on the Sabbath.[50a]

28. According to the basic *halachah*, if the seventh day of mourning falls on the Sabbath, the mourner is permitted to receive an *aliyah*.[51] But the custom is not to receive one during *Shacharis* (the Morning Service), but only during *Minchah* (the Afternoon Service).[52] If he has an obligation to receive an *aliyah* (for example, if he has a *yahrzeit*), some rule that he is permitted to receive it during *Shacharis*.[53]

29. The mourner is permitted to be the one honored to raise up the Torah Scroll at the end of the reading, or to roll it closed, tie and cover it (*hagba'ah u'gelilah*). Likewise, he can be the one honored to take the Torah Scroll out of, and return it to, the Ark (*hotza'ah ve'hachnasah*).

---

49. The *gaon* R' Zalman Margolios (*Aveilus* §13 and *Biurim* there).

50. *Aruch HaShulchan* 400:9. And see responsa *Minchas Yitzchak* IX:§130.

50a. *Sdei Chemed*, s.v. *chasan vekallah* §16. Moreover, he writes there that in congregations where the custom is to read the passage beginning, *And Abraham was old*. . . (Genesis 24:1), in honor of the bridegroom, the bridegroom who is in mourning should also be given this *aliyah*, and should be treated in all respects like any other bridegroom.

51. See *Da'as Torah* (§400), who cites *Ikrei HaDat* (*Yoreh De'ah* 36:19) as giving this ruling in the name of *Ashdos HaPisgah* (§12). The same ruling is given by *Zera Emes* (part 2 §115).
    Responsa *Shemesh Tzedakah* (§10) likewise permits the mourner to receive an *aliyah* on the seventh day. He notes that *Taz* (402:§§5) forbids the mourner to receive an *aliyah*, at least during *Shacharis*. However, he explains that this ruling of *Taz* is based on the custom that people do not come to console the mourner on the seventh day of mourning. But according to our current custom, by which comforters may come on the morning of the seventh day before *Shacharis*, their departure signals the end of *shivah*. (This is because part of the seventh day is counted as the whole day.) Under this circumstance, the mourner may certainly receive an *aliyah* afterwards, during *Shacharis*. This is the reasoning of *Shemesh Tzedakah*.
    Sdei Chemed (*Aveilus* §29) likewise states that the consensus of the *Acharonim* is that the mourner may receive an *aliyah* during *Shacharis*. He cites *Zachur LeAvraham* (175b, s.v. *miktzas*); and *Misgeres HaShulchan* (§395). The latter mentions that in some congregations, the custom is also to give the mourner an *aliyah* during *Shacharis* when the seventh day of mourning falls on Monday or Thursday.

52. *Kol Bo Al Aveilus* p. 339; *Chazon LaMo'ed* 17:1:1; *Gesher HaChaim* 21:14:2.
    Chazon LaMo'ed (loc. cit., note 2) cites *Teshuvah Me'Ahavah* as ruling that if the mourner goes to a synagogue other than his regular one, he is permitted to receive an *aliyah* there, even during *Shacharis*). The same ruling is given by *Elyah Rabbah* (133:§§3).
    Responsa *Be'er Moshe* (II:§111) writes that if the prayer-service is held in the mourner's home on his seventh day of mourning, he is permitted to receive an *aliyah*.

53. See *Kol Bo Al Aveilus* loc. cit.; and *Gesher HaChaim* loc. cit.

(This applies on a weekday also. See above, 16:24.)[54]

◄§ The *Gabbai,* and *Mi Shebeirach*

30. If the *gabbai* of the synagogue is a mourner, he is permitted to perform his usual function of calling people to the Torah-reading and reciting the customary *Mi Shebeirach* . Moreover, one may recite a *Mi Shebeirach* for a mourner or include him among those for whom a *Mi Shebeirach* is recited.[55]

◄§ *Kel Malei Rachamim*

31. During *shivah* , one may recite the memorial prayer, אֵ־ל מָלֵא רַחֲמִים, "God, full of mercy. . ." This applies even on the Sabbath before Rosh Chodesh (*Shabbos Mevorchim*), when this prayer usually is not recited.[56]

The Conclusion of the Sabbath

◄§ Preliminary Psalms Before *Maariv*

31a. Some Authorities write that at the conclusion of the Sabbath, one omits the psalms many recite in the mourner's home before *Maariv* . These are Psalms 144, 29 and 67.[56a]

◄§ Removing Shoes and Changing Clothes

32. At the conclusion of the Sabbath, the mourner removes his shoes after *Borchu* ("Bless Hashem, the Blessed One,")[57] at *Maariv* , but if he is serving as the *chazzan* (leader of the service), he removes his shoes just before *Borchu* .

Before removing his shoes, he should say בָּרוּךְ הַמַּבְדִּיל בֵּין קוֹדֶשׁ לְחוֹל, "Blessed is He Who separates between holy and secular," without mentioning Hashem's Name or Kingship.[58]

---

54. See *Drishah* (§385), who is also cited by *Taz* ad loc. §§1.

55. Responsa *Yehudah Ya'aleh* , *Orach Chaim* §20.

56. *Magen Avraham* (284:§§7) writes: "On *Shabbos Mevorchim* , one does not recite *Hazkaras Neshamos* [prayers for the deceased], except for someone who was buried that same week (*Maharil*)."

56a. ArtScroll *Siddur* p. 592. *Chazon LaMo'ed* 16:note 17, in the name of *Bigdei Yesha* ; *Shmiras Shabbos Kehilchasah* chapter 65 note 154.

57. This is the ruling of *Rama* (*Orach Chaim* 553:2), regarding Tishah B'Av. *Mishnah Berurah* (ad loc. §§6) writes that it is forbidden to show any sign of mourning on the Sabbath. He adds that the mourner should not touch his shoes with his hands, since this would obligate him to wash his hands; but if he did touch them, then after the fact (*bediavad*), he should wipe his hands with anything [such as a handkerchief or other object] which would clean them.
   See also *Chazon LaMo'ed* §17:note 52.

58. *Rama* loc. cit. And see *Mishnah Berurah* (ad loc. §§7). He explains why the mourner who is leading the services removes his shoes before *Borchu* : It is to avoid the distraction (*teiruf*) which might confuse his prayer if he removed them after *Borchu* . But since he should not show any sign of affliction [e.g., going without shoes] on the Sabbath, he first notes the conclusion of the Sabbath by reciting, הַמַּבְדִּיל בֵּין קוֹדֶשׁ לְחוֹל 'Who separates between holy and secular,' without mentioning Hashem's Name or Kingship (*Pri Megaddim*).

Some have the custom of delaying the recitation of *Maariv* until after the conclusion of the Sabbath. In such cases, a mourner should recite בָּרוּךְ הַמַּבְדִּיל בֵּין קוֹדֶשׁ לְחוֹל, "Blessed is He Who separates between holy and secular,"change his clothes, and remove his shoes before *Maariv* even if he is not serving as the *chazzan*. [59]

ᴥᔤ Passages After *Maariv*

33. In some congregations, the verse וִיהִי נֹעַם, 'May the pleasantness. . .,' is not recited in the mourner's home at the end of the *Maariv* service at the conclusion of the Sabbath. Instead, one begins with יֹשֵׁב בְּסֵתֶר עֶלְיוֹן, 'Whoever sits in the refuge of the Most High. . .'. [60]

Others also omit the entire passage beginning יֹשֵׁב בְּסֵתֶר עֶלְיוֹן, 'Whoever sits in the refuge of the Most High. . .' They recite only the last verse, beginning, אֹרֶךְ יָמִים אַשְׂבִּיעֵהוּ, 'With long life will I satisfy him. . .'[61]

However, in most congregations the custom in the mourner's home is to recite וִיהִי נֹעַם, 'May the pleasantness. . .,' as well as יֹשֵׁב בְּסֵתֶר, 'Whoever sits in the refuge. . .'[62]

As for the passages beginning וְיִתֶּן לְךָ, 'And may God give you. . .' some rule that it should be recited,[63] but others rule to the contrary.[64]

34. After *Maariv* at the departure of the Sabbath, Psalm 16, מִכְתָּם לְדָוִד, 'A Michtam by David', is recited, instead of Psalm 49, לַמְנַצֵּחַ לִבְנֵי קֹרַח, 'For the Conductor, by the sons of Korach', which is recited in the mourner's home on other weekdays.[65]

---

59. *Zeh HaShulchan* (*Orach Chaim*, §559), regarding Tishah B'Av. And see *Gesher HaChaim* ch. 20 note 6.

60. *Magen Avraham* (beginning of §295). *Levushei Srad* explains why וִיהִי נֹעַם, "May the pleasantness. . .," is omitted: The end of this verse beseeches G-d to grant success to מַעֲשֵׂה יָדֵינוּ, "our handiwork . . .," and the mourner is forbidden to work.

61. *Kol Bo Al Aveilus* (p. 281) writes: "*Abudraham* (*Hilchos Brachos*) states: 'At the conclusion of the Sabbath one does not recite וִיהִי נֹעַם, 'May the pleasantness. . .,' nor יֹשֵׁב בְּסֵתֶר עֶלְיוֹן, 'Whoever sits in the refuge of the Most High. . .' Instead, one begins, אֹרֶךְ יָמִים אַשְׂבִּיעֵהוּ, 'With long life will I satisfy him. . .' The same ruling is given by other *Acharonim* (*Ginzei Yosef* §148)."

62. *Kol Bo Al Aveilus* (loc. cit.) writes: "However, Rabbeinu Shlomo Kluger, in responsa *HaElef Lecha Shlomo* (*Orach Chaim* §119) states that one should recite וִיהִי נֹעַם, 'May the pleasantness. . .'"

The same ruling is given by *Gesher HaChaim* (20:3:9), who writes: "As is stated in *Kaf HaChaim* (ad loc. §§3), in most congregations the custom is to recite both, וִיהִי נֹעַם, 'May the pleasantness. . .,' and יֹשֵׁב בְּסֵתֶר עֶלְיוֹן, 'Whoever sits in the refuge of the Most High. . .,' since these verses refer to the community as a whole."

63. *Tanya Rabbasi* (*Hilchos Avel* §28) rules that one should recite it. The same ruling is given by *Shibolei HaLeket* (§22), and by *Pri Megaddim* (§295 *Mishbetzos Zahav* §§3). He explains that even though this passage is omitted on Tishah B'Av, that is because the mourning of that day is extremely intense. The same ruling is given by *Chazon LaMo'ed* 17:11.

64. *Chazon LaMo'ed* citing *Bigdei Yesha*. The same ruling is given by *Gesher HaChaim* loc. cit.

65. *Chazon LaMo'ed* ch. 16 loc. cit.

Gesher HaChaim (20:3:12) states that Psalm 16 מִכְתָּם לְדָוִד, 'A Michtam by David', is substituted

◄§ *Havdalah*

35. If the mourner is the one reciting *Havdalah*, he omits the joyous introductory verses, הִנֵּה אֵ־ל יְשׁוּעָתִי, "Behold! God is my salvation," etc., and begins with the blessings over wine, fragrant spices, and the lights of the fire.[66]

Some rule that the mourner does not recite the blessing over fragrant spices.[67] But the prevalent custom is that he does recite it.[68]

36. Some rule that upon the departure of the Sabbath, one who is mourning for his parent must be careful to immediately change out of his Sabbath clothes; otherwise, he must perform *kri'ah* on them.[69] But others disagree.[70] (See also above, 6:20.)

---

for Psalm 49 לַמְנַצֵּחַ לִבְנֵי קֹרַח , '*For the Conductor, by the sons of Korach*', on every day on which one does not recite *Tachanun*.

66. *Pischei Teshuvah* 391:§§1 in the name of responsa *Har HaKarmel* §20.

67. *Pri Megaddim* (§297 *Eshel Avraham* §§5) writes: "*Knesses HaGedolah*, in his glosses on *Tur*, cites *Rada*, *zal*, as stating that the mourner does not recite the blessing over fragrant spices."

The same ruling is given by *Birkei Yosef* (§2) in the name of *Mahari Faraghi*. He states that the mourner does not recite the blessing over fragrant spices at the conclusion of the Sabbath. But he comments that this ruling is "not indisputable," and that this is one of those issues which should be decided by observing the prevalent custom among the people [וּפוֹק חֲזִי עַמָּא דְבַר].

68. See *Kaf HaChaim* (297:§§8), citing *Sefer Mareis Ayin* (*Likutim* 7:4).

The same ruling is given by responsa *Maharam Shick* (*Yoreh De'ah* §363); and by *Gesher HaChaim* (20:3:10), and *Chazon LaMo'ed* (16:12).

69. *Kol Bo Al Aveilus* p. 30 note 19, citing *Chikkekei Lev* §51.

70. See *Minchas Shlomo* (by the gaon, R' Shlomo Zalman Auerbach, *shlita*) §73. He writes that from the plain meaning of the *Gemara* and *Poskim* one may infer that one need not hurry to change clothes at the conclusion of the Sabbath. He explains: As long as it is clear that one's special clothes are still worn for the honor of the Sabbath, one is not obligated to perform *kri'ah* on them.

CHAPTER TWENTY-NINE
The Seventh Day of Mourning

---

1. On the morning of the seventh day of *shivah*, after *Shacharis* (the Morning Prayer), the mourners sit for a short time on a low seat (as they did throughout the seven days). The comforters console them and then tell them, "Arise."[1]

Some have the custom that at this conclusion of the seven days, the comforters add the following two verses: לֹא־יָבוֹא עוֹד שִׁמְשֵׁךְ, וִירֵחֵךְ לֹא יֵאָסֵף, כִּי ה' יִהְיֶה־לָּךְ לְאוֹר עוֹלָם, וְשָׁלְמוּ יְמֵי אֶבְלֵךְ, 'No more will your sun set, nor your moon be darkened, for Hashem will be an eternal light for you, and your days of mourning will end' (Isaiah 60:20). כְּאִישׁ אֲשֶׁר אִמּוֹ תְּנַחֲמֶנּוּ, כֵּן אָנֹכִי אֲנַחֶמְכֶם, וּבִירוּשָׁלַיִם תְּנֻחָמוּ, 'Like a man whose mother consoles him, so shall I console you, and you will be consoled in Jerusalem' (ibid. 66:13).[2]

Some have the custom of placing a stone on the place where the mourners sat.[3]

Some follow a custom of formally terminating the *shivah* by having the mourners walk outside together —or around the corner — accompanied by the comforters.[3a] Symbolically, this is explained as representing the mourner's re-emergence into society from which he had withdrawn during the *shivah* week. Others ascribe kabbalistic significance to this practice.

2. The first part of this seventh day is counted as a whole day. Therefore, as soon as the comforters depart, the restrictions of the *shivah* are removed.[4] Likewise, the mourner may change out of the garment in which he made a tear (*kri'ah*), even if he is mourning for his parent.[5]

3. If there are no comforters present, the restrictions of *shivah* are removed from the time when comforters ordinarily come, namely, after the morning service in the synagogue.[6]

---

1. *Nachamu Ami* 21:12
2. *Chazon LaMo'ed* 20:2.
3. *Nachamu Ami*, citing the *gaon* R' Moshe Bergman, author of *Zibula Basraisa* et al.
3a. While this custom is practiced in many communities, we have not found a written *halachic* source for this. [Ed.]
4. *Shulchan Aruch* 395:1.
5. See *Mishmeres Shalom os kuf* §85; and *Da'as Torah*, in the notes to the passage printed in 340:15.
6. *Rama* 395:1.

✥ On the Sabbath

4. If the seventh day of mourning falls on the Sabbath, when comforters do not come, the basic *halachah* would be that the mourning of the first seven days would cease after sunrise (*neitz hachamah*). (This refers, of course, to those aspects of mourning which apply even on the Sabbath.) However, since during the week the custom is to end the mourning after *Shacharis*, it was instituted that on the Sabbath, too, the mourning restrictions of the first seven days ends after the morning prayers, i.e., *Mussaf*.[7] See above, 28:20 regarding reviewing the weekly *Sidrah* when the Sabbath is the seventh day.

    For the question whether the mourner may be called up to the Torah-reading on the Sabbath, see above, 28:24-29.

5. Some rule that the principle, "the first part of the day is counted as all of it," does not apply to the prohibition against marital relations; hence, marital relations are forbidden during the entire seventh day of mourning.[8] But others disagree.[9]

6. We have mentioned the principle that "the first part of this seventh day is counted as a whole day." It is universally interpreted by all *halachic* authorities to mean that *shivah* ends on the morning of the seventh day. However, since *halachically*, the twenty-four-hour day begins at nightfall (for example, the Sabbath begins on Friday night), some rule that, *in case of extreme need*, the above principle may be interpreted to mean that "the first part of the *night* is counted as the entire [24-hour] day." That is, the restrictions of *shivah* end at the beginning of the night preceding the seventh day. Thus, if mourning began on Tuesday, it would end, *in cases of extreme need*, after consultation with a competent *halachic* authority, at the beginning of Sunday night.[10] However, it is emphasized that the

---

7. *Taz* 402:§§5, and *Shach* §§4.

    See also responsa *Minchas Elazar* (part II:§26). He rules that the mourner is permitted to immerse in the *mikveh* on the seventh day of mourning, if it occurs on the Sabbath. But he states that it is even preferable, if possible, to arrange a *minyan* in the mourner's home for *Shacharis*, so that he can go to the *mikveh* before the Torah-reading.

8. *Taz* (*Orach Chaim*, §555) writes: "*Sefer Chassidim* states that marital relations are forbidden to the mourner during the entire seventh day of mourning; and the same ruling is given by responsa of *Maharam* §549."

    Biurei Maharshal on *Tur* (§395; cited by *Prishah* there §§2) rules the same.

9. See *Aruch HaShulchan* 395:3.

    The same ruling may be inferred from Responsa *Radbaz* part III:§559; *Chochmas Adam* in *Matzeivas Moshe* §6; *Sdei Chemed* (*Aveilus* §25) citing *Be'er HaMayim* §52; *Mishmeres Shalom os tav* §63; *Be'ur HaGra* ad loc. §1. The same ruling may be inferred from *Taz* and *Shach* on §402 (cited above, footnote 7). They both rule that the inconspicuous restrictions of mourning (*devarim shebetzin'a*) are removed on the seventh day.

10. *Tur* (ad loc.) writes: "Some rule that the principle, 'the first part of the day is counted as all of it,' refers specifically to the daytime; that is, one must observe mourning for part of the daytime; observing mourning for part of the nighttime is not counted as the whole day. Others rule [to the contrary], that even part of the nighttime is counted as the whole [24-hour] day. . .and Rabbeinu Tam ruled that, in case of pressing need, the mourner is permitted to bathe on the night of the seventh day."

    Beis Yosef comments on this: "As for the practical *halachah*, we follow Rabbeinu Meir [of

a
aspects of this ruling are very complex, and a competent rabbinic authority should be consulted should the need arise. See note 10.

⋈ Mending the *Kri'ah* Garment

7. As explained above (chapt. 6), the mourner must perform kri'ah on his garment.

For all family members for whom one is required to mourn, except one's parent, one is permitted to mend the tear unevenly (*lishlol*, i.e., baste) after *shivah*.[11] (See above, 6:29 and note 89 there.)

⋈ Visiting the Cemetery

8. The custom is to go to the cemetery on the seventh day of mourning to visit the deceased, recite memorial prayers, and pray for him.[12] (This custom is described in more detail in chapt. 42.)

9. Some follow the custom of the *Arizal* to erect the monument on the seventh day of mourning.[13]

Rotenburg, who rules that the principle refers specifically to the *daytime*], since he came after the other *Poskim*, and his reasoning is convincing." This is also the ruling given in *Shulchan Aruch*. And see *Pischei Teshuvah* (ad loc. §§1), citing responsa of *Radbaz* (part III:§559). See also *Chochmas Adam* in *Matzeivas Moshe* par. 6.

11. *Shulchan Aruch* 340:15.

12. Ibid. 344:20.

13. *Chazon LaMo'ed* (25:2). And in note 1 he refers to *Sha'ar HaMitzvos* (p. 11a), cited by *Pesora DeAbba* (part II:§12). Based on this source, the conclusion is reached by *Kuntres HaYechieli* (p. 55b and 56b) that one should erect the monument on the seventh day of mourning itself.

Chut HaMeshulash writes that this was the practice followed by the author of *Chasam Sofer* when he set up the monument for his wife. *Minchas Yitzchak* (part IV:§107) states that this was also the practice followed by *Maharsham*.

For more on this subject and other customs of when the monument should be erected, see below, chapt. 41.

CHAPTER THIRTY

If *Shivah* Was Not Observed

◄§ Making Up for Missed Observance

1. If one either intentionally or unintentionally failed to observe *shivah* at the correct time, he may make up for it by observing *shivah* during the first thirty days from death.[1]

After the first thirty days, he need not make up for the missed *shivah*. Even if he had already begun to make up for the *shivah* two or three days before the end of the thirty days, he need not continue, once the thirty days have ended. For example, death occurred on the first day of Av and *shivah* was not observed. The mourner began to make up for the missed *shivah* on the twenty-seventh of Av. On the thirtieth of Av (thirty days after the death), he may stop observing *shivah*.[1a]

For the *halachah* in case one did not learn of the death until after the day of burial, see below, 31:9. The above does not apply to the *mitzvah* of performing

---

1. *Shulchan Aruch* 396:1.

Are the thirty days counted from the death or from the burial? *Gesher HaChaim* (21:15:1) writes that the same answer applies here as in the question about receiving news of the death within thirty days (*shmu'ah krovah*). For details see below, 31:3, where it is explained that the custom is to be lenient and count from the day of death.

Consider the following case: A person received news of the death within thirty days of its occurrence (*shmu'ah krovah*). He did not begin to observe *shivah*, and thirty days passed from the death, but this was still within thirty days of receiving the news. Is he required to make up for the omitted period of sitting *shivah*?

Responsa *Beis Shlomo* (*Orach Chaim* §109 §§3) writes that in such a case the person must make up for the omitted *shivah*, since the day of receiving the news is equivalent to the day of the death. His ruling is cited by *Mishmeres Shalom* (*os zayin* §4). The same ruling is given by *Zera Emes* (part II:§155), cited by *Sdei Chemed* (*Aveilus os* 63); and by *Chochmas Shlomo* (by the *gaon* Moharshak), *Yoreh De'ah* §396.

Tiferes LeMoshe (ad loc.) also raises this same question, writing: "It seems reasonable that one should have to make up for the omitted *shivah* within the entire thirty days from receiving the news; otherwise, the lax would be rewarded for his laxity." However, responsa *Chaim Sha'al* (by the *gaon* the Chida) part I:§47 writes that [if thirty days have passed from the death] one need not make up for the omitted *shivah*. And see *Mishmeres Shalom* (loc. cit.), who comments on this: "In matters of mourning, we follow the lenient opinion, even if it is that of the minority. And afterwards I saw that this is also the ruling of the *gaon* the Rav of Brod, *zal* (author of *Machazeh Avraham*), in his approbation for *Eivel Yachid*."

1a. *Tiferes LeMoshe* ad loc.

kri'ah on one's garment. If one did not perform *kri'ah* at the height of grief (i.e., during the first seven days), the rule is as follows:

   (a) For the death of any family member other than one's parent, one may not perform *kri'ah* later.

   (b) For one's parent, one must perform *kri'ah* later, no matter how long after burial.[2] (See above, 6:7.)

2. All the above applies only if the mourner failed to observe the entire *shivah*. If he failed to mourn only some of the days — even the very first ones[3] — he does not have to make up for the missed days. In such a case, *shloshim* is counted from when he should have started sitting *shivah*.[4]

---

2. *Shulchan Aruch* 396:1.

3. Ibid. 396:2; *Gesher HaChaim* 21:15 note 15.

   Responsa *Igros Moshe* (*Yoreh De'ah* part III:§158) writes that if one did not observe mourning on the first day, he must make up for it. This ruling requires study.

4. *Shulchan Aruch* loc. cit.

   Tiferes LeMoshe (ad loc.) writes: "The following question requires study: If one omitted the majority of the seven days of mourning, is this considered as if he had omitted the entire seven days?"

   Da'as Kedoshim (ad loc. §§1) writes: "Logically, if one omitted the majority of the seven days, it is as if he had omitted the entire seven days, and he should have to make up for them. All the same, the matter requires study."

   It would seem that the opposite conclusion is implied by the wording of the responsum of *Rosh* upon which *Shulchan Aruch* based his ruling. *Rosh* writes: "*Ravad*'s statement applies only if the person failed to observe mourning for the entire seven days — similar to the case where one failed to practice *kefi'as hamitah* (overturning the bed)." Hence, the opinion of *Da'as Kedoshim* requires study.

   This conclusion — that missing the majority of the seven days is *not* equivalent to missing all of them — is also implied in the responsa of R' Akiva Eiger (*Tinyana* §23). He writes of a case in which a person received news of a death. He was told that it had occurred more than thirty days previously (*shmu'ah rechokah*), whereas actually it had occurred within thirty days (*shmu'ah krovah*). At the end of this responsum, R' Akiva Eiger writes that, since the person thought he had received a *shmu'ah rechokah*, he must certainly have observed mourning for at least a short part of one day. Therefore the halachah is similar to the case in *Shulchan Aruch* (396:2): that if one observed part of the seven days, but neglected to observe the remainder, he need not make up for it. Clearly, then, according to R' Akiva Eiger's understanding of *Shulchan Aruch*, there is no need to make up the seven days if one observed even a short part of one day.

   This is also the ruling of *Chazon Ish* (*Yoreh De'ah* §212), who likewise bases his conclusion on the above responsum of R' Akiva Eiger.

   See also responsa *Sho'el U'Meshiv* (part 1 §78), cited by *Sdei Chemed* (Aveilus §11). He writes: "It is possible that if one neglected to observe part of the practices of mourning during the days that he observed mourning, one has not fulfilled the obligation [of the *shivah* at all], since one did not observe it in its entirety. This is not to be compared with the last day of *Yom Tov* [in the Diaspora], which counts as one of the seven days of mourning even though one observes only part of the practices of mourning — namely, the inconspicuous ones. In that case, one is not obligated to observe any other practices; but in the ordinary case, one is obligated to observe all the practices [; therefore, if he omits part of them, it is as if he did not sit *shivah* at all]."

   It would seem that the ruling of R' Akiva Eiger, cited above, implies otherwise; for in the case of a *shmu'ah rechokah*, too, only part of the practices of mourning are observed (as is explained in *Shulchan Aruch* 402:2); yet he rules that if one observed the practices required in the case of a *shmu'ah rechokah*, it is as if he had observed part of the seven days, and he need not make up for the *shivah*.

If one failed to observe the mourning of *shloshim*, he does not have to make up for it afterwards. This applies even if he omitted the entire *shloshim*.[5]

◈ After Recovering from Illness

3. If one failed to observe *shivah* because he was sick during those seven days, and then he recovered during the *shloshim*, some rule that he must make up the missed *shivah*.[6] Others rule that he need not make it up.[7]

◈ Mourning Erroneously Stopped

4. A person was told that a family member died, and he began to observe mourning. Then he was told that the family member did not die, so he stopped mourning. Afterwards, he was told that the original announcement was correct, so he resumed mourning. In this case, he counts his period of mourning from

---

5. *Tiferes LeMoshe* loc. cit.

6. Responsa *Nachlas Shivah* (§17), discussing the case of a woman who had just given birth and was therefore unable to observe mourning. The same ruling is given by the responsa of the *gaon* Maharar Shimon Shapira of Prague. Both these authorities are cited by *Beis Lechem Yehudah* (396:§§2), and by his responsa in *Kuntres Acharon* on §396; and *Beis Lechem Yehudah* adds his concurrence, rejecting the contrary ruling of *Shevus Yaakov*.

The same ruling — that one must make up the missed *shivah* — is given by responsa *Chasam Sofer* (*Yoreh De'ah* §342), cited by *Pischei Teshuvah* (ad loc. §§3); by responsa *Tuv Ta'am VaDa'as* (*mahadura* 3 §221), who writes that the *halachah* on this question follows the opinion of *Nachlas Shivah*; and by responsa *Sho'el U'Meshiv* (*mahadura kamma* part I:§75). The latter explains that we do not say that one who omitted a *mitzvah* through circumstances beyond his control is considered as if he had performed it.

This ruling is also given by *Knesses HaGedolah* in his responsa (*Yoreh De'ah* §243).

7. *Elyah Rabbah* (*Orach Chaim* 132:2) cites the ruling of *Nachlas Shivah* (mentioned at the beginning of our previous footnote), and comments: "However, it seems to me that the *halachah* in this case is that [there is no need to make up for the omitted mourning,] not even for the first seven days of mourning. . .and I presented this for the consideration of great authorities, and they ruled accordingly in practice."

The same ruling is given by *Shevus Yaakov* (§88), cited by *Ikrei HaDat* (*Yoreh De'ah* 36:25), who writes: "*Or Ne'elam* (§11) is another authority who did not agree with the ruling of *Nachlas Shivah*; since [the woman whose case was discussed by *Nachlas Shivah*] was able to observe part of the practices of mourning, this was sufficient."

The same ruling is given by *Da'as Kedoshim* (ad loc. §§3), for the reason just mentioned. This ruling is also given by *Aruch HaShulchan* (ad loc. par. 3), who explains: "It is impossible that [the sick person], even on his sickbed, did not observe at least one practice of mourning for at least a short time during the seven days, if his mental faculties were intact." The same ruling — that the sick person need not make up for the omitted mourning — is cited by *Menachem Aveilim* (§8 s.v. *choleh*), in the name of *P'nei Mevin* (part II p. 45); by *Teshuvah MeAhavah* (part III), who concludes that the *halachah* follows the opinion of *Shevus Yaakov*; and by *Gesher HaChaim* (21:15:4).

Yeshuos Yaakov (*Orach Chaim* 548:§§7) also disagrees with the ruling of *Nachlas Shivah*.

Even Yaakov (§39) writes: "Since we have the rule, 'the *halachah* follows the lenient opinion in matters of mourning,' there is room to be lenient on this issue; for we may accept the testimony of the *gaon Shevus Yaakov* that the following ruling was accepted by all the halachic authorities, and was also the practice observed among the people: In the case of a sick person, or a woman who has just given birth, it is sufficient that the person knew of the death, and observed at least some aspect of mourning; this fulfills his obligation of mourning."

the time of the original announcement, even if he missed several days in the interim.[8]

✥ A Minor Who Comes of Age

5. A minor (under the age of *bar-* or *bas mitzvah*) is not required to observe mourning.[9] If he becomes a *bar mitzvah* during the period of mourning — even during the *shivah* — *Shulchan Aruch* rules that he is exempt from all the laws of mourning.[10] But some rule that in the case of mourning for a parent, he is

---

8. This *halachah* is mentioned by *Shulchan Aruch* (340:26) with regard to the *mitzvah* of tearing the garment (*kri'ah*). He rules that in a case of this sort, the original *kri'ah* fulfills the obligation [and one need not tear again]. *Shach* (ad loc. §§40) writes: "As regards *shivah*, it would be logical to conclude that since the obligation of mourning applied to him, and he did observe mourning, this fulfills his obligation, even though he unintentionally omitted some of the days. Hence, the omitted mourning need not be made up. However, the matter requires study."

The *Acharonim* have decided this question by ruling that one counts the seven days from the time of the original announcement. See *Pischei Teshuvah* (396:§§1), who cites this ruling in the name of *Radbaz HeChadashos* (part III §521). *Radbaz* writes that even if the person did not begin to observe mourning at all, the first days [which he erroneously omitted to mourn] are counted as part of the seven.

Aruch HaShulchan (ad loc. par. 4) rules similarly. However, he states that this applies only if the person began to observe mourning. *Aruch HaShulchan* adds that even if the seven days had already passed before the person learned that the original announcement had been correct, he need observe no further *shivah*, since he observed at least the first day.

As for *Radbaz*'s ruling in the case where the person did not begin to observe mourning at all, see *Da'as Torah* (ad loc.), who cites *Yoseif Da'as* as arguing against *Radbaz*'s ruling. *Da'as Torah* concludes: "The ruling [of *Yoseif Da'as*] seems to be the correct one."

See also *Gesher HaChaim* (21:15:3 and note 16), who writes at length to explain the ruling of *Radbaz*.

9. *Nekudos HaKesef* (§340), commenting on *Taz* (§§15). The same ruling is given by by *Dagul MeiRevavah* (ad loc.). He writes that the *mitzvah* of *chinuch* (training the child in *mitzvos*) does not apply to mourning, since it would prevent the child from studying Torah. *Beis Hillel* (§381) and *Sha'arei De'ah* rule the same. The same ruling — that a minor is not obligated to observe mourning — is given by *Levushei Srad* (§340, commenting on *Taz* (§§15); by *Chochmas Adam* (152:17); and by *Magen Avraham* (551:§§38).

See also *Cheker Halachah* (*Hilchos Aveilus* I:§§3), who discusses this topic at length. And see *Mishmeres Shalom os ches* §26; and in *os kuf* §59 he writes: "I found it explicitly written in *Roke'ach* (*Hilchos Aveilus* §314): 'A child who is not yet aged thirteen years and one day is not required to sit in mourning.' "

See also *Chiddushei R' Akiva Eiger* (*Orach Chaim* §616). He writes that even if a boy is aged thirteen years and one day, if he has not yet grown at least two pubic hairs there is reason to rule leniently as regards mourning.

On the other hand, some authorities rule that one must train the child in the *mitzvah* of mourning, as in other *mitzvos*. See *Drishah* (§340), cited by *Taz* (§§15).

Kol Bo Al Aveilus (p. 272) writes: "*Kesav Sofer* (*Yoreh De'ah* §172) notes an apparent contradiction between two passages in *Taz*; and concludes that one is obligated to train a minor in the laws of mourning" [by having the child observe mourning if he is of educable age and a family member dies].

Sheivet Yehudah takes it as an obvious fact that a minor must observe mourning, even if this means interrupting his Torah studies. And see the commentary *Imrei Baruch* on *Dagul MeiRevavah* (§340). He writes that, even according to the opinion of *Shach*, one is obligated to train a child in the laws of mourning by having him observe those aspects of mourning which do not preclude Torah-study; for example, the prohibition against wearing shoes, and the like.

10. *Shulchan Aruch* 396:3. The same ruling is given by *Chochmas Adam* (168:6); *Aruch HaShulchan* (396:5); *Kitzur Shulchan Aruch* (216:2); and by *Ikrei HaDat* (*Yoreh De'ah* 36:48).

nevertheless obligated to observe those practices which apply after the *shloshim*, until the end of the first twelve months, since these stem purely from the *mitzvah* of honoring parents.[11]

Others rule that if he became a *bar mitzvah* during the *shivah*, he must observe mourning for the remainder of the *shivah*.[12]

Still others rule that he is obligated to observe an entire period of mourning, counting the *shivah* and *shloshim* from the day he became *bar mitzvah*. However, if he became *bar mitzvah* after the thirtieth day from death, the *halachah* is the same as for someone who did not hear of the death until more than thirty days after death (*shmu'ah rechokah*). In that case, he observes mourning only for a short time on the day he became *bar mitzvah*. Nevertheless, he is obligated to observe those practices which apply after the *shloshim*, until the end of the first twelve months. The twelve months are counted from the day of burial.[13]

---

11. *Chochmas Adam* (loc. cit.), cited by *Pischei Teshuvah*, §§4. The same ruling is given by *Aruch HaShulchan* (ad loc.). But *Gesher HaChaim* (19:3:3) cites *Chochmas Adam*, and then adds: "However, one who is lenient in this matter also has authorities on whom to rely." He does not cite his source.

12. See *Ikrei HaDat* (36:48), who writes: "*Yad Eliahu* (§93) refutes the reasoning of *Taz*."

The same ruling is given by *Chadrei De'ah* (*Yoreh De'ah* 396:3). According to him, it is obvious that, once the minor becomes *bar mitzvah*, he must observe mourning for the remaining days.

Tiferes LeMoshe also remarks that in fact *Rosh* does not mention the case where the child becomes a *bar mitzvah* during the first seven days of mourning. But *Tiferes LeMoshe* goes on to say: "One must conclude that *Tur* interpreted *Rosh* as follows: The Sages instituted seven days of mourning, connecting their enactment with a verse. Therefore, in a case where the person cannot sit in mourning for seven days, he is exempt entirely; for the Sages instituted seven days, and no less." He concludes that if there are adults who began mourning immediately at burial, the minor must mourn with them from the day he becomes *bar mitzvah* until the seventh day from the burial. This ruling of *Tiferes LeMoshe* is cited by *Mishmeres Shalom* (os kuf §60).

Gesher HaChaim (loc. cit.) writes: "In the case of a minor who becomes *bar mitzvah* during the first seven days of mourning, the custom of the majority is that he does not observe seven days of mourning from when he becomes *bar mitzvah*, but only for the remainder of the seven days [from when the mourning should have begun]. The plain meaning of *Tur* and *Shulchan Aruch* (§396 based on *Rosh*) is that he is exempt even from those remaining days, as *Taz* rules. . .but the majority of the *Acharonim* follow the ruling of *Yad Eliyahu* (§93), who states that he mourns only for the remainder of the seven days."

13. This is the ruling of Rabbeinu Meir of Rotenburg, cited by *Rosh* at the end of *Mo'ed Katan*. The same ruling is given by *Bach* ad loc. *Shach* (ad loc. §§3) agrees with *Bach*.

CHAPTER THIRTY-ONE

Delayed News of a Death

I. *Shmu'ah Krovah* / "Recent" News

✎§ Definition

1. The term *shmu'ah krovah* refers to news of a death that is heard within thirty days. (The question whether these thirty days are counted from the time of death or of burial is discussed below.) The news is deemed "recent" *(shmu'ah krovah)* even if it arrives at the end of the thirtieth day.[1]

If there is a difference in time zone between the place the death occurred and the place where the mourner is, the end of the thirty days is calculated according to the place of the mourner.[1a]

In case of a *shmu'ah krovah*, the mourner is required to observe *shivah* from the day when he was informed of the death. Likewise, the first thirty days of mourning are counted from that day.

For a mourner who was aware when interment took place, the laws of mourning apply from the time of interment. For one who did not know of the interment, the day when the *shmu'ah krovah* reaches the mourner is regarded as the day of interment.[2]

✎§ The Day of Hearing the News

2. On the day when he learns of the death, the mourner is obligated to perform *kri'ah*; see above, chapt. 6.[3] He is also obligated by the laws of the first

---

1. *Shulchan Aruch* 402:1.

   Rif (*Perek Elu Megalchin*) cites two opinions on this question, but rules that the news is called "recent" *(shmu'ah krovah)* even if it arrives on the thirtieth day. The same ruling is given by *Rambam*, *Ramban*, and *Tur*.

   Prishah (ad loc. §§1) explains why, in this instance, we do not apply the rule, מְקְצָת הַיּוֹם כְּכֻלּוֹ, "Part of the day counts as all of it." He writes: "[That rule applies] in cases where one had already started mourning. Here, however, the person had not begun to mourn, and since the beginning occurs within thirty days, he must sit [in mourning] for seven days."

1a. *Kol Bo Al Aveilus* p. 311.

2. *Shulchan Aruch* loc. cit.

3. Ibid.

   It is true that [for the death of a family member other than one's father or mother] someone who

meal[4] (se'udas havraah; see above, chapt. 14). He is forbidden to put on tefillin[5] (see above, 13:2-11).

However, he does not observe the laws applying to an onen (one whose deceased is not yet buried; see above, chapt. 5).[5a]

◄§ Calculating the Thirty Days

3. As stated above, news of death is called "recent" (shmu'ah krovah) if it arrives within thirty days. How are these thirty days calculated?

If burial did not take place on the day of death, some rule that the thirty days are calculated from the day of death.[6]

Others rule that they are calculated from the day of burial.[7]

---

does not perform kri'ah within seven days of the death is not required to perform kri'ah afterwards. But this is because after [seven days] the original grief (chimum) has subsided. That does not apply, however, when the person did not previously know of the death. In this case, the day of hearing the news is the height of his grief (Gesher HaChaim 24:1:8).

4. Rosh (cited by Be'er HaGolah §§3) states: "It [a shmu'ah krovah] is subject to the law of se'udas havra'ah and all the laws of mourning, like the day of burial."

5. Taz (§§1) writes: "Beis Yosef (ad loc.) states in the name of Ramban that on the day of a shmu'ah krovah one should not wear tefillin, just as [one does not wear them] on the day of burial." Nekudos HaKesef (ad loc.) infers the same ruling from Shulchan Aruch (402:2).

5a. Gesher HaChaim (loc. cit.) writes: "The laws of aninus (i.e., exempting the bereaved from mitzvos, and so on) are for the honor of the deceased, because the family member is obligated to attend to the burial. This certainly is not applicable on the day of hearing belated news of the death."

6. Shach (§§5), in the name of Bach and Drishah (§399), who in turn cite Maharshal.

The same ruling is given by Taz (ad loc. §§6); Chochmas Adam (171: 6), and Elyah Rabbah (Orach Chaim §548), cited by Pri Megaddim (Mishbetzos Zahav §5). He states: "One counts from the day of death, not from burial."

Mishmeres Shalom (os shin §38) states that the same ruling is given by responsa Tiferes Tzvi (Yoreh De'ah end of §56); and by Shevus Yaakov (II end of §100), who mentions as an obvious fact that one counts from the day of death; and responsa of Mahari'a (Yehudah Ya'aleh), Yoreh De'ah §371, writes: "You ask whom the halachah follows. The gaon, author of Teshuvah MeAhavah (Yoreh De'ah §402), cites Shach §§5 (in Nekudos HaKesef), and Dagul MeiRevavah, in the name of Mahariv, as taking it as obvious that one counts from the day of burial. On this he [Teshuvah MeAhavah] comments: "Nevertheless, it is possible to be lenient, since we have the rule that in matters of mourning we rule leniently." And Sdei Chemed (Aveilus §54) writes: "It would seem possible to rely on the opinion of the previously mentioned holy rabbis who rule that one counts from the day of death; for since the issue is disputed, the rule about following the lenient opinion in matters of mourning applies to the Poskim as well [as the Talmud]."

The same ruling — to count from the day of death — is given by Chazon LaMo'ed (22:1). And Gesher HaChaim (24:1:1) writes: "If one wishes to be lenient [i.e., count from the day of death], he has authorities upon whom he may rely."

7. Shach (in Nekudos HaKesef, commenting on his own citation from Bach) writes: "His [Bach's] conclusion is not indisputable. In addition, the matter requires study, since Maharshal based his conclusion [that one counts from the day of death] on the writings of 'Rabbeinu Yerucham and Poskim,' and yet Rabbeinu Yerucham himself explicitly writes the opposite about this halachah. In nesiv 28, part II he writes: 'A shmu'ah rechokah means that one heard of the death of one's family member, and heard about it more than thirty days from the burial.' Thus we see explicitly that one counts from the day of burial. The matter requires study." (It should be noted that Chochmas Adam loc. cit. offers a solution to the problem raised by Shach. He suggests that Rabbeinu Yerucham

Some rule that in any case, even according to the second opinion, on the thirtieth day from burial we apply the principle, "part of the day counts as all of it." Therefore, if the news arrives during the thirtieth day, it is considered too late to be a *shmu'ah krovah*. This is on condition that thirty full days have passed from the day of death.[8]

The customary current practice is to be lenient and follow the first opinion — to count from the day of death.[9] The news is considered a *shmu'ah rechokah* ["deferred news"] if it arrives after the thirtieth day from death, even though it arrived within thirty days of burial.

✃ Doubt About the Thirty Days

4. If a person hears of the death of a family member, and he does not know whether thirty days have passed, some rule that he is obligated to observe mourning as for a *shmu'ah krovah*.[10] Others rule that he need not do

---

mentioned the day of burial because usually death and burial are both on the same day.)

Even HaEzer (ad loc.) comments on the ruling of *Maharshal*: "In my humble opinion, this is a surprising ruling; for it is explained by *Rosh* and *Mordechai* that a *shmu'ah krovah* is counted from the day of burial; and the *Poskim* agree with their ruling."

Dagul MeiRevavah (loc. cit.) writes that he found the same ruling in responsa of *Mahari* Weill (§16), who also takes it as obvious that one counts from the day of burial. The same ruling is given by responsa of *P'nei Yehoshua* (§9), cited by *Ikrei HaDat* (*Yoreh De'ah* §36 os 43) and by *Da'as Torah* (ad loc.).

Mishmeres Shalom (loc. cit.) cites *Hagahos VeChiddushim* by the gaon, author of *Heishiv Moshe* (§402). He in turn cites *Nekudos HaKesef* and *Tiferes LeMoshe* as ruling that the news of death is not called a *shmu'ah rechokah* unless it arrives more than thirty days from the day of burial. He concludes: "And that is clear."

The same ruling is given by *Siddur R' Yaakov Emden* (*Hilchos Aveilus* §§22); and by *Tiferes Yisrael* (*Mo'ed Katan* ch. 3 and in his *chiddushim* there).

Chazon LaMo'ed writes: "This [that one counts from the day of burial] is also the ruling of *Yavetz*. And responsa of *Rabaz* (Shparn) §85 derives this ruling from the commentary of *Rabbeinu Channanel* on *Mo'ed Katan* 20b." The same ruling is given by *Aruch HaShulchan* (402:10).

8. Responsa *To'afos Re'em* (§57), cited by *Da'as Torah* and *Mishmeres Shalom*.

   Gesher HaChaim (loc. cit. par. 3) writes: "If one received the news on the thirty-first day from the death, and this was the thirtieth day from burial, this is considered a *shmu'ah rechokah*. This applies even according to the *Poskim* who rule that one counts from the day of burial; for in this case one may also take into consideration the opinion cited by *Rif*, that even regarding news of death, one may apply the rule, 'Part of the day counts as all of it.' "

9. *Sdei Chemed*, responsa of *Mahari'a* (*Yehudah Ya'aleh*), and *Gesher HaChaim*, as cited above, footnote 6.

10. See *Taz* (397:§§2). He writes that this question is raised·by *Maharam Mintz* (§95), who concludes, after discussion, that he has no clear proof as to whether one is obligated to mourn. "However," *Taz* states, "responsa of *Mahari* Ben-Lev rules that in this case one is obligated to mourn. . .and that is also the ruling of my teacher and father-in-law [*Bach*], ad loc." The same ruling is given by *Shach* (ad loc. §§1).

   Mishmeres Shalom (os samech §33) cites responsa *Chavos Ya'ir* as ruling that one must observe mourning. And his ruling is cited by *Beis Lechem Yehudah* (§§1).

   See also *Pischei Teshuvah* (ad loc. §§1), who cites responsa *Yerios HaOhel* (§38) as concluding in favor of the *Poskim* who rule that one is obligated to mourn. The same ruling is given by responsa *Radbaz HeChadashos* (§62); responsa *Yad Eliahu* (§44); *Bechor Shor* (in his *chiddushim* on *Mo'ed Katan* 20b); *Noda BiYehudah* (*mahadura kamma Even Ha'ezer* §31, and *mahadura tinyana Yoreh*

so.[11] The *Acharonim* write that one should be lenient on this question [and not treat the news as a *shmu'ah krovah*].[12] However, one authority states that in our day, when it is possible to easily clarify the matter by telegram or telephone, one should be strict until it is clarified.[13]

◄§ Cases of Error

5. A person heard that his family member died, and did not know whether the news was "recent" or "deferred." Relying on the lenient ruling cited in the previous section, he treated the news as not being a *shmu'ah krovah*. Afterwards, he found out that in fact it had been a *shmu'ah krovah*. However, by the time he found this out, thirty days had passed from the time of death.

In this case some rule that, as long as seven days have not yet passed from the original moment of hearing the news, he must observe mourning until the end of seven days from that moment.[14] Others disagree.[15] The *Acharonim* write that one

---

De'ah §208); and *Sha'ar HaMelech* (*Hilchos Ishus* 4:17). See also *Binas Adam* (*Sha'ar Rov VeChazakah* §44) and *Chochmas Adam* (168:8), who rules that one is obligated to mourn. The same ruling is given by *Ohel Yosef* (§46), cited by *Ikrei HaDat*. And see *Nahar Shalom* (*Orach Chaim* §71 §§1), who concludes that the *halachah* follows *Radbaz* and his supporters.

11. *Taz* loc. cit.

12. See *Mishmeres Shalom* (os samech §33), who writes: As for the *halachah*, it would seem that one should rely on those who rule leniently. These are *Taz*; *Shevus Yaakov* (I:§98); *Chacham Tzvi* (§3); and his son, in *She'elas Yavetz* (§128). These last two both indicate their agreement with the ruling of *Taz*. In addition, *Maharikash* (in his *Hagahos* on §402) writes: "The prevalent custom does not follow the ruling [of *Maharibal*, *Rashdam*, and their supporters]; and it is known that, even in a dispute among the *Poskim*, 'The *halachah* in matters of mourning follows the lenient opinion.' [This is evident from *Beis Yosef* (§396); and the same ruling is given by responsa *Toras Chaim* (III:§56); and *Divrei Emes* (responsa §2). Moreover, *Mahari Zain*, in responsa *Ginas Veradim* (*Yoreh De'ah klal 5* §9) applies this rule even to recent *Poskim*, writing: "This rule, that 'The *halachah* in matters of mourning follows the lenient opinion,' is valid even [when the lenient ruling is that of] a single individual in opposition to a majority." A number of *Acharonim* hold the lenient position, and also *Machaneh Efrayim* (*Hilchos Ishus* end of §3) writes: "If there is a question if the news of death is considered a *shmu'ah krovah* or a *shmu'ah rechokah*, we are lenient." Therefore, we follow the lenient opinion.

See also *Ikrei HaDat* (*Yoreh De'ah* 36:§§2). He refers to *Chikrei Lev* (§116), who proves that in such a case the *halachah* remains in doubt, and therefore: "One should rule leniently, as did *Yavetz* in an actual case. . .In addition, *Kol Eliahu* also comes to the defense of *Taz*. . ."

And see responsa *Besamim Rosh* (§385), who answers a query from someone who [heard that] his daughter had died, and did not know whether thirty days had passed. *Besamim Rosh* rules that the father is not required to observe mourning. This ruling is cited by *Chida*, zal, in his *Tov Ayin* (9:9). He in turn is cited by *Ikrei HaDat* (ad loc.).

13. Responsa *Sheivet HaLevi* (by the gaon R' Shmuel HaLevi Vosner, shlita), *Yoreh De'ah* §213.

14. Responsa of R' Akiva Eiger *tinyana* §23. And see what he writes there in the name of *Tiferes LeMoshe*.

15. *Taz* (397:§§2) cites *Maharam Mintz*, who raises this question and concludes that it "requires study to determine whether one is obligated to observe mourning." *Taz* comments: "In my humble opinion, there is no [need to observe] mourning in this case, since thirty days have now passed since the day of death. Here there is no less reason for exemption than in the case of one who mistakenly or purposely failed to observe mourning until thirty days had passed. In that case, he certainly has no further obligation to observe mourning, since thirty days have now passed from the day of death." *Shach*, in *Nekudos HaKesef*, agrees with *Taz*. The same ruling is given by *Shulchan Gevoha* (402:§§3).

should be lenient on this question [and not observe mourning].[16]

The same applies if, on first hearing of the death, he was incorrectly informed that thirty days had already passed. Then he found out that the moment of hearing the news had actually been within thirty days; but by the time he found this out, thirty days had passed from the time of death. In this case, too, he need not observe mourning.[17]

6. A person learned of a death on the thirtieth day. He mistakenly observed mourning for only a short time on that day, as is the *halachah* when the news is not a *shmu'ah krovah*. After the thirtieth day, he found out that he should have observed mourning as for a *shmu'ah krovah*. In this case, he need not observe any further mourning.[18]

7. A person was informed of the death of a family member. He completed observing *shivah*. Afterwards, he found out that the family member had not died then, but now has died.

In this case, he must again observe *shivah*.[19]

8. A person was informed that one of his sisters had died, and he observed *shivah* for her. Afterwards, he learned that she was alive, but the one who had died was a different sister of his.

In this case, he must again observe the seven days of mourning.[20]

◄§ Failure to Observe Mourning After Hearing a *Shmu'ah Krovah*

9. If a person heard a *shmu'ah krovah* but did not immediately begin to observe mourning, he is required to begin mourning, as long as thirty days have not yet passed from when he heard the news. This applies even if thirty days have already passed from the time of death.

However, some rule that if thirty days have already passed from the time of death, he is not required to observe mourning.[21]

---

16. *Chochmas Adam* 168:8. The same ruling is given by *Chazon Ish, Yoreh De'ah* §212.

17. *Sdei Chemed* (*Aveilus* §67) cites responsa *Pnei Yehoshua* as ruling that in this case one is required to observe mourning, but *Sdei Chemed* himself rules to the contrary. The same ruling [not to require mourning] is given by *Gesher HaChaim* (24:2:9). He explains that this is comparable to the case of one who observed mourning for part of the seven days; in that case, one is not required to make up the missing days. [Here, too, since mourning was observed for a short time on the day of receiving the news, there is no need to make up any further period of mourning.]

This reasoning of *Gesher HaChaim* would seem to point to an even greater leniency: Even if the correct information is received within thirty days from the death, but more than seven days from the original announcement, one would not have to observe mourning. The matter requires study.

18. See responsa of R' Akiva Eiger, end of responsum 23. See also a comment on this responsum in *Chazon Ish, Yoreh De'ah* §212.

19. *Mishmeres Shalom os shin* §34. He finds this *halachah* stated explicitly in *Teshuvos HaRosh* §27.

20. See ibid. §33. He finds this *halachah* stated explicitly by an early *halachic* work: *Eshkol, Hilchos Aveilus* §51.

21. See *Sdei Chemed* (*Aveilus* §63), who reasons that the day of hearing the news is equivalent to the day of death. He distinguishes between our case and the one mentioned by *Taz* and *Nekudos*

← If One Was Informed After He Had Already Recited *Maariv*

10. If a person hears a *shmu'ah krovah* after having recited the Evening Prayer (*Maariv*) — even if he recited *Maariv* and heard the *shmu'ah krovah* during the daytime — his seven days of mourning are counted from the next day, and the day when he heard the news does not count as one of the seven.[22]

For example, he recited *Maariv* before sundown on Wednesday. After praying, and still before sundown, he heard a *shmu'ah krovah*, and began observing mourning. Nevertheless, Wednesday is not counted in his seven days of mourning. Instead, Thursday is counted as the first day of the seven.

All the same, he must put on *tefillin* the next day (in our example, Thursday), but without reciting the accompanying blessing.[23]

On the other hand, if he had not yet recited *Maariv*, the day of hearing the *shmu'ah krovah* counts as the first of the seven, even if his congregation had already recited *Maariv* during the daytime, before he heard the *shmu'ah krovah*.[24]

11. If, on the thirtieth day, and after having recited *Maariv* during the daytime, a person hears of the death, this is considered a *shmu'ah krovah*, and that day

---

HaKesef at the end of §397. They state there that once thirty days have passed from the day of death, there is no further requirement to mourn. There, however, the person did not definitely know whether news of the death had reached him within thirty days; he was in a state of doubt regarding how long ago the death had occurred. In our case, by contrast, he definitely knew that the death had occurred within the past thirty days, but he neglected to observe mourning. Therefore, as long as thirty days have not yet passed from the time when he heard the news, he remains obligated to observe mourning (*Zera Emes* II:§155).

The same ruling — that in this case one is required to observe mourning — is given by *Hagahos Chochmas Shlomo;* and by *Mishmeres Shalom (os zayin* §4), citing responsa *Beis Shlomoh (Orach Chaim,* 109:§§3).

This same question is raised by *Tiferes LeMoshe* (§397). He states: "Reason dictates that the person must make up for the missed period of mourning [as soon as possible] within thirty days from when the death became known to him. Otherwise, anyone who sinned [neglected to mourn] would receive a reward [exemption from mourning]. The same ruling is given by *Gesher HaChaim* (24:1:7).

However, responsa *Chaim Sha'al* (by the *gaon Chida*) I:§47 rules that in our case one is not required to observe mourning; and *Mishmeres Shalom* (loc. cit.) comments on this: "In matters of mourning, we follow the lenient opinion, even when a single individual disputes a number of other authorities. Afterwards, I found that this is also the ruling of the *gaon*, the Rav of Brod, author of *Machazeh Avraham*, in his approbation to *Eivel Yachid*."

See also responsa *Betzel HaChochmah* (I:§66). He writes of the following case: A person heard of the death on the thirtieth day. Through circumstances beyond his control, he could not observe mourning until that evening. By that time, it was already more than thirty days from the death. Nevertheless, this authority rules, the person is required to observe mourning.

22. *Shulchan Aruch* 402:11. The reason is explained by *Taz* (ad loc. §§7): Let us assume, for example, that the period between 6:00 and 6:30 p.m. on Wednesday was still daytime. But in order to be allowed to recite *Maariv*, one was lenient and regarded it as if it were already Thursday. Then, during this same period of time, one was informed of the death. In order to be lenient and end the period of mourning sooner, one wishes to consider it as Wednesday again. One is not allowed to do so, because this would constitute תרי קולא דסתרי אהדדי, "two leniencies which contradict each other."

23. See *Pischei Teshuvah* 388:§§2.

24. See *Shach* 375:§§14.

is counted as the first of the seven days of mourning.[25] However, some rule that even though this is considered a *shmu'ah krovah*, the day when he heard the news does not count as one of the seven days of mourning.[26]

⋖§ During Twilight

11a. The twilight period between sundown (*sh'ki'ah*) and nightfall (*tzeis hakochavim*) is called *bein hashmashos*. If one hears a *shmu'ah krovah* during this period, it is considered to have been heard on the day which is just ending, and that day is counted as the first of the seven days of mourning.[27]

For example, a *shmu'ah krovah* was heard during the twilight period between Tuesday and Wednesday. In this case, Tuesday is counted as the first of the seven days of mourning.

⋖§ Sabbath and *Yom Tov*

12. If one hears a *shmu'ah krovah* on the Sabbath, the Sabbath counts as the first day of mourning. After the Sabbath ends, he performs *kri'ah*. Friday is his seventh day of mourning.[28]

If one hears a *shmu'ah krovah* on the Sabbath which is also the day before *Yom Tov*, that Sabbath counts as one day of mourning, since inconspicuous mourning practices are observed (see above, 28:18). The Festival then cancels the remainder of *shivah*.[29]

13. If the Sabbath or Festival is the thirtieth day from the death, and news of the death is heard that day, the *halachah* is the same as for a *shmu'ah rechokah* "deferred" news; see below, par. 19). Accordingly, mourning is observed for only a short time at the conclusion of the Sabbath or Festival.[30] Nevertheless, on that Sabbath or Festival itself, the inconspicuous practices of mourning are observed (see above, chapt. 28).[31] The same applies if news of a death is heard on the

---

25. *Taz* ad loc. §§7.

26. *Chiddushei HaGershuni* ad loc.

27. *Pischei Teshuvah* (375:§§5), in the name of responsa *Radbaz HeChadashos* (§268). And see *Sdei Chemed* (*Aveilus* §15).

   Regarding the *halachah* if one receives news of death *bein hashmashos* on the thirtieth day, see *Chazon LaMo'ed* (22:note 2). He writes that "study is required to determine whether this period may be considered nighttime in order to treat the news as a *shmu'ah rechokah*, as is found in a similar situation in Tractate *Shabbos* (34a)."

28. *Shulchan Aruch* 402:11.

29. Ibid. 402:10; and *Shach* ad loc. §§8.

30. *Shulchan Aruch* 402:5.

31. *Shulchan Aruch* loc. cit. and *Orach Chaim* 548:17. And see *Chiddushei R' Akiva Eiger* ad loc.

   He writes: "If one hears a *shmu'ah krovah* on the first day of the Festival, and this is the twentiety-eighth day from the death; and on the third day of the Festival it becomes a *shmu'ah rechokah* [i.e., it is already more than thirty days from the death], one might rule that from the third day [of the Festival] on, [even] the inconspicuous practices of mourning דְּבָרִים שֶׁבְּצִינְעָא (see above, 28:18)] need not be observed. This is comparable to the case of one who hears a *shmu'ah rechokah* during a Festival, as discussed in 402:6. But to determine the *halachah* requires study."

thirtieth day from death, and this is also the Diaspora's second day of *Yom Tov* .[32]

One authority writes that if a resident of *Eretz Yisrael* is visiting in the Diaspora and hears news of a death on the thirtieth day from the death, which is also the Diaspora's second day of *Yom Tov*, this is considered a *shmu'ah krovah*. After *Yom Tov*, he must observe six more days of mourning.[33]

✎ Sabbath Eve

14. If a man is informed of a death on Sabbath Eve [i.e., Friday evening] after he has already accepted the Sabbath upon himself — or, in the case of a woman, after she has already kindled the Sabbath candles — some Authorities rule that they are considered to have heard the news on the Sabbath. Thus, if that Sabbath is the thirtieth day from the death, they need observe mourning only for a short time after the Sabbath ends. However, other Authorities disagree.[34]

✎ Purim

15. Some rule that if one hears of a death on Purim, and it is the thirtieth day from the death, mourning need be observed only for a short time on the day after Purim.

Likewise if news of the death is heard on the Sabbath, which is the twenty-ninth day from the death, and Purim is the following day, mourning need be observed only for a short time on the day after Purim.[35]

✎ The Bridegroom and Bride

16. One authority writes that if a bridegroom or bride hears a *shmu'ah krovah* during the seven days of feasting (*sheva brachos*) following the wedding, and these days end more than thirty days after the death, the *halachah* is the same as for

---

32. *Elyah Rabbah*, ad loc. He explains: "Even though it [the Diaspora's second day of *Yom Tov*, usually] counts as one of the seven [days of mourning], this does not give it any more weight than the Sabbath. The Sabbath, too, [usually] counts as one of the seven days of mourning, and yet [if the news arrives on a Sabbath which is the thirtieth day from the death,] the *halachah* followed is that of a *shmu'ah rechokah*. This is because only the inconspicuous practices of mourning are observed on the Sabbath. Therefore the day does not have sufficient weight [as a day of mourning] to bring about a seven-day mourning period."

[If the Sabbath were given full weight as a day of mourning, we would say that the seven days of mourning had begun on the Sabbath, which was within thirty days of the death. Therefore the news would be a *shmu'ah krovah*, and a full seven-day mourning period would be required (i.e., another six days in addition to the Sabbath). However, the Sabbath is not given full weight as a day of mourning. It is given only partial weight — enough to be counted as one of the seven days under other circumstances; but not enough to be considered a full-fledged day of mourning by itself, and hence to make the news a *shmu'ah krovah*. The same applies to the Diaspora's second day of *Yom Tov*.]

33. Responsa *Betzel HaChochmah* I:§66.

34. See *Mishmeres Shalom os shin* §18. However, *Kol Bo Al Aveilus* (footnote on p. 265) writes: "See responsa *Binyan David* (§40), who rules strictly in this matter, requiring a full seven-day mourning period."

35. *Hagahos Chochmas Shlomo Orach Chaim* §696.

36. *Kol Bo Al Aveilus* p. 68. He does not give any source for this ruling.

a *shmu'ah rechokah*; that is, mourning is observed for only a short part of the day following the days of the *sheva brachos*.[36]

✑ Following a Festival

17. If, ten days after the end of Succos, one hears of a death which occurred on the day before the Festival, this is considered a *shmu'ah krovah*, and one must observe *shivah*. It is true that if one were to count a short time on the day before the Festival as canceling *shivah*, add the seven days of the festival as canceling seven more, count the *Yom Tov* of *Shemini Atzeres* as canceling yet another seven days (see below, 32:12), and then add the ten subsequent days which passed before the news was heard, one would have a total of thirty-one days. However, the Festivals are counted as canceling seven days of mourning only if one observed at least a short time of mourning before the Festival (see below, 32:2). In our case, where the person did not even know of the death before the Festival, the Festival does not cancel mourning.[37]

✑ Priority in Reciting *Kaddish* and Leading the Prayer-Service

18. Generally, one who is in *shivah* has precedence in reciting *Kaddish* in a place where the custom is for only one person at a time to recite it. Similarly, he has precedence in leading the prayer service. However, even though one who hears a *shmu'ah krovah* must observe the seven days of mourning, he does not have precedence in reciting *Kaddish*, as would someone who began mourning immediately after the burial.[38]

II. *Shmu'ah Rechokah* / "Deferred" News

✑ Definition of *Shmu'ah Rechokah*

19. If a person hears of the death beyond thirty days — even on the night immediately following the thirtieth day[39] — it is deemed "deferred" news *(shmu'ah rechokah)*. In this case, he observes mourning only for a short time on the day he hears the *shmu'ah rechokah*.[40]

---

37. *Shulchan Aruch* (402:8 and *Orach Chaim* 548:20). *Shach* (§§5) adds: "He begins counting the seven and the thirty days [of mourning] from the time when he heard the news."

38. *Mateh Efrayim* 1:§7.

39. *Shulchan Aruch* 402:1. In this case, he observes mourning for a short time that night, and then he is not required to observe any further mourning. This is in contrast to the case of one who has already mourned for six days; there, a short amount of mourning on the night of the seventh day is not counted as the whole day. In our case, however, the *halachah* is more lenient. Since it is a *shmu'ah rechokah*, there is no requirement of a seven-day mourning period. Hence a short time, even during the night, is enough to fulfill the obligation *(Beis Yosef* §395, citing R' Meir of Rotenburg).

40. *Shulchan Aruch* loc. cit. *Gesher HaChaim*, *Chazon LaMo'ed*, et al. explain that the word שָׁעָה *(sha'ah)* used here by *Shulchan Aruch* simply means "a short amount of time," not literally an hour.

Regarding the question whether these thirty days are counted from the time of death or of burial, see above, par. 3.

◆§ The Day of Hearing the News / One Mourning Act

20. During the short time that one observes mourning on the day of the *shmu'ah rechokah*, he need not observe all the laws of mourning. It is sufficient to perform one act of mourning, such as removing his shoes. He need not wrap his head or overturn the bed (see above, chapt. 22), and he is permitted to work, to bathe, to use lotions, to have marital relations, and to study Torah.

If he is not wearing shoes when he hears the *shmu'ah rechokah*, he must overturn the bed, or wrap his head, since he must do one thing which is visibly an act of mourning.

If the *shmu'ah rechokah* arrives while he is studying Torah, working, bathing, or applying lotion, he must interrupt the activity for the sake of mourning. A short interruption is sufficient. An exception is *tefillin*; if he is wearing them when he hears the news, he need not remove them.[41]

Interrupting these activities is not in itself enough to fulfill the obligation of mourning. He must also perform one positive act which is visibly for the sake of mourning, such as removing his shoes, overturning the bed, or wrapping the head. However, any one of these by itself is sufficient.[42]

◆§ During *Shacharis* / *Tefillin* / *Tachanun*

21. If, during *Shacharis*, the *shmu'ah rechokah* reaches him in synagogue while he is in the midst of the Introductory Psalms (*Pesukei DeZimrah*) or the like, he should not remove his *tefillin*, but should simply remove his shoes and continue praying with the congregation. But if the news of the death causes him to weep, he must remove his *tefillin*.[43]

A congregant who has received a *shmu'ah rechokah* does not recite *Tachanun*. If the congregation is praying in his home, they also do not recite *Tachanun*. If the mourner is a woman, the congregation recites *Tachanun* even in her home.[44]

◆§ Meal of Condolence / *Kri'ah* / *Dayan HaEmes* / Haircut

22. In the case of a *shmu'ah rechokah*, the mourner's neighbors do not have to provide him with a Meal of Condolence (*se'udas havra'ah*; see above, chapt. 14).[45] Likewise, for any family member except a parent, the mourner does not

---

41. *Shulchan Aruch* 402:2. And *Shach* (§§2), citing *Ramban*, explains the reason: Even during *shivah*, one puts on *tefillin*, except for the first day (see above, chapt. 13). It would not make sense for the *halachah* to be more strict for a *shmu'ah rechokah* than for the second day of regular mourning.

42. *Shulchan Aruch* loc. cit.

43. *Mishnah Berurah* 38:§§16.

44. *Sdei Chemed (Aveilus* §183), citing *Vaya'an Yosef* (p. 30b). The same source states: "In the case of a woman, *Tachanun* is recited, since they are not praying in the place where the deceased lived, and the time for mourning has already passed, and she is not praying with them.'"

45. *Shulchan Aruch* 402:3.

perform *kri'ah* for a *shmu'ah rechokah*.[46] However, he *does* recite the blessing *Dayan HaEmes* (". . .the True Judge").[47] If he did not recite it immediately upon hearing of the death, he must do so during the next twenty-four hours. If he did not recite it during those twenty-four hours, some rule that he can no longer recite it.[48]

For a *shmu'ah rechokah* regarding one's parent — no matter how long after the death — one performs *kri'ah* on all one's garments (see above, 6:15).[49]

In a situation where one is not required to perform *kri'ah*, he is forbidden to do so.[50]

23. If one did not observe the required act of mourning upon hearing a *shmu'ah rechokah*, he must do so afterwards.[51]

24. If the *shmu'ah rechokah* is about one's parent, he is forbidden to have a haircut or shave "until his friends reprimand him for his unkempt appearance."[52] (For the definition of this time-limit, see above, 24:19-22.) He must observe the mourning practices of the Twelve Months (i.e., the practices in effect *after* the

---

46. *Shulchan Aruch* 402:4.

    Sdei Chemed (*Aveilus* §183) cites *Emek She'elah* (a commentary on *She'iltos*) as stating that according to the *Geonim* (in *She'iltos* and *Halachos Gedolos*), one does perform *kri'ah*. The author of *Emek She'elah* writes at length to explain the reasoning of these *Geonim*. Obviously, however, since the *Poskim* make no mention at all of this ruling, they must have been convinced that the more lenient ruling is to be followed.

    Kol Bo Al Aveilus (p. 364) cites an opinion that one should perform *kri'ah*, but without reciting the accompanying blessing [*Dayan HaEmes*, ". . .the True Judge"].

47. This is in accord with the general *halachah* that one recites this blessing upon hearing bad news [see *Shulchan Aruch Orach Chaim* §222].

48. *Gesher HaChaim* (24:2:3) explains: "Since he is not observing mourning at all, it is assumed that after twenty-four hours his grief has subsided. Therefore he can no longer recite the blessing. And even though above (chapt. 6 note 27) we cited the ruling of *Chida* that within three days from hearing the news one may recite the blessing, this would logically apply to someone who is observing mourning. However, the *halachah* regarding this matter depends on one's feeling grief."

49. *Shulchan Aruch* (loc. cit.) and *Gesher HaChaim* (loc. cit.).

50. *Rama* (ad loc.). *Shach* (§§3) comments: "An exception is made for one's father or mother, or for a great scholar who was accustomed to pose difficult questions in *halachah*, and with whom one feared to disagree. If one wishes to perform an extra act of mourning in honor of such a person, one is permitted to do so. This is what *Bach* writes in 340:25, citing *Or Zarua*."

51. *Ma'aseh Eliahu* (§67). The same ruling is given by responsa *Tzitz Eliezer* (part VII:§49:10:2).

52. *Shulchan Aruch* 402:1. And see *Chiddushei R' Akiva Eiger* (ad loc.). He writes that *Shiurei Knesses HaGedolah* records disagreement among the *Poskim Acharonim* concerning the case where one's friends reprimand him within thirty days [from his hearing the *shmu'ah rechokah*].

    Da'as Torah (ad loc.) writes: "See *Orach LaTzaddik* (§12-§18). He discusses whether the reprimand must be *after* thirty days or whether this applies even if the reprimand comes *within* thirty days. [That is, once thirty days have passed, may one rely on the reprimand which he received earlier, or must he wait for another reprimand?] The author of *Orach LaTzaddik* rules stringently on this question [i.e., that one must wait until reprimanded again after the thirty days]. At the end, he cites a responsum by the author of *Knesses HaGedolah*, who rules that according to the basic *halachah*, one may be lenient on this question, but the custom is to be strict; therefore the custom should be investigated."

    See also *Zachur LeAvraham* (*Hilchos Avel* §300). And see responsa *Mayim Rabbim* (§72 and §73), who rules that the [first] reprimand is effective only after thirty days [from receiving the news].

shloshim) until the end of Twelve Months, from the day of the burial, not from the day of the *shmu'ah rechokah*.[53]

✥ *Shmu'ah Rechokah* on the Sabbath or Festival

25. If one hears a *shmu'ah rechokah* on the Sabbath or Festival, he does not observe any mourning at all that day — not even the inconspicuous practices. At the conclusion of the Sabbath or Festival, he observes mourning for a short time (as described above, par. 20-22), and that is sufficient.[54]

> For the *halachah* regarding *kri'ah* on *Chol HaMo'ed* for a *shmu'ah krovah* or *shmu'ah rechokah*, see below, 32:3.

✥ Hearing of Two Deaths

26. If one hears two *shmu'os rechokos* on the same day, he observes mourning only for a short time (see above, paragraphs 20-22), as for a single *shmu'ah rechokah*. This applies even if the two deaths did not occur on the same day.[55]

If one hears two *shmu'os krovos*, or if two family members were buried on the same day and he is aware of the burials on the day they occur, he counts the *shivah* and *shloshim* for both decedents at the same time.

If he hears of one death one day, and of the other death the next day, he counts the *shivah* and *shloshim* for the second deceased from the day of hearing the second *shmu'ah krovah*.[56]

✥ Notification After Twelve Months Have Passed

27. If one hears of a death only after twelve months, the *halachah* is as follows:

> For the death of one's parent, one observes mourning only for a short time on the day of receiving the news, as explained above, par. 20-22. In this case, the single act of mourning may even be one of those applying during the Twelve Months (the period after the first thirty days of mourning).[57]

For the death of a family member other than one's parents, some rule that one is not required to observe mourning even for a short time.[58] Others rule that one must observe mourning only for a short time on the day of receiving the news.[59]

---

53. *Shulchan Aruch* loc. cit.. The ruling that the twelve months are counted from the day of the burial is given by *Gesher HaChaim* (loc. cit.), and is obvious, since it is consistent with the *halachah* for other mourners.

54. *Shulchan Aruch* 402:6.

55. Ibid. 402:9; *Be'er Hagolah*; *Shach* ad loc. §§6.

56. *Shulchan Aruch* 402:7. *Shach* writes: "The same *halachah* applies if two of one's family members die, one after the other, as explained above, §375."

57. *Shulchan Aruch* 402:1; *Shach* ad loc. §§1.

58. See *Da'as Torah* ad loc.

59. See *Sdei Chemed Aveilus* §182. The same ruling is implied by *Gesher HaChaim* 24:2:4.

28. If one is in doubt as to whether twelve months have passed from the day of burial, some rule that, because of doubt, he must observe the laws of mourning which apply during the twelve months of mourning (i.e., after the end of the first seven days). But one who is lenient on this matter forfeits nothing.[60]

⋙ Credibility of the Reporter

29. If death is reported by one of the following sources, one must accept the report as reliable and observe mourning:

(a) A single witness[61]

(b) One who did not see the death, but heard about it from another (*eid mi'pi eid*).[62]

(c) A non-Jew who mentions the death without being aware that his Jewish listener needs the information for halachic purposes (*meisiach le'fi tumo*).[63] In this case, the *shivah* and *shloshim* are counted from the day when the mourner heard of the death.[64]

If two witnesses state that death occurred, and two others state that it did not occur, one does not observe mourning.[65]

---

60. *Kol Bo Al Aveilus* p. 364. He writes there, citing *Zachur LeAvraham* (§300), that one who is lenient on this matter forfeits nothing.

He also writes there: "If one heard a *shmu'ah rechokah* about one's father or mother after eleven and a half months, the following question arises: Must he complete thirty days even though twelve months [from burial] will have passed [before the end of the thirty days]? See *Zachur LeAvraham* (*Yoreh De'ah* §300). He rules that once twelve months have passed, one may have a haircut as soon as one's friends reprimand him for his long hair. Likewise, if a Festival (*regel*) occurs during thirty days from the *shmu'ah rechokah*, it is possible that one is permitted to have a haircut on the day before the Festival, if one's friends reprimand him" (cited in the name of *Knesses HaGedolah* loc. cit.).

61. *Shulchan Aruch* 397:1. *Shach* (§§1) comments: "*Ramban* gives the rule: 'The same types of witnesses who are accepted to confirm a woman's permissibility for remarriage are also accepted to confirm that one must mourn.' This ruling is also given by *Bach*. And see *Even HaEzer* §17, concerning the types of witnesses who are accepted to confirm a woman's permissibility for marriage."

62. *Beis Hillel* (ad loc.) writes: "As for the ruling that one must accept the testimony of someone who [merely] heard [the information] from another witness, this means even if the person simply says: 'I heard of it from a witness,' even if he is not acquainted with that witness and does not mention his name, but gives the report without these details. This is the *halachah* found in *Even HaEzer* §17."

63. *Shulchan Aruch* loc. cit.

Taz (ad loc. §§1) cites a responsum of *Or Zarua* as ruling that this type of evidence is not acceptable for purposes of mourning. The same ruling is given by *Zachur LeAvraham*, citing a number of *Poskim*. However, *Gesher HaChaim* (19:9:1) writes that we follow the ruling of *Shulchan Aruch*.

64. *Chiddushei R' Akiva Eiger* ad loc. This applies only in a case where the family members had not yet given up hope of finding their relative alive (*Rikash*). And see responsa *Zekan Aharon* (§94).

65. *Shulchan Aruch* 397:2. *Shach* (ad loc. §§2) explains that [in the absence of uncontradicted testimony] a man is presumed to be alive. *Taz* (ad loc. §§2) gives a different explanation: Since the matter is in doubt, one rules leniently.

Gesher HaChaim (loc. cit.) states that the same *halachah* applies if a single witness states that death occurred, and another states that it did not.

◄§ Obligation to Inform About a Death

30. If one is unaware that his family member has died, others are not obligated to inform him, even of the death of his parent. To this the verse applies: '*He who speaks gossip is a fool*' (*Proverbs* 10:18).[66]

As long as the person remains unaware of the death, the laws of mourning do not apply to him. One is permitted to invite him to a wedding feast or other celebrations.[67] However, if the person asks about his family member, one should not lie to him and say that he is alive, for it is written, '*Keep far from falsehood*' (*Exodus* 23:7).[68]

Nonetheless, the custom is to inform a son of his parent's death, so that he can recite *Kaddish*. But there is no custom at all to inform a daughter.[69]

---

66. *Shulchan Aruch* 402:12.

Responsa *Maharam Shick* (*Orach Chaim* §26) — discussing the case of a man who did not know that his sister had died — rules that the man should not be informed, even if he is praying for her recovery in his daily prayers. He states that even though the sister died, praying for her is not a transgression. Moreover, the rule in *halachah* is that one does not tell one person to commit a transgression [in this case, to unnecessarily inform someone of a death] for the benefit of another [i.e., to prevent him from uttering a pointless prayer]. True, *Rama* rules that one must inform a son about his father's death so that the son will recite *Kaddish*. But there, another factor enters in: the command to save a Jew who is in danger: '*Do not stand by the blood of your fellow Jew*' (*Leviticus* 19:16). The purpose of *Kaddish* is to redeem the deceased from Gehinnom. If we are commanded to save a person's body from danger, how much more so his soul.

67. *Shulchan Aruch* loc. cit. The reason is that the person does not know of the death.

Chiddushei HaGershuni (ad loc.) writes about the case where a husband knows of the death of his wife's family member, for whom she would be required to mourn. If the wife does not know of the death, her husband is permitted to have marital relations with her, since the laws of mourning do not apply until the mourner hears of the death. This, he writes, is the ruling given by *Sefer Chassidim* (§800) and *Gilyon Maharsha*. *Chiddushei HaGershuni* adds, in the name of *Maharash* HaLevi (*Yoreh De'ah* §27), that this is not a violation of the prohibition against causing someone else to sin: '*Do not put a stumbling-block in front of the blind*' (*Leviticus* 19:14).

68. *Shulchan Aruch* loc. cit.

Taz (ad loc. §§8) writes: "It would seem that one may answer with an ambiguous expression, not stating explicitly that the person has died, but using language which could be interpreted either for life or death. A support for this is found in the incident of R' Chiya, when he inquired of R' Abba. . . [*Pesachim* 4a]."

69. *Rama* ad loc.

See also *Kol Bo Al Aveilus* (p. 262). He cites responsa *Maharash* Engel (part 6 §10) as writing: "I know for certain that the *gaon*, author of *Baruch Ta'am*, ruled in practice that if one son is saying *Kaddish* it is not necessary to inform the other sons. It is true that this is contrary to the prevalent custom, but in a number of instances I have observed that when a *tzaddik* died, they did not inform all his sons until after thirty days."

Regarding the case where a person is within the Twelve Months of mourning for one of his parents, and then the other parent dies, *Sdei Chemed* (*Aveilus* §53) writes: "It would seem that one need not inform [the son]. Since he is already saying *Kaddish* for his father or mother, the one *Kaddish* counts for both of them. However, one must question this reasoning: Perhaps the one *Kaddish* counts for both of them only if intended for both of them; or if recited without specific intent. But if he specifically intends the *Kaddish* for only one of his parents, perhaps it does not count for the other. And if he only knows about the death of one parent, this means that he is intending the *Kaddish* for that parent alone. Therefore it is possible that one must inform him."

One authority rules that during a Festival one should not inform a son of his parent's death, since this would prevent rejoicing on *Yom Tov*;[70] and this authority rules that the same applies on Purim.[71]

See also *Chazon LaMo'ed* (chapt. 22). He states that if one knows the sons will not observe mourning, one should not inform them until after thirty days.

70. *Pischei Teshuvah* (ad loc. §§2), citing responsa *Panim Me'iros* (part II:§191). The reason is that if one were to inform the son, he would have to observe the inconspicuous practices of mourning.

71. *Pischei Teshuvah* (loc. cit.), citing responsa *Panim Me'iros* (loc. cit. §99). He rules that the son should not be informed until after Purim.

CHAPTER THIRTY-TWO

Shivah and *Shloshim* Canceled by a Festival

---

1. A Festival (*Yom Tov*) interrupts and cancels the mourning of *shivah* and *shloshim*.[1] For this purpose, "Festival" means Pesach, Shavuos, Succos, Rosh Hashanah, and Yom Kippur.[2]

✎ Conditions of Cancelation

2. If death occurs before a Festival so that one is obligated to observe mourning[3] — and if he did in fact observe mourning before the Festival, even for a moment — then the Festival exempts him from the laws of *shivah*.[4]

This applies only if he actually mourned for at least a short time before the Festival; even if, during that short time, he observed only inconspicuous mourning practices (*devarim shebetzin'a*). An example of this could occur, for example, if one heard a *shmu'ah krovah*[5] [see previous chapter] on a Sabbath which was the day before a Festival.

However, if he intentionally or unintentionally failed to observe mourning altogether, or if he did not have time to observe mourning because he only became obligated to do so immediately before nightfall,[6] the Festival does not cancel the mourning.

---

1. *Shulchan Aruch* (*Yoreh De'ah* 399:1, and *Orach Chaim* 548:7).

   Responsa *Chasam Sofer* (*Yoreh De'ah* §348) explains that the Festival annuls the Heavenly judgment upon the soul of the deceased. This explains why a wedding does not cancel the mourning of a bridegroom, even though the wedding is a personal festival for him.

2. *Shulchan Aruch* 399:6.

3. Concerning the exact time when one becomes obligated to observe mourning, see above, chapt. 13.

4. See *Mishnah Berurah* (548:§§26). He writes: "See *Pri Megaddim*, who states that the act of mourning performed need not necessarily be removing one's shoes. It could also be overturning the bed (see above, chapt. 22), or any other practice which is required during *shivah*. Any such act makes it possible for the Festival to cancel *shivah*."

5. For the definition of *shmu'ah krovah*, see above, chapt. 31.

6. See *Birkei Yosef*, who states that this *halachah* applies only if he came to ask the rabbi during the period just before sundown, when one has accepted the laws of the Festival upon oneself in order to "take from the non-sacred and add it to the sacred"; or if he came during the period called *bein hashmashos*, between sundown and nightfall; or if he knew the *halachah* that one should not observe mourning during these periods. However, if he mourned during these periods, by performing some act

If he did not know of the death before the Festival began, the Festival certainly does not cancel the mourning.

In these cases in which the mourning is not canceled, the bereaved observes the inconspicuous mourning practices during the Festival, and when it ends he begins the seven days of mourning (shivah).[7]

If one's failure to observe mourning before the Festival was due to circumstances beyond his control — for example, if the mourner was sick or had just given birth — the Festival cancels shivah, since the mourner knew of the death.[8]

3. If death occurs on the day before the Festival and the family members are afraid that there will not be enough time to complete the burial before nightfall, when the Festival will commence, they may request non-Jews to take the deceased to burial. Once the non-Jews left the town and are no longer visible to the family, the laws of shivah begin to apply. If this is even a short time before Yom Tov, and they observe mourning during this brief time, the Festival cancels their shivah. This applies even if the non-Jews perform the burial on Yom Tov.[9]

☙ A Bridegroom During His Days of Feasting

4. During the seven days of feasting (sheva brachos) following a wedding, the bridegroom is exempt from the laws of mourning (see below, 35:2). If his relative dies during the seven days of the sheva brachos, and a Festival also begins during those same seven days, some rule that the Festival does not cancel shivah, since the bridegroom had not yet become obligated to mourn. But others rule to the contrary [i.e., that shivah is canceled].[10]

---

of mourning then because he thought he was permitted to do so, the Festival cancels shivah (Mahari, responsa Beis Yehudah part II:§57). See also responsa Maharanach (§51).

7. Shulchan Aruch 399:6.

8. Mishnah Berurah 548:§§53. For more details about such circumstances, see above, chapt. 30.

9. Shulchan Aruch 399:14; Dagul MeiRevavah §375.

10. Chiddushei R' Akiva Eiger (§342) cites Knesses HaGedolah (Likutim §17), who in turn cites
    responsa Eidus BeYaakov (§11) as ruling that the Festival does cancel shivah. He comments: "In my humble opinion, this requires study. The most apparent conclusion would be that since the laws of mourning had not yet begun applying to [the bridegroom], the Festival does not cancel [the mourning]. The actual text of the responsum is not available to me for examination. As for the practical halachah, study is required."

Gilyon Maharsha (ad loc.) also writes that, logically, the Festival should not cancel the mourning, and the bridegroom should be obligated to observe the seven-day mourning period after the Festival. He compares this situation to that of two consecutive Festivals — Succos and Shemini Atzeres. If one did not observe mourning for at least a short time before Succos, Shemini Atzeres does not cancel the mourning. Subsequently, however, Gilyon Maharsha also cites Knesses HaGedolah's ruling that the mourning is canceled. He explains the reasoning of Knesses HaGedolah as follows: The bridegroom's seven days of feasting are not comparable to a Festival, but to the Sabbath. On the Sabbath, one is considered to have observed mourning, and therefore the Festival cancels the mourning.

Gesher HaChaim (19:7:2) writes that, according to the consensus of the Acharonim, the Festival does not cancel shivah.

❧ Laundering and Bathing on the Day Before the Festival

5. If one observed even a brief time of mourning before the Festival, and the Festival will therefore cancel the mourning, he is permitted to launder his clothes on the day before the Festival (*erev Yom Tov*); but he may not wear them until the night, when *Yom Tov* commences. Preferably, on *erev Yom Tov* he should be careful not to launder until after the middle of the day (*chatzos hayom*), so as to make it obvious that he is laundering for the sake of the Festival.[11] But some rule that he is forbidden to launder until the end of the afternoon.[12]

Bathing, even in cold water, is forbidden until the night of the Festival.[13] But some rule that the mourner is permitted to bathe, even in hot water, once he has recited *Minchah* in the late afternoon,[14] and this second ruling is the prevalent custom (but see footnote).[15]

Other practices of mourning, such as sitting on [or near] the floor, and not wearing shoes, apply until nightfall. But some rule more leniently, placing the time-limit for these matters at two hours before evening.[16] An exception is the day

---

11. *Shulchan Aruch* (399:5, and *Orach Chaim* 548:10).

　　Mishnah Berurah (ad loc. §§36) explains: The Sages took into consideration that when night comes and the Festival begins, one cannot launder. Hence, for the sake of the Festival, they permitted one to launder the day before.

12. *Mishnah Berurah* loc. cit. §§37, in the name of the *Rama*.

13. *Shulchan Aruch* loc. cit.

　　Mishnah Berurah (ad loc. §§38) explains: "This means [that one may not bathe] even in cold water, since at night [when the Festival begins] it is possible to bathe in cold water. And during *Chol HaMo'ed*, one is permitted [to bathe] even in hot water, since the laws of *shivah* have been canceled for him."

14. *Shulchan Aruch* loc. cit.

15. *Rama* (*Yoreh De'ah* ad loc.). But in *Orach Chaim* (ad loc.) he writes: "However, in accordance with our [Ashkenazic] custom of prohibiting bathing during *shloshim*, one may not bathe; for the Festival only cancels the restrictions of *shivah* [not those of *shloshim*]. The same principle applies to laundering, in a community where the custom is to prohibit laundering for the entire *shloshim*."

　　See also *Mishnah Berurah* (ad loc. §§42), who writes: "Nevertheless, the custom is to be lenient in this regard [and permit bathing in the late afternoon, even in hot water], as *Rama* writes in *Yoreh De'ah* 399:5. But some of the *Acharonim* rule that one can be lenient only to the extent of bathing in cold water, but not hot. (Nevertheless, during *Chol HaMo'ed* one may certainly rely on the lenient opinion [and bathe even in hot water].) But it should be noted that, even according to the lenient opinion which permits bathing in hot water, this applies only on the day before the Festival, and likewise during *Chol HaMo'ed*, for the honor of the Festival. Once the Festival is over, one is forbidden to bathe or launder until the end of *shloshim*; for the Festival does not cancel the restrictions of the thirty days. See *Hagahos Imrei Baruch* §399."

16. *Mishnah Berurah* (loc. cit. §§39). And see ibid. §§40, where he writes, citing *Yeshuos Yaakov*, that the time limit is "just before dark, i.e., *bein hashmashos* (between sundown and nightfall). And it is possible that even during the period of *tosefes Yom Tov* [the late afternoon when one may accept *Yom Tov* upon oneself], [the laws of mourning] do not apply. And see *Bach* (§261), who states that the time when one may accept the Sabbath upon oneself begins two hours before evening."

　　Sha'ar HaTziyun (ad loc.) writes: "*Elyah Rabbah* cites *Ravan* as ruling that all the restrictions of *shivah* are removed, from the time of the *Minchah* prayer on [i.e., from about two-and-a-half hours before evening; the exact time varies with the seasons]. A similar conclusion may be inferred from the words of *Shach* (§§14), who explains the permission to launder on the day before *Yom Tov* by stating:

before Pesach, when the restrictions of mourning are removed after midday (*chatzos hayom*), since the afternoon before Pesach is considered to be *Yom Tov*.[17]

∞ When the Sabbath Coincides With *Erev Yom Tov*

6. If a person's family member dies on Friday, and that Sabbath coincides with *erev Yom Tov* (the eve of a Festival), some rule that in this case he is permitted to bathe in hot water on Friday in the late afternoon, in honor of the Festival. Others rule that he is permitted to bathe only in cold water. If one sees that a person wishes to rely on the lenient opinion [and bathe in hot water], one should not object.[17a]

∞ *Erev* Yom Kippur

7. On *erev* Yom Kippur, the mourner is permitted to bathe and immerse in a *mikveh* in the late afternoon, one or two hours before nightfall, even if he has not yet recited *Minchah*.[18] And some permit him the leniency of sitting on a chair or bench to eat the *Se'udah Mafsekes* (the last meal before Yom Kippur).[19] He is also permitted to go to the synagogue to recite *Minchah*.[20]

Calculating *Shloshim* if a Festival Cancels *Shivah*

∞ Pesach

8. In the Diaspora, if one observed mourning for even a moment before Pesach, that short time is counted as *shivah*. Adding the eight days of the Festival yields fifteen days. Thus, the restrictions of the *shloshim* (the period from the end of the seventh until the end of the thirtieth day of mourning) must be observed for another fifteen days.

'The restrictions of *shivah* are already canceled.' This implies that from the time when laundering is permitted, the restrictions of the seven-day mourning period do not apply."

17. *Chochmas Adam klal* 169:3. This ruling is based on the *Darkei Moshe* in the name of *Tashbatz*, and he concludes that one may rely on it.

17a. *Terumas HaDeshen* (§287) rules that one is permitted to bathe even in hot water. He is cited by *Shach* (ad loc. §§16) and by *Magen Avraham* (*Orach Chaim* loc. cit. §15).
    Be'ur Halachah (ad loc.) cites opposing opinions on this question, but concludes: "If a person wishes to rely on the lenient opinion, certainly one should not object, since *Shach*, *Magen Avraham*, and *Derech HaChaim* cite the opinion of *Terumas HaDeshen* as halachah. As for the objection of *Elyah Rabbah*, it is based only on the custom cited there by *Darkei Moshe*, who states that it is customary to be strict on this question."

18. *Mateh Efrayim* (606:16). The same ruling is given by *Mishnah Berurah* (ad loc. §§25).

19. *Pischei Teshuvah* (387:§§1), citing responsa *Divrei Yosef* (§61). This is contrary to the opinion of *Magen Avraham*, who in §606 implies that he rules strictly on this question. The lenient ruling is also given by *Mateh Efrayim* loc. cit. And *Elef HaMagen* (ad loc.) writes that this is the custom.

20. *Darkei Moshe* §384, citing *Kol Bo*.

In *Eretz Yisrael*, the calculation is as follows: The short time before Pesach counts as the first seven days. The seven days of the Festival bring the total to fourteen. Hence the *shloshim* end after another sixteen days.[21]

⇜ Shavuos

9. If one observed mourning for even a moment before Shavuos, that short time is counted as the first seven days. The Festival of Shavuos is only one day (in *Eretz Yisrael*) or two (in the Diaspora). However, in Temple times, if one did not offer the Festival sacrifice on the *Yom Tov* day of Shavuos, he could make up for it during the following six days. Therefore, Shavuos is counted as seven days. This brings the mourner's total to fourteen days. Hence the *shloshim* end in another sixteen days. In the Diaspora, the second day of *Yom Tov* counts as one of these last sixteen days.[22]

⇜ Rosh Hashanah

10. If one observed mourning for even a moment before Rosh Hashanah, the laws of *shivah* are canceled due to Rosh Hashanah. Betwen Rosh Hashanah and Yom Kippur, he observes the restrictions which apply after *shivah*. Then, when Yom Kippur arrives, it cancels all the remaining days of the *shloshim*.[23]

⇜ Yom Kippur

11. If one observed mourning for even a moment before Yom Kippur, the laws of *shivah* are canceled. Between Yom Kippur and Succos, he observes the restrictions which apply after *shivah*. Then, when Succos arrives, it cancels all the remaining days of the *shloshim*.[24]

⇜ Succos / Shemini Atzeres

12. Observance of even a moment of mourning before Succos, combined with the seven days of Succos, counts as the first fourteen days of mourning. The day of Shemini Atzeres counts as another seven days, yielding twenty-one. The next day, which is the second day of Shemini Atzeres in the Diaspora, counts as one day, yielding twenty-two. Hence, the *shloshim* end after another eight days.[25]

---

21. *Shulchan Aruch* (*Yoreh De'ah* 399:7 and *Orach Chaim* 548:12).

22. *Shulchan Aruch* (*Yoreh De'ah* 399:8 and *Orach Chaim* 548:13).

23. *Shulchan Aruch* (*Yoreh De'ah* 399:9 and *Orach Chaim* 548:14).

24. *Shulchan Aruch* (*Yoreh De'ah* 399:10 and *Orach Chaim* 548:15).

25. *Shulchan Aruch* (*Yoreh De'ah* loc. 399:11 and *Orach Chaim* 548:16). *Mishnah Berurah* (ad loc. §§46) explains: Shemini Atzeres is counted as a *Yom Tov* on its own. True, this Festival is different from Shavuos, in that the sacrifices of Shemini Atzeres cannot be made up during the following week. Nevertheless, the Torah equates all the Festivals to each other, by stating at the end of the relevant passage: '*These are the Festivals of Hashem*' (*Leviticus* 23:37). Therefore, the same *halachah* [regarding mourning] applies to all of them.

It is customary to visit the grave on the seventh and thirtieth day of mourning. How to fulfill this custom when a Festival cancels *shivah* or *shloshim* is explained below, chapter 42.

❧ Canceling *Shloshim*

13. If a Festival occurs after one has observed *shivah*, the Festival cancels the entire laws of mourning of *shloshim* (the period from the end of the seventh until the end of the thirtieth day of mourning). This applies even if the seventh day of mourning occurs on the day before a Festival.[26] Thus, one is permitted to take a haircut and shave (when mourning for relatives other than his parent), to launder and iron one's clothes, and to bathe, in the late afternoon prior to the Festival after having recited *Minchah*.[27] Some rule more leniently, permitting these activities after midday (*chatzos hayom*). Under difficult circumstances (*sha'as hadechak*), it is possible to follow the more lenient ruling.[28]

On the day before Pesach, according to all opinions, one may bathe and launder after midday. And taking a haircut or shave is permitted even before midday (but see below, par. 16).[29]

14. If one's eighth day of mourning occurs on a Sabbath which is the day before a Festival (i.e., the first day of the Festival is Sunday), he may launder and bathe on Friday, even before *Minchah*.[30] Some rule that he may return to his regular seat in the synagogue as soon as this Sabbath begins (see above, chapt. 27). Nevertheless, he is forbidden to attend a joyous feast (see above, chapt. 25) on this Sabbath.[31]

---

26. *Shulchan Aruch (Yoreh De'ah* 399:3 and *Orach Chaim* 548:8).

27. *Rama (Yoreh De'ah* 399:3 and *Orach Chaim* 548:8). This leniency is granted for the honor of the Festival. Our statement that it applies "after having recited *Minchah*" is cited from *Be'ur Halachah* (ad loc. s.v. *she'mutar*). He writes that one should wait until this time, ". . .so it will be obvious that it is for the honor of the Festival."

28. See *Sha'ar HaTziyun* (ad loc. §§23), who writes: "The words of the *Mechaber* [R' Yosef Karo, author of *Shulchan Aruch*], below 548:10, imply that it is enough [sufficiently stringent] if one launders and irons his clothes after midday. . .and in time of urgent need (*sha'as hadechak*) it is possible that one might rely on the lenient opinion, as stated by the *Mechaber*."

Be'ur Halachah (ad loc.) writes: "One should be aware that *Rama*'s statement that the permission applies only 'in the late afternoon' is in accord with the first opinion cited in 548:10. [We cited this opinion above, in par. 10.] According to that opinion, the permission [regarding *shivah*] applies only when night arrives. Hence [regarding the *shloshim*], it applies 'in the late afternoon.' But according to the more lenient opinion there [regarding the *shivah*], which permits bathing in the late afternoon, the permission [regarding the *shloshim*] applies even before midday. This is what *Gra* writes, and it is obvious."

29. *Rama (Yoreh De'ah* 399:3) and *Mishnah Berurah* (ad loc. §§31).

30. *Shulchan Aruch* loc. cit. Our statement that the permission applies "even before *Minchah*" is cited from *Be'ur Halachah* (ad loc.) who writes: "It would seem that in this case one need not wait until after the *Minchah* Prayer. There [in the case of *shivah*] one must make it obvious that the permission is for the honor of *Yom Tov*. Here [in the case of *shloshim*] this is not necessary."

31. *Sha'arei Teshuvah* (ad loc.), citing responsa *Bach HeChadashos* (§12). *Sha'arei Teshuvah* adds: "The same ruling is given by *Beis Hillel (Yoreh De'ah* §399). However, *Shevus Yaakov* (part I:§90) refutes *Beis Hillel* and rules that one may not return to his regular seat in the

15. With regard to mourning for someone other than one's parent:

If [shivah ends before a Festival, but] the mourner did not have a haircut or shave on the day before the Festival, he is permitted to do so after the Festival, since the Festival canceled the restrictions of the shloshim. However, he is forbidden to have a haircut or shave during Chol HaMo'ed, since he could have done so before the Festival.

On the other hand, if his seventh day of mourning occurred on a Sabbath which was the day before a Festival, he is permitted to take a haircut or shave during Chol HaMo'ed, since he had no possibility of doing so before the Festival.[32]

16. The permission to take a haircut or shave on the day before Yom Tov applies only in the case of mourning for someone other than one's parent. If one is mourning for his parent, he is forbidden to have a haircut or shave until his friends reprimand him for his unkempt appearance (see above, 24:19-21). Thus, even if a Festival occurs after the first thirty days of mourning, the mourner is forbidden to have a haircut.[33] If the Festival occurs within the thirty days, the mourner is forbidden to shave.

⇜ Which Mourning Practices Are Affected

17. The halachah that the Festival cancels shivah and shloshim includes only those practices stemming from the obligation to mourn. Those stemming from the obligation to show respect for the deceased are not canceled. Therefore, the flame which is customarily left burning in the mourner's home throughout the first seven days after death [see above, 16:3] should remain burning also during the Festival. However, during a Festival one should not place this flame in the room where people eat. All the more so, one should not place it in the room where the death occurred, since this might lead one to eulogize the deceased. One is not allowed to light this flame on Yom Tov. Hence, if he did not kindle it before Yom Tov, he should have a non-Jew kindle it on Yom Tov.[34]

Likewise, the Festival does not cancel one's rights of precedence in reciting

---

synagogue. . .Nonetheless, since Bach rules permissively on this matter, which is only a question of custom, it would seem that one who instructs someone to follow the permissive ruling cannot be called 'in error,' as Shevus Yaakov writes; for the permissive ruling has support among the Poskim."

32. Shulchan Aruch (Orach Chaim 548:8). And see Mishnah Berurah (ad loc. §§33). He writes: "Obviously, the same applies to laundering."

33. Shulchan Aruch (Yoreh De'ah 399:4 and Orach Chaim 548:9). Levushei Srad (ad loc.) explains that the Festival cancels only those aspects of mourning which apply specifically to shivah or shloshim [in contrast to the prohibition against having a haircut, which, in the case of mourning for one's parent, applies until one's friends reprimand him for his long hair; see above, 24:20-22].

Mishnah Berurah (ad loc. §§34) writes that if one's friends reprimand him within the first thirty days, one may have a haircut. He gives the source as Elyah Rabbah. However, Elyah Rabbah writes that the permission applies if one's friends reprimand him on the thirtieth day. The matter requires study. Afterwards, I saw that Shoneh Halachos (ad loc.) states that this is a printing error in Mishnah Berurah; and in the newly printed edition of Mishnah Berurah the passage is corrected. The same correction is made in Igros Moshe Yoreh De'ah part III:§157.

Kaddish in the synagogue (see below, 39:39-48). Thus, as long as one is within seven or thirty days from the death, one has the rights of precedence corresponding to the actual number of days that have passed, even if a Festival has occurred in the meantime.[35]

The effect of the Festival on the laws of tearing one's garment (kri'ah) is discussed above, 6:30.

---

34. *Mishnah Berurah* loc. cit. §§3.
35. *Mateh Efrayim* 1:3.

CHAPTER THIRTY-THREE

Yom Tov and *Chol HaMo'ed*

The laws of the period before burial (*aninus*) during *Yom Tov* and *Chol HaMo'ed* are discussed above, chapter 5.

◌§ *Kri'ah*

1. One does not rend one's garment (perform *kri'ah*; see chapt. 6) on *Yom Tov*, not even on the Diaspora's second day of *Yom Tov*, and not even if the deceased is a member of one's family,[1] since performing *kri'ah* on *Yom Tov* is a desecration of the Festival. Nevertheless, if one *did* perform *kri'ah* on a *Yom Tov*, the obligation of *kri'ah* has been fulfilled and he would not be obligated to perform *kri'ah* again after the Festival.[2]

2. Those family members of the deceased who are obligated to mourn for him are permitted to perform *kri'ah* during *Chol HaMo'ed*.[3] However, some rule that this is forbidden. The custom in Ashkenazic communities is not to perform *kri'ah* during *Chol HaMo'ed*, except for one's parent. For other family members, one performs *kri'ah* after the Festival week. But in a community where there is no established custom, one *should* perform *kri'ah* during *Chol HaMo'ed* for any family member.[4]

When does this apply? If the death or burial occurred during *Chol HaMo'ed*. But if death and burial occurred on *Yom Tov*, one performs *kri'ah* after the Festival week.[5]

---

1. *Shulchan Aruch* 340:31.

2. This is similar to the *halachah* with regard to performing *kri'ah* on *Shabbos*. Ibid. 340:28.

3. *Shulchan Aruch* (340:31, and *Orach Chaim* 547:6). *Mishnah Berurah* (ad loc. §§11) writes: "If one is not obligated to perform *kri'ah*, but wishes to do so in order to show respect for the deceased, this is forbidden."

4. *Rama* (ad loc.). And he concludes: "Where no custom has been established, one should perform *kri'ah* for any family member"; for according to the basic *halachah*, [this ruling] is the one to be followed (*Mishnah Berurah* ad loc. §16).

   Kaf HaChaim (ad loc. §§30) writes: "This [to perform *kri'ah* only for one's parent during *Chol HaMo'ed*] is the custom in the Holy City of Jerusalem; and this is also the custom of Izmir and Salonika. But *Shach* writes, citing *Masas Binyamin*, that in the Kingdom of Poland the custom is to perform *kri'ah* for any family member."

5. Since the deceased died and was buried on *Yom Tov*, *Chol HaMo'ed* is neither the moment of most intense grief (*sha'as chimum*) nor the moment of hearing the news (*sha'as shmu'ah*). Therefore, *kri'ah* is put off until after the Festival (*Magen Avraham* §§3, citing *Maharam MiLublin*; *Pischei Teshuvah* ad loc. §§11, citing *Mishneh LaMelech*, *Hilchos Avel* 11:1).

   Chazon LaMo'ed (ch. 6 note 19) writes: "If one did not perform *kri'ah* on that day [the day of death or burial], it might be said that he should not afterwards perform *kri'ah* during *Chol HaMo'ed*.

3. If, on *Chol HaMo'ed*, one hears of a death which occurred within the preceding thirty days (*shmu'ah krovah*), the same *halachah* applies as when a death occurs during *Chol HaMo'ed* (see previous paragraph).[6] If *Chol HaMo'ed* is within thirty days of the death, but after the Festival more than thirty days will already have passed, one performs *kri'ah* during *Chol HaMo'ed*, even for a family member other than one's parent; and this applies according to all the opinions mentioned in the previous section.[7]

However, in the case of a *shmu'ah rechokah* (more than thirty days from the death), one does not perform *kri'ah* during *Chol HaMo'ed*, even for one's parent.[8] Instead, [for one's parent,] one performs *kri'ah* after the Festival week.[9]

◄§ The Blessing, *Dayan HaEmes*

4. Even for those family members for whom one does not perform *kri'ah* during *Chol HaMo'ed*, one must nevertheless recite the blessing, *Dayan HaEmes* ("...the True Judge"; see above, 6:6) during *Chol HaMo'ed*.[10] If one did not recite it at its proper time, some rule that one may not recite it later when performing *kri'ah* after the Festival week, if by then more than three days have elapsed since hearing of the death.[11]

◄§ Festival Garments

5. Following a burial during *Chol HaMo'ed*, one must change out of the garments on which one performed *kri'ah*.[12] Likewise, one must change out of the

---

However, I later saw in *Maharil* (*Hilchos Chol HaMo'ed* p. 73): 'It once happened that a certain person did not perform *kri'ah* for his father on the bitter day [of death or burial] during *Chol HaMo'ed*. And during that same *Chol HaMo'ed* he happened to come to the city of *Maharash*, who instructed him to perform *kri'ah* then.' "

6. Responsa of *Maharam MiLublin* (loc. cit.). The same ruling is given by *Shach* (§§44). He states that in this regard there is no difference between the day of burial and the day of hearing a *shmu'ah krovah*.

7. *Shulchan Aruch* (340:32). *Shach* (§§47) comments: "Even according to our custom, mentioned above, 340:31, that one should not perform *kri'ah* during *Chol HaMo'ed* for any relative except one's parent, this applies only if one will be able to perform *kri'ah* after *Chol HaMo'ed*; but if, after the Festival, more than thirty days will already have passed, and therefore one will not be able to perform *kri'ah*, the custom does not apply; in such a case, one must follow the *halachah* as determined by the majority of the *Geonim*."

8. *Shach* (ad loc. §§47), citing *Maharshal* and *Bach*. The same ruling is given by *Mishnah Berurah* (547:§§14). However, *Magen Avraham* (ad loc. §§3) cites *Rit* (§5) as ruling that one does perform *kri'ah*.

9. *Pri Megaddim* (ad loc. *Eshel Avraham* §§3).

10. This blessing was instituted to be recited for bad news. It is not dependent upon the beginning of mourning, nor even upon *kri'ah*, if *kri'ah* is performed several days after one first heard of the death (*Gesher HaChaim* 4:26).

11. See above, chapt. 6 footnote 27.

12. This is for the honor of the Festival. It is similar to the *halachah* which applies on the Sabbath during *shivah*. Then, too, one must change out of the torn garment, as is explained in *Shulchan Aruch* (400:1). On *Chol HaMo'ed*, as on the Sabbath, conspicuous mourning is forbidden.

ordinary weekday clothes worn for the funeral. Immediately on the evening following the termination of the Festival (*motza'ei Yom Tov*), one must again don the *kri'ah* garments, so as not to have to perform *kri'ah* on the garments one wore on *Yom Tov* (see above, 6:20).

The laws regarding conducting a funeral on *Yom Tov* are presented above, chapter 11.

⋖§ Eulogy / *Tzidduk HaDin* / *Kaddish*

6. It is forbidden to deliver a eulogy during *Chol HaMo'ed*, even for a sage whose body is present and not yet buried.[13] Therefore, the bier should not be left stationary in the street, since that would present a stimulus for eulogy. Likewise, the deceased should not be taken to the cemetery until the grave is completely ready.[14]

7. *Shulchan Aruch* states: "[During *Chol HaMo'ed*] one recites *Tzidduk HaDin* and *Kaddish* in the usual manner. The same applies on the [Diaspora's] second day of *Yom Tov*. But on the first day of *Yom Tov*, since one is not permitted to occupy oneself with the funeral, one cannot recite [*Tzidduk HaDin* and *Kaddish*]."

Rama comments: "Some disagree, ruling that *Tzidduk HaDin* should not be recited during *Chol HaMo'ed*; and this is the prevalent custom in these [Ashkenazic] lands — *Tzidduk HaDin* is not recited on days when *Tachanun* is not recited."[15]

⋖§ Interment

8. All the work necessary for burial may be performed on *Chol HaMo'ed*. This includes sewing burial wrappings (*tachrichim*), even if the sewing is the type requiring a professional. If someone is making the coffin, this should be done in the courtyard of the same building where the deceased is, so that it will be clear that it is being done for him. If boards for the coffin are not on hand, it is permitted to bring

---

13. *Be'ur Halachah* (§547). And see *Igros Moshe* (*Orach Chaim* part I:§165). He expresses doubt as to whether the mourner himself might be permitted to deliver a eulogy.

14. *Shulchan Aruch* (*Yoreh De'ah* 401:1, and *Orach Chaim* 547:1). But see *Kaf HaChaim* (ad loc.), who writes: "It would seem that this applied in Talmudic times, when the custom was to deliver the eulogies at the cemetery. But according to the current custom of delivering the eulogies in the [funeral] home, it is proper to take the body out of the home at soon as possible, so as not to present a stimulus for eulogy."

15. *Shulchan Aruch* and *Rama* (401:6). *Gesher HaChaim* (16:6:4) writes: "At those times when one does not recite *Tzidduk HaDin*, one also does not recite *Kaddish HaGadol*. Then, instead of *Tzidduk HaDin*, one recites Psalm 16 (*Michtam LeDavid*), and instead of *Kaddish HaGadol*, one recites the regular Mourner's *Kaddish*." (The *Kaddish* mentioned by the *Poskim* together with *Tzidduk HaDin* refers to *Kaddish HaGadol*, the *Kaddish* containing the addition: בְּעָלְמָא דִּי הוּא עָתִיד לְאִתְחַדָּתָא, '. . . *in the world which will be renewed.*' See Appendix.)

Mishnah Berurah (ad loc. §§26) writes: "At those times when one does not recite *Tzidduk HaDin*, one does not speak of the praises of the deceased; for this, too, would be a stimulus to eulogy. Therefore, one is forbidden to deliver a speech about the deceased, unless the deceased is a sage whose body is present and not yet buried. Delivering such a speech is all the more forbidden on *Yom Tov*. In our time, no one is defined as a 'sage' with regard to this *halachah*."

wood and saw it to the needed dimensions, but this should be done unobtrusively, inside the house.

If it cannot be done unobtrusively, it may even be done in public.

If the deceased was a well-known personality, the work can even be done in the marketplace.

Where the Jewish community is small, and everyone knows when someone has died, the *halachah* is the same as for a well-known personality.[16]

9. During *Chol HaMo'ed*, one should not pluck up grass or herbage nor pick up earth to throw over one's shoulder, as is customarily done after the burial on an ordinary day (see above, 10:23).[17]

10. During *Chol HaMo'ed*, as on an ordinary day, after the burial the participants form two parallel rows (the *shurah*; see above, 10:22) to console the mourners. However, the mourners do not remove their shoes.[18]

∞§ The Mourner's Meal of Condolence (*Se'udas Havraah*)

11. The requirement that the neighbors provide the mourner with his first meal (*se'udas havra'ah*, see above, chapt. 14) is not practiced on *Yom Tov*, not even on the Diaspora's second day of *Yom Tov*. During *Chol HaMo'ed* it is practiced; however, the mourner sits on a chair to eat the meal, since the requirement to sit on or near the floor does not apply during *Chol HaMo'ed*.[19]

In Jerusalem, the custom is not to provide the *se'udas havraah* during *Chol HaMo'ed*, except in the case of mourning for one's parent.[20]

If the *se'udas havraah* is provided during *Chol HaMo'ed*, it should not consist of eggs or lentils, as is customary on an ordinary day. Instead, it should consist of cakes or the like.[21]

∞§ Count of *Shivah* and *Shloshim*

12. If burial takes place on *Yom Tov* or during *Chol HaMo'ed*, the restrictions of the first seven days of mourning (*shivah*) do not apply. One begins counting

---

16. *Shulchan Aruch Orach Chaim* 547:10. See above, end of chapt 11.

17. *Shulchan Aruch* (*Orach Chaim* loc. cit. §12). *Elyah Rabbah* writes that *Shulchan Aruch*'s prohibition only refers to plucking up grass, herbage and earth for the needs of the cemetery; but it is permitted to pull them up after the burial, as an allusion to the Resurrection of the Dead. However, *Ma'amar Mordechai* disputes this point, writing that *Elyah Rabbah*'s ruling does not fit the plain meaning of *Shulchan Aruch*. And the custom is not to pluck up grass, herbage, or earth during *Chol HaMo'ed* (*Mishnah Berurah* ad loc. §§25).

18. The *halachah* that the participants form the *shurah* is mentioned in a *mishnah*, *Mo'ed Katan* 27a.
   The mourners do not remove their shoes because one does not observe [conspicuous] mourning during *Chol HaMo'ed*.

19. *Shulchan Aruch* (*Yoreh De'ah* 401:4, and *Orach Chaim* 547:8).

20. *Kol Bo Al Aveilus* (p. 273), citing *Mizbach Adamah* (*Orach Chaim* §547). And *Yikrei DeChayei* (§17) comments: "But then [when giving the *se'udas havra'ah* to the sons or daughters of the deceased], one also gives it to the other family members who are present."

21. *Chochmas Adam* in *Kuntres Matzeivas Moshe* par. 2.

the first seven days of mourning only after the Festival.[22]

However, the restrictions of the *shloshim* (the first thirty days of mourning) do apply. Therefore the *shloshim* are counted from the day of burial.[23]

For example, if burial occurred on Pesach (15 Nissan), *shloshim* would extend from 15 Nissan through 14 Iyar. However, *shivah* would be observed from 22 Nissan through 28 Nissan.

13. In the Diaspora, where two days of *Yom Tov* are observed, the second day of the final part of *Yom Tov* is counted as the first day of *shivah*,[24] even though the restrictions of *shivah* are not observed that day. Since the observance of the second day of *Yom Tov* in the Diaspora is a Rabbinic institution, it is counted in the *shivah*, and the restrictions of the *shivah* are observed only for the six days following the Festival.

The same applies to the second day of Rosh Hashanah; it counts as the first day of *shivah*, even though the restrictions of the *shivah* are not observed that day. This applies whether burial was performed on the first day of Rosh Hashanah (by non-Jews) or on the second day.[25]

◄§ Mourning Practices

14. Inconspicuous, private mourning practices (*devarim shebetzin'a*) apply on *Yom Tov* and *Chol HaMo'ed*. Therefore, the mourner is forbidden to bathe in hot water, and is also forbidden to have marital relations.[26] However, he is permitted to bathe in hot water in preparation for the final *Yom Tov* day of the Festival. Likewise, he is permitted to change underwear in honor of *Yom Tov*.[26a]

Some rule that Torah-study is also forbidden.[27] But others rule that it is permitted.[28] The prevalent custom is to follow the lenient opinion [and permit Torah-study].[28a] In any case, it is preferable (*lechatchilah*) that during the Festival the mourner should not be included among those called up to the Torah-reading.[29]

---

22. *Shulchan Aruch* (*Orach Chaim* 548:1). *Mishnah Berurah* (ad loc. §§2) explains that the rejoicing of the Festival is a *mitzvah* incumbent upon the entire people, while the mourning for this particular deceased is a *mitzvah* incumbent only upon certain individuals. Therefore the rejoicing takes precedence over the mourning.

23. *Shulchan Aruch* loc. cit.

24. However, the second of the first two days of *Yom Tov* is not counted as part of the *shivah*; for it has no less status than *Chol HaMo'ed*, which is not counted as part of the *shivah* (*Mishnah Berurah* ad loc. §§6).

25. *Shach* (399:§§8). The same ruling is given by *Mishnah Berurah* (ad loc. §§8).

26. *Shulchan Aruch* (*Yoreh De'ah* 399:2, and *Orach Chaim* 548:4), and *Mishnah Berurah* (ad loc. §§16).

26a. *Be'urei Maharshal* (§389).

27. *Magen Avraham* (ad loc. §§5) writes: "It seems to me that it is forbidden to review the passages which are read in public during the Festival."

28. *Pischei Teshuvah* (ad loc. §§1). The same ruling is given by *Sha'arei Teshuvah* (ad loc. §§5). He cites *Chacham Tzvi* (§100), who ruled in the case of a certain scholar who was accustomed to review *mishnayos* by memory. *Chacham Tzvi* instructed him that he was "permitted to do so during the entire Festival, even though inconspicuous practices of mourning do apply on *Yom Tov* and *Chol*

15. Even in circumstances where a non-mourner would ordinarily be permitted to shave or take a haircut during *Chol HaMo'ed*, the mourner is forbidden to do so. Likewise, he is forbidden to wear new clothes.[30]

He is permitted to wear newly laundered garments,[31] and also to wear *Yom Tov* clothes.[32]

16. Work performed during *Chol HaMo'ed* in order to prevent financial loss (*davar ha'aveid*) is permitted to the mourner just as it is to other people.[33]

In a community where the custom is for everyone to keep his store open during *Chol HaMo'ed*, the mourner is also permitted to do so.[34] Similarly, if he is a paid worker in a job which is visible to the public, some rule that he may engage in his work during *Chol HaMo'ed*.[35]

Regarding work which is not performed for the pupose of preventing a loss, but which is permitted for some other reason, others may perform it for the mourner on their own premises during *Chol HaMo'ed*. If he has servants, they may work for him in an inconspicuous manner within his home.[36]

17. We explained above (par. 12) that the restrictions of *shivah* do not begin until after the Festival. Thus a case could happen that although seven or more days have elapsed since the death, the restrictions of *shivah* are still in effect. In this case,

---

HaMo'ed . . ." *Sha'arei Teshuvah* concludes: "If so, obviously if one also wishes to review the public Torah-reading, one is permitted to do so, even if there is no obligation to do so; for this is no less permissible than other kinds of Torah-study."

Elyah Rabbah rules the same. Likewise, *Yad Eliahu* (Ragolar) rules that Torah-study is permitted. The same ruling is given by *Aruch HaShulchan*, in the name of *Shitah Mekubetzes*, who in turn cites *Talmidei Rabbeinu Yonah*.

28a. *Shmiras Shabbos Kehilchasah* (ch. 65 note 175), in the name of the *gaon*, R' Shlomo Zalman Auerbach, *shlita*.

29. *Mishnah Berurah* (ad loc. §§16).

Regarding being called up to the Torah-reading on Simchas Torah, see below, chapt. 34.

30. *Shulchan Aruch* (399:1). The reason is that the restrictions of the *shloshim* (the first thirty days of mourning) apply during *Chol HaMo'ed*.

31. *Sdei Chemed* (*Aveilus* §41), citing responsa *Pnei Yehoshua* (part II, end of §39). Moreover, this is no less permissible than on the Sabbath, when some authorities permit wearing newly laundered garments. And *Kitzur Shulchan Aruch* (219:7) even permits wearing newly ironed garments.

32. *Magen Avraham* (ad loc. §§5); see also *Pri Megaddim* (ad loc.). He considers the possibility that this leniency might even apply to a new garment.

33. *Rama* (399:2).

34. *Sdei Chemed* (*Aveilus* §35). The reason is that closing his store would constitute conspicuous mourning. But if there are people in that community who close their stores during *Chol HaMo'ed*, the mourner is forbidden to open his.

35. *Sdei Chemed* (loc. cit.), citing *Be'eros HaMayim*. The same source is also cited by *Kaf HaChaim* (§542 §§15). *Kaf HaChaim* also cites *Ikrei HaDat* (26:§5), who writes that he permitted someone to work in a case of this kind. The implication is that in these circumstances the mourner may work even if he is not poor, since not working would constitute conspicuous mourning.

36. *Rama* (loc. cit.). But *Chiddushei R' Akiva Eiger* (ad loc.) writes that this applies only after seven days from burial.

the mourner may have others work for him on their premises. This applies even if the work is not necessary to prevent loss (davar ha'aveid).[37] Likewise, once seven days have elapsed since the death, the mourner's servants may work for him in an inconspicuous manner within his home.[38]

If a partner in a store becomes a mourner during a Festival, some rule that the halachah is the same as for any case of mourning (see above, 18:24): The other partner(s) must close the store until after the third day of mourning. But some authorities, more leniently, permit the non-mourning partner(s) to open the store after seven days have passed from the burial.[38a]

18. In chapter 27, we presented the laws regarding changing one's seat in the synagogue, noting that in some congregations the custom is that the mourner change his seat even on the Sabbath and Yom Tov. But even in those congregations, if death occurred on Yom Tov or Chol HaMo'ed, one does not change one's seat then, because the conspicuous practices of mourning do not begin until after the Festival.[39]

If the mourner is the permanent chazzan (leader of the prayer-services), he may continue to serve in this capacity during the Festival.[40]

In the Diaspora, where the Kohanim ascend the duchan to recite the Priestly Blessing (Bircas Kohanim) only on Yom Tov, a kohen who is a mourner may not recite the blessing.[41] However, if there is no other kohen present, or if only one other kohen is present, the mourner must ascend to recite the Priestly Blessing.[41a] If two or more other kohanim are present, the mourner should leave the synagogue before the chazzan begins the blessing רְצֵה ("Be favorable...") and should not return until the end of the Priestly Blessing. [See above 16:25 and footnote there; and below, 36:7.]

In Eretz Yisrael, according to some Poskim, a mourner may recite the blessing.[42]

---

37. It is true that any mourner may have others work for him in their homes, as is stated in Shulchan Aruch (Yoreh De'ah 380:18). However, there the leniency is restricted to kablanus (a "contractor" relationship whereby someone is paid by the job rather than by the hour, day, or other time unit), and only if the work was assigned before the mourning began [see, for example, above, 18:19-23]. In our case, the leniency applies even if the work is assigned during shivah.

38. Shulchan Aruch (Yoreh De'ah 399:1, and Orach Chaim 548:6).

38a. The gaon Maharash MiPrague rules that the other partner must close the store until after the third day of mourning, as in any other case regarding the partner of a mourner. The same ruling is given by Ba'er Heitev, citing Eliahu Zuta. However, Chochmas Adam (Hilchos Aveilus 169:2) cites Elyah Rabbah as ruling leniently on this point, stating that if the death occurred on the first day of Chol HaMo'ed, the non-mourning partner may open the store immediately after Yom Tov (Mishnah Berurah ad loc. §§24).

39. Mishnah Berurah ad loc. §§15.

40. Gilyon Maharsha ad loc.

41. Magen Avraham Orach Chaim 128:§§66. Responsa Sha'ar Efrayim (§92). It is proper for the kohen to leave the synagogue before the Priestly Blessing is recited, so that his failure to recite the blessing will not constitute conspicuous mourning (Chasam Sofer Yoreh De'ah §352).

41a. Mishnah Berurah 128:§§159.

42. Gesher HaChaim 23:1:5.

Other Laws

◄§ Consoling Mourners

19. One is permitted to console mourners during a Festival.[43] Therefore, the seven days during which comforting the mourners is *obligatory* are counted from the day of burial [even though the mourners do not observe most *shivah* restrictions during the Festival]. Nevertheless, one should pay a regular *shivah* visit during their *shivah* observance.[44]

For example (in the Diaspora), a burial occurred during the week of Pesach, on 19 Nissan. From the 19th through the 22nd of Nissan (four days), the restrictions of *shivah* did not apply, yet comforting the mourners was permitted. The *shivah* extends from the 23rd through the morning of the 29th of Nissan, but comforting the mourners is *obligatory* only through the morning of the 25th, since four days of comforting had been possible during the Festival. Nevertheless, one should visit the mourners until their *shivah* is completed, on the morning of the 29th.

Ordinarily, the custom in Ashkenazic communities is for the congregation to console the mourners in the synagogue on Sabbath Eve before the recitation of *Mizmor Shir L'Yom HaShabbos* ("a psalm, a song for the seventh day") during *shivah* (see above, 17:9). However, this practice is not followed in a case where death occurred during a Festival, if the Sabbath occurring during *shivah* is more than seven days after the death.[45]

If the final day of *Yom Tov* is Friday, the congregation should not console the mourners in the synagogue, because that would constitute conspicuous mourning on *Yom Tov*.[46] This applies even if seven days have not yet passed since the death.

◄§ *Hallel*

20. If prayer-services are conducted in a mourner's home during *Chol HaMo'ed*, *Hallel* is recited, since mourning is not observed during *Chol HaMo'ed*.[47]

---

43. *Shulchan Aruch* (*Yoreh De'ah* 399:1, and *Orach Chaim* 548:6).

   Gesher HaChaim (20:5:2) writes: "In our day, the Ashkenazic custom is not to go to the mourner's home on either the Sabbath or Festival. However, on *Chol HaMo'ed . . . Ashkenazim* do console mourners, just as on *Chol HaMo'ed* they follow the custom of consoling the mourners as they walk through the *shurah* [the double row of comforters at the cemetery; see above 10:22]."

44. *Shulchan Aruch* 399:2.

45. *Mishnah Berurah* (ad loc. §§25).

   See also *Pri Megaddim* (ad loc. *Mishbetzos Zahav* par. 5). He discusses the practice of comforting the mourners in the synagogue on Friday evening, and expresses doubt about whether it should be observed in the case of one who did not know of the death when it occurred, but was informed within thirty days (*shmu'ah krovah*). In our case in the text, where the mourner knew of the death, it may be assumed that he comforted himself in the meantime, and he need not be comforted publicly on *erev Shabbos*. In the case of a *shmu'ah krovah*, on the other hand, more than seven days may have passed from the time of death; but since the mourner did not know of the death, he could not have been comforted about it. Therefore there might be reason to observe the practice of comforting the mourners on *erev Shabbos*.

46. *Pri Megaddim* (loc. cit.), citing *Elyah Rabbah*.

47. *Mishnah Berurah* 131:§§20.

Some authorities rule that even the mourner himself should recite *Hallel,* even if he prays at home, and all the more so if he prays in the synagogue.[48]

✌ Leading the Prayer-Service

21. The custom is not to have a mourner lead the prayer-services *Yom Tov* or *Chol HaMo'ed,*[49] even for *Minchah* or *Maariv.*[50] In the case of mourning for one's parent, this applies during the entire twelve months of mourning; in other cases, for the thirty days. However, if no one else is available, the mourner may lead the service.[51]

✌ Mourning Lamp

22. The flame which is customarily left burning in the mourner's home throughout *shivah* (see above, 16:1-3 and 32:17) should remain burning also on *Yom Tov* and *Chol HaMo'ed,* even though mourning is not observed then.[52]

---

48. *Mishmeres Shalom (os he* §37) writes, citing *Sefer HaChaim* (on *Orach Chaim* §526): "All the more so, [the mourner should recite *Hallel* during *Chol HaMo'ed*] when he prays in the synagogue; for some rule that even on Rosh Chodesh or Chanukah he should recite *Hallel* with the public in the synagogue, certainly so during *Chol HaMo'ed*" (See there §40).

49. *Rama* 376:4.

50. *Pri Megaddim* (§671 *Mishbetzos Zahav* par. 8) writes: "During *Chol HaMo'ed,* which is like *Yom Tov,* I have on occasion not permitted mourners to lead the *Minchah* or *Ma'ariv* services."

51. *Magen Avraham* 581:§§4.

52. *Mishnah Berurah* (548:§§3). He adds: "However, it should not be lit where one eats, and all the more so it should not be lit in the room where the death occurred, since this might cause people to eulogize the deceased. Instead, it should be lit someplace where people do not eat. But since one derives no benefit at all from this light, one should not light it himself on *Yom Tov,* but should have a non-Jew light it" (*Pri Megaddim* §132, and *Chiddushei R' Akiva Eiger* §514).

CHAPTER THIRTY-FOUR

The Festival Cycle and the Mourner

The Days of Awe

⤳ Selichos

1. During *shivah*, the mourner is not permitted to leave his home in order to recite *Selichos* [prayers of supplication recited in conjunction with the Days of Awe and the Ten Days of Repentance] with the congregation in the synagogue.

This applies even after the first three days of mourning, and even on the first day of *Selichos*.[1] However, in his home the mourner is permitted either to recite *Selichos* by himself or to gather a *minyan* of ten or more men to recite them.[2]

On the day preceding Rosh Hashanah, the *Selichos* are especially numerous. In some congregations, the same is true on the day preceding Yom Kippur. Therefore, on the day preceding Rosh Hashanah (and, in those congregations, also on the day preceding Yom Kippur),[3] the mourner is permitted to go to the synagogue in order to recite *Selichos* with the congregation.[4] He may also remain in order to recite the rest of the prayer-service along with the congregation. Nevertheless, if it is possible to gather a *minyan* in his own home and recite the *Selichos* there calmly and with concentration, he should do so rather than go to the synagogue.[5]

---

1. *Rama*, *Orach Chaim* 581:1; *Mateh Efrayim* ad loc. 581:22.

2. *Elef LaMateh* (ad loc. §§44) writes: "The *Poskim* say that *Vidui* (Confession) and *Tachanun* should not be recited in the house of mourning, so as not to intensify the Attribute of Strict Justice. This applies even if the mourner is not in the place where the death occurred. (This is the ruling of *Pri Megaddim*, in *Mishbetzos Zahav*, contrary to the ruling of *Yeshuos Yaakov*; and see *Elyah Rabbah*.) Hence, for the recitation of *Selichos* it is proper to choose a house other than that in which the death occurred . . . Nevertheless, [the rest of] the prayer service should be conducted in the place where the death occurred; for this is of benefit to the soul of the deceased, as is explained in the Kabbalistic works."

3. *Magen Avraham* (ad loc. §§5), citing *Knesses HaGedolah*. The same ruling is given by *Mateh Efrayim* and *Mishnah Berurah* (ad loc.).

4. See *Machatzis HaShekel* (ad loc.). He explains that the large number of *Selichos* is generally considered a very important matter in the eyes of the public; and if the mourner were unable to attend, it would cause him great distress. Therefore the *halachah* is lenient on this point.

5. *Mateh Efrayim* ad loc.

◆§ Leading the Prayer-Service

2. During *shivah*, one should not serve as *chazzan* for the *Selichos* — and this certainly applies on the day preceding Rosh Hashanah. The reason is that during *shivah* one is under the influence of the Attribute of Strict Justice. However, afterwards — during the Twelve Months for one's parent, or *shloshim* for some other family member — one may serve as *chazzan* even on the day preceding Rosh Hashanah and during the Ten Days of Repentance.[6]

◆§ Rosh Hashanah and Yom Kippur

3. The following two laws apply during the Twelve Months of mourning for one's parent, and during *shloshim* for any other family member:[7]

(a) He is forbidden to lead the prayer-services on Rosh Hashanah or Yom Kippur. However, if no one else of his stature is available, he is permitted to do so.[8]

(b) He should not be appointed to blow the *shofar*, unless this has been his established responsibility for several years, or there is no one else as qualified.[9]

4. If one's family member dies on Rosh Hashanah, one does not observe mourning during the two days of Rosh Hashanah. This applies whether the burial occurred on the first day of Rosh Hashanah and burial was performed by non-Jews, or whether burial occurred on the second day of Rosh Hashanah. Nevertheless, in either case the second day of Rosh Hashanah counts as the first day of *shivah*.[10]

---

6. Ibid. 581:23; and responsa *Noda BiYehudah* (*mahadura kamma Orach Chaim* §32). The same ruling is given by *Mishnah Berurah* (ad loc. §§7).

7. See *Pri Megaddim* (ad loc. *Eshel Avraham* §§ 4), who writes: "*Darkei Moshe* states in the name of *Maharil* (*Hilchos Yom Tov*) that *Maharash* ruled that a mourner could lead the prayer-services after *shivah*. Therefore, even if the death occurred less than seven days before the festival, (and the festival canceled *shivah*,) he ruled that the mourner could lead the services. But it must be that in that case no one more qualified was available to lead the services . . . [One could reason] that if death occurred seven days before Rosh Hashanah, and Rosh Hashanah canceled the thirty-day mourning period, according to all opinions the mourner may lead the services, even if someone more qualified is available. . . However, there is reason to rule [to the contrary], that the mourner is under the influence of the Attribute of Strict Justice (*Midas HaDin*), and therefore it is not fitting for him to lead the services during the Days of Awe (*Yomim Nora'im*). Therefore, even if Rosh Hashanah cancels *shloshim* [the mourner should not lead the services]; for with regard to *Kaddish*, the Festivals do not interrupt mourning." *Mateh Efrayim* also writes that even if *shloshim* is canceled, one is forbidden to lead the services.

8. *Magen Avraham* (ad loc. §§4). See *Mateh Efrayim* (ad loc.).

9. *Mateh Efrayim* (585:7). And see *Elef HaMagen* (ad loc. §§ 18). He explains that since the mourner is in grief, there is concern that he might make a mistake in the *shofar*-blasts (*Elyah Rabbah*). But if the mourner does not want to give up the privilege of blowing the *shofar*, and it has been his established duty in the past, one should not get involved in a quarrel over this issue. (Responsa *Olas Shmuel* §85, cited by *Pischei Teshuvah*.)

10. See above 33:13 and footnote 25 there.

Laws applying to an *onen* (one whose deceased is not yet buried) on Rosh Hashanah is explained above, 5:30.

◌৯ *Kittel*

5. During the Twelve Months of mourning for one's parent, or during *shloshim* for any other family member, one is permitted to wear a *kittel* (white outer garment) on Yom Kippur. However, in some congregations the custom is that a mourner does not wear a *kittel*.[11] The prevalent custom today is that he does not wear it.[11a]

Regarding whether a mourner during *shivah* or during the Twelve Months of mourning should recite *Yizkor* is discussed below, chapter 43.

Succos

◌৯ Dwelling in a *Succah*

6. The mourner is obligated by the *mitzvah* of dwelling in the *succah*.[12]

Some rule that if the deceased is so dear to the mourner that he cannot take his mind off him, and he suffers while sitting in the *succah*, he is exempt from the *mitzvah*.[13]

◌৯ *Hakafos* With a *Lulav*

7. During the Twelve Months of mourning for one's parent, or during *shloshim* for any other family member, some rule that one should not perform the customary *hakafos* (circling the central platform, or *bimah*) with the *lulav* [i.e, the Four Species]. Others disagree.[14] A third group permits this, but only on the first day of

---

11. *Rama* (§610) states: "Some have written that the custom is to wear clean, white garments on
    Yom Kippur, in imitation of the Ministering Angels. And this is the accepted custom: to wear the
    kittel, which is white and clean. In addition, it is the clothing of the deceased, and this subdues and
    breaks a person's heart."
    Taz (ad loc. §§3) writes: "There is a practical difference between these two reasons, with regard to a
    mourner. According to the first reason [that it resembles the angels], he is forbidden to wear the *kittel*.
    But according to the second reason [that it subdues and breaks the heart], he is permitted. And it would
    seem that one who relies on the second reason and wears [the *kittel*] will not lose thereby."
    Elyah Rabbah (ad loc.) writes: "The custom in these lands is that the mourner does not wear a *kittel*.
    The reason may be that his heart is already subdued, or that it is considered like a Sabbath garment."
    However, *Mateh Efrayim* (ad loc.) writes: "The mourner, too, should wear [a *kittel*]."

11a. The *gaon* R' Moshe Feinstein, in *Kovetz Am HaTorah* (*kovetz* 12:7).

12. *Shulchan Aruch* (640:5). The Talmud (*Succah* 25b) explains: Normally, a person is exempt from
    dwelling in the *succah* if he suffers or is in discomfort. This applies only when the discomfort is
    caused by the conditions of dwelling in the *succah*. However, in the case of the mourner, whose
    suffering is [not caused by the *succah*, but is] from within, it is incumbent upon him to compose his
    mind in order to fulfill the *mitzvah* of the *succah*.

13. *Magen Avraham* (ad loc. §§10), citing *Tanya*. *Mishnah Berurah* (ad loc. §§31) writes: "See
    Yeshuos Yaakov, who disagrees with *Tanya* on this point." *Sha'ar HaTziyun* (ad loc. §§46)
    writes: "I also did not find this ruling among the other *Rishonim* (early *halachic* authorities)."

14. *Beis Yosef* (§660) states: "*Kol Bo* (§114) writes that the custom of Narvonne is that if mourning
    comes upon a person during the Succos Festival, he does not perform the *hakafos*. . .neither he

Succos and on Hoshana Rabbah.[15]

If Twelve Months of mourning for one's parent have passed, one is permitted to perform *hakafos* during Succos. This applies even if it was a leap-year (of thirteen months), and the *yahrzeit* (anniversary of the death) has not yet arrived.[16]

When the mourner refrains from performing *hakafos*, he should honor someone who does not have a *lulav* by letting him carry the *lulav* to perform the *hakafos*.[17] While the others are circling, it is a good practice for the mourner to stand on or next to the *bimah* holding the Torah scroll.[18]

Some rule that if the mourner is the rabbi of his community, he must perform the *hakafos*.[18a]

◆§ Simchas Beis HaSho'eivah

8. During *Simchas Beis HaSho'eivah*, the mourner may take part in the recitation of *Psalms* (*Shir HaMa'alos*), but not in the dancing.[19]

---

nor those mourning with him." [For the meaning of "those mourning with him," see above, 15:11-15.] On this, *Beis Yosef* comments: "This is a surprising statement. Why should they miss out on the *hakafos*? Thus, the accepted custom is that even the mourner himself performs the *haka-fos*."

However, *Darkei Moshe* (by Rama) writes (ad loc.): "But we [Ashkenazic Jewry] have the custom that the mourner does *not* perform *hakafos* as long as he is in mourning, even during the Twelve Months of mourning for one's parent." *Rama* writes similarly in his glosses on *Shulchan Aruch* (loc. cit.).

15. *Kaf HaChaim* (ad loc. §§18) cites *Siddur Yavetz* as writing: "On *Yom Tov* and Hoshana Rabbah, it would seem obvious that we should tell the mourner, 'Perform the *hakafos*,' so he should not display any sign of mourning in public. During *Chol HaMo'ed*, too, one may say that if he refrains from performing the *hakafos*, he forfeits thereby; nevertheless, all follow the custom [of the mourner's congregation]."

Gesher HaChaim (part II, 17:5:4) writes that even if one follows the strict custom in accordance with the ruling of *Rama*, he may perform *hakafos* by himself with his *lulav*, either before or after those performed by the congregation; but on Hoshana Rabbah he is permitted to perform the *hakafos* with the congregation.

16. *Pri Megaddim* (ad loc.). He explains that once Twelve Months have elapsed, the mourning is over.

17. See *Sha'arei Teshuvah* (ad loc. §§1). He writes: "See also *Elyah Rabbah*, who states: 'If the mourner has a *lulav*, he should honor someone who does not have one, by letting him carry the *lulav* to perform the *hakafos*. This is in case the correct *halachah* is in accordance with the opinion that the mourner should perform the *hakafos*, and if he fails to perform them, he is acting incorrectly.' One might add another reason: If the mourner holds the *lulav* in his hand and does not perform the *hakafos*, this seems more like mourning in public [than if he is not holding a *lulav*]."

18. My father and teacher, *zatzal*, in his manuscript work, *Zichron Eliahu*. The reason is as mentioned in the previous footnote: to avoid publicizing the mourning.

18a. Responsa *Minchas Yitzchak* (part 6:62) writes: "In a community where the custom is that the rabbi always goes at the head of the line, and if he were missing from his place it would certainly publicize the mourning, he should perform the *hakafos* on *Yom Tov* and Hoshana Rabbah."

The *gaon* R' Moshe Feinstein (in *Kovetz Am HaTorah kovetz* 12) rules similarly, but without stipulating that it applies only on *Yom Tov* and Hoshana Rabbah, as distinct from the other days of the Festival. He concludes: "The matter still requires study."

19. *Gesher HaChaim* 23:3:7.

❧ Tikkun Leil Hoshana Rabbah

9. Regarding the *Tikkun Leil Hoshana Rabbah* (special compendium of passages from Scriptures and *Zohar* which is read on the seventh night of Succos): If one's family member dies during Succos, the *halachah* depends on one's custom in other years. If one is accustomed to recite the *Tikkun* every year, one may recite it in this circumstance as well. However, if one sometimes omits reciting the *Tikkun* in other years, one is forbidden to recite it in this circumstance.[20]

❧ The Weekly Torah Portion

9a. It is a *mitzvah* to review the weekly Torah portion, twice in Hebrew and once in the Aramaic translation (see *Shulchan Aruch Orach Chaim* §285). If one's family member dies during Succos, one is permitted to read *Parashas VeZos HaBrachah* in this manner.[21]

❧ Simchas Torah

10. During the Twelve Months of mourning, one is permitted on Simchas Torah to hold a Torah Scroll and circle the *bimah*, but not to dance.[22] However, some rule that even circling with a Torah Scroll is forbidden.[23]

❧ Chasan Torah / Chasan Bereishis

11. The person called up to the Torah for the final verses of the Book of Deuteronomy is called the *Chasan Torah* ("Bridegroom of the Torah"), and the one called up for the opening verses of Genesis is the *Chasan Bereishis*

---

20. *Sha'arei Teshuvah* 664:§§1.

21. This is in accord with the *halachah* that any mourner is permitted to read the weekly Torah portion in this manner on the Sabbath that falls during *shivah*. It is all the more permissible in our case, where some rule that Torah-study is altogether permitted (see above, 33:14). The same ruling [that the mourner is permitted to read *Parashas VeZos HaBrachah* twice in Hebrew and once in the Aramaic translation] is offered by *Sdei Chemed* (*Aveilus os* 34), citing R' Chaim Falaghi in his work, *Lev Chaim*.

   Regarding the correct time to read the *parashah*, *Sdei Chemed* writes that one should do so on the day of Simchas Torah [in the Diaspora; *Shemini Atzeres* in *Eretz Yisrael*] since this is the most appropriate way of reading it "along with the congregation." *Sha'arei Teshuvah* (285:§§4) cites *Birkei Yosef*, who states in the name of the *Ari, zal* that the *parashah* should be read on the day of Hoshana Rabbah. This is also the ruling given by *Mishnah Berurah* (ad loc. §§18). But in 669:§§4, he cites the *Poskim* as ruling that one should read the *parashah* on the night of Simchas Torah.

22. *Kaf HaChaim* (669:§§33) writes: "If death occurred during the Festival, is the mourner permitted to perform the seven *hakafos* (circlings) with the Torah Scroll on Simchas Torah? *Zachur LeAvraham* (*Yoreh De'ah, end of* §300 in *Hilchos Avel*) writes that the mourner is permitted to sit in the synagogue on the night of Simchas Torah, during the twelve months of mourning for his father; and [the congregation] dance and clap in front of him. And the permission also applies to the *hakafos*."

   The same ruling is given by *Gesher HaChaim* (23:3:7): that the mourner is permitted to perform the *hakafos*, but not to dance. And see there (part 2, 17:4:2), where he explains the distinction between the *hakafos* of Simchas Torah [which are permitted] and the *hakafos* with the *lulav* [which are forbidden]. See also responsa *Minchas Yitzchak* (VI:§62).

23. Responsa *Chelkas Yaakov* (III:§75).

("Bridegroom of Genesis"). If one had been chosen for one of these honors, and then one of his family members dies during the festival, he should go to a different synagogue for Simchas Torah, and his congregation should choose someone else to be the Chasan. Or he can transfer the honor to someone else as a gift, if the custom in his congregation permits doing so.[24]

◄§ Aliyah on Simchas Torah

11a. A mourner whose family member died during Succos is permitted to be called up to the Torah on Simchas Torah.[25] However, some authorities rule that he should not be called up, but should step out of the synagogue during the Torah-reading. If he cannot step outside — for example, if he is needed to complete the minyan of ten men — even these authorities rule that he is permitted to be called up to the Torah.[26]

12. After shloshim for one's parent, one is permitted to eat at the Festive meal given by the Chasan Torah and Chasan Bereishis.[27]

◄§ Shemini Atzeres

13. If death occurs during the Succos Festival, Shemini Atzeres does not cancel shivah.[28] [One must observe shivah beginning the day after Shemini Atzeres (or, in the Diaspora the day after Simchas Torah).] Moreover, Shemini Atzeres is counted as only one day of shloshim.[29] But some rule that it is counted as seven

---

24. The gaon R' Zalman Margolios (Aveilus §19); Mishmeres Shalom (os shin §52); and see Sdei Chemed (Aveilus §188).

25. Pischei Teshuvah (399:§§1). The same ruling is given by Mishmeres Shalom (os he §54); and by Gesher HaChaim (23:3:7). The reason offered is that it is an ancient custom that everyone in the synagogue is called up to the Torah on Simchas Torah. If the mourner would not be called up, it publicizes the mourning.

26. Sdei Chemed, Aveilus §30.

27. Mishnah Berurah (669:§§8), citing Bikurei Yaakov. And see Bikurei Yaakov (ad loc. §§7). He writes: "Responsa Maharam Mintz, cited by Shach (Yoreh De'ah §246), permits the mourner, after shloshim, to eat at a siyum in celebration of completing a tractate. It is true that Bach forbids this, but Beis Lechem Yehudah explains that [Bach] only [forbids it] when the mourner himself did not study the tractate, but simply wishes to celebrate the siyum along with the others. In our case, however, all Israel have completed the Torah, and the mourner has a share in the rejoicing of the mitzvah."

28. Shulchan Aruch (399:2). And Taz (ad loc. §§4) explains: "One might have thought that, since Shmini Atzeres is a festival unto itself, it cancels the mourning, as in the cases mentioned above, at the beginning of §399 [see above, chapt. 32]. But Shulchan Aruch here informs us that this is not so. Shmini Atzeres effectively cancels only when the mourner had already observed at least a short part of the mourning before Succos, causing Succos to cancel the shivah, and Shemini Atzeres to be counted as an additional seven days toward shloshim. This is not the case here [where the death occurred during Succos]."

29. This is the ruling given by Beis Yosef (ad loc.), in the name of Hagahos Maimonios. He states that the effectiveness of Shmini Atzeres [in being counted as seven days of the thirty] is only when the burial [and some form of mourning practice; see above chapt. 32] took place prior to the Festival. But if the death occurred during the Festival, Shemini Atzeres counts as only one day of the thirty-day

days.[30] Therefore, some rule that in a case where the restrictions on bathing involve suffering or similar difficulties, one may be lenient [and count Shemini Atzeres as seven days with regard to bathing]. The same possibility of leniency applies with regard to women having a haircut, since in any case some authorities rule leniently and permit a woman to have a haircut after *shivah*.[31]

Chanukah

14. On the first night of Chanukah, the mourner should not be the one to kindle the *Menorah* in the synagogue and recite the blessing of *shehecheyanu*.[32] But at home he kindles the *Menorah* and recites *shehecheyanu*.[33]

After *shloshim*, some rule that the mourner is permitted to take part in a festive meal of Chanukah. Others forbid this.[34]

15. During Chanukah, a mourner may lead the services for *Minchah* and *Ma'ariv*. For *Shacharis*, he may do so until *Hallel*.[35] However, some have the custom that a mourner may not lead the services during Chanukah.[36]

---

mourning period. The same ruling is cited by the following *Poskim*: *Bach*; *Taz* (§§4); *Shach* (§§7); *Magen Avraham* (548:§§1); and *Mishnah Berurah* (ad loc. §§4). In *Sha'ar HaTziyun* (ad loc.), he states that *Birkei Yosef* cites the responsa of *Ri Migash* as giving the same ruling as *Taz* and *Magen Avraham*. He adds that in this case one should *not* apply the rule that "in matters of mourning, the *halachah* follows the lenient opinion." The same ruling [to count Shemini Atzeres as only one day] is given by responsa *Igros Moshe* (*Yoreh De'ah* §246).

30. *Maharshal* (responsa §5), cited by *Taz* (loc. cit.).
    Shach (§§7) writes that this ruling is affirmed by responsa *Masas Binyamin* (§71). This also seems to be the ruling of *Drishah*. And *Nekudos HaKesef* (ad loc.) appears to hold the same opinion. This ruling is also given by *Beis Lechem Yehudah* (ad loc. §§11).
    Teshuvah MeAhavah (part 2, *Orach Chaim*) writes that the halachic conclusion of *Shach* seems to be that Shemini Atzeres, even in this case, counts as seven days. He adds that this ruling is affirmed by the *gaon*, author of *Korban Nesanel*, in his responsa *Toras Nesanel* (§39), contrary to the ruling of *Taz* and *Magen Avraham*.
    The same ruling (that Shemini Atzeres should be counted as seven days) is cited by *Kerem Shlomo on Yoreh De'ah*; and by responsa *Zera Emes* (*Yoreh De'ah* §161).
    Even Yaakov (§60), after citing all the opinions, writes: "From everything that has been said, it seems clear, in my humble opinion, that it is obviously possible to give the lenient ruling in this matter and count Shemini Atzeres as seven days of the thirty-day mourning period, even if burial occurred during *Chol HaMo'ed*. This is in accordance with the rule, 'In matters of mourning, the *halachah* follows the lenient opinion.' And the *gaon*, author of *Aruch HaShulchan*, testifies that this [to count Shemini Atzeres as seven days] is indeed the accepted custom."

31. *Chochmas Adam* (169:2). And *Gesher HaChaim* (23:2:12) writes that in case of pressing need, one may rely on the ruling of *Maharshal*.

32. *Mishnah Berurah* (671:§§44). [See below, footnote 54a.]

33. Ibid. The reason is that there is no prohibition against a mourner's reciting *shehecheyanu*.

34. See Chapter 25 footnotes 68 and 69.

35. *Taz* (671: §§8) writes that the mourner may lead the *Ma'ariv* services. *Pri Megaddim* (ad loc.) rules that he may do so for *Minchah* and *Ma'ariv*, and for *Shacharis* until *Baruch She'amar*. *Knesses HaGedolah* rules that he may serve as *sheliach tzibbur* until Hallel.

36. *Be'ur Halachah* (§132) rules that on the days when one does not recite *LaMenatze'ach* ('For the Conductor; a psalm of David. May Hashem answer you on the day of distress . . .') and *Kel Erech*

Hallel is not recited in the mourner's home during Chanukah; but those who prayed there must recite it afterwards in their homes. Some rule differently: that those praying in the mourner's home should recite *Hallel*, but the mourner himself should not.[36a] Others rule that even the mourner says *Hallel*.[36b]

16. During the eight days of Chanukah, eulogies are forbidden,[37] except for a Torah sage whose body is present and not yet buried.[38] However, on the day preceding Chanukah, eulogies are permitted.[39]

Purim

The *halachah* regarding a funeral on Purim is discussed above, 10:5.

⋈ Eulogies

17. Eulogies are forbidden on Purim, except for a Torah sage whose body is present and not yet buried. [This prohibition includes the Purim of both the walled and the unwalled cities, i.e., both the fourteenth and the fifteenth of Adar.] In a leap year, this prohibition also includes Purim Katan, i.e., the fourteenth and the fifteenth of Adar I.[40] However, on the day preceding Purim, eulogies are permitted.[41]

18. In some communities, the custom is [that a group of people] go to the grave on the seventh day of mourning and lament. This is forbidden on Purim. Instead, only the mourner should go, along with a *chazzan,* and he should recite *hashkavah* (memorial prayers for the deceased).[42] The custom of lamenting is also forbidden on the day preceding Purim.[43]

Apayim ('*O God, slow to anger.* . .'), the mourner should not lead the services. This is the custom followed by the *Chassidim*.

36a. *Magen Avraham* (131:§§10) and *Mishnah Berurah* (131:§§20) write that *Hallel* should not be recited in the mourner's home, but those who prayed there must recite it afterwards in their homes. However, *Pri Chadash* and *Elyah Rabbah* write that Hallel *should* be recited in the mourner's home. The same ruling is cited in *Sha'arei Teshuvah* §683, that it obviously *should* be recited. On this, *Mishnah Berurah* (131:§§20 and 683:§§1) comments: ". . .but the mourner himself should certainly *not* recite it."

36b. *Shulchan Aruch HaRav, Orach Chaim* 131:5; *Gesher HaChaim* 20:3:7; *Chazon LaMo'ed* 16:18.

37. *Shulchan Aruch* §670:1.

38. Ibid. (*Yoreh De'ah* §401:5). He adds that the day when one hears of the death is equivalent [in this respect] to the day of death before the body is buried. This applies even if the news arrived more than thirty days from the death (*shmu'ah rechokah*).

39. *Mishnah Berurah* (681:§§1). He mentions that according to some *Poskim*, it is forbidden to fast on the day preceding Chanukah. In *Sha'ar HaTziyun* he states that the *halachah* is more lenient about eulogies than about fasting. Hence, even those *Poskim* would permit eulogies; and this is the ruling given by *Bach*.

40. *Shulchan Aruch* 696:3 and 697:1.

41. The explanation cited above (footnote 39), regarding the day preceding Chanukah, applies here as well.

42. *Magen Avraham* (696:5) because it is forbidden to eulogize on Purim.

43. Ibid.

◄§ Mourning Practices

19. The conspicuous mourning practices of *shivah* [for example, sitting on a low stool or not wearing shoes] do not apply on Purim.[44] This exemption includes both the fourteenth and the fifteenth of Adar, in both walled and unwalled cities, but not Purim Katan.[45] It applies even if death and burial occurred on Purim.[46]

The inconspicuous, private mourning practices (*devarim shebetzin'a*, for example, the prohibition of marital relations,) *are* observed on Purim.

Some rule that if death and burial occurred on Purim, all the mourning practices of *shivah* apply.[47]

Even though one is exempt from mourning on Purim, the two days count as part of the *shivah*.[48]

The mourner is permitted to change clothes on Purim without performing *kri'ah* on the clothes he changes into.[49] However, he must minimize his celebration of the holiday.[50]

If the fifteenth of Adar falls on the Sabbath, the walled cities observe a "Triple Purim" (*Purim Meshulash*), meaning that the Purim feast is held on the sixteenth. In such a case, some rule that the practices of *shivah* do not apply on the sixteenth; but others rule that they do apply.[51]

---

44. *Rama* (*Orach Chaim* 696:4); and the same ruling is given by *Shulchan Aruch* (*Yoreh De'ah* 401:7).

45. *Rama* (loc. cit.). He explains that the exemption applies on both the fourteenth and the fifteenth, in both walled and unwalled cities. However, *Mishnah Berurah* (ad loc. §§16) cites *Derech HaChaim* as ruling that on the fifteenth of Adar [in the unwalled cities], the mourner should not leave his home to go to the synagogue, even for the purpose of reciting *Shacharis*. Nevertheless, he states, the *Poskim* imply that even on the fifteenth he may wear shoes, and need not sit on the floor.

46. *Rama* loc. cit.

47. *Shulchan Aruch* (*Orach Chaim* 696:4) writes: "All the laws of mourning apply on Chanukah and Purim." But in *Yoreh De'ah* (401:7), it is written: "If death occurs before Purim, and Purim falls [during *shivah*, it does not cancel [the count of the seven days]. Nevertheless, mourning is not observed, neither on the fourteenth nor the fifteenth [of Adar]."

To resolve the apparent contradiction, *Shach* (ad loc. §§4) cites *Drishah* as explaining that in *Orach Chaim*, *Shulchan Aruch* is referring to the case when death occurs on Purim, while in *Yoreh De'ah* he is referring to the case when it occurs before Purim. The same interpretation is given by responsa *Zera Emes* (I:§102).

48. *Rama* (*Orach Chaim*, 696:4); *Shulchan Aruch* (*Yoreh De'ah* 401:7).

49. Wearing the torn clothes would publicize the mourning, and that is forbidden on Purim. One is required to change clothes in the same manner as for the Sabbath.

50. See *Mishnah Berurah* (696:§§12). See *Sha'ar HaTziyun* (§§11), who states that *Magen Avraham* forbids seeing any type of celebration, but *Elyah Rabbah* questions this ruling. *Derech Chaim* cites the ruling of *Elyah Rabbah*.

Yesodei Semachos; Appendix, p. 146 cites *HaGaon Rav Moshe Feinstein zatzal*, that a mourner should eat the festive meal only with his family and should not participate in a masquerade; also, that a teacher may remain at a Purim or a Chanukah party but should refrain from participating in the singing and dancing.

51. See *Mikra'ei Kodesh* (p. 178), who writes that mourning is not observed on the sixteenth. The same ruling is given by *Chazon LaMo'ed* (chapt. 17). However, *Purim Meshulash*, by R' Sh. Dublitzky, (2:27) cites many opinions on this issue.

◈§ The *Megillah*

20. On Purim night, if a mourner during *shivah* has a *minyan* in his home, he should pray and hear the reading of the *Megillah* there. If he does not have a *minyan* at home, he should pray at home and then go to hear the *Megillah* in the synagogue. But if not for the purpose of going out to hear the *Megillah*, he should not leave his home.[52]

If Purim occurs on the evening following a Sabbath, and the mourner had gone to the synagogue on the Sabbath, he is permitted to remain there for the prayer-service and the *Megillah* reading.[53]

21. If the mourner is the only one in the synagogue who knows how to read the *Megillah* with the correct vocalization, melody and precise pronunciation, he is permitted to be the Reader.[54]

Even after *shloshim* [for one's parent], if the mourner is the one who reads the *Megillah*, someone else should recite the accompanying blessings. But some rule leniently, permitting the mourner to recite them [even during *shivah*].[54a]

22. On Purim day, the mourner is permitted to go to the synagogue to hear the *Megillah*-reading even if he has a *minyan* in his home.[55]

Some rule that he is also permitted to go to the synagogue to pray.[56] Others forbid this.[57] If one chooses to follow the lenient ruling, he forfeits nothing. But all

---

52. *Mishnah Berurah* (696:§§16). See *Da'as Torah* (*Orach Chaim* §696, and in the note there). He cites R' David Jungreis, *zatzal*, as ruling that on Purim night (in contrast to the day) one must observe all the laws of mourning, since the Book of *Esther* (9:22) specifically calls Purim "days" of feasting and rejoicing. However, he cites the *gaon* R' Shlomo Zalman Auerbach, *shlita*, as ruling that no distinction should be made between the night and the day of Purim, at least with regard to the prohibition against wearing shoes and the requirement to sit on the floor.

53. *Shulchan Aruch* (696:5).

54. *Mishnah Berurah* (ad loc. §§12, citing responsa *Binyan Olam* §35).

54a. The reason for having someone else recite the blessings is so that the mourner should not recite *shehecheyanu*. Although the mourner himself is permitted to recite this blessing, he should not be the one to recite it on behalf of the congregation. However, after someone else recites the blessings, the mourner reads the *Megillah* (*Mishnah Berurah* 692:§§2, citing *Derech HaChaim*).

   Luach Eretz Yisrael cites the *gaon*, *HaAderes*, *zatzal*, as remarking that, through error, it was printed in a number of places that the mourner does not recite the blessings [for the *Megillah*. However, he *should* recite them, and] this is not comparable to the recitation of *shehecheyanu* on Chanukah (see above, par. 14). In the latter case, the mourner would be reciting the blessing purely on behalf of the congregation. But here, in the case of the *Megillah*, he recites it on his own behalf, as well.

   The *Luach* adds, in the name of the *gaon*, R' Y. Canelle, *z"l*: "[With regard to Chanukah,] *Chayei Adam* explains that the mourner should not kindle the lights [in the synagogue] because the congregants are in joy as they recite *shehecheyanu*. This implies that the determining factor is not the blessing, but the fact that the congregants are in joy. And on Purim, too, they are in joy. And see *Noda BiYehudah*, *mahadura tinyana* §141."

55. *Mishnah Berurah* 696:§§16.

56. *Magen Avraham* (ad loc. §§5), based on an inference from *Tur*.

57. *Taz* (ad loc. §§2). He explains that absence from the prayer service is not considered publicizing the mourning, since it is not obviously due to mourning.

agree that he may not leave his home for a purpose which is not a *mitzvah* .[58]

On the fifteenth of Adar in the unwalled cities, and on the fourteenth in the walled cities, the mourner may not go to the synagogue to pray, even for the Morning Prayer (*Shacharis*).[59]

◄§ *Kri'ah*

23. The *mitzvah* of kri'ah (tearing the garment — see above, chapt. 6) is performed on Purim, even for someone other than one's parent. But after performing *kri'ah*, one must change out of the torn garment(s).[60] The *mitzvah* requiring the neighbors to provide the mourner his first meal after the burial (*se'udas havra'ah* — see above, chapt. 14) applies on Purim. But instead of the usual *se'udas havra'ah* of eggs or lentils, the mourner should be given meat and wine.[61]

If the first day of mourning is on Purim, some rule that the mourner is permitted to put on *tefillin* .[62] Others forbid doing so.[63] But if death occurs on the day before Purim, and burial on Purim night, the mourner should put on *tefillin* , but without reciting the accompanying blessing.[64]

◄§ Leading the Prayer-Service

24. The mourner is permitted to lead the prayer-services on Purim.[65] However, some rule strictly on this point, forbidding him to do so.[66]

25. The Ashkenazic custom on an ordinary Friday Eve is that, before the congregation recites "*A psalm, a song for the Sabbath day* ," the mourner enters the synagogue, and the *shamash* announces, "Come forth towards the mourner." Then the congregation consoles him. (See above, 17:9.) If Friday is

---

58. *Mishnah Berurah* loc. cit. §§13 and 16.

59. See above, footnote 45.

60. In this respect, the *halachah* for Purim is the same as for the Sabbath, since conspicuous mourning is forbidden on Purim, too.

61. *Chochmas Adam, Kuntres Matzeivas Moshe* par. 2.

62. *Elyah Rabbah*; but *Pri Megaddim* writes that in terms of determining *halachah*, the matter requires further study.

63. *Magen Avraham* (ad loc. §§16); *Derech HaChaim*; *Chayei Adam* .

64. *Mishmeres Shalom os pe* §3. In our case, there is a compound doubt: First, the *halachah* might follow *Maharitatz*, who rules that on the day of burial [when it is not the same as the day of death], the mourner is obligated to wear *tefillin*. Second, it might follow *Elyah Rabbah*, who rules that a mourner is required to wear *tefillin* on Purim. Hence, the mourner should put on *tefillin*. But he should not recite the accompanying blessing, since the *mitzvah* is valid even without the blessing.

65. *Zachur LeAvraham* , *Yoreh De'ah, Hilchos Avel* §300.

66. The reason is the same as explained above, footnote 36, regarding Chanukah. And see *Aliyos Eliyahu* (*Ma'alos HaSulam* , *Kuntres Acharon* §§6). He relates that, one Purim, a mourner wished to lead the *Minchah* service in the *beis midrash* of the Gaon of Vilna, *z'l*. When the mourner put the *tallis* over his head in preparation for leading the prayer, the Gaon indicated to him that he was not permitted to lead the service. As to the fact that the mourner had already wrapped his head in the *tallis* , the Gaon commented with a characteristically apt phrase: אָבֵל וַחֲפוּי רֹאשׁ, '. . .in mourning, and with covered head' (Esther 6:12).

Purim, this custom should not be observed, since mourning should not be announced in public on Purim.[67] This also applies on the fifteenth of Adar in an unwalled city.[68]

✥ Mishlo'ach Manos / Matanos LaEvyonim

26. The mourner is obligated by the mitzvos of sending food portions (mishlo'ach manos) to a friend and giving gifts to the poor (matanos la'evyonim), even during shivah.[69] However, he should not send things which are associated with joy (simchah).[70]

Other people should not send mishlo'ach manos to the mourner. This applies during the entire Twelve Months of mourning for one's parent, and during the shloshim for some other family member. And the prohibition includes even sending things not associated with joy.[71] However, a woman is permitted to send mishlo'ach manos to the mourner's wife.[71a]

If there is no one else in one's town to whom one can send mishlo'ach manos except the mourner, one is obligated to fulfill the mitzvah by sending to him, unless he indicates that he does not wish to receive mishlo'ach manos.[72]

If the mourner is poor, one may send him money, since this is no less permissible than giving him charity.[73]

One authority writes that it is permissible to send mishlo'ach manos to the community's rabbi even if he is in mourning.[73a]

If a person's parent died on Purim, one is permitted to send the person mishlo'ach manos the following year — even things associated with joy, and even though Purim is the yahrzeit (anniversary of the death).[74]

---

67. *Taz* (ad loc. §§2).

68. *Sha'arei Teshuvah* (ad loc. §§7), citing *Elyah Rabbah*.

69. *Shulchan Aruch* (loc. cit. sif 6), and *Mishnah Berurah* (ad loc. §§17). The reason is that the mourner is obligated by all the mitzvos.

70. *Magen Avraham* (ad loc. §§1), citing *Sefer Chassidim*.

71. *Rama* (696:7). The sending of mishlo'ach manos is forbidden because it is considered similar to asking about the mourner's welfare (see above, 21:10 ff).

71a. I heard this ruling from the gaon, R' Y. Sh. Elyashiv, shlita. It is true, he explained, that anything acquired by the wife belongs to the husband. However, in this situation the husband is not at all forbidden to acquire the item. There is simply a prohibition against sending it to him. And since the mishlo'ach manos is not sent to him, it is permitted. See the discussion of this topic in responsa *Yaskil Avdi* (VIII:§20).

72. *Rama* (696:7). *Mishnah Berurah* (ad loc. §§22) explains why one is exempt if the mourner indicates that he does not wish to receive mishlo'ach manos. It is an instance of the general rule that "one does not give a person a gift against his will."

73. *Magen Avraham* (696:§§11).

73a. *Divrei Malkiel* (part 5 §237).

74. *Magen Avraham* (696:§§11), citing *Sefer Chassidim*. *Levushei Srad* (ad loc.) notes that, according to *Rama* in *Yoreh De'ah*, all the stringencies observed during the first twelve months of mourning apply on the first yahrzeit, even though it occurs after the twelve months are completed.

Pesach

◄§ The Mourner's First Meal

27. The *mitzvah* of giving the mourner the *se'udas havra'ah* (the first meal after the burial — see above, chapt. 14) should not be performed on the day preceding Pesach, from the time when *chametz* becomes forbidden.[75]

◄§ *Seder* Practices

28. After *shivah*, the mourner is obligated by the *mitzvah* of *heseibah* (i.e., he must recline at the table during parts of the *Seder* meal).[76] Nevertheless, it is proper for the mourner not to recline on the specially luxurious couch he uses for Pesach. Instead, he should perform the *mitzvah* somewhat differently from the usual manner: That is, he should sit on an ordinary couch with only one pillow under his head, or he should recline on a friend's knees.[77]

The accepted custom is that a mourner does not wear the *kittel* (white outer garment) on Pesach. However, if he does wear it, people should not tell him not to do so.[78]

On Pesach night, a mourner recites *Hallel*, even if he is in the midst of *shivah*.[79]

[Usually, if he had begun observing *shivah* before Pesach, the arrival of the *Yom Tov* would cancel *shivah*. Thus, he could not be "in the midst of *shivah*" on Pesach night. However, this could occur if the burial occurred late in the afternoon on the day preceding Pesach, and he did not have time to accept the laws of mourning upon himself before *Yom Tov*. In that case, the *Yom Tov* would not cancel *shivah*.]

Shavuos

29. *Tikkun Leil Shavuos* is a special compendium read on Shavuos night. If one is accustomed to read it every year, he may do so even if Shavuos occurs during

---

Nevertheless, explains *Levushei Srad*, the *halachah* is lenient in the matter of *mishlo'ach manos* on Purim.

75. *Beis Yosef* (*Yoreh De'ah* §378); *Ba'er Heitev* (*Orach Chaim* 471:§§9), citing *Maharshal*. And see *Sha'ar HaTziyun* (ad loc. §§26) who adds that the *se'udas havra'ah* may be given until the time when *chametz* becomes forbidden.

76. *Chok Yaakov*, *Shulchan Aruch HaRav*, and *Derech HaChaim*, contrary to the ruling of *Bach* and *Magen Avraham*, who rule that the mourner is exempt from this *mitzvah* (*Sha'ar HaTziyun* 472:§§15).

77. *Mishnah Berurah* (ad loc. §§13).

78. *Mishnah Berurah* loc. cit.; and the same ruling is given by the *gaon* R' Moshe Feinstein, *zatzal*, in *Kovetz Am HaTorah* (*choveres* 12:7).

79. *Sdei Chemed* (*Aveilus* §214), citing *Machazik Brachah* (§685). The same ruling is given by *Shulchan Aruch HaRav* (§472); *Zachur LeAvraham* (*Hilchos Aveilus*, s.v. *Hallel*); and *Beis Oved* (*Dinei Hallel*).

shivah. But if in other years he sometimes omits it, he is forbidden to read it during *shivah*.[80]

Tishah B'Av

30. On Tishah B'Av, the mourner goes to the synagogue for both the evening and morning services, remaining until the end of the *Kinnos*. However, some rule that during the first three days of mourning he should go only in the morning, not at night.[81]

31. On Tishah B'Av, the mourner is not required to change his place in the synagogue[82] (see above, chapt. 27).

32. At the Morning Service (*Shacharis*) on Tishah B'Av, the mourner is permitted to be called up to the reading of the Torah or the *haftarah*, even during *shivah*. This is because only sorrowful passages are read, and because the entire congregation is forbidden to study Torah, just as he is.[83]

Some rule that the mourner is also permitted to be the *ba'al korei* (the one who reads the Torah) during *Shacharis*.[84]

At *Minchah*, he is forbidden to be called up to the Torah or to serve as *ba'al kri'ah*.[85]

33. On Tishah B'Av, it is permitted to deliver eulogies for a Torah sage.[86]

---

80. See above, footnote 20, regarding *Tikkun Leil Hoshana Rabbah*. The same *halachah* applies here.

81. See above, 26:9, and footnote there.

82. See above, 27:5.

83. *Sha'arei Teshuvah* (554:§§1), cited by *Kaf HaChaim* ad loc.

84. *Chazon LaMo'ed* 17:6.

85. See *Kaf HaChaim* 559:§§56.

86. *Mishnah Berurah* (559:§§17). He writes: "Even though [Tishah B'Av] is called a *mo'ed* (festival), [this is permitted,] since the entire day is intended for weeping and eulogy." He implies that the leniency applies even if burial has already taken place.

CHAPTER THIRTY-FIVE

The Bridegroom and Bride

---

1. If a wedding is planned, but before the *chupah* takes place the bridegroom or bride loses one of the family members for whom mourning is required, the wedding must be postponed. The seven days of mourning (*shivah*) are observed,[1] and on the seventh day, the *chupah* may take place, followed by the seven days of feasting (*sheva brachos*).[2]

2. If the wedding and the first instance of marital relations took place before the death, the seven days of feasting are observed first, and then the seven days of mourning.

---

1. If the deceased is a family member other than one's parent, this *halachah* is a law of the Talmud; it applies even if the wedding feast has already been prepared, and will spoil if the wedding is not held. Since there is someone [i.e., the parents] who will prepare a second feast afterwards, the Sages did not permit a person to have his wedding while he is an *onen* (one whose deceased is not yet buried). All the more so, they did not permit him to have his wedding once the status of mourner already applies to him [i.e., once burial has been completed].

However, if the deceased is the bridegroom's father or the bride's mother, the law of the Talmud is different. The Talmud (*Kesubos* 3b) states: "If a person's bread [for the wedding feast] is already baked, and his animals already slaughtered, and his wine mixed, and then the father of the bridegroom [who had to arrange the wedding feast; see *Rashi*] or mother of the bride [who provided the bride with her trousseau; see *Rashi*] dies, the deceased should be brought into a room, and the bridegroom and bride should go under the *chupah*. The bridegroom should perform the first act of marital relations, which is a *mitzvah*, and then separate from his wife. The seven days of the wedding feasts should be observed, and then the seven days of mourning. . ." Thus, by the law of the Talmud, in such a situation, the seven days of feasting are observed before *shivah*. Nevertheless, *Shach* (§342 in *Nekudos HaKesef*) writes: "It seems that in our day, even if the deceased is one's parent, the *halachah* is the same as for [the death of] other family members [i.e., and the wedding is postponed]". The same ruling is offered by *Chochmas Adam* (154:3).

See *Igros Moshe* (*Yoreh De'ah* §226). He writes: "If a parent died, and due to error they performed the wedding and the first act of marital relations, the seven days of feasting should be observed first [before *shivah*]. But if, due to their grief, they wish to observe *shivah* first, the bride can [relinquish her right to the wedding feasts]. . .and they can observe *shivah*. And logic indicates that the seven days of feasting should not be observed afterwards, since the time for them will already have passed."

2. *Tur* cites *Rosh* as writing: "He [the bridegroom] should postpone the *chupah* until after the entire thirty days [of mourning], unless he has small children, or has not yet fulfilled the *mitzvah* of procreation, as will be explained below." But *Ramban* writes that the *chupah* should not be postponed thirty days, since [the bridegroom] had gone to great effort, and the wedding was prevented by circumstances beyond his control. *Beis Yosef* states that the same ruling is given by *Rambam*, and concludes: "As for the *halachah*, we follow the lenient opinion in matters of mourning." He gives the same ruling [i.e., that the wedding may be held immediately at the end of *shivah*] in *Shulchan Aruch* (loc. cit.).

If the *chupah* took place before the death, but as yet there had been no marital relations, the *halachah* is a matter of disagreement among the *Poskim* (see footnote).[3]

3. In cases where the seven days of feasting are to be held first — and likewise if the death occurs during the seven days of feasting — the following *halachos* apply:

    (a) The laws of *aninus* (the period between death and burial; see chapt. 5) are not observed.[4]

    (b) The *mitzvah* of *kri'ah* (tearing the garment) is not performed.[5] But some Authorities maintain that if the mourning is for the person's parent, *kri'ah* is required. However, after performing it, one must change out of the torn garments.[6]

---

3. Many *Poskim* rule that the wedding ceremony itself [without the first act of marital relations] is not sufficient to postpone the observance of mourning. Therefore, *shivah* must be observed first, and then the seven days of the wedding feasts. Those who rule this way include: *Taz* (342:§§1); and *Shach* (in *Nekudos HaKesef*, ad loc.), citing Rabbeinu Yerucham, who cites *Rosh*. This conclusion is also implied by *Dagul Meirevavah* (ad loc.). The same ruling is given by *Chochmas Adam* (154:3); the *gaon* R' Zalman Margolios (*Onen* §33, and *Biurim* ad loc.); *Pachad Yitzchak*, cited by *Ikarei HaDat* (36:12); and other *Acharonim* (see *Sdei Chemed*, *Aveilus* §216).

On the other hand, most of the great Sefardic *Poskim* (*Zera Emes*, *Pri Chadash*, et al. — see *Sdei Chemed* loc. cit.) rule that the *chupah*, even without the first act of marital relations, is sufficient to postpone the mourning. This is because the *chupah* ceremony by itself is enough to initiate the bridegroom's personal festival. Therefore, they rule that the first act of marital relations should be performed, the seven days of wedding feasts should be held, and afterwards *shivah* should be observed.

Still others (*She'elas Yavetz* et al.) rule that, even though the seven days of feasting should be held first, the bridegroom is forbidden to perform the first act of marital relations [until after *shivah*]. They explain that if the death [of the parents] occurred before the *chupah* ceremony, there is danger that if the wedding is postponed, it might be canceled altogether. [Therefore, the *halachah* places the entire wedding process, including the first act of marital relations, before the mourning.] But our case is different. The *chupah* already took place before the death. Hence there is no danger that the wedding will be canceled. In this case, marital relations are forbidden.

4. *Kol Bo Al Aveilus* (p. 133); *Gesher HaChaim* (19:7:10); *Chazon LaMo'ed* (2:29). And see *Gesher HaChaim* (part II, 15:3), who writes at length on this point. He states that even before the burial, the bridegroom and bride are permitted to eat meat and drink wine, and are obligated by all the *mitzvos* of the Torah.

5. *Maharil* (*Hilchos Semachos*); *Knesses HaGedolah*; *Sdei Chemed* (loc. cit.), citing *Beis Oved* and responsa *Zera Emes*. The same ruling is given by *Moharash Flazhi* in a responsum cited by *Chaim BeYad* (§108); and this is also the opinion of the author of *Chaim BeYad* himself.

Yafeh LaLeiv (III:§342) cites *Vayomer Yitzchak* as ruling that the bridegroom or bride should perform *kri'ah* immediately. But the author of *Yafeh LaLeiv* himself disagrees, stating that the correct ruling is that of the authorities just noted, who rule that *kri'ah* should not be performed. "And this is what I instructed in a case which came before me."

The same ruling is given by *Chochmas Adam* (loc. cit. §4), and by *Gesher HaChaim* (loc. cit.). They rule that *kri'ah* is postponed until the beginning of the mourning period. The same ruling is given by *Chazon LaMo'ed* (loc. cit.), and by *Kitzur Shulchan Aruch* (§213). He explains that the bridegroom is even permitted to launder and iron clothes and to take a haircut, since it is written (*Isaiah* 33:17): 'Your eyes shall behold the king in his beauty' [and the bridegroom is comparable to a king].' All the more so, he should not rend his clothes or be seen in torn garments.

6. *Yavetz* (II:§185). He reasons that *kri'ah* is no less obligatory in this situation than during *Chol HaMo'ed*.

Ikrei HaDat (*Yoreh De'ah* 36:12), citing *Devar Moshe*, writes: "[The bridegroom and bride] are

(c) The blessing of *Dayan HaEmes* is recited.[7]

(d) The bridegroom and bride do not take part in the funeral procession.[8] But some rule that he or she should attend the funeral,[9] but not go to the cemetery.[10]

4. Some rule that if the bridegroom is a *kohen*, he is forbidden to become *tamei* (ritually contaminated) for his family members (see above, chapter 7).[11]

5. One Authority writes that the bridegroom should put on *tefillin* even on the first day of mourning.[12]

6. One Authority discusses the following situation: Death occurred during the days of the wedding feasts. The bridegroom (or bride) mistakenly began mourning. In this case, he rules, he must complete the seven days of mourning. If, by mistake, he

---

obligated to perform *kri'ah*, since their days of feasting are not equivalent to a *Yom Tov* of the Torah. . .But if the bridegroom is Sefardic, their custom is not to perform *kri'ah* [during *Chol HaMo'ed*] for any family member except a parent. Therefore, he should follow their custom in this matter, too."

Gesher HaChaim (loc. cit.) writes: "If one wishes to follow the opinion of those *Poskim* who rule that the bridegroom performs *kri'ah* for his parent, as during *Chol HaMo'ed*, he has authorities on whom to rely. However, he should perform *kri'ah* in private, after first changing out of [his wedding clothes], and then immediately put on his wedding clothes again. He does not need to perform *kri'ah* again upon changing into his wedding clothes, for they are comparable to Sabbath clothes. Moreover, during the entire seven days of feasting he should not be seen in torn clothes. However, it is preferable to follow the ruling of *Maharil*, and postpone the *kri'ah*."

7. *Gesher HaChaim* (loc. cit. par. 6). He explains that if the blessing were postponed until the beginning of *shivah*, it would be inappropriate, following, as it would, the seven days of feasting.

8. *Maharil*. *Sdei Chemed* (loc. cit.) writes: "It seems from the words of *Beis Oved* that even *Yavetz* agrees on this point. . .Furthermore, from the words of *Mishnas R' Eliezer* (part II:§35), it is quite clear that the bridegroom should not go to the cemetery."

The same ruling is given by *Chochmas Adam* (loc. cit.). *Pis'chei Teshuvah* (ad loc. §§2) cites *Shevus Yaakov* as stating that a bride should not go [to the funeral], but a bridegroom should go. However, *Sdei Chemed* (loc. cit.) rejects this ruling, based on the statement of *Maharil*.

9. See *Aruch HaShulchan* (342:8), who cites the ruling of *Shevus Yaakov* mentioned in our previous footnote. He explains that, due to the principle of modesty, the custom was that the bride did not leave her home until the first Sabbath after the wedding. . .therefore, if she were to attend her father's funeral like the other mourners, this would constitute conspicuous mourning, which is forbidden during the [personal] festival [of *sheva berachos* week]. But in our time, as is known, states *Aruch HaShulchan*, the bride customarily goes out of the house immediately after the wedding. Therefore, she is certainly obligated to attend the funeral, if it is the custom in her community that women attend funerals.

10. *Gesher HaChaim* (loc. cit. par. 7) writes: "However, in my opinion, those who object [to the ruling that the bride or bridegroom may attend the funeral] did not notice the words of *Maharil*, who writes explicitly, '. . .however, they should not go to the cemetery.' But they are certainly permitted to accompany their parent as they are taken out of the house. (This applies in communities where the custom is that the son accompanies his father; and all the more so, it applies to accompanying the mother.) And even the bride, if she is troubled by the thought of not accompanying her parent, is permitted to walk with the funeral procession for a few steps."

11. *Gesher HaChaim*, citing *Zekan Aharon* (§108). And in part II (15:3:2), *Gesher HaChaim* supports his ruling with the commentary of *Ritva* on *Kesubos*. But he also mentions there that some reject this proof. And see above, 7:7.

12. *Gesher HaChaim* (loc. cit.). This matter is discussed above, 13:7.

did not do so, but resumed the feasting, he must begin the entire seven-day mourning period again.

Thus, if he had observed two or three days of mourning, then interrupted the mourning and completed the seven days of feasting, he must afterwards observe a full seven days of mourning. The two or three days of mourning which had originally been observed do not count.[13]

7. Throughout all the days of feasting — even the seventh day[14] — the bridegroom (or bride) does not observe any of the laws of mourning. He is even permitted to launder and iron clothes, and to take a haircut.[15] There is one exception: The prohibition against marital relations must be observed.[16] However, he is permitted to be secluded with the bride.[17]

8. In general, the requirement to observe seven days of rejoicing applies if neither the bridegroom nor the bride has been married before. If, for example, a widower is marrying a widow, only three days of rejoicing are observed. But in this case, too, all the laws mentioned above, with regard to mourning, apply. The three days of rejoicing are observed first, and then the seven days of mourning.[18]

9. The days of the wedding feasts do not count as part of the first thirty days of mourning. The count of the thirty days begins when mourning is first begun.[19] Even if the wedding took place just before a Festival, and the death occurred during Chol HaMo'ed, the wedding feasts held during the Festival do not count as part of the thirty days.[20]

10. If a Festival occurs during the seven days of the wedding feasts, the Festival does not cancel shivah. However, some rule to the contrary.[21]

---

13. Responsa Sheivet HaLevi, by the gaon R' Shmuel Wosner, shlita (Yoreh De'ah §213).
14. This is because the seven days of feasting must be complete. Therefore, the seventh day of feasting does not count as the first day of mourning. Kol Bo Al Aveilus (p. 66), citing Shiurei Knesses HaGedolah; Sha'arei De'ah (§342); Zachur LeAvraham (§8 and 9); and other Acharonim.
15. Shulchan Aruch (§342). And see Shach (ad loc. §§11).
16. Shulchan Aruch (loc. cit.). The reason is that this prohibition is one of the inconspicuous practices of mourning.
17. Shulchan Aruch 383:2. And see Mishmeres Shalom (os nun §44). He writes about the case of a man who married a woman who was a niddah. Before the couple could have marital relations, the husband became a mourner. He had already fulfilled the mitzvah of procreation (piryah u'reviyah). Mishmeres Shalom concludes that marital relations are permitted after shivah.
18. Chiddushei R' Akiva Eiger ad loc. The same ruling is given by Gesher HaChaim: "It has been determined that even in the case of a widower who is marrying a widow, the three days of feasting are observed first."
19. Shulchan Aruch (loc. cit.). Shach (§§8) writes: "It is true that [if death occurs] during a Festival, the halachah, as explained in §399, is that the days of the Festival following the death are counted [as part of the first thirty days of mourning]. But that is different, because in that case, even during the Festival the mourner observes those laws of mourning which apply throughout the entire thirty days of mourning. In our case, this is not so. The bridegroom or bride is even permitted to launder and iron clothes or to have a haircut (Ramban and other Poskim)."
20. Taz (399:§§2); Mishnah Berurah (548:§§27).
21. See above, 32:4.

CHAPTER THIRTY-SIX

Shloshim: The First Thirty Days of Mourning

For the reader's convenience, this chapter summarizes the main laws and customs of the *shloshim*. The finer details and corollary *halachos* are set forth in other chapters, each in its appropriate place.

1. After the first seven days of mourning (*shivah*), one is still considered a mourner until the thirtieth day. This second period (the twenty-three days from the end of the *shivah* until the thirtieth day) is referred to as the *shloshim*. During *shloshim*, one observes certain practices of mourning.[1]

[The additional mourning practices, which apply for Twelve Months to one mourning the loss of a parent, are treated below, chapt. 38.]

❧ Cutting Hair and Fingernails

2. Taking a haircut or shave is forbidden, according to the basic *halachah*, during the entire *shloshim*. This includes not only the hair of the head, but also any body hair, even in concealed areas (such as the underarms). Regarding a mustache, or the hair at the sides of the mouth, one is forbidden to cut it during

---

1. *Rambam (Hilchos Avel* 6:1) writes: "It is a Rabbinic Enactment (*divrei sofrim*) that the mourner must observe certain practices of mourning for the entire thirty days. On what did the Sages base the thirty days? On the verse, '*She shall weep for her father and mother for a month*' (*Deut.* 21:13). This implies that a mourner grieves for an entire thirty days."

    Ravad criticizes *Rambam*'s statement, writing: "The *Gemara* cites the command, רָאשֵׁיכֶם אַל־תִּפְרָעוּ, '*You shall not grow your hair long*' (*Leviticus* 10:6). And the root, פרע, here is associated with the same root in the passage about the nazarite." [*Ravad* is referring to the derivation and parallelism of phrases which we cited above (chapt. 24 note 1) regarding the prohibition of the nazirite and mourner cutting the hair for thirty days.]

    Radbaz comments: "It is surprising that our teacher [*Rambam*] ignored our [Babylonian] Talmud and based himself on the Jerusalem Talmud; and this is what *Ravad*, *zal*, means by his criticism. But the explanation is as follows: From the passage about the nazarite we can only derive the law about letting one's hair grow long. Whence would we derive the other laws [of mourning]? Therefore, [*Rambam*] based himself on the Jerusalem Talmud, which refers to the verse about [the captive woman's] crying for her parents; for there is written, '*. . .and she shall uncover her hair, and let her nails grow, and remove the gown in which she was captured*' (*Deut.* 21:12-13). From this it is correct to derive all the types of deprivation which apply during the thirty days. This is also implicit in the wording of [*Rambam*], who writes: 'This implies that a mourner grieves for an entire thirty days.' "

shivah. Thereafter, one is permitted to cut it if it interferes with eating.[2] (Details of this halachah, as well as circumstances in which one is permitted to have a haircut or shave, are presented above, chapt. 24.)

Cutting fingernails with an instrument such as scissors, trimmer, knife, etc. is forbidden during the entire shloshim. But trimming them by hand, or with one's teeth, is permitted even during shivah.[3]

◅§ Garments Newly Laundered, Ironed, or Purchased

3. One is forbidden to wear freshly ironed clothes during the entire shloshim.

Regarding clothes which are laundered but not ironed, the custom is not to wear those laundered with soap or other laundering agents. But those laundered only in water are permitted.

Even freshly ironed clothes may be worn during the shloshim if someone else puts them on first, even for a short time. One is also forbidden to wear new clothes. But if this is a necessity, it is permitted after someone else first wears them for two or three days.[4]

(Details of these laws are explained above, chapt. 23.)

◅§ Bathing and Use of Cosmetics

4. According to the basic halachah, the prohibition against bathing [or showering] applies only during shivah. However, the custom is to prohibit bathing during the entire shloshim. One should not depart from this custom, for it is an ancient one, established by early Sages.[5]

As regards bathing the entire body at once, some forbid this even in cold water. Others permit it in cold water.

(Details of these halachos are presented above, chapt. 19.)

Likewise, a woman is forbidden to use eyeshadow or facial makeup during the entire shloshim. However, a married woman may use them after shivah, so that she should not be unattractive to her husband. And one authority rules that a married woman is permitted to bathe after shivah.[6]

◅§ Mopping the Floor

5. During shloshim, one is permitted to mop the floor in honor of the Sabbath.[6a]

---

2. Shulchan Aruch (390:1). And see above, chapt. 19 note 1, for differing rulings about this law.

3. See above, chapt. 24.

4. See Shulchan Aruch §399.

5. Rama 381:1.

6. This matter is explained above, chapt. 19.

6a. Kerem Shlomo (Yoreh De'ah §381). However, responsa Meshiv Devarim (Yoreh De'ah §215) writes that this is forbidden. The same ruling is given by responsa Divrei Sofrim (§146). Apparently [since the dispute here is about the shloshim], this implies that it is forbidden during shivah, according to all opinions. This matter requires study. However, R' Wosner shlita writes that during the shloshim, it is definitely permitted to wash the floors. But, if someone permits the washing of the floor during the

✺ Participating in Festive Meals

6. During the *shloshim*, one is forbidden to attend a festive meal.[7] (Details of this *halachah* — including circumstances when attending a special meal is permitted — are presented above, 25:11.)

✺ Priestly Blessing / *Bircas Kohanim*

7. The custom in the Diaspora is that a *kohen* who is in mourning during the Twelve Months for a parent, or *shloshim* for another relative, may not recite the blessing of the *kohanim*.[7a] He should leave the synagogue before the *chazzan* begins the blessing of רְצֵה ("Be favorable") and should not return until after the end of the Priestly Blessing.[7b] However, if there are not two other *kohanim* besides the mourner, he must go up and recite the Priestly Blessing.[7c]

✺ Hakafos with the *Lulav*

8. During Succos, the mourner is forbidden to perform the *hakafos* with the *lulav*.[8]

✺ Exchanging Greetings

9. The mourner is permitted to inquire about another's welfare [*sh'ilas shalom*; lit. "inquiry of shalom"], since they are in a state of well-being. All the more so, he may reply to someone who unwittingly inquires about his welfare. But others are not permitted to ask about his welfare, since he is not in a state of well-being. After the *shloshim* (if the mourning is for any family member except a parent), there are no restrictions about exchanging greetings.[9]

✺ Sending *Mishlo'ach Manos* or Other Gifts

10. One is not permitted to send gifts to a mourner during the *shloshim* or during the Twelve Months for a parent, since this is comparable to extending greetings of peace.[10]

On Purim, the mourner is obligated to send portions of food [*mishlo'ach manos*] to others, but others are not permitted to send *mishlo'ach manos* to him.[11] [See above, 34:26.]

---

shivah because it is dirty, he should not be reprimanded for it.

See also responsa *Divrei Sofrim* (loc. cit.), who rules that the mourner is permitted to polish his shoes during the *shloshim*. It is true, he writes, that *Shevilei David* forbids polishing shoes during *Chol HaMo'ed*, since this is comparable to laundering. Nevertheless, for the mourner [during the ordinary days of the year] it is permitted. *Divrei Sofrim* explains there why this is so.

7. *Shulchan Aruch* §391.

7a. *Rama* (*Orach Chaim* 128:43), and *Mishnah Berurah* (128:§§159).

7b. *Mishnah Berurah* (loc. cit. §§12).

7c. *Mishnah Berurah* (loc. cit. §§159). See above, 33:18.

8. *Rama* (*Orach Chaim* 660:2). See above, 34:7.

9. *Shulchan Aruch* (§385). And see above, 21:10-11.

10. *Rama* (385:3).

11. *Shulchan Aruch* (*Orach Chaim* 696:6). And see above, 34:26.

◄§ Belated Consolations

11. If one did not console the mourner during *shivah*, one may comfort him during the entire *shloshim*. After the *shloshim*, one does not comfort him in the usual manner, but simply tells him: תִּתְנַחֵם, "Be consoled."

If the mourning is for a parent, one may console him in the usual manner during the entire Twelve Months.[12]

◄§ Marrying

12. During the entire *shloshim*, the mourner is forbidden to marry. (Details of this *halachah* — including circumstances when marrying is permitted — are presented below, chapt. 37.)

◄§ Changing One's Seat in the Synagogue

13. The mourner must move from his usual place in the synagogue. In case of mourning for one's parent, this applies during the entire Twelve Months; in case of mourning for some other family member, it applies during the entire *shloshim*.

(Regarding whether this applies on the Sabbath, and for other details of this *halachah*, see above, chapt. 27.)[12a]

◄§ Business Trips

14. During the entire *shloshim*, in case of mourning for any family member other than one's parent, the mourner is forbidden to travel a great distance for business purposes. This is because such a trip is extremely conspicuous. It is also similar to a celebration, since it involves joining a large group of travelers, who rejoice a lot along the way.

In case of mourning for one's parent, such a trip is forbidden until one's friends reprimand him [for not traveling] and tell him, "Come with us." (See footnote.)[13]

---

12. *Shulchan Aruch* (380:2). And see above, chapt. 17.

12a. Regarding changing one's seat in the *Beth Midrash*, see *Emek Brachah* (Pomeranzig).

13. These are the words of *Shulchan Aruch* (380:25). But see *Aruch HaShulchan* (380:33), who writes that *Shulchan Aruch* was referring to traveling in a large caravan, as was done in early times. Taking part in such a caravan would be extremely noticeable. It would also be similar to a celebration, because the members of such a caravan rejoice a lot along the way. "But in our time [when it is not customary to travel in large caravans], this *halachah* is not applicable."

Aruch HaShulchan also writes there that from the words of *Rambam* (*Hilchos Avel* §6), it is clear that during *shloshim* it is proper to minimize one's business activities, if this is possible — in other words, if it would not involve a monetary loss (*davar ha'aveid*). See above, chapt. 18 paragraphs 7 and 8 and relevant footnotes for further examples of *davar ha'aveid*.

Gesher HaChaim (21:7:9) first cites these words of *Aruch HaShulchan*, and then writes: "According to this, the mourner also should not take part in tours involving a caravan during the first thirty days of mourning. . .since he is forbidden to take part in pleasurable gatherings, even if they do not include a meal. (Such a tour is no more permissible than a large caravan, which is forbidden simply because they rejoice along the way, not because they eat together.) Therefore [*Bach* and *Taz* (end of §385, and cited also by *Ba'er Heitev* in the name of Rabbeinu Yehudah)] write that during *shloshim* one should not

Similarly, one should refrain from pleasure strolls during the entire *shloshim*. In case of mourning for one's parent, one should refrain from pleasure strolls during the entire Twelve Months.[14] [See below, 38:6.]

~§ Social Gatherings

15. During *shloshim*, a mourner is forbidden to invite others, or to accept an invitation, to a social gathering, even if it does not involve a meal. In case of mourning for one's parent, this is forbidden during the entire Twelve Months.[15]

Likewise, the mourner should not make a social visit as a friendly gesture on *Yom Tov*. However, on *Yom Tov* and *Chol HaMo'ed*, during *shloshim*, he may visit those individuals whom he regularly visits during Festivals. Not doing so now would be like publicizing his mourning.[16]

~§ Making Up for Missed Observance of *Shloshim*

16. If one failed to observe the mourning practices of *shloshim*, he is not required to make up for it afterwards.[17]

~§ The Prohibition Against Excessive Grieving

17. One is forbidden to mourn excessively. The first three days are for weeping, the first seven for eulogy, and the first thirty for refraining from haircutting and laundering. One should not grieve more than this.[18]

---

invite friends, nor accept invitations from them. [The other *Poskim* and *Acharonim* do not cite this *halachah*. It may be that 'inviting friends' means inviting them to drink. This would be similar to what *Ba'er Heitev* adds there in the name of *Maharil*. Likewise, it would be forbidden to invite the mourner to a pub. But this matter somewhat requires study.]

"It would also seem," continues *Gesher HaChaim*, "that during the Twelve Months, the mourner should not make social visits, as is usually done on *Yom Tov*. [That is, he should not make such visits on an ordinary day, nor during a Festival] However, if there are specific individuals whom he is regularly accustomed to visit on *Yom Tov* and *Chol HaMo'ed*, he may do so during the Twelve Months [but only during the Festival]. Not doing so then would be like publicizing his mourning."

14. *Yoseif Ometz* (p. 330) presents proof for this *halachah*. And see our previous footnote.

15. See *Taz* (385:§§1), citing *Bach*.

Responsa *Binyan Olam* (*Yoreh De'ah* §62) explains the ruling of *Taz*: "Sometimes people invite their friends and relatives [to their home], as on the Sabbath and *Yom Tov*, and serve them pastries and sweets. In such a case, the prohibition involving a festive meal does not apply, since [no bread is eaten, and therefore] this is not considered a meal at all. But [*Taz*] is informing us that, nevertheless, [the mourner] is forbidden [to invite people in this manner], because it is a form of celebration. Likewise, the mourner is forbidden to be invited to someone else's home in this manner.

"Alternatively, it is possible that *Taz* is referring to the common custom of receiving people in one's home in the morning during the Festivals. He informs us that the mourner may not drop in on others in this manner, nor may they drop in on him."

And see above, footnote 13.

16. See above (footnote 13, in the name of *Gesher HaChaim*), and footnote 15.

17. *Tiferes LeMoshe* 396:1.

18. *Shulchan Aruch* (394:1).

18. The foregoing applies to ordinary people. For a Torah scholar (*talmid chacham*), the mourning should be in proportion to the degree of his wisdom. Nevertheless, it is forbidden to weep for him more than thirty days,[19] or to eulogize him more than twelve months.

If news of a sage's death arrives after more than twelve months, it is forbidden to eulogize him, even on the day the news arrives.[20]

☙ The Mourner's Attitude

19. For the entire first three days, the mourner should feel as if a sword is poised over his neck; from the third until the seventh day, as if it is pointed at him from a corner of the room; from the seventh until the thirtieth day, as if it is going in front of him in the street. And during the entire first year, the whole family is undergoing judgment. But if a male child is born, the whole family is healed.[21]

If a group of men study together, and one of them dies, the whole group should worry.[22]

20. Anyone who does not mourn in the manner commanded by the Sages is cruel. Instead, he should be apprehensive, troubled, investigate his conduct, and repent.[23]

☙ The Thirtieth Day

21. To determine the thirtieth day, one counts from the day of burial.[24]

22. If the thirtieth day falls on the Sabbath, the mourner is permitted to bathe on Friday. The reason is that the basic *halachah* permits bathing after *shivah*; the prohibition against bathing during the entire thirty days is only a custom. Therefore, in this circumstance, for the honor of the Sabbath, it is permitted. Likewise, in this circumstance, at Sabbath Eve services one may resume sitting in his regular seat in

---

19. *Shulchan Aruch* (394:2). According to *Beis Yosef*, this law is derived from the verse, '*And the people of Israel wept for Moses in the plains of Moab for thirty days, and the days of weeping of the mourning for Moses were completed*' (*Deut.* 34:8).

20. *Shulchan Aruch* (loc. cit.), and *Shach* §§1.

21. *Shulchan Aruch* (394:4), based on the Jerusalem Talmud, *Mo'ed Katan*.

Prishah (loc. cit. §§6) writes: "This may be compared to a stone arch. [If one stone slips out, the whole arch is in danger of falling. But] when a new stone is inserted in place of the one that fell, the void is filled and the arch is again firm. It may be inferred that even if the deceased was a female, [the family] is healed only by the birth of a male; for, once the structure is shaken, it requires something strong to repair what was ruined."

22. *Shulchan Aruch* (394:5), based on the Talmud, *Shabbos* 106a, which adds: "Some say this means if the greatest one dies (*Rashi*: They should worry, since the Attribute of Strict Justice held sway over the head of the household); and some say it means if the least of them dies" (*Rashi*: Because punishment begins with the least).

23. *Shulchan Aruch* (394:6). *Shulchan Aruch* is citing the exact words of *Rambam* (*Hilchos Avel* 13:12). *Kesef Mishneh* comments: "These words of our teacher (*Rambam*) are appropriate to his [high status]."

24. *Shach* (402:§§5).

synagogue. Changing one's seat during the first thirty days of mourning is also only a custom.[25]

On the other hand, some things — such as taking a haircut and the like — are forbidden by the basic *halachah* [not just custom] during the first thirty days of mourning. Such things are forbidden on Friday, even if the thirtieth day falls on the Sabbath.[26]

23. In chapter 29 we explained that on the seventh day of mourning, the beginning of the day is counted as the whole day. The same applies to the thirtieth day.[27] Therefore, the mourning of the thirty days ends after sunrise (*neitz hachamah*) on the thirtieth day.[28]

24. On the thirtieth day, one goes to the cemetery and visits the grave, and recites commemorative passages for the deceased.[29]

---

25. *Rama* (400:2)
26. *Dagul MeiRevavah* (ad loc.), in the name of *Tosafos*. See what we write on this subject above, chapt. 24.
27. *Shulchan Aruch* (395:1).
28. Since there are no comforters on the thirtieth day, the mourning ends immediately after sunrise (*Shach* ad loc. §§1).
29. *Shulchan Aruch* (344:20).

CHAPTER THIRTY-SEVEN
Marrying During *Shloshim*

---

1. During the entire first thirty days of mourning (*shloshim*), the mourner is forbidden to marry,[1] even without a feast.[2] But if *Yom Tov* occurs during the *shloshim*, he is permitted to marry after *Yom Tov*.[3]

2. After *shloshim*, the mourner is permitted to marry, even if the mourning is for his father or mother. He is also permitted to hold a wedding feast.[4]

A woman mourner is likewise permitted to marry after the *shloshim*.[5] One authority rules that one is permitted to remarry his divorced wife even during the *shloshim*, but without a feast.[6]

3. If the mourner has not yet fulfilled the *mitzvah* of procreation (*piryah u'reviyah*),[6a] he is permitted to marry after *shivah*, even if the mourning is for his parent.[7] Nevertheless, if the date has not already been set, it is preferable (*lechatchilah*) to set it for after the *shloshim*.[8]

4. Likewise, if a man has small children, or if he has no one to care for his needs, he is permitted to marry during the *shloshim*. However, he is forbidden to have marital relations until after the *shloshim*.[9]

---

1. *Shulchan Aruch* (392:1). The source is a *baraisa* cited in *Mo'ed Katan* 23b: "The entire thirty days [are prohibited] for marriage."
2. Ibid. The reason, as explained by *Beis Yosef* and *Bach* (ad loc.), is that a wedding is a joyful occasion even without a feast.
3. *Mishmeres Shalom* (os nun §39).
4. *Beis Yosef* (ad loc.).
5. *Da'as Torah* (ad loc.). And see responsa *Zera Emes* (II:§159), cited by *Ikrei HaDat* (36:22). This is also the conclusion reached by *Mishmeres Shalom* (os nun §38).
6. *Aruch HaShulchan* (392:1).
6a. For the criteria as to when one has fulfilled this *mitzvah*, see *Shulchan Aruch*, *Even HaEzer* §1.
7. *Shulchan Aruch* and *Rama* (392:2). However, during *shivah* he is forbidden to marry. And see responsa *Igros Moshe*, *Yoreh De'ah* §227.
8. According to *Gesher HaChaim* (21:9, and footnote there), this is because some authorities disagree and rule that even if the mourner has not yet fulfilled the *mitzvah* of procreation, he is forbidden to marry until after the *shloshim*. The same explanation is also given by *Kol Bo Al Aveilus* (p. 356), who adds that if the wedding feast is already prepared, even if the date has not yet been set, it is permissible (*lechatchilah*) to go ahead with the wedding. And in footnote 19, he writes: "But after the fact (*bediavad*), it is permissible even if the wedding feast is not yet prepared, and the date has not been set."
9. *Shulchan Aruch* 392:2.

5. Matchmaking (*shiduchim*) is permitted during *shivah*, even on the day of the death.[10]

6. In circumstances when it is permitted to marry during the *shloshim*, the bridegroom or bride is permitted to launder clothes, to wear freshly laundered clothes, and to bathe for the wedding.[11] Likewise, he is permitted to take a haircut on his wedding day.[12]

7. At the wedding feast of a mourner, even during the *shloshim*, dancing and playing musical instruments are permitted.[13] Likewise, in communities where the custom is to lead the bridegroom through the streets on the way to the *chupah*, accompanied by musical instruments, this is permitted even for a bridegroom who is a mourner.[14]

The wedding is followed by the seven days of wedding feasts (*sheva brachos*). After these seven days, the mourner completes the *shloshim*.[15] The seven days of the wedding feasts, in this case, are counted as part of the *shloshim*.[15a]

8. If a man who had not yet fulfilled the *mitzvah* of procreation (*piryah u'reviyah*) became engaged to marry, and after he had prepared the wedding feast, his fiancee's brother died — he may proceed with the wedding and have marital relations after *shivah*.[16]

If a man's wife dies, leaving young children, and her sister agrees to marry the widower, he may hold the wedding immediately. This is because she feels more compassion for her sister's children than another woman would. However, marital relations are prohibited until after the *shloshim*.[17] This applies even if a Festival occurs during the *shloshim*.[17a]

৵৽ A Widower

9. A man whose wife dies is forbidden to remarry until three Festivals have passed.[18] However, the prohibition against attending a feast, as well as the other laws of mourning, apply for only thirty days, as for the death of any other family

---

10. *Shach* (§§1), citing *Bach*.

11. See responsa *Chasam Sofer*, *Yoreh De'ah* §348.

12. Ibid. But see above, note to 24:12, where we cite an opinion that this is forbidden.

13. This question is raised by *Imrei Baruch* (§392), and he concludes that these things are permissible. The same ruling is given by responsa *Sheivet HaLevi* (*Yoreh De'ah*, §213).

14. Responsa *Yehudah Ya'aleh*, *Orach Chaim* §91.

15. See responsa *Chasam Sofer*, *Yoreh De'ah* §348.

15a. *Tiferes LeMoshe* §399.

16. *Shulchan Aruch* (392:3).

17. *Rama* (ad loc.), and *Taz* §§7.

17a. *Mishmeres Shalom* (os nun §40).

18. *Shulchan Aruch* (392:2). This prohibition is not an extension of the laws of mourning. Its purpose is that the memory of the widower's first wife fade from his mind by the time he is with his second wife. Through the rejoicing of the Festivals, his memory of his first wife is lessened (*Shach* ad loc. §§2).

member [except father or mother].[19]

[Pesach, Shavuos, and Succos are classified as "Festivals" for this purpose; Rosh Hashanah and Yom Kippur are not.[20] Rabbinic festivals, such as Chanukah, are also not classified as "Festivals" for this purpose. Some rule that Shemini Atzeres counts as a separate Festival,[21] but others disagree.[22]

10. If a man's wife dies, he is permitted in certain cases to remarry immediately after *shivah*. These cases are:

    (a) He has not yet fulfilled the *mitzvah* of procreation (*piryah u'reviyah*), or

    (b) He has young children, or

    (c) He has no one to care for his needs.[23]

However, he is forbidden to have marital relations until after the *shloshim*. An exception is case (a), where he is permitted to have marital relations after *shivah*.[24]

Some rule that even if a man is wealthy and can afford servants and maidservants, he may remarry after *shivah*. They reason that, unless, for example, his daughter is available to wash his hair,[25] or give other kinds of help which he would be embarrassed to receive from others, he is classified as having "no one to care for his needs." The same applies, they rule, in all similar situations. Because of this ruling, the custom is that many are lenient in this matter, and remarry before three Festivals have passed.[26] However, a man who is on a high spiritual level (*ba'al nefesh*) should be careful about this.[27]

◈ A Widow

11. If a woman's husband dies, she observes mourning for only thirty days.[28] However, she is forbidden to remarry for three months. This is a precaution to

---

19. *Rama* (ad loc.), in the name of *Tur*; *Shach* §§3.

20. *Shulchan Aruch* 392:2.

21. *Dagul MeiRevavah* (ad loc.). And *Sdei Chemed* (*Aveilus* §9) writes that this ruling is stated explicitly by *Agudah*. The same ruling is given by *Gesher HaChaim* (21:9:3).

22. Responsa *Chasam Sofer* (§350) cites R' Akiva Eiger as writing that, based on the words of *Rosh* (*Perek Elu Megalchin* §95), it would not seem [that Shemini Atzeres is counted as a separate Festival for this purpose]. *Sdei Chemed* (*Aveilus* §9) writes: "It would seem there is some basis for inferring the same conclusion from *Piskei Tosafos* (*Mo'ed Katan* 3:§123), since Shemini Atzeres is not mentioned there at all. . ." The same ruling is given by *Kitzur Shulchan Aruch*.

23. *Shulchan Aruch* (392:2). *Kol Bo Al Aveilus* (p. 357) cites *Naharei Afarsemon* (*Yoreh De'ah*, §156) as stating that in case (c), the permission applies only after the first thirty days of mourning — even though this does not seem to be implied by *Shulchan Aruch* §392.

24. *Shulchan Aruch* (392:2).

25. See *Chiddushei R' Akiva Eiger* (ad loc.), and Responsa of *Beis Yosef* §135.

26. *Rama* (ad loc.), citing *Piskei Mahara'i* §3.

27. *Pischei Teshuvah* (ad loc. §§3), in the name of *Shevus Yaakov*. And see *Dagul MeiRevavah*, ad loc.

28. See *Taz* (ad loc. §§3), who writes: "The custom of women is to mourn for a full year for a deceased husband. But I do not know of any basis or proof for the validity of their custom. Perhaps

prevent cases of doubtful parentage.[29] [If she were to remarry immediately and give birth after seven months, doubt would arise as to whether it was the child of the first husband after a nine-month pregnancy, or of the second husband after a seven-month pregnancy.]

---

they do this for the sake of their children, who [are required to] mourn [for their father] twelve months."
And see the comment of *Gilyon Maharsha* (ad loc.) on *Shach* §§2.

29. *Taz* (ad loc. §§3), and *Shach* (ad loc. §§2).

CHAPTER THIRTY-EIGHT

Yud-Beis Chodesh:
The Twelve Months of Mourning

For the reader's convenience, this chapter summarizes the main laws and customs of *Yud-beis Chodesh*, the Twelve Month extended mourning period for one's parent. The finer details and corollary *halachos* are set forth in other chapters, each in its appropriate place.

1. In mourning for one's parent, certain laws apply for an entire Twelve Months. This is an aspect of the *mitzvah* of honoring father and mother.[1]

◆§ Haircuts

2. The mourner is forbidden to take a haircut until his friends reprimand him for his appearance. It is considered that after three months,[2] one's friends would reprimand him. [Therefore, after this period of time, he may take a haircut even if his friends have not yet reprimanded him.] For details of this *halachah*, see above, 24:19.

◆§ Festive Meals

3. For the entire Twelve Months, the mourner is forbidden to attend a festive meal.

The custom is not to eat at any group meal at all outside one's home during this period.[3] The laws and customs regarding this prohibition are presented above, chapter 25.

◆§ Wearing New Clothes

4. The custom is not to wear new clothes for the entire Twelve Months. However, the mourner finds it necessary to wear new clothes, he may do so after first having someone else wear them for two or three days.[4]

---

1. *Shach* 344:§§9. Therefore he writes there (citing *Mahariv*) that if one's father or mother commanded him not to observe the mourning of the Twelve Months (i.e., the period following the *shloshim*), it is a *mitzvah* to obey. This is because the laws of the Twelve Months do not apply in the case of the death of other family members, but only for one's father or mother, in order to honor them.
2. *Shulchan Aruch* and *Rama* 390:4.
3. *Shulchan Aruch* and *Rama* 391:1, 2, and 3.
4. *Rama* (389:3); and *Be'er HaGolah* (ad loc.), citing *Kol Bo*.
   Regarding old clothes which have been newly sewn, see *Emek Brachah* (Pomeranzig). See also responsa *Igros Moshe* (part 3 §79).

He is permitted to wear new clothes whose purpose it is to absorb perspiration (for example, undershirts, socks), even without having someone else wear them first.[5]

❧ Buying New Utensils

5. It is permitted to buy and use new utensils and furniture, and it is not necessary to have someone else use them first.

It is also permitted to paint one's house.[6]

❧ Business Trips / Pleasure Strolls

6. The mourner should not go on long business trips, since this is extremely conspicuous. It is also similar to a celebration, since it involves joining a large group of travelers who rejoice a lot along the way. Such a trip is forbidden until one's friends reprimand him [for not traveling] and tell him, "Come with us."[7] See chapter 36, note 13.

Likewise, one should refrain from pleasure strolls during the entire Twelve Months.[8] See above, 36:14.

❧ Social Gatherings and Visits

7. During the entire Twelve Months, the mourner is forbidden to invite others, or to accept an invitation, to a social gathering, even if it does not involve a meal.[9]

Likewise, the mourner should not make a social visit as a friendly gesture on *Yom Tov*. However, on *Yom Tov* and *Chol HaMo'ed*, he may visit those individuals whom he regularly visits during Festivals. Not doing so now would be like publicizing his mourning.[10]

❧ Extending Greetings / Giving Gifts to a Mourner

8. During the entire Twelve Months, one should not inquire about the mourner's welfare [*sh'ilas shalom* lit. "inquiry of Shalom"]. However, some rule more leniently and permit welfare inquiries after *shloshim*, as long as one does not use the term *shalom*, but instead uses expressions like "Good morning."[11]

---

5. See above, chapt. 23.

6. This *halachah* is also discussed above, loc. cit. And see *Da'as Kedoshim* 389:§§1.

7. *Shulchan Aruch* 380:25.

8. *Yoseif Ometz* (p. 33 *Laws of Shloshim and the Twelve Months*). He writes: "A major proof for this is the custom that on the Sabbath the mourner does not leave his home except to go to the synagogue. [It seems that this was the custom there, and I have not seen any sources that comment on this (Ch.G.)] Now, this is difficult to understand. Can it be that one observes more mourning on the Sabbath than during the week? But one is forced to conclude that during the week the mourner is permitted to leave his home only because it may be assumed that his purpose is to earn his living. This is not the case on the Sabbath, and therefore going out just for a stroll on the Sabbath is forbidden. All the more so, then, it must be forbidden during the week." See above, chapt. 31 note 13, citing *Gesher HaChaim*.

9. See above 36:14.

10. See above, loc. cit. and note there.

11. See above, chapt. 21.

Likewise, during the entire Twelve Months one should not send the mourner gifts, since this is comparable to asking about his welfare.[12]

However, in the case of an engagement, some rule that one may give an engagement ring to a fiancee who is a mourner,[12a] and a mourner may give an engagement ring to a fiancee.

∞§ *Mishlo'ach Manos*

On Purim, the mourner is obligated to send portions of food (*mishlo'ach manos*) to others, but others may not send *mishlo'ach manos* to him.[13]

∞§ Belated Consolations

9. If one did not console a mourner for a parent during *shivah*, one may console him during the entire Twelve Months.[14]

∞§ Changing One's Seat in Synagogue

10. During the entire Twelve Months, the mourner should not sit in his regular place in the synagogue.

Regarding the question whether this applies on the Sabbath, and for other laws about changing one's seat, see above, chapter 27.

∞§ Priestly Blessing

11. The custom in the Diaspora is that a *kohen* who is in mourning for his father or mother does not recite the Blessing of the *Kohanim*.[14a] For more details, refer to 33:18 and 36:7.

∞§ *Hakafos* with the *Lulav*

12. On Succos during the Twelve Months, the mourner does not perform the *hakafos* (circling the central platform in the synagogue) with the *lulav*.[15]

∞§ Wearing a *Kittel*

13. Some have the custom that during the Twelve Months they do not wear the *kittel* (white outer garment) during Rosh Hashanah, Yom Kippur, and the

---

12. *Rama* 385:3.

12a. The *gaon* Rav Moshe Feinstein, *zatzal*, cited in *Yesodei Semachos* p. 110. The reason that she is permitted to receive this gift as a mourner is because it is considered in her case as a betrothal gift [סִבְלֹנוּת], and the formalization of the *shidduch*.

13. See 34:26. [Regarding the mourner within Twelve Months publicly reading the *Megillah*, see above 34:21; leading the prayer-services: 34:24; sending *mishloach manos* to a rabbi: 34:26; participating in the Purimmeal: chapt. 34 footnote 50.]

14. *Shulchan Aruch* 385:2.

14a. *Rama* (*Orach Chaim* 128:§§43).

15. See above, 34:7.

night of the Pesach *Seder*. However, others are more lenient, and do wear it.[16]

◌§ Mentioning the Name of One's Deceased Parent

14. During the entire Twelve Months, when one mentions the name of one's parent, one should add: (מִשְׁכָּבָה) מִשְׁכָּבוֹ כַּפָּרַת הֲרֵינִי [*hareini kaparas mishkavo* (fem.:*mishkavah*)], "I am atonement for his (her) resting place."[17] After the Twelve Months, one substitutes: לִבְרָכָה (זִכְרוֹנָה) זִכְרוֹנוֹ [*zichrono (zichronah) livrachah*], ". . .of blessed memory."[18]

The custom is to be strict during the Twelve Months and follow this practice also when writing, by adding the abbreviation: הכ"מ.[19]

One of the *Rishonim* writes that this *halachah* applies only when quoting one's parents on a halachic matter; but when quoting their ordinary conversation, one need not add the extra words, "I am atonement for his (her) resting place."[20]

The same *halachah* applies to one's Torah teacher. On mentioning his name during the Twelve Months following his demise, one adds: *hareini kaparas mishkavo*.[21]

---

16. See above, 34:5 and 28.

17. *Shulchan Aruch* (*Yoreh De'ah* 240:9), based on the Talmud (*Kiddushin* 31). *Rashi* there explains the phrase as meaning: "If anything bad is due to come upon his soul, may it come upon me." He adds: "But after twelve months, the soul has already received what it received. [Even] for the wicked, the judgment does not last more than twelve months."

   Yoseif Ometz (*Dinei Shneim'asar Chodesh*) writes that *hareini kaparas mishkavo* should be said for only eleven months.

18. See *Taz* (ad loc. §§13), who writes: "The *Gemara* states [that one should say] לְחַיֵּי לִבְרָכָה זִכְרוֹנוֹ הַבָּא הָעוֹלָם (*zichrono livrachah lechayei ha'olam haba*), '. . .of blessed memory for the life of the World to Come,' and this is the expression printed in some editions of *Tur*. Those who add only ז"ל (*zichrono livrachah*), 'of blessed memory,' are leaving out words; the proper addition is זללה"ה (*zichrono livrachah lechayei ha'olam haba*), '. . .of blessed memory for the life of the World to Come.' "

   And see *Shach* (ad loc. §§13), who writes: "Even during the Twelve Months, one can say, '. . .of blessed memory.' But after the Twelve Months, one should not say, 'I am atonement for his resting place,' since [even] for the wicked, punishment in Gehinnom only lasts Twelve Months. And this is the prevalent custom."

   However, *Taz* (ad loc. §§12) implies that during the Twelve Months one should not say, ". . .of blessed memory," since "the deceased may not yet have achieved the World to Come [i.e., his period of punishment may not be completed]; hence this would involve a falsehood."

19. *Rama* (ad loc.) cites a ruling that "if, during the Twelve Months, one mentions one's father in writing, one need not add, 'I am atonement for his resting place,' but simply, '. . .of blessed memory,' since the writing lasts more than Twelve Months. But some rule strictly, [requiring one to add, 'I am atonement for his resting place,'] even in writing; and this [stricter ruling] is the prevalent custom."

   Be'ur HaGra (ad loc.) also implies that he agrees with the stricter ruling.

20. *Tosefos Ri HaZaken* on *Kiddushin* 31b. And see *Darkei Moshe* (240:§§4). He cites Rabbeinu Yonah as ruling that one should use the expression in all instances, not just for a halachic quotation. And see the lengthy discussion of this topic by the *gaon* R' Moshe Halberstam, *shlita*, in *Yagdil Torah* (London) p. 103.

21. *Shulchan Aruch Yoreh De'ah* 242:28.

◦§ Count of the Twelve Months

15. The Twelve Months' mourning period is counted from the day of burial.[22]

◦§ A Leap Year

16. Even in a leap year, one observes mourning for only Twelve Months. No laws of mourning are observed in the thirteenth month.[23] For example, if death occurred on 1 Cheshvan in a leap year, the Twelve Months would end on 29 Elul the following year, even though this is a month before the *yahrtzeit*.

◦§ The Conclusion of the Twelve Months

17. At the end of the Twelve Months, the principle that "part of the last day counts as the whole day" does not apply. Therefore, all the prohibitions of the Twelve Months remain in force throughout the last day.[24] Moreover, the custom is that on the following day, i.e., the *yahrtzeit*, these prohibitions are also observed.[25]

18. On the last day of the Twelve Months (even in a leap year), the mourners visit the grave and recite commemorative passages and prayers for the deceased.[26]

19. Some have the custom that on the last day of the Twelve Months [even though it is not the *yahrtzeit*] the mourner leads the prayer-service and recites *Kaddish*.[27] However, he does not fast on that day.[28] But some rule that he should fast.[29]

> The *halachah* regarding the mourner's reciting *Kaddish* and leading the prayer-services during the Twelve Months are presented below, chapters 39 and 40.

---

22. Responsa *Mas'as Binyamin*, citing *Maharshal*, and quoted by *Taz* (402:§§9). The same ruling is given by the following authorities: *Shach* in *Nekudos HaKesef* (ad loc.); *Chiddushei HaGershuni* (ad loc.); *Mishnah Berurah* (568:§§44); and *Chazon LaMo'ed* (ch. 27 footnote 2), citing *Yavetz*.

23. *Shulchan Aruch* (391:2). The same ruling is given by responsa *Meggidos* (by the author of *Pri Megaddim*) §82.

   However, *Leket Yosher* (*Minhagei Terumas HaDeshen*) writes: "One need not observe mourning for thirteen months. Nonetheless, he [the author of *Terumas HaDeshen*] commanded that the mourner should make some slight observance, such as not sitting in his regular seat [in synagogue] until the [anniversary of the] day when his father died. This is what he heard from others. On another occasion, he said: 'When one finishes the Twelve Months, he does not need to mourn any more at all.' "

24. *Shulchan Aruch* (395:3).

25. *Rama* (395:). This *halachah* is discussed below, chapt. 44.

26. *Shulchan Aruch* 344:20.

27. This custom is discussed below, chapt. 44.

28. *Ma'amar Mordechai* (*Orach Chaim* §568). And see below, chapt. 44.

29. Responsa *Rav Pe'alim* (part 4 *Orach Chaim* §11).

CHAPTER THIRTY-NINE

Kaddish During the First Year

◄§ Eleven Months

1. The custom is to recite *Kaddish* for one's parent for eleven months.

The Midrash speaks of the great benefit of reciting *Kaddish*. It states that by doing so, one redeems one's parent from *Gehinnom*. [1]

---

1. *Rama* §376, citing *Kol Bo* and others. His source is the story about R' Akiva (some say Rabban Yochanan ben Zakkai) which is cited, with minor variations, in a number of places. Here we shall recount the story in the familiar version found in *Or Zarua*. It is also cited, with slight variations in *Menoras HaMa'or* (*Ner* 1, 1:1), who quotes one version from *Midrash Tanchuma*, *Parashas Noach*.

Once, R' Akiva saw a bizarre man with a complexion black as coal. On his head, he was carrying a load heavy enough for ten men, and he was running swiftly as a horse. R' Akiva ordered him to stop.

'Why do you do such hard work?' R' Akiva asked.

The apparition answered, 'Do not detain me lest my supervisors be angry with me.'

'I am a dead man,' he replied. 'Every day I am punished anew by being sent to chop wood for a fire in which I am consumed.'

'What did you do in life, my son?' asked R' Akiva.

'I was a tax-collector. I would be lenient with the rich and oppress the poor.'

R' Akiva persisted. 'Have you heard if there is any way to save you?'

'I heard that if only I had left a son who would stand before the congregation and call out בָּרְכוּ אֶת ה' הַמְבֹרָךְ, *Bless HASHEM, the blessed One* — to which the people would respond בָּרוּךְ ה' הַמְבֹרָךְ לְעוֹלָם וָעֶד, *Blessed is HASHEM, the blessed One, for all eternity!* And if only I had left a son who could proclaim to the congregation, יִתְגַּדַל וְיִתְקַדַּשׁ שְׁמֵהּ רַבָּא, *May His great Name be exalted and sanctified* — to which the people would respond . . . יְהֵא שְׁמֵהּ רַבָּא מְבָרַךְ, *May His great Name be blessed!* If I had such a son I would be released from my punishment. But I left no son . . . When I died, my wife was pregnant; but even if she had a son, there would be no one to teach him.'

That moment R' Akiva resolved to discover if a boy had been born and, if so, to teach him until he could lead the congregation in prayer. He went to Ludkia and inquired after the despised tax-collector. 'May the bones of the wicked one be pulverized!' the people spat out. To R' Akiva's inquiries about the widow, they responded, 'May her memory be obliterated from the earth!' And his child — 'He is not even circumcised.'

R' Akiva took the child, had him circumcised, and personally taught him Torah and the order of prayers. When he was ready, R' Akiva appointed him to lead the congregation in prayer. When he said, '*Borchu es HASHEM* . . .' the people blessed Him; '*Yisgadal V'yiskadash shmei rabba*. . .' and the people responded, '*Yehei shmei rabba*. . .'

Instantly the tortured soul was freed from its punishment. That very night, it appeared to R' Akiva in a dream and blessed him. 'May it be God's will that your mind be at ease in Paradise, for you have rescued me from the judgment of *Gehinnom*.'

R' Akiva cried out to God, 'May You be known as HASHEM [the Attribute of Mercy] forever; HASHEM is Your appellation throughout the generations.'

Yesh Nochalin cites the version of this story in *Zohar Chadash*, according to which the deceased

On that basis, it would be logical to recite *Kaddish* during the entire Twelve Months, since the punishment of the wicked in *Gehinnom* lasts for twelve months. However, one does not wish to assume that one's parent was wicked; therefore, the custom is to recite *Kaddish* for only eleven months.[2]

Some rule that *Kaddish* should be recited until one week before the end of the Twelve Months.[3]

If one knows for certain that one's parent is among those who are punished for Twelve Months in *Gehinnom* — for example, if they did not observe the Sabbath —

---

afterwards came [to R' Akiva] in a dream and told him: "When my son read the *Haftarah* they lightened my punishment in *Gehinnom*; and when my son led the public prayer-service and recited *Kaddish*, they completely tore up my sentence. And when he became wise and acquired Torah, they gave me a portion in *Gan Eden*."

The earliest source which mentions that mourners recite *Kaddish* (for the benefit of the soul of the deceased) is Tractate *Sofrim* (19:12), which states: "After the *chazzan* finishes the *Mussaf* prayer, he goes behind the door of the synagogue. . . There he finds the mourners and all the relatives of [the deceased] and recites a blessing over them. Then he recites *Kaddish*." And *Rama* (*Orach Chaim* 132:2) writes: "They recite the Mourner's *Kaddish* (*Kaddish Yasom*) after *Aleinu*. The *Kaddish* for the mourner is mentioned by the *Geonim* and the *Rishonim*" (*Gesher HaChaim* 30:3:1).

2. *Ba'er Heitev* (*Orach Chaim* §132:§§5) writes: "For example, if the death occurred on the third of Shevat, the last day of reciting *Kaddish* should be the second of Teves. The reason for stopping [after eleven months] is so as not to assume that one's father was wicked. If one were to recite *Kaddish* on the third of Teves, this would be the first day of the twelfth month, and this day would be counted as if it were a whole month. Thus, it would be as if one had recited *Kaddish* for the entire twelve months. Therefore, one should recite it on the second of Teves, and that should be the last day. Then, on the third of Shevat, he should observe the *yahrzeit*." The same ruling is given by *Shevus Yaakov* (part 2:§129); *Machatzis HaShekel* (ad loc.); and *Chayei Adam* (32:18).

Mishmeres Shalom (*os kuf* §43) cites *Yad Shaul* (*Yoreh De'ah* §376), who writes that one should stop one day before the end of eleven months. [In the above example, this would be the first of Teves.] *Mishmeres Shalom* adds: "The laws of *Kaddish* written by the author of *Pri Megaddim* have been published. There it states that 'one should stop two days before [the end of the eleven months]; but this is not the accepted custom.' Likewise, the section on the laws of *Kaddish* in *Derech HaChaim* cites *Knesses Yechezkel* (§15), who writes: 'The custom is only to recite *Kaddish* for one day less than eleven months.' See *Sdei Chemed* (*Aveilus* §162), who indeed notes that the above passage from *Derech HaChaim* implies that on the last day of the eleven months one should not recite *Kaddish*. . . He comments: 'But this is not the truth, for there is no reason not to recite it on that day. . . and it has already been stated that one should not attempt to study *halachah* from digests.' Now, it appears that *Machatzis HaShekel* understood this to be a misprint in the digest of *Derech HaChaim*. But in my humble opinion, this is not so; it was a deliberate ruling; and I have already cited (the same ruling) from *Yad Shaul*. . . However, the *Mishmeres Shalom* concludes the correct practice is like the *Sdei Chemed* who says that on the last day of the eleventh month one should say *Kaddish*. Moreover, *Responsa Megiddos* (by the author of *Pri Megaddim*) states that there must be a full thirty days between the last day of reciting *Kaddish* and the *yahrzeit*." [In the above example, one would stop on the first of Teves, since Teves has only 29 days.]

3. *Shiurei Brachah* (§376). *Kol Bo Al Aveilus* (p. 369 note 19) writes that the same ruling is given by *Zachur LeAvraham* (*Avel* 100:27). He adds: "*Kol Bo* likewise implies that one should recite *Kaddish* for twelve months. *Pachad Yitzchak* (s.v. *Kaddish*) also states that the custom is to recite it for twelve months. The *gaon Ksav Sofer* recited *Kaddish* for his father, the author of *Chasam Sofer*, for one week less than twelve months."

Gesher HaChaim (30:9:3) writes that a few individuals follow this custom.

one is obligated to recite *Kaddish* for the full Twelve Months.[4]

Kaddish is recited even on the Sabbath and Festivals, although the deceased are not punished on the Sabbath.[4a]

⋖§ Twelfth Month

2. If one's father commanded him to recite *Kaddish* for him during the twelfth month — or, in a leap-year, during the thirteenth month — until the *yahrzeit* (anniversary of the death), one should obey, even if one's father was a scholar and a *tzaddik*.[5]

⋖§ Parent's Wishes

3. If one's father commanded him not to recite *Kaddish* for him, some rule that he should obey; but others disagree.[6]

⋖§ Belated News of Death

4. If one did not hear of the death of one's parent until long after the burial — for example, in the eleventh month, or even on the last day of the eleventh

---

4. *Rama* 376:4 and see *Pischei Teshuvah* (ad loc. §§9), who writes in the name of *Chomos Yerushalayim* (§257): "If a person knows that his parent was in the category of those who must remain in *Gehinnom* for twelve months, it is both proper and obligatory for him to recite *Kaddish* for twelve months. And see responsa *Chasam Sofer (Even HaEzer* 1:69). Concerning someone who committed suicide (God save us), he states that one can recite *Kaddish* for the entire twelve months, since that person put himself in the category of the wicked; moreover, [the deceased] prefers [that *Kaddish* be said for him for the entire twelve months] since this gives him atonement. And may Hashem, Who is good, grant him atonement." The same ruling is given by *HaGaon* R' Moshe Feinstein, *zatzal*, in *Kovetz Am HaTorah choveres* XII:6.

4a. *Rama* 376:4. The reason is given by *Shiurei Brachah* (ad loc.): *Kaddish* is effective in raising the spiritual level of the departed soul. The same ruling is given by *Elef LaMateh* (commentary on *Mateh Efrayim*) 4:§§2, in the name of the *Ari Zal*: "Even though there is no punishment in *Gehinnom* on the Sabbath, by reciting *Kaddish* one adds merit to one's parents, raising them, level by level, to *Gan Eden*."

5. *Mishmeres Shalom* (os tzadi §26). *Yad Eliahu* (Ragolar), in the testament included in that work, instructs: "Be careful to recite *Kaddish* and lead the prayer-services throughout the Twelve Months, and for an additional eleven days (to make up for the difference between the lunar and solar year); and in a leap year, for thirteen months. This involves no risk of appearing to consider one's father wicked." See *Sheivet HaLevi* (*Yoreh De'ah tinyana* §161) that one should not say *Kaddish* during the twelfth month based on an assumption that that would be the will of his parents.

My father, master, and teacher, *zatzal*, writes in his manuscript work, *Zichron Eliahu*, that some instruct their children to pay someone to recite *Kaddish* during the twelfth month. He wrote the same in his will.

Sheivet HaLevi (§165) rules that if his father did not instruct him to do so, the son should not hire someone to recite *Kaddish* during the twelfth month. "Since the son requests the other person to recite *Kaddish*, this gives the impression that he considers his father wicked [just as if he were to recite *Kaddish* himself]. And this is obvious."

6. *Pischei Teshuvah* (344:§§1) writes: "See responsa *Even Shoham* (§72), who states that if someone commands that his son should not recite *Kaddish* for him, he should be obeyed. However, responsa *Chelkas Yaakov* (part 2 §93) writes that if someone releases his son from the obligation of reciting *Kaddish* for him, the son need not obey, even if the father explicitly commanded him [not to recite *Kaddish*]. *Even Yaakov* (§47) concludes that, at least in most such cases, it is logical to rule that the son is not obligated to obey his father, and is definitely permitted to recite *Kaddish* for the elevation of the soul."

month— one should, nevertheless, recite *Kaddish* only until the end of the eleventh month, counting from the day of burial.[7]

5. If the mourner heard of the death in the twelfth month, one authority writes that he should recite *Kaddish* during the whole twelfth month, except for the last day. And if he heard on the last day of the twelfth month, he should recite *Kaddish* that day.[8]

If he heard after the Twelve Months, he should not recite *Kaddish*.[9]

6. If one is in doubt as to whether Twelve Months have passed since the burial, one authority rules that he should not recite *Kaddish*.[10]

Another authority rules to the contrary, that he should recite *Kaddish*; but the mourner who is in doubt cannot take precedence over another mourner who is certain that Twelve Months have not yet passed.[11] [The question of precedence could arise if both mourners wish to lead the prayer-service. Or it could arise in a congregation where the custom is that only one person at a time may recite *Kaddish*.]

If a person in doubt wishes to follow the lenient ruling and not recite *Kaddish*, those present should not protest.[12]

◄§ If a Second Death Occurs

7. If, during the Twelve Months, a second family member dies (Heaven protect us), the mourner would need to recite *Kaddish* for the second deceased during the twelfth month of the first deceased. In such a case, some rule that he should recite *Kaddish* throughout the twelfth month.[13] But one authority rules that he should refrain from reciting *Kaddish* on the first and last day of the twelfth month.[14]

◄§ End of the Eleven Months

8. Some rule that if the eleven months end on a Friday, the mourner should recite *Kaddish* on the Sabbath. This is because there is no punishment in *Gehinnom* on the Sabbath, and the purpose of *Kaddish* then is only to raise the soul of the deceased to higher and higher levels. On the other hand, if the eleven months end

---

7. *Gesher HaChaim* (30:9:5), as inferred from *Nekudos HaKesef* (end of §402).

8. *Gesher HaChaim* (loc. cit. par. 6) states this ruling on his own authority.

9. The *Acharonim* rule that he need not recite *Kaddish*, since after twelve months there is no punishment for the deceased. But *Kol Bo Al Aveilus*, p. 378, states that he should recite it.

10. *Da'as Kohen* §217.

11. *Gesher HaChaim* 30:9:13.

12. Ibid. This is because, according to some *Poskim*, once it is known that the father died, it is reasonable to assume that he died more than twelve months ago.

13. *Chazon LaMo'ed* (24:5), in the name of *Nezirus Shimshon* (*Orach Chaim* §132). The same ruling is given by *Gesher HaChaim* (loc. cit. note 11), in the name of *Kanaf Rananah* (§8).

14. *Gesher HaChaim* loc. cit. In this way, he makes it obvious that he does not need to recite *Kaddish* for the first deceased for twelve months. But if the first or last day of the twelfth month falls during *shivah* for the second deceased, he should recite *Kaddish* on that day as well.

on the day preceding a Festival, he should not recite *Kaddish* on the Festival, since there is punishment in *Gehinnom* on the Festival.[15]

9. The eleven months are counted from the day of burial, even if a long time elapsed between death and burial.[16]

Some rule that the eleven months are counted from the day of death; but they add that, nevertheless, if the mourner wishes to recite *Kaddish* for eleven months from the day of burial, he is permitted to do so, and he has the same rights of precedence regarding *Kaddish* as any other mourner.[17]

> The question whether to say *Kaddish* when in doubt as to whether the parent died is discussed above, 12:15.

✥ *Kaddish DeRabbanan* / The Rabbis' *Kaddish*

10. The above was in reference to the Mourner's *Kaddish* (*Kaddish Yasom*). As for the Rabbis' *Kaddish* (*Kaddish DeRabbanan*), recited after learning in a *minyan* of ten or more men, the mourner is permitted to recite it even after the eleven months. Likewise, he may recite it during the twelfth month, following Mishnah study for the benefit of the deceased's soul.[18] However, some rule that during the twelfth month, the mourner may not recite *Kaddish DeRabbanan* after Mishnah study for the deceased.[19]

Some rule that during the twelfth month the mourner is also forbidden to recite *Kaddish DeRabbanan* after study which is part of the synagogue service: for example, after the *Baraisa* of R' Yishmael which is recited before *Shacharis*, and the like; or after regularly scheduled public Mishnah study.[19a]

---

15. *Sdei Chemed* (*Aveilus* §162), citing responsa *Agudas Ezov*. (This ruling requires study; for if it is correct, why isn't one required to recite *Kaddish* each Sabbath during the twelfth month?) Responsa *Sheivet HaLevi* (*Yoreh De'ah tinyana* §165) writes that since the other *Poskim* say nothing about this, it may be inferred that they do not rule this way. He also states that one could fulfill the ruling of *Sdei Chemed* by reciting *Kaddish DeRabbanan* on that Sabbath.

16. *Be'ur Halachah* (§132) who cites *Rama, Yoreh Deah* 376:14, that the primary judgment of the deceased commences with burial. The same ruling is given by the *gaon* R' Moshe Feinstein, *zatzal*, in *Kovetz Am HaTorah* (XII:19).

See also *Gesher HaChaim* (loc. cit. par. 11), who writes: "If the deceased was killed or drowned, and his body was not found, or if the family heard that he was killed, but the body was not found, and the family gave up hope of finding it, the obligation to recite *Kaddish* [and observe mourning] begins from the day they gave up hope of finding the body. In that case, the count of the eleven or twelve months begins from the day they gave up hope and began to recite *Kaddish*. Even if the body was subsequently found and brought to burial, the months are not counted from the day of burial, but from the day of giving up hope."

17. *Mateh Efrayim* (*Dinei Kaddish Yasom* 4:1).

18. Responsa *Rav Pe'alim* (part 4 *Yoreh De'ah* §32). The same ruling is given by my master, father, and teacher, *zatzal*, in his manuscript work, *Zichron Eliahu*; and by the following authorities: *Gesher HaChaim* (loc. cit. §3); responsa *Sheivet HaLevi* (*Yoreh De'ah tinyana* §165); responsa *Maharitz* (§31).

19. *Even Yaakov* (§49).

19a. The *gaon* R' Moshe Feinstein, *zatzal*, in *Kovetz Am HaTorah* (12:17).

◆§ *Kaddish* by Someone Other than a Son

11. If *Kaddish* is recited for the deceased by someone other than his son, it may be recited even during the twelfth month.[20] Nevertheless, some have the custom that in this case, too, *Kaddish* is recited for only eleven months.[21]

◆§ Points in the Prayer Services When *Kaddish* Is Recited

12. Many have followed the custom of commanding their sons to recite *Kaddish* eight times a day.[22]

The custom is for the mourner to recite *Kaddish* at the following points in the daily prayers:

Morning Service:

(a) After רַבִּי יִשְׁמָעֵאל אוֹמֵר, "Rabbi Yishmael says. . .". [*Kaddish DeRabbanan*].[22a]

(b) After . . .מִזְמוֹר שִׁיר חֲנֻכַּת, "A psalm, a song for the inauguration of the Temple" (in the Ashkenaz version).[22b]

(c) After עָלֵינוּ [*Aleinu*], "It is our duty to praise. . .".[22c]

(d) After the שִׁיר שֶׁל יוֹם, *Song of the Day.* [22d]

(e) After אֵין כֵּאלֹהֵינוּ [*Ein Kelokeinu*], "There is none like our God" [during the week in the *Sefard* version; on the Sabbath in all versions; *Kaddish DeRabbanan*].[22e]

Afternoon Service:

(a) After עָלֵינוּ [*Aleinu*], "It is our duty to praise. . .".[22f]

---

20. Responsa *Meshiv Devarim* (*Yoreh De'ah* §213), cited by *Even Yaakov* (loc. cit.). He writes: "One who recites *Kaddish* for someone else can recite *Kaddish DeRabbanan* for the entire twelve months." The same ruling is given by *Gesher HaChaim* (30:9:4). He states: "Of course, someone else [other than the son] can recite *Kaddish* even during the twelfth month; and it is proper to do this; that is, if someone else recites the *Kaddish* (whether for pay or without pay), he should recite it for twelve months."

See *Kovetz Am HaTorah* (XII:16), which cites the *gaon* R' Moshe Feinstein, *zatzal*, as ruling that directors of institutions who accept the responsibility of reciting *Kaddish* should have recited it for twelve months.

21. *Gesher HaChaim* (loc. cit.) writes: "Many have the custom that not only the son, but even someone else reciting *Kaddish* for the elevation of the soul of the deceased, recites it for only eleven months." *Sheivet HaLevi* (*Yoreh De'ah tinyana* §165) writes: "If the son requests another person to recite *Kaddish* for pay [during the twelfth month], this gives the impression that the son considers his parents wicked; therefore this should not be done. And this is obvious."

22. *Shiurei Berachah* (§376), based on the statement of the holy *Zohar* that *Kaddish* is effective for "an hour and a half." Thus, states *Shiurei Berachah*, they recite *Kaddish* eight times, in order to save the deceased from punishment for twelve hours. "However, Rabbeinu R'Chaim Vital, *zatzal*, revealed the secret that 'an hour and a half' (*sha'ata u'falga*) is not intended in its plain meaning, but refers to a level in *Gehinnom* which is called *sha'ata u'falga*."

22a. ArtScroll Ashkenaz *Siddur* p. 52.

22b. Ibid. p. 56.

22c. Ibid. p. 160.

22d. Ibid. p. 162*ff*.

22e. ArtScroll Sefard *Siddur* pp. 184; 518.

22f. Ibid. Ashkenaz p. 254.

Evening Service:

> (a) After שִׁיר הַמַּעֲלוֹת [*Shir HaMa'alos*], "A song of ascents. . ." (in the Sefardic version).[22g]
>
> (b) After עָלֵינוּ [*Aleinu*], "It is our duty to praise. . ."[22h]

Moreover, the mourner recites "*Borchu*. . ." at the end of the Morning Service, after אֵין כֵּאלֹהֵינוּ, "There is none like our God," and at the end of the Evening Service (in *Eretz Yisrael*, and in the Diaspora in those congregations where *Borchu* is recited at these points of the service, and by someone other than the *chazzan*).

13. One authority writes that the custom should be instituted that sons who are in mourning for their parents recite some Psalms each day, followed by *Kaddish*.[23]

14. One authority writes that the Half-*Kaddish* after the Torah-reading should be recited by the mourners.[24] If no mourner is present, it should be recited by the one who read the Torah, even if his father and mother are living.[25]

15. On Sabbath during Pesach, Song of Songs (*Shir HaShirim*) is read in the synagogue; on Shavuos, the Book of Ruth is read; and on the Sabbath during Succos, the Book of Ecclesiastes (*Koheles*). After each of these Scroll-readings, the mourner recites the Mourner's *Kaddish*.[26]

16. On Sabbath Eve, the mourner recites *Kaddish* after *Kabbalas Shabbos*.[26a]

In the Ashkenazic version, after the Mishnah, *Bameh Madlikin* ["With what may we light?"],[26b] he recites *Kaddish DeRabbanan*.[27]

22g. Ibid. Sefard p. 282.

22h. Ibid. Ashkenaz p. 278.

23. *Shiurei Berachah* (loc. cit.), citing *Vayakhel Moshe*. He tells of an awesome incident concerning a certain spirit. There it is stated that, for defense against harmful spirits, nothing is so effective as reciting *Kaddish* after Psalms. Therefore he recommends instituting this daily custom.

24. *Sdei Chemed* (*Aveilus* §163) writes in the name of responsa *Agudas Ezov*: "His custom is that the *Kaddish* after the Torah-reading should be recited for the merit of the one who, in accord with the true *halachah*, is entitled to *Kaddish*." He derives this ruling from a responsum of *Rashbatz* (3:§171), who rules that this *Kaddish* does not belong to the *chazzan*, nor to the one who reads the Torah, but to the mourners.

Kol Bo Al Aveilus (p. 374) writes that on this basis the custom in a number of places is that on a weekday the mourner is called up third to the Torah-reading, and on the Sabbath he is called up last (if there is also a mourner to be called up for *maftir*), and he then recites the *Kaddish*. *Elef HaMagen* (commentary on *Mateh Efrayim*) 3:§§3 writes: "This implies that even if [the mourner] is not called up third [on a weekday] or last [on the Sabbath], he can still recite the *Kaddish* after the Torah-reading." However, the *Sha'ar Ephraim* 10:9 writes that the *Kaddish* should be recited by the one who reads the Torah. If the person who is called up last is a mourner, or is observing a *yahrzeit*, he customarily says the *Kaddish*.

25. *Elef HaMagen* (loc. cit.), and *Kol Bo Al Aveilus* (loc. cit.). The same ruling is given by *Gesher HaChaim* (30:8:2).

26. *Gesher HaChaim* (loc. cit. par. 4).

26a. ArtScroll Ashkenaz *Siddur* p. 322.

26b. Ibid.

27. These *Kaddishim* are considered part of the Sabbath prayer-service (*Ba'er Heitev* §132 §§5, in the name of *Knesses Yechezkel*). Therefore, if two men are observing a *yahrzeit*, one on Friday

◄§ Other Times

17. Other times when the mourner recites *Kaddish* are:

(a) After a Torah discourse. This includes an aggadic (non-halachic) discourse.

(b) After a eulogy that included a Torah talk.

(c) After reciting Psalms.

In all cases, *Kaddish* is recited only in a *minyan* of ten or more men.

The *Acharonim* write that one should not recite *Kaddish* excessively.[28]

18. When there is no mourner in the synagogue, the *Kaddish* after *Aleinu* is recited by someone whose parent is not living.[29] Some rule that in a congregation where this is the custom, a mourner in the twelfth month is likewise permitted to recite that *Kaddish* [if there is no mourner who is in the eleven month period].[30]

When a mourner is present in the synagogue, no one else is allowed to recite *Kaddish*.[31]

19. If he will not have an opportunity to recite *Kaddish* afterwards, a mourner, or someone observing a *yahrzeit*, is permitted to recite *Kaddish* in the midst of *Pesukei D'zimrah*. He should do so where there is a break in the subject matter in a Psalm, or between one Psalm and the next.[32]

The regular order of the morning prayer-service is that the *Shemoneh Esrei* prayer is followed by *Uva L'Tzion* ("A redeemer shall come to Zion. . ."), which includes *Kedushah* ("Holy, holy, holy. . ."). This is followed by *Kaddish Tiskabel*

---

and one on the Sabbath, these *Kaddishim* are recited by the one whose *yahrzeit* is observed on the Sabbath.

28. *Gesher HaChaim* (loc. cit. par. 5).

29. *Rama* (*Orach Chaim* 132:2).

30. *Elef HaMagen* (*Dinei Kaddish Yasom* §4). In this case, reciting *Kaddish* after the eleventh month does not give the disrespectful impression that the mourner considers his parent wicked. This is because he is simply following the established custom [that if no mourner who is in the eleven months is present, someone else recites this *Kaddish*]. The same ruling is given by *Leket Yosher* p. 99.

31. *Mateh Efrayim* (*Dinei Kaddish Yasom* 4:3). "There are some sons who cannot lead the prayer-service to recite *Kaddish* and *Borchu* for the benefit of their parent. This is the case when the son is under the age of *bar mitzvah*, and sometimes even when he is a grown man, but for some other reason cannot lead the services. From the incident of R' Akiva [see above, footnote 1], we know the great benefit that [the son's recitation of *Kaddish* and *Borchu*] has for the deceased. Therefore, it was enacted that this *Kaddish* [after *Aleinu*] should be reserved for mourners, whether under or over the age of *bar mitzvah*."

Elef HaMagen (loc. cit. §§8) writes in the name of *Ma'avar Yabok*: "At the end of the prayer-service, *Pitum HaKetores* ("The Incense Mixture") is recited, and then *Aleinu* ("It is our duty to praise. . ."). After *Pitum HaKetores*, *Kaddish DeRabbanan* is recited, to cool *Gehinnom* for all the deceased of the world in general, through the recitation of this passage. . .and the *Kaddish* after *Aleinu* is called the Mourner's *Kaddish* (*Kaddish Yasom*). A son recites it for his parent, for it cools the fire of *Gehinnom* for an hour and a half" (*sha'ata u'falga*; but see above, footnote 22).

32. My master, father, and teacher, *zatzal*, in his manuscript work, *Zichron Eliahu*, citing *Orchos Chaim* (§132), in the name of *Yehudah Ya'aleh*. The same ruling is given by *Elef HaMagen* (commentary on *Mateh Efrayim*) *sha'ar* 4.

(Full *Kaddish*, which contains the phrase, תִּתְקַבֵּל צְלוֹתְהוֹן וּבָעוּתְהוֹן דְּכָל [בֵּית] יִשְׂרָאֵל, "May the prayers and supplications of the entire [Family of] Israel be accepted. . .").

Some rule that if the mourner arrives late to the prayer-service, and he does not have time to recite the *Shemoneh Esrei* prayer before the congregation reaches the *Kedushah* of *Uva L'Tzion*, he may lead the service from *Uva L'Tzion* and *Kaddish Tiskabel*[33] and the rest of the prayer service to the end. Then the mourner recites his own prayers in the usual order, individually, from the Morning Blessings.

◆§ Primary Benefit of *Kaddish* Is When Recited by Son

20. The main benefit of *Kaddish* for the deceased is derived when his or her own son recites it.[34]

◆§ *Kaddish* by a Daughter

21. If the deceased left only daughters, although some have permitted a daughter to recite *Kaddish* at a prayer-service in her home,[35] virtually all the other *Poskim* disagree and rule that a daughter should not recite *Kaddish*, even in her home, and even if her father commanded her to do so. If she wishes to benefit the soul of her father, she should be careful at all times, whether praying at the synagogue or at a prayer-service in her home, to listen attentively to *Kaddish* and answer *Amen* with the proper concentration. He Who knows the thoughts of all will consider this as if she had recited *Kaddish* in compliance with her father's command.[36]

---

33. *Zichron Eliahu*, citing *Pachad Yitzchak* (*os kuf* "*Kaddish*"). Responsa *Chelkas Yaakov* (part 2 §138) writes that if someone comes to the synagogue when the mourners are beginning to recite the *Kaddish* after *Aleinu*, he may join them in reciting *Kaddish*, even though he was not with them when they recited *Aleinu*.

34. That the son — rather than other relatives — is the primary one who should say *Kaddish* for the deceased, may be inferred from the story of R' Akiva (see above, footnote 1). Moreover, the Sages said (*Sanhedrin* 104a): "The son gives merit to the father." Likewise, *Rama* (§376) rules: "This *Kaddish* is only to be recited for one's parent, but not for other family members." The same ruling is given by responsa *Binyamin Zev* (§201). He points out that if this were not so, R' Akiva would not have had to seek out the son; he could simply have paid someone else to recite *Kaddish*.

35. *Shevus Yaakov* (part 2 §93). The same ruling is recorded by *Sdei Chemed* (*Aveilus* §160), citing responsa *Knesses Yechezkel*.

36. *Mishmeres Shalom* (*os kuf* §51) cites *Beis Lechem Yehudah* (376:§§5), who states in the name of *Sefer Chassidim*: "There is no halachic basis for a daughter's reciting *Kaddish*, and [such a practice] is ridiculous nonsense [שטות וכחוכא ואיטלולי]." The same ruling is cited by *Sdei Chemed* (*Aveilus* §160), citing many *Acharonim*.

See also *Pischei Teshuvah* (ad loc. §§3), citing *Chavos Ya'ir* (§222), who answers a question about someone who disappeared [and was presumed dead] without leaving a son. The father had commanded that his daughter should recite *Kaddish*. *Chavos Ya'ir* states: "According to the basic law, she should recite *Kaddish*, for [the recitation of *Kaddish*] by a daughter also gives benefit and satisfaction to the soul [of the departed]. Nevertheless, there is danger that this practice would weaken the customs of the Jewish people. And since it is a conspicuous matter, one should protest against it."

Sdei Chemed (loc. cit.) states that the same ruling is given by the following authorities: *Sha'arei Tzedek* (p. 190c); *Kiryas Chanah* (§35), and responsa *Knesses Yechezkel* cited there; *Kerem Shlomo* (p. 55b); and *Kemach Soless* (p. 169d). "The implication is that a daughter should not recite *Kaddish* at all, neither in the synagogue nor in her home." The same ruling is given by *Mateh Efrayim* (*Dinei Kaddish Yasom* 4:8), who states that even if the father had commanded his daughter [to recite

In some congregations, the custom is that if no sons were left, and the daughter is not yet *bas mitzvah*, they permit her to recite *Kaddish*, even in the synagogue. She does so after *Aleinu* and after the Song of the Day; or before the initial blessing of *Pesukei D'zimrah*, שֶׁאָמַר בָּרוּךְ, "Blessed is He Who spoke. . ."[37]

◄§ When There Is a Surviving Parent

21a. The custom is to recite *Kaddish* for one's mother even if one's father is living. The father does not have the right to prevent this.[38]

◄§ *Kaddish* by a Young Child

22. A child who has lost a parent must recite *Kaddish*, even if he has not reached *gil chinuch*, the age at which he can be taught to do *mitzvos*.[39] If an adult says the words of *Kaddish* aloud so that the child can repeat after him word by word, one must answer *Amen* to the child's recitation.[40]

If this adult is also a mourner, and is reciting *Kaddish* on his own behalf, as well

---

Kaddish], the command should not be obeyed, and one should protest against such a practice, even in a prayer-service in the daughter's home. "All the more so, she should not be allowed to recite any of the *Kaddishim* included in the prayer-service. This applies even if she is unmarried; and, all the more so, if she is married, God forbid that she should make her voice heard in public through reciting *Kaddish*, whether in the synagogue or in a *minyan* [elsewhere]. Instead, if she wishes to benefit the soul of her father, she should be careful at all times, whether praying at the synagogue or at a prayer-service in her home, to listen attentively to *Kaddish* and answer *Amen* with the proper concentration. He Who knows the thoughts of all will consider this as if she had recited *Kaddish* in compliance with her father's command."

37. *Chazon LaMo'ed* (chapt. 24 note 4). He writes: "And this is the custom followed by my teacher and father-in-law, *zal*" *Gesher HaChaim* (30:8:5).

38. *Rama* (376:4), citing *Beis Yosef*. The same ruling is given by *Pischei Teshuvah* (240:§§14), citing *Yam Shel Shlomo* (*Kiddushin* 1:§63). The reason is that the father would be violating the command '*You shall love your fellow-Jew as yourself*' [*Leviticus* 19:18]. However, *Be'er HaGolah* (§§8) writes: "In this *siman*, *Beis Yosef* cites *Kol Bo* . . .as stating that the father does have the right to prevent [his son from reciting *Kaddish*]; and he cites this same ruling at the end of *Hilchos Yoreh De'ah*, in the name of *Tashbatz*. . .but there he writes: 'However, the custom is that [the son] recites *Kaddish* even during the father's lifetime.' And this is the ruling cited by *Darkei Moshe* (ad loc. §§9)."

   Mishmeres Shalom (os kuf §42) writes: "See *Ribash* (§115), cited by *Magen Avraham* (§132 end of §§2). He states that the *mitzvah* of honoring one's father takes precedence, and therefore the son should not recite *Kaddish* [if the father protests]. See also *Teshuvah MeAhavah*, who rules that our custom is in accord with the opinion of *Yam Shel Shlomo*. And see *Birkei Yosef* for the correct explanation of our custom."

39. *Kol Bo Al Aveilus* (p. 373 note 29) writes: "It is obvious that a child, even below educable age [*gil chinuch*], must recite *Kaddish*. It could almost be said that the enactment of reciting *Kaddish* [at the end of the prayer-service] was instituted only for children — and certainly, also for children. See *Maharil* (*Hilchos Tefillah*), who states: 'If the child has lost a parent, he repeats [*Kaddish*] after someone, word by word.' And see *Rama*, end of §376. See also *Gesher HaChaim*, who writes: 'One should realize that when the great *Poskim* object to a child being allowed to recite *Kaddish*, they are only referring to the *Kaddishim* usually recited by the *chazzan*, such as the *Kaddish* after *Yishtabach*, or the one after the *Shemoneh Esrei*, or *Kaddish Tiskabel*. But the *Kaddishim* at the end [or beginning] of the prayer-service are recited even by a child.' "

40. *Kol Bo Al Aveilus* (loc. cit.), citing responsa *Matas Yado* (*Orach Chaim* §9).

as helping the child, one answers *Amen* to the adult, if he finishes first. [If, after a short interval, the child finishes, one must answer *Amen* to the child as well. But] if the child finishes almost simultaneously with the adult, one should not answer *Amen* to the child.[41] The determining time interval is a measure known as *k'dei dibbur*, defined as the time required to say, "*Shalom Aleichem Rebbe*" (approximately one or two seconds).

◆§ *Kaddish* by Grandsons and Other Relatives

23. If the deceased has no living sons, but has son's sons, these grandsons recite *Kaddish*.[42] If he has no son's sons, but has daughter's sons, some rule that these grandchildren have no rights to recite *Kaddish* where other mourners are present.[43] (See above, par. 6.) But others rule that they have the same rights as son's sons.[44]

24. If the deceased left no sons, some rule that his son-in-law is required to recite *Kaddish*.[45] Others disagree.[46]

25. If the deceased left neither sons nor grandsons, some rule that his father should recite *Kaddish*.

In this case, if someone else in the synagogue is in mourning for his own parent, the following agreement should be made: The mourning father recites one-third of

---

41. Ibid. He also discusses the case where the adult and the child are brothers. The adult is reciting *Kaddish* on his own behalf, but has the child recite it with him in order to train him, so that the child will be able to recite it even when the adult is not in the synagogue. In that case, rules *Kol Bo Al Aveilus*, one should answer *Amen* to the adult, but not to the child.

42. *Pischei Teshuvah* (376:§§7), citing *Ba'er Heitev* (by *Maharit*) §§11, who in turn cites the responsa of *Rama*. The same ruling is given by *Sdei Chemed* (*Aveilus* §158), citing *Shevus Yaakov* (part 2 §95). *Sdei Chemed* states that the *Acharonim* confirm this ruling of *Shevus Yaakov*. But *Pischei Teshuvah* (loc. cit.) cites *Knesses Yechezkel* as ruling that the son's son is not given the priority of a *ben shivah*, *ben shloshim*, or *yahrzeit*.

43. *Pischei Teshuvah* (loc. cit.), citing *Kiryas Chanah* (§35), who in turn cites *Mahari*, the author of *Knesses Yechezkel*. He rules that the daughter's son — and all the more so, the daughter herself — has no rights of precedence at all to recite *Kaddish* in the synagogue over other mourners; but if they wish to gather a *minyan* in their home, then the daughter's son — or someone whom they pay to recite *Kaddish* — is permitted to recite it for the deceased.

44. *Pischei Teshuvah* (loc. cit.) citing *Ba'er Heitev* (by *Maharit*). The same ruling is given by *Kaf HaChaim* (55:28), who cites *Knesses HaGedolah* (§403) as stating: "What is more, the custom now is to recite *Kaddish* for one's maternal grandfather or grandmother — [even] during the lifetime of one's parent — if the grandparents left no sons. One need fear no harmful consequences of reciting *Kaddish* during one's parents' lifetimes, since 'There is no sorcery in Jacob' [*Numbers* 23:23]."

45. *Sdei Chemed* (*Aveilus* §159), citing *Zera Emes* (part II, end of §148). And see *Mishmeres Shalom* (os kuf §58).

46. *Kiryas Chanah* (§35), cited by *Sdei Chemed* (loc. cit.). He explains that, although a son-in-law is required to honor his father-in-law, the obligation to recite *Kaddish* is not based on the requirement to honor one's parent (or parent-in-law). Rather, the obligation to recite *Kaddish* is based upon the fact that it gives merit to the departed soul. As the Talmud states: "The son gives merit to the father" (*Sanhedrin* 104a). Since a son-in-law does not give the merit which a son would give, the son-in-law is not obligated to recite *Kaddish*.

the *Kaddishim*, and the mourning son recites two-thirds of them. But the Mourner's *Kaddish* after *Aleinu* is recited only by the other mourner.[47]

Others rule, however, that the father has no rights of *Kaddish* if another mourner is present.[48]

As explained below, paragraph 37, in many congregations in our time, the custom is that all the mourners recite *Kaddish* simultaneously at the points in the prayer-service listed above (paragraph 12). In that case, the question of rights of precedence does not arise.

If the deceased's father is not living, *Kaddish* should be recited by a brother[49] or other relative.[50]

~§ Paying Someone to Recite *Kaddish*

26. If the deceased has no relatives to recite *Kaddish* for him, someone should be hired to do so. It brings more merit to the deceased if the person takes payment than if he does not.[51]

In the morning, before praying, this person should state: "All the *Kaddishim* I recite today are for the benefit of the soul of. . .(naming the deceased)." Then he should add (*Psalms* 90:17): וִיהִי נֹעַם ה' אֱלֹהֵינוּ עָלֵינוּ וּמַעֲשֵׂה יָדֵינוּ כּוֹנְנָה עָלֵינוּ וּמַעֲשֵׂה יָדֵינוּ

---

47. *Mateh Efrayim* (4:7); and *Shevus Yaakov* part 2:§93. The same ruling is given by *Mishmeres Shalom* (*os kuf* §52), citing *Tosafos* (*Sotah* 10b). This ruling is also cited by *Sdei Chemed* in the name of *Kemach Soless* (p. 170b, s.v. *av*).

  Sdei Chemed also cites *Be'er HaMayim* (§54) as ruling that a father should recite *Kaddish* for his child. He understands *Kaddish* to be a form of prayer, and relates this to the story of King David when he mourned over the death of his son, Avshalom [*II Samuel* 19:1, 5]. "And even if [the deceased] left brothers, it is more fitting for the father to recite *Kaddish* for his son or daughter, for his soul is bitterly grieved, and his soul mourns over the death of his son or daughter (may the Merciful One save us)" (*Elef HaMagen*, on *Mateh Efrayim* 4:§§13).

  Sdei Chemed also states: "If the deceased is an elder son, and hence the other sons were obligated to honor him during his lifetime, [the *halachah* is as follows]: If the father does not want the brothers of the deceased to recite *Kaddish* while he is living, then obviously the father should be the one to recite it, not the sons. However, if the father does not mind whether the sons recite *Kaddish*, then the question who should recite it is a matter of doubt."

48. *Noda BiYehudah* (*tinyana Orach Chaim* §8).

49. If one left a son-in-law as well as a brother, some rule that the brother takes precedence (*Elef HaMagen* loc. cit.). The same ruling is given by *Sdei Chemed* (*Aveilus os* 159), citing *Zera Emes* (as mentioned above, footnote 45). However, *Mishmeres Shalom* (*os kuf* §58) disagrees with *Sdei Chemed* and rules that the son-in-law takes precedence.

50. *Rama* 376:4.

51. *Kaf HaChaim* (55:30), based on *Beis Yosef* (end of §403), who states that the custom is to pay someone to recite *Kaddish* if the deceased did not leave a son. This ruling is also cited in *Ben Ish Chai* (*Parashas Vayechi* §15).

  Magen Avraham (132:§§2) writes that *Beis Yosef* implies that it gives more merit to the deceased to pay someone to recite *Kaddish* than to have someone else recite it without payment.

  Pischei Teshuvah (376:§§7) cites responsa *Chasam Sofer* (§345) as ruling that someone reciting *Kaddish* for payment has no rights to say *Kaddish* if there are other mourners.

  See also the responsa of *Rama MiPano* (§89), cited by *Pischei Teshuvah* (*Even HaEzer* 89:§§2). He rules that a husband is not obligated to pay someone to recite *Kaddish* for his wife.

כּוֹנְנֵהוּ, *'May the pleasantness of my Lord, our God, be upon us — may He establish our handiwork for us; our handiwork may He establish.'*[52]

27. One may accept payment to say *Kaddish* for a number of people. If he does so, some rule that he should recite [at least] one *Kaddish* a day for each deceased. Therefore, the number of people for whom he can recite *Kaddish* is limited by the number of *Kaddishim* he can recite each day.[53] However, some rule, to the contrary, that he may recite one *Kaddish* for a number of people.[54]

28. One authority writes that, during the year of mourning for one's parent, one may accept payment to recite *Kaddish* for someone else as well. If one does so, it is good to use part of the money to purchase additional candles for the soul of his parent. During the twelfth month of mourning for his parent, he should not recite *Kaddish* for someone else, even if this means financial loss. To recite *Kaddish* during this month would be disrespectful toward his parent.[55]

◄§ For Whom Does One Recite *Kaddish*?

29. [The purpose of Kaddish is to serve as a merit for the deceased to shield him from the judgment of *Gehinnom*. Theoretically, therefore, if the deceased were not required to undergo such judgment, there would be no need for *Kaddish* to be recited on his behalf. Nevertheless,] *Kaddish* is recited even for a *tzaddik* who was famous from youth for his Torah knowledge and piety; and likewise for someone martyred in sanctification of the Divine Name (*kiddush Hashem*).[56]

30. *Kaddish* is recited for a child if he had reached the age of understanding what a sin is (*bar da'as*), even if he had not reached the age of receiving Divine punishment for sins.[57]

If someone recites *Kaddish* for a child who was one year old or less, he should

---

52. *Kaf HaChaim* 55:30.

53. See responsa *Igros Moshe* (*Yoreh De'ah* §254): "He can accept payment from several people to recite *Kaddish*. However, he should recite one *Kaddish* per day for each one. It is good if he keeps a written record for himself, noting which *Kaddish* is for which person."

"All this is on the assumption that no one misunderstands the arrangement. But if the relative who is paying for the *Kaddish* thinks that the person being paid is reciting many *Kaddishim* for this deceased, it may be that this is exactly what he is paying for. In that case, there is a risk of committing fraud (*gezel*)." [I.e., if the one paying the money believes that the recipient is reciting many *Kaddishim* for his relative each day, but in fact he is reciting only one per day, the recipient may be defrauding the one who pays.] For more on this subject, see *Kol Bo Al Aveilus* (p. 376).

54. *Even Yaakov* (§50). The same ruling is given by responsa *Be'er Moshe* (the Debreciner Rav, *shlita*) IV:§97. He states that one and the same *Kaddish* can count for several people. He disputes the ruling of *Igros Moshe* cited in our previous footnote.

55. Responsa *Chelkas Yaakov* (III:§157).

56. Responsa of *Maharil* (§99). *Darkei Moshe* (376:§§9) confirms that "this is the custom."

57. *Sdei Chemed* (*Aveilus* §151), and *Pischei Teshuvah* (376:§§3). The same ruling is given by *Gesher HaChaim*, and by *Kol Bo Al Aveilus* (p. 371); and by responsa *Teshuras Shai* (*mahadura kamma* §61). They rule that one must recite *Kaddish* even for someone who died before the age of twenty.

not be prevented. However, he does not have rights of precedence over other mourners.[58] (And see above, pars. 6 and 25.)

31. If a *mumar* (one who rejected the Torah; see above 6:2) is killed by non-Jews, some rule that his sons should recite *Kaddish* for him.[59]

32. If one's Torah teacher dies without leaving sons, one should make an effort to recite *Kaddish* for him. However, this does not give one any rights of precedence over other mourners.[60]

◄§ Intent in Reciting *Kaddish*

33. When one recites *Kaddish*, leads the prayer-services, or recites *Borchu* ("Bless Hashem"), one should not intend thereby to protect or benefit the departed soul.[61] Instead, one's entire intent should be to sanctify the great Name of Hashem, Blessed is He. By this merit (that the name of Heaven is

---

58. *Gesher HaChaim* (30:8:9). The same ruling is given by responsa *Tzitz Eliezer* (part 7 ch. 6:7). He cites responsa *Vayitzbor Yosef* as ruling that it is correct to recite *Kaddish* even for a baby, and also to observe the *yahrzeit* and light a candle for the soul.

59. *Rama* (end of §376). And see *Taz* (ad loc. §§6), and *Shach* (ad loc. §§15). They state that this applies only if the *mumar* is killed, since being killed gives him atonement; but if he died in his bed, [i.e., of natural causes, his sons do not recite *Kaddish* for him].

And see *Gesher HaChaim*, who states that if the deceased was a non-believer (*poker*) and threw off the yoke of observance, or if he committed suicide (in such a manner that it is clear that his suicide was deliberate), his sons may recite *Kaddish* for him only in a *minyan* where there are no other mourners. But if other mourners are present, the sons of that person may not say *Kaddish* (See *Chasam Sofer* §326, and *Shach* 345:§§1).

Gesher HaChaim also writes, in the name of *Chasam Sofer*, that even where no other mourners are present, the sons of a non-believer cannot recite *Kaddish HaGadol* (the Great *Kaddish*, containing the passage beginning, בְּעָלְמָא דִּי הוּא עָתִיד לְאִתְחַדָּתָא, "in the world which will be renewed. . .").

60. *Sdei Chemed* (*Aveilus* §157), citing responsa *Chasam Sofer* (*Orach Chaim* §164). The same ruling is given by responsa *Kiryas Chanah* (§35). Responsa *Knesses Yechezkel* cites *Lechem HaPanim*, who found it written that a *talmid muvhak* (primary disciple) recites *Kaddish* for his *rav*. *Kiryas Chanah* interprets this as informing us that there is no objection to the disciple's reciting *Kaddish* for his *rav*; but he does not have permission to recite *Kaddish* if other mourners are present. And see *Sdei Chemed* (loc. cit.), who further explains this ruling.

61. In the testament included in *Yad Eliahu* (Ragolar), we find: "Also, when reciting *Kaddish*, praying, or reciting *Borchu*, and when reciting the prayers at the conclusion of the Sabbath . . . God forbid that one should allow ulterior motives to enter into one's thoughts: [for example,] that one is giving satisfaction to [the departed] soul, saving it from the punishment of *Gehinnom* and the sufferings of the grave. God forbid that one should recite these things with such thoughts in mind — one should not even entertain such thoughts before the recitation [of *Kaddish*] or before the prayers. This would destroy all the effort, the prayer, and the sanctity; for the rule in Heaven is that they do not tolerate any foreign intent, but only that all should be for the sake of heaven." The same ruling is given by *Gesher HaChaim* (chapt. 30 note 2).

However, *Olas Tamid*, by the gaon R' Sh. Huminer, zatzal, (ch. 23) writes, citing *Darkei Chaim*: "However, in two places one may have intent to benefit the soul of the deceased. One place is [in *Kaddish*, at the passage:] יְהֵא שְׁלָמָה רַבָּא, '*May there be abundant peace. . .upon all Israel.*' Here one may intend to include the 'soul of the deceased, X ben Y.' The other place is [in the final passage of *Kaddish*:] עֹשֶׂה שָׁלוֹם בִּמְרוֹמָיו, '*He Who makes peace in His heights. . .*' Here, too, one may include 'the soul of X ben Y — may he have a blessing of peace from Hashem, Who makes peace in His heights.' "

sanctified because of the deceased), the soul will be saved from the punishment of *Gehinnom*. [62]

◄§ Laws of Reciting *Kaddish*

34. *Kaddish* can be recited only in the presence of ten male Jews who have reached the age of *bar mitzvah* (thirteen years and a day). The one reciting *Kaddish* is counted among the ten. Such a group of ten is called a *minyan*. This requirement of a *minyan* applies whether the *Kaddish* is recited during prayer, after Torah-study, or after the recitation of Psalms. [63]

If fewer than a *minyan* prayed or learned together, and afterwards were joined by enough men to make up a *minyan*, the correct thing to do is to recite a chapter of Psalms or read three [or more] verses of Scripture, and then recite *Kaddish*. [64]

Kaddish DeRabbanan [the Rabbis' *Kaddish*] can be recited even if fewer than ten men — even only one or two — studied, as long as a *minyan* is present when it is recited.

It can even be recited by someone other than the ones who studied. [64a] However, some rule that this applies only to learning which is usually conducted in a congregation — for example, the *baraisa of R' Yishmael* which is recited before *Shacharis*, and the like; but for other kinds of learning, *Kaddish DeRabbanan* may be recited only by one of those who took part in the learning. [64b]

---

62. *Gesher HaChaim* (loc. cit.).

   Sefer HaChaim, by the brother of *Maharal MiPrague*, (2:8) writes: "The Torah itself alludes to *Kaddish* and its great benefit, in the words of Balaam: '*May my soul die the death of the just*' (*Numbers* 23:10). The last word of this phrase, יְשָׁרִים, forms the initials of the response to *Kaddish*, יְהֵא שְׁמֵהּ רַבָּא מְבָרַךְ, '*May His great Name be blessed . . .*'.

   "The main reason for reciting *Kaddish* seems to be as follows. Death only happens to those who sin, and most people die because of the sin of *chillul Hashem* (desecration of the Name), for which atonement is not complete until one dies; and when the Holy One, Blessed is He, punishes the sinner, His Name is sanctified. . .Therefore, the son of this deceased sinner stands up before the congregation and recites, '*May His great Name be magnified and sanctified . . .*' — that is to say: 'I am comforted for my father's death, since through his death the Name of my Father Who is in heaven is magnified and sanctified.' Immediately, the sin of *chillul Hashem* which the father committed is atoned for."

63. *Shulchan Aruch* (*Orach Chaim* 55:1,4).

64. *Mishnah Berurah* (55:§§2), citing "the consensus of the *Acharonim*." He also cites *Taz*, who
   rules that even if they recited [Psalms or the Torah passage] without a *minyan*, it is sufficient that a *minyan* be present when *Kaddish* is recited. *Magen Avraham* (§69 and §234) rules to the contrary. And from the commentary of *Gra* on §234, it is clear that he agrees with *Magen Avraham*. And see *Pri Megaddim* (*Mishbetzos Zahav os* 3), from which it is clear that, regarding *Pesukei D'zimrah* and the *Maariv* prayer, *Magen Avraham* agrees with *Taz*. See also *Gesher HaChaim* (30:8:11), who writes: "After the fact (*bediavad*), if it is difficult to arrange for the *minyan* to recite [Psalms or the Torah passage] with him, one may rely on the ruling of *Taz*, who rules that the individual may recite *Kaddish* after Torah-study or the recitation of Psalms, as long as there is a *minyan* to answer to the *Kaddish*."

64a. *Be'ur Halachah* (§155).

64b. The *gaon* R' Moshe Feinstein, *zatzal* (*Kovetz Am HaTorah* 12:8).

35. If *Kaddish* is begun in the presence of ten men, and then one or more leave, the *Kaddish* which had already been started should be completed[65] — as long as the majority of the ten remain.[66] Nevertheless, those who leave are committing a transgression. To them applies the verse, 'Those who abandon *Hashem* will perish' (Isaiah 1:28).[67] But if ten will remain, others are permitted to leave.[68]

✥ Bowing During Kaddish

36. One who recites *Kaddish* should bow at the following points:

(a) יִתְגַּדֵּל [*Yisgadeil*][68a] [or: *Yisgadal*], "May His great Name grow exalted and sanctified. . ."

(b) יְהֵא שְׁמֵהּ רַבָּא [*Y'hei sh'mei rabba*], "May His great Name be blessed. . ."

(c) יִתְבָּרַךְ [*Yisbarach*], "Blessed, praised, glorified. . ."

(d) בְּרִיךְ הוּא [*B'rich hu*], "Blessed is He."

(e) אָמֵן [*Amen*].

However, some have the custom not to bow at all during *Kaddish*.[69]

✥ Recitation in Unison

37. In our day, the custom in most congregations is that when there is more than one mourner, all recite each *Kaddish* together,[69a] regardless whether one

---

65. *Shulchan Aruch* (55:2). And *Mishnah Berurah* (loc. cit. §§9) writes: "If the *Kaddish* is the one before *Borchu*, *Derech HaChaim* writes, in the name of *Elyah Rabbah*, that one may also recite *Borchu*, since these form one unit. But *Ma'amar Mordechai* disagrees."

66. Sometimes the *halacha* requires not just a simple majority (six), but *ruba demincara*, "a majority that is apparent to the eye" (seven). *Mishnah Berurah* (citing *Pri Megaddim*) states that in our case, six are sufficient.

67. *Rama* (loc. cit.). And *Mishnah Berurah* (ad loc. §§12) writes: "It seems to me that this means if one does not wait until the congregation completes a particular section of the prayer-service. But if he waits until they complete the section, this is sufficient. For example, if someone is the tenth man for the recitation of *Borchu*, he is not required to wait until the *chazzan* finishes reciting the *Shemoneh Esrei* aloud; for that is a different section of the prayer-service. But if he is the tenth man when the *chazzan* begins repeating the *Shemoneh Esrei* aloud, he must remain until they finish the whole *seder kedushah* (*Ashrei* through *Uva L'Tzion*), as well as the whole *Kaddish* (*Kaddish Tiskabel*) which follows. And the *halacha* is similar for other sections of the prayer-service."

68. *Rama* (loc. cit.). However, *Mishnah Berurah* (§§14) writes that they may do so only if they have already heard *Kedushah*, and the subsequent *Kaddishim*, until *Aleinu* ("It is our duty to praise. . ."). See *Be'ur Halacha* (ad loc. s.v. *mikol makom*), who writes: "If the tenth man violated the *halachah* and left, one might ask: Is the ninth man permitted to leave? — since in any case the ten men required for the *Shechinah* (Divine Presence) are not there, and the congregation will be able to complete the *Kaddish* which had already been started, even if he leaves. This question requires study." See also *Be'ur Halacha* (ad loc. s.v. *aval im nish'aru*).

68a. *Shulchan Aruch* (56:4). And *Kaf HaChaim* (§38, citing *Yad Aharon*) states that one should bow at each *Amen*.

69. This is in accord with the ruling of *Gra* (ad loc.). He writes that one should not bow, since one should not add to the bowings enumerated by the Sages (*Gesher HaChaim* 30:6:10).

69a. See *Pischei Teshuvah* (376:§§6). He cites responsa *Divrei Iggeres* (§7). "He, of blessed memory, enacted in his land that all the mourners recite *Kaddish*; and there he explains his

has a higher level of obligation than another. Even someone who is not a mourner, but is reciting *Kaddish* for payment, recites it with the mourners. Some authorities have objected to this custom.[70]

---

reasons. And in *Siddur Beis-Kel Amudei Shamayim*, by *Yavetz* (p. 174b), he writes: 'As for the detailed laws of the Ashkenazic community regarding precedence in reciting *Kaddish*, I shall not discuss them here, for they are purely a matter of custom. And the Sefardic custom in this matter is very good and right: If there are a number [of mourners in the congregation], all of them have the right to recite *Kaddish*, and they recite it in unison. This eliminates disputes and endless arguments about a matter which has no root or basis.' "

See also *Kaf HaChaim* (55:31), who writes that if a congregation has studied Oral Torah or recited Psalms, and they all wish to recite *Kaddish*, they are permitted to do so. "This," he states, "may be inferred from the words of *Mahari Eish* in *Bnei Yehudah* (§3). The same ruling is given by *Rav Pe'alim* (part 2:§14), and in *Ben Ish Chai* (*Parashas Vayechi* §16). But he writes: 'It is preferable (*lechatchilah*) to be careful that one of the congregation should not recite *Kaddish*, but answer the others.' But in my humble opinion, if this is the case, then two should answer, since וְאָמְרוּ אָמֵן, 'Now respond, *Amen*,' is a plural form."

The same ruling is given by responsa *Minchas Yitzchak* (part 4 §30). He states that it is only the *Kaddishim* recited during the prayer-service that require nine to answer, but for the Mourner's *Kaddish* (*Kaddish Yasom*) this is not required, since it is a voluntary *Kaddish* and those reciting it are not serving as proxies to fulfill an obligation of the congregation. But he writes: "In any case, they should try to make sure that two members of the congregation are answering to the *Kaddish*."

70. See *Chasam Sofer* (§159). He cites the words of *Yavetz* (quoted in our previous footnote), and comments: "It would seem that this is a good custom, and it is better for a *mitzvah* to be done by many than by an individual. And I am surprised at [the custom of] our forefathers, for whom the Torah was an eternal inheritance, as *Rosh* writes in a responsum cited by *Beis Yosef* (*Yoreh De'ah*, end of §82). How could we suspect them of going wrong and twisting the path? Moreover, at first glance it would seem difficult to understand the custom that the *ben shivah* [a mourner in the first seven days] has precedence over the *ben shloshim* [one in the first thirty days]. . .

"But [the answer is] that the principal benefit of *Kaddish* for the deceased is not in the fact that the person recites the words, but that he gives the congregation the merit of answering *Amen* many times, as well as answering, יְהֵא שְׁמֵהּ רַבָּא, 'May His great Name be blessed forever and ever. . .' — which is a very powerful utterance — and בָּרוּךְ ה' הַמְבֹרָךְ לְעוֹלָם וָעֶד, 'Blessed is Hashem, the blessed One, for all eternity.' By acting as an intermediary for the congregation, [the one reciting *Kaddish*] gives merit to his parents. Thus, our custom [that only one person at a time recites *Kaddish*] is well-founded; for if many recite *Kaddish* at the same time, only one of them is causing [the congregation to answer]. The rest are only accessories, which is insubstantial. If so, each one would rush to be first, so that the congregation would answer to him and not to someone else.

"Thus it follows that the aforementioned rules of precedence are also valid, for without doubt, the congregants also receive great merit, since they cause merit to those deceased. . .Thus, the greater the level of need of the deceased — i.e., [in descending order] one within *shivah*, one within *shloshim*, and one whose *yahrzeit* is being observed — the more merit the congregants receive for helping him by responding to the *Kaddish* recited for him, as opposed to others' *Kaddishim*. Therefore, the congregants certainly do not prefer someone who is in the Twelve Months to recite *Kaddish*, thereby causing them to lose the great merit [they would have had for answering to a deceased with a higher level of need]. . ."

Chazon LaMo'ed (26:§§11) writes: "Responsa *Yaskil Avdi* (V:§23) states that if someone repeats *Kaddish* along with the *chazzan*, word by word, the *Amen* answered by the congregation applies to his recitation as well. 'And this was the custom instituted in the Chassidic congregation of Beth Kel. The *chazzan* would recite *Kaddish* with the kabbalistic intentions (*kavanos*) prescribed by the *Ari zal*, and were someone else to recite it aloud with him, it would confuse him and interfere with the *kavanos*. Therefore, the rabbis there instituted that whoever needed to recite *Kaddish* would recite it in a whisper along with the *chazzan*, and this, with God's help, is effective.'

"The same ruling is offered by responsa *Bnei Tzion* (§122), who writes: 'The Ashkenazic custom is

In some congregations, the custom is that all recite *Kaddish* together, except for the *Kaddish* after *Aleinu*, which is recited only by the mourner with the highest level of obligation.

38. In congregations where the custom is for all the mourners to recite each *Kaddish*, they must be careful to recite it in unison.[71]

If one finishes before another, the *halachah* of answering *Amen* depends upon the time interval between them. The determining measure is *k'dei dibbur*, the time required to say *Shalom Aleichem Rebbe* (about one or two seconds). If the interval between the first and last to finish is less than *k'dei dibbur*, one may answer to either the first or the last, and one's answer counts for all of them. If the interval between two people reciting *Kaddish* is more than *k'dei dibbur*, one must answer *Amen* to each of them.[72]

✺ Precedence in *Kaddish*

39. There are five categories of mourners regarding the recitation of *Kaddish*:[73]

---

better: that each individual recites *Kaddish*, in accord with the law and his custom. . .and although the Sefardim recite it all together, let them follow their custom.' The same ruling is given by *Gesher HaChaim*, who writes: 'It is more desirable that each individual should recite only one *Kaddish*, enunciating it slowly and clearly, and the congregation should listen to each recitation of *Kaddish* and answer it correctly. This is better than having many *Kaddishim* recited simultaneously, in such a way that none achieves the desired result.'

"See also Responsa *Tirosh Veyitzhar Tiferes Banim* (§28), who writes: 'Regarding the *Kaddishim*, there is no objection to having all recite it together. But in some places, the custom is for only one person to recite it, and they cast lots [to determine who recites it]. Possibly, this custom was instituted because sometimes there is just barely a *minyan* for prayer, and under that circumstance it is correct that only one person should recite *Kaddish*. . .In any case, it is proper that there should be as many *minyanim* in the synagogue as there are people who need to recite *Kaddish*. Each person should recite it for his *minyan*, and each *minyan* should hear their mourner.' "

71. This eliminates the problem of doubts about whom to answer, and also the problem that the congregation does not properly hear the *Kaddish*. In addition, responsa *Ma'adnei Asher* (§119) writes that he saw it written in the name of the *gaon* R' Nassan Adler, that if all recite *Kaddish* together, word by word, the rules of precedence mentioned by *Rama* do not apply. However, some also question this custom. See *Kol Bo Al Aveilus* (p. 373), in the name of *Shomer Tzion HaNe'eman* (p. 333). He also cites *Minchas Kena'os* by the *gaon* Maharatz Chayus (§7), who states: "The *chazzan* stands on the *bimah* (central platform) and recites *Kaddish*, and the mourners repeat after him. . ." But he states that *Binyan Tzion* raises objections to this custom.

72. *Pischei Teshuvah* (ad loc. §§6), citing responsa *Halachos Ketanos* (2:§48).

73. *Be'ur Halachah* (§132 *Kuntres Maamar Kaddishin*) explains the difference between the levels of obligation. "It would seem that the Sages established [these different levels] based on the degree of [the Attribute of Strict Justice] prevailing over the deceased. The *Kaddish* is to defend [the deceased] from punishment]. Thus, during *shivah*, the deceased needs more mercy and merit; and during *shloshim*, he needs more mercy than during the Twelve Months.

"Concerning the *yahrzeit*, there are two considerations: either the fact that on that day the usual protective forces (*mazal*) of the mourner were weakened, as *Levush* writes in *Yoreh De'ah* (402:12); or in order to give spiritual satisfaction (*nachas ruach*) to one's father or mother, to protect them, and to atone for their souls.

"As for the final day of reciting *Kaddish* (*yom hafsakah*), the custom is that the mourners [who are in the Twelve Months] allow him all the *Kaddishim*. This is because the custom is to stop reciting

(a) a mourner during *shivah* (*ben shivah*).[74]

(b) a mourner during *shloshim* (*ben shloshim*).

(c) a mourner during the Twelve Months of mourning (*ben yud-beis chodesh*).

(d) a mourner on his final day of reciting *Kaddish* (*ben yom hafsakah*).

(e) one observing a *yahrzeit*, anniversary of the death.

40. A mourner in *shivah* takes precedence over one in *shloshim*.[75]

Kaddish a month before [the end of the Twelve Months]. Thus, in effect, he is forgoing [his rights to all the *Kaddishim* he would have taken] during an entire month. Therefore, they grant him this precedence. This is why [the *ben yom hafsakah*] has no rights of precedence over a *ben shloshim* or someone with a *yahrzeit*; they benefit nothing from [his forgoing the twelfth month], since in any case they would have had precedence over him."

And see the responsa of R' Shlomo Eiger (*Yoreh De'ah* §47) who states that being a *Kohen* or *Levi* does not in itself give a mourner precedence over another mourner.

See also *Emek Berachah* (Pomeranzig), who states that if a person has precedence over someone else in reciting *Kaddish* or serving as *chazzan*, he should not try to be kind to the other person by forgoing his right of precedence; for the right belongs to the deceased. However, if the other person would otherwise suffer greatly, one may forgo the right of precedence.

74. *Be'ur Halachah* (loc. cit.) clarifies the following points:

A person is defined as a *ben shivah* during the first seven days from burial. This applies even if the person saying *Kaddish* is not observing the seven days of mourning — for example, if a Festival canceled *shivah* (see above, chapt. 34). Since *Kaddish* is not a matter of mourning, but of giving honor to the deceased, the Festival does not cancel the recitation of *Kaddish*, even though it cancels the observance of mourning.

With regard to counting these seven days — and likewise the thirty days — from burial [for the purpose of reciting *Kaddish*], we do not apply the rule that "part of the [last] day is counted as a whole day." Therefore, the mourner in *shivah* or mourner in *shloshim* has his rights of precedence even at the *Minchah* Prayer of the seventh or the thirtieth day.

If news of the death was received sometime within the first thirty days from burial (*shmu'ah krovah*), one must observe *shivah* and *shloshim* from the day of hearing the news (see above, chapt. 31). Nevertheless, one's rights of precedence in reciting *Kaddish* are counted only from the day of the burial [not from the day one began to observe mourning].

75. *Be'ur Halachah* (loc. cit.) states the following rules:

If a mourner in *shivah* who has reached at least the age of *bar mitzvah* goes to the synagogue on the Sabbath, he has the right to recite all the *Kaddishim*. This applies even if he [did not go to the synagogue] during the *shivah* week, but had a *minyan* in his home. At the synagogue on the Sabbath, he takes precedence over a mourner in *shloshim*, a *yahrzeit*, and, all the more so, a mourner in the Twelve Months. This applies to the *Kaddishim* during the main part of the prayer-service. However, the *Kaddish* recited after the Song of the Day (*Shir Shel Yom*), of those recited after the recitation of Psalms, should be divided as follows: Someone observing a *yahrzeit* should receive one *Kaddish* without having to take part in a drawing of lots. For the other *Kaddishim* recited after Psalms, the one observing a *yahrzeit* should draw lots with the other mourners.

If a mourner in *shivah* who is under the age of *bar mitzvah* goes to the synagogue during all the seven days, he has the right to recite all the *Kaddishim* which are a regular part of the prayer-service. He even takes precedence completely over a mourner in *shloshim*. However, someone observing a *yahrzeit* should be given one *Kaddish*. If the number of people observing *yahrzeit* is equal to the number of *Kaddishim* in the prayer-service, these people take precedence completely over the mourner in *shivah* who is under the age of *bar mitzvah*.

The rules in the previous paragraph, which apply to a mourner in *shivah* who is under the age of *bar mitzvah*, also apply to the following persons:

(a) someone over the age of *bar mitzvah* who goes to the synagogue during *shivah*;

A mourner in *shloshim* takes precedence over anyone except one in *shivah* .[76]

Mourners who are in the Twelve Months customarily allow the mourner on his final day of reciting *Kaddish* to recite all the *Kaddishim* that day, and also to lead the services during that day.

One observing a *yahrzeit* takes precedence over a mourner in the Twelve Months in reciting all the *Kaddishim* and leading the services that day.[77]

41. If two mourners are present and only one of them is capable of leading the services, the one who leads the services does not thereby forfeit his rights to any of the *Kaddishim* .

The same applies if both are capable of leading the service, but only one of them does so, because he is acceptable to the congregation while the other mourner is not.[78]

42. If several brothers are among the mourners, each one has rights equal to any other mourner, even though all the brothers are reciting *Kaddish* for the same father.[79]

43. If two mourners have the same level of obligation (see above, par. 39), but one of them is a resident of the community[80] and the other is a visitor, the resident

---

(b) someone over the age of *bar mitzvah* who goes to the synagogue on *Yom Tov* because the Festival canceled his *shivah* ;

(c) one whose family member died during a Festival. Since he goes to the synagogue during the seven days, he has the same rights of precedence as a mourner in *shivah* who is under the age of *bar mitzvah* .

76. However, the *Kaddishim* recited after Psalms, after the Song of the Day, and after *Mizmor Shir Chanukas*. . . ('A psalm, a song for the inauguration of the Temple. . .' the introductory psalm to *Pesukei D'zimrah*) are given to mourners who are in the Twelve Months.

If a mourner in *shloshim* and a *yahrzeit* are both present, the *yahrzeit* should recite the *Kaddish* after *Maariv* , and the mourner in *shloshim* should recite two *Kaddishim* , one during *Shacharis* and one during *Minchah* . If the one observing the *yahrzeit* will not be coming to the synagogue for *Maariv* , he should recite the first *Kaddish* of *Shacharis* . But if there are many people observing *yahrzeit* , they take precedence completely over the mourner in *shloshim* .

If a mourner in *shloshim* and a mourner on his final day of reciting *Kaddish* are both present, the mourner in his final day of reciting *Kaddish* recites only one *Kaddish* , and the mourner in *shloshim* recites the rest.

If a person is a mourner in *shloshim* for his father and also a mourner in the Twelve Months for his mother, he has only the rights of precedence of a mourner in *shloshim* , since the *Kaddishim* he recites count for both his father and mother. But if there are many people observing *yahrzeiten* , so that they take precedence completely over the mourner in *shloshim* , he can in any case recite one of the *Kaddishim* after Psalms, like any other mourner in the Twelve Months (*Be'ur Halachah*, §132).

77. However, for the *Kaddishim* recited after Psalms, after the Song of the Day, and after *Mizmor Shir Chanukas*. . . ('A psalm, a song for the inauguration of the Temple. . .' the introductory psalm to *Pesukei D'zimrah*), the one observing the *yahrzeit* cannot take precedence over the mourners (ibid.).

78. Ibid.

79. *Rama* (376:4). *Gilyon Maharsha*, commenting on *Shach* (ad loc. §§12), explains the reason: either because each brother is obligated to honor his father; or because of the merit of the father, who merited to have more than one son.

80. "Resident" is defined as one who lives in the town. This includes not only those who pay taxes or are employed by the community, but also those poor who [do not pay taxes or work, but]

takes full precedence over the visitor. This includes the right to lead the services and the right to recite *Kaddish*.[81]

Nevertheless, if both of them are within the Twelve Months, the visitor on his first day in the community takes precedence over the resident. This includes the right to lead the services and the right to recite *Kaddish*.

Likewise, the visitor has the right to lead the services once, and recite *Kaddish* once every thirty days.[82]

44. The following are possible situations of precedence in *Kaddish*:

    (a) Two mourners are present in a community. One is a resident who has a *yahrzeit*. The other is a visitor who is within *shloshim*. The resident should recite the first and second *Kaddish*, and the visitor, the third.

    (b) A visitor has a *yahrzeit*. A resident is within *shloshim* or within the Twelve Months. The visitor recites only one *Kaddish*, namely, the first one.

    (c) The visitor is within *shloshim* and the resident, within Twelve Months. They equally divide the *Kaddishim*, as well as the opportunities to serve as *sheliach tzibbur*.[83]

45. If a person who regularly prays at a certain synagogue comes to a different synagogue in the same town to recite *Kaddish*, the mourners in that synagogue can prevent him from reciting *Kaddish*, even if the newcomer is within *shivah*. His rights are less than those of a visitor, since he has a place to pray.[84]

46. If a person gathers a *minyan* at a synagogue, and without his efforts the *minyan* would not have assembled, he has more rights to *Kaddish* than one within *shloshim*, someone who has a *yahrzeit*, and the like.[85]

---

permanently reside there.

    If a resident employs a tutor, or houses yeshivah students, or employs a hired servant [who lives with him], these are considered residents, if they are unmarried. But if they have a wife and children in another town, they are considered non-residents (visitors).

    If the deceased left sons who live in another town, and they come to their father's town, the fact that their father was a resident does not give them the status of resident, even if the father is buried in the town cemetery (*Be'ur Halachah* loc. cit.).

81. *Be'ur Halachah*.

82. Ibid.

83. Consider the following case: Three mourners are present. One is a resident who is a mourner in *shloshim*. The second is also a resident, and is observing a *yahrzeit*. The third is a visitor who is observing a *yahrzeit*.

    In this case, the visitor has the right to recite one *Kaddish*. The resident who is observing a *yahrzeit* cannot tell the visitor, "I take precedence over you," because the visitor could answer: "I'm not taking the *Kaddish* from you, but from the mourner in *shloshim*."

    Therefore, the resident who is observing a *yahrzeit* should recite the first *Kaddish*; the visitor should recite the second one; and the mourner in *shloshim*, the third one (ibid.).

84. Ibid.

85. *Elef HaMagen* (commentary on *Mateh Efrayim*) I:§§3, citing *Kuntres Oveir Orach* (a work appended to *Orchos Chaim*). Evidence for this ruling is cited from *Sifrei* (*Parashas Pinchas*), which states that the Holy One, Blessed is He, said to Moshe Rabbeinu, may peace be upon him: "He who guarded the fig tree should eat its fruit. . ." *Elef HaMagen* adds that a number of *geonim* confirmed this ruling. "And it seems to me, on this basis, that the same would apply to someone who volunteered

47. According to the above rules, it could happen that some mourners, either residents or visitors, might not have an opportunity to recite *Kaddish* during a given prayer-service. If so, they are permitted to recite additional Psalms at the end of the service, and then recite *Kaddish*.[86]

48. One must be careful not to quarrel in the synagogue over the right to lead the services or to recite *Kaddish*. The main purpose of *Kaddish* is to repair the sin of desecrating the Divine Name (*chilul Hashem*), and to consecrate the Name of Heaven. Through quarreling, one causes *chilul Hashem*.[87] If there is danger of quarreling, God forbid, it is preferable that all recite *Kaddish* in unison.[88]

49. If a person preempts another's right to recite *Kaddish*, he neither benefits himself nor deprives the other person. The *Kaddish* is counted for the merit of the soul for whom it should have been recited.[89]

50. On the final day of reciting *Kaddish*, a person should be called up to the Torah.[90]

---

his house so that a *minyan* could pray there; for this same reason, he should have precedence over other mourners in reciting *Kaddish*. The same would apply to one who delivers a Torah talk or teaches others; the custom is to recite *Kaddish DeRabbanan* afterwards [and the person who spoke or taught should have precedence in reciting this *Kaddish*]. The same would apply to the one who reads the Torah, after which Half-*Kaddish* is recited. All these should have precedence over other mourners."

It would seem that this ruling applies only if the one who read the Torah is a mourner. Otherwise, as is clarified above, par. 14, the *Kaddish* after the Torah-reading should be recited by the mourners, not by the one who reads the Torah.

86. *Ner LeEliahu* (*Minhagei Kedimah* §34).

87. Ibid. §11.

88. *Kitzur Shulchan Aruch* (26:18). Responsa *Bnei Tzion* (§122) writes: "In our age there are many mourners, and it is impossible to give each one even one *Kaddish*. Therefore, the custom prevails that all [the mourners] recite the *Kaddishim* simultaneously."

89. *Pischei Teshuvah* (376:§§7), citing *Chasam Sofer* (§345), who heard this ruling in the name of *Heshev Yaakov*. *Chasam Sofer* explains that this is based on the statement of the Talmud (*Bava Kamma*): "If someone steals someone else's *olah* (the animal intended for a burnt offering) and sacrifices it, he is exempt [from paying for it] because the original owner is credited as if he sacrificed it." And see responsa *Maharam* Shick (*Orach Chaim* §57).

90. *Kol Bo Al Aveilus* (p. 370) citing *Duda'ei HaSadeh* (§4). See the note by the *gaon* M. Ginz at the end of that work.

CHAPTER FORTY

Leading the Prayer-Service

1. The custom is that the mourner leads the prayer-service during the entire eleven months [during which he recites *Kaddish*].[1] Leading the services is even more effective [in benefiting the soul of the deceased] than reciting the Mourner's *Kaddish*, which was originally instituted only for children [since they cannot lead the services].[2]

If one is unable to serve as leader for the entire prayer-service, he should do so from *Ashrei* and *Uva L'Tzion* to the end of the services.[3] One should especially make an effort to lead the *Maariv* services at the conclusion of the Sabbath, since this is the time when the souls return to *Gehinnom*.[4] Likewise, one should make an effort to lead the services every day for *Maariv*, since this is a time when the Attribute of Strict Justice is particularly powerful.[5]

2. It is a *mitzvah* for the congregation to allow the mourner to serve as leader, for this gives spiritual satisfaction to the deceased and rescues him from the

---

1. *Rama* (376:4). *Mateh Efrayim* (4:2) writes that it is possible to lead the services [for the benefit of the deceased] even after eleven months. However, *Rama* (loc. cit.) implies the contrary. See *Sheivet HaLevi* (*Yoreh De'ah tinyana* §161), who states that one may lead the services intermittently during the twelfth month. The *gaon* R' Moshe Feinstein, *zatzal* (*Kovetz Am HaTorah kovetz* 12:14) writes that one should lead the services during the twelfth month, even though one is not obligated to do so.

2. *Rama* (376:4.).

   Aruch HaShulchan (376:12) writes: "If a person is able to lead the services, he should recite the *Kaddishim* that occur *during* the prayer-service, for they are the primary ones. As for the *Kaddishim* that occur at the *end* of the prayer-service, he should leave them for the children, and not 'grab' them. Many unlearned people make the mistake of thinking that the main *Kaddish* is the one at the end of the prayer-service, which is called the Mourner's *Kaddish* (*Kaddish Yasom*). [Those who make this mistake are like the unlearned who] (*Jonah* 4:11) 'do not know their right from their left.' "

3. *Rama* (loc. cit.).

4. *Rama* (loc. cit.).

   She'arim MeTzuyanim BeHalachah (§26) writes: "In some communities, the custom is that when someone has a *yahrzeit* during the week, he leads the *Maariv* services at the conclusion of the preceding Sabbath. [However, if a mourner is present,] the mourner certainly has precedence. But my teacher, *Maharash* Engel, (part V §43) writes that, nevertheless, if a town has an established custom that the one observing the *yahrzeit* should lead the services even in the presence of mourners, and if the majority of the congregation did not object to this custom when it was first instituted, and now too they do not wish to abolish it, the mourner does not have the power to override the custom."

5. *Kitzur Shulchan Aruch* (26:1).

punishment of *Gehinnom*. Nevertheless, if the mourner cannot pronounce the letters [correctly], or has some similar difficulty, he should not lead the services.

If one of the by-laws of the synagogue stipulates that mourners are not allowed to lead the services throughout the week, but instead the permanent *chazzan* should continue as usual, this by-law should not be abolished.[6]

3. If a person — whose *nusach* (version of the prayers) is *Nusach Ashkenaz* — is leading the services in a synagogue where *Nusach Sefard* is used, or the reverse,[7] he should use his regular *nusach* for the whispered (i.e., silent) prayer; but when he repeats the prayer aloud (*chazaras hashatz*), he should read from a prayerbook and use the *nusach* of the synagogue.[8]

4. If a mourner, or someone observing a *yahrzeit*, arrives late to the synagogue, but wishes to lead the services, he must at least recite *Baruch She'amar* ("Blessed is He Who spoke. . ."), *Ashrei* ("Praiseworthy are they who dwell in Your house. . ."), and *Yishtabach* ("May Your Name be praised forever. . .") [before reciting *Borchu*].[9]

---

6. *Mishnah Berurah* (53:§§60). He explains that the bylaw was instituted because of unlearned congregants who do not know and understand the blessings and prayers, and who make mistakes. To have such people lead the services would be disrespectful. Therefore, in order to prevent arguments, they instituted that even the learned should not lead the services.

7. *Kol Bo Al Aveilus* (p. 367 note 8) writes that one is permitted to change his *nusach* in order to serve as leader.

8. *She'arim HaMetzuyanim BeHalachah* (26:§§3) cites this *halachah* in the name of responsa *Sho'el U'Meshiv* (mahadura III part 1:§247). He adds: "The same ruling is given by the *Netziv* in responsa *Meshiv Davar* (§17). He states that for the whispered prayer, one is forbidden to depart from one's regular *nusach*; but when he repeats the prayer aloud, he should use the *nusach* of the congregation. The same ruling is given by responsa *Shivas Tzion* (§5).

"*Igros Moshe* (*Orach Chaim* part 2 §29) writes that the *chazzan* is forbidden to use one *nusach* for the 'silent' *Amidah* and a different one when he repeats the *Amidah* aloud. He explains that the purpose of the silent *Amidah* is to familiarize himself with the text that he will be reciting aloud, as *Magen Avraham* writes (124:§§3). Thus, if the *chazzan's* personal prayer is of a different *nusach*, he may confuse the two versions when he prays aloud.

"Strangely, *Igros Moshe* does not cite the rulings of the *geonim* cited above. Moreover, *Rama* (§100) writes that when one uses a prayerbook, he does not need to rehearse the prayer, since he has it before his eyes; and this applies even to the festival prayers, which are not recited every week and hence are less familiar. Furthermore, *Magen Avraham* himself (128:§§31 and 585:§§9) writes that in our day, when we pray with prayerbooks, [a *kohen* who is serving as *chazzan* may interrupt his prayer to recite the Priestly Blessing, since he] is assured of finding his place in the prayer afterwards, and we need not worry that he might make a mistake. In addition, the *gaon*, author of *Sha'ar Ephraim*, of Vilna (end of §13) writes: 'Post-facto (*bediavad*), the differences in wording between *nusach Ashkenaz* and *nusach Sefard* do not invalidate the *Amidah* prayer. Although some have counted the words in each blessing [and say that these totals have mystical significance — so that if one mixes different versions one will not have the correct numerical totals according to either version], this has no basis in the Talmud.' And this same ruling (that, *bediavad*, the differences in wording between *nusach Ashkenaz* and *nusach Sefard* do not invalidate the *Amidah* prayer) is given by *Eshel Avraham*."

[See also R' David Cohen, *G'vul Yavetz* pp. 146-8.]

9. *Mishnah Berurah* (53:§§4).

5. Whoever has precedence in reciting *Kaddish* also has precedence in leading the services,[10] if he is acceptable to the congregation.[11] (The laws of precedence are presented above, 39:39-49.)

When two mourners are present in a synagogue, the congregation should not split into two *minyanim*. Instead, [if the two mourners are of equal precedence,] one should lead the services until [and including] *Tachanun*, and the other should serve for the remainder of the prayer-service (i.e., from *Ashrei and U'va L'Tziyon*).[11a] This applies even if the two are not brothers.

6. Some rule that a man whose beard has not yet grown in should not continually lead the services, even if he is a mourner; he should only serve intermittently.[12] Others rule that we need not be particular about this restriction.[13] With regard to the *Maariv* prayer, one should follow the lenient opinion.[14]

7. [On a day when he is performing a circumcision, a *mohel* usually takes precedence over other congregants in leading the services. However,] a

---

10. *Be'ur Halachah* (§134).

11. *Darkei Moshe* (376:§§9) cites *Maharik* as writing that the mourner's rights of precedence apply only to the recitation of *Kaddish*. With regard to leading the services, everyone is equal, since this depends solely upon the will of the congregation. The prayer is theirs, and it is inappropriate that their representative should be someone not of their choice. Therefore, the one they prefer should lead the services.

However, *Chazon LaMo'ed* (26:9) states, in the name of *Hagahos Chasam Sofer* (on *Orach Chaim*), that the ruling of *Maharik* refers only to Talmudic times, when the prayer obligation of the congregation was fulfilled through the *sheliach tzibbur* (leader; literally, representative of the congregation); and the rule is that one person cannot serve as the representative of another against his will. In our time, by contrast, the congregation has no power to annul the mourner's right to lead the services, as long as he has no halachic disqualification or speech defect.

And see *Mishnah Berurah* (53:§§61), who writes: "Regarding the *Maariv* service, which does not correspond to the Continual Offerings (*Temidin*), but to the [burning of the] remains of the sacrifices [on the Altar during the night], it is possible that the consent of those who bring the sacrifice is not required, and the congregation cannot prevent the mourner leading the *Maariv* service, since it is a *mitzvah* that the son of the deceased should lead the services. Nevertheless, one certainly should not quarrel with the congregation over any *mitzvah*, as is mentioned below, §§65."

11a. The *gaon* R' Moshe Feinstein *zatzal* (*Kovetz Am HaTorah mahadura 2 kovetz* 12:4-5).

12. *Pri Megaddim* (in *Eshel Avraham* 132:§§2), cited by *Biur Halachah* (§53 s.v. *yuchal*).

13. *Shivas Tzion* (§18). He writes: "However, it has become the prevailing custom among us not to be particular about this. The custom is to allow youth who are in mourning for their father or mother to lead the services on all the ordinary weekdays during their year of mourning, even if they are not eighteen and have no beard. The explanation is that the congregation relinquishes [its right to have a *chazzan* who is old enough to grow a beard]. According to this custom, one is permitted to lead the services as soon as he reaches the age of thirteen; for at that time he is considered an adult according to *halachah*, as is stated by *Magen Avraham*."

14. *Be'ur Halachah* (loc. cit.). The reason is that for the *Maariv* prayer, the *chazzan* does not repeat the *Shemoneh Esrei* prayer aloud, and "as is known, *Rambam* distinguishes between *prisas Shema* (reciting the blessings of the *Shema*) and leading the prayer-service... In addition, in the absence of any indication to the contrary, it may be assumed that the congregation agrees that the mourner may lead the services..."

mourner takes precedence over a *mohel*.[15] But some disagree [and rule that the *mohel* takes precedence].[16] In any case, someone observing a *yahrzeit* takes precedence over both a mourner and a *mohel*.[17]

8. The custom is that the one who leads the services for *Selichos* also leads the services for the remainder of the day,[18] and even for the previous *Maariv* prayer.[19] The *halachah* is that this person takes precedence over a mourner, a *mohel*, or someone observing a *yahrzeit*.[20] But some rule that he does not take precedence over someone observing a *yahrzeit*, if the latter is fasting.[21]

Nevertheless, the mourner should be allowed to lead the services for the last part of the prayer-service, from *Ashrei* and *Uva L'Tziyon* to the end.[22] One authority writes that in our day the custom is not to have one who lead *Selichos* serve for the remainder of the day. Therefore, the mourner, or someone observing a *yahrzeit*, has precedence as usual.[22a]

✦ Sabbath and Festivals

9. The custom is that a mourner does not lead the services on the Sabbath[23]

---

15. *Shach* (265:§§23) writes, in the name of *Maharam* Mintz: "The mourner is not to be prevented from leading the services for this reason on the day of a circumcision. Preventing the mourner [from leading the services] is comparable to preventing a person from doing a *mitzvah*, and to stealing from the deceased — unless there is an established custom to the contrary, instituted by the sages. . ." *Shach* adds: "*Hagahos Minhagim* cites [*Maharam* Mintz's] ruling in brief, but there is a copyist's error there, and as a result the custom has become prevalent that the *mohel* takes precedence over the mourner — and this is not correct."

This ruling of *Shach* is also cited by *Chiddushei R' Akiva Eiger* (*Orach Chaim* §53), in the name of *Derech HaChaim*. The same ruling is given by *Chazon LaMo'ed*, in the name of *Yavetz*.

16. *Magen Avraham* (§53) cites the passage from *Hagahos Minhagim* mentioned in our previous footnote, ruling that the *mohel* takes precedence over the mourner. But he concludes: "Nevertheless, if the congregants prefer that the mourner serve as *chazzan*, he has the right to do so." The same ruling is given by *Mishnah Berurah* (ad loc. §§60), citing *Magen Avraham*.

17. *Magen Avraham* (§53) writes: "It seems to me that someone observing a *yahrzeit* takes precedence over the *mohel*, unless the congregation objects; for, according to *Rama*, even the mourner takes precedence." The same ruling is cited by *Mishnah Berurah* (loc. cit.) — that someone with a *yahrzeit* takes precedence over both the *mohel* and the mourner. Nevertheless, the congregation has the right to choose whichever of the three they prefer.

18. The reason is that "When one begins a *mitzvah*, we tell him: 'Finish' " (*Rama* §581, citing *Kol Bo*).

19. *Mishnah Berurah* (581:§§14). But the following *Maariv* does not belong to this person.

20. *Mishnah Berurah* (loc. cit.), citing *Magen Avraham*. The reason is that the congregants have the right to choose their representative in prayer.

21. *Mishnah Berurah* (loc. cit.) states that *Elyah Rabbah* questions the ruling that the one who led the *Slichos* service has precedence. *Elyah Rabbah* rules that the one observing the *yahrzeit* has precedence if he is fasting.

22. *Mishnah Berurah* loc. cit.

22a. *Mateh Efraim* 581:31.

23. *Rama* (376:4). And *Da'as Torah* (ad loc.) cites responsa *Sha'arei Tzedek* (*Orach Chaim* §8) as ruling that on the Sabbath the mourner is forbidden to lead the services, even for the section from

or Festivals,[24] even though, according to the basic *halachah*, this is not forbidden.

Regarding the question whether a mourner who is observing a *yahrzeit* is permitted to lead the services on the Sabbath, see below, Chapter 44. A mourner who is a bridegroom [i.e., during the *sheva brachos*, the seven days of the wedding feasts,] can lead the services.[24a]

◆§ The Days of Awe / Rosh Hashanah and Yom Kippur

10. During the Days of Awe (*Yomim Nora'im*), a mourner does not lead the services.[25] Nevertheless, if there is no one better qualified, he is permitted to do so.[26]

For this purpose, the term "Days of Awe" refers only to Rosh Hashanah and Yom Kippur. It does not include the days [preceding Rosh Hashanah] when *Selichos* are recited, nor the days between Rosh Hashanah and Yom Kippur, known as the Ten Days of Repentance. Therefore on these days the mourner is permitted to lead the prayer-services and *Selichos*.[27]

Pesukei D'zimrah until *Shochen Ad*.

Levushei Mordechai (*Yoreh De'ah* §20) writes that the mourner is permitted to lead the services on the Sabbath for the preliminary section until the Mishnah chapter about the sacrifices, *Eizehu Mekoman*. He also states that if the deceased was a Sabbath desecrator, those mourning for him are permitted to lead the services even on the Sabbath, since in that case he is punished in *Gehinnom* even then. On this, *Da'as Torah* comments: "See *Zohar Chadash* (*Bereishis*, on the verse, 'These are the generations of the heavens and the earth. . .'), [which states] the contrary: that Sabbath desecrators are not punished on the Sabbath, but are punished doubly on Friday."

Da'as Torah also states that the mourner should not lead the *Minchah* service on the Sabbath, since this prayer includes the words: "Abraham exults, Isaac rejoices. . ." and "Cause us to rejoice in Your salvation."

24. *Da'as Torah* states, citing *Bach*, that on *Yom Tov* the mourner may not lead the services even if no one else is available. This is because the prayers of *Yom Tov* include jubilant rejoicing.

24a. *Igros Moshe* (*Orach Chaim*, part IV §21:10).

25. *Pri Megaddim* (§581 in *Eshel Avraham* par. 4) writes: "*Darkei Moshe* cites *Maharil* (*Hilchos Yom Tov*), who mentions a ruling of *Maharash* that the mourner may lead the services once seven days have passed from the day of the death. Therefore, even if the death occurred less than seven days before the Festival, the Festival canceled *shivah*." *Pri Megaddim* comments: "One must explain that this is referring to the situation where there is no one better qualified; see *Yoreh De'ah*, *Shach* 376:§§14. According to this, if the death occurred seven days before Rosh Hashanah, and Rosh Hashanah canceled *shloshim*, one might say that, according to all opinions, the mourner is permitted to lead the services even if someone better qualified is present. . .[On the other hand,] one could explain [to the contrary:] that the mourner is under the influence of the Attribute of Strict Justice, and therefore it is not appropriate for him to lead the services during the Days of Awe (*Yamim Nora'im*). If so, even in a case where Rosh Hashanah cancels *shloshim*, nevertheless [he is] still [under the influence of the Attribute of Strict Justice]. . . for, regarding *Kaddish*, the festivals do not cancel the priority of *ben shloshim*."

26. *Shach* (ad loc. §§14).

27. This *halachah* is presented above, chapt. 34, regarding Rosh Hashanah.

✦ Rosh Chodesh

11. On Rosh Chodesh, the mourner leads the services until the recitation of *Hallel.* But some have the custom that he does not lead the services for *Shacharis.*[28] However, see below, paragraph 14.

✦ Chanukah

12. Some rule that during Chanukah the mourner is permitted to lead the entire prayer-service, except *Hallel.* However, some have the custom that he does not do so even for *Minchah* or *Maariv.*[29] However, see below paragraph 14.

✦ Purim

13. Some rule that the mourner does not lead the services on Purim, even for *Minchah.*[30]

✦ Special Days

14. Some have the custom that the mourner does not lead the services on days when one omits the recitation of *LaMenatze'ach* ("For the Conductor — a psalm of David. . .") and *Kel Erech Apayim* ("O God, slow to anger. . ."). These days are:

    (a) Rosh Chodesh;

    (b) Chanukah;

    (c) Purim (including both the fourteenth and the fifteenth of Adar, Adar I, and Adar II);

    (d) *Erev* Pesach.

However, on *erev* Yom Kippur the custom is that the mourner does lead the services.[31]

---

28. *Mishnah Berurah* (581:§§7) writes: "Likewise, on the days when *Tachanun* is not recited, [the mourner] is permitted to lead the services for *Shacharis*, as long as someone else leads the services for *Hallel.* (And the mourner should recite the *Kaddish* after *Hallel*, since it belongs to the one who repeated the *Shemoneh Esrei* prayer aloud.)" But *Chayei Adam* writes: "It seems to me that the *Gra* did not permit [a mourner] to lead the services even for *Shacharis* on Rosh Chodesh. However, if no one else is available, all agree that he may lead the services, even for *Mussaf*."

29. This *halachah* is presented above, chapt. 34, regarding Chanukah.

30. *Aliyos Eliahu* (17:6) relates that the *Gra* did not permit a mourner to lead the services for *Minchah* on Purim. The author relates that it once happened that a particular mourner had already enwrapped his head in the prayer shawl, ready to lead the services, when, with characteristic wit, the *Gra* remarked (quoting *Esther* 6:12), 'in mourning, and with covered head.'
    The same ruling [that the mourner may not lead the services on Purim] is given by *Knesses Yehudah* (§44).

31. *Be'ur Halachah* (§132 in *Kuntres Ma'amar Kaddishin*).

⌐⌐ Customs for the Benefit of the Deceased

15. The custom is that the mourner is called up for *Maftir*.[32] This applies during his entire Twelve Months of mourning.[33]

16. Some have the custom of kindling a light in the home of the deceased during the first thirty days of mourning, and in the synagogue during the entire Twelve Months.[34]

17. The custom is to study *mishnayos* for the benefit of the soul of the deceased during the entire Twelve Months of mourning.[35] And many have the custom

---

32. *Rama* (376:4), citing *Kol Bo*. His source is the story about R' Akiva related in *Zohar Chadash* (see above, chapt. 39 footnote 1). In the story, the deceased came to R' Akiva in a dream and told him: "When my son read the *Haftarah*, they lightened my punishment in *Gehinnom*."

Yad Eliahu (Ragolar), in the testament included in that work, commands his sons to read the *Haftarah* of the Prophets; and to be particular to read it from a parchment scroll (not just a printed book). *Yalkut David* (*Yoreh De'ah* §376) explains that the mourner reads the *Haftarah* of the Prophets, because the blessings accompanying this reading include prayer for the Redemption of Israel and the sanctification of the Name of Hashem, Blessed is He, as in *Kaddish*. See also see responsa *Tzitz Eliezer* (16:§38).

Ma'aseh Eliahu (§294) writes that the mourner during the first year of mourning takes precedence over someone observing a *yahrzeit* that week. And see below (chapt. 44) for more on the question of precedence.

33. *Mateh Efrayim* (*Dinei Kaddish Yasom* 4:2). The same ruling is given by *Chazon LaMo'ed*, citing *Yavetz*.

34. In the testament of R' Naftali Katz, *zatzal*, he writes that a light should burn in his home throughout the first thirty days [of mourning], and in the synagogue until after the *yahrzeit*. And this is cited by *Chazon LaMo'ed* (ch. 13 note 7). The same ruling is given by *Ma'avar Yabok* (2:1), who states that the light should burn in the synagogue throughout the first twelve months of mourning.

Yoseif Ometz (p. 329) writes: "The custom regarding the light is that it is kindled in the room where the death occurred, and burns there throughout the first seven days of mourning. Also, the custom is to kindle a light in the synagogue from the end of the seven days until the end of the eleven months, and it burns all day and night. I have not found any source that mentions these two customs, not even in the works of very recent authorities. Moreover, I have heard that in the land of Italy there is no custom to have a light burning continually, but only that it should burn during the time of public prayer; and after the prayer, they extinguish it. And even though one should not depart from our custom, which was instituted by our forefathers. . .nevertheless, there is no obligation to exert oneself excessively for this matter, to kindle wax candles. . .; and, all the more so, if the light goes out on the Sabbath, one is severely forbidden to tell a non-Jew to kindle it."

35. At the end of *Elef HaMagen*, the author writes: "The kabbalistic works state that Mishnah-study for the soul of the deceased is of great benefit for him. The Sages said that Asher, the son of the Patriarch Jacob, may peace be upon him, sits at the entrance to *Gehinnom* and rescues anyone who studies Mishnah. (And the same applies to anyone for whom others study Mishnah.) This is indicated by the verse (*Genesis* 49:20): *Asher's bread is rich*. The word for 'rich' (שְׁמֵנָה) is spelled with the same letters as 'Mishnah' (מִשְׁנָה). That is, 'Asher's bread is Mishnah.' Likewise, reciting Psalms for the deceased is of great benefit to him, as explained in the kabbalistic works.".

Torah Or writes: "Mishnah-study is an [even] greater remedy than leading the prayer-service." *Yoseif Ometz* (p. 331) states: "Concerning leading the services for the prayers and the *Kaddishim*, this remedy is only for the unlearned; but Torah-study is many times more effective than [leading] the prayers; through Torah-study, one brings the deceased into *Gan Eden*. And if the son discovers new

that, during the entire Twelve Months, they give charity for the benefit of the departed soul. They also study one chapter of *mishnayos* a day, as well as Tractate *Mikva'os* Chapter 7, *mishnayos* 4-7 [*see Appendix*]. The initial letters of these four *mishnayos* spell נְשָׁמָה (*neshamah*, "soul") .[36]

18. Some have the custom that, during the entire Twelve Months of mourning, on the conclusion of the Sabbath, they study *Mishnayos Kelim* Chapter 24,[37] in the home of the deceased. If it is not possible to do this in the home of the deceased, they do so anywhere.[38] Afterwards, they study *Mikva'os* Chapter 7.[39]

19. [If three or more males, aged thirteen or older, participate in a meal, a leader (*mezamen*) is appointed to formally invite the others to join him in the recitation of the Grace After Meals.] The mourner, during the entire Twelve Months, should make an effort to serve as the *mezamen*, since this is of benefit to the departed soul.[40]

Torah insights (*chiddushim*), inestimable honor is given to his father in the heavenly yeshivah; this can be proven from *Midrash HaNe'elam*."

Kav HaYashar (chapt. 35) writes: "If a person merited to marry his daughter to a Torah scholar, when his son-in-law discovers new and correct insights into the Torah, the father-in-law and mother-in-law are crowned with many diadems."

Sha'arei Teshuvah (290:§§2) cites *Da'as Chochmah*, who quotes the *Arizal* as saying that if one reveals new Torah insights on the Sabbath, one's fathers are crowned in the other world; and this is why honoring parents is placed next to the Sabbath [in the verse, '*Every man shall fear his father and his mother; and you shall keep My Sabbaths*' (*Leviticus* 19:3)].

36. *Zichron Eliahu* (manuscript). He cites *Mishnah Berurah* (§§19), who writes: "It is logical that if the son contributes charity for his father's benefit, this in every case helps to lighten [the father's] punishment; for 'the son gives merit to the father.' "

37. This Mishnah chapter is extremely effective, because it contains seventeen *mishnayos*, each ending with the phrase, "completely pure." The whole chapter ends with the phrase, "pure, both inside and outside."

38. *Zichron Eliyahu*.

39. Ibid. *Atzei Eden U'ma'aseh Oreg* states: "We received it from our teacher, and our teacher from Eliyahu, *zal*, that this chapter (*Mikva'os* Chapter 7) raises the soul of the deceased to its place. Therefore the mourner should study it throughout the twelve months, in order to remedy the soul of his father or mother, relatives, or friends; and he should do the same on the *yahrzeit*. The initial letters of the first three *mishnayos* of this chapter (the initials of the words, יֵשׁ, אֵלּוּ, and הַצִּיחַ) spell אַיֵּה. The initial letters of the last four *mishnayos* (the initials of the words נָפַל, שְׁלוֹשָׁה, מִקְוֶה and הַטְבִּיל) spell נְשָׁמָה (*neshamah*, 'soul'). When studying these *mishnayos*, one should intend to raise the *neshamah* to the supernal constellation called אַיֵּה. (The letters of this word, in reverse order, spell the initials of הָאָרַת יְסוֹד אַבָּא, 'the illumination of the foundation of Father.') This is stated in *Kehillas Yaakov*."

Ma'aseh Oreg gives a detailed kabbalistic explanation of this matter. He adds: "The fourth *mishnah* begins with the word נָפַל (*nafal*, 'fell'). The letters of this word are the initials of the verse, '*He gave generously to the poor*' (פִּזַּר נָתַן לָאֶבְיוֹנִים) (*Tehillim* 112:9). Upon reaching this *mishnah*, one should set aside *tzeddakah*, so that, by means of the *tzeddakah*, the soul of the deceased will be raised up from its 'fall.' For one's father or mother, one should study this chapter every *motza'ei Shabbos*, after *Havdalah*, throughout the Twelve Months, and on the *yahrzeit*, and on Friday before *Minchah*, in case of need, 'to give life to the soul of every living being.' "

40. *Shevus Yaakov* (part 1 §102), *Pischei Teshuvah* (§375:§§3). *Yoseif Ometz* also writes that this raises the deceased from *Gehinnom*. And see *She'eilas Yavetz* (I:§74).

20. The children of the deceased should donate books to the synagogue, inscribing the name of the deceased in the books. Whenever people use these books to study, it will give spiritual satisfaction (*nachas ru'ach*) to the departed soul.[41]

21. Even though the recitation of *Kaddish* and leading the services are of benefit to the soul of one's parent, there is a greater benefit that children can confer. The greatest service that children can offer is to conduct themselves proper, in a manner that will be pleasing to God and man. In this way, they are a credit to their departed parents not only during the services, but all their waking hours. Furthermore, one should command his children to be especially fastidious in the performance of some particular *mitzvah*; and if they fulfill it, this too will be even more effective than reciting *Kaddish*.[42]

---

41. *Ahavas Chessed* (II:15 note).

42. *Kitzur Shulchan Aruch* (26:22), citing the holy *Zohar* (end of *Parashas Bechukosai*).

Responsa *Chaim Be Yad* (*Yoreh De'ah* §116) writes: "In addition, it would seem true to say that when the son exerts himself in Torah and *mitzvos*, does *tzedakah*, and supports Torah scholars for the elevation of the souls of his parents and relatives, even if they were pious and righteous people, the son merits through this that they, in their righteousness in the upper world, pray for him, that he should have a long and full life, wealth, and honor, and that an abundant influence of salvation and mercy will flow upon him from above."

CHAPTER FORTY-ONE

The Monument

◄§ The Obligation

1. Erecting a monument over the grave is an ancient Jewish custom.[1] The Sages used the word *nefesh* (lit., "soul") to refer to the monument.[2]

The obligation to erect a monument is incumbent upon the family of the deceased, since it is one of the needs of burial,[3] and is included in the *mitzvah* of honoring the deceased.[4]

---

1. Thus we find: '*And Jacob placed a monument upon her grave; this is the monument of the grave of Rachel*' (*Genesis* 35:20). And Mishnah *Shekalim* (2:5) states: "With the remainder of the money collected for the needs of the deceased, they build a *nefesh* for him on his grave." *Bartinura* (ad loc.) and *Sefer Chassidim* (§738) explain that *nefesh* means a monument.

2. "The word *nefesh* refers to the fact that the *nefesh* of the deceased hovers over the place where the body was buried, even after the *neshamah* [another aspect of the soul] departs from it" (*Gesher HaChaim*).

   "The holy *Zohar* and the writings of the *Ari zal* explain that the three aspects of the soul are the *nefesh*, *ru'ach*, and *neshamah*. The *nefesh* remains constantly hovering over the grave, except on the Sabbath and *Yom Tov*, and certain other times, when it goes up to take pleasure in the paradise of the souls (*nefashos*). In honor of the *nefesh*, in order to give it a defined place to dwell, we mark the grave, or build a structure over it. The *ru'ach* clothes itself in the person's Torah knowledge and service of God, in the place where the person performed his service when alive. The *neshamah* is the part which goes up to enjoy the Divine radiance and to progress to ever greater achievements" (*Ta'amei HaMinhagim* p. 476).

3. *Tur* (§348) writes: "The heirs can be forced [by the Torah court] to pay for all the needs of burial, as well as everything normally done for the members of that family — even the stone which is placed on the grave." And *Beis Yosef* (ad loc.) cites *Teshuvos HaRosh* (§13): "As for your question whether the stone which is placed on the grave is considered part of the needs of burial, the answer is: The stone is one of the needs of burial."

   See also *Ikrei HaDat* (*Yoreh De'ah* 35:§§19), who states: "It is said that one does not make a *nefesh* for a *tzaddik*. However, this only means that one does not make an elaborate structure; but a simple stone should be placed on the graves of *tzaddikim*, too."

   Teshuvos Rashba (§56) states that a husband is obligated to place a monument on his wife's grave; and this applies if it is the custom of his family, even if it is not the custom of her family.

4. *Chazon LaMo'ed* (25:1). *Ma'avar Yabok* states (*Imrei No'am* §40): "The monument on the graves of *tzaddikim* helps the living. When they see the monument of an important man, they are aroused to stop at his grave and ask for mercy upon the living and the dead. Undoubtedly, the righteous are pleased when people do this. Moreover, this gives them merit, since they are counted among those who beseech mercy for the entire generation, and because of him [the *tzaddik*], people request mercy for all the departed of the Jewish nation."

◆§ Time to Erect

2. Some have the custom to erect the monument [at least in unfinished form] immediately after *shivah*,[5] and they are particular that it should be completed by the *shloshim*.[6] Others rule that it should be erected after the Twelve Months.[7]

◆§ Inscribing the Name and the Date of Death

3. The custom is to engrave or write on the monument the name of the deceased and the name of his father [e.g., *"Binyamin ben Yaakov"*]; similarly, for a female, one writes her name and the name of her father [e.g., *"Dinah bas Yaakov"*]. This is the same form used when reciting memorial prayers [e.g., *Yizkor* and *Kel Malei Rachamim*].

The Sefardic custom, for either a male or a female, is to write the person's name and the name of his or her mother [e.g., *"Binyamin ben Rachel"*; *"Dinah bas Leah"*]. This is in accord with the Sefardic custom for memorial prayers.[8]

4. Sometimes, if a person becomes seriously ill, he is given an additional name. If he recovers, and people become accustomed to using his new name for at least thirty days, this additional name is included in the monument inscription when he dies. This applies, all the more so, if he had been called up to the Torah by this new name, or had signed a document with it. However, if he does not recover from the

---

5. But not *during shivah* (*Naggid U'Mitzvah*, *Aveilus*). He explains the reason for this custom, according to Kabbalah. It is based on the teaching of the *Ari zal*, *Sha'ar HaMitzvos* (p. 10a), cited by *Pesora D'Abba* (II:§12).

 Chut HaMeshulash writes that this was the custom followed by *Chasam Sofer* in placing a monument for his wife. *Minchas Yitzchak* (IV:§107) states that this was the custom followed by the *gaon Maharshak*.

 Gesher HaChaim (28:2:1) writes that this is the custom of Jerusalem. He also states there: "The custom is to inscribe the monument after the *shloshim*, or later, during the Twelve Months; and some do it even later."

 Kol Bo Al Aveilus (p. 379) cites *Pele Yo'etz* (s.v. *kevurah*): "Included in the needs of burial and rest for the deceased is the placement of a stone monument on the grave immediately after *shivah*. . .and if one cannot erect the monument immediately, one should do so as soon as possible." And the same *halachah* is cited by *Kol Bo Al Aveilus* in the name of *Minchas Elazar* (III:§37) — contrary to those whose custom is not to place the monument until after the Twelve Months. "This [erecting the monument immediately after *shivah*] was done by the *gaon Divrei Chaim* of Sanz; and the same was done by the *gaon*, author of *Darkei Teshuvah*, for his father, the *gaon*, *zatzal*."

6. *Even Yaakov* §46.

7. *Beis Lechem Yehudah* (§376) cites *Lechem HaPanim* as stating, in the name of *Ma'aneh Lashon*:

 "The prevailing custom in most places is not to place the monument until after the Twelve Months." The same ruling is given by *Chiddushei R' Akiva Eiger*. He explains that the monument is a sign of importance, and this is inappropriate during the first Twelve Months [because] the deceased is suffering; or, alternatively, the purpose of the monument is to make sure that the person will not be forgotten, and [this is not necessary during the Twelve Months, because] the memory of the deceased stays fresh in people's minds until after Twelve Months. *Kol Bo Al Aveilus* states that *Elyah Rabbah* (§224) mentions these same explanations, but *Kol Bo Al Aveilus* questions the validity of these explanations.

8. *Gesher HaChaim* (28:3:1).

illness, the new name is not taken into account, and only his original name is inscribed on the monument.[9]

5. The date of death is also inscribed on the monument. For this purpose, only the Jewish calendar is used, not the civil calendar.[10]

6. The custom is to inscribe the abbreviation ת.נ.צ.ב.ה. on the monument. It stands for תְּהֵא נִשְׁמָתוֹ (נִשְׁמָתָהּ) צְרוּרָה בִּצְרוֹר הַחַיִּים ("May his/her soul be bound up in the Bond of Life").[11]

✺ Praises

7. One should not inscribe excessive praises on the monument.[12]

It is proper to place a monument of average value, and not spend excessively on it. Instead, one should increase one's expenditures for charity.[13]

8. If one replaces the monument, one should not inscribe fewer praises on the new one than were on the previous one.[14]

---

9. *Gesher HaChaim* (loc. cit.), and see responsa *Chelkas Yaakov* (I:§165).

10. *Gesher HaChaim* (loc. cit.). The same ruling is given by *Kol Bo Al Aveilus* (p. 381), citing responsa *Maharam* Shick (*Yoreh De'ah* §171). *Kol Bo Aveilus* adds: "Since [writing this], I also found that *Chasam Sofer* writes in *Sefer HaDrashos* . . .'not like the groundless innovation of those who give the date according to the birth of the Christians' Messiah; for, the House of Israel will certainly be shamed for this treachery.' And the *gaon* R' Meir Ash, in his *Imrei Yosher*, gives the same ruling, as do responsa *Sha'arei Tzeddek* (§199) and responsa *Pri HaSadeh* (I:§3)."

11. *Otzar Kol Minhagei Yeshurun* (§20) writes that this phrase is based on the verse (*I Samuel* 25:29): '*May my master's soul be bound up in the Bond of Life with Hashem.*' He explains that the abbreviation of this verse, spoken by Avigail to King David, was chosen "because we believe in the coming of *Mashiach*, and in the destined kingship of the House of David, and in the Resurrection of the Dead, and that Hashem rewards the actual doing of a *mitzvah*, and that He also rewards a good thought; and all these five principles of faith, found in *Rambam*'s Thirteen Principles, are included in this abbreviation. . ."

12. *Chazon LaMo'ed* (loc. cit.). And in note 3 he writes: "This was also the command of the *gaon* R' Naftali Katz, *zatzal*; and the *gaon Maharshak*, *zatzal*, wrote: 'No praises or titles should be inscribed [on the monument]. . .for what profit is there in having one's praises sung in one's eulogy or on the monument?' Likewise, the *gaon* R' Akiva Eiger, *zatzal*, commanded that his monument should be inscribed: 'Here is buried R' Akiva Eiger.' "

13. See *Ahavas Chessed* (II:15, in the note). He writes: "I would like to mention here another important matter. There are people who wish to create a memorial for the eternal commemoration of their parents' souls; so they make them a monument of expensive marble, artistically engraved with gilded letters and the like, and drawings, and many flowers..They spend a great deal of money on these things, thinking that in this way they are giving much spiritual satisfaction to the soul of the deceased. In such thoughts, these people are making a number of errors. The truth is that the soul of the deceased, after departing this world, recognizes there, in the World of Truth, the intended purpose of Torah and *mitzvos* . . .

"It would be better for them if they would place a less expensive monument, with regular letters instead of gilded ones. . .and with the remainder of the money that they would have spent on this, would buy a copy of the Talmud and donate it to the *Beth Midrash*, inscribing it for the commemoration of the souls of their parents. Alternatively, they could establish a permanent free loan fund for the commemoration of their parents' souls. In this way, their souls would be elevated very high; for with each and every loan, [the children] would acquire another *mitzvah* of the Torah; and this would inevitably add merit to their parents as well. . ."

14. Responsa *Igros Moshe* (*Yoreh De'ah* §225).

◄§ Eulogy at the Time of Placing the Monument

9. The custom is to eulogize the deceased at the time of formally erecting the monument.[15] Therefore, some rule that the monument should not be placed on one of the days when eulogy is forbidden.[16] (For the list of these days, see above, 8:10.)

10. If the deceased commanded his children not to erect a monument for him, they should not obey, but should place a small one.[17]

---

15. *Kol Bo Al Aveilus* (p. 381), citing *Levushei Mordechai* (*tinyana Yoreh De'ah* §140).

16. Responsa *Minchas Yitzchak* (III:§51). He also writes: "Likewise, responsa *Levushei Mordechai* is cited as stating that one should not set up the monument within thirty days before a Festival." And in §52, he writes that the placing of the monument should not be carried out on one of the days when *Tachanun* is not recited.

Chazon LaMo'ed (loc. cit.) also writes that one should not set up the monument on Rosh Chodesh, Chanukah, or Purim.

17. *Mishmeres Shalom*, citing *Zachur LeAvraham*, who gives his source as *Chaim Sha'al* (part I §71 §§6). He explains that the sons are required to set up a monument for their father; and if the deceased had known that the monument is of benefit to the soul, he would have commanded his children accordingly.

CHAPTER FORTY-TWO

Visiting the Grave

---

1. The custom is to visit the graves of one's parents and forefathers.[1] It benefits the deceased when their children and friends come to their graves to pray for them and to ask Hashem to grant good to their souls.[2]

◆§ During the First Year

2. One should not visit the grave during the first year to pray for a sick person's recovery, or for other matters, because during this time the deceased is still going through his time of judgment. Instead, one should pray only for the elevation of the departed soul.[3] Many have the custom to minimize visiting the grave during the first year, even to pray for the deceased.[4] If one goes on a distant journey, and it will be

---

1. The earliest mention of visiting graves is found in the Midrash, which states that when Joseph was taken down to Egypt, he visited the grave of his mother on the way, and wept. Rachel answered him that Hashem would save him from every tribulation (*Sefer HaYashar*). Jacob said of Rachel, *'I buried her there, on the road to Efrath'* (*Genesis* 48:7). *Rashi* explains that Jacob did this by Divine command, so that she would be of help to her sons when Nevuzaradan would exile them, and they would pass that way. Then, Rachel would come out by her grave and weep, begging Hashem to have mercy on them, as it is said, *'A voice is heard in Ramah. . .Rachel weeps for her children'* (*Jeremiah* 31:14). And the Holy One, Blessed is He, answers her: *'There is reward for your deed. . .and the children will return to their border'* " (ibid. verses 15-16).

About Caleb it is written: *'He came to Hebron'* (*Numbers* 13:22). The Talmud (*Sotah* 34a) explains: "Rava said: This teaches us that Caleb withdrew from the scheme of the spies and went to pray at the tombs of the Patriarchs. He said to them: 'My fathers, beseech Hashem to have mercy on me, that I may be saved from the scheme of the spies.' " (*Nachamu Ami* 33:1)

2. Proof that this is of benefit to the deceased may be drawn from the request of Barzilai the Giladite (*II Samuel* 19:38): *'Let me die in my city.'* He desired this so that his relatives could come to his grave (*Ner Eliyahu*, in the name of *Ma'avar Yabok*, 3:23).

In the *Zohar* (*Parashas Vayechi* p. 217) we find: "R' Yitzchak requested three things of R' Yehudah. One of them was that for all seven days [after his death] the latter would go to his grave and pray for him."

An allusion to this matter is also found in Tractate *Semachos* (4:11): "When Ben Yehotzadak died, his brother Yochanan came from the Galil, arriving after the tomb had already been sealed. . .They said, 'Do not become *tamei* [ritually contaminated] for him; but open [the gate of the cemetery] near the tomb, and he shall see the tomb' " (*Gesher HaChaim*).

3. *Zichron Eliyahu*, citing the *Zohar* (*Parashas Vayechi*). But *Darkei Chaim VeShalom* states that if the deceased was a great man, one is permitted [to pray for a sick person or other matters even during the first year].

4. *Zichron Eliyahu*. The same ruling is given by responsa *Melamed LeHo'il* (*Yoreh De'ah* §144).

impossible for him to visit his parents' graves later, one may visit them even during the first year.[5]

◆§ Visiting the Same Grave Twice

3. One should not visit the same grave twice in the same day.[6]

If it is impossible to leave the cemetery without passing the grave again, some have the custom of stopping at the grave and requesting permission to return to it.[7]

Some have the custom that when they visit the cemetery on their parents' *yahrzeit* (anniversary of death), they do not visit other graves that day.[8]

If a *kohen* has *yahrzeit*, and goes near the cemetery in order to see the grave, this is considered as if he had visited the grave itself, and is of great benefit.[8a]

◆§ Eating Before Visiting a Grave

4. Some are careful not to eat before going to the cemetery.

Some have the custom to taste a little food, but not to have a meal.

---

5. Responsa *Melamed LeHo'il* (loc. cit.).

6. *Zichron Eliyahu*, citing *Tzeva'as R' Yehudah HeChassid* and *Magen Avraham* (§581 §§16). The same ruling is given by *Kitzur HaShelah*, and also by *Ta'amei HaMitzvos*, by Rabbeinu Chaim Vital (*Parashas Vayechi*).
  The citation from *Tzeva'as R' Yehudah HeChassid* (§12) is as follows: "One should not visit the same grave twice in one day; instead, one should request everything one wishes to request, and not go back again until the next day." *Even Yaakov* (44:4) deduces from these words that "this restriction applies only if, at the first visit, one already knew all the things one wanted to request. In that case, one should not divide his supplications between two visits on the same day. . .But this implies that if one has reason to make a new request, about which one had not known during the previous visit, one is permitted to visit the grave again, even that same day."
  He writes that a similar conclusion was reached by responsa *Ginzei Yosef* (26:§§4), in the name of *Yismach Lev*, who records the following halachic query: A certain person was regularly sent by others to pray at certain graves, and on one occasion, he had gone there in the morning as someone's emissary. Afterward, someone else asked him to go [to the same graves] and pray for him. [Was he allowed to go a second time that same day?] The ruling was in the affirmative; for the words of R' Yehudah HeChassid imply that the restriction applies only if one goes to pray for oneself. In that case, one should not divide his supplications between two visits on the same day. But this does not apply if, when he went the first time, he did not yet know that his presence would be required a second time. This would seem especially true since one could also say that we apply the restriction to the sender, not the emissary.
  Even Yaakov (loc. cit.) gives yet another reason to rule permissively under such circumstances. He bases it on the commentary *Damesek Eliezer*, who explains that the reason why one should not go twice on the same day is because doing so would give the impression that he suspects the deceased of not praying for him the first time; this would be an insult to the deceased, implying that he considers them uncompassionate. However, this reason would not apply to this case where one went the second time because of a new supplication [about which one had not known before], or because someone else subsequently sent him.

7. *Zichron Eliyahu*. And the point made in our previous footnote, in the name of *Even Yaakov*, applies here as well.

8. Ibid.

8a. *Chazon LaMo'ed* (27:4), citing *Duda'ei HaSadeh* (§21).

However, many are not particular about this point [i.e., they may even have a meal].⁹

ᴥᔑ Ritual Impurity

5. Some refrain from visiting graves, except for a funeral.

Some authorities caution against going to a cemetery if one is impure due to *tumas keri* (i.e., has had marital relations or a seminal emission), until one has immersed in the *mikveh*. Otherwise, negative spiritual forces become attached to him.¹⁰ Likewise, one should not visit the graves of the wicked; for they are harmful.¹¹

ᴥᔑ Women

6. Women should not enter the cemetery when in the *niddah* state, until they have gone to the *mikveh*.¹² Some rule more leniently, and permit them to go to the cemetery during their Seven Clean Days.¹³

---

9. *Gesher HaChaim* (29:3) writes: "Some are careful to go to the cemetery only *before* eating." And in his note 6, he quotes the following passage from *Ma'aneh Lashon Yashan*:
"It is an ancient custom to go to the cemetery on fast-days (as stated in *Taanis* 17b, and *Tur* and *Shulchan Aruch* 579:10). And even when visiting the cemetery on an ordinary day, one should go there before one eats. I have searched the [halachic] works and the commentaries on *Shulchan Aruch*, and have not found anyone who cites this custom as *halachah*. Afterwards, I saw *Kuntres Mo'ed Kol Chai*, written by a contemporary author, R' Yosef HaKohen Schwartz, *rav* of the city of Banihad. He writes (p. 5): 'People are careful not to eat before visiting the cemetery. However, some have the custom of tasting a little food before going, so as not to be in the category of those who "starve themselves and then sleep over in the cemetery" (since in this case one would be starving oneself because he needs to go to the cemetery, but this is not to be compared to a fast-day, when one starves oneself for a different reason). The kabbalistic works explain that one may have only a light snack before going, not one's usual full meal.'
"However, if one does not follow this custom, and eats [a regular meal] before going to the cemetery, there is no objection, since the custom [of not eating] has no basis [in the halachic literature]."

10. *Magen Avraham* (559:§§14) cites *Kisvei HaArizal* as stating that one should not go to the cemetery except for a funeral — "especially if one has not remedied the sin of seminal emission; for negative spiritual forces (*chitzonim*) cling to him." And see *Iggeres HaGra* (known as *Alim LiTrufah*), which the Gaon of Vilna wrote to his family as he set out to go to *Eretz Israel*. He states: "Be careful not to go to the cemetery at all; for there the *klipos* (negative forces) cling very much to people; and this [warning] applies, all the more so, to women. All the troubles and sins result from this."

11. *Chayei Adam* (138:5).

12. Ibid. (3:38). He writes: "It seems to me that [women] should not enter the cemetery until they have gone to the *mikveh*." The same ruling is given by *Pischei Teshuvah* (*Yoreh De'ah* 195:§§19), citing *Chamudei Daniel* (manuscript). He states: "Women have the custom not to go [to the cemetery until they have been to the *mikveh*]; and this is correct."

13. *Beis Baruch*, commenting on the passage from *Chayei Adam* quoted in our previous footnote, writes, in the name of *Leket HaKemach HeChadash*: "In case of great need, a woman is permitted to go to the cemetery during the Seven Clean Days (*yemei libun*)." This is also implied by the wording of *Pischei Teshuvah* (see our previous footnote), who says that the restriction applies "during the days of *niddah*" [which would seem to imply only during the days of actual *niddah*, but not during the Seven Clean Days]. *Shulchan Melachim*, in *Shalom Ve'emes* (§§5), also disputes the statement of *Chayei Adam*, objecting: "If so, an unmarried girl, a widow, or a divorcee, who do not go to the *mikveh* would be always forbidden to go to the cemetery. But, certainly [this *halachah*] is no stricter than [that

7. On certain days, women are permitted to go to the cemetery even during the time of menstrual flow. These days are:

    (a) The day of formally dedicating the monument.

    (b) The *yahrzeit*.

    (c) The days when *Selichos* are recited, through Yom Kippur.[14]

৵১ Special Days for Visiting the Grave

8. The custom is to visit the grave on the following days:

    (a) On the seventh day, after ending the restrictions of *shivah*.

    (b) On the thirtieth day of mourning.

    (c) On the completion of the first Twelve Months of mourning. This applies even if that day is not the *yahrzeit*; for example, in a leap-year.[15] However, some have the custom not to visit the grave at the end of the Twelve Months unless it is the *yahrzeit*.[15a]

    (d) On the *yahrzeit*, every year.[16]

9. If the seventh day of mourning falls on the Sabbath or a *Yom Tov*, one visits the grave the following day.[17]

The same applies if *Yom Tov* occurs during *shivah*, and *Yom Tov* cancels the *shivah* (see above, chapt. 32). Whether it is a seven- [in the Diaspora, eight-]day Festival (Pesach and Succos), or a one- or two-day Festival (Shavuos, Rosh

---

regarding] the sanctity of the synagogue, where the custom is to permit women to enter during their Seven Clean Days."

14. *Shulchan Melachim* (*Dinei Niddah VeYoldos* §§5).

15. *Shulchan Aruch* (344:20). *Shulchan Aruch* states: "At the completion of the Twelve Months, they visit [the deceased] and recite *Hashkavos* [memorial prayers] for him." This implies that the custom applies at the end of the Twelve Months, even if this does not coincide with the *yahrzeit* — as in a leap-year. And this is the ruling given by *Chazon LaMo'ed* (20:5).

The same may be deduced from *Beis Yosef* (*Orach Chaim* §547), who writes, regarding the *halachah* that a person should not eulogize his deceased within thirty days before a festival: "It seems to me that this applies only according to the custom during Talmudic times. . .but as for the custom in our time, that at the completion of the year [of mourning] we eulogize the deceased and recite memorial prayers, this is permitted [even less than thirty days before the festival], even according to Shmuel, since this does not arouse the memory of the deceased in such a way that it will not be forgotten for thirty days. On the contrary, their purpose [in performing this custom at the completion of the year of mourning] is to conclude the mourning. Before this, they wear black, and after this they remove the black clothing and put on good clothes." This implies that the custom was to go to the cemetery upon completion of the mourning; and the visit to the grave concludes the mourning. And this could not apply to the *yahrzeit*, but only to the end of the Twelve Months [since the *yahrzeit* does not necessarily coincide with the last day of mourning].

15a. I have heard that certain major authorities of our time have given this ruling.

16. The custom of visiting the grave on the day of the *yahrzeit* is mentioned by *Rashi* on *Yevamos* 122a, s.v. *tlasa riglei*. There *Rashi* states that he found, in a responsum of the *Geonim*: "'All these festivals of the *Amora'im*' — this refers to the anniversary of the death of a great man. They establish it as a day of honor, and each year when that day arrives, the Torah scholars gather from all around and visit his grave, along with the rest of the people, to study Torah by his grave."

17. It is not possible to visit the grave on Friday, since this would still be during the first seven days of mourning.

Hashanah, or Yom Kippur), one visits the grave the day after *Yom Tov* — even if it is still within seven days of the death.[18]

However, some rule that this visit should be made only on the seventh day after the death [or later].[19] [For example, if the death occurred a day before Shavuos, and the Festival canceled the remainder of *shivah*, one would not visit the grave until the seventh day from the death.]

The same principle applies to the visit made on the thirtieth day of mourning: That is, if a Festival occurs during *shivah* or during *shloshim*, the Festival cancels some of the days of mourning, with the result that the restrictions of the *shloshim* end less than thirty days after the death. Nevertheless, one visits the grave on the day the restrictions of the *shloshim* end, not on the thirtieth day from the death.[19a]

10. If one of the days for visiting the grave (see above, par. 8) falls on Rosh Chodesh, one should postpone the visit until after Rosh Chodesh. The same applies to Chanukah.[20]

However, some have the custom of visiting even on Rosh Chodesh or Chanukah — and, all the more so, on other days when *Tachanun* is not recited (e.g., Lag B'Omer, the fifteenth of Av, Tu Bishvat, and the like). During a visit which falls on one of these days, they recite Psalms for the elevation of the departed soul, and recite *Kaddish*. However, they omit the memorial prayers customarily recited on an ordinary day.[21]

11. Some have the custom not to visit the grave during the month of Nissan. If one has a *yahrzeit* during Nissan, one visits the grave the day before Rosh Chodesh Nissan. Nevertheless, if one did not visit then, and the *yahrzeit* occurs during Nissan, he may visit on the day of the *yahrzeit*. However, one should not recite the supplications (*techinos*) which are customarily recited on an ordinary day.[22]

On the other hand, some have the custom that there is no objection to visiting the

---

18. *Zichron Eliyahu* (manuscript). The same ruling is given by *Gesher HaChaim* (29:6); and it may also be deduced from *Magen Avraham* (696:§§5), cited below, footnote 25.

19. *Chazon LaMo'ed* (ch. 20 in the notes at the end of the book), contrary to the ruling of *Gesher HaChaim*.

19a. This means that if the Festival occurs during *shloshim*, one goes to the cemetery after *Yom Tov*.
    If the Festival occurs during *shivah*, *Yom Tov* reduces the length of the *shloshim* to fewer than thirty days, as explained above (32:8-12). In that case, one goes to the cemetery as soon as the restrictions of the *shloshim* cease (*Zichron Eliahu*, manuscript).
    As mentioned in the present section and in our previous footnote, *Chazon LaMo'ed* rules that if the Festival occurs during *shivah*, one goes to the cemetery on the seventh day from the death. Theoretically, he would rule similarly regarding *shloshim* — i.e., that one goes on the thirtieth day after the death, even if the restrictions of the *shloshim* ended earlier. On the other hand, he might draw a distinction between *shloshim* and *shivah*.

20. [The *halachah* regarding Rosh Chodesh is found in] *Kol Bo*, *Hilchos Avel*, cited by *Ba'er HaGolah* (344:§§28). *Gesher HaChaim* (29:6) infers that the same applies to Chanukah.

21. *Gesher HaChaim* (loc. cit.). He writes that *Kol Bo*, who forbids going to the cemetery on Rosh Chodesh, only intended that one should not go there in order to recite the funeral dirge (*lekonnen*); "but in order to pray, one could say that this is permissible even according to him."

22. Responsa *Melamed LeHo'il* (*Yoreh De'ah* §144).

grave during Nissan.[23]

12. If the seventh day of mourning falls on Purim, one does not visit the grave with other people. Instead, the mourner goes alone, with one *chazzan*, to recite memorial prayers.[24] The same applies if the seventh day of mourning occurs on the day before Purim.[25]

13. One does not visit the cemetery on the Sabbath. If the thirtieth day of mourning occurs on the Sabbath, some advance the visit to Friday.[26] Others postpone it until Sunday.[27]

However, if Rosh Chodesh occurs on Friday, and the *yahrzeit* is on the Sabbath, all postpone the visit until Sunday. Likewise, if Rosh Chodesh falls on Sunday, all perform the visit on Friday.[28]

14. One does not visit the cemetery during *Chol HaMo'ed*.

If one's *yahrzeit* occurs on the first day of Pesach or of Succos, one advances the visit to the day before the Festival. If the *yahrzeit* falls on the seventh day of Pesach or the last day of Succos, one postpones the visit until after the Festival.

If the *yahrzeit* falls during *Chol HaMo'ed*, many do not visit at all.[28a]

15. The custom is to visit graves on Tishah B'Av,[29] the day before Rosh Hashanah,[30] and the day before Yom Kippur.[31] However, some do not do so

---

23. *Gesher HaChaim* loc. cit.

24. *Magen Avraham* (696:§§5).

25. Ibid.

26. *Ikrei HaDat* (*Yoreh De'ah* 36:35). He writes: "If the *yahrzeit* of one's parent occurs on the Sabbath, following *Isru Chag HaPesach* [i.e., *Isru Chag*, the day after the last day of Pesach, is Friday], one should fast [for the *yahrzeit*] on Sunday [instead of on the Sabbath]. But as regards visiting the cemetery to recite memorial prayers and *Kaddish*, and to study Torah [for the benefit of the deceased], it is better to do this on the Friday [in this case, *Isru Chag*] preceding [the *yahrzeit*] (*Devar Moshe* I:§68)."

27. *Zichron Eliyahu* (manuscript) writes: "Some advance the visit to Friday; but many have the custom of postponing the visit until after the Sabbath." *Gesher HaChaim* writes similarly: "Some advance the visit, others postpone it."

28. *Gesher HaChaim* (32:5). But the words of *Ikrei HaDat* cited above, footnote 26, seem to imply the contrary. He spoke of a case in which Friday was *Isru Chag* [which, like Rosh Chodesh, is a semi-festival], and yet he wrote that the visit to the cemetery should be performed on Friday [not postponed to Sunday]. This requires study.

However, if Rosh Chodesh falls on Sunday, all agree that the visit is put ahead to Friday.

28a. *Gesher HaChaim* loc. cit.

29. *Rama* (559:10) writes: "[On Tishah B'Av], we go to the cemetery immediately after leaving the synagogue [after the morning prayers]." *Mishnah Berurah* (ad loc. §§41) explains: "[This refers to a] Jewish [cemetery]. [We go there] so that [the deceased] should request mercy for us. If there is no Jewish cemetery, we go even to a non-Jewish one, as if to say that we are like the dead. All this refers to going up to a distance of four *amos* [about eight feet] from the [nearest grave]; but one should not actually enter a cemetery — not even a Jewish one — since there is danger that negative spiritual forces (*chitzonim*) might cling. . .Moreover, it would seem that if going to the cemetery means that one would have to wear shoes, it is better not to go at all."

30. *Rama* (581:4).

31. *Mateh Efrayim* (§604-605:14). He adds: "One should not recite too many prayers, but only those prescribed by the early authorities; for *Tachanun* is not recited on this day, since it is

on the day before Yom Kippur, but go a day or two earlier.[32]

Some also visit the graves of the righteous on the day before Rosh Chodesh, and on the fifteenth of each Jewish month.[33] They are especially particular to do so onthe day before Rosh Chodesh Elul and the day before Rosh Chodesh Nissan.[34] Likewise, during the month of Elul it is customary to visit the graves of one's parents and forefathers, and of the righteous.[35]

◆§ Visiting Graves to Pray in Situations of Trouble

16. The custom is to go to the graves of forefathers, relatives, and the righteous to pray in any situation of trouble, G-d forbid, which befalls the individual or the community; and likewise, to pray for the sick.[36]

◆§ Washing Hands

17. When visiting the cemetery, one should wash hands before praying at the graves. And one should wash hands again after leaving the cemetery.[37]

Some also have the custom of washing the face after leaving the cemetery.[38]

---

considered like *Yom Tov*."

32. *Elef HaMagen* (on *Mateh Efrayim* ad loc. §§39) writes: "See the *Siddur of Yavetz*, where the author expresses surprise at the communities that follow this custom: How could they choose the day before Yom Kippur [as the time to visit the cemetery], since it is like *Yom Tov*? Therefore, it is well to go two or three days before Yom Kippur." And the same ruling is given by *Shulchan Gevoha*.

33. *Elef HaMagen* (on *Mateh Efrayim* 581:§§110) writes: "The holy books state that the propitious time for visiting the graves of *tzaddikim* is on the day before Rosh Hashanah, the day before Rosh Chodesh, and the fifteenth of each [Jewish] month (except on the Sabbath, Festival, and Rosh Chodesh, when one should not go). It is very good and beneficial, in a number of ways, to visit the graves of *tzaddikim*. By doing so, one can truly achieve repentance, and be saved from all troubles, on both the material and spiritual level."

34. *Zichron Eliyahu* (manuscript) writes: "Likewise, the custom among the Near-Eastern communities [*Eidos HaMizrach*: Sefardic, Yemenite, etc.] is to visit [the cemetery] on the day before Rosh Chodesh Elul and the day before Rosh Chodesh Nissan; for these are times when prayer is especially desirable. Some have the custom to walk around the perimeter of the cemetery on the day before Rosh Chodesh Nissan, with a *minyan* of men, reciting *tehillim* and various prayers. And some have the custom that when they visit a grave, they circle it, reciting *tehillim* and prayers."

35. *Mishmeres Shalom* (os kuf §2).

36. Ibid. He writes: "We find in *Sotah* (34b): 'Rava said: This teaches us that Caleb withdrew from the scheme of the spies and went to pray at the tombs of the Patriarchs. He said to them: "My fathers, beseech Hashem to have mercy on me, that I may be saved from the scheme of the spies." '

"And see *Tosafos* (ad loc. s.v. *avosai*): 'You might object that in Chapter *Mi She'meiso* (*Brachos* 18a) the *Gemara* says that "the dead are not conscious of anything." And the conclusion reached there is that this applies even to the Patriarchs. The answer is that by means of the prayer which one prays [when visiting the grave], they are informed that such-and-such has been prayed for.' Thus, the *Gemara* says in the second chapter of *Taanis* (16a): 'Why do we go to the cemetery? In order that [the deceased] should ask for mercy for us.' Likewise, *Pirkei Chassidim* relates the story of R' Manni, who visited the [burial] cave of the Patriarchs."

Mishmeres Shalom adds: "This is the source of the custom of visiting one's parents' graves."

37. *Magen Avraham* (4:§§20), citing *Maharil* (§23). The reason for washing hands upon leaving the cemetery is that evil spirits (*ruchos ra'os*) accompany those who are leaving.

38. *Mishnah Berurah* (ad loc. citing *Artzos HaChaim*).

◦§ The Blessing אֲשֶׁר יָצַר אֶתְכֶם בַּדִּין /
". . .Who Created You with Justice. . ."

18. If one has not seen Jewish graves for thirty days, one recites:

בָּרוּךְ אַתָּה ה׳ אֱלֹהֵינוּ מֶלֶךְ הָעוֹלָם, אֲשֶׁר יָצַר אֶתְכֶם בַּדִּין, וְזָן וְכִלְכֵּל אֶתְכֶם בַּדִּין, וְהֵמִית אֶתְכֶם בַּדִּין, וְיוֹדֵעַ מִסְפַּר כֻּלְּכֶם בַּדִּין, וְהוּא עָתִיד לְהַחֲיוֹתְכֶם וּלְקַיֵּם אֶתְכֶם בַּדִּין. בָּרוּךְ אַתָּה ה׳ מְחַיֵּה הַמֵּתִים. אַתָּה גִּבּוֹר לְעוֹלָם אֲדֹנָי, מְחַיֵּה מֵתִים אַתָּה, רַב לְהוֹשִׁיעַ. [מַשִּׁיב הָרוּחַ וּמוֹרִיד הַגֶּשֶׁם / מוֹרִיד הַטָּל] מְכַלְכֵּל חַיִּים בְּחֶסֶד, מְחַיֵּה מֵתִים בְּרַחֲמִים רַבִּים, סוֹמֵךְ נוֹפְלִים, וְרוֹפֵא חוֹלִים, וּמַתִּיר אֲסוּרִים, וּמְקַיֵּם אֱמוּנָתוֹ לִישֵׁנֵי עָפָר. מִי כָמוֹךָ בַּעַל גְּבוּרוֹת, וּמִי דּוֹמֶה לָּךְ, מֶלֶךְ מֵמִית וּמְחַיֶּה וּמַצְמִיחַ יְשׁוּעָה, וְנֶאֱמָן אַתָּה לְהַחֲיוֹת מֵתִים.

"Blessed are You, Hashem, our God, King of the universe, Who fashioned you with justice, nourished and sustained you with justice, took your lives with justice, knows the sum total of all of you with justice, and Who in the future will resuscitate you and restore you with justice. Blessed are You, Hashem, Who resuscitates the dead." Then one says [the second blessing of the *Shemoneh Esrei* prayer]: *"You are eternally mighty, my Lord. You resuscitate the dead, You are great in salvation. He causes the wind to blow and the rain to fall"* [In summer, in place of *"the wind to blow and the rain to fall,"* Nusach Sefard substitutes: *"the dew to come down."* But those who pray in the Nusach Ashkenaz do not recite either phrase during the summer]. *He nourishes the living with kindness, resuscitates the dead with abundant mercy, supports the fallen, heals the sick, releases the imprisoned, and maintains His faith with those asleep in the dust. Who is like You, O Master of mightiness, and who resembles You, O King Who causes death and restores life and causes salvation to sprout? And You are trustworthy to resurrect the dead."* (One stops here, omitting the closing phrase of the blessing.)[39]

19. If one sees graves from a rooftop or a window, at a distance, one does not recite this blessing. Likewise, one does not recite it if one again visits a cemetery within thirty days of the present visit.[40]

For the question whether one should recite this blessing when accompanying the deceased to burial, see above, 10:14.

---

39. *Shulchan Aruch* (224:12). And see *Gesher HaChaim*, who writes: "Even though one is forbidden to recite other blessings within four *amos* (about eight feet) [of a grave], just as one is forbidden to study Torah there, the *halachah* regarding this blessing is different, since it relates to the deceased. It is for this same reason that the custom is to permit reciting Psalms and *Kaddish* also within four *amos* [of a grave]."

40. *Gesher HaChaim* (29:17).

✒ Placing One's Hand on the Grave; Reciting Verses

20. Upon reaching the grave,[41] it is customary to place one's left hand on the monument and recite the following verses:

וְנָחֲךָ ה' תָּמִיד וְהִשְׂבִּיעַ בְּצַחְצָחוֹת נַפְשֶׁךָ, וְעַצְמֹתֶיךָ יַחֲלִיץ, וְהָיִיתָ כְּגַן רָוֶה וּכְמוֹצָא מַיִם אֲשֶׁר לֹא יְכַזְּבוּ מֵימָיו: וּבָנוּ מִמְּךָ חָרְבוֹת עוֹלָם, מוֹסְדֵי דוֹר־וָדוֹר תְּקוֹמֵם וְקֹרָא לְךָ גֹּדֵר פֶּרֶץ מְשׁוֹבֵב נְתִיבוֹת לָשָׁבֶת,

'Hashem will guide you always, sating your soul in thirsty places, and rescuing your bones; and you shall be like a watered garden, and like a never-failing spring of water. From you, the ancient ruins will be rebuilt; you will re-establish the structures of the generations; they will call you, "the one who repairs the breach and resettles the ways of civilization"' (Isaiah 58:11-12).

Then one says:

תִּשְׁכַּב בְּשָׁלוֹם עַד בֹּא מְנַחֵם מַשְׁמִיעַ שָׁלוֹם,

'Lie in peace until the coming of the Consoler Who will announce peace.'

When placing one's hand on the grave, one should think of the verse, וְנָחֲךָ, 'Hashem will guide you always,' quoted above, which contains fifteen words, like the number of joints on the hand[42] (See footnote).

✒ Placing a Pebble on the Grave

21. It is written in *Drashos Maharash* that when he visited a grave, he would say:

יְהִי רָצוֹן שֶׁתְּהֵא מְנוּחָתוֹ שֶׁל פְּלוֹנִי פֹּה בְּכָבוֹד וּזְכוּתוֹ יַעֲמוֹד לִי,

'May it be Your will that [the name of the deceased] rest here in honor, and may his merit defend me.'

It is customary to leave a small stone or piece of grass on the grave, in honor of the deceased, to show that one visited his grave.[43]

---

41. *Zichron Eliahu* writes, in the name of *Likutei Eitzos* (§71): "When one visits the graves of one's parents and forefathers, as is the custom, it is good to state that one requests that the deceased buried in the vicinity of one's relatives or parents should inform them that their son or daughter has come and has made such-and-such requests. In *Tehillah LeMoshe*, the introduction to *Yismach Moshe* on *Nach*, it is related that the holy *rav*, author of *Yismach Moshe*, once sent two men to the grave of our holy teacher, the author of *Noam Elimelech*, to pray for his son. He told the emissaries: 'When you come to the courtyard of the cemetery, say: We vow a coin (*prutah*) to *tzedakah* on behalf of the soul who will go and tell the soul of the *Rav*, R' Elimelech, that we have come to his grave to pray to Hashem.' It may be that this is the source of the custom followed by some, that when they go to the cemetery and do not find the grave where they wanted to pray, they say: I hereby vow a *prutah* (or a specific number of *prutos*) to *tzedakah*, on behalf of the soul who will inform (here one gives the name of the deceased and the name of his father) that I have come to his grave to pray to Hashem.'"

42. Ibid. citing *Birkei Yosef* and *Sha'arei Teshuvah* (*Orach Chaim* 224:§8). See *Kaf HaChaim* (ad loc. §§42), who quotes *Kemach Soless* who asks that the above verse contains seventeen words.

43. *Ba'er Heitev* (*Orach Chaim* 224:§§8).

◄§ Reciting Psalms at Graveside

22. [There is a prohibition against "ridiculing the helpless" (*lo'eg larash*), i.e., flaunting one's ability to perform *mitzvos* in the presence of the deceased who can no longer perform *mitzvos*.] Nevertheless, it is permissible to recite Psalms at graveside, even within four *amos* [about eight feet] of it, and likewise to study Torah and deliver a Torah discourse in honor of the deceased. These things are not considered *lo'eg larash*.[44]

◄§ The Order of Psalms

23. As mentioned above (par. 8), the custom is to visit the cemetery on the day when the *shivah* and *shloshim* end, and on the *yahrzeit*. Among Ashkenazic congregations, the custom during these visits is to recite the following seven Psalms for the elevation of the departed soul: 33, 16, 17, 72, 91, 104, and 130. Then one recites those letters from *Psalm* 119 which spell the name of the deceased, and also those that spell the word נְשָׁמָה (*neshamah*, "soul"). [*Psalm* 119 is arranged in alphabetical order. The first eight verses begin with *alef*; the next eight with *beis*, and so on. Thus, for example, to spell the name, דָּוִד, "David," one would recite verses 25-32, then verses 41-48, and then again verses 25-32.] Afterwards, one recites the prayer beginning אָנָּא (*Ana*, "Please. . ."),[44a] followed by the Mourner's *Kaddish* and the *Kel Malei* memorial prayer.

The prayer beginning *Ana*, and *Kel Malei*, are recited only on those days when *Tachanun* is included in the prayer-service. The Mourner's *Kaddish* is recited only in the presence of a *minyan*.[45]

Some recite the *Kel Malei* in the cemetery, even on days when *Tachanun* is not included in the prayer-service.[45a]

◄§ Correct Intent in Praying at the Grave

24. When one prays at the graves of one's parents, forefathers, and relatives, or at other graves, one should not direct their prayers *to* the deceased, nor request anything from them. One should pray only to the Holy One, Blessed is He. One should not direct one's efforts towards the deceased, so that one will not be in the category of those who seek favors from the dead (*doresh el hameisim*).

When one prays at the graves of *tzaddikim*, one should request of Hashem, Blessed is He, that He have mercy upon oneself through the merit of the righteous ones who dwell in the dust.[46]

---

44. *Sdei Chemed (Aveilus* §115).

44a. ArtScroll Ashkenaz *Siddur* p. 808.

45. *Ner LeEliahu (Minhagei Beis HaKevaros* §11).

45a. *Chazon LaMo'ed* (9:6).

46. *Ba'er Heitev* (581:§§17). However, *Gesher HaChaim* writes: "But many permit addressing the deceased and saying to him: 'Be our representative and pray for us to Hashem, Blessed is He.' Since one asks the deceased to pray to Hashem, Blessed is He, this is not considered directing one's

25. Some have the custom that if a person has not visited his parent's grave during the past ten years, he should not visit it any more.[47]

⋖ Decorum at the Cemetery

26. One is forbidden to treat the cemetery lightly.[48] Thus, one may not relieve oneself there, nor may one eat or drink there. One is forbidden to makecalculations of accounts there, even for the needs of the community. One may not pasture animals there, nor have an irrigation ditch pass through the cemetery. One may not use the cemetery as a shortcut to get from one place to another. One may not gather grass or plants there. If one did gather plants, even for the needs of the cemetery, one must burn them on the spot.[49]

27. One may pick fruit from trees planted in the cemetery, as long as the trees are not growing on the graves themselves.[50]

28. One is forbidden to derive any kind of benefit from a structure which serves as a tomb. However, one is not forbidden to derive benefit from the earth of a

---

efforts towards the deceased himself. It is like asking a living *tzaddik* to pray for one." And see responsa *Maharam Shick* (*Orach Chaim* §293).

47. See *Mishmeres Shalom (os hei* §32), who states: "Some say that the time limit is ten years; others, seven years. And see *Yoseif Da'as, zal*, who writes that there is no time limit. As proof, he points out that Caleb visited the tomb of the Patriarchs. [See above, footnote 1.] I have seen that *Kuntres Eser Tzachtzachos* writes: The *Rav* . . . related in the name of his grandfather, the *Rav* of Sanz, *zatzal*, that he was once in the city of Premisla and said, 'I have heard it said that if one has not visited one's parent's graves for ten years, one should not go any more. . .' As for the issue itself, I have heard that the prohibition applies only if the person had once visited the grave, and later stopped visiting it for a period of ten years; but if he had never been to his parent's grave, there is no prohibition, even after many years. If so, this would refute the proof of the *gaon* of Levov, based on the story of Caleb. The matter requires study."

    Gesher HaChaim (29:16) writes: "It is true that some have written that if one has not visited his parent's grave for ten years, he should not visit it; nevertheless, one need not observe this prohibition — see the statement of *Duda'ei HaSadeh* (§38) on this matter."

    Even Yaakov (44:5) writes: "If one takes these words literally, one would certainly think that this is the conclusion reached by *Duda'ei HaSadeh*, to whom [*Gesher HaChaim*] refers. . .but this is not so. *Duda'ei HaSadeh* does indeed cite *Yoseif Da'as*, who ridicules this custom; but he himself [*Duda'ei HaSadeh*] writes that one could say, regarding the graves of one's own parents, that one should visit for the sake of honoring one's parent. If a long time has passed, and one has not gone there, it may be assumed that one's parents are upset about this, and will not lend a receptive ear to relay one's prayers on high. . .Likewise, regarding the graves of one's parents, it makes a difference whether [one's absence] was avoidable or unavoidable. If it was unavoidable, there is no prohibition, and one may go, even after many years."

48. *Shulchan Aruch* (*Yoreh De'ah* 368:1). *Shach* (ad loc. §§1) explains that this is in order to show respect for the dead. *Pischei Teshuvah* (ad loc. §§1) writes: "See responsa *Chasam Sofer* (§335), who writes that the prohibition applies even in a place which is not over a grave, but has been set aside as a public cemetery; it takes on the sanctity of a cemetery, with the appropriate prohibitions."

49. *Shulchan Aruch* (loc. cit. par. 1).

50. Ibid. par. 2, and *Shach* §§20.

grave.[51] One is forbidden to sit on a monument,[52] or to lean on it.[53]

One is forbidden to walk on a grave, but for the needs of a *mitzvah*, this is permitted. Sitting or leaning on it is forbidden, even for the needs of a *mitzvah*.[54] It is customary to request the deceased's forgiveness if one must walk on the grave.[55]

29. One should not walk in a cemetery,[56] or within four *amos* (about eight feet) of a deceased person,[57] with *tefillin* on one's head. This applies even if the deceased

---

51. Ibid. 364:1.

52. *Rama* (ad loc.) cites a dispute on this issue. See *Taz* (§§1), who states, citing *Rashal*, that the prevalent custom is to forbid sitting on a grave.

53. *Taz* (loc. cit.). The same ruling is given by *Shach* (§§3), citing *Hagahos Asheri*.

54. *Taz* and *Shach* (ad loc.), citing *Hagahos Asheri*.

Responsa *Yad Eliahu* (§54), cited by *Pischei Teshuvah* (ad loc. §§2), and *Chiddushei R' Akiva Eiger* (ad loc.), who states that there are two reasons to forbid (sitting on a grave): First, one is forbidden to get any benefit from a grave (*issur hana'ah*); second, it is disrespectful to the dead. The difference between these two reasons has a practical application. Walking over a grave to get somewhere else gives one no benefit, since one could walk even more easily if there were no grave there. Thus, walking over the grave is forbidden only because it is disrespectful. Therefore, if one wants to walk over a grave in order to do a *mitzvah* [such as performing a burial], this would be permissible; [for in this case, it is not considered disrespectful]. On the other hand, sitting on a monument gives one benefit: It is more comfortable to sit on a stone than on the ground. And even if one's purpose is to do a *mitzvah*, it is still forbidden to derive benefit from a grave.

Misgeres HaShulchan (*Yoreh De'ah*) writes: "In our day, it is impossible to take the deceased to burial without stepping on graves. The same is true in the case of someone who wants to visit the grave of his parents and pray there, as is customary. In these cases, if the path is narrow and there is no room [to get to the grave without stepping on other graves], one may rely on those who rule that this is permissible. . .but regarding anything unnecessary — such as leaning or sitting on a monument, or a situation where it is possible to get to the grave without stepping on other graves — one should be careful [not to step on them]. . . Moreover, I have noticed that people lean on the monuments and are not careful in this matter. One who is strict about this will be blessed." This ruling is also cited by *Even Yaakov* (§30).

55. *Zichron Eliahu* (manuscript).

56. *Shulchan Aruch* (*Yoreh De'ah* 367:2, and *Orach Chaim* 45:1).

See also *Mishnah Berurah* (ad loc. §§1), who writes: "[Wearing *tefillin*] is forbidden even within four *amos* of the place where the graves begin, unless there is a partition (*mechitzah*) between [the person and the graves].

"Now, it will be noticed that *Shulchan Aruch* wrote two separate statements [(1) 'One should not walk in a cemetery,' (2) '. . . or within four *amos* of a deceased person'], instead of combining them into one statement such as: 'One should not walk within four *amos* of a grave or a deceased person.' In the opinion of *Magen Avraham*, *Shulchan Aruch* chose this wording in order to indicate that, inside a cemetery, one is forbidden [to wear *tefillin*] even if one is more than four *amos* from the nearest grave. But other *Poskim* rule leniently on this point. And see *Be'ur Halachah* that, in the midst of the cemetery, in the proximity of many graves, it would seem that one should be strict [and not wear *tefillin*], even if one is four *amos* or more from the nearest grave. This is not the case at the edge of the cemetery, where there are no graves, but the ground has simply been designated for graves. In that case, according to the basic *halachah*, one need not be strict. Nevertheless, it is proper not to go inside the cemetery fence at all with *tefillin* on one's head, since one might accidentally come within four *amos* of a grave."

57. *Mishnah Berurah* (ad loc. §§2) writes: "*Ateres Zekeinim* states that the entire room where the deceased is lying is considered equivalent to 'within four *amos*'; but *Magen Giborim* disagrees, ruling that the prohibition applies only literally within four *amos*.

"Even by the grave of a child who had not reached the age of performing *mitzvos*, one should not

is a woman or child.[58] Doing so would violate the prohibition of *lo'eg larash*[59] (see above, par. 22). But if the *tefillin* and straps are covered, this is permitted.[60]

Likewise, one should not walk in a cemetery, or within four *amos* of a deceased person, while carrying a Torah Scroll and reading from it,[61] or while praying.[62] One is also forbidden to recite Torah from memory, except for the honor of the deceased.[63]

30. In Talmudic times, men attached *tzitzis* to the ordinary garments they wore.[64] Under those circumstances, people were permitted to walk in a cemetery, or

---

go within [four *amos*] with *tefillin* on one's head, because of the prohibition of *lo'eg larash*" [see above, par. 22].

58. See *Pischei Teshuvah* (367:§§1), who writes: "See responsa *Maharitatz*, in his *chiddushim* on Chapter *Eizehu Neshech* (p. 12), who states that the prohibition against learning Torah or wearing *tefillin* within four *amos* of the deceased applies only if the deceased had been obligated by these *mitzvos* when alive, and now, after death, has been released from these *mitzvos*. In such a case, one violates the prohibition of *lo'eg larash* [see footnote 59, below]. But if the deceased was a woman or child, and hence was exempt from these *mitzvos* when alive, this is not considered *lo'eg larash*.

"But see *Tzelach* (*Berachos* p. 3a and p. 18), who assumes it to be obvious that the prohibition of *lo'eg larash* applies even if the deceased was a woman or child. And see what the *gaon* of Levov writes about this in his *Yeshuos Yaakov* (*Orach Chaim* 71:§§6)."

Mishnah Berurah (23:§§5) writes: "One should be strict about the prohibition of *lo'eg larash* even at the grave of a child, since he might have had the soul of a grown man. But by the grave of a woman, who was exempt [from these *mitzvos*] even when alive, *lo'eg larash* does not apply (*Elyah Rabbah* and *Pri Megaddim*)."

Shoneh Halachos (ad loc. par. 3) writes that the prohibition applies even if the deceased was a woman. Regarding the statement of *Mishnah Berurah* that there is no prohibition in that case, *Shoneh Halachos* points out that this is based on the ruling of *Maharitatz*; but in fact, *Maharitatz* concludes that one should be strict even if the deceased was a woman. *Pri Megaddim*, he says, did not see the text of *Maharitatz*, but only the citation of it in *Elyah Rabbah*. *Shoneh Halachos* states that this point is also made by *Kehillos Yaakov* (IX:§9); and *Sdei Chemed* (*Aveilus os* 113), who cites *Maharitatz* and expresses surprise at the passage in *Pischei Teshuvah* (cited at the beginning of this footnote), because he did not quote *Maharitatz*'s final conclusion. Thus, *Sdei Chemed* concludes that the prohibition of *lo'eg larash* applies even if the deceased was a woman or a child.

59. One would appear to be taunting the dead about the fact that they cannot perform *mitzvos* (*Mishnah Berurah* 23:§§1 quoting the *Tur*).

60. *Mishnah Berurah* (45:§§3). He adds: "Therefore, although one is permitted to go there wearing only the *tefillin* of the arm, since it is covered, one must be careful also to cover the strap which is wrapped around one's finger (*Taz*)."

61. See *Pischei Teshuvah* (ad loc. §§2), who writes: "See responsa *Noda BiYehudah* (*tinyana*, *Orach Chaim* §109). He was asked: 'If there is a time of trouble, and the people go to pray at the graves of the *tzaddikim*, is it correct to take a Torah Scroll with them into the cemetery?'

"The reply was: 'In the works of the Talmud and *Poskim*, there is no explicit ruling as to whether just holding the Torah Scroll [as opposed to holding and reading it] is forbidden. But from the wording of *Rambam* in *Hilchos Sefer Torah*, one may infer that this is forbidden. In any case, far be it from us to do such a thing, for the *Zohar* (*Parashas Acharei*) states that if, God forbid, the Scroll is missing even a single letter, this would cause great harm, God forbid. Since this is the case, [one cannot take a Torah Scroll into a cemetery,] for we [cannot be completely] sure that a letter has not been left out or added.' "

62. *Shach* (§§3) writes, in the name of *Maharshal*, that for the recitation of *Kaddish*, too, one must be at least four *amos* from the nearest grave. This ruling is cited by *Drishah*. The same ruling is given by *Bach*.

63. *Shulchan Aruch* loc. cit.

64. In those days, their clothes were made with four corners (*Mishnah Berurah* 23:§§2).

within four *amos* of a deceased person or a grave, while wearing *tzitzis*, as long as the *tzitzis* did not drag on the graves. If they did drag on the graves, this was forbidden, because of *lo'eg larash*.[64a]

In our time, when four-cornered garments are worn only for the sake of the *mitzvah*, wearing *tzitzis* in such places is forbidden even if the *tzitzis* do not drag on the graves. This prohibition applies if the *tzitzis* are uncovered; but if they are covered, one is permitted to wear them.[65]

31. Some have the custom that when they go into a cemetery, they tie together the two *tzitzis* on each side of the garment. But this does not help.[66]

32. If one goes at least four *amos* (about eight feet) away from the cemetery, one is permitted to read Torah or pray, even if he can see the graves. If there is a partition (*mechitzah*), one is permitted to read Torah or pray behind the *mechitzah*, even within four *amos* of the cemetery.[67]

64a. See note 59 above.

65. "For example, [it is permissible] to wear the *tallis gadol* (prayer shawl) if the *tzitzis* (fringes) are hidden under one's clothes. For the same reason, the *tallis katan* [small four-cornered fringed garment] which one wears under one's clothes does not violate the prohibition of *lo'eg larash*, since it is covered — unless one is not wearing any garment on top of it; in that case, it, too, is forbidden, unless one hides the *tzitzis* in one's clothes. (And *Pri Megaddim* implies that one should be strict about the *tallis gadol* [and not wear it in the cemetery], even if the *tzitzis* are hidden, since the *tallis gadol* is worn especially for praying. However, *Beis Yosef* implies the opposite. And *Derech HaChaim* also states, without limitation, that [wearing the *tallis*] is permissible if the *tzitzis* are covered.)" (*Mishnah Berurah* loc. cit. §§3).

66. "Even though they tie them together, this does not cancel the *mitzvah* of *tzitzis*, since it is not a permanent knot, but the intention is to untie it immediately upon leaving the cemetery — similar to what [*Shulchan Aruch*] writes in 10:3. Moreover, according to their opinion that tying the *tzitzis* cancels the *mitzvah*, this means that they are wearing [a four-cornered] garment without *tzitzis*" (*Mishnah Berurah* ad loc. §§4).

67. *Shulchan Aruch Yoreh De'ah* 367:6.

CHAPTER FORTY-THREE

Memorial Prayers:
Yizkor and *Kel Malei Rachamim*

---

1. The custom is to memorialize the deceased[1] after the Torah-reading[2] on the Sabbath[3] and *Yom Tov*.[4] On the Sabbath, the memorial prayer is *Kel Malei*

---

1. *Beis Yosef* (*Orach Chaim* §284), in the name of Rabbeinu Shneur, comments on the custom of reciting memorial prayers and pledging charity for the deceased. As evidence that this is of benefit to the deceased, he quotes *Sifrei* (*Parashas Devarim* §21): " '*Atone for Your people Israel*' (*Deut.* 21:8) — this refers to the living. '. . .*whom You have redeemed*' (ibid.) — this refers to the dead. It teaches us that the dead need atonement." *Beis Yosef* adds: "It seems that this custom is based on a statement in *Kiddushin* (31a): During the first Twelve Months [of mourning] one says: הֲרֵינִי כַּפָּרַת מִשְׁכָּבוֹ, 'I am atonement for his resting place' [see above, 38:14]. This implies that, through the physical life [of the living], the dead receive atonement. And the same applies to their money." [That is, when the living give *tzedakah*, this too brings atonement for the dead.]

   Similarly, *Kaftor VaFerach* quotes *Pesikta*: "Great is *tzedakah*, for it saves people from the punishment of *Gehinnom*, as it is said: '*Atone for Your people Israel*': One might think that once a person dies, *tzedakah* cannot help him. But the Torah says: '*Atone. . .*' "

   Sefer Chassidim (§170) tells of a certain pious man who used to pledge charity for the benefit of the souls of his relatives. Afterwards, he would pledge everything for the benefit of all souls in general. When asked why he did this for the benefit of all souls, he replied: "There are those among them from whose merit I benefit; and I do not wish to be ungrateful. Besides, because of them, it will likewise be good for me." *Perush Al Sefer Chassidim* (ad loc.) explains: "They, too, will not wish to be ungrateful, so they will pray for me, and on their merit, Hashem, Blessed is He, will do good to me."

   See also *Pesikta Rabbasi* (*pesikta* 20 *Matan Torah*): "One might think that once a person goes down to *Gehinnom*, nothing can be done for him. But [the truth is that] when people pray for mercy for him, he is thrown out of *Gehinnom* like an arrow shot from a bow" (*Tanchuma*, beginning of *Parashas Ha'azinu*). And see *Tashbatz* §289.

2. The point is that this memorial prayer is to follow directly after the Torah-reading — not after *Ashrei* ('Praiseworthy are those who dwell in Your house. . .') which precedes the *Mussaf* prayer. After this *Ashrei*, one should not recite anything. The *Kaddish* recited by the *chazzan* just before the *Mussaf* prayer is based on this preceding *Ashrei*. Therefore, there should be no interruption between *Ashrei* and *Kaddish*. The passage beginning *Yehallelu* ('Let them praise the name of Hashem. . .'), which is recited while returning the Torah Scroll to the Ark, is not considered an interruption (*Mishnah Berurah* 284:§§15).

3. *Rama* (*Orach Chaim* 284:6).

   Why was the Sabbath chosen as the time to recite this memorial prayer? *Beis Yosef* states: "Rabbeinu Binyamin writes: 'the Sabbath is the Day of Rest, modeled on the world to come. It is a day on which the dead, too, rest, and are not punished. Therefore it is a fit time to memorialize them for rest and blessing, and to pray for them.' "

   See also responsa *Zecher Yehosef* (§94), who cites responsa *Binyan Olam* (beginning of §62) as ruling that "a son may recite memorial prayers [*Kel Malei Rachamim*] for his father on the Sabbath. . .and it is preferable for the son to recite it himself than for the *chazzan* to do so, since 'the son gives merit to the father.' "

4. *Shulchan Aruch* (*Orach Chaim*, Laws of Yom Kippur 621:6,) writes: "The custom is to pledge charity on Yom Kippur for the benefit of the deceased, and to recite *Yizkor* for them — since the

Rachamim ("O God, full of mercy. . ."); on *Yom Tov*, it consists of both *Yizkor* (recited by each individual) and *Kel Malei Rachamim*. In both distinct cases, the recitations are referred to as *Hazkaras Neshamos* (lit., "Recalling of the Souls").

In some congregations the custom is to recite memorial prayers [*Kel Malei Rachamim*] each Monday and Thursday, after the Torah-reading.[5]

2. For the deceased, the primary merit achieved by the memorial prayer derives from the contributions one makes to charity for the elevation of his soul.[6]

3. If the *yahrzeit* occurs on a weekday, one should recite the *Kel Malei Rachamim* on the preceding Sabbath — even if the *yahrzeit* occurs on Monday and Thursday, when there is a Torah-reading.[7]

If the *yahrzeit* occurs on Monday or Thursday, and the custom of one's congregation is to recite *Kel Malei Rachamim* on those days (see above, par. 1), one should recite it not only on the Sabbath, but also on the day of the *yahrzeit*.

In addition, it is customary to recite the *Kel Malei Rachamim* at the grave.[8]

4. The leader of the prayer-service is permitted to recite the memorial prayers for others even if his own father and mother are alive.[9]

---

dead, too, receive atonement on Yom Kippur." *Rama* (*Yoreh De'ah* 249:16) likewise states: "It is a custom of the early sages to pledge charity for the benefit of the deceased, and this helps their souls (*Roke'ach* §217)."

Gesher HaChaim (31:1) writes: "It seems that, originally, the custom was to recite memorial prayers only on Yom Kippurim, as indicated by *Midrash Tanchuma*, *Mordechai*, and *Shulchan Aruch*. *Mahariv* writes that the day is called 'Yom HaKippurim' [lit., 'Day of Atonements,' in the plural] because it brings atonement for both the living and the dead. Afterwards, the custom was instituted to recite memorial prayers each Sabbath, as is mentioned by *Rama*, *Orach Chaim* §284."

5. *Sha'arei Efrayim* (10: 27). The same custom is mentioned by *Gesher HaChaim* (loc. cit.).

However, *Nimukei Orach Chaim* (§284) states that in his city and the surrounding areas, there is no custom at all to recite memorial prayers on a weekday.

6. See above, footnotes 1 and 4. And *Rabbeinu Bachyai* (commenting on the verse, '*Atone for Your people Israel,*' *Deut.* 21:8) writes: "From this we learn that the pledges given by the living for the sake of the dead are of benefit to the dead. And, all the more so, when their son pledges [*tzedakah*] in their name, this gives merit to them." See also *Beis Yosef* §621.

Pri Megaddim (ad loc.) comments: "If the person recited the confession (*vidui*) before his death, it may be said that he received atonement and should be considered a *tzaddik*."

Mishnah Berurah (ad loc. §§19) writes: "It stands to reason that if the son gives for the benefit of his father, this helps in every case to lighten the punishment [even if the father was not meritorious], since, 'the son gives merit to the father.' "

7. *Mishmeres Shalom* (*os yud* §13), citing *Ge'ulas Israel*, in the name of the holy *rav* R' Pinchas of Koretz, *zal*.

8. *Shulchan Aruch* (*Yoreh De'ah* 344:20) states: "At the end of the Twelve Months, one visits [the grave] and puts him to rest [the word for 'putting to rest' is *Hashkavah*]." And *Be'er HaGolah* (ad loc.) explains: "One recites memorial prayers, and prays for the deceased. And there is a prescribed prayer for this, called *Hashkavah* [by Sefardic Jews, corresponding to the *Kel Malei Rachamim* of Ashkenazic Jews]."

9. *Kol Bo Al Aveilus* (p. 399), in the name of the *gaon* R' Wolf Boskovitch, cited by *Tzafnas Paane'ach* (23) and by *Yad Yitzchak* (§80).

It is permitted to memorialize many souls in one memorial prayer.[10] In that case, after mentioning all their names, one continues: שֶׁהָלְכוּ לְעוֹלָמָם . . . בְּעַד הַזְכָּרַת נִשְׁמָתָם . . ., ". . .who went on to *their* world. . .I shall contribute to charity in remembrance of *their* souls. . ." — and one continues the prayer in the plural, concluding: וְיָנוּחוּ בְּשָׁלוֹם עַל מִשְׁכָּבָם, ". . .and may *they* repose in peace on *their* resting place."[11]

5. The Ashkenazic custom is to use the name of the deceased and the name of his or her father (for example: '*Binyamin ben Yaakov*'; '*Dinah bas Yaakov*'). The Sefardic custom is to use the name of the deceased and the name of his or her mother (for example: '*Binyamin ben Rachel*'; '*Dinah bas Leah*').[12]

6. Some rule that in *Kel Malei Rachamim* the correct wording is עַל, '. . .upon (not: תַּחַת, '*under*') כַּנְפֵי הַשְׁכִינָה, the wings of the Shechinah (Divine Presence).'[13] Others say: בְּצֵל כַּנְפֵי הַשְׁכִינָה, ". . .in the shade of the wings of the Shechinah. . ."[14] Still others rule that the correct phrase is: תַּחַת, '. . .under (not: עַל, '*upon*') the wings of the Shechinah.'[14a]

7. One should not recite memorial prayers in any language except Hebrew.[15]

8. The memorial prayer is recited even for someone who committed suicide.[16]

9. In some congregations, the custom is not to recite memorial prayers for anyone who was under the age of thirteen.[17] However, the prevalent custom is to recite

---

10. Ibid., in the name of *Arugas HaBosem* (*Orach Chaim teshuvah* 211). He cites a number of geonim who were asked about this, and all ruled that it is permissible to include all the souls together. "Nevertheless," he continues, "the *Admor*, *zatzal*, had doubts about mentioning all the names of the deceased in one commemoration, and cited proof. . ." But he concludes that [mentioning each of the deceased separately] would be burdensome to the congregation (*tircha d'tzibbura*) and would lead to idle conversation and other [problems]. Thus he agreed with his questioner that one may include [all the deceased] together. However, if one of the deceased was a very great man, it would be proper, out of respect for him, to mention him separately. And see responsa *Tzitz Eliezer* (XVI:§35), who discusses this subject at length.

11. *Gesher HaChaim* (31:2:3).

12. Ibid. par. 10.

13. The *Shelah HaKadosh* (*Maseches Shavuos*) writes that in the *Kel Malei* prayer one should not say תַּחַת כַּנְפֵי הַשְׁכִינָה, "under the wings of the *Shechinah*," because this is dangerous for the soul of the deceased, God forbid, since it brings him down . . . Rather, one should say: עַל כַּנְפֵי הַשְׁכִינָה, "upon the wings of the Shechinah."

14. *Gesher HaChaim* (loc. cit.).

14a. *Sha'ar HaKollel* (ch. 26). The same ruling is given by *Ma'avar Yabok*.

15. Responsa *Mahari Shteif* (§255). See also *Magen Avraham* (end of §284).

16. Responsa *Yehudah Ya'aleh* (§355). He writes: "This is no disgrace to the living [who recite memorial prayers for their relative]. On the contrary, it is to their credit, and is considered an act of kindness to the deceased, just as it is no disgrace to the *tzaddikim* who, when they die, pass by Gehinnom in order to raise up from there a number of souls of the wicked. . ."

17. *Ikrei HaDat* (*Yoreh De'ah* 36:11). He writes: "The reason seems to be that a person under the age of *bar mitzvah* is not liable to punishments; so what need is there to pray that the Attribute of Strict Justice should be ameliorated for him?"
Ikrei HaDat points out that this reason is somewhat questionable; for if this is the case, memorial prayers would not be recited for anyone under twenty, since until that age one is not liable to

them even for someone who was under the age of thirteen, if he was *bar da'as* (capable of understanding).[18] Some recite memorial prayers even for a child who had not reached the age of *bar da'as*.[19]

10. One is permitted to recite memorial prayers for one's first wife, even after having remarried.[20]

☙ Days When Memorial Prayers Are not Recited

11. On the following days, one does not recite the *Kel Malei Rachamim* memorial prayer:

    (a) Rosh Chodesh.

    (b) Chanukah.

    (c) Tu B'Shvat.

    (d) The fourteenth and fifteenth of Adar, Adar I, or Adar II.

    (e) The entire month of Nissan.[21]

    (f) The fourteenth of Iyar [Pesach Sheni in some communities].

    (g) Lag B'Omer.

    (h) From Rosh Chodesh Sivan through the day after Shavuos. Some congregations do not say through the thirteenth of that month.

    (i) The fifteenth of Av.

    (j) Erev Rosh Hashanah.

    (k) Erev Yom Kippur.

---

punishment at the hands of the Heavenly Court; so what need is there to pray that the punishment should be ameliorated?

But see *Sdei Chemed* (*Aveilus* §212), who cites these words of *Ikrei HaDat* and writes: "If the reader will examine what I wrote in *Kuntres HaKlalim* (*HaAlef* §19), he will see clearly that this question [raised by *Ikarei HaDat*] presents no difficulty. In the first place, although the Sages mention an opinion that the heavenly court does not punish anyone under the age of twenty, many hold that they did not mean that this is the decisive ruling." He concludes: "Therefore, certainly, since it is not a clear-cut ruling that [the heavenly court] does not punish anyone under the age of twenty, it is fit and correct to recite memorial prayers for such a person."

18. *Gesher HaChaim* (loc. cit.). He explains: "In certain respects, even children are punishable once they are *bar da'as*. This may be inferred from the commentary of *Tosafos* on the Torah passage about the death of Er and Onan (*Genesis* 38:6-10), who received this punishment because they were *bar da'as* — even though they were under the age of *bar mitzvah*."

19. Ibid. "Many have this custom, because children have previous accounts [i.e., punishments] from other incarnations."

20. See *Kol Bo Al Aveilus* (p. 404), who cites *Duda'ei HaSadeh* as stating that one should not do so.

However, he cites the *gaon* R' Moshe Ginz, in *Kuntres Gesher LeDuda'im*, as permitting this. Since one prays for the first wife in a whisper, and no one hears, there is no objection. The same permissive ruling is given by *Gesher HaChaim* (loc. cit.). He adds: "This is not comparable to the statement of the Sages (*Mo'ed Katan* 21b) that 'if a person's wife dies and he remarries, one should not speak words of consolation to him.' We must distinguish [between the situation of comforting a mourner and that of reciting memorial prayers]."

21. *Mishnah Berurah* (429:§§8).

(l) Between Yom Kippur and Succos.

(m) The day after Succos. Some communities do not resume until the month of Cheshvan.

Likewise, one does not recite memorial prayers on a day when there is a circumcision in the synagogue; or if the father, the *mohel*, or the *sandak* are praying in one's synagogue —even if the *bris* is performed elsewhere. One also does not recite memorial prayers if one of the congregation is a bridegroom on his wedding day or during the seven days of feasting (*sheva brachos*) following the wedding.[22]

12. In addition, the memorial prayer is not recited on *Shabbos Mevarchim* (the Sabbath before Rosh Chodesh) — not even during the time of the *Omer*-count, when *Av Harachamim* ("Father of compassion. . .") is recited.

For someone who died that week, the memorial prayer is recited on *Shabbos Mevarchim*.[23] But some rule that the memorial prayer is never recited on *Shabbos Mevarchim*.[24]

During the Sabbaths leading up to the month of Nissan, four special Torah-portions are read (*Shekalim*, *Zachor*, *Parah*, and *HaChodesh*), each on its designated Sabbath. On these Sabbaths, memorial prayers are not recited.[25]

When Tishah B'Av falls on the Sabbath, memorial prayers are recited, even though *Tzidkascha Tzedek* ("Your righteousness is an everlasting righteousness. . .") is not recited.[26] But when Tishah B'Av occurs on a weekday, memorial prayers are not recited.[27]

✥ Yizkor

13. The custom is to recite the *Yizkor* prayers four times a year: on Yom Kippur, Shemini Atzeres, the seventh day of Pesach (outside of *Eretz Yisrael*, the eighth day of Pesach), and Shavuos (outside of *Eretz Yisrael*, the second day of Shavuos).

Each individual recites *Yizkor* for the elevation of the souls of his parents or other relatives, then recites *Kel Malei Rachamim*.[28]

---

22. *Sha'arei Efrayim* (10:27). The same ruling is given by *Gesher HaChaim*, who states that this is because *Tachanun* is not recited on these days.

Responsa *Zecher Yehosef* (§94) writes that on the days when memorial prayers are not recited, one does not recite it even if it is the Sabbath preceding the *yahrzeit*.

23. *Magen Avraham* (284:§§4).

24. *Mishnah Berurah* (ad loc. §§17) states: "*Pri Megaddim* writes: 'It seems that one does not recite memorial prayers at all [on *Shabbos Mevarchim*].' "

25. *Maharil*, cited by *Mishnah Berurah* (685:§§18).

26. *Mishnah Berurah* (284:§§16), in the name of *Pri Megaddim*.

27. *Gesher HaChaim*. This follows those who rule that even *Tzidduk HaDin* is not recited when Tishah B'Av occurs on a weekday.

28. *Zichron Eliahu* (manuscript). See responsa of *Rashban* (*Orach Chaim* §292). He remarks:

"During the Festivals, our duty is purely to rejoice in the Festival. Only on the Diaspora's last day of *Yom Tov* is it customary to recite memorial prayers; and one should not depart from the custom. The exception to this rule is that *Yizkor* is said on Shemini Atzeres instead of Simchas Torah. This is because of the honor of the Torah." This responsum is cited by *Kol Bo Al Aveilus* (p. 403).

The memorial prayers [including *Yizkor*] are recited even if these days fall on the Sabbath.[29]

✺§ Residents of *Eretz Yisrael*

13a. A resident of *Eretz Yisrael* who is visiting the Diaspora may recite *Yizkor* on the second day of *Yom Tov* there.[29a]

The following is the *halachah* regarding someone who lives outside *Eretz Yisrael* and intends to return to the Diaspora, but is presently in *Eretz Yisrael*, and is praying with a congregation consisting of residents of *Eretz Yisrael*:

> (a) If he will be able to pray with a *minyan* of visitors from the Diaspora on the second day of *Yom Tov*, he should not recite *Yizkor* on the first day of *Yom Tov* with the residents of *Eretz Yisrael*. Instead, he should recite it on the second day, with the others who came from the Diaspora.
>
> (b) If he will not be able to pray with a *minyan* of visitors from the Diaspora on the second day of *Yom Tov*, some rule that he should recite *Yizkor* on the first day of *Yom Tov*.[29b]

✺§ Those With Parents Leave The Synagogue

14. If both of one's parents are living, one should step out of the synagogue during the recitation of *Yizkor*. Therefore, the *shamash* announces: "*Yizkor!*" before the recitation of the memorial prayers.[30]

✺§ *Yizkor* During the First Year

15. *Yizkor* is recited during the first year of mourning, and even during the first week.[31] However, some have the custom not to recite it during the first year;

---

29. See *Kol Bo Al Aveilus* (loc. cit.). He states that in some communities the custom is not to recite memorial prayers if these days occur on the Sabbath. But he writes: "There are no grounds for this custom." See *Pischei She'arim* on *Sha'arei Efrayim* (*sha'ar* 10 §§31), who writes that memorial prayers should be recited even if these days fall on the Sabbath.

29a. *Igros Moshe Orchos Chaim* III:§92.

29b. *Yom Tov Sheni Kehilchaso* (13:2). The same ruling is given by responsa *Riv'vos Efrayim*.

30. The *Acharonim* explain that the reason for leaving the synagogue during *Yizkor* is to prevent *ayin hara* ("evil eye") [i.e., it is not fitting to remain present when the death of parents is the topic of prayer]. Another explanation is that if part of the congregation recited the prayer while others remained silent, it would give the impression of splitting into factions (See *Pischei She'arim* §§32 and other *Acharonim*).

31. See *Kol Bo Al Aveilus* (p. 404), who cites *Succas Shalom* (6:1) as writing: "[The custom not to recite *Yizkor* during the first year of mourning] is a bad custom, without any foundation. . .and if one does not [recite *Yizkor*], this is classified as stealing from the dead."

Chamishah Maamaros, by the *Gaon* of Munkatsch (in the part called *Divrei Torah* p. 12) states: "In some communities, the custom is not to recite *Yizkor* prayers during the first Twelve Months of mourning. This has no foundation or real justification. On the contrary, then [during the first Twelve Months] the deceased have the greatest need for mercy, and for people to memorialize and pray for them in the synagogue. The reasons put forth to explain this custom [of not reciting memorial prayers during the Twelve Months] are valueless. They argue that they do not wish to arouse their grief to the

when *Yizkor* is announced, they go out of the synagogue.[32]

16. *Yizkor* and *Kel Malei Rachamim* are primarily intended to be recited in a *minyan*. However, even if a person is praying alone in his home, he should recite *Yizkor* on the appropriate days (see above, par. 13). *Kel Malei Rachamim* may also be recited by someone praying alone. Likewise, if there is no *minyan* at the cemetery, one may nonetheless recite the memorial prayers.[33]

17. An integral part of the memorial prayer is the pledge to give *tzedakah* for the elevation of the soul of the deceased (see above, par. 2). It is a *mitzvah* to fulfill this pledge immediately the next day.[34]

⋖§ Kindling Lights

18. At the four times a year when one recites *Yizkor* (see above, par. 13), many follow a custom to kindle lights for the benefit of the souls of the parents or other relatives for whom one prays.[35]

---

point of weeping and wailing, which would distract the other congregants. They also claim that it would be damaging to mourn on *Yom Tov* (*Orchos Chaim* 668). But these arguments are without any trace of validity. Therefore, certainly [the recitation of memorial prayers] is extremely necessary during the first Twelve Months, for during that time the deceased is judged. And this is clear and obvious.

"Moreover, I know from our forefathers and rabbis, the holy *geonim*, that they ruled that memorial prayers *should* be recited even during the first Twelve Months, and they were very emphatic about it. 'The lips of truth will stand firm forever.' "

The *gaon*, author of *Duda'ei HaSadeh* (§85), castigates this practice [of not reciting memorial prayers during the first Twelve Months], terming it an erroneous custom. He states that one may infer from *Shach* and *Pri Megaddim* that memorial prayers should be recited during the first year — "and this is stated explicitly in *Levush* (*Yoreh De'ah* §347). And our custom is to recite it, even if it is the first time, even during a Festival."

The same ruling is given by *Zichron Eliyahu*. Likewise, *Gesher HaChaim* writes: "It is obvious that also during the first year after the death, one recites memorial prayers." And responsa *Be'er Moshe* (V:§152) writes: "In a place where the custom is not to recite memorial prayers during the first year, one should step outside and recite it there."

32. *Kitzur Shulchan Aruch* (133:21). And *Kerem Shlomo* (§668) explains that they do not wish to arouse their grief to the point of weeping and wailing, which would distract the other congregants.

Nachamu Ami (29:§12) states: "Some have the custom that if the death occurred during the past year, they remain in the synagogue, but without reciting memorial prayers (*Sefer HaMinhagim Chabad*)." He also writes there (note 11) that if the deceased is not yet buried, all agree that one does not recite memorial prayers (since the main judgment of the deceased begins after burial). But *Dinim VeHanhagos* quotes the *Chazon Ish* as stating that one should not recite memorial prayers during the first year.

33. *Gesher HaChaim*, citing *Duda'ei HaSadeh* (§12), states that the recitation of memorial prayers is not a procedure of special sanctity which requires the presence of ten adult male Jews.

34. *Kol Bo Al Aveilus* (part II p. 151) states that it was said of the *gaon Terumas HaDeshen*, that on the day after reciting memorial prayers he would not taste any food before paying the *tzedakah* he had pledged (*Mekor Yisrael Hadras Kodesh* p. 9).

35. *Rama* (610:4) writes, regarding *Yom Kippur*, that it is correct to kindle a memorial light (*ner neshamah*) for one's parents. See *Gesher HaChaim* (31:2:5), who states that this is the custom on all four of the Festivals when memorial prayers are recited. He also states there that if olive oil is available, one should light with it. If it is not available, one lights with a tallow candle. If that also is unavailable, one lights with kerosene (*neft*). If even kerosene is unavailable, but there is an electric light, one lights the electric light (The electric light would have to be lit before *Yom Tov*).

Some have the custom to kindle these lights in the synagogue; and since they burn in the synagogue, it is possible even for a Jew to light them on *Yom Tov* (as long as he kindles them from an already burning light, as is always required on *Yom Tov*). This applies to the three Festivals (Shemini Atzeres, Pesach, and Shavuos).

Others have the custom to kindle these lights in their home. In that case, they should be lit before *Yom Tov*. But if one needs to light them on *Yom Tov* night, they must be placed where they will give people light.[36]

◆§ *Kel Malei Rachamim* Under the *Chupah*

19. If the parents of the bridegroom and bride are not living, some have the custom to recite *Kel Malei Rachamim* for them under the *chupah*.[37]

---

36. *Be'ur Halachah* (§514 s.v. *ner batalah*) writes: "Furthermore, one should be aware that if one did not kindle the *yahrzeit* light before *Yom Tov*, one should at least light it in the room where people eat, so that it will add light to the room. And it is good to light it in the synagogue, for this avoids the danger of its being a *ner batalah* (a light which is not used, and which one is therefore forbidden to light on *Yom Tov*). But in a situation of pressing need, it is possible that one could permit lighting it anywhere [even where no one will benefit from it], since it is comparable to a *mitzvah* light, because it is for the honor of one's parents. This is explained in responsa *Kesav Sofer*."

37. Responsa *Chelkas Yaakov* (II:§114). He cites R' Sar-Shalom, *zatzal*, as pointing out that *Rashi* interprets the blessing, ". . .Who created everything for His glory" (*she'hakol bara lich'vodo*), which is recited under the *chupah*, as: ". . .not part of the order [of the other blessings recited there], but refers to the gathering of the people who are gathered there to bestow kindness [on the bridegroom and bride]. . ." R' Sar-Shalom explains that when the bridegroom and bride stand under the *chupah*, their parents who are in the world of truth are given permission to take part in their children's rejoicing. This is what *Rashi* means by "the gathering of the people who are gathered." He is referring to those who have already been "gathered" from the world, but are now taking part in the rejoicing. This being the case, it is fit to mention them for rest and blessing, even though a bridegroom and bride are present.

CHAPTER FORTY-FOUR

The *Yahrzeit*

~§ The Sabbath Before the *Yahrzeit*

1. The custom is that a man who will observe a *yahrzeit* (anniversary of his parent's death) during the week is called up to the Torah-reading for *maftir* on the preceding Sabbath.[1] Even if the *yahrzeit* is on the Sabbath, he is called up on the preceding Sabbath.[2]

2. There are a number of customs regarding a person who will observe a *yahrzeit* during the coming week. Various congregations have adopted one or more of the following:

(a) The person leads the prayer-services on the Sabbath before the *yahrzeit*, for all the prayer-services including *Kabbalas Shabbos*.

(b) He also recites the *Kaddish* following *Mizmor Shir LeYom HaShabbos* ('A psalm, a song for the Sabbath day . . .').[3]

---

1. *Birkei Yosef* (284:§§1) writes: "In our time the custom has become prevalent in some places that when the anniversary of the passing of one's father or mother approaches, one is called up as *maftir* on the preceding Sabbath." The same ruling is given by *Sha'arei Efrayim* (9:42), and by responsa *Nishmas Kol Chai* (*Yoreh De'ah* §72), et al. But see responsa *Duda'ei HaSadeh* (§4), who writes: "We have not found at all that one observing a *yahrzeit* is required [to be called up to the Torah] unless the *yahrzeit* actually falls on the Sabbath."

   With regard to rights of precedence in this matter, see *Birkei Yosef* (loc. cit.), who was asked: If one person is observing the *yahrzeit* of his father, and another is observing the *yahrzeit* of his mother, which takes precedence? He replied: "The one who is observing the *yahrzeit* of his father takes precedence, since a man is subject to more laws and obligations than a woman" [and therefore needs more assistance with his judgment in the next world]. Likewise, *Sha'arei Efrayim* (loc. cit.) states that this [giving precedence to the one observing the *yahrzeit* of his father] is the custom in some places; but where there is no established custom, the question of precedence should be decided by lottery.

   If one person is observing the *yahrzeit* of his father and mother, and another the *yahrzeit* of only his father, *Birkei Yosef* (loc. cit.) writes that the one observing the *yahrzeit* of his father and mother has precedence.

2. Responsa *Nishmas Kol Chai* (loc. cit.), and responsa *Ma'aseh Avraham* (*Yoreh De'ah* §56). The latter writes that even more important than reading the *Haftarah* on the Sabbath of the *yahrzeit* is reading it on the Sabbath *preceding* the *yahrzeit*, in order to give merit to the soul of the deceased before its day of judgment. The same is stated by the following authorities: *Sefer HaChaim* (25:19); responsa *Meleches Shlomo* (*Yoreh De'ah* §14); responsa *Ma'aseh Eliahu* (§92). And see below, footnote 22.

3. *Kaf HaChaim* (53:§§23) writes: "The custom is that when the *yahrzeit* falls during the weekdays, one recites *Kaddish* in the *Maariv* prayer of the preceding Sabbath, even though the custom of the

(c) He leads the *Mussaf* prayer.[4]

(d) He recites the *Kaddish DeRabbanan* before *Aleinu* [4a]

Regarding whether a mourner [within the Twelve Months of mourning for his parent] is permitted to lead the services on the Sabbath before the [first] *yahrzeit*, there are differing opinions. Each congregation follows its custom.[5]

⋙ Leading the *Maariv* Service

The custom is to lead the prayer-service for *Maariv* at the conclusion of the Sabbath before the *yahrzeit*.[6]

Ari zal was that one recites *Kaddish* only on the day of the *yahrzeit* itself, as I noted in §§20.

"It seems to me that this custom [of reciting *Kaddish* the previous Sabbath] is based on what the *Rav*, zal, writes in *Sha'ar HaMitzvos* (*Parashas Vayechi*): 'Regarding the soul, the Sages said that throughout the Twelve Months, the soul of [the deceased] ascends and descends; and after the Twelve Months, it ascends but does not again descend. I heard in the name of my teacher, that even if the person died in the middle of the week, and the Twelve Months therefore also conclude [in the middle of the week] — nonetheless, on the Sabbath preceding the conclusion of the Twelve Months, the soul ascends and does not again descend. The explanation is as follows: On the Sabbath, even during the Twelve Months, all the souls ascend to the supernal *Gan Eden*, as is known. For this *neshamah*, a few days are lacking to complete the Twelve Months. Nevertheless, since it has already ascended [on the Sabbath, as always], it does not have to descend again for the sake of those three or four days which are lacking from the Twelve Months.' *Gesher Chaim* (ch. 32) cites this explanation and adds: 'Perhaps this is the reason why it is customary also to recite *Kaddish* at the beginning of the Sabbath, during the Evening Prayer of the Sabbath preceding the *yahrzeit*. But this applies only in the absence of anyone else who is obligated to recite *Kaddish*. If someone else with such an obligation is present, no rights of precedence are given to the one who has a *yahrzeit* during the coming week.' "

4. *Kol Bo Al Aveilus* (p. 401) writes: "However, the prevalent custom is to lead the services only for *Mussaf* — and one does this even if he was not called up to the Torah for *maftir*." The same ruling is given by *Gesher HaChaim* (32:2); and by *Mishmeres Shalom* (os yud §13), in the name of *Sefer Mor Uk'tzia*.

4a. Responsa *Duda'ei HaSadeh* (§23).

5. Responsa *Divrei Malkiel* (VI:§23) writes: "The mourner should not be permitted to lead the services [even] if he has a *yahrzeit* on the Sabbath or *Yom Tov*."

Even Yaakov (§48) permits the mourner to lead the services, even on the Sabbath before the *yahrzeit*. The same ruling is given by *Sheivet HaLevi* (*Yoreh De'ah tinyana* §161) that "the mourner is not forbidden to lead the services [on the *yahrzeit* or the Sabbath before the *yahrzeit*], even during the first year, as long as the congregants do not object."

Responsa *B'Tzeil HaChachmah* (IV:§129) distinguishes between the first *yahrzeit* [when the mourner is not permitted to lead the services] and the other years [when one who will be observing a *yahrzeit* in the coming week may lead the services on the Sabbath].

Responsa *Minchas Yitzchak* (IX:§134) rules that this matter depends on the custom in each community.

6. *Gesher HaChaim* (loc. cit.). In his note 6 ad. loc., he writes: "We have heard an explanation from the rav R' Baruch Zeldovitch, zatzal, as to why one leads the services at the conclusion of the Sabbath before the *yahrzeit*: [On the Sabbath, a person receives an extra soul, the *neshamah yeseirah*.] At the conclusion of every Sabbath, the *neshamah yeseirah* departs from him, with the intention of returning on the following Sabbath. At the conclusion of the final Sabbath of a person's life, it leaves him, without intending to return. Thus, at the conclusion of the Sabbath before a person dies, it is like the death of his *neshamah yeseirah*. Therefore, that Sabbath's conclusion is also like a *yahrzeit*."

Chazon LaMo'ed, in his notes at the end of his book, raises an objection to this line of reasoning: It

✥ Prayers and *Kaddishim*

3. The son leads the services on the day of the *yahrzeit* for all three prayers (*Maariv*, *Shacharis*, and *Minchah*), and recites the *Kaddishim*.[7]

Regarding the laws of precedence when more than one person has a *yahrzeit*, or when mourners are present — see above, chapters 39 and 40.

✥ Trips at the Time of *Yahrzeit*

4. It is preferable (*lechatchilah*) not to set out on a trip on the day of the *yahrzeit* or the day before, if one knows that when traveling he will be unable to recite the *Kaddishim*. However, if the trip is urgent, and postponing it will probably result in financial loss, one is permitted to travel.[8]

5. If someone is traveling on the day of the *yahrzeit* and cannot reach a settlement where there are ten Jews in order to recite *Kaddish*, he is not required to spend extravagantly for this purpose [that is, to hire a faster means of transportation]. He is simply required to spend as much as he can afford.

Likewise, if he is traveling as part of a group, and the other members of the group are unwilling to stop long enough for him to recite *Kaddish*, he is required to do whatever he can to persuade them, and to plead with them to stop for him so that he can recite *Kaddish*. One who acts this way thereby honors his father and mother.[9]

✥ Missed *Kaddish*

6. If one missed reciting *Kaddish* because he was traveling on the day of the *yahrzeit*, and then reaches a town in time for the *Maariv* belonging to the day

---

applies only if the person died on a weekday, but not if he died on the Sabbath.

Ner Eliyahu (*Minhagei Yom HaZikaron* §17) writes: "However, in the holy city of Jerusalem, may it be rebuilt and established, many follow the custom of the *gaon* R' Shmuel Salant, *zatzal*. He opposed letting the sons lead the *Maariv* services at the conclusion of the Sabbath before the *yahrzeit*. The reason one generally leads the services at the Sabbath's conclusion is because that is the time when the wicked return to *Gehinnom*. By leading the services [at the Sabbath's conclusion], one gives the impression of considering one's parents wicked. Thus, one should not lead the services then, just as one does not lead the services after the first eleven months" [see above, beginning of chapt. 39].

7. *Rama* (376:4) writes: "The custom is that on the day of the *yahrzeit* of one's father or mother, every year, he recites the Mourner's *Kaddish* (*Kaddish Yasom*) for them; and if he knows how to lead the entire prayer-service, he should do so." The same ruling is given by *Darkei Moshe* (ad loc. §§9).

8. *Mateh Efrayim* (3:3). And see the comment of *Elef LaMateh* (ad loc. §§3). See also *Mishmeres Shalom* (*os yud* §15), who writes: "Therefore, whoever has fear of Hashem in his heart will not set out on a business trip on the day of the *yahrzeit*, even if it is very necessary. [He will refrain,] either because [he realizes that] he will not succeed [in his business dealings] that day (since it is a day of misfortune for him), or because of respect for his father and mother. For, if he is at home, he can better observe the *yahrzeit*, by studying *mishnayos*, reciting *Kaddish*, leading the services, going to the cemetery, and dispensing charity to the extent of his ability for the merit of their souls. He contemplates the fact that his parents, who troubled themselves for him their whole life long, are worth commemorating at least one day a year, for the amelioration of their souls."

9. *Mateh Efrayim* (loc. cit.).

after the *yahrzeit*, he should recite *Kaddish* after that *Maariv*. The same applies to someone who missed reciting *Kaddish* for some other unavoidable reason. However, at this *Maariv* he has no precedence over others who need to recite *Kaddish*, since the time for his *Kaddish* has already passed.[10]

7. Some rule that if one forgot to recite *Kaddish* on the day of the *yahrzeit*, he should recite it another day. Then, in all subsequent years, he should also recite *Kaddish* on the day before the *yahrzeit*.[11]

◄§ Grandparents' *Yahrzeit*

8. Some have the custom of leading the services and reciting *Kaddish* on the *yahrzeits* of their grandparents, both paternal and maternal, if the grandparents' children are no longer alive. But a person who is doing so has no rights of precedence whatever over any mourners who may be present.[12]

◄§ Early *Maariv* Before *Yahrzeit*

9. One authority writes that when a person has a *yahrzeit*, he should not lead the services for *Maariv* before nightfall.

However, on Friday one may be lenient on this point, since the Torah commands us to begin observing the Sabbath before nightfall. Nevertheless, where possible, one who is observing a *yahrzeit* should not lead the services for *Maariv* before nightfall, even on Sabbath eve.[13]

◄§ *Onen* Who Has *Yahrzeit*

10. Some rule that an *onen* (one whose deceased relative is not yet buried) who has a *yahrzeit* is permitted to go to the synagogue and recite *Kaddish*.[14] Others rule that he is forbidden to do so.[15] However, on the Sabbath he is permitted to do so.[16]

◄§ Mourner Who Has *Yahrzeit* Leading the Sabbath Services

11. If a person is in the Twelve Months of mourning for his father or mother, or in *shloshim* for some other family member, and he has a *yahrzeit* which falls on the Sabbath, some rule that he is permitted to serve as leader of the services on the

---

10. Ibid. (par. 4), cited by *Be'ur Halachah* (§132).

11. *Ikrei HaDat* (*Orach Chaim* 29:34), in the name of *Kikar LaAden* (*Likutim* 5:11).

12. *Mateh Efrayim* (3:1).

13. Responsa *Chelkas Yaakov* (III:§149).

14. Responsa *Avodas Gershuni* (§62), cited by *Elyah Rabbah* (132:§§4); and also cited by *Gilyon Maharsha* (*Yoreh De'ah* §341). See also responsa *Arba'ah Turei Even* (§10), cited by *Pischei Teshuvah* (341:§§9).

15. *Pischei Teshuvah* (loc. cit.); *Pri Megaddim* (*Orach Chaim* §132, in *Mishbetzos Zahav* §2); responsa *Megiddos* (§21), by the author of *Pri Megaddim*. The same ruling is given by *Birkei Yosef* (§341); *Beis Lechem Yehudah* (ad loc.); *Michtam LeDavid* (§1), cited by *Ikrei HaDat* (36:44); and responsa *Maharam Shick* (*Yoreh De'ah* §342).

16. *Birkei Yosef* (loc. cit.).

Sabbath.[17] Others rule that he is forbidden to do so.[18]

⋞ Being Called Up to the Torah / *Kel Malei Rachamim*

12. The custom is that a person who is observing a *yahrzeit* is called up to the Torah-reading that day.[19] If he is the third person called up on a weekday, or the last person [before *maftir*] on the Sabbath, he also recites the *Kaddish* that follows the Torah-reading.[20]

If the *yahrzeit* falls on a day when there is no Torah-reading, some have the custom to be called up on the nearest preceding day on which the Torah is read.[21]

If the *yahrzeit* occurs on the Sabbath, the person observing it is called up to be the *maftir* (the one who reads the portion from the Prophets).[22] But some are particular

---

17. Responsa *Me'ir Nesivim* (§80); responsa *Levushei Mordechai* (telisai *Yoreh De'ah* 16:4); responsa *Duda'ei HaSadeh* (§44); responsa *Betzel HaChachmah* (IV:§129); and *Gesher HaChaim* (23:4:8). The latter writes: "Even when the seventh day of mourning falls on the Sabbath, the mourner can lead the Sabbath morning prayers if he is observing a *yahrzeit*."

See also *Even Yaakov* (§48), who states that the *gaon* R' Tzvi Pesach Frank was asked about this and replied: "*Toras Mordechai* (§166) concludes that in practice [the mourner who has a *yahrzeit*] is permitted to lead the services without fear of prohibition. And that book was written by a great man whose words are authoritative."

See also responsa *Minchas Yitzchak* (IX:§134).

18. Responsa *Divrei Malkiel* (VI:§23).

19. *Leket Yosher* (Minhagei *Terumas HaDeshen*), p. 99, writes: "I recall that he [the author of *Terumas HaDeshen*] said it is good to purchase an *aliyah* to the Torah on the *yahrzeit* of one's parent, since this means that one will have the opportunity to recite *Borchu* over the Torah Scroll."

Mishmeres Shalom (os *yud* §16) cites a responsa which states: "It is the custom of all Israel — a custom which has the force of Torah — that one who is observing a *yahrzeit* has an obligation to be called up to the Torah. And see *Levush* (*Orach Chaim* §133); and this is a valid custom; one should not depart from it."

See also *Mishnah Berurah* (153:§§7), who states that if two people are observing *yahrzeits* on the same day, and one of them is called up to the Torah, the other should be honored with *hagbahah* (lifting up the Scroll after the reading). [The reference is to a weekday when only one person is called up after the *Kohen* and *Levi*, and it is forbidden to call more than these three to the Torah. Otherwise (e.g., on the Sabbath) both of those observing a *yahrzeit* could be called to the Torah.]

20. *Mateh Efrayim* (3:1). Regarding this *Kaddish*, see above (39:14).

21. *Gesher HaChaim* (32:2); *Chazon LaMo'ed* (27:8).

22. *Sha'arei Efrayim* (9:42); responsa *Ma'aseh Avraham* (§56). The same ruling is given by *Gesher HaChaim* (32:2).

If one must choose between being called up to *maftir* on the Sabbath before the *yahrzeit* or the Sabbath of the *yahrzeit*, which is preferable? Responsa *Ma'aseh Avraham* (loc. cit.) writes that in his city the custom is to tell people that they should give higher priority to being called up to *maftir* on the Sabbath before the *yahrzeit* than on the Sabbath of the *yahrzeit*. This is in order to give merit to the soul of the deceased before its day of judgment. The same ruling is given by *Sefer Chaim* (§25 os 19); and by *Masa Chaim* (Minhagim 10:100). Responsa *Meleches Shlomoh* (*Yoreh De'ah* §14) offers proof that this is the correct ruling, based on *Shalmei Tzibbur* [see also footnote 2 above].

But see *Yechaveh Da'as* (§59), who disputes this ruling and writes that it is preferable to be called up to *maftir* on the day of the *yahrzeit*. He states that the custom of the author of *Minchas Elazar* was to be called up sixth to the Torah every Sabbath; and on the Sabbath preceding the *yahrzeit* of his parents, he would be called up to *maftir*. But if the *yahrzeit* fell on the Sabbath, he would be called up sixth on the preceding Sabbath.

to be called up as one of the seven who are called up before the *maftir*.[23]

Likewise, one recites *Kel Malei Rachamim* after the Torah-reading on the day of the *yahrzeit*; and if the *yahrzeit* falls on a day when there is no Torah-reading, *Kel Malei Rachamim* is recited on the nearest preceding day on which the Torah is read.[24]

◦§ Mishnah Study

13. It is customary on the *yahrzeit* to study *mishnayos* for the elevation of the soul of the deceased.[25] The custom is to study chapters whose initial letters spell the/name of the deceased. Then one studies the last four *mishnayos* of the seventh chapter of Tractate *Mikvaos*, whose initial letters spell נְשָׁמָה (*neshamah*, "soul"),[26] followed by the prayer beginning אָנָא, "Please. . .".[27] The sons of the deceased then recite *Kaddish DeRabbanan*. Many also have the custom of studying chapter 24 of Tractate *Kelim*, which is especially beneficial to the departed soul.[28]

On those days when *Tachanun* is not recited, *Ana* also is not recited.[28a]

14. If the *yahrzeit* falls on the Sabbath or *Yom Tov*, the custom is to study *mishnayos* that day.[29] However, some have the custom to advance the study of *mishnayos* to *erev Shabbos* or *erev Yom Tov*.[30]

---

23. My master, teacher, and father, *zatzal*, in his work *Zichron Eliyahu* (manuscript).

24. See above, chapt. 43.

25. In Tractate *Yevamos* (122a), *Rashi* cites *Teshuvos HaGeonim*, *zal*, stating: " 'All these festivals of the *Amora'im*. . .' — This refers to the day on which a great man died. They set it as a time to honor him; and every year, when that day arrives, the Torah scholars gather from all around and come to his grave, together with the rest of the people, in order to sit and learn there."

And see *Zer HaTorah* (in *Revid HaZahav* §§48), who writes, in the name of the *gaon* R' Tzvi Pesach Frank, *zatzal*, that for a child who was under thirteen years old, one does not observe the *yahrzeit* nor recite *Kaddish*. "However, I know that our teacher, the *gaon* R' Yosef Chaim Sonnenfeld, *zatzal*, was called up to *maftir* and led the *Mussaf* prayer for his son who was an infant of six weeks."

26. [ArtScroll Ashkenaz *Siddur* pp. 802-810.] *Ma'aseh Oreg* states: "We have a tradition from Elijah the Prophet that these *mishnayos* raise up the soul of the deceased to its place in *Gan Eden*."

27. [ArtScroll ibid. p. 808.] *Chazon LaMo'ed* (27:6) writes: "In the prayer *Ana*, some simply say: וְתַצִּיל אוֹתוֹ מִכָּל הַדִּינִים, '. . .and save him from all the punishments,' instead of the list of punishments written there."

He also cites *Tzvi LaTzaddik* as writing: "Here in the holy city of Jerusalem, may it be rebuilt speedily in our days, some people say only the following brief version [instead of *Ana*] after Torah-study [for the deceased]: הַמְרַחֵם יְרַחֵם עַל נִשְׁמַת פב"פ, 'May the Merciful One have mercy on the soul of [here they say the name of the deceased].' "

28. There are seventeen *mishnayos* in this chapter. Seventeen is the numerical value of the word טוב (*tov*, "good"). Every *mishnah* in the chapter ends with the phrase: "completely pure." The chapter concludes with the words: "pure, both inside and outside." This is an allusion to the holy soul (R' Yisrael, *zal*, of Ruzhin).

Responsa Sho'el U'Meishiv (II:182) writes that the halachic literature mentions that one should study Tractate *Chaggigah* for the *yahrzeit*.

28a. *Gesher HaChaim* (loc. cit.) et al.

29. *Gesher HaChaim* (32:3).

30. *Sdei Chemed* (*Aveilus* §96).

◆§ The *Yahrzeit* Memorial Lamp (*Ner Neshamah*)

15. The custom is to kindle a light for the day of the *yahrzeit*. It should burn for the entire 24-hour day. One does not extinguish this light, even if it burns for more than twenty-four hours.[31] Many authorities write that it is propitious to kindle it in the synagogue.[32]

If the *yahrzeit* falls on the Sabbath, and one forgot to kindle the light the preceding afternoon, and only remembered during the twilight period called *bein hashmashos*, one is permitted to ask a non-Jew to kindle it then.[33]

If the *yahrzeit* falls on *Yom Tov*, and one forgot to kindle the light the preceding afternoon, one should kindle it from an existing flame in the manner permitted on *Yom Tov* in the room where people eat, so that they will benefit from the light. But it is more correct to kindle it in the synagogue; however, under pressing circumstances, it is possible to permit kindling it anywhere.[34]

---

31. See *Elef HaMagen*, a commentary on *Mateh Efrayim* (*sha'ar* 3 in the note). He writes: "The explanation for kindling a *yahrzeit* memorial light is as follows: It is known that the *neshamah* is happy for lights to be kindled. And it derives pleasures of splendor and joy, and spreads out and expands from the enjoyment of the light; for the *neshamah* itself is a portion of light drawn from the light of intelligent awareness (*sechel*). . .This is why King Solomon, may peace be upon him, compared the holy *neshamah* to a light, as it is said (*Proverbs* 20:27): נֵר ה׳ נִשְׁמַת אָדָם, *'Man's soul is a lamp of Hashem.'* Therefore, every year on the anniversary of the passing of one's parent, or other relatives, one kindles a light, called the *yahrzeit lamp*, in the synagogue; for on this day, the *neshamah* has permission to travel about in the world. It comes to the synagogue and sees the light burning for it, and receives spiritual satisfaction (*nachas ru'ach*) from this."

Regarding whether it is permissible to use an electric light for this purpose, see *Hadras Kodesh* (p. 18). He permits using an electric light, basing his ruling on the words of *Beis Yitzchak* (*Yoreh De'ah* I:§120:5), who rules that it is possible to use electric lights to fulfill the obligation of kindling the Sabbath lights. But *Hadras Kodesh* (p. 64) cites one scholar as objecting that the *yahrzeit* light is not comparable to Sabbath lights. The purpose of the Sabbath lights is so that people can see where they are going and not bump into things. However, the *yahrzeit* light is for the benefit of the *neshamah*. Thus it might be that the latter can only be of oil or wax.

See also *Mo'ed LeChol Chai* (p. 10), who writes in favor of the ruling of *Beis Yitzchak*, to permit using an electric light — as well as a light of gas, kerosene, or tallow. The same ruling is given by *Yechaveh Da'as* (§60). However, responsa *Meshaneh Halachos* (V:§70) cites the words of the *Gaon* of Tschebin (printed in *HaBe'er*; year 15:§58). He was asked about this question and ruled strictly [i.e., that one may not use an electric light], since the purpose is to benefit the *neshamah*, and [is based on the concept that] נֵר ה׳ נִשְׁמַת אָדָם, *'Man's soul is a lamp of Hashem.'* Moreover, he states that *Maharil*, cited by *Magen Avraham* (§610), writes that the word *ner* (נֵר, "lamp") consists of the initials of the words *neshamah, ru'ach* (נְשָׁמָה, רוּחַ, "soul, spirit"). The numerical value (*gematria*) of *ner* is 250, corresponding to the 248 limbs of the body, plus 2, representing the two spiritual components, *neshamah* and *ru'ach*. And *Maharal*, in his *Nesivos Olam*, states that an object is only termed *ner* if it has the three components of vessel, wick, and oil. "Therefore," concludes the *Gaon* of Tschebin, "one cannot fulfill the obligation with an electric light. However, if the deceased is a woman, it is possibly permissible."

Leket Yosher (*Hilchos Shabbos* p. 49) writes: "However, on the Sabbath in the synagogue, or on the father's *yahrzeit*, the best way to fulfill the *mitzvah* (*mitzvah min hamuvchar*) is with a wax candle."

32. Responsa *B'Tzeil HaChachmah* (IV:§29).

33. *Magen Avraham* (*Orach Chaim* 261:§6), citing *Maharshal*.

34. *Bi'ur Halachah* (§514 s.v. *ner shel batalah*).

If the *yahrzeit* falls on a Sabbath which is the day after *Yom Tov*, one is permitted on *Yom Tov* to ask a non-Jew to light it.[35]

16. One authority writes that if the *yahrzeit* of both one's parents is on the same day, one should kindle two lamps; if one does not kindle a separate lamp for each parent, one would appear negligent in honoring them.[36]

If several sons or daughters of the deceased reside in one house, it is sufficient to kindle one light. Nevertheless, it is better that each son or daughter should kindle his or her own light.[37]

17. It is customary also to kindle a flame that will burn while one is leading the prayer-services.[38]

18. If one forgot to kindle a *yahrzeit* memorial lamp (*ner neshamah*), one should calculate how much it would have cost to do so, and give the money to a poor person.[39]

19. A woman should not kindle a *yahrzeit* memorial lamp for her first husband, especially in the presence of her present husband.[40] Likewise, it is incorrect for a husband to do so for his first wife in the presence of his present wife.[41]

20. As stated (above, par. 15), it is good to kindle a light in the synagogue to burn for twenty-four hours for the elevation of the soul of the deceased. Some rule that one is permitted to make use of this light.[42] Others rule that one is forbidden to

---

35. *Duda'ei HaSadeh* (§17 and §34). He states there that, if possible, it is better for the non-Jew to go to a dark place and kindle the light there, and afterwards one may use that light for the *yahrzeit*.

36. *Kol Bo Al Aveilus* (p. 398). But *Rama* (610:4), regarding Yom Kippur, implies that one light is sufficient. Perhaps there is a distinction between *Rama*'s topic and ours. And see *Elyah Rabbah* (ad loc.).

37. *Kol Bo Al Aveilus* (loc. cit.), citing *Mo'ed LeChol Chai* (p. 34), who states that one light is sufficient. He adds: "However, there is no doubt that it is seen as an honor to the parents if each individual kindles a light, even when they are all in the same house (*HaPosek* 5705 p. 825). And, obviously, when they are not in the same house, each one should kindle a light."

38. *Mishmeres Shalom* (*os yud* §6 and *os nun* §26). The same ruling is given by *Minhagei Chasam Sofer* (in *Likutei HaBach* part 3).

39. Responsa *Yehudah Ya'aleh* (*Yoreh De'ah* §315).

40. The author of *Zichron Moshe* (a biography of the *Chasam Sofer*) relates that once the *Chasam Sofer* was present when his third wife (the widow of the author of *Tiv Gittin*) kindled a light on the twenty-fifth of Tishrei, the *yahrzeit* of her first husband.
    "When he saw her do this, the *Chasam Sofer* was taken aback. He was a very particular man; but, in his righteousness, he did not say anything to her. Since he did not want to hurt her feelings, he did not tell her that it was not proper for her to do so, especially in the presence of her present husband. However, he himself groaned over the matter. And, unfortunately for the Jewish people, he afterwards died on that very date, the twenty-fifth of Tishrei."

41. *Kol Bo Al Aveilus* (p. 404).
    Regarding the recitation of memorial prayers for one's first wife, see above, 43:10.

42. *Sha'arei Teshuvah* (154:§§20) writes: ". . .However, one may permit [using] the *yahrzeit* light which burns for the entire twenty-four-hour day." This ruling is cited by *Mishnah Berurah* (ad loc. §§56).

do so.[43] However, if one kindled the light at home, he may use it according to both opinions.

One may not recite the *Havdalah* blessing (". . .Who created the illumination of the fire") at the conclusion of the Sabbath over this light.[43a]

◄§ Visiting the Grave

21. The custom is to visit the graves of one's parents on their *yahrzeit*. If one does not live in the city where they are buried, one should visit other Jewish graves on that day.[44]

Details of laws and customs of visiting the grave are discussed in chapter 42.

◄§ Mourning Practices

22. On the day of the first *yahrzeit*, although the Twelve Months have already concluded, one observes all the practices of mourning which applied during the Twelve Months (see above, chapt. 38).[45] However, if the *yahrzeit* occurs on a Sabbath or during a Festival, one observes no mourning.[46] [Reciting *Kaddish* and memorial prayers are separate practices, in order to honor and benefit the deceased, and are not included in the category of mourning.]

In a leap-year, when the *yahrzeit* falls in the thirteenth month, one does not observe mourning on the *yahrzeit*.[47]

23. On the night of the *yahrzeit* of one's father or mother, one is forbidden to take part in a group meal.[48] Likewise, one is forbidden to do so on the day of

---

43. *Kaf HaChaim* (ad loc. §96).

43a. *Mishnah Berurah* (298:§§30). The reason is that this light was not kindled to illuminate the room, but only to commemorate the soul of the deceased.

44. *Kav HaYashar* (§71) first mentions that Caleb visited the tomb of the Patriarchs to pray that he would be saved from the scheme of the spies (see above, chapt. 42 footnote 1). He then writes: "This is the source of the custom that on our parents' *yahrzeit* we go to their graves to pray. And even if one is in another city on the day of the *yahrzeit*, nevertheless, when he goes to other Jewish graves to pray, this arouses all the souls in *Gan Eden*; for 'the earth is all one block.' The Holy One, Blessed is He, has decreed that the souls of the righteous be present in the cemeteries, for the benefit of Israel, so that [those souls] may hear the prayers at the graves" [and carry them heavenward].

45. *Rama* (395:3) writes: "The custom is that also on the date on which one's parent died, one observes the restrictions of the Twelve Months. And this [custom] is correct."

46. *Leket Yosher* (p. 98) writes that, "if the *yahrzeit* occurs on an ordinary day, one should refrain from changing clothes, as a sign of sorrow. However, if [the *yahrzeit*] falls on the Sabbath or a Festival, one changes one's clothes, since one also does not fast then." The same ruling is given by *Bach* (§395); but he adds: "If burial took place the day after the death, one must observe the restrictions of the Twelve Months [on the *yahrzeit*], even [if it falls] on the Sabbath, since in this case the *yahrzeit* is the last day of the twelfth month."

47. *Bach* (loc. cit.) writes: "If it is a leap-year, one is permitted to attend a feast after Twelve Months, as is mentioned above, §391. In that case, one does not observe the restrictions of the Twelve Months on the *yahrzeit*. Even though one does fast on the *yahrzeit*, nevertheless since one is already permitted to attend feasts and has ceased one's mourning, one does not return to it."

48. *Rama* (391:3 and 402:12).

the *yahrzeit*, even if one is not fasting.[49] However, on the following night, one is permitted to take part in such a meal.[50] [Thus, if the *yahrzeit* falls on Wednesday, one is forbidden to take part in a group meal on Tuesday night or Wednesday, but permitted on Wednesday night.]

Some rule that this prohibition applies only to a wedding feast; but other meals are permitted, whether or not they are *mitzvah* meals.[51] Others rule that the meal of a *bris milah* (circumcision) is also forbidden.[51a]

Some rule that this prohibition applies only on the first *yahrzeit*.[52]

Some authorities have written that the officiating rabbi (*mesader kiddushin*) of a

---

49. Obviously, the same *halachah* applies during the day as on the preceding night; for there is no reason to distinguish between the two. The *Poskim* specifically mention the night, because in any case one does not eat during the day, because one is fasting. But if one is not fasting, the *halachah* is the same for the day as for the night. And this is the ruling given by *Chazon LaMo'ed* (27:11).

50. The *gaon* R' Zalman Margolios (*Aveilus* §24). The same ruling is given by responsa *She'eilas Yavetz* (part 2 §184). He points out that one is permitted to take part in a group meal on the night after the gathering of bones (*likut atzamos*; reinterment), and he reasons that the night after the *yahrzeit* should not be any stricter than that.

51. *Pischei Teshuvah* (391:§§8) writes: "See responsa *Mekom Shmuel* (§80), who writes that the prohibition applies only to a wedding feast, which includes the celebrations of bridegroom and bride, and involves rejoicing. But the meal of a circumcision, *pidyon haben*, or a *siyum* after completing a Tractate is permitted." Likewise *Pri Megaddim* (§444 in *Mishbetzos Zahav* §§9) rules that on the night of the *yahrzeit* one is permitted to take part in the meal of a *siyum*; this would seem to apply even to one who did not take part in the learning of the tractate.

She'eilas Yavetz (II:§184) also rules that, except for a wedding feast, group meals are permitted, even if the meal is not for the sake of a *mitzvah* — and all the more so if it is a *mitzvah* meal. *Chochmas Adam* (171:11) and *Kitzur Shulchan Aruch* (221:7) rule similarly.

However, the wording of *Rama* — "It is forbidden to eat at a *se'udah* (group meal)" — implies that *any* type of group meal is forbidden. This is also implied by the words of *Taz* and *Shach* in §395.

51a. *Chochmas Adam* (171:11).

52. *Lechem HaPanim* (in his *Kuntres Acharon*) states: "*Ma'aneh Lashon* and many *Poskim* draw a distinction between the first year, when this prohibition applies, and all subsequent years, when it does not apply. And I also heard [halachic authorities] giving this ruling in practice, based on the ruling of my teacher and father-in-law, the *Magen Avraham*." This passage is cited by *Beis Lechem Yehudah* (end of §391), and in his gloss to §376 he proves that, according to the opinion of the *Ari zal*, the correct ruling is that of *Ma'aneh Lashon*: that in all subsequent years, one is permitted to take part even in a wedding feast.

See also *Chochmas Adam* (§171), who cites this passage from *Beis Lechem Yehudah*. The same ruling is given by *Mishmeres Shalom (os yud* §8). However, *Taz* and *Shach* (on 395:3) write that the prohibition applies every year. A similar ruling is given by the *gaon* R' Zalman Margolios (*Aveilus* §24). He states that in every year except the first, a wedding feast is forbidden, but other kinds of group meals are permitted.

It would seem, according to the *Poskim* who permit attending any type of group meal in all except the first year, that this leniency applies even in the first year, if it is a leap-year, since in that case mourning is not observed on the *yahrzeit* (see above, footnote 47).

Afterwards, I saw that *Ba'er Heitev* (395:§§3) writes: "However, even according to those who rule leniently on this matter, as *Levush* writes, nevertheless in the first year, even if it is a leap-year, one should not eat at the meal of a celebration."

wedding is permitted to take part in the feast even if it is the night of his parent's yahrzeit.[53]

⋅§ Fasting

24. It is a *mitzvah* to fast on the *yahrzeit* of one's father or mother.[54] In the *Minchah* prayer of the fast, one recites *Aneinu* ("Answer us. . .") [in the blessing, *Shome'a tefillah* "Who hears prayer")], as always during an individual fast.[55]

It is desirable to accept the fast upon oneself during the previous day's *Minchah* prayer, in accord with the law of an individual fast. If one forgot to do so, but one customarily fasts on the *yahrzeit*, one is still required to fast. But if one does not customarily fast on this day, the fast is not valid unless one accepted it upon oneself before sundown.[56]

If one fasted on the first *yahrzeit* without stipulating that he did not intend this practice to have the force of a vow, it is nevertheless considered a vow. If one subsequently decides not to fast on the *yahrzeit*, one must be released from the vow.[57]

25. It is good to fast on the *yahrzeit* of one's primary teacher (*rabbo muvhak*), since one is obligated to honor him even more than one's father.[58]

26. If one forgot and ate, one is still obligated to fast for the rest of the day. One is not required to fast on a different day in order to make up for breaking the fast. Even if one wishes to make it up, this is not possible.[59]

Even if one is suffering greatly from the fast, one cannot release oneself by donating charity instead.[60]

27. If the *yahrzeit* falls on the Sabbath or Rosh Chodesh,[61] some rule that the fast should be postponed until the following day.[62] Others rule that it should be

---

53. Responsa *Levushei Mordechai* (*tinyana* §137), citing responsa *Naharei Afarsemon* (§54), writes that the *mesader kiddushin* is someone needed by the public (*rabim tzrichim lo*), and is therefore permitted to take part in the meal.

54. *Rama* (376:4 and 402:12); *Shulchan Aruch* (*Orach Chaim* 568:7). Some suggest that one fasts on the *yahrzeit* because on that day one's *mazal* (fortune) was bad (*Maharam* Mintz §9; *Levush, Yoreh De'ah* 402:12; *Leket Yosher* p. 98, citing the author of *Terumas HaDeshen*). Others explain that the fast is to gain atonement for one's parent, since every year their soul undergoes a small amount of judgment (*Maharam* Mintz, §9; *Levush* loc. cit.; *Leket Yosher* loc. cit.).

55. *Kitzur Shulchan Aruch* (loc. cit.).

56. *Gesher HaChaim* (32:6).

57. *Chochmas Adam* (171:11); *Kitzur Shulchan Aruch* (221:1); *Gesher HaChaim* (loc. cit. par. 7).

58. *Mishnah Berurah* (568:§§46), citing *Shelah*.

59. *Shulchan Aruch* (568:11). This is because the *yahrzeit* is a specific date on which the person fasts. *Mishnah Berurah* (ad loc. §§2). And see *Sha'ar HaTziyun* (ad loc. §§2).

60. *Be'ur Halachah* (ad loc. s.v. *yachol*).

61. See *Kaf HaChaim* (ad loc. §97), who writes: "It seems that if [the *yahrzeit*] falls on Rosh Chodesh Nissan or Rosh Chodesh Av, one can fast that very day, and need not postpone the fast until the next day, since some rule that it is a *mitzvah* [even without a *yahrzeit*] to fast on those days, as is written below, at the end of §573 and in §580 (*Yafeh LaLeiv* ad loc.). However, *Chochmas Adam* (141:11) writes that even on the public fast-days of Rosh Chodesh Nissan or Rosh Chodesh Av one should not fast for a *yahrzeit*, since it is already the established custom [not to fast]."

62. *Shulchan Aruch* (568:9).

advanced to the previous day.[63] But *Rama* rules that the custom is not to fast at all if the *yahrzeit* falls on one of these days.[64]

28. If the *yahrzeit* falls on Chanukah, one does not fast. And if one did fast, one must fast again after Chanukah [to atone for having fasted on Chanukah].[64a]

Some rule that fasting is also forbidden on the day before Chanukah.[65]

Fasting is forbidden on Purim, both the fourteenth and the fifteenth of Adar.[66] It is also forbidden on Purim Katan, both the fourteenth and the fifteenth of Adar I.[67]

Throughout the whole month of Nissan,[68] and likewise during the days between Yom Kippur and Succos, fasting is forbidden.[69]

It is also forbidden to fast on other days when *Tachanun* is not recited.[70]

29. If the first *yahrzeit* falls on Friday, one need not continue the fast through the end of the day; instead, as soon as one leaves the synagogue on Sabbath Eve [after *Maariv*], one is permitted to eat, even if this is before sundown. But it is preferable (*lechatchilah*) that when initially accepting the fast upon oneself, one should stipulate that one does not in the future intend to make a practice of fasting until the end of the day.[71]

If the first *yahrzeit* fell on Friday, and one fasted until the end of the day, one is obligated for the rest of one's life to fast until the end of the day when the *yahrzeit* falls on Friday.[72]

---

63. *Lechem HaPanim* (in his *Kuntres Acharon*). The same ruling is cited by *Kaf HaChaim* (ad loc. §94), in the name of *Kevod Chachomim*, who writes that [if the *yahrzeit* occurs on the Sabbath] one should fast on Friday.

64. *Rama* (loc. cit.). *Mo'ed Kol Chai* (§1) writes that the prevalent custom in this case is not to fast at all, neither before nor after the *yahrzeit*. The same ruling is cited by *Kaf HaChaim* (ad loc. §§94), in the name of *Leket HaKemach*, stating that: "Since it cannot be observed at its proper time, it is not observed at all" (הוֹאִיל וְאִידְחַי אִידְחַי).

64a. *Rama* (670:3), and *Mishnah Berurah* (ad loc. §§11).

65. Responsa *Har HaKarmel* (§10). He adds that even if a person has [fasted on the day before Chanukah] for many years, this has the status of an erroneous vow [and therefore one can discontinue the practice without having the vow annulled].

Shulchan Aruch (686:1) writes that it is permissible to fast the day before or the day after Chanukah or Purim. However, *Mishnah Berurah* (ad loc. §§1) cites *Bach* and *Pri Chadash* who rule that it is forbidden to fast on the day before Chanukah.

66. *Shulchan Aruch* (696:3).

67. Ibid. 697:1.

68. *Rama* (429:2).

69. *Mishnah Berurah* (624:§§14).

70. *Rama* (568:9).

71. *Rama* (*Yoreh De'ah* 402:12). And *Mishnah Berurah* (*Orach Chaim* 249:§§21) explains that it is preferable (*lechatchilah*) that when initially accepting the fast upon oneself, one should stipulate that he will not fast until the end of the day. But post-facto (*bediavad*), even if one did not make such a condition, one is permitted to eat as soon as one leaves the synagogue.

72. *Mishnah Berurah* (ad loc.), citing *Magen Avraham*. Unless one explicitly stipulates that he does not intend always to fast until the end of the day, it is assumed that he did intend to do so. But if the first *yahrzeit* does occur on a Friday, it is preferable (*lechatchilah*) not to continue the fast until the end of the day.

If the first *yahrzeit* fell on some other weekday, and one fasted until the end of the day, some rule that one must do so even when the *yahrzeit* falls on Friday — unless he originally stipulated that he did not intend always to fast until the end of the day. Others rule to the contrary [that even if one did not stipulate this, he need not fast until the end of Friday]. And, in this case, if a person is suffering from the fast, he may rely on the more lenient ruling, and eat immediately upon leaving the synagogue [following *Maariv*], even if this is before sundown.[73]

30. If the *yahrzeit* occurs on the day before Yom Kippur, one should not fast on that day at all.[74]

If it occurs on the day before Tishah B'Av, one should fast until the final meal (*Se'udah Mafsekes*) before Tishah B'Av. But it is good to stipulate, on the very first *yahrzeit*, that one will only fast until *chatzos hayom*, then pray *Minchah Gedolah*, and eat.[75] [*Chatzos hayom* is the middle of the day. The exact hour varies with the season, but it is usually within half an hour before or after 12:00 noon Standard Time. *Minchah Gedolah* is the earliest time for the Afternoon Prayer, half an hour after *chatzos hayom*.]

If the *yahrzeit* falls the day before or after one of the public fast-days, and it is difficult to fast for two successive days, one should fast only until *chatzos hayom* on the day of the *yahrzeit* [and then observe the public fast-day as usual].[76]

[Some have the custom of fasting on a designated Monday, Thursday, and Monday in the months of Cheshvan and Iyar. This fast is called *Taanis Behab*.] If the *yahrzeit* falls on the day before one of the fast-days of *Taanis Behab*, and one regularly fasts on the *yahrzeit*, one should fast on the *yahrzeit*, not on the *Taanis Behab*.[77]

If the *yahrzeit* falls on the day after one of the fast-days of *Taanis Behab*, and one has already accepted upon oneself the *Taanis Behab*, one should observe the *Taanis Behab*. But if one has not yet accepted it upon oneself, one should fast for the *yahrzeit* instead, since it is more important.[78]

If one regularly fasts on the *yahrzeit* of his mother, and later his father died on the day after the mother's *yahrzeit*, some write that he should fast on his mother's *yahrzeit* [only], since this was already his established practice [if fasting for two successive days would be too difficult].[79]

---

73. *Mishnah Berurah* loc. cit.
74. *Orchos Chaim* (548:10); *Yalkut David* (p. 54).
75. *Mishnah Berurah* (552:§§29).
76. *Yalkut David* (p. 53), citing responsa *Pri HaSadeh* (part 2 §4).
77. *Yoseif Da'as* (§402) was asked about this, and ruled that the questioner [should fast on the *yahrzeit* but] was permitted to eat on the *Taanis Behab*.
78. Responsa *Pri HaSadeh* (loc. cit.).
79. Responsa *Vayitzbor Yosef* (§1). He also mentions this ruling in his *Mo'ed Kol Chai* (p. 22).
    However, he also states that if one parent died the day after the other, one could conclude that the fast should be observed on the date of the second death, on the basis of the Talmud's rule (*Berachos* 13): "More recent sorrows make one forget the earlier ones."

31. Some rule that if a person is ill or infirm, and cannot fast and lead the services himself, he can pay someone else to do so in his stead. Since the rule is that "a man's agent is equivalent to himself," this is counted as if he himself had fasted.[80]

32. If one's son has a *bris milah* or *pidyon haben* on the day of one's parent's *yahrzeit*, one need not fast. But, if he wishes, he may fast until *Minchah Gedolah* (about half an hour after midday; see above, par. 30).[81] Some rule that if the *mohel* or the *sandak* has a *yahrzeit* that day, he also need not fast.[82]

Some rule that the officiating *kohen* at a *pidyon haben* (redemption of the firstborn) must fast for the entire day if he has a *yahrzeit*.[83] Others rule that the *kohen* is permitted to eat at the meal celebrating the *pidyon haben*, even if the *pidyon haben* was postponed until after the thirtieth day from birth.[84]

A bridegroom, during the seven days of feasting (*sheva brachos*) following the wedding, does not fast for a *yahrzeit*.[85]

One authority writes that the same applies to a boy on the day of his *bar mitzvah*.[85a]

33. On the day of the *yahrzeit*, one is even forbidden to eat at a *siyum* (celebration of finishing a tractate).[86] But some rule that, if he was one of those who studied the tractate, he may eat at the *siyum*.[87]

---

80. *Yad Yitzchak* (III:§75), cited by *Kol Bo Al Aveilus* (p. 393). But see *Mo'ed Kol Chai*, who cites responsa *Olas Shmuel* (§61) as writing that it is not effective to pay someone to fast in his stead, because one cannot become an agent to suffer. Were this not so, he argues, someone who was sentenced to a lashing could pay someone else to be lashed in his stead.

81. *Mishnah Berurah* (568:§§46). The *halachah* regarding *pidyon haben* is explained in *Sha'arei Teshuvah* (ad loc. §§19).

82. *Sha'arei Teshuvah* (loc. cit.), citing *Be'er Yaakov*. The same ruling is given by *Pischei Teshuvah* (*Yoreh De'ah* 402:§§5); and by responsa *Har HaKarmel* (*Orach Chaim* §10). The latter writes that it is perfectly proper to agree to be *sandak* or *mohel* on a day when one has a *yahrzeit*. The same ruling is given by *Gesher HaChaim* (32:7). However, *Pri Megaddim* (ad loc. in *Mishbetzos Zahav* §§5) rules that the *sandak* and *mohel* must fast if they have a *yahrzeit* on the day of the *bris milah*.

83. *Pischei Teshuvah* (402:§§4), citing *Panim Me'iros* (II:§98). He writes that although it is customary to have the *kohen* recite the blessing over wine, in this case someone else should recite it. He is cited by *Sha'arei Teshuvah* (*Orach Chaim* 568:§§19).

84. *Sha'arei Teshuvah* (loc. cit.).

85. *Sha'arei Teshuvah* (loc. cit.), citing *Pri Megaddim*, who in turn cites responsa *Devar Moshe*. This ruling is also cited by *Pischei Teshuvah* 402:§§4.

85a. *Purim HaMeshulash* p. 147.

86. *Shach* (246:§§27), citing *Maharil*. The same ruling is given by *Pri Megaddim* (*Orach Chaim* §444 in *Mishbetzos Zahav* §§9).

87. *Beis Lechem Yehudah* (ad loc.). The same ruling is given by responsa *Maharam Shick* (*Yoreh De'ah* §367). He adds: "This applies if the *siyum* is celebrated on time [i.e., on the day when the learning is completed], as is written in *Elyah Rabbah* (551:§§25)." Likewise, *Gesher HaChaim* (ch. 32) writes: "Many are lenient, permitting him not to fast, if he finished the tractate that very day."

◦§ Leniency Regarding Fasting

34. There are *Poskim* who are lenient about fasting on the day of the *yahrzeit*,[88] especially in our time, when the generations are weak and do not have strength to fast. Therefore, the *tzaddikim* of the age have instituted that on the *yahrzeit* one should perform the *mitzvos* of giving *tzedakah* and providing for guests — activities which everyone can do.[89] This is the custom among the Chassidim. They also have the custom that after the [morning] prayer on the day of the *yahrzeit*, one gives the congregation brandy and cakes [*tikkun*] for the elevation of the soul of the deceased.[90]

Even if one is unable to fast, the custom is not to eat meat or drink wine on the day of the *yahrzeit*.[90a]

◦§ Determining the Date of the *Yahrzeit*

35. The *yahrzeit* is the date of death, not the date of burial,[91] even the first year.[92]

---

88. See *Be'ur HaGra* (*Yoreh De'ah* 376:§§7). On the statement of *Rama* there that it is a *mitzvah* to fast on the *yahrzeit*, he comments that this would seem to be implied by the Talmud at the beginning of the third chapter of *Shevuos*, which discusses the case of one who took an oath to fast "as on the day his parent died." He adds: "However, I have seen some commentaries who interpret this as referring to the actual day they died" [not the *yahrzeit*]. *Chut HaMeshulash* (p. 30a) states that the wife of the *Chasam Sofer* (the daughter of the *gaon* R' Akiva Eiger, *zatzal*) commanded that her children should not fast on her *yahrzeit*, and the *Chasam Sofer* ruled that they should obey her command. His son, the *Ksav Sofer*, *zal* made it his custom to complete a tractate every year on that day, so that he could eat at a *mitzvah* meal [the *siyum*]; and he ate only dairy foods. Likewise, R' Akiva Eiger commanded in his will that his children should not fast on his *yahrzeit*, but instead should learn Torah during that whole twenty-four-hour day, or pay others to do so.

89. *Mishmeres Shalom* (os yud §15), citing *Chessed LeAvraham*, in his introduction to *Mishnayos Zera'im*. The same ruling is given by responsa *Duda'ei HaSadeh* (§45), in the name of *Segulos Yisrael* (s.v. *yahrzeit*). He cites a number of *tzaddikim* as advising not to fast, but instead to seek out other *mitzvos*, such as *gemilus chessed* (doing kindness to others) to the extent of one's ability, and the study of *Mishnayos*.

90. See responsa *Minchas Yitzchak* (VI:§135), who writes: "Regarding the *tikkun* ('rectification' — i.e., the cake and liquor) which one gives out on the day of the *yahrzeit*, and people wish the person 'LeChaim!': This is because his [the son's] *mazal* was bad on that day. Likewise, people drink to sweeten the judgment of the one observing the *yahrzeit*. This is based on...what our teacher, the *Ateres Tzvi* of Zeditchov, wrote: that when Israel drink and wish each other 'LeChaim!' the Holy One, Blessed is He, forgives the sins of Israel. He also writes that if there is danger that someone might bring non-kosher liquor, the custom should be instituted that [the one observing the *yahrzeit*] gives *tzedakah* for the benefit of the departed soul; for in fact the *tikkun* also is based on giving *tzedakah* [i.e., serving refreshments is an act of kindness to the congregation]."

It is related in the name of R' Eliezer of Komarna that the *tzaddik*, R' Tzvi of Zeditchov, *zatzal*, once forgot the *yahrzeit* of his mother. She came to him [in a dream] at night and told him: "My son, I forgive you for the *Kaddish*, and also for the *mishnayos* I forgive you. But that you did not give the *tikkun* to revive the spirits of Israel — for that I cannot forgive you." He was frightened, and immediately instructed his chassidim to study *mishnayos*. He did not recite *Kaddish*, but he gave out the *tikkun* to them.

90a. *Ner LeEliyahu* in the name of *Ran* on *Nedarim* (p. 12).

91. *Shulchan Aruch* (*Orach Chaim* 568:8) writes: "One need fast only on the anniversary of one's parent's death, not on the anniversary of the burial." The same ruling is given by *Rama* (*Yoreh De'ah* §402) — "unless one was present at the burial but not at the death (tradition received from a venerable elder, *Moharam* Landau)."

92. See *Taz* (ad loc. §§9). See also *Mishnah Berurah* (568:§§44) and *Sha'ar HaTziyun* (ad loc. §§42). He states that *Elyah Rabbah* and *Chayei Adam* ruled that the *yahrzeit* should be observed

However, some apply the following rules:

(a) If burial took place three or four days or more after the death, the first *yahrzeit* should be observed on the date of burial, and in all subsequent years it should be observed on the date of death.

(b) If burial took place the day after the death, even the first *yahrzeit* should be observed on the date of death.[93]

(c) If burial took place two days after the death, see footnote.[94]

In a leap-year, when the *yahrzeit* is in the thirteenth month, it is always observed on the date of the death, even if burial took place a number of days after the death.[95]

36. If the death occured in Adar of a regular year, the author of the *Shulchan Aruch* [R' Yosef Caro] rules that in a leap-year one should fast in Adar II.[96]

---

on the date of the death, even if this means that the Twelve Months of mourning will not end until after the *yahrzeit* [i.e., if the burial was two days or more after the death]. And this is the ruling given unequivocally by *Be'ur Halachah* (§132) and by *Aruch HaShulchan*.

93. *Shach* (ad loc. §§3). And *Gesher HaChaim* (32:8) writes that "many follow this ruling."

94. On this matter, the words of *Shach* (loc. cit.) are ambiguous. At the beginning of the passage, he states that if the burial was three or four days after the death, the *yahrzeit* [in the first year] is on the date of the burial. This implies that if burial was only two days after the death, the *yahrzeit* is on the date of the death. But at the end of the passage, he writes that if burial was the day after death, the *yahrzeit* is on the date of the death. This implies that if burial was two days after death, the *yahrzeit* is on the date of the burial.

Responsa *Chelkas Yaakov* (I:§132) concludes that if burial was two days after death, the *yahrzeit* is on the date of the death, even in the first year. He explains that the main determining factor is *Shach's* explanation that if burial was three days after death, the *yahrzeit* is on the day of the burial, because it is uncommon for this to happen [i.e., for there to be such a great delay between death and burial]. Based on that, writes *Chelkas Yaakov*, if burial was two days after death, the *yahrzeit* should be on the date of the death, since a two-day delay is more common (for example, when death occurs before the Sabbath, so that burial cannot be performed until Sunday).

However, he cites responsa *Levushei Mordechai* as stating that even if burial occurs only two days after death, the *yahrzeit* in the first year is on the date of burial. This authority follows *Shach's* explanation that if burial occurred three days after death, and the *yahrzeit* were observed on the date of death, the Twelve Months of mourning would not end until after the *yahrzeit*, which could lead people to err. This problem, says *Levushei Mordechai*, would arise even if burial occurred only two days after death; for in that case, too, the Twelve Months of mourning would not end until after the *yahrzeit*.

The same ruling [that if burial occurs two days after death, the *yahrzeit* is observed on the date of burial] is given by responsa *Igros Moshe* (*Yoreh Deah* III:§160). It may also be inferred from the words of *Pischei Teshuvah* cited in our next footnote.

95. *Pischei Teshuvah* (*Orach Chaim* 568:§§3). The reason is that the mourning was already completed in the twelfth month. Therefore, no error can arise from observing the *yahrzeit* on the date of the death. However, *Igros Moshe* (*Yoreh Deah* part III:§160) writes that if the death occurred in Adar of a regular year, and the following year is a leap year, the *yahrzeit* should be observed in Adar I on the date of the burial and in Adar II on the date of the death.

96. *Shulchan Aruch* (*Orach Chaim* 568:7). The same ruling is given by responsa *Chasam Sofer* (*Orach Chaim* §163).

If death occurred in Adar in a regular year, and the following year is a leap-year, *Beis Yosef* (*Yoreh De'ah* §403) states, in the name of *Tashbatz*, that in the first year one should fast and recite *Kaddish* in Adar I, but in subsequent years one should observe the *yahrzeit* in Adar II. *Beis Yosef* explains that this

Rama comments: "But some rule that one should fast in Adar I. . .and that is the custom: to fast in Adar I. However, some are strict, and fast in both [Adar I and Adar II]." He adds that if the death occurred in a leap-year in Adar II, the custom is to fast in Adar II.[97]

37. If death occurred on the first day of Rosh Chodesh Adar II (i.e., the thirtieth of Adar I), the *yahrzeit* in a regular year should be observed on the first day of Rosh Chodesh Adar — i.e., the thirtieth of Shevat, not the twenty-ninth of [Adar]. This is because Adar of a regular year always corresponds to Adar II of a leap-year.[98]

If the death occurred on the twenty-ninth of Adar I in a leap-year, one should fast on the twenty-ninth of Adar in a regular year.[99]

38. The months of Cheshvan and Kislev sometimes have thirty days, sometimes twenty-nine. If death occurred on the first day of Rosh Chodesh Kislev (i.e., the thirtieth of Cheshvan), or on the first day of Rosh Chodesh Teves (i.e., the thirtieth of Kislev)· in a year when Cheshvan or Kislev had thirty days, some rule that the *yahrzeit* should be observed on Rosh Chodesh even

---

is because the first year of mourning ends after twelve months. As the Talmud says, "[Even] the wicked of Israel are judged in *Gehinnom* for [only] twelve months." The Talmud does not say, "for a year," but "for twelve months." Therefore, one counts twelve months [even if the year has thirteen months].

And see responsa *Chasam Sofer* (*Orach Chaim* §14), who states that this only applies if the death occurred in Adar, since in this case the twelfth month has the same name as the month when the death occurred — i.e., both are called "Adar." [But if death occurred in another month, and the following year is a leap-year, the *yahrzeit* is observed in the thirteenth month. For example, if death occurred on 10 Nissan in a regular year, and the following year is a leap-year, the *yahrzeit* would be observed on 10 Nissan, even though this is thirteen months after the death. Similarly, if death occurred on 10 Shevat in a leap-year, the *yahrzeit* is observed on 10 Shevat, even though this would be thirteen months after the death.] And see below, par. 42.

97. *Rama* (ad loc.). *Mishnah Berurah* (ad loc. §§42) writes: "See *Magen Avraham*, who concludes that if one made a vow to fast on the *yahrzeit* of his father or his teacher, he is obligated to fast on both [Adar I and Adar II], for this is the correct *halachah*; and this is also the ruling of *Gra*. However, if one did not make an explicit vow, but only accepted the custom, because it is a custom to fast on the *yahrzeit* of one's father or mother, then one need only fast on the day on which one fasted in the first leap-year after the death; for this was his intention when he accepted the custom upon himself. However, if he comes [to a rabbi] to ask what to do in the first leap-year, the correct thing to tell him is to fast on both [Adar I and Adar II]. But if it is difficult for him to fast on both days, it would seem that it is better for him to choose the first day [Adar I]; for this is the custom. All the same, [if he observes the *yahrzeit* in both Adars] the mourners only have to allot him a *Kaddish* in one of them."

Gesher HaChaim (loc. cit. par. 10) writes: "If he once fasted in both [Adar I and Adar II], he must always do so."

98. *Mishnah Berurah* (loc. cit.). But responsa *Igros Moshe* (part III:§159) rules that the *yahrzeit* should be observed on Rosh Chodesh Nissan.

99. This is to exclude the supposition that one might fast on the twenty-ninth of Shevat (*Sha'arei Teshuvah* ad loc. §§16, citing responsa *Givas Shaul* §73).

in a year when the month [Cheshvan or Kislev] has only twenty-nine days.[100]

Others rule that one reckons [not according to the year of the death, but] according to the year of the first *yahrzeit*. If the first *yahrzeit* was in a year when the month had twenty-nine days, the *yahrzeit* should always be observed on the twenty-ninth of the month.[101] If it was in a year when the month had thirty days, the *yahrzeit* should always be observed on Rosh Chodesh.

The prevalent custom follows this second opinion.[102]

If death occurred on Rosh Chodesh Kislev in a year when Rosh Chodesh was only one day, then, in a year when Rosh Chodesh is two days, one should observe the *yahrzeit* on the second day of Rosh Chodesh.[103]

39. If the death occurred in the twilight period known as *bein hashmashos*,[103a] [and accordingly it is doubtful whether the date should be that of the day that is ending or the day that is beginning] — in this case, if no other mourners are present in the congregation, one should lead the services on both days. If this is

---

100. *Sha'arei Teshuvah* (loc. cit.), citing responsa *Panim Me'iros*. He explains that, usually, the *molad* (day of the new moon) occurs thirty days from the previous Rosh Chodesh. Therefore, even when the month has only twenty-nine days, the *yahrzeit* should be observed on Rosh Chodesh, which is thirty days from the previous Rosh Chodesh. The same ruling is given by *Bigdei Yesha*.

   Aruch HaShulchan also rules this way, explaining that the name "Rosh Chodesh" is the determining factor [i.e., since the death occurred on Rosh Chodesh, the *yahrzeit* should also be on Rosh Chodesh]. The same ruling is given by *Igros Moshe* (loc. cit.). He expresses surprise at *Magen Avraham*, who writes that the *yahrzeit* should be observed on the twenty-ninth [i.e., the day before Rosh Chodesh]. *Igros Moshe* maintains that this cannot be correct, since the parent had still been alive on the twenty-ninth. As for the statement of *Mishnah Berurah* that "the custom is to follow the ruling of *Magen Avraham* [in this matter]," *Igros Moshe* states that the term "custom" cannot apply to a situation which only rarely occurs.

101. *Mateh Efrayim* (3:§7) writes that even in a year when the relevant month has thirty days, the *yahrzeit* should be observed on the twenty-ninth, even though it would be possible to observe it on the thirtieth. And *Elef LaMateh* (ad loc. §§7) writes that this is to be inferred from the statement of *Magen Avraham*. *Elef LaMateh* explains the reasoning of *Magen Avraham*: Since the *yahrzeit* was observed on the twenty-ninth in the first year, it should be observed on this date every year. But *Elef LaMagen* writes that this is not necessarily correct. He concludes that one should not depart from the ruling of *Taz* and *Magen Avraham*, and should observe the *yahrzeit* on the twenty-ninth; and on this day one has [the regular] rights of precedence [of one observing a *yahrzeit*] to recite *Kaddish*. Nevertheless, if one wishes, one may be strict and also recite *Kaddish* and serve as *sheliach tzibbur* on the first day of Rosh Chodesh, if there is no one else in the congregation [i.e., mourners or others observing a *yahrzeit*] who are obligated to do these things.

   Gesher HaChaim (32:11) writes: "Whenever there are two days of Rosh Chodesh, the *yahrzeit* is observed on the first day of Rosh Chodesh, corresponding to the day of the death." It is surprising that he does not mention the above discussion among the *Poskim*. The matter requires study.

102. *Magen Avraham* (ad loc. §§20), cited by *Mishnah Berurah* (568:§§42), who states that this is the prevalent custom. And *Gesher HaChaim* (loc. cit.) also writes that this is the ruling to be followed.

103. *Sha'arei Teshuvah* (ad loc. §§16). The same ruling is given by *Mateh Efrayim* (loc. cit.).

103a. If the death occurred during the day [before sundown], the *yahrzeit* is observed on that day only, even if the death occurred after the congregation recited *Maariv*. [Some congregations recite *Maariv* before sundown.] *Pischei Teshuvah* (375:§§6).

not possible, one authority rules that one should observe the *yahrzeit* on the earlier day.[104] But some rule that one should observe it on the later day.[105]

As regards fasting, one authority rules that one should fast on the day of one's choice.[106] Another rules that one should fast on the earlier day.[107] Another rules that, in the first year, one should fast on the later day.[108]

If one is in doubt whether the death occurred on the fourth or the fifth of the month, and one has brothers who know when the *yahrzeit* is, but one cannot find out, one should observe all the practices of the *yahrzeit* on the fourth of the month, and none on the fifth. If one does not have brothers, or if they, too, are in doubt, one should observe all the practices of the *yahrzeit*, except the fast, on both the fourth and the fifth. One should fast on the fourth, and on the fifth one [need not fast, but] should increase one's Torah-study and religious service.[109]

If one knows the month of the *yahrzeit*, but not the day, one should observe it on the last day of the month.[109a]

If the deceased was found dead, and the day of death is not known, one should assume that it occurred on the last possible day. For example, if the death could have occurred any time between the ninth and the thirteenth of the month, the *yahrzeit* is observed on the thirteenth.[109b]

40. If the death occurred on the first of the month, but the sons were in a place where it was already the second of the month (or the reverse), one authority

---

104. *Gesher HaChaim* (32:12).

105. Responsa *Duda'ei HaSadeh* (§99). The same ruling is given by *Igros Moshe* (*Yoreh De'ah* part III:§159), because on the earlier day the parent had been alive the whole day. He mentions the ruling of *Chasam Sofer* regarding the case where one [knows that the *yahrzeit* is on one of two successive days, but] does not know which day. In that case, *Chasam Sofer* rules that the *yahrzeit* should be observed on the earlier day. But *Igros Moshe* explains that our present question is not comparable to that case.

See also *Chazon LaMo'ed* (§28 note 4), who writes: "I heard of a case in which death occurred *bein hashmashos* [at the end of] the Sabbath. The *Gaon* of Tchebin, *zatzal*, answered that the *yahrzeit* should be observed on the Sabbath, since [during *bein hashmashos*] the entire Jewish people were still observing the Sabbath."

106. *Chazon LaMo'ed* (28:20), citing *Yalkut David* (p. 55).

107. *Gesher HaChaim* (loc. cit.).

108. *Sheivet HaLevi* (*Yoreh De'ah* §213) rules this way because the later day was possibly the day of death, and certainly the day of burial. But this ruling applies only in the first year. Regarding subsequent years, *Sheivet HaLevi* states that the matter requires study.

109. Responsa *Chasam Sofer* (*Orach Chaim* §161).

109a. *Chochmas Adam* (171:11). The reason is that we presume the person was alive as long as it is possible to presume so. Hence, we presume that he died on the last day of the month. For this same reason, *Chayei Adam* (132:37) writes that if one is in doubt whether [the death occurred] in Adar I or Adar II, one should fast in Adar II, since we presume the person was alive as long as it is possible to presume so.

109b. *Igros Moshe* (loc. cit.).

writes that the *yahrzeit* should be observed according to the date where the sons were.[110] But some rule that it should be observed according to the date where the death occurred.[111]

41. If one does not know the date of his father's or mother's death, he should select a date on which to observe the *yahrzeit*. But he cannot take precedence over other mourners in reciting *Kaddish*.[112]

If one does not know the date of his father's death, he should not select the same date as his mother's *yahrzeit*.[113] Likewise, if both dates are unknown to him, he should select a separate date to observe each *yahrzeit*, unless he has reasonable grounds for thinking that both parents died on the same day.[114]

42. Some rule that the customs of the *yahrzeit* — special Torah-study, recitation of *Kaddish*, being called up to the Torah for *maftir*, and the like — should also be observed at the conclusion of the Twelve Months of mourning, even if this does not coincide with the *yahrzeit* (for example, in a leap-year); but the fast should be observed only on the day of the *yahrzeit*.[115] Others rule that one should

---

110. *Kol Bo Al Aveilus* (p. 396) analyzes this question. He writes that the ruling depends on the differing explanations about why one fasts on the *yahrzeit*. According to the explanation that the son fasts because it is a day when his *mazal* (fortune) was bad, the fast should be observed on the date at the son's location. But according to the explanation that the fast is to gain atonement for the deceased, the fast should be observed on the date at the location where the death occurred.

He cites *Duda'ei HaSadeh* (p. 39) as ruling that the *yahrzeit* should be observed on the date at the son's location. However, if one fasts on the date at the location of the death, this is also good, since the main purpose of the fast is in honor of the deceased, to lighten his judgment and give merit to his soul.

He concludes: In any case, if, for example, one in America whose parents are buried in Europe has a *yahrzeit* on a certain day of the month, there is no doubt that he should recite *Kaddish* also at the *Minchah* prayer on the preceding day because in Europe it is already the *yahrzeit* when *Minchah* is recited in America.

111. *Gesher HaChaim* (32:14). The same ruling is given by responsa *Chelkas Yaakov* (II:§97). His reason is that it may be inferred from the responsum of *Chasam Sofer* that the purpose of the *yahrzeit* is atonement for the deceased. But if one also is concerned about the other reason — that the son fasts because it is a day when his *mazal* (fortune) was bad — the fast should also be observed according to the date at the son's location.

The same ruling is given by responsa *Be'er Moshe* (part II:§114): that all depends on the date at the place where the death occurred.

112. *Mateh Moshe* (V:§767). The same ruling is given by *Mishnah Berurah* (568:§§42), citing *Rashal*.

113. Responsa *Teshuras Shai* (*mahadura kamma Yoreh De'ah* §585). The reason is that on the date of his mother's *yahrzeit* he is in any case obligated to fast.

114. Responsa *Minchas Yitzchak* (I:§183).

115. See the citation from *Beis Yosef* (above, footnote 96). The ruling cited in our text is also given by *Nishmas Kol Chai* (I:§72): that, regarding the fast, one should be lenient [and not fast at the end of the Twelve Months of mourning]; for the fast is to be observed in the thirteenth month, because that is the date when the son's *mazal* was bad. But regarding the recitation of *Kaddish*, the reading of the *Haftarah*, and the study of *mishnayos* for the elevation of the departed soul, the most

even fast at the end of the Twelve Months.[116]

As regards visiting the grave at the end of the Twelve Months, see above, chapter 42.

---

important time is at the conclusion of the Twelve Months; for these things are in order to save one's father or mother from the judgment of *Gehinnom* — and why should their atonement be delayed? He discusses this matter at length.

See also *Sdei Chemed* (*Aveilus* §92). And see *Ma'amar Mordechai* (568:§§7), who writes: "I have heard people say that [if the first year is] a leap-year, the fast should be observed the month before the month when the death occurred; but this seems to me a custom based on ignorance, requiring no refutation." And see *Mateh Efrayim* (3:9), and responsa *Beis HaYotzer* (*Orach Chaim* §45). The *gaon* R' Eliezer Yehudah Waldenberg, author of *Tzitz Eliezer*, also wrote to me confirming the ruling given in our text.

116. Responsa *Rav Pe'alim* (IV:4 *Orach Chaim*, §41). There he answers the objection of *Ma'amar Mordechai* cited in our previous footnote. He also cites this ruling in the name of *Divrei Yosef* (§57).

CHAPTER FORTY-FIVE

Reinterment (*Likut Atzamos*)

Throughout this chapter, the term "reinterment" refers to the entire process of removing the remains from their first grave and interring them in a different grave. "Disinterment" means removing the remains from the first grave. "Reburial" means reinterring them in the second grave.

1. If one disinters his father or some other family member for whose death he is obligated to mourn, he must mourn that entire day [until evening]. He must observe all the restrictions of a mourner, including the prohibitions against wearing shoes, marital relations, bathing, and the use of lotions.[1]

2. The status of mourning begins as soon as one starts to remove the remains from the first grave and continues to nightfall even if the disinterment was not concluded by nightfall.[2] If one was in the midst of disinterment when evening arrived, no restrictions of mourning apply the next day. Therefore, to prevent a situation where one would not observe mourning rites for the disinterment of one's parents, it is forbidden to begin too close to nightfall.[3]

However, some rule that the status of mourning begins only after one finishes disinterring the remains. [And, according to this opinion, if one finished the reinterment after nightfall, he must observe mourning throughout the next day.][4]

---

1. *Shulchan Aruch* (403:1).

2. This is the ruling given by *Kesef Mishneh* (*Hilchos Avel* 12:8). And *Chazon LaMo'ed* (loc. cit. note 1) cites support for this ruling from the words of *Tur*, citing Tractate *Semachos*. The same conclusion is reached by *Gesher HaChaim* (part II:22:2). This ruling is also given by *Mishpetei Uziel* (*mahadura tinyana Yoreh De'ah* §130). He states that the mourning begins as soon as they begin to remove the remains from the first grave, and ceases when it gets dark.

3. *Shulchan Aruch* (loc. cit.).

4. *Chazon Ish* (*Yoreh De'ah* 213:4) writes: "According to *Rosh*, it seems that, for reinterment, the obligation of mourning begins when the reinterment is completed. Even if the head and most of the skeleton have been reburied, the *mitzvah* is not finished as long as there are still more remains to rebury, and therefore the mourning does not begin. This is comparable to mourning [for a death], which begins only upon completion of burial, i.e., when the grave is filled with earth. (As for the statement of *Kesef Mishneh*, *Hilchos Avel* §12, that the mourning starts as soon as one begins to remove the remains from the first grave — this requires study.) And if the reinterment began in the daytime and finished at night, mourning is observed throughout the next day."

Some rule that the subsequent reburial is an independent cause of mourning. Thus, even if reburial occurs on a day when disinterment is not a cause of mourning, one mourns on the day of reburial, until evening.[5]

If a widow remarried, and then her first husband was reinterred, she should not mourn.[6]

3. The status of *aninus* (one whose deceased is not yet buried) does not apply to reinterment. Instead, the mourning begins immediately at the beginning of disinterment. But, since there is no *aninus*, one is permitted to eat meat and drink wine. Regarding whether one is exempt from *mitzvos*, see footnote.[6a]

◌ᣚ *Kri'ah*

4. If the person whose remains are being reinterred is someone for whom one would be obligated to rend one's garment, he is also obligated to rend at the reinterment.[6b] Likewise, if one would not be allowed to sew (*le'achos*) the garment after having performed *kri'ah* for the death, one also is not allowed to sew it after having performed *kri'ah* for the reinterment (See above, chapt. 6).

◌ᣚ Reinterment of a Coffin

5. Even if the disinterred remains are in an iron coffin, and will be reburied in the same coffin, this is considered reinterment (*likut atzamos*).[7] However, some rule

---

5. *Chazon Ish* (loc. cit. par. 1). He writes: "The reburial of the remains from the world of life to their resting place is the essence of reinterment, and mourning is observed that day." This is also the ruling of the *gaon* R' Moshe Feinstein *zatzal*, *Igros Moshe Yoreh De'ah* §260. But *Chazon LaMo'ed* (loc. cit. note 6) writes: "From the words of *Maharil Diskin* it may be inferred that mourning is not observed on the day of burying [the remains]." *Gesher HaChaim* (part I:26:3:8) likewise rules that mourning is not observed on the day of burying the remains.

6. Responsa *Chasam Sofer* (*Yoreh De'ah* §355), cited by *Pischei Teshuvah* (ad loc. §§2).

6a. *Rama* (ad loc. par. 1); *Shach* (ad loc. §§1). See *Chazon Ish* (*Yoreh De'ah* §213), who writes: "However, the *halachah* that an *onen* [one whose deceased is not yet buried] is exempt from the *mitzvos* because he is preoccupied with the *mitzvah* of burial, certainly applies also to reinterment; for the person is obligated to rebury the remains." Similarly, responsa *Chasam Sofer* (§353) writes: "Anyone who knows that his family member is to be reinterred on a particular day is exempt from all the *mitzvos* until the remains are brought to their rest." See also *Noda BiYehudah mahadura kamma Yoreh De'ah* (§88).

However, *Chelkas Yaakov* (II:§46) writes that one who reinters a family member is exempt from the *mitzvos*, not because of *aninus* (for there is no *halachah* of *aninus* with regard to reinterment), but simply because he is preoccupied with the *mitzvah* [of burying the remains]. Therefore, the exemption only applies while the person is actually occupied with the reinterment. He also understands this to be the intent of *Chasam Sofer* in the statement just quoted. The same ruling [that with regard to reinterment there is no status of *aninus* giving one an overall exemption from *mitzvos*] is given by responsa *Cheshev HaEfod* (II:§83); *Erech Shai* (§403); and *Igros Moshe* (*Yoreh De'ah* III:§161).

6b. *Shulchan Aruch* (loc. cit. par. 2). And see *Chazon LaMo'ed* (30:2), who writes: "If he did not tear his garment then [at the reinterment], he should do so the next day, as long as he is still wearing that garment (responsa *Maharil Diskin*, in his *Kuntres Acharon* §200)." And see responsa *Betzel HaChachmah* (II:§65:6).

7. *Chazon Ish* (loc. cit.) writes: "It makes no difference whether the remains are removed from the burial shrouds and coffin and reburied, or whether the coffin and shrouds themselves are [dis-

that the *halachos* of *likut atzamos* apply only if the remains were in the first grave without a coffin, even if they were reburied in a coffin; or if they were in a coffin in the first grave and were reburied without a coffin; or, all the more so, if both the first and second burial were without a coffin. But, according to these authorities, if the remains were in a coffin in both graves, the *halachos* of *likut atzamos* do not apply.[8]

☙ If One Is Informed of the Reinterment

6. If one of the family members for whom one is obligated to mourn is reinterred,
    and one hears of it on the day it happens, he is required to mourn, even if he was not present at the reinterment. But if he hears about it the next day, he is not required to mourn.[9]

One should not inform the family members when the reinterment will take place.[10]

☙ The *Shurah* / Meal of Condolence / Dirges

7. The custom of forming a *shurah* (two parallel lines of comforters; see above,
    10:22) is not practiced at a reinterment. However, the mourners speak words of consolation to each other.[11]

For a reinterment, the *se'udas havra'ah* (the mourner's first meal after the burial; see above, chapt. 14) is given to the mourner in his home.

Funeral dirges (*lekonnen*) and lamentations (see above, 8:3) are not recited for reinterment, but praises are recited; that is, the deceased is praised according to his traits and deeds. But some rule that "praises" means praising the Holy One, Blessed is He, Who kills and resurrects.[12]

---

interred and] reburied [with the remains in them]. . . However, if the coffin is made of stone [and is reinterred without removing the remains], [the Sages] said that this is not considered reinterment. If the coffin is made of metal, the matter requires study. Does this follow the same *halachah* as for stone? Logic would indicate that [the exception applies] only [to] stone; for stone is more like earth [than metal is]."

The same ruling is given by *Igros Moshe* (*Yoreh De'ah* §260). Likewise, *Chazon LaMo'ed* (loc. cit. note 6) writes: "In our land, it is already a well-known fact that we follow the strict ruling of *Chazon Ish* [i.e., to apply the *halachos* of reinterment (*likut atzamos*) even if the remains are in an iron coffin when removed from the grave and also are in this coffin when reburied] — as is known to every *chevra kaddisha* (burial society)."

8. *Har Tzvi* (*Yoreh De'ah* §296). The same ruling is given by *Minchas Elazar* (IV:§12); and *Gesher HaChaim* (loc. cit. par. 12).

9. *Shulchan Aruch* and *Rama* (loc. cit. par. 5).

10. Responsa *Chasam Sofer* (*Yoreh De'ah* §353), cited by *Pischei Teshuvah* (ad loc. §§1). He writes: "It is good to institute a law to forbid informing anyone on the day that his family member is being reinterred. . . This is included in [the *mitzvah*] of *gemilus chessed*, doing kindness to others; for the Torah is concerned for the welfare of Israel, that they should not have to lose time."

11. *Shulchan Aruch* (loc. cit. par. 3). His source is Tractate *Semachos* (ch. 12). There we find: "We do not form the *shurah* for them, nor recite the blessing of mourners over them, nor speak the consolations of mourners; but they speak consolations to each other." This is also the quotation given by *Tur*.

12. *Tur* (loc. cit.). And *Rambam* (*Hilchos Avel* 12:6) writes: ". . .but praises of the Holy One, Blessed is He, are spoken there, and also words of exhortation (*divrei kibushim*)."

◈ Reinterment on Festivals

8. Reinterment of one's father — and, all the more so, of other family members — is not performed during a Festival.[13]

◈ Children Reinterring Parents

9. A son is not permitted to personally reinter his father if flesh is still on the bones.
And even after the flesh is decomposed, it is not proper for the son to reinter the remains.[14]

◈ A *Kohen*

10. A *kohen* is forbidden to become *tamei* for a family member unless the body is complete (see above, chapt. 7). Therefore, a *kohen* is forbidden to take part in the reinterment of his father, since the body might be found to be incomplete.[15]

◈ Exemption from Performing *Mitzvos*

11. One who is reinterring the remains, watching over a deceased, or moving the remains from one place to another, is exempt from reciting the *Shema*, from praying, from putting on *tefillin*, and from all other *mitzvos* of the Torah.

This applies during the weekdays as well as on the Sabbath; whether or not the remains are those of a relative; whether on shipboard or on the road.

Even if several people are working together to reinter the remains, this exemption applies to each of them. But with regard to watching over the remains, if several people are watching over them [and it is time to recite the *Shema*], they should take turns, one watching over the remains while the others recite the *Shema*.

Even if the exempt person wishes to recite the *Shema* or perform some other commandment, he should not do so. The intent of this *halachah* is to ensure that proper respect is given to the remains, and this supersedes an individuals desire to perform a commandment.[16]

◈ Respect for the Remains

12. A person transporting the remains from one place to another should not put them in a sack and sit on them, or treat them in any other disrespectful manner. But he is permitted to transport them in a compartment near his person. If he is afraid they will be stolen, he is permitted [to sit on the sack].[17]

※ ※ ※

---

13. *Shulchan Aruch* (loc. cit. par. 4). The reason is that the reinterment would impair the rejoicing of the Festival.

14. Ibid. par. 7. The reason is that refraining from reinterring the father is a sign of respect for him.

15. *Shach* (loc. cit. §§1), citing *Drishah*.

16. *Shulchan Aruch* (loc. cit. par. 9); and *Shach* (ad loc. §§3).

17. *Shulchan Aruch* (loc. cit. par. 10). The example used in the *Shulchan Aruch* is that "one should not put them in a sack or saddlebag on the donkey's back and sit on them, because this is disrespectful. But he is permitted to hang them behind him on the donkey. And if he is afraid of thieves or highwaymen, he is permitted."

בִּלַּע הַמָּוֶת לָנֶצַח
וּמָחָה אֲדֹנָי יֱהֹוִה דִּמְעָה מֵעַל כָּל פָּנִים.

May He swallow up death forever;
may HASHEM God wipe away tears
from every face.
(Isaiah 25:8)

ᘒ Appendix

Prayer for the Sick

Viduy /Confession

Mesiras Moda'ah /Declaration of Intent

The Short Version of *Viduy*

The Long Version of *Viduy*

Sefardic *Viduy*

Dayan HaEmes and *Kri'ah*

Prayer at the Cemetery

Tzidduk HaDin

Kaddish HaGadol After a Burial

The *Shurah*

Psalms When Visiting a Grave

Upon Visiting the Grave of a Father

Upon Visiting the Grave of a Mother

On Erev Rosh Hashanah and Erev Yom Kippur
at the Graves of Parents and Forebares

Study of Mishnah In Memory of the Deceased

The Rabbis' *Kaddish*

Prayer After Mishnah

Transliteration of *Kaddish:*
Kaddish HaGadol / Mourner's *Kaddish* / The Rabbis' *Kaddish*

⋖§ Prayer for the Sick

Among the Psalms commonly recited for the sick are: 20, 6, 9,13,16,17,18, 22, 23, 28, 30, 31, 32, 33, 37, 38, 39, 41, 49، 55, 56, 69, 86, 88, 89, 90, 91, 102, 103, 104, 107, 116, 118, 142, 143, 148. (Alternatively, some or all of the following psalms are recited: 20, 30, 121, 130, 142.) Afterwards, verses whose initial letters spell the patient's Hebrew name are recited. Psalm 119 (see below, page 451) is used customarily for this purpose because it consists of twenty-two sets of eight verses. All the verses in each set begin with the same Hebrew letter and the sets are arranged in alphabetical order. If, for example, the sick person's name is יַעֲקֹב the eight verses (73-80) which begin with the letter י are recited first, then the verses which begin with the letters ע, ק, and ב. Some continue the same pattern spelling out בֶּן/בַּת son/daughter, and the name of the patient's mother. Following this, the words קְרַע שָׂטָן, Tear away Satan, are spelled out by the same method of reciting the eight verses which correspond to the respective letters. Some add the following supplication. The first paragraph, in parentheses, is recited only if a minyan is present.

(HASHEM, HASHEM, God, Merciful and Compassionate, Slow to Anger, and Abundant in Kindness and Truth. Preserver of Kindness for thousands of generations, Forgiver of Iniquity, Transgression and Sin. He Who Erases.)

לְךָ Yours, HASHEM, is the greatness, the strength, the splendor, the triumph, and the glory; for everything in heaven and on earth is Your Kingdom; HASHEM, Who is elevated above every leader. And in Your hand is the soul of every living thing and the spirit of all mankind. And in Your hand is the strength and the power to make great, to strengthen and to cure every man, even he who is crushed, crushed to the very depths of his soul. Nothing is unknown to You, and in Your hand is the soul of every living thing. Therefore may it be Your will, O Trustworthy God, Merciful Father, Healer of all illnesses of Your people, Israel, even those near the very gates of death; the One Who binds His beloved ones with healing preparations, and Who redeems His devout ones from the pit of destruction, and Who delivers the souls of His servants from death — You, O Trustworthy Healer — please send healing, cure, and remedy, with abundant kindness, graciousness, and compassion to [patient's Hebrew name] the son/daughter of [patient's mother's Hebrew name]. Restore his/her unfortunate spirit and soul, so that he/she should not descend to the grave. May You be filled with mercy upon him/her to restore him/her to health, to cure, strengthen, and invigorate him/her as is the wish of all of his/her relatives and friends. May all his/her merits and charitable deeds appear before You and may You cast into the depths of the sea all of his/her sins. May Your mercy suppress Your anger against him/her and may You send him/her a complete recovery, a spiritual recovery, and a physical recovery. Renew his/her youth like the eagle's; send him/her and all sick people a lasting cure, a blessed cure,

(יהוה יהוה אֵל רַחוּם וְחַנּוּן אֶרֶךְ אַפַּיִם וְרַב חֶסֶד וֶאֱמֶת נֹצֵר חֶסֶד לָאֲלָפִים נֹשֵׂא עָוֹן וָפֶשַׁע וְחַטָּאָה וְנַקֵּה:)

לְךָ יהוה הַגְּדֻלָּה וְהַגְּבוּרָה וְהַתִּפְאֶרֶת וְהַנֵּצַח וְהַהוֹד כִּי כֹל בַּשָּׁמַיִם וּבָאָרֶץ לְךָ יהוה הַמַּמְלָכָה וְהַמִּתְנַשֵּׂא לְכֹל לְרֹאשׁ: וְאַתָּה בְּיָדְךָ נֶפֶשׁ כָּל חַי וְרוּחַ כָּל בְּשַׂר אִישׁ. וּבְיָדְךָ כֹּחַ וּגְבוּרָה לְגַדֵּל וּלְחַזֵּק וּלְרַפְּאוֹת אֱנוֹשׁ עַד דַּכָּא עַד דִּכְדּוּכָה שֶׁל נֶפֶשׁ. וְלֹא יִפָּלֵא מִמְּךָ כָּל דָּבָר וּבְיָדְךָ נֶפֶשׁ כָּל חַי. לָכֵן יְהִי רָצוֹן מִלְּפָנֶיךָ הָאֵל הַנֶּאֱמָן אַב הָרַחֲמִים הָרוֹפֵא לְכָל תַּחֲלוּאֵי עַמְּךָ יִשְׂרָאֵל הַקְּרוֹבִים עַד שַׁעֲרֵי מָוֶת. וְהַמְחַבֵּשׁ מָזוֹר וּתְעָלָה לִידִידָיו וְהַגּוֹאֵל מִשַּׁחַת חֲסִידָיו וְהַמַּצִּיל מִמָּוֶת נֶפֶשׁ מְרוּדָיו. אַתָּה רוֹפֵא נֶאֱמָן שְׁלַח מַרְפֵּא וַאֲרוּכָה וּתְעָלָה בְּרוֹב חֶסֶד וַחֲנִינָה וְחֶמְלָה לְנֶפֶשׁ (שם החולה) בֶּן/בַּת (שם אמו/אמה) [לְרוּחוֹ וְנַפְשׁוֹ/לְרוּחָהּ וְנַפְשָׁהּ] הָאוּמְלָלָה וְלֹא תֵרֵד [נַפְשׁוֹ/נַפְשָׁהּ] לִשְׁאוֹלָה וְהִמָּלֵא רַחֲמִים עָלָיו לְהַחֲלִימוֹ וּלְרַפֹּאותוֹ לְהַחֲזִיקוֹ וּלְהַחֲיוֹתוֹ/עָלֶיהָ לְהַחֲלִימָהּ וּלְרַפֹּאתָהּ לְהַחֲזִיקָהּ וּלְהַחֲיוֹתָהּ] כִּרְצוֹן כָּל [קְרוֹבָיו וְאוֹהֲבָיו/ קְרוֹבֶיהָ וְאוֹהֲבֶיהָ]. וְיֵרָאוּ לְפָנֶיךָ [זְכִיּוֹתָיו וְצִדְקוֹתָיו/זְכִיּוֹתֶיהָ וְצִדְקוֹתֶיהָ] וְתַשְׁלִיךְ בִּמְצוּלוֹת יָם כָּל [חֲטֹאתָיו/חֲטֹאתֶיהָ] וְיִכְבְּשׁוּ רַחֲמֶיךָ אֶת כַּעַסְךָ [מֵעָלָיו/מֵעָלֶיהָ] וְתִשְׁלַח [לוֹ/לָהּ] רְפוּאָה שְׁלֵמָה רְפוּאַת הַנֶּפֶשׁ וּרְפוּאַת הַגּוּף וּתְחַדֵּשׁ כַּנֶּשֶׁר [נְעוּרָיו/נְעוּרֶיהָ] וְתִשְׁלַח [לוֹ/לָהּ] וּלְכָל חוֹלֵי יִשְׂרָאֵל מַרְפֵּא אֲרוּכָה מַרְפֵּא בְרָכָה

a gracious, compassionate cure, a merciful cure, with peace and life and lengthy days and years. May there be fulfilled for him/her and for every patient the verse recorded by Your servant Moses, the most trustworthy of Your House: And he [Moses] said: 'If you diligently listen to the voice of HASHEM, your God, and you do what is fair in His eyes, and you give ear to His commandments and you observe all His statutes — any sickness that I have brought upon Egypt I will not bring upon you, for I am HASHEM your healer.' And you shall serve HASHEM, your God, and He shall bless your bread and your water, and I shall remove sickness from among you. None shall miscarry nor be barren in your land; I will fill out the number of your days. And HASHEM will remove from you all sickness, and He will not place upon you any of the evil diseases of Egypt, of which you know, but He will bring them upon all your enemies. And through Your servants, the prophets, the following is written: And you shall eat in plenty and be satisfied and you will praise the Name of HASHEM, your God, Who treated you wondrously, and My people shall never be ashamed. I have seen his ways and I will heal him, I will guide him and bestow consolations upon him and upon his mourners. I will create a new expression of the lips: 'Peace, peace, to thousands who are far and near,' says HASHEM, 'and I will heal him.' For you who fear My Name, there will shine a sun of righteousness, with healing in its wings. Then your light shall burst out like the dawn and your health shall sprout speedily. Heal us, HASHEM — then we will be healed; save us — then we will be saved, for You are our praise. Bring complete recovery for all the ailments of Your people, the family of Israel, and particularly to [patient's Hebrew name] the son/daughter of [patient's mother's Hebrew name], a complete recovery to [for a male: his two hundred and forty-eight organs and to his three hundred and sixty-five sinews / for a female: to all her organs and to all her sinews]. Cure him/her like Hezekiah, king of Judah, from his sickness, and like Miriam the prophetess from her leprosy. Employ the sacred names which emanate from the verses containing Your Thirteen Attributes of Divine Mercy. Please, O God, heal [patient's Hebrew name] the son/daughter of [patient's mother's Hebrew name] and raise him/her from his/her sickbed. Grant lengthy days and years to him/her so that he/she may serve You with love and fear. And grant him/her a life of mercy, a life of health, a life of peace, a life of blessing, as it is written: For length of days and years of life and peace shall they add to you. Amen, Selah.

מַרְפֵּא תְרוּפָה וּתְעָלָה מַרְפֵּא חֲנִינָה וְחֶמְלָה מַרְפֵּא יְדוּעִים וְגָלוּיִם מַרְפֵּא רַחֲמִים וְשָׁלוֹם וְחַיִּים מַרְפֵּא אוֹרֶךְ יָמִים וְשָׁנִים טוֹבִים. וִיקֻיַם [בּוֹ/בָּהּ] וּבְכָל חוֹלֵי יִשְׂרָאֵל מִקְרָא שֶׁכָּתוּב עַל יְדֵי מֹשֶׁה עַבְדְּךָ נֶאֱמַן בֵּיתֶךָ וַיֹּאמֶר אִם שָׁמוֹעַ תִּשְׁמַע לְקוֹל יהוה אֱלֹהֶיךָ וְהַיָּשָׁר בְּעֵינָיו תַּעֲשֶׂה וְהַאֲזַנְתָּ לְמִצְוֹתָיו וְשָׁמַרְתָּ כָּל חֻקָּיו כָּל הַמַּחֲלָה אֲשֶׁר שַׂמְתִּי בְמִצְרַיִם לֹא אָשִׂים עָלֶיךָ כִּי אֲנִי יהוה רֹפְאֶךָ: וַעֲבַדְתֶּם אֵת יהוה אֱלֹהֵיכֶם וּבֵרַךְ אֶת לַחְמְךָ וְאֶת מֵימֶיךָ וַהֲסִרֹתִי מַחֲלָה מִקִּרְבֶּךָ: לֹא תִהְיֶה מְשַׁכֵּלָה וַעֲקָרָה בְּאַרְצֶךָ אֶת מִסְפַּר יָמֶיךָ אֲמַלֵּא: וְהֵסִיר יהוה מִמְּךָ כָּל חֹלִי וְכָל מַדְוֵי מִצְרַיִם הָרָעִים אֲשֶׁר יָדַעְתָּ לֹא יְשִׂימָם בָּךְ וּנְתָנָם בְּכָל שֹׂנְאֶיךָ: וְעַל יְדֵי עֲבָדֶיךָ הַנְּבִיאִים כָּתוּב לֵאמֹר וַאֲכַלְתֶּם אָכוֹל וְשָׂבוֹעַ וְהִלַּלְתֶּם אֶת שֵׁם יהוה אֱלֹהֵיכֶם אֲשֶׁר עָשָׂה עִמָּכֶם לְהַפְלִיא וְלֹא יֵבֹשׁוּ עַמִּי לְעוֹלָם: דְּרָכָיו רָאִיתִי וְאֶרְפָּאֵהוּ וְאַנְחֵהוּ וַאֲשַׁלֵּם נִחֻמִים לוֹ וְלַאֲבֵלָיו: בּוֹרֵא נִיב שְׂפָתָיִם שָׁלוֹם שָׁלוֹם לָרָחוֹק וְלַקָּרוֹב אָמַר יהוה וּרְפָאתִיו: וְזָרְחָה לָכֶם יִרְאֵי שְׁמִי שֶׁמֶשׁ צְדָקָה וּמַרְפֵּא בִּכְנָפֶיהָ: אָז יִבָּקַע כַּשַּׁחַר אוֹרֶךָ וַאֲרֻכָתְךָ מְהֵרָה תִצְמָח: רְפָאֵנוּ יהוה וְנֵרָפֵא הוֹשִׁיעֵנוּ וְנִוָּשֵׁעָה כִּי תְהִלָּתֵנוּ אָתָּה וְהַעֲלֵה רְפוּאָה שְׁלֵמָה לְכָל מַכּוֹת עַמְּךָ יִשְׂרָאֵל וּבִפְרָט לְ(שם החולה) בֶּן/בַּת (שם אמו/אמה) רְפוּאָה שְׁלֵמָה [לִרְמַ״ח אֵבָרָיו וּשְׁסַ״ה גִידָיו/לְכָל אֵבָרֶיהָ וּלְכָל גִידֶיהָ] לְרַפֵּא [אוֹתוֹ/אוֹתָהּ] כְּחִזְקִיָּהוּ מֶלֶךְ יְהוּדָה מֵחָלְיוֹ וּכְמִרְיָם הַנְּבִיאָה מִצָּרַעְתָּהּ (בְּשֵׁמוֹת הַקְּדוֹשִׁים הַיּוֹצְאִים מִפְּסוּקִים שֶׁל שְׁלֹשׁ עֶשְׂרֵה מִדּוֹתֶיךָ): אֵל נָא רְפָא נָא לְ(שם החולה) בֶּן/בַּת (שם אמו/אמה) לְהָקִים [אוֹתוֹ מֵחָלְיוֹ/ אוֹתָהּ מֵחָלְיָהּ] וּלְהַאֲרִיךְ עוֹד יְמֵי [חַיָּיו/ חַיֶּיהָ] כְּדֵי [שֶׁיַּעֲבוֹד/שֶׁתַּעֲבוֹד] לָךְ בְּאַהֲבָה וּבְיִרְאָה וְתִתֵּן [לוֹ/לָהּ] חַיִּים שֶׁל רַחֲמִים חַיִּים שֶׁל בְּרִיאוּת חַיִּים שֶׁל שָׁלוֹם חַיִּים שֶׁל בְּרָכָה כְּדִכְתִיב כִּי אֹרֶךְ יָמִים וּשְׁנוֹת חַיִּים וְשָׁלוֹם יוֹסִיפוּ לָךְ אָמֵן סֶלָה:

⋖ Viduy / Confession (see chapter 2)

Prayer for Recovery composed by R' Saadya Gaon

If possible, the patient should recite the following prayer for recovery prior to his viduy/confession. [See 2:4].
If the patient is unable to recite the prayer on his own, someone should assist him or recite it on his behalf:

רְפָאֵנִי *Heal me, Hashem, and I shall be healed. Save me, and I shall be saved. Bandage my brokenness, heal my wound, and shelter me in Your great peace. Please, give me more time to keep Your mitzvos and uphold Your statutes, so that I may be among those who take shelter in the shadow of Your wings, who quench their thirst with the abundance of Your house, and whom You give to drink from the stream of Your delights. May I merit the abundant goodness that You have stored away for those who fear You, that You created for those who take refuge with You; for with You is the source of life; in Your light shall we see light. When someone requests of You, though he ask but a little, You answer his request doubly, many times over, for Your servant asks in accord with his own strength and his spiritual inadequacy, but You, O God, bestow upon us in accord with Your arm and the might of Your hand, O God of our salvation Selah! And we give thanks to You forever; generation after generation, we shall relate Your praise. Blessed are You forever, Amen and Amen.*

רְפָאֵנִי יהוה וְאֵרָפֵא הוֹשִׁיעֵנִי וְאִוָּשֵׁעַ
חֲבוֹשׁ שִׁבְרִי וּמְחַץ מַכָּתִי
וְסוֹכְכֵנִי בִּשְׁלוֹמְךָ הַגָּדוֹל אָנָּא סַפֵּק נָא עוֹד
עַל יָדַי לִשְׁמוֹר מִצְוֹתֶיךָ וּלְהָקִים חֻקֶּיךָ
וְאֶהְיֶה מִבְּנֵי הָאָדָם אֲשֶׁר בְּצֵל כְּנָפֶיךָ
יֶחֱסָיוּן, יִרְוְיוּן מִדֶּשֶׁן בֵּיתֶךָ וְנַחַל עֲדָנֶיךָ
תַשְׁקֵם, וְאֶזְכֶּה לְרַב טוֹב אֲשֶׁר צָפַנְתָּ
לִירֵאֶיךָ פָּעַלְתָּ לַחוֹסִים בָּךְ, כִּי עִמְּךָ מְקוֹר
חַיִּים בְּאוֹרְךָ נִרְאֶה אוֹר; וְשׁוֹאֵל, אִם
יִשְׁאָלְךָ מְעַט, תַּעֲנֵהוּ בְכֶפֶל שְׁאֵלָתוֹ
לְהַרְבֵּה מְאֹד, כִּי עַבְדְּךָ לְפִי כֹחוֹ וּבְקֹצֶר
רוּחוֹ יִשְׁאָל, וְאַתָּה כְּפִי זְרוֹעֲךָ וּכְעֶצֶם יָדְךָ
תַּעֲמָס לָנוּ הָאֵל יְשׁוּעָתֵנוּ סֶלָה, וְנוֹדֶה לְךָ
לְעוֹלָם לְדוֹר וָדוֹר נְסַפֵּר תְּהִלָּתֶךָ בָּרוּךְ
אַתָּה לְעוֹלָם, אָמֵן אָמֵן.

⋖ Mesiras Moda'ah / Declaration of Intent (see 2:4)

Me'il Shmuel (Hilchos Aveilus U'Misah, par. 10) writes that when a person's soul departs, the Accuser stands at his right side to impede him, and urge him to deny Hashem, the God of Israel. The soul refuses, but it is possible, God forbid, that [through suffering and confusion] it might be brought to affirm the apostasy. Therefore, a person should act in time, while he still has his faculties, to pray to Hashem before the time of evil arrives. [The halachah of court procedure provides that if a person knows in advance that he may be forced into making a statement against his will, he may prepare an abrogation beforehand and entrust it to a Torah court, in case it should be needed. Such an advance abrogation is called a moda'ah. Regarding his final moments, too,] a person should prepare a moda'ah. The procedure is as follows. Ten men [constituting a beis din, or court] are assembled in the presence of the sick person, and he makes the following declaration (moda'ah):

יְהִי רָצוֹן *May it be Your will, Hashem, my God and God of my fathers — the great, mighty, and awesome God, Who holds in His hand the soul of every living being and the spirit of all men — after long length of days and years of serving Him, Blessed is His name, the time will come for Him to single me out with pure good will, with His mercy, kindness, and pity on me, to take my soul from me. May it be Your will that when that time comes, my mind will be clear and settled, with faculties intact as of old. May I cleave to Him and His unity, Blessed is He, not to stray from fearing and loving Him, up to and including the moment when my soul departs.*

יְהִי רָצוֹן מִלְּפָנֶיךָ יהוה אֱלֹהַי וֵאלֹהֵי
אֲבוֹתַי, הָאֵל הַגָּדוֹל הַגִּבּוֹר
וְהַנּוֹרָא, אֲשֶׁר בְּיָדוֹ נֶפֶשׁ כָּל חַי וְרוּחַ כָּל
בְּשַׂר אִישׁ, שֶׁכְּשֶׁיַּגִּיעַ לְאַחַר אֲרִיכוּת יָמִים
וְשָׁנִים בַּעֲבוֹדָתוֹ יִתְבָּרֵךְ שְׁמוֹ, עֵת פְּקֻדָּתִי
בְּרָצוֹן הַטּוֹב וְהַפָּשׁוּט בְּרַחֲמָיו וַחֲסָדָיו
וּבְחֶמְלָתוֹ עָלַי לִטּוֹל מִמֶּנִּי נִשְׁמָתִי שֶׁאֶהְיֶה
בָּעֵת הַזֹּאת בְּדַעַת צְלוּלָה וּמְיֻשֶּׁבֶת עָלַי
וּבְשִׂכְלִי כְּמֵאָז וָקֶדֶם לִהְיוֹתִי דָּבוּק בּוֹ
וּבְאַחְדּוּתוֹ בָּרוּךְ הוּא שֶׁלֹּא לָזוּז מִיִּרְאָתוֹ
וּמֵאַהֲבָתוֹ עַד יְצִיאַת נִשְׁמָתִי עַד וְעַד
בִּכְלָל.

I accept upon myself the yoke of His indivisible and all-encompassing kingship. Hashem is One and His Name is One.

May my mind also be clear and settled to acknowledge the righteousness of His judgment, Blessed is He. He is true, His decrees are true, and all is done to me with mercy and kindness, and I shall do His will, Blessed is He, with fear and love, for He is the Master and the Ruler.

If it should be the will of the Creator, Blessed is He — His good and pure will, after long length of days and years of serving Him, Blessed is His Name — if He should see fit, when that time comes, to give me severe suffering; and if my mind should become, God forbid, crazed and confused, I hereby acknowledge the righteousness of His holy and pure judgment of kindness and mercy upon me. You are righteous in all that comes upon me, for You have acted truthfully, and I have acted wickedly.

If at that time, however, the Tempter and Destroyer, the great Accuser should come, God forbid, to tempt, entice, and trick me (God forbid, far, far be it from me), to deny the One Who made, fashioned, and created me, the King Who reigns over all kings, or to deny, God forbid, His holy Torah, or any of His commandments, whether Scriptural, Prophetic, Rabbinic, or any precautionary enactment, or any secondary precautionary enactment, God forbid, — I hereby make this declaration with the concurrence of the Holy One, Blessed is He, and His Divine Presence (Shechinah), and in your presence, you holy congregation [referring to the ten men assembled]. It is a completely valid declaration, in accord with all the pertinent requirements enacted by the Sages. I declare that trickery and enticement to be null and void, like a broken shard.

Moreover if, God forbid, I should submit to the Accuser, far, far be it from me, through suffering, confusion, and mental derangement, that admission is hereby retroactively nullified and canceled. It shall have no force or validity, as if it never existed; for a person cannot be blamed for what he says in his suffering. But in truth I unreservedly acknowledge in front of you that I believe in my God, the Creator, Blessed is His Name — I believe that He is all-encompassing, indivisible, and unique. Hashem is One and His name is One. I accept upon myself the yoke of His kingship. Hear, O Israel, Hashem is our God, Hashem, the One and Only. Blessed is the Name of His glorious kingdom for all eternity. Hashem, God, is true.

וּמְקַבֵּל אֲנִי עַל מַלְכוּתוֹ וְאַחְדּוּתוֹ עָלַי, יהוה אֶחָד וּשְׁמוֹ אֶחָד.

וִיהִי גַם כֵּן דַּעְתִּי צְלוּלָה וּמְיֻשֶּׁבֶת עָלַי לְהַצְדִּיק דִּינוֹ בָּרוּךְ הוּא, הוּא אֱמֶת וּגְזֵרוֹתָיו אֱמֶת וְהַכֹּל בְּחֶסֶד וּבְרַחֲמִים עָלַי, וְאֶעֱשֶׂה רְצוֹנוֹ בָּרוּךְ הוּא בְּיִרְאָה וּבְאַהֲבָה כִּי רַב וְשַׁלִּיט הוּא.

וּבְאִם שֶׁיִּהְיֶה רְצוֹן הַבּוֹרֵא בָּרוּךְ הוּא רְצוֹנוֹ הַטּוֹב וְהַפָּשׁוּט לְאַחַר אֲרִיכוּת יָמִים וְשָׁנִים בַּעֲבוֹדָתוֹ יִתְבָּרֵךְ שְׁמוֹ כְּשֶׁיַּגִּיעַ עֵת הַזֹּאת לְיַסְּרֵנִי בְּיִסּוּרִים קָשִׁים; וְיִהְיֶה לִי בִּלְבּוּל וְטֵרוּף הַדַּעַת, חַס וְשָׁלוֹם, הֲרֵינִי מַצְדִּיק אֶת דִּינוֹ הַקָּדוֹשׁ וְהַטָּהוֹר שֶׁל חֶסֶד וְרַחֲמִים עָלַי; וְאַתָּה צַדִּיק עַל כָּל הַבָּא עָלַי כִּי אֱמֶת עָשִׂיתָ וַאֲנִי הִרְשַׁעְתִּי.

אָמְנָם בְּאִם שֶׁיָּבֹא חַס וְשָׁלוֹם בָּעֵת הַהִיא הַמֵּסִית וְהַמַּדִּיחַ הַמְקַטְרֵג הַגָּדוֹל לְהַסִית וּלְהַדִּיחַ וּלְפַתּוֹת אוֹתִי חַס וְשָׁלוֹם, חָלִילָה וְחָלִילָה, לִכְפּוֹר בְּעוֹשִׂי יוֹצְרִי וּבוֹרְאִי מֶלֶךְ מַלְכֵי הַמְּלָכִים, אוֹ בְּתוֹרָתוֹ הַקְּדוֹשָׁה, אוֹ בְּאַחַת מִמִּצְוֹתָיו, הֵן מִצְוֹת דְּאוֹרַיְיתָא, אוֹ מִדִּבְרֵי קַבָּלָה אוֹ מִדְּרַבָּנָן, אוֹ מֵאֵיזֶה סְיָג וְגֶדֶר וּמִשְׁמֶרֶת לְמִשְׁמֶרֶת הֲרֵינִי מוֹסֵר מוֹדָעָה בְּצֵרוּף קוּדְשָׁא בְּרִיךְ הוּא וּשְׁכִינְתֵּיהּ לִפְנֵיכֶם עֵדָה קְדוֹשָׁה בְּמוֹדָעָה גְּמוּרָה בְּכָל דִּינֵי מְסִירוּת מוֹדָעָה שֶׁתִּקְּנוּ חֲזַ״ל, שֶׁיִּהְיֶה הַפִּתּוּי וְהַהֲסָתָה הַהִיא כְּאֶפֶס וּכְאַיִן וְכַחֶרֶס הַנִּשְׁבָּר.

וּבְאִם חַס וְשָׁלוֹם אוֹדֶה לוֹ חָלִילָה וְחָלִילָה מִתּוֹךְ צַעַר וּבִלְבּוּל וְטֵרוּף דַּעַת וְשֵׂכֶל, הַהוֹדָעָה הַהִיא תִּהְיֶה מֵעַתָּה וּמֵעַכְשָׁיו בְּטֵלָה וּמְבֻטֶּלֶת לָא שְׁרִירָא וְלָא קַיָּמֶת, וְהָיְתָה כְּאִלּוּ לֹא הָיְתָה מֵעוֹלָם כִּי אֵין אָדָם נִתְפָּס עַל צַעֲרוֹ, אֲבָל בֶּאֱמֶת מוֹדֶה אֲנִי לִפְנֵיכֶם בְּהוֹדָעָה גְּמוּרָה שֶׁאֲנִי מַאֲמִין בֵּאלֹהַי, הַבּוֹרֵא יִתְבָּרֵךְ שְׁמוֹ שֶׁהוּא אֶחָד יָחִיד וּמְיֻחָד, יהוה אֶחָד וּשְׁמוֹ אֶחָד, וַאֲנִי מְקַבֵּל עָלַי עֹל מַלְכוּתוֹ, שְׁמַע יִשְׂרָאֵל יהוה אֱלֹהֵינוּ יהוה אֶחָד, בָּרוּךְ שֵׁם כְּבוֹד מַלְכוּתוֹ לְעוֹלָם וָעֶד, וַיהוה אֱלֹהִים אֱמֶת.

Moses, His servant, the most trustworthy of His household is true, and His Torah is true, both the Oral and the Written Torah. All the mitzvos, Scriptural, Prophetic, and Rabbinic, are true, and all the fine details of the mitzvos are true. I believe in them with complete faith — praised be God — wholeheartedly, eagerly, and willingly. The One God, Master of all creatures, Blessed is He, spoke them.

I do not deny — far, far be it from me — any of the mitzvos, minor or major, Scriptural, Prophetic, or Rabbinic. I fear God, and I love the Creator, Blessed is His Name, and I love His teachings and His commandments. I believe in the Thirteen Principles of Faith, generally and specifically. I believe that the Creator, Blessed is His Name, is the First and the Last, and besides Him there is no God; that there is goodly reward in the World to Come for the righteous, and there is evil, bitter punishment for the wicked; that there will be a resurrection of the dead when the Creator, Blessed is His Name, wills it; that He has the power to kill and to keep alive. I believe in the coming of the Messiah; that the Creator, Blessed is His Name, is not a body nor the semblance of a body, and that He is [in a spiritual sense] * a very great and awesome light, a holy and pure light, a primal, ever-existing light, a clear light, a bright light, a lucid, shining light, an unfathomable and hidden light, a pure and infinite light, Blessed is He. He is living and existing; Hashem is the Source of living waters, and from Him come all the forms of life. May the verse be fulfilled through me: "You who cling to Hashem, your God, are alive all you today" [Deut. 4:4]; and also the verse: "In Me your days will be multiplied, and years of life will be added to you" [Proverbs 9:11]. God of life, inscribe me for good life and peace, Amen. May the words of my mouth and the expressions of my heart find favor before You, Hashem, my Rock and Redeemer.

מֹשֶׁה עַבְדּוֹ נֶאֱמַן בֵּיתוֹ אֱמֶת וְתוֹרָתוֹ אֱמֶת, שֶׁבִּכְתָב וְשֶׁבְּעַל פֶּה, וְכָל מִצְוֹת דְּאוֹרַיְתָא וְדִבְרֵי קַבָּלָה מִדְרַבָּנָן אֱמֶת וְכָל דִּקְדוּקֵי הַמִּצְוֹת אֱמֶת, וַאֲנִי מַאֲמִין בָּהֶם בֶּאֱמוּנָה שְׁלֵמָה תְהִלָּה לָאֵל בְּלֵב שָׁלֵם וּבְנֶפֶשׁ חֲפֵצָה, אֵל אֶחָד אֲדוֹן כָּל הַמַּעֲשִׂים בָּרוּךְ הוּא אֲמָרָם.

וְאֵינֶנִּי כוֹפֵר חָלִילָה וְחָלִילָה בְּשׁוּם מִצְוָה מֵהַמִּצְוֹת קְטַנָּה אוֹ גְדוֹלָה דְּאוֹרַיְתָא וְדִבְרֵי קַבָּלָה וּדְרַבָּנָן רַק אֶת הָאֱלֹהִים אֲנִי יָרֵא וַאֲנִי אוֹהֵב אֶת הַבּוֹרֵא יִתְבָּרֵךְ שְׁמוֹ וְתוֹרוֹתָיו וּמִצְוֹתָיו, וַאֲנִי מַאֲמִין בִּשְׁלֹשׁ עֶשְׂרֵה עִקָּרִים בִּכְלָל וּבִפְרָט, וְשֶׁהַבּוֹרֵא יִתְבָּרֵךְ שְׁמוֹ הוּא רִאשׁוֹן וְהוּא אַחֲרוֹן וּמִבַּלְעָדָיו אֵין אֱלֹהִים, וְיֵשׁ שָׂכָר טוֹב לַצַּדִּיקִים לָעוֹלָם הַבָּא וְעֹנֶשׁ רַע וּמַר לָרְשָׁעִים וְשֶׁתִּהְיֶה תְּחִיַּת הַמֵּתִים בְּעֵת שֶׁיַּעֲלֶה רְצוֹן הַבּוֹרֵא יִתְבָּרֵךְ שְׁמוֹ, וּבְיָדוֹ לְהָמִית וּלְהַחֲיוֹת וּבְבִיאַת הַמָּשִׁיחַ וְשֶׁהַבּוֹרֵא יִתְבָּרֵךְ שְׁמוֹ אֵינוֹ גּוּף וְלֹא דְּמוּת הַגּוּף וְהוּא * אוֹר גָּדוֹל וְנוֹרָא מְאֹד, אוֹר קָדוֹשׁ וְטָהוֹר אוֹר קַדְמוֹן, אוֹר צַח אוֹר מְצֻחְצָח אוֹר זַךְ וְנָקִי, אוֹר טָמִיר וְנֶעְלָם, אוֹר פָּשׁוּט אֵין סוֹף בָּרוּךְ הוּא, וְהוּא חַי וְקַיָּם מְקוֹר מַיִם חַיִּים יהוה וּמִמֶּנּוּ תּוֹצְאוֹת הַחַיִּים וִיקֻיַּם בִּי מִקְרָא שֶׁכָּתוּב וְאַתֶּם הַדְּבֵקִים בַּה' אֱלֹהֵיכֶם חַיִּים כֻּלְּכֶם הַיּוֹם, וְנֶאֱמַר כִּי בִי יִרְבּוּ יָמֶיךָ וְיוֹסִיפוּ לְךָ שְׁנוֹת חַיִּים לְחַיִּים טוֹבִים וּלְשָׁלוֹם תִּכְתְּבֵנִי אֱלֹהִים חַיִּים אָמֵן, יִהְיוּ לְרָצוֹן אִמְרֵי פִי וְהֶגְיוֹן לִבִּי לְפָנֶיךָ יהוה צוּרִי וְגוֹאֲלִי.

The following two paragraphs is to be recited only by a male.

From your honors [addressing the ten men assembled], I would like to make an additional request. Since in our day there is no one in the world who is so righteous that he has never experienced an impure emission and the wasting of seed in one way or another, and those drops consider me their father, and they wish to benefit from me and from my bier after my death, since they claim: 'You are our father' — therefore I ask your honors' forgiveness that you help me to ask the King Who reigns over

גַּם אֲנִי מְבַקֵּשׁ מִמַּעֲלַתְכֶם מֵאַחַר שֶׁאֵין צַדִּיק בָּאָרֶץ בַּזְּמַן הַזֶּה אֲשֶׁר לֹא קָרָה לוֹ מִקְרֶה בִּלְתִּי טָהוֹר בְּהוֹצָאַת זֶרַע לְבַטָּלָה יִהְיֶה בְּאֵיזֶה אֹפֶן שֶׁיִּהְיֶה וְאוֹתָן הַטִּפּוֹת הֵמָּה חוֹשְׁבִין אוֹתִי לָהֶם לְאָב וְרוֹצִים לֵהָנוֹת מִמֶּנִּי וּמִמִּטָּתִי אַחַר מִיתָתִי בְּאָמְרָם כִּי אַתָּה אָבִינוּ בְּכֵן אֲבַקֵּשׁ מִמַּעֲלַתְכֶם מְחִילָה שֶׁתַּעַזְרוּנִי לְבַקֵּשׁ אֶת פְּנֵי מֶלֶךְ מַלְכֵי

*The expressions that follow refer to lofty spiritual concepts, and are not to be taken in a literal sense.

kings, the Holy One, Blessed is He, to return to holiness all those drops that came out of me needlessly, whether under duress or willingly, by mistake or on purpose, awake or asleep. May their return to holiness be accomplished by means of the holy name contained in the verse, "He swallowed riches and regurgitated them" [Job 20:15], in combination with the Name, הׄ-ו-יׄ-הׄ, with the vocalization of *shuruk*, as follows: (one must be careful not to pronounce this Holy Name) יׄ-הׄ-חׄ-בׄ-יׄ-וׄ-הׄ.

Moreover, I hereby pronounce a ban and excommunication upon the evil spirits, and destructive forces created by the drops of seminal emission and my [wasted] seed — all of them are included [in the ban]. May they not touch me, my bier, nor my clothes, nor accompany me to my grave. And your honors, I ask you, too, to join with the Divine Presence (Shechinah) and pronounce a ban upon them, so that they will have no power to follow my bier nor, all the more so, to touch me, my clothes, my body, or my soul.

הַמְּלָכִים הַקָּדוֹשׁ בָּרוּךְ הוּא לְהַכְנִיס לִקְדֻשָּׁה כָּל אוֹתָן הַטִּפִּין שֶׁיָּצְאוּ מִמֶּנִּי לְבַטָּלָה הֵן בְּאֹנֶס הֵן בְּרָצוֹן הֵן בְּשׁוֹגֵג הֵן בְּמֵזִיד הֵן עֵר הֵן יָשֵׁן עַל יְדֵי שֵׁם הַקָּדוֹשׁ הַיּוֹצֵא מִפָּסוּק חַיִל בָּלַע וַיְקִיאֶנּוּ בְּשִׁלּוּב שֵׁם הֲוָיָה בְּנִקּוּד שׁוּרֶק כָּזֶה:

(one must be careful not to pronounce this Holy Name)

(יְהַחְבְּוֶהׁ):

גַּם הִנְנִי מַחֲרִים וּמְנַדֶּה אוֹתָם הַמַּזִּיקִים וְשֵׁדִין וְרוּחִין וְלֵילִין שֶׁנִּבְרְאוּ מִטִּפּוֹת קֶרִי וְזֶרַע שֶׁלִּי כֻּלָּם בִּכְלָל שֶׁלֹּא יִגְּעוּ בִּי אוֹ בְּמִטָּתִי אוֹ בִּבְגָדַי וְלֹא יְלַוּוּ אוֹתִי לְקִבְרִי וְאַתֶּם גַּם אַתֶּם תְּצָרְפוּ עִמָּכֶם הַשְּׁכִינָה וְהַחֲרִימוּ אוֹתָם בְּאֹפֶן שֶׁלֹּא יִהְיֶה לָהֶם כֹּחַ לֵילֵךְ אַחַר מִטָּתִי וּמִכָּל שֶׁכֵּן לִגַּע בִּי וּבִבְגָדַי אוֹ בְּגוּפִי אוֹ בְנַפְשִׁי.

The ten men assembled there, seated as a *beis din* (Torah court), reply:

בְּצֵרוּף In conjunction with the Holy One, Blessed is He, and His Divine Presence (Shechinah), we have accepted the declaration (moda'ah) by which [patient's Hebrew name] the son/daughter of [patient's mother's Hebrew name] has given over his body, life, spirit, and soul to the Source of all sources, the Cause of all causes. Anything that he does from this day on in contradiction to that declaration, in deed, speech, or thought, we hereby nullify, in conjunction with the Holy One, Blessed is He, and His Divine Presence (Shechinah). [Any such deed] will have no effect whatever.

בְּצֵרוּף קוּדְשָׁא בְּרִיךְ הוּא וּשְׁכִינְתֵּיהּ קִבַּלְנוּ הַמְּסִירַת מוֹדָעָה אֲשֶׁר מָסַר (שם החולה) בֶּן/בַּת (שם אמו/אמה) גּוּפוֹ נַפְשׁוֹ רוּחוֹ וְנִשְׁמָתוֹ לְעִלַּת כָּל הָעִלּוֹת וְסִבַּת כָּל הַסִּבּוֹת וְכָל מַה שֶּׁיַּעֲשֶׂה מֵהַיּוֹם נֶגֶד מְסִירַת הַמּוֹדָעָה הַזֹּאת הֵן בְּמַעֲשֶׂה הֵן בְּדִבּוּר הֵן בְּמַחֲשָׁבָה אֲנַחְנוּ מְבַטְּלִים אוֹתוֹ הַמַּעֲשֶׂה בְּצֵרוּף קֻדְשָׁא בְּרִיךְ הוּא וּשְׁכִינְתֵּיהּ; וְלֹא יַעֲשֶׂה שׁוּם רֹשֶׁם כְּלָל.

The following is said only for a male patient:

We, the beis din, in conjunction with the Holy One, Blessed is He, and His Divine Presence (Shechinah), also pronounce a ban on all the drops of seed that have ever been needlessly emitted from [patient's Hebrew name], the son of [patient's mother's Hebrew name] from the beginning of time until this day, including those emitted in previous incarnations; and also on any which are emitted from this day until after his death — they shall not touch [patient's Hebrew name] the son of [patient's mother's Hebrew name], neither him himself, nor his body, nor his clothing, nor his bier, nor shall they accompany him from his home to his grave. May his righteousness appear before You, and may the glory of Hashem gather him in, and may he lie on his resting place in peace, Amen.

גַּם מַחֲרִימִים אֲנַחְנוּ בֵּית דִּין בְּצֵרוּף קֻדְשָׁא בְּרִיךְ הוּא וּשְׁכִינְתֵּיהּ כָּל טִפּוֹת זֶרַע שֶׁיָּצְאוּ מִן (שם החולה) בֶּן (שם אמו) לְבַטָּלָה מֵעוֹלָם עַד הַיּוֹם הַזֶּה גַּם אֲשֶׁר יָצְאוּ מִמֶּנּוּ בַּגִּלְגּוּלִים הַקּוֹדְמִים גַּם אֲשֶׁר יָצָא לְבַטָּלָה מֵהַיּוֹם עַד אַחַר מִיתָתוֹ שֶׁלֹּא יִגְּעוּ בְּ(שם החולה) בֶּן (שם אמו) הֵן בּוֹ בְּעַצְמוֹ אוֹ בְּגוּפוֹ הֵן בִּבְגָדוֹ הֵן בְּמִטָּתוֹ וְלֹא יְלַוּוּ אוֹתוֹ מִבֵּיתוֹ לְקִבְרוֹ, וְצִדְקוֹ לְפָנֶיךָ יְהַלֵּךְ וּכְבוֹד יהוה יַאַסְפֵהוּ, וְיָנוּחַ עַל מִשְׁכָּבוֹ בְּשָׁלוֹם אָמֵן סֶלָה.

◈ The Short Version of *Viduy*

If it is difficult for the patient to recite a complete confession [as below],
he should recite the following abridged version:

מוֹדָה *I acknowledge before You, Hashem, my God and God of my fathers, that my recovery or death is in Your hands. May it be Your will that You heal me completely; but if I die, may my death be an atonement for all the mistakes, sins, and rebellions I have erred, sinned, and rebelled before You. May my portion be in Gan Eden, and may You allow me to be in the World to Come, which lies in store for the righteous.*

מוֹדָה אֲנִי לְפָנֶיךָ, יהוה אֱלֹהַי, וֵאלֹהֵי אֲבוֹתַי, שֶׁרְפוּאָתִי וּמִיתָתִי בְּיָדֶךָ. יְהִי רָצוֹן מִלְּפָנֶיךָ שֶׁתִּרְפָּאֵנִי רְפוּאָה שְׁלֵמָה; וְאִם אָמוּת תְּהֵא מִיתָתִי כַּפָּרָה עַל כָּל חֲטָאִים, וַעֲוֹנוֹת, וּפְשָׁעִים, שֶׁחָטָאתִי, וְשֶׁעָוִיתִי, וְשֶׁפָּשַׁעְתִּי לְפָנֶיךָ. וְתֵן חֶלְקִי בְּגַן עֵדֶן, וְזַכֵּנִי לָעוֹלָם הַבָּא הַצָּפוּן לַצַּדִּיקִים.

◈ The Long Version of *Viduy*

מוֹדָה *"I acknowledge before You, Hashem, my God and God of my fathers, God of Abraham, Isaac and Jacob, God of gods and Lord of lords — in the heavens above and on the earth below there is no other — Who makes the heavens and the earth, does kindness, judgment and righteousness on earth; Who was, is and will be; Who gives life to all, that my recovery is in Your hand or my death is in Your hand. May it be Your will, Hashem, my God and God of my fathers, that You heal me completely, for You are God, the Merciful Healer; but if — may it be far from us — I die, may my death be an atonement for all the mistakes, sins, and rebellions I have erred, sinned and rebelled before You, and may my portion be in Your Torah and in Gan Eden, and allow me to take part in the World to Come, which lies in store for the righteous.*

"I acknowledge and believe that You exist and are the Absolute Existence; that You are One, and not like individual beings; and are the Source of all existing beings; that You are not a physical being nor a physical force; and are not subject to physical events and forces; nor can You be described in physical terms; that Your existence precedes all existing things; that You are to be worshiped and exalted; that You are the One Who puts prophecy in the mouth of all the prophets; and that the prophecy of Your servant and prophet, Moses, is above all the prophets; that through him, You gave us from heaven the perfect, soul-reviving Torah; that this is the holy Torah that is found among us; that it reached [Moses] from the mouth of the Almighty; that this Torah is eternal and unalterable; that You know

מוֹדָה אֲנִי לְפָנֶיךָ יהוה אֱלֹהַי וֵאלֹהֵי אֲבוֹתַי, אֱלֹהֵי אַבְרָהָם יִצְחָק וְיַעֲקֹב, אֱלֹהֵי הָאֱלֹהִים וַאֲדוֹנֵי אֲדוֹנִים, בַּשָּׁמַיִם מִמַּעַל וְעַל הָאָרֶץ מִתָּחַת אֵין עוֹד, עוֹשֶׂה שָׁמַיִם וָאָרֶץ, עוֹשֶׂה חֶסֶד מִשְׁפָּט וּצְדָקָה בָּאָרֶץ, הָיָה וְהֹוֶה וְיִהְיֶה, מְחַיֶּה אֶת הַכֹּל, שֶׁרְפוּאָתִי בְיָדֶךָ וּמִיתָתִי בְּיָדֶךָ. יְהִי רָצוֹן מִלְּפָנֶיךָ, יהוה אֱלֹהַי וֵאלֹהֵי אֲבוֹתַי, שֶׁתִּרְפָּאֵנִי רְפוּאָה שְׁלֵמָה, כִּי אַתָּה אֵל רוֹפֵא רַחֲמָן, וְאִם בַּר מִינָן אָמוּת תְּהֵא מִיתָתִי כַּפָּרָה עַל כָּל חַטֹאותַי, וַעֲוֹנוֹתַי, וּפְשָׁעַי, שֶׁחָטָאתִי, וְשֶׁעָוִיתִי, וְשֶׁפָּשַׁעְתִּי, לְפָנֶיךָ, וְתֵן חֶלְקִי בְּתוֹרָתֶךָ וּבְגַן עֵדֶן. וְזַכֵּנִי לָעוֹלָם הַבָּא הַצָּפוּן לַצַּדִּיקִים.

וַאֲנִי מוֹדֶה וּמַאֲמִין כִּי אַתָּה נִמְצָא מְצִיאוּת גְּמוּרָה, וְאַתָּה אֶחָד וְלֹא כָאֲחָדִים, וְרֹאשׁ לְכָל הַנִּמְצָאִים, וְאֵינְךָ גוּף וְלֹא כֹּחַ בְּגוּף וְלֹא יַשִּׂיגוּךָ מַשִּׂיגֵי הַגּוּף וּמִקְרָיו, וְאֵין בְּךָ דָּבָר מִתָּאֲרֵי הַגּוּפִים, וְאַתָּה קַדְמוֹן לְכָל הַנִּמְצָאִים, וְאַתָּה רָאוּי לְהֵעָבֵד וּלְהָרִים, וְאַתָּה הַנּוֹתֵן נְבוּאָה בְּפִי כָל הַנְּבִיאִים וּנְבוּאַת מֹשֶׁה עַבְדְּךָ נְבִיאֶךָ לְמַעְלָה מִכָּל הַנְּבִיאִים. וְאַתָּה נָתַתָּ לָנוּ עַל יָדוֹ מִן הַשָּׁמַיִם תּוֹרָה שְׁלֵמָה וּמְשִׁיבַת נֶפֶשׁ, וְהִיא זֹאת הַתּוֹרָה הַקְּדוֹשָׁה הַמְּצוּיָה בֵּינֵינוּ, וְהִגִּיעָה אֵלָיו מִפִּי הַגְּבוּרָה, וְלֹא תִהְיֶה זֹאת הַתּוֹרָה נֶעֱדֶרֶת וְלֹא נְסוּחָה, וְאַתָּה יוֹדֵעַ

the thoughts of all human beings and overlook nothing; that it is Your way to pay goodly reward to the righteous and punish the wicked; and that You will bring our beloved Mashiach and resurrect our dead.

   May the words of my mouth and the thoughts of my heart find favor in front of You, my Rock and Redeemer.

מַחְשְׁבוֹת בְּנֵי אָדָם וְלֹא תִתְרַשֵׁל בָּהֶם, וְדַרְכְּךָ לִגְמוֹל טוֹב לַצַּדִּיקִים וּלְהַעֲנִישׁ לָרְשָׁעִים וְתָבִיא מְשִׁיחֵנוּ הָאָהוּב וּתְחַיֶּה מֵתֵינוּ.

יִהְיוּ לְרָצוֹן אִמְרֵי פִי וְהֶגְיוֹן לִבִּי לְפָנֶיךָ יהוה צוּרִי וְגוֹאֲלִי.

◆§ Sefardic *Viduy*

This version of *Viduy* is cited in *Beis Oved* (see 2:11).

רבון Ruler of the worlds, Master of forgiveness and mercy — may it be Your will, Hashem my God and God of my fathers, that I be remembered for the good before Your throne of glory. Look upon my suffering, for there is no unblemished place in my flesh because of Your anger; no peace in my bones because of my sins. And now, God of forgiveness, turn Your kindness towards me, and do not enter into judgment against Your servant. If the time is drawing near for me to die, Your unity will never depart from my mouth, as it is written in Your Torah: 'Hear, O Israel: Hashem is our God, Hashem, the One and Only.' Blessed is the Name of His glorious kingdom for all eternity. I acknowledge before You, Hashem, my God and God of my fathers, God of the spirits of all flesh, that my recovery is in Your hands, and all the events of my life are in Your hands. May it be Your will to heal me completely; may I be remembered by You, and may my prayer be remembered in front of You like the prayer of Hezekiah when he was ill. But if the time has drawn near for me to die, may my death be atonement for all the mistakes, sins, and rebellions I have erred, sinned, and rebelled before You, from the day I came into being on earth until this moment. Grant that my portion be in Gan Eden; may I merit the World to Come, which awaits the righteous. Cause me to know the path of life, satiety of joys with Your countenance, pleasantness in Your right hand forever. Blessed is the One Who hears prayer.

   We beg You! With the strength of Your right hand's greatness, untie the bundled sins. Accept the prayer of Your nation; strengthen us, purify us, O Awesome One. Please, O Strong One — those who foster Your Oneness, guard them like the pupil of the eye. Bless them, purify them, show them pity, may Your righteousness always recompense them. Powerful Holy One, with Your abundant goodness guide Your congregation. One and only Exalted One, turn to Your nation which proclaims Your holiness. Accept our en-

רִבּוֹן הָעוֹלָמִים בַּעַל הַסְּלִיחוֹת וְהָרַחֲמִים יְהִי רָצוֹן מִלְּפָנֶיךָ יהוה אֱלֹהַי וֵאלֹהֵי אֲבוֹתַי שֶׁאֶעֱלֶה זִכְרוֹנִי לִפְנֵי כִסֵּא כְבוֹדְךָ לְטוֹבָה וּרְאֵה בְעָנְיִי כִּי אֵין מְתוֹם בִּבְשָׂרִי מִפְּנֵי זַעְמֶךָ, אֵין שָׁלוֹם בַּעֲצָמַי מִפְּנֵי חַטָּאתִי, וְעַתָּה אֱלוֹהֵי סְלִיחוֹת הַטֵּה אֵלַי חֲסָדֶיךָ וְאַל תָּבוֹא בְמִשְׁפָּט אֶת עַבְדֶּךָ, וְאִם קָרְבָה עֵת פְּקֻדָּתִי לָמוּת, אַחְדוּתְךָ לָעַד מִפִּי לֹא תָמוּשׁ כַּכָּתוּב בְּתוֹרָתֶךָ שְׁמַע יִשְׂרָאֵל יהוה אֱלֹהֵינוּ יהוה אֶחָד; בָּרוּךְ שֵׁם כְּבוֹד מַלְכוּתוֹ לְעוֹלָם וָעֶד. — מוֹדֶה אֲנִי לְפָנֶיךָ יהוה אֱלֹהַי וֵאלֹהֵי אֲבוֹתַי אֱלֹהֵי הָרוּחוֹת לְכָל בָּשָׂר שֶׁרְפוּאָתִי בְיָדְךָ וְעִתּוֹתַי בְּיָדֶךָ יְהִי רָצוֹן מִלְּפָנֶיךָ שֶׁתִּרְפָּאֵנִי רְפוּאָה שְׁלֵמָה וְיַעֲלֶה זִכְרוֹנִי וּתְפִלָּתִי לְפָנֶיךָ כִּתְפִלַּת חִזְקִיָּהוּ בַּחֲלוֹתוֹ וְאִם קָרְבָה עֵת פְּקֻדָּתִי לָמוּת תְּהֵא מִיתָתִי כַּפָּרָה לְכָל חֲטָאוֹתַי וּלְכָל עֲוֹנוֹתַי וּלְכָל פְּשָׁעַי שֶׁחָטָאתִי וְשֶׁעָוִיתִי וְשֶׁפָּשַׁעְתִּי לְפָנֶיךָ מִיוֹם הֱיוֹתִי עַל הָאֲדָמָה עַד הַשָּׁעָה הַזֹּאת וְתֵן חֶלְקִי בְּגַן עֵדֶן וְזַכֵּנִי לָעוֹלָם הַבָּא הַצָּפוּן לַצַּדִּיקִים וְתוֹדִיעֵנִי אֹרַח חַיִּים שֹׂבַע שְׂמָחוֹת אֶת פָּנֶיךָ נְעִימוֹת בִּימִינְךָ נֶצַח, בָּרוּךְ שׁוֹמֵעַ תְּפִלָּה.

אָנָּא בְּכֹחַ גְּדֻלַּת יְמִינְךָ תַּתִּיר צְרוּרָה, קַבֵּל רִנַּת עַמְּךָ שַׂגְּבֵנוּ טַהֲרֵנוּ נוֹרָא, נָא גִבּוֹר דּוֹרְשֵׁי יִחוּדְךָ כְּבָבַת שָׁמְרֵם בָּרְכֵם טַהֲרֵם רַחֲמֵם צִדְקָתְךָ תָּמִיד גָּמְלֵם, חֲסִין קָדוֹשׁ בְּרֹב טוּבְךָ נַהֵל עֲדָתֶךָ, יָחִיד גֵּאֶה לְעַמְּךָ פְּנֵה זוֹכְרֵי קְדֻשָּׁתֶךָ, שַׁוְעָתֵנוּ קַבֵּל

treaty and hear our cry, O Knower of mysteries. Blessed is the Name of His glorious kingdom for all eternity.

May the pleasantness of my Lord, our God, be upon us — may He establish our handiwork for us; our handiwork may He establish.

And it came to pass, in the thirtieth year, on the fifth of the fourth month, when I was in the midst of the Exile, on the River K'var, the heavens were opened, and I saw Divine visions (Ezekiel 1:1). "In the year of the death of King Uziahu, I saw Hashem sitting on a high and exalted throne, and its lower emanation filled the Temple. Fiery angels were standing above him. Each one had six wings. With two he would cover his face, with two he would cover his feet, and with two he would fly. Each one called to the other and declared: 'Holy, holy, holy is Hashem of hosts, His glory fills all the earth' (Isaiah 6:1). Hear, O Israel: Hashem is our God, Hashem, the One and Only. Hashem is God. Hashem is God. Hashem reigns, Hashem reigned, Hashem will reign forever and ever. Moses is true and his Torah is true. I hope for Your salvation, Hashem. May the soul of Your servant rejoice, for I lift up my soul to You, Hashem. Into Your hand I entrust my spirit. You have redeemed me, Hashem, the true God. May the words of my mouth and the thoughts of my heart find favor in front before You, my Rock and Redeemer."

וּשְׁמַע צַעֲקָתֵנוּ יוֹדֵעַ תַּעֲלוּמוֹת, בָּרוּךְ שֵׁם כְּבוֹד מַלְכוּתוֹ לְעוֹלָם וָעֶד.

וִיהִי נֹעַם אֲדֹנָי אֱלֹהֵינוּ עָלֵינוּ וּמַעֲשֵׂה יָדֵינוּ כּוֹנְנָה עָלֵינוּ וּמַעֲשֵׂה יָדֵינוּ כּוֹנְנֵהוּ.

וַיְהִי בִּשְׁלֹשִׁים שָׁנָה בָּרְבִיעִי בַּחֲמִשָּׁה לַחֹדֶשׁ וַאֲנִי בְתוֹךְ הַגּוֹלָה עַל נְהַר כְּבָר נִפְתְּחוּ הַשָּׁמַיִם וָאֶרְאֶה מַרְאוֹת אֱלֹהִים. בִּשְׁנַת מוֹת הַמֶּלֶךְ עֻזִּיָּהוּ וָאֶרְאֶה אֶת יהוה יוֹשֵׁב עַל כִּסֵּא רָם וְנִשָּׂא וְשׁוּלָיו מְלֵאִים אֶת הַהֵיכָל. שְׂרָפִים עוֹמְדִים מִמַּעַל לוֹ שֵׁשׁ כְּנָפַיִם שֵׁשׁ כְּנָפַיִם לְאֶחָד בִּשְׁתַּיִם יְכַסֶּה פָנָיו וּבִשְׁתַּיִם יְכַסֶּה רַגְלָיו וּבִשְׁתַּיִם יְעוֹפֵף. וְקָרָא זֶה אֶל זֶה וְאָמַר קָדוֹשׁ קָדוֹשׁ קָדוֹשׁ יהוה צְבָאוֹת מְלֹא כָל הָאָרֶץ כְּבוֹדוֹ. שְׁמַע יִשְׂרָאֵל יהוה אֱלֹהֵינוּ יהוה אֶחָד. יהוה הוּא הָאֱלֹהִים יהוה הוּא הָאֱלֹהִים. יהוה מֶלֶךְ יהוה מָלָךְ יהוה יִמְלֹךְ לְעוֹלָם וָעֶד. מֹשֶׁה אֱמֶת וְתוֹרָתוֹ אֱמֶת. לִישׁוּעָתְךָ קִוִּיתִי יהוה. שָׂמַח נֶפֶשׁ עַבְדֶּךָ כִּי אֵלֶיךָ יהוה נַפְשִׁי אֶשָּׂא. בְּיָדְךָ אַפְקִיד רוּחִי פָּדִיתָה אוֹתִי יהוה אֵל אֱמֶת. יִהְיוּ לְרָצוֹן אִמְרֵי פִי וְהֶגְיוֹן לִבִּי לְפָנֶיךָ יהוה צוּרִי וְגֹאֲלִי.

◄§ Dayan HaEmes and Kri'ah

The mourners recite the following blessing when they perform kri'ah on their garments (see 6:6):

בָּרוּךְ Blessed are You, HASHEM, our God, King of the universe, the true Judge.

בָּרוּךְ אַתָּה יהוה אֱלֹהֵינוּ מֶלֶךְ הָעוֹלָם, דַּיַּן הָאֱמֶת.

◄§ Prayer at the Cemetery

Those who have not seen Jewish graves for thirty days recite the following blessing (see 42:18)

בָּרוּךְ Blessed are You, HASHEM, our God, King of the universe, Who fashioned you with justice, nourished and sustained you with justice, took your lives with justice, knows the sum total of all of you with justice, and will restore and resuscitate you with judgment. Blessed are You, HASHEM, Who resuscitates the dead.

You are eternally mighty, my Lord, the Resuscitator of the dead are You; abundantly able to save. [In the winter: He makes the wind blow and He makes the rain descend.] [Nusach Sefard in the summer: He makes the dew descend.]

בָּרוּךְ אַתָּה יהוה אֱלֹהֵינוּ מֶלֶךְ הָעוֹלָם, אֲשֶׁר יָצַר אֶתְכֶם בַּדִּין, וְזָן וְכִלְכֵּל אֶתְכֶם בַּדִּין, וְהֵמִית אֶתְכֶם בַּדִּין, וְיוֹדֵעַ מִסְפַּר כֻּלְּכֶם בַּדִּין, וְהוּא עָתִיד לְהַחֲיוֹתְכֶם וּלְקַיֵּם אֶתְכֶם בַּדִּין. בָּרוּךְ אַתָּה יהוה, מְחַיֶּה הַמֵּתִים.

אַתָּה גִבּוֹר לְעוֹלָם אֲדֹנָי, מְחַיֶּה מֵתִים אַתָּה, רַב לְהוֹשִׁיעַ. [בחורף: מַשִּׁיב הָרוּחַ וּמוֹרִיד הַגֶּשֶׁם.] [נוסח ספרד בקיץ: מוֹרִיד הַטָּל.]

He sustains the living with kindness, resuscitates the dead with abundant mercy, supports the fallen, heals the sick, releases the confined, and maintains His faith to those asleep in the dust. Who is like You, O Master of mighty deeds, and who is comparable to You, O King Who causes death and restores life and makes salvation sprout. And You are faithful to resuscitate the dead.

מְכַלְכֵּל חַיִּים בְּחֶסֶד, מְחַיֵּה מֵתִים בְּרַחֲמִים רַבִּים, סוֹמֵךְ נוֹפְלִים, וְרוֹפֵא חוֹלִים, וּמַתִּיר אֲסוּרִים, וּמְקַיֵּם אֱמוּנָתוֹ לִישֵׁנֵי עָפָר. מִי כָמוֹךָ בַּעַל גְּבוּרוֹת, וּמִי דּוֹמֶה לָּךְ, מֶלֶךְ מֵמִית וּמְחַיֶּה וּמַצְמִיחַ יְשׁוּעָה, וְנֶאֱמָן אַתָּה לְהַחֲיוֹת מֵתִים.

❧ *Tzidduk HaDin*

When the deceased is brought to the cemetery, the following is recited (see 10:15).
However, it is omitted on days when *Tachanun* is not recited (see 10:18).

הַצוּר *The Rock! — perfect is His work, for all His paths are justice; a God of faith without iniquity, righteous and fair is He.*

The Rock! — perfect in every work. Who can say to Him, 'What have You done?' He rules below and above, brings death and resuscitates, brings down to the grave and raises up.

The Rock! — perfect in every deed. Who can say to Him, 'What do You do?' O He Who says and does, do undeserved kindness with us. In the merit of him [Isaac] who was bound like a lamb, hearken and act.

O righteous One in all His ways, O Rock who is perfect — slow to anger and full of mercy — take pity and please spare parents and children, for Yours, O master, are forgiveness and mercy.

Righteous are You, HASHEM, to bring death and to resuscitate, for in Your hand is the safekeeping of all spirits. It would be sacrilegious for You to erase our memory. May Your eyes mercifully take cognizance of us, for Yours, O Master, are mercy and forgiveness.

A man, whether he be a year old, or whether he lives a thousand years, what does it profit him? — As if he has never been shall he be. Blessed is the true Judge, Who brings death and resuscitates.

Blessed is He, for His judgment is true, He scans everything with His eye, and He recompenses man according to his account and his just sentence. All must give His Name acknowledgment.

We know, HASHEM, that Your judgment is righteous, You are righteous when You speak and pure when You judge; and there is no complaining about the attribute of Your judgment. Righteous are You, HASHEM, and Your judgments are fair.

O true Judge, Judge of righteousness and truth. Blessed is the true Judge, for all of His judgments are righteous and true.

הַצוּר תָּמִים פָּעֳלוֹ, כִּי כָל דְּרָכָיו מִשְׁפָּט, אֵל אֱמוּנָה וְאֵין עָוֶל, צַדִּיק וְיָשָׁר הוּא.

הַצוּר תָּמִים בְּכָל פְּעַל, מִי יֹאמַר לוֹ מַה תִּפְעָל, הַשַּׁלִּיט בְּמַטָּה וּבְמַעַל, מֵמִית וּמְחַיֶּה, מוֹרִיד שְׁאוֹל וַיָּעַל.

הַצוּר תָּמִים בְּכָל מַעֲשֶׂה, מִי יֹאמַר אֵלָיו מַה תַּעֲשֶׂה, הָאוֹמֵר וְעֹשֶׂה, חֶסֶד חִנָּם לָנוּ תַּעֲשֶׂה, וּבִזְכוּת הַנֶּעֱקַד כְּשֶׂה, הַקְשִׁיבָה וַעֲשֵׂה.

צַדִּיק בְּכָל דְּרָכָיו הַצוּר תָּמִים, אֶרֶךְ אַפַּיִם וּמָלֵא רַחֲמִים, חֲמָל נָא וְחוּס נָא עַל אָבוֹת וּבָנִים, כִּי לְךָ אָדוֹן הַסְּלִיחוֹת וְהָרַחֲמִים.

צַדִּיק אַתָּה יהוה לְהָמִית וּלְהַחֲיוֹת, אֲשֶׁר בְּיָדְךָ פִּקְדוֹן כָּל רוּחוֹת, חָלִילָה לְּךָ זִכְרוֹנֵנוּ לִמְחוֹת, וְיִהְיוּ נָא עֵינֶיךָ בְּרַחֲמִים עָלֵינוּ פְקוּחוֹת, כִּי לְךָ אָדוֹן הָרַחֲמִים וְהַסְּלִיחוֹת. אָדָם אִם בֶּן שָׁנָה יִהְיֶה, אוֹ אֶלֶף שָׁנִים יִחְיֶה, מַה יִּתְרוֹן לוֹ, כְּלֹא הָיָה יִהְיֶה, בָּרוּךְ דַּיַּן הָאֱמֶת, מֵמִית וּמְחַיֶּה.

בָּרוּךְ הוּא, כִּי אֱמֶת דִּינוֹ, וּמְשׁוֹטֵט הַכֹּל בְּעֵינוֹ, וּמְשַׁלֵּם לְאָדָם חֶשְׁבּוֹנוֹ וְדִינוֹ, וְהַכֹּל לִשְׁמוֹ הוֹדָיָה יִתֵּנוּ.

יָדַעְנוּ יהוה כִּי צֶדֶק מִשְׁפָּטֶךָ, תִּצְדַּק בְּדָבְרֶךָ וְתִזְכֶּה בְּשָׁפְטֶךָ, וְאֵין לְהַרְהֵר אַחַר מִדַּת שָׁפְטֶךָ, צַדִּיק אַתָּה יהוה, וְיָשָׁר מִשְׁפָּטֶיךָ.

דַּיַּן אֱמֶת, שׁוֹפֵט צֶדֶק וֶאֱמֶת, בָּרוּךְ דַּיַּן הָאֱמֶת, שֶׁכָּל מִשְׁפָּטָיו צֶדֶק וֶאֱמֶת.

The soul of all the living is in Your hand, righteousness fills Your right hand and Your power. Have mercy on the remnant of the sheep of Your hand, and say to the Angel [of Death], 'Hold back your hand!'

נֶפֶשׁ כָּל חַי בְּיָדֶךָ, צֶדֶק מָלְאָה יְמִינְךָ וְיָדֶךָ, רַחֵם עַל פְּלֵיטַת צֹאן יָדֶךָ, וְתֹאמַר לַמַּלְאָךְ הֶרֶף יָדֶךָ.

Great in counsel and abundant in deed, Your eyes are open upon all the ways of the children of man, to give man according to his ways and according to the fruit of his deeds.

גְּדֹל הָעֵצָה וְרַב הָעֲלִילִיָּה, אֲשֶׁר עֵינֶיךָ פְקֻחוֹת עַל כָּל דַּרְכֵי בְּנֵי אָדָם, לָתֵת לְאִישׁ כִּדְרָכָיו וְכִפְרִי מַעֲלָלָיו.

To declare that HASHEM *is just, my Rock, in Whom there is no wrong.*

לְהַגִּיד כִּי יָשָׁר יהוה, צוּרִי וְלֹא עַוְלָתָה בּוֹ.

HASHEM *gave and* HASHEM *took, Blessed be the Name of* HASHEM.

יהוה נָתַן, וַיהוה לָקָח, יְהִי שֵׁם יהוה מְבֹרָךְ.

He, the Merciful One, is forgiving of iniquity and does not destroy, frequently withdrawing His anger, not arousing His entire rage.

וְהוּא רַחוּם, יְכַפֵּר עָוֹן וְלֹא יַשְׁחִית, וְהִרְבָּה לְהָשִׁיב אַפּוֹ, וְלֹא יָעִיר כָּל חֲמָתוֹ.

⋙ *Kaddish HaGadol* After a Burial

The male mourners recite the following *Kaddish* [a transliteration of this *Kaddish* appears on page 468]:
This *Kaddish* is omitted on days when *tachanun* is not recited (see 10:20).

יִתְגַּדַּל *May His great Name grow exalted and sanctified (Cong.— Amen) in the world which will be renewed, and where He will resuscitate the dead and raise them up to eternal life, and rebuild the city of Jerusalem and complete His Temple within it, and uproot alien worship from the earth, and return the service of Heaven to its place and where the Holy One, Blessed is He, will reign in His sovereignty and splendor, [Nusach Sefard: and cause His salvation to sprout, and bring near His Messiah (Cong.— Amen)], in your lifetimes and in your days, and in the lifetimes of the entire Family of Israel, swiftly and soon. Now respond: Amen. (Cong.— Amen.)*

יִתְגַּדַּל וְיִתְקַדַּשׁ שְׁמֵהּ רַבָּא. (.אָמֵן – Cong.) בְּעָלְמָא דִּי הוּא עָתִיד לְאִתְחַדָּתָּא, וּלְאַחֲיָאָה מֵתַיָּא, וּלְאַסָּקָא יָתְהוֹן לְחַיֵּי עָלְמָא, וּלְמִבְנֵא קַרְתָּא דִי יְרוּשְׁלֵם, וּלְשַׁכְלְלָא הֵיכְלֵהּ בְּגַוַּהּ, וּלְמֶעְקַר פָּלְחָנָא נָכְרָאָה מִן אַרְעָא, וְלַאֲתָבָא פָּלְחָנָא דִי שְׁמַיָּא לְאַתְרֵהּ, וְיַמְלִיךְ קֻדְשָׁא בְּרִיךְ הוּא בְּמַלְכוּתֵהּ וִיקָרֵהּ, [נוסח ספרד: וְיַצְמַח פֻּרְקָנֵהּ וִיקָרֵב מְשִׁיחֵהּ. (.אָמֵן – Cong.)] בְּחַיֵּיכוֹן וּבְיוֹמֵיכוֹן וּבְחַיֵּי דְכָל בֵּית יִשְׂרָאֵל, בַּעֲגָלָא וּבִזְמַן קָרִיב. וְאִמְרוּ: אָמֵן. (.אָמֵן – Cong.)

Cong., then mourner:
May His great Name be blessed forever and ever.
Mourner continues: *Blessed, praised, glorified, exalted, extolled, mighty, upraised, and lauded be the Name of the Holy One, Blessed is He (Cong.—Blessed is He) — (Between Rosh Hashanah and Yom Kippur add: exceedingly) beyond any blessing and song, praise and consolation that are uttered in the world. Now respond: Amen. (Cong.— Amen.)*
May there be abundant peace from Heaven, and good life, upon us and upon all Israel. Now respond: Amen. (Cong.— Amen.)
Take three steps back. Bow left and say, 'He Who makes peace . . .'; bow right and say, 'may He . . .'; bow forward and say, 'and upon all Israel . . .'
He Who makes [Between Rosh Hashanah and Yom Kippur some add: the] peace in His heights, may He make peace upon us, and upon all Israel. Now respond: Amen. (Cong.— Amen.)
Mourner remains standing in place for a few moments, then takes three steps forward.

Cong., then mourner:
יְהֵא שְׁמֵהּ רַבָּא מְבָרַךְ לְעָלַם וּלְעָלְמֵי עָלְמַיָּא.
Mourner continues – **יִתְבָּרַךְ** וְיִשְׁתַּבַּח וְיִתְפָּאַר וְיִתְרוֹמַם וְיִתְנַשֵּׂא וְיִתְהַדָּר וְיִתְעַלֶּה וְיִתְהַלָּל שְׁמֵהּ דְּקֻדְשָׁא בְּרִיךְ הוּא. (Cong. – בְּרִיךְ הוּא.)
(Between Rosh Hashanah and לְעֵלָּא מִן כָּל° –
Yom Kippur °לְעֵלָּא וּלְעֵלָּא מִכָּל) בִּרְכָתָא וְשִׁירָתָא תֻּשְׁבְּחָתָא וְנֶחֱמָתָא, דַּאֲמִירָן בְּעָלְמָא. וְאִמְרוּ: אָמֵן. (.אָמֵן – Cong.)
יְהֵא שְׁלָמָא רַבָּא מִן שְׁמַיָּא, וְחַיִּים עָלֵינוּ וְעַל כָּל יִשְׂרָאֵל. וְאִמְרוּ: אָמֵן. (.אָמֵן – Cong.)
(Between Rosh Hashanah and Yom עֹשֶׂה שָׁלוֹם
Kippur some substitute – הַשָּׁלוֹם) בִּמְרוֹמָיו, הוּא יַעֲשֶׂה שָׁלוֹם עָלֵינוּ, וְעַל כָּל יִשְׂרָאֵל. וְאִמְרוּ: אָמֵן. (.אָמֵן – Cong.)

◄§ The *Shurah* / Prayer of Consolation

Those present at the burial form a *shurah* : two parallel two rows of comforters through which the mourners walk. As the mourners pass, those forming the rows recite the traditional Prayer of Consolation (see 10:22).

הַמָּקוֹם *May the Omnipresent console you among the other mourners of Zion and Jerusalem.*

הַמָּקוֹם יְנַחֵם אֶתְכֶם בְּתוֹךְ שְׁאָר אֲבֵלֵי צִיּוֹן וִירוּשָׁלָיִם.

As the participants leave the cemetery, they should tear out some blades of grass and toss them over their right shoulders as they recite:

וְיָצִיצוּ *May they blossom forth from the city like the grass of the earth. Remember that we are but dust.*

וְיָצִיצוּ מֵעִיר כְּעֵשֶׂב הָאָרֶץ. זָכוּר כִּי עָפָר אֲנַחְנוּ.

After leaving the cemetery, one washes his hands ritually (see 42:17) and recites:

בִּלַּע *May He swallow up death forever, and may HASHEM the God wipe away tears from every face and remove the scorn of His people from throughout the world, for HASHEM has spoken.*

בִּלַּע הַמָּוֶת לָנֶצַח, וּמָחָה אֲדֹנָי יֱהוִֹה דִּמְעָה מֵעַל כָּל פָּנִים, וְחֶרְפַּת עַמּוֹ יָסִיר מֵעַל כָּל הָאָרֶץ, כִּי יהוה דִּבֵּר.

◄§ Psalms When Visiting a Grave

[Those who have not seen Jewish graves for thirty days recite the blessing אֲשֶׁר יָצַר (p. 444).]
The following Psalms are recited (see 42:23):

33. *Sing joyfully, O righteous, because of HASHEM; for the upright, praise is fitting. Give thanks to HASHEM with the harp, with the ten-stringed lyre make music to Him. Sing Him a new song, play well with sounds of deep emotion. For the word of HASHEM, is upright and all His deeds are done with faithfulness. He loves righteousness and justice, the kindness of HASHEM fills the earth. By the word of HASHEM the heavens were made, and by the breath of His mouth all their host. He assembles like a mound the waters of the sea, He places the deep waters in vaults. Fear HASHEM, all the earth; be in dread of Him all inhabitants of the world. For He spoke and it came to be, He commanded and it stood firm. HASHEM annuls the counsel of peoples, he thwarts the designs of nations. The counsel of HASHEM will endure forever, the designs of His heart throughout the generations. Praiseworthy is the people whose God is HASHEM, the nation He chose for His own heritage. From heaven HASHEM looks down, He sees all mankind. From His dwelling place He oversees all inhabitants of the earth, He Who fashions their hearts together, Who comprehends all their deeds. A king is not saved by a great army, nor is a hero rescued by great strength. Illusory is the horse for salvation; despite its great strength it provides no escape. Behold, the eye of HASHEM is on those who fear Him, upon those who await His kindness. To rescue their soul from death, and to sustain them in famine. Our soul longed for HASHEM — our help and our shield is He.*

לג רַנְּנוּ צַדִּיקִים בַּיהוה, לַיְשָׁרִים נָאוָה תְהִלָּה. הוֹדוּ לַיהוה בְּכִנּוֹר, בְּנֵבֶל עָשׂוֹר זַמְּרוּ לוֹ. שִׁירוּ לוֹ שִׁיר חָדָשׁ, הֵיטִיבוּ נַגֵּן בִּתְרוּעָה. כִּי יָשָׁר דְּבַר יהוה, וְכָל מַעֲשֵׂהוּ בֶּאֱמוּנָה. אֹהֵב צְדָקָה וּמִשְׁפָּט, חֶסֶד יהוה מָלְאָה הָאָרֶץ. בִּדְבַר יהוה שָׁמַיִם נַעֲשׂוּ, וּבְרוּחַ פִּיו כָּל צְבָאָם. כֹּנֵס כַּנֵּד מֵי הַיָּם, נֹתֵן בְּאוֹצָרוֹת תְּהוֹמוֹת. יִירְאוּ מֵיהוה כָּל הָאָרֶץ, מִמֶּנּוּ יָגוּרוּ כָּל יֹשְׁבֵי תֵבֵל. כִּי הוּא אָמַר וַיֶּהִי, הוּא צִוָּה וַיַּעֲמֹד. יהוה הֵפִיר עֲצַת גּוֹיִם, הֵנִיא מַחְשְׁבוֹת עַמִּים. עֲצַת יהוה לְעוֹלָם תַּעֲמֹד, מַחְשְׁבוֹת לִבּוֹ לְדֹר וָדֹר. אַשְׁרֵי הַגּוֹי אֲשֶׁר יהוה אֱלֹהָיו, הָעָם בָּחַר לְנַחֲלָה לוֹ. מִשָּׁמַיִם הִבִּיט יהוה, רָאָה אֶת כָּל בְּנֵי הָאָדָם. מִמְּכוֹן שִׁבְתּוֹ הִשְׁגִּיחַ, אֶל כָּל יֹשְׁבֵי הָאָרֶץ. הַיֹּצֵר יַחַד לִבָּם, הַמֵּבִין אֶל כָּל מַעֲשֵׂיהֶם. אֵין הַמֶּלֶךְ נוֹשָׁע בְּרָב חָיִל, גִּבּוֹר לֹא יִנָּצֵל בְּרָב כֹּחַ. שֶׁקֶר הַסּוּס לִתְשׁוּעָה, וּבְרֹב חֵילוֹ לֹא יְמַלֵּט. הִנֵּה עֵין יהוה אֶל יְרֵאָיו, לַמְיַחֲלִים לְחַסְדּוֹ. לְהַצִּיל מִמָּוֶת נַפְשָׁם, וּלְחַיּוֹתָם בָּרָעָב. נַפְשֵׁנוּ חִכְּתָה לַיהוה, עֶזְרֵנוּ וּמָגִנֵּנוּ הוּא.

For in Him will our hearts be glad, for in His Holy Name we trusted. May Your kindness, HASHEM, be upon us, just as we awaited You.

16. *A Michtam by David. Protect me O God, for I have sought refuge in You. You have said to HASHEM, 'You are my Master, I have no claim to Your benefit.' For the sake of the holy ones who are interred in the earth and for the mighty — all my desires are fulfilled because of them. Their sorrows will multiply, those who rush after other [gods]; I shall not pour their blood libations, nor carry their names upon my lips. HASHEM is my allotted portion and my share, You guide my destiny. Portions have fallen to me in pleasant places, even the inheritance is beautiful to me. I will bless HASHEM Who has advised me, also in the nights my own intellect instructs me. I have set HASHEM before me always; because He is at my right hand I shall not falter. For the following reason does my heart rejoice and my soul is elated, my flesh, too, rests in confidence: Because You will not abandon my soul to the grave, You will not allow Your devout one to witness destruction. You will make known to me the path of life, the fullness of joys in Your Presence, the delights that are in Your right hand for eternity.*

17. *A prayer of David: Hear, HASHEM, what is righteous, attend to my entreaty, give ear to my prayer — which is not from deceitful lips. May my judgment go out from before You, Your eyes behold uprightness. You examined my heart, You searched at night; You tested me — You found not; my thoughts do not transgress the words of my mouth. So that [my] human deeds accord with the word of Your lips, I guarded myself from the paths of the lawless, supporting my strides in Your pathways, my footsteps did not falter. I have called out to You, because You will answer me, O God; incline Your ear to me, hear my utterance. Demonstrate clearly Your kindnesses, You Who saves with Your right hand those who seek refuge [in You] from those who arise [against them]. Guard me like the apple of the eye; shelter me in the shadow of Your wings, from the wicked who have plundered me, my mortal enemies who surround me. In their fat they enclose themselves; with their mouths they speak with arrogance. As we step forth they immediately surround us, they fix their gaze to spread over the land. His appearance is like a lion that yearns to tear asunder; and like a young lion lurking in hiding. Rise up HASHEM, confront him and bring him to his knees; rescue my soul from the wicked one, who is Your sword. O to be among those who die by Your hand, HASHEM, who die of old*

כִּי בוֹ יִשְׂמַח לִבֵּנוּ, כִּי בְשֵׁם קָדְשׁוֹ בָטָחְנוּ. יְהִי חַסְדְּךָ יהוה עָלֵינוּ, כַּאֲשֶׁר יִחַלְנוּ לָךְ.

טז מִכְתָּם לְדָוִד, שָׁמְרֵנִי אֵל כִּי חָסִיתִי בָךְ. אָמַרְתְּ לַיהוה, אֲדֹנָי אָתָּה, טוֹבָתִי בַּל עָלֶיךָ. לִקְדוֹשִׁים אֲשֶׁר בָּאָרֶץ הֵמָּה, וְאַדִּירֵי כָּל חֶפְצִי בָם. יִרְבּוּ עַצְּבוֹתָם אַחֵר מָהָרוּ; בַּל אַסִּיךְ נִסְכֵּיהֶם מִדָּם, וּבַל אֶשָּׂא אֶת שְׁמוֹתָם עַל שְׂפָתָי. יהוה מְנָת חֶלְקִי וְכוֹסִי, אַתָּה תּוֹמִיךְ גּוֹרָלִי. חֲבָלִים נָפְלוּ לִי בַּנְּעִמִים, אַף נַחֲלָת שָׁפְרָה עָלָי. אֲבָרֵךְ אֶת יהוה אֲשֶׁר יְעָצָנִי, אַף לֵילוֹת יִסְּרוּנִי כִלְיוֹתָי. שִׁוִּיתִי יהוה לְנֶגְדִּי תָמִיד, כִּי מִימִינִי, בַּל אֶמּוֹט. לָכֵן שָׂמַח לִבִּי וַיָּגֶל כְּבוֹדִי, אַף בְּשָׂרִי יִשְׁכֹּן לָבֶטַח. כִּי לֹא תַעֲזֹב נַפְשִׁי לִשְׁאוֹל, לֹא תִתֵּן חֲסִידְךָ לִרְאוֹת שָׁחַת. תּוֹדִיעֵנִי אֹרַח חַיִּים, שֹׂבַע שְׂמָחוֹת אֶת פָּנֶיךָ, נְעִמוֹת בִּימִינְךָ נֶצַח.

יז תְּפִלָּה לְדָוִד; שִׁמְעָה יהוה צֶדֶק, הַקְשִׁיבָה רִנָּתִי, הַאֲזִינָה תְפִלָּתִי, בְּלֹא שִׂפְתֵי מִרְמָה. מִלְּפָנֶיךָ מִשְׁפָּטִי יֵצֵא, עֵינֶיךָ תֶּחֱזֶינָה מֵישָׁרִים. בָּחַנְתָּ לִבִּי, פָּקַדְתָּ לַּיְלָה, צְרַפְתַּנִי בַל תִּמְצָא; זַמֹּתִי בַּל יַעֲבָר פִּי. לִפְעֻלּוֹת אָדָם בִּדְבַר שְׂפָתֶיךָ, אֲנִי שָׁמַרְתִּי אָרְחוֹת פָּרִיץ. תָּמֹךְ אֲשֻׁרַי בְּמַעְגְּלוֹתֶיךָ, בַּל נָמוֹטוּ פְעָמָי. אֲנִי קְרָאתִיךָ כִי תַעֲנֵנִי, אֵל; הַט אָזְנְךָ לִי, שְׁמַע אִמְרָתִי. הַפְלֵה חֲסָדֶיךָ, מוֹשִׁיעַ חוֹסִים, מִמִּתְקוֹמְמִים בִּימִינֶךָ. שָׁמְרֵנִי כְּאִישׁוֹן בַּת עָיִן, בְּצֵל כְּנָפֶיךָ תַּסְתִּירֵנִי. מִפְּנֵי רְשָׁעִים זוּ שַׁדּוּנִי, אֹיְבַי בְּנֶפֶשׁ יַקִּיפוּ עָלָי. חֶלְבָּמוֹ סָגְרוּ, פִּימוֹ דִּבְּרוּ בְגֵאוּת. אַשֻּׁרֵנוּ עַתָּה סְבָבוּנוּ, עֵינֵיהֶם יָשִׁיתוּ לִנְטוֹת בָּאָרֶץ. דִּמְיוֹנוֹ כְּאַרְיֵה יִכְסוֹף לִטְרוֹף, וְכִכְפִיר יֹשֵׁב בְּמִסְתָּרִים. קוּמָה יהוה, קַדְּמָה פָנָיו הַכְרִיעֵהוּ, פַּלְּטָה נַפְשִׁי מֵרָשָׁע חַרְבֶּךָ. מִמְתִים יָדְךָ | יהוה, מִמְתִים מֵחֶלֶד,

age — whose portion is eternal life, and whose belly You fill with Your concealed treasure; they are sated with sons and they bequeath their abundance to their babes. And I — because of righteousness I shall behold Your face, upon awakening I will be sated by Your image.

72. For Solomon. O God, give Your judgments to the king and Your righteousness to the king's son. May he judge Your nation with righteousness, and Your poor with justice. May mountains bear peace to the nation, and hills — through righteousness. May he judge the nation's poor, save the children of the destitute, and crush the oppressor. So that they will fear You as long as the sun and moon endure, generation after generation. May [his words] descend like rain upon cut vegetation, like showers, waterer of the earth. May the righteous flourish in his days with abundant peace beyond the days of the moon. May he dominate from sea to sea, and from river to the ends of the earth. May nobles kneel before him, and may his foes lick the dust. The kings of Tarshish and the isles shall return tribute, the kings of Sheba and Seba shall offer gifts. All the kings shall prostrate themselves before him; all the peoples shall serve him. For he will deliver the destitute one who cries out, and the poor one with none to help him. He will pity the impoverished and destitute, and the souls of destitute ones he will save. From fraud and from violence he will redeem their soul, and their blood will be precious in his eyes. And he will live, and he will give him of the gold of Sheba; and he will pray for him continually and bless him every day. May an abundance of grain be in the land on the mountaintops — its fruit will rustle like the [cedars of] Lebanon; may [people] blossom forth from the city like the grass of the earth. May his name endure forever, may his name be perpetuated as long as the sun; and all peoples will bless themselves by him — they will praise him. Blessed be HASHEM, God, the God of Israel, Who alone does wondrous things. Blessed be His glorious Name forever; and may all the earth be filled with His glory. Amen and Amen. The prayers of David, the son of Jesse, are ended.

91. Whoever sits in the refuge of the Most High — he shall dwell in the shadow of the Almighty. I will say of HASHEM, 'He is my refuge and my fortress, my God, I will trust in Him.' For He will deliver you from the ensnaring trap, from devastating pestilence. With His pinion He will cover you, and beneath His wings you will be protected; shield and armor is His truth. You shall not fear the terror of night; nor of the arrow that flies by day; nor the pestilence that walks in gloom; nor the destroyer who lays waste at noon. Let a

חֶלְקָם בַּחַיִּים וּצְפוּנְךָ תְּמַלֵּא בִטְנָם; יִשְׂבְּעוּ בָנִים, וְהִנִּיחוּ יִתְרָם לְעוֹלְלֵיהֶם. אֲנִי בְּצֶדֶק אֶחֱזֶה פָנֶיךָ, אֶשְׂבְּעָה בְהָקִיץ תְּמוּנָתֶךָ.

עב לִשְׁלֹמֹה, אֱלֹהִים מִשְׁפָּטֶיךָ לְמֶלֶךְ תֵּן, וְצִדְקָתְךָ לְבֶן מֶלֶךְ. יָדִין עַמְּךָ בְצֶדֶק, וַעֲנִיֶּיךָ בְמִשְׁפָּט. יִשְׂאוּ הָרִים שָׁלוֹם לָעָם, וּגְבָעוֹת בִּצְדָקָה. יִשְׁפֹּט עֲנִיֵּי עָם, יוֹשִׁיעַ לִבְנֵי אֶבְיוֹן, וִידַכֵּא עוֹשֵׁק. יִירָאוּךָ עִם שָׁמֶשׁ, וְלִפְנֵי יָרֵחַ, דּוֹר דּוֹרִים. יֵרֵד כְּמָטָר עַל גֵּז, כִּרְבִיבִים זַרְזִיף אָרֶץ. יִפְרַח בְּיָמָיו צַדִּיק, וְרֹב שָׁלוֹם עַד בְּלִי יָרֵחַ. וְיֵרְדְּ מִיָּם עַד יָם, וּמִנָּהָר עַד אַפְסֵי אָרֶץ. לְפָנָיו יִכְרְעוּ צִיִּים, וְאֹיְבָיו עָפָר יְלַחֵכוּ. מַלְכֵי תַרְשִׁישׁ וְאִיִּים מִנְחָה יָשִׁיבוּ, מַלְכֵי שְׁבָא וּסְבָא אֶשְׁכָּר יַקְרִיבוּ. וְיִשְׁתַּחֲווּ לוֹ כָל מְלָכִים, כָּל גּוֹיִם יַעַבְדוּהוּ. כִּי יַצִּיל אֶבְיוֹן מְשַׁוֵּעַ, וְעָנִי וְאֵין עֹזֵר לוֹ. יָחֹס עַל דַּל וְאֶבְיוֹן, וְנַפְשׁוֹת אֶבְיוֹנִים יוֹשִׁיעַ. מִתּוֹךְ וּמֵחָמָס יִגְאַל נַפְשָׁם, וְיֵיקַר דָּמָם בְּעֵינָיו. וִיחִי, וְיִתֶּן לוֹ מִזְּהַב שְׁבָא, וְיִתְפַּלֵּל בַּעֲדוֹ תָמִיד, כָּל הַיּוֹם יְבָרְכֶנְהוּ. יְהִי פִסַּת בַּר בָּאָרֶץ בְּרֹאשׁ הָרִים, יִרְעַשׁ כַּלְּבָנוֹן פִּרְיוֹ, וְיָצִיצוּ מֵעִיר כְּעֵשֶׂב הָאָרֶץ. יְהִי שְׁמוֹ לְעוֹלָם, לִפְנֵי שֶׁמֶשׁ יִנּוֹן שְׁמוֹ; וְיִתְבָּרְכוּ בוֹ, כָּל גּוֹיִם יְאַשְּׁרֻהוּ. בָּרוּךְ יהוה אֱלֹהִים אֱלֹהֵי יִשְׂרָאֵל, עֹשֵׂה נִפְלָאוֹת לְבַדּוֹ. וּבָרוּךְ שֵׁם כְּבוֹדוֹ לְעוֹלָם, וְיִמָּלֵא כְבוֹדוֹ אֶת כָּל הָאָרֶץ, אָמֵן וְאָמֵן. כָּלּוּ תְפִלּוֹת, דָּוִד בֶּן יִשָׁי.

צא יֹשֵׁב בְּסֵתֶר עֶלְיוֹן, בְּצֵל שַׁדַּי יִתְלוֹנָן. אֹמַר לַיהוה: מַחְסִי וּמְצוּדָתִי, אֱלֹהַי אֶבְטַח בּוֹ. כִּי הוּא יַצִּילְךָ מִפַּח יָקוּשׁ, מִדֶּבֶר הַוּוֹת. בְּאֶבְרָתוֹ יָסֶךְ לָךְ, וְתַחַת כְּנָפָיו תֶּחְסֶה; צִנָּה וְסֹחֵרָה אֲמִתּוֹ. לֹא תִירָא מִפַּחַד לָיְלָה, מֵחֵץ יָעוּף יוֹמָם. מִדֶּבֶר בָּאֹפֶל יַהֲלֹךְ, מִקֶּטֶב יָשׁוּד צָהֳרָיִם.

thousand encamp at your side and a myriad at your right hand, but to you it shall not approach. You will merely peer with your eyes and you will see the retribution of the wicked. Because [you said]: 'You, HASHEM, are my refuge,' you have made the Most High your dwelling place. No evil will befall you, nor will any plague come near your tent. He will charge His angels for you, to protect you in all your ways. On palms they will carry you, lest you strike your foot against a stone. Upon the lion and the viper you will tread; you will trample the young lion and the serpent. For he has yearned for Me and I will deliver him; I will elevate him because he knows My Name. He will call upon Me and I will answer him, I am with him in distress; I will release him and I will bring him honor. With long life will I satisfy him, and I will show him My salvation.

104. Bless HASHEM, O my soul. HASHEM, my God, You are very great; You have donned majesty and splendor; covering with light as with a garment, stretching out the heavens like a curtain. He Who roofs His upper chambers with water; He Who makes clouds His chariot; He Who walks on winged wind. He makes the winds His messengers, the flaming fire His attendants. He established the earth upon its foundations, that it falter not forever and ever. The watery deep, as with a garment You covered it; upon the mountains, water would stand. From Your rebuke they flee, from the sound of Your thunder they rush away. They ascend mountains, they descend to valleys, to the special place You founded for them. You set a boundary they cannot overstep, they cannot return to cover the earth. He sends the springs into the streams, they flow between the mountains. They water every beast of the field, they quench the wild creatures' thirst. Near them dwell the heaven's birds, from among the branches they give forth song. He waters the mountains from His upper chambers, from the fruit of Your works the earth is sated. He causes vegetation to sprout for the cattle, and plants through man's labor, to bring forth bread from the earth; and wine that gladdens man's heart, to make the face glow from oil, and bread that sustains the heart of man. The trees of HASHEM are sated, the cedars of Lebanon that He has planted; there where the birds nest, the chassidah with its home among cypresses; high mountains for the wild goats, rocks as refuge for the gophers. He made the moon for festivals, the sun knows its destination. You make darkness and it is night, in which every forest beast stirs.

יִפֹּל מִצִּדְּךָ אֶלֶף, וּרְבָבָה מִימִינֶךָ, אֵלֶיךָ לֹא יִגָּשׁ. רַק בְּעֵינֶיךָ תַבִּיט, וְשִׁלֻּמַת רְשָׁעִים תִּרְאֶה. כִּי אַתָּה יהוה מַחְסִי, עֶלְיוֹן שַׂמְתָּ מְעוֹנֶךָ. לֹא תְאֻנֶּה אֵלֶיךָ רָעָה, וְנֶגַע לֹא יִקְרַב בְּאָהֳלֶךָ. כִּי מַלְאָכָיו יְצַוֶּה לָּךְ, לִשְׁמָרְךָ בְּכָל דְּרָכֶיךָ. עַל כַּפַּיִם יִשָּׂאוּנְךָ, פֶּן תִּגֹּף בָּאֶבֶן רַגְלֶךָ. עַל שַׁחַל וָפֶתֶן תִּדְרֹךְ, תִּרְמֹס כְּפִיר וְתַנִּין. כִּי בִי חָשַׁק וַאֲפַלְּטֵהוּ, אֲשַׂגְּבֵהוּ כִּי יָדַע שְׁמִי. יִקְרָאֵנִי וְאֶעֱנֵהוּ, עִמּוֹ אָנֹכִי בְצָרָה; אֲחַלְּצֵהוּ וַאֲכַבְּדֵהוּ. אֹרֶךְ יָמִים אַשְׂבִּיעֵהוּ, וְאַרְאֵהוּ בִּישׁוּעָתִי.

קד בָּרְכִי נַפְשִׁי אֶת יהוה; יהוה אֱלֹהַי גָּדַלְתָּ מְּאֹד, הוֹד וְהָדָר לָבָשְׁתָּ. עֹטֶה אוֹר כַּשַּׂלְמָה, נוֹטֶה שָׁמַיִם כַּיְרִיעָה. הַמְקָרֶה בַמַּיִם עֲלִיּוֹתָיו; הַשָּׂם עָבִים רְכוּבוֹ, הַמְהַלֵּךְ עַל כַּנְפֵי רוּחַ. עֹשֶׂה מַלְאָכָיו רוּחוֹת, מְשָׁרְתָיו אֵשׁ לֹהֵט. יָסַד אֶרֶץ עַל מְכוֹנֶיהָ, בַּל תִּמּוֹט עוֹלָם וָעֶד. תְּהוֹם כַּלְּבוּשׁ כִּסִּיתוֹ, עַל הָרִים יַעַמְדוּ מָיִם. מִן גַּעֲרָתְךָ יְנוּסוּן, מִן קוֹל רַעַמְךָ יֵחָפֵזוּן. יַעֲלוּ הָרִים, יֵרְדוּ בְקָעוֹת, אֶל מְקוֹם זֶה יָסַדְתָּ לָהֶם. גְּבוּל שַׂמְתָּ בַּל יַעֲבֹרוּן, בַּל יְשֻׁבוּן לְכַסּוֹת הָאָרֶץ. הַמְשַׁלֵּחַ מַעְיָנִים בַּנְּחָלִים, בֵּין הָרִים יְהַלֵּכוּן. יַשְׁקוּ כָּל חַיְתוֹ שָׂדָי, יִשְׁבְּרוּ פְרָאִים צְמָאָם. עֲלֵיהֶם עוֹף הַשָּׁמַיִם יִשְׁכּוֹן, מִבֵּין עֳפָאיִם יִתְּנוּ קוֹל. מַשְׁקֶה הָרִים מֵעֲלִיּוֹתָיו, מִפְּרִי מַעֲשֶׂיךָ תִּשְׂבַּע הָאָרֶץ. מַצְמִיחַ חָצִיר לַבְּהֵמָה, וְעֵשֶׂב לַעֲבֹדַת הָאָדָם; לְהוֹצִיא לֶחֶם מִן הָאָרֶץ. וְיַיִן יְשַׂמַּח לְבַב אֱנוֹשׁ, לְהַצְהִיל פָּנִים מִשָּׁמֶן, וְלֶחֶם לְבַב אֱנוֹשׁ יִסְעָד. יִשְׂבְּעוּ עֲצֵי יהוה, אַרְזֵי לְבָנוֹן אֲשֶׁר נָטָע. אֲשֶׁר שָׁם צִפֳּרִים יְקַנֵּנוּ, חֲסִידָה בְּרוֹשִׁים בֵּיתָהּ. הָרִים הַגְּבֹהִים לַיְּעֵלִים, סְלָעִים מַחְסֶה לַשְׁפַנִּים. עָשָׂה יָרֵחַ לְמוֹעֲדִים, שֶׁמֶשׁ יָדַע מְבוֹאוֹ. תָּשֶׁת חֹשֶׁךְ וִיהִי לָיְלָה, בּוֹ תִרְמֹשׂ כָּל חַיְתוֹ יָעַר.

The young lions roar after their prey, and to seek their food from God. The sun rises and they are gathered in, and in their dens they crouch. Man goes forth to his work, and to his labor until evening. How abundant are Your works, HASHEM; with wisdom You made them all, the earth is full of Your possessions. Behold this sea — great and of broad measure; there are creeping things without number, small creatures and great ones. There ships travel, this Leviathan You fashioned to sport within. All of them look to You with hope, to provide their food in its proper time. You give to them, they gather it in; You open Your hand, they are sated with good. When You hide Your face, they are dismayed; when You retrieve their spirit, they perish and to their dust they return. When You send forth Your breath, they are created, and You renew the surface of the earth. May the glory of HASHEM endure forever, let HASHEM rejoice in His works. He looks toward the earth and it trembles, He touches the mountains and they smoke. I will sing to HASHEM while I live, I will sing praises to my God while I endure. May my words be sweet to Him — I will rejoice in HASHEM. Sinners will cease from the earth, and the wicked will be no more — Bless HASHEM, O my soul. Halleluyah!

130. *A song of ascents. From the depths I called You, HASHEM. My Lord, hear my voice, may Your ears be attentive to the sound of my pleas. If You preserve iniquities, O God, my Lord, who could survive? For with You is forgiveness, that You may be feared. I put confidence in HASHEM, my soul put confidence, and I hoped for His word. I yearn for my Lord, among those longing for the dawn, those longing for the dawn. Let Israel hope for HASHEM, for with HASHEM is kindness, and with Him is abundant redemption. And He shall redeem Israel from all its iniquities.*

הַכְּפִירִים שֹׁאֲגִים לַטָּרֶף, וּלְבַקֵּשׁ מֵאֵל אָכְלָם. תִּזְרַח הַשֶּׁמֶשׁ יֵאָסֵפוּן, וְאֶל מְעוֹנֹתָם יִרְבָּצוּן. יֵצֵא אָדָם לְפָעֳלוֹ, וְלַעֲבֹדָתוֹ עֲדֵי עָרֶב. מָה רַבּוּ מַעֲשֶׂיךָ יהוה, כֻּלָּם בְּחָכְמָה עָשִׂיתָ, מָלְאָה הָאָרֶץ קִנְיָנֶךָ. זֶה הַיָּם, גָּדוֹל וּרְחַב יָדָיִם; שָׁם רֶמֶשׂ וְאֵין מִסְפָּר, חַיּוֹת קְטַנּוֹת עִם גְּדֹלוֹת. שָׁם אֳנִיּוֹת יְהַלֵּכוּן, לִוְיָתָן זֶה יָצַרְתָּ לְשַׂחֶק בּוֹ. כֻּלָּם אֵלֶיךָ יְשַׂבֵּרוּן, לָתֵת אָכְלָם בְּעִתּוֹ. תִּתֵּן לָהֶם, יִלְקֹטוּן; תִּפְתַּח יָדְךָ, יִשְׂבְּעוּן טוֹב. תַּסְתִּיר פָּנֶיךָ, יִבָּהֵלוּן; תֹּסֵף רוּחָם יִגְוָעוּן, וְאֶל עֲפָרָם יְשׁוּבוּן. תְּשַׁלַּח רוּחֲךָ יִבָּרֵאוּן, וּתְחַדֵּשׁ פְּנֵי אֲדָמָה. יְהִי כְבוֹד יהוה לְעוֹלָם, יִשְׂמַח יהוה בְּמַעֲשָׂיו. הַמַּבִּיט לָאָרֶץ וַתִּרְעָד, יִגַּע בֶּהָרִים וְיֶעֱשָׁנוּ. אָשִׁירָה לַיהוה בְּחַיָּי, אֲזַמְּרָה לֵאלֹהַי בְּעוֹדִי. יֶעֱרַב עָלָיו שִׂיחִי, אָנֹכִי אֶשְׂמַח בַּיהוה. יִתַּמּוּ חַטָּאִים מִן הָאָרֶץ, וּרְשָׁעִים עוֹד אֵינָם, בָּרְכִי נַפְשִׁי אֶת יהוה, הַלְלוּיָהּ.

קל שִׁיר הַמַּעֲלוֹת, מִמַּעֲמַקִּים קְרָאתִיךָ יהוה. אֲדֹנָי שִׁמְעָה בְקוֹלִי, תִּהְיֶינָה אָזְנֶיךָ קַשֻּׁבוֹת לְקוֹל תַּחֲנוּנָי. אִם עֲוֹנוֹת תִּשְׁמָר יָהּ, אֲדֹנָי מִי יַעֲמֹד. כִּי עִמְּךָ הַסְּלִיחָה, לְמַעַן תִּוָּרֵא. קִוִּיתִי יהוה קִוְּתָה נַפְשִׁי, וְלִדְבָרוֹ הוֹחָלְתִּי. נַפְשִׁי לַאדֹנָי; מִשֹּׁמְרִים לַבֹּקֶר, שֹׁמְרִים לַבֹּקֶר. יַחֵל יִשְׂרָאֵל אֶל יהוה; כִּי עִם יהוה הַחֶסֶד, וְהַרְבֵּה עִמּוֹ פְדוּת. וְהוּא יִפְדֶּה אֶת יִשְׂרָאֵל, מִכֹּל עֲוֹנוֹתָיו.

119.

This psalm, known as תְּמַנְיָא אַפִּין, *eight facets,* is an alphabetical arrangement describing the ceaseless striving to faithfully live a true life of Torah, regardless of time, place, circumstances, or social environment. The psalm consists of twenty-two sets of verses; each set containing eight verses beginning with the same letter. It is customary to spell the name of the deceased by reciting the sets of verses corresponding to the letters of his name. Then one recites the sets of letters that spell the word נְשָׁמָה, *soul* (see 42:23).

א *Praiseworthy are those whose way is perfect, who walk with the Torah of HASHEM. Praiseworthy are those who guard His testimonies, they seek Him whole-heartedly. They have also done no iniquity, for they have walked in His ways. You have issued Your precepts to be kept diligently.*

א אַשְׁרֵי תְמִימֵי דָרֶךְ, הַהֹלְכִים בְּתוֹרַת יהוה. אַשְׁרֵי נֹצְרֵי עֵדֹתָיו, בְּכָל לֵב יִדְרְשׁוּהוּ. אַף לֹא פָעֲלוּ עַוְלָה, בִּדְרָכָיו הָלָכוּ. אַתָּה צִוִּיתָה פִקֻּדֶיךָ, לִשְׁמֹר מְאֹד

These are my prayers: may my ways be firmly guided to keep Your statutes. Then I will not be ashamed, when I gaze at all Your commandments. I will give thanks to You with upright heart, when I study Your righteous ordinances. I will keep Your statutes, O, do not forsake me utterly.

ב *How can a youngster purify his path? By observing Your word. With all my heart I sought You, do not let me stray from Your commandments. In my heart I have stored Your word, so that I would not sin against You. Blessed are You,* HASHEM, *teach me Your statutes. With my lips I recounted all the ordinances of Your mouth. I rejoiced over the way of Your ennobling testimonies as much as in all riches. Of Your precepts I speak and I look at Your paths. I occupy myself with Your statutes, I will not forget Your word.*

ג *Bestow upon Your servant that I should live, that I may keep Your word. Unveil my eyes that I may perceive wonders from Your Torah. I am a sojourner in the world, hide not Your commandments from me. My soul is shattered with yearning for Your ordinances always. You rebuked the accursed willful sinners who stray from Your commandments. Remove from upon me scorn and contempt, for I have guarded Your testimonies. Though princes sat and spoke against me, Your servant discusses Your statutes. Indeed, Your testimonies are my preoccupation, they are my counselors.*

ד *My soul has clung to the dust, revive me in accordance with Your word. I have recounted my ways and You answered me, teach me Your statutes. Let me understand the way of Your precepts, that I may discuss Your wonders. My soul drips away from sorrow, sustain me in accordance with Your word. Remove from me the way of falsehood, and graciously endow me with Your Torah. I have chosen the way of unshakeable truth, I have placed Your ordinances [before me]. I have clung to Your ennobling testimonies, O* HASHEM, *put me not to shame. I will run on the way of Your commandments, for You will broaden my understanding.*

ה *Teach me, O* HASHEM, *the way of Your statutes, and I will cherish it to the utmost. Grant me understanding so that I may cherish Your Torah, and keep it with all my heart. Lead me on the path of Your commandments, for that is my desire. Incline my heart toward Your ennobling testimonies and not to greed. Avert my eyes from seeing futility, through Your ways preserve me. Fulfill Your word to Your servant for the purpose of fearing You. Remove*

אַחֲלַי, יִכֹּנוּ דְרָכָי לִשְׁמֹר חֻקֶּיךָ. אָז לֹא אֵבוֹשׁ, בְּהַבִּיטִי אֶל כָּל מִצְוֹתֶיךָ. אוֹדְךָ בְּיֹשֶׁר לֵבָב, בְּלָמְדִי מִשְׁפְּטֵי צִדְקֶךָ. אֶת חֻקֶּיךָ אֶשְׁמֹר, אַל תַּעַזְבֵנִי עַד מְאֹד.

ב בַּמֶּה יְזַכֶּה נַּעַר אֶת אָרְחוֹ, לִשְׁמֹר כִּדְבָרֶךָ. בְּכָל לִבִּי דְרַשְׁתִּיךָ, אַל תַּשְׁגֵּנִי מִמִּצְוֹתֶיךָ. בְּלִבִּי צָפַנְתִּי אִמְרָתֶךָ, לְמַעַן לֹא אֶחֱטָא לָךְ. בָּרוּךְ אַתָּה יהוה, לַמְּדֵנִי חֻקֶּיךָ. בִּשְׂפָתַי סִפַּרְתִּי, כֹּל מִשְׁפְּטֵי פִיךָ. בְּדֶרֶךְ עֵדְוֹתֶיךָ שַׂשְׂתִּי, כְּעַל כָּל הוֹן. בְּפִקּוּדֶיךָ אָשִׂיחָה, וְאַבִּיטָה אֹרְחֹתֶיךָ. בְּחֻקֹּתֶיךָ אֶשְׁתַּעֲשָׁע, לֹא אֶשְׁכַּח דְּבָרֶךָ.

ג גְּמֹל עַל עַבְדְּךָ, אֶחְיֶה וְאֶשְׁמְרָה דְבָרֶךָ. גַּל עֵינַי וְאַבִּיטָה, נִפְלָאוֹת מִתּוֹרָתֶךָ. גֵּר אָנֹכִי בָאָרֶץ, אַל תַּסְתֵּר מִמֶּנִּי מִצְוֹתֶיךָ. גָּרְסָה נַפְשִׁי לְתַאֲבָה, אֶל מִשְׁפָּטֶיךָ בְכָל עֵת. גָּעַרְתָּ זֵדִים אֲרוּרִים, הַשֹּׁגִים מִמִּצְוֹתֶיךָ. גַּל מֵעָלַי חֶרְפָּה וָבוּז, כִּי עֵדֹתֶיךָ נָצָרְתִּי. גַּם יָשְׁבוּ שָׂרִים בִּי נִדְבָּרוּ, עַבְדְּךָ יָשִׂיחַ בְּחֻקֶּיךָ. גַּם עֵדֹתֶיךָ שַׁעֲשֻׁעָי, אַנְשֵׁי עֲצָתִי.

ד דָּבְקָה לֶעָפָר נַפְשִׁי, חַיֵּנִי כִּדְבָרֶךָ. דְּרָכַי סִפַּרְתִּי וַתַּעֲנֵנִי, לַמְּדֵנִי חֻקֶּיךָ. דֶּרֶךְ פִּקּוּדֶיךָ הֲבִינֵנִי, וְאָשִׂיחָה בְּנִפְלְאוֹתֶיךָ. דָּלְפָה נַפְשִׁי מִתּוּגָה, קַיְּמֵנִי כִּדְבָרֶךָ. דֶּרֶךְ שֶׁקֶר הָסֵר מִמֶּנִּי, וְתוֹרָתְךָ חָנֵּנִי. דֶּרֶךְ אֱמוּנָה בָחָרְתִּי, מִשְׁפָּטֶיךָ שִׁוִּיתִי. דָּבַקְתִּי בְעֵדְוֹתֶיךָ, יהוה אַל תְּבִישֵׁנִי. דֶּרֶךְ מִצְוֹתֶיךָ אָרוּץ, כִּי תַרְחִיב לִבִּי.

ה הוֹרֵנִי יהוה דֶּרֶךְ חֻקֶּיךָ, וְאֶצְּרֶנָּה עֵקֶב. הֲבִינֵנִי וְאֶצְּרָה תוֹרָתֶךָ, וְאֶשְׁמְרֶנָּה בְכָל לֵב. הַדְרִיכֵנִי בִּנְתִיב מִצְוֹתֶיךָ, כִּי בוֹ חָפָצְתִּי. הַט לִבִּי אֶל עֵדְוֹתֶיךָ, וְאַל אֶל בָּצַע. הַעֲבֵר עֵינַי מֵרְאוֹת שָׁוְא, בִּדְרָכֶךָ חַיֵּנִי. הָקֵם לְעַבְדְּךָ אִמְרָתֶךָ, אֲשֶׁר לְיִרְאָתֶךָ. הַעֲבֵר

my disgrace, which I feared, for Your judgments are good. Behold, I yearn for Your precepts, through Your righteousness preserve me.

ו May Your kindness come to me, HASHEM, Your salvation, as You promised. I shall offer a response to those who scorn me, for I have trusted in Your word. Do not remove from my mouth the word of utmost truth, because I have yearned for Your ordinances. I will safeguard Your Torah constantly, forever and ever. And I will walk in broad pathways, for I have sought Your precepts. I will speak of Your testimonies before kings and I will not be ashamed. I will be preoccupied with Your commandments which I love. I will lift my hands to Your commandments, which I love, and I will discuss Your statutes.

ז Remember the assurance to Your servant, by which You gave me hope. This is my comfort in my affliction, for Your promise preserved me. Willful sinners taunted me exceedingly, but I did not swerve from Your Torah. I remembered Your judgments of old, HASHEM, and I was comforted. Trembling seized me because of the wicked who forsake Your Torah. Your statutes were music to me, in my dwelling place. In the night I remembered Your Name, O HASHEM, and I kept Your Torah. All this came to me because I guarded Your precepts.

ח My portion is HASHEM; I have pledged to keep Your words. I pleaded before You wholeheartedly, favor me according to Your promise. I considered my ways and returned my feet to Your testimonies. I hastened and I did not delay to keep Your commandments. Bands of wicked men plundered me, but I did not forget Your Torah. At midnight I arise to thank You for Your righteous judgments. I am a friend to all who fear You, and to those who keep Your precepts. Your kindness, HASHEM, fills the earth, teach me Your statutes.

ט You have done good to Your servant, HASHEM, according to Your word. Teach me good reasoning and knowledge, for I have been faithful to Your commandments. Before I was afflicted I erred, but now I keep Your word. You are good and beneficent, teach me Your statutes. Willful sinners have piled false accusations upon me, but I guard Your precepts with all my heart. Their heart grew thick as fat, but for me, Your Torah is my preoccupation. It is good for me that I was afflicted, so that I might learn Your statutes. I prefer the Torah of Your mouth more than thousands in gold and silver.

חֶרְפָּתִי אֲשֶׁר יָגֹרְתִּי, כִּי מִשְׁפָּטֶיךָ טוֹבִים. הִנֵּה תָּאַבְתִּי לְפִקֻּדֶיךָ, בְּצִדְקָתְךָ חַיֵּנִי.

ו וִיבֹאֻנִי חֲסָדֶךָ יהוה, תְּשׁוּעָתְךָ כְּאִמְרָתֶךָ. וְאֶעֱנֶה חֹרְפִי דָבָר, כִּי בָטַחְתִּי בִּדְבָרֶךָ. וְאַל תַּצֵּל מִפִּי דְבַר אֱמֶת עַד מְאֹד, כִּי לְמִשְׁפָּטֶךָ יִחָלְתִּי. וְאֶשְׁמְרָה תוֹרָתְךָ תָמִיד לְעוֹלָם וָעֶד. וְאֶתְהַלְּכָה בָרְחָבָה, כִּי פִקֻּדֶיךָ דָרָשְׁתִּי. וַאֲדַבְּרָה בְעֵדֹתֶיךָ נֶגֶד מְלָכִים, וְלֹא אֵבוֹשׁ. וְאֶשְׁתַּעֲשַׁע בְּמִצְוֹתֶיךָ אֲשֶׁר אָהָבְתִּי. וְאֶשָּׂא כַפַּי אֶל מִצְוֹתֶיךָ אֲשֶׁר אָהָבְתִּי, וְאָשִׂיחָה בְחֻקֶּיךָ.

ז זְכֹר דָּבָר לְעַבְדֶּךָ, עַל אֲשֶׁר יִחַלְתָּנִי. זֹאת נֶחָמָתִי בְעָנְיִי, כִּי אִמְרָתְךָ חִיָּתְנִי. זֵדִים הֱלִיצֻנִי עַד מְאֹד, מִתּוֹרָתְךָ לֹא נָטִיתִי. זָכַרְתִּי מִשְׁפָּטֶיךָ מֵעוֹלָם | יהוה, וָאֶתְנֶחָם. זַלְעָפָה אֲחָזַתְנִי מֵרְשָׁעִים, עֹזְבֵי תוֹרָתֶךָ. זְמִרוֹת הָיוּ לִי חֻקֶּיךָ, בְּבֵית מְגוּרָי. זָכַרְתִּי בַלַּיְלָה שִׁמְךָ יהוה, וָאֶשְׁמְרָה תוֹרָתֶךָ. זֹאת הָיְתָה לִּי, כִּי פִקֻּדֶיךָ נָצָרְתִּי.

ח חֶלְקִי יהוה, אָמַרְתִּי לִשְׁמֹר דְּבָרֶיךָ. חִלִּיתִי פָנֶיךָ בְכָל לֵב, חָנֵּנִי כְּאִמְרָתֶךָ. חִשַּׁבְתִּי דְרָכָי, וָאָשִׁיבָה רַגְלַי אֶל עֵדֹתֶיךָ. חַשְׁתִּי וְלֹא הִתְמַהְמָהְתִּי, לִשְׁמֹר מִצְוֹתֶיךָ. חֶבְלֵי רְשָׁעִים עִוְּדֻנִי, תוֹרָתְךָ לֹא שָׁכָחְתִּי. חֲצוֹת לַיְלָה אָקוּם לְהוֹדוֹת לָךְ, עַל מִשְׁפְּטֵי צִדְקֶךָ. חָבֵר אָנִי לְכָל אֲשֶׁר יְרֵאוּךָ, וּלְשֹׁמְרֵי פִּקּוּדֶיךָ. חַסְדְּךָ יהוה מָלְאָה הָאָרֶץ, חֻקֶּיךָ לַמְּדֵנִי.

ט טוֹב עָשִׂיתָ עִם עַבְדְּךָ, יהוה כִּדְבָרֶךָ. טוֹב טַעַם וָדַעַת לַמְּדֵנִי, כִּי בְמִצְוֹתֶיךָ הֶאֱמָנְתִּי. טֶרֶם אֶעֱנֶה אֲנִי שֹׁגֵג, וְעַתָּה אִמְרָתְךָ שָׁמָרְתִּי. טוֹב אַתָּה וּמֵטִיב, לַמְּדֵנִי חֻקֶּיךָ. טָפְלוּ עָלַי שֶׁקֶר זֵדִים, אֲנִי בְּכָל לֵב אֶצֹּר פִּקּוּדֶיךָ. טָפַשׁ כַּחֵלֶב לִבָּם, אֲנִי תוֹרָתְךָ שִׁעֲשָׁעְתִּי. טוֹב לִי כִי עֻנֵּיתִי, לְמַעַן אֶלְמַד חֻקֶּיךָ. טוֹב לִי תוֹרַת פִּיךָ, מֵאַלְפֵי זָהָב וָכָסֶף.

י Your hands made me and prepared me; grant me understanding so that I may learn Your commandments. Those who revere You shall see me and they will rejoice, because I hoped in Your word. I know, HASHEM, that Your judgment is righteous, and that You afflicted me in faithfulness. May Your kindness comfort me, as Your promise to Your servant. May Your mercies come upon me so that I may live, for Your Torah is my preoccupation. May the willful sinners be shamed, for they have maligned me with lies — but I will discuss Your precepts. May they return to me those who fear You, and who know Your testimonies. May my heart be perfect in Your statutes, so that I be not shamed.

כ My soul pines for Your salvation, for Your word I hope. My eyes pine for Your promise, saying, 'When will You comfort me?' Though I have been like a wineskin dried in smoke, I did not forget Your statutes. How many are Your servant's days? When will You execute judgment upon my pursuers? Willful sinners dug pits for me, in violation of Your Torah. All Your commandments teach truthfulness; they pursue me with lies — help me! They had almost destroyed me on earth, but I did not forsake Your precepts. In accordance with Your kindness preserve me, and I will keep the testimony of Your mouth.

ל Forever, HASHEM, Your word stands firm in heaven. Your faithfulness endures from generation to generation, You established the earth and it endures. To fulfill Your decree they stand until this day, for all are Your servants. Had Your Torah not been my preoccupation, then I would have perished in my affliction. I will never forget Your precepts, for through them You have preserved me. I am Yours, save me, for I have sought Your precepts. The wicked hoped to destroy me, but I contemplate Your testimonies. To every goal I have seen an end, but Your commandment is exceedingly broad.

מ O how I love Your Torah! All day long it is my conversation. [Each of] Your commandments makes me wiser than my enemies, for it is ever with me. From all my teachers I grew wise, for Your ennobling testimonies are my conversation. From wise elders I gain understanding, because I have guarded Your precepts. From every evil path I restrained my feet, so that I might keep Your word. From Your ordinances I did not turn aside, for You have taught me. How sweet to my palate is every one of Your words, more than honey to my mouth. From Your precepts I acquire understanding, therefore I hate every path of falsehood.

י יָדֶיךָ עָשׂוּנִי וַיְכוֹנְנוּנִי, הֲבִינֵנִי וְאֶלְמְדָה מִצְוֹתֶיךָ. יְרֵאֶיךָ יִרְאוּנִי וְיִשְׂמָחוּ, כִּי לִדְבָרְךָ יִחָלְתִּי. יָדַעְתִּי יהוה כִּי צֶדֶק מִשְׁפָּטֶיךָ, וֶאֱמוּנָה עִנִּיתָנִי. יְהִי נָא חַסְדְּךָ לְנַחֲמֵנִי, כְּאִמְרָתְךָ לְעַבְדֶּךָ. יְבֹאוּנִי רַחֲמֶיךָ וְאֶחְיֶה, כִּי תוֹרָתְךָ שַׁעֲשֻׁעָי. יֵבֹשׁוּ זֵדִים כִּי שֶׁקֶר עִוְּתוּנִי, אֲנִי אָשִׂיחַ בְּפִקּוּדֶיךָ. יָשׁוּבוּ לִי יְרֵאֶיךָ, וְיֹדְעֵי עֵדֹתֶיךָ. יְהִי לִבִּי תָמִים בְּחֻקֶּיךָ, לְמַעַן לֹא אֵבוֹשׁ.

כ כָּלְתָה לִתְשׁוּעָתְךָ נַפְשִׁי, לִדְבָרְךָ יִחָלְתִּי. כָּלוּ עֵינַי לְאִמְרָתֶךָ, לֵאמֹר מָתַי תְּנַחֲמֵנִי. כִּי הָיִיתִי כְּנֹאד בְּקִיטוֹר, חֻקֶּיךָ לֹא שָׁכָחְתִּי. כַּמָּה יְמֵי עַבְדֶּךָ, מָתַי תַּעֲשֶׂה בְרֹדְפַי מִשְׁפָּט. כָּרוּ לִי זֵדִים שִׁיחוֹת, אֲשֶׁר לֹא כְתוֹרָתֶךָ. כָּל מִצְוֹתֶיךָ אֱמוּנָה, שֶׁקֶר רְדָפוּנִי, עָזְרֵנִי. כִּמְעַט כִּלּוּנִי בָאָרֶץ, וַאֲנִי לֹא עָזַבְתִּי פִקֻּדֶיךָ. כְּחַסְדְּךָ חַיֵּנִי, וְאֶשְׁמְרָה עֵדוּת פִּיךָ.

ל לְעוֹלָם יהוה, דְּבָרְךָ נִצָּב בַּשָּׁמָיִם. לְדֹר וָדֹר אֱמוּנָתֶךָ, כּוֹנַנְתָּ אֶרֶץ וַתַּעֲמֹד. לְמִשְׁפָּטֶיךָ עָמְדוּ הַיּוֹם, כִּי הַכֹּל עֲבָדֶיךָ. לוּלֵי תוֹרָתְךָ שַׁעֲשֻׁעָי, אָז אָבַדְתִּי בְעָנְיִי. לְעוֹלָם לֹא אֶשְׁכַּח פִּקּוּדֶיךָ, כִּי בָם חִיִּיתָנִי. לְךָ אֲנִי הוֹשִׁיעֵנִי, כִּי פִקּוּדֶיךָ דָרָשְׁתִּי. לִי קִוּוּ רְשָׁעִים לְאַבְּדֵנִי, עֵדֹתֶיךָ אֶתְבּוֹנָן. לְכָל תִּכְלָה רָאִיתִי קֵץ, רְחָבָה מִצְוָתְךָ מְאֹד.

מ מָה אָהַבְתִּי תוֹרָתֶךָ, כָּל הַיּוֹם הִיא שִׂיחָתִי. מֵאֹיְבַי תְּחַכְּמֵנִי מִצְוֹתֶךָ, כִּי לְעוֹלָם הִיא לִי. מִכָּל מְלַמְּדַי הִשְׂכַּלְתִּי, כִּי עֵדְוֹתֶיךָ שִׂיחָה לִי. מִזְּקֵנִים אֶתְבּוֹנָן, כִּי פִקּוּדֶיךָ נָצָרְתִּי. מִכָּל אֹרַח רָע כָּלֵאתִי רַגְלָי, לְמַעַן אֶשְׁמֹר דְּבָרֶךָ. מִמִּשְׁפָּטֶיךָ לֹא סָרְתִּי, כִּי אַתָּה הוֹרֵתָנִי. מַה נִּמְלְצוּ לְחִכִּי אִמְרָתֶךָ, מִדְּבַשׁ לְפִי. מִפִּקּוּדֶיךָ אֶתְבּוֹנָן, עַל כֵּן שָׂנֵאתִי כָּל אֹרַח שָׁקֶר.

נ נֵר לְרַגְלִי דְבָרֶךָ, וְאוֹר לִנְתִיבָתִי.
נִשְׁבַּעְתִּי וָאֲקַיֵּמָה, לִשְׁמֹר מִשְׁפְּטֵי צִדְקֶךָ.
נַעֲנֵיתִי עַד מְאֹד; יהוה, חַיֵּנִי כִדְבָרֶךָ.
נִדְבוֹת פִּי רְצֵה נָא, יהוה; וּמִשְׁפָּטֶיךָ לַמְּדֵנִי.
נַפְשִׁי בְכַפִּי תָמִיד, וְתוֹרָתְךָ לֹא שָׁכָחְתִּי.
נָתְנוּ רְשָׁעִים פַּח לִי, וּמִפִּקּוּדֶיךָ לֹא תָעִיתִי.
נָחַלְתִּי עֵדְוֹתֶיךָ לְעוֹלָם, כִּי שְׂשׂוֹן לִבִּי
הֵמָּה. נָטִיתִי לִבִּי לַעֲשׂוֹת חֻקֶּיךָ לְעוֹלָם
עֵקֶב.

ס סֵעֲפִים שָׂנֵאתִי, וְתוֹרָתְךָ אָהָבְתִּי. סִתְרִי
וּמָגִנִּי אָתָּה, לִדְבָרְךָ יִחָלְתִּי. סְוּרוּ מִמֶּנִּי
מְרֵעִים, וְאֶצְּרָה מִצְוֹת אֱלֹהָי. סָמְכֵנִי
כְאִמְרָתְךָ וְאֶחְיֶה, וְאַל תְּבִישֵׁנִי מִשִּׂבְרִי.
סְעָדֵנִי וְאִוָּשֵׁעָה, וְאֶשְׁעָה בְחֻקֶּיךָ תָמִיד.
סָלִיתָ כָּל שׁוֹגִים מֵחֻקֶּיךָ, כִּי שֶׁקֶר
תַּרְמִיתָם. סִגִים הִשְׁבַּתָּ כָל רִשְׁעֵי אָרֶץ,
לָכֵן אָהַבְתִּי עֵדֹתֶיךָ. סָמַר מִפַּחְדְּךָ בְשָׂרִי,
וּמִמִּשְׁפָּטֶיךָ יָרֵאתִי.

ע עָשִׂיתִי מִשְׁפָּט וָצֶדֶק, בַּל תַּנִּיחֵנִי
לְעֹשְׁקָי. עֲרֹב עַבְדְּךָ לְטוֹב, אַל יַעַשְׁקֻנִי
זֵדִים. עֵינַי כָּלוּ לִישׁוּעָתֶךָ, וּלְאִמְרַת צִדְקֶךָ.
עֲשֵׂה עִם עַבְדְּךָ כְחַסְדֶּךָ, וְחֻקֶּיךָ לַמְּדֵנִי.
עַבְדְּךָ אָנִי הֲבִינֵנִי, וְאֵדְעָה עֵדֹתֶיךָ. עֵת
לַעֲשׂוֹת לַיהוה, הֵפֵרוּ תּוֹרָתֶךָ. עַל כֵּן
אָהַבְתִּי מִצְוֹתֶיךָ, מִזָּהָב וּמִפָּז. עַל כֵּן
כָּל פִּקּוּדֵי כֹל יִשָּׁרְתִּי, כָּל אֹרַח שֶׁקֶר
שָׂנֵאתִי.

פ פְּלָאוֹת עֵדְוֹתֶיךָ, עַל כֵּן נְצָרָתַם נַפְשִׁי.
פֵּתַח דְּבָרֶיךָ יָאִיר, מֵבִין פְּתָיִים. פִּי
פָעַרְתִּי וָאֶשְׁאָפָה, כִּי לְמִצְוֹתֶיךָ יָאָבְתִּי.
פְּנֵה אֵלַי וְחָנֵּנִי, כְּמִשְׁפָּט לְאֹהֲבֵי שְׁמֶךָ.
פְּעָמַי הָכֵן בְּאִמְרָתֶךָ, וְאַל תַּשְׁלֶט בִּי כָל
אָוֶן. פְּדֵנִי מֵעֹשֶׁק אָדָם, וְאֶשְׁמְרָה פִּקּוּדֶיךָ.
פָּנֶיךָ הָאֵר בְּעַבְדֶּךָ, וְלַמְּדֵנִי אֶת חֻקֶּיךָ.
פַּלְגֵי מַיִם יָרְדוּ עֵינָי, עַל לֹא שָׁמְרוּ
תוֹרָתֶךָ.

נ *Your word is a lamp for my feet and a light for my path. I have sworn — and I will fulfill — to keep Your righteous ordinances. I am exceedingly afflicted; O HASHEM, preserve me in accordance with Your word. Please accept with favor the offerings of my mouth, HASHEM, that You should teach me Your ordinances. My life is constantly in danger, but I did not forget Your Torah. The wicked laid a snare for me, but I did not stray from Your precepts. I have taken Your ennobling testimonies as my eternal heritage, for they are the joy of my heart. I have inclined my heart to perform Your statutes, forever, to the utmost.*

ס *I hate the freethinkers, but I love Your Torah. You are my concealment and my shield, I put hope in Your word. Depart from me, You evildoers, and I will guard the commandments of my God. Support me according to Your promise that I may live, disgrace me not in my hope. Sustain me that I may be saved, and I will always be engrossed in Your statutes. You trampled all who stray from Your statutes, for their deceit is falsehood. Like dross, You purged all the wicked of the earth, therefore I have loved Your testimonies. My flesh shuddered from dread of You, and I feared Your judgments.*

ע *I practiced justice and righteousness, abandon me not to those who exploit me. Be Your servant's guarantor for good, let not willful sinners exploit me. My eyes pine for Your salvation, and for Your promised righteousness. Treat Your servant according to Your kindness, and teach me Your statutes. I am Your servant, grant me understanding, so that I may know Your testimonies. For it is a time to act for HASHEM, they have voided Your Torah. Therefore I have loved Your commandments, more than gold, even more than fine gold. Therefore I have declared the fairness of every precept regarding everything! I have hated every path of falsehood.*

פ *Your ennobling testimonies are wonders, therefore my soul has guarded them. The introduction of Your words illuminates, making simpletons understand. I opened my mouth and swallowed deeply, because I crave for Your commandments. Turn to me and favor me, as is Your practice to those who love Your Name. Ready my steps in Your word, and do not give iniquity dominion over me. Redeem me from human exploitation, and I will keep Your precepts. Cause Your face to shine upon Your servant, and teach me Your statutes. My eyes shed streams of water, because they did not keep Your Torah.*

צ Righteous are You, HASHEM, and each of Your judgments is fair. You commanded the justice of Your testimonies, and great faithfulness. My zeal has consumed me, for my oppressors have forgotten Your words. Your word is very pure, and Your servant loves it. I am young and despised, yet I do not forget Your precepts. Your righteousness is an everlasting righteousness, and Your Torah is truth. Distress and anguish have overtaken me, Your commandments are my preoccupation. Your ennobling testimonies are righteous forever, grant me understanding so that I may live.

ק I called with all my heart, answer me, O HASHEM, I will guard Your statutes. I called You, save me, and I will keep Your testimonies. I arose before dawn and I cried out, I hoped for Your word. My eyes preceded the night watches, to discuss Your word. Hear my voice in accordance with Your kindness — O HASHEM, preserve me in accordance with Your practice. The pursuers of sinful counsel have nearly attained it, they are far from Your Torah. Yet You are nearby, HASHEM, and all Your commandments are true. From the start I gained knowledge from Your testimonies, because You established them forever.

ר See my affliction and release me, for I have not forgotten Your Torah. Champion my cause and redeem me, preserve me that I may fulfill Your word. Salvation is far from the wicked, for they sought not Your statutes. Your mercies, HASHEM, are abundant, preserve me as is Your practice. Many were my pursuers and tormentors, but I did not swerve from Your ennobling testimonies. I saw traitors and I quarreled with them, because they kept not Your word. See that I have loved Your precepts — O HASHEM, preserve me in accordance with Your kindness. Your very first utterance is truth, and every ordinance of Your righteousness is valid for all time.

ש Princes have pursued me without cause, but my heart has feared Your utterance. I rejoice over Your word, like one who finds abundant spoils. I have hated falsehood and abhorred it, Your Torah I love. Seven times a day I have praised You for Your righteous ordinances. There is abundant peace to the lovers of Your Torah, and there is no stumbling block for them. I hoped for Your salvation, HASHEM, and I performed Your commandments. My soul kept Your testimonies, and I loved them very much. I have kept Your orders and Your testimonies, because all my ways are before You.

צ צַדִּיק אַתָּה יהוה, וְיָשָׁר מִשְׁפָּטֶיךָ. צִוִּיתָ צֶדֶק עֵדֹתֶיךָ, וֶאֱמוּנָה מְאֹד. צִמְּתַתְנִי קִנְאָתִי, כִּי שָׁכְחוּ דְבָרֶיךָ צָרָי. צְרוּפָה אִמְרָתְךָ מְאֹד, וְעַבְדְּךָ אֲהֵבָהּ. צָעִיר אָנֹכִי וְנִבְזֶה, פִּקֻּדֶיךָ לֹא שָׁכָחְתִּי. צִדְקָתְךָ צֶדֶק לְעוֹלָם, וְתוֹרָתְךָ אֱמֶת. צַר וּמָצוֹק מְצָאוּנִי, מִצְוֹתֶיךָ שַׁעֲשֻׁעָי. צֶדֶק עֵדְוֹתֶיךָ לְעוֹלָם, הֲבִינֵנִי וְאֶחְיֶה.

ק קָרָאתִי בְכָל לֵב, עֲנֵנִי יהוה; חֻקֶּיךָ אֶצֹּרָה. קְרָאתִיךָ הוֹשִׁיעֵנִי, וְאֶשְׁמְרָה עֵדֹתֶיךָ. קִדַּמְתִּי בַנֶּשֶׁף וָאֲשַׁוֵּעָה, לִדְבָרְךָ יִחָלְתִּי. קִדְּמוּ עֵינַי אַשְׁמֻרוֹת, לָשִׂיחַ בְּאִמְרָתֶךָ. קוֹלִי שִׁמְעָה כְחַסְדֶּךָ; יהוה, כְּמִשְׁפָּטֶךָ חַיֵּנִי. קָרְבוּ רֹדְפֵי זִמָּה, מִתּוֹרָתְךָ רָחָקוּ. קָרוֹב אַתָּה יהוה, וְכָל מִצְוֹתֶיךָ אֱמֶת. קֶדֶם יָדַעְתִּי מֵעֵדֹתֶיךָ, כִּי לְעוֹלָם יְסַדְתָּם.

ר רְאֵה עָנְיִי וְחַלְּצֵנִי, כִּי תוֹרָתְךָ לֹא שָׁכָחְתִּי. רִיבָה רִיבִי וּגְאָלֵנִי, לְאִמְרָתְךָ חַיֵּנִי. רָחוֹק מֵרְשָׁעִים יְשׁוּעָה, כִּי חֻקֶּיךָ לֹא דָרָשׁוּ. רַחֲמֶיךָ רַבִּים | יהוה, כְּמִשְׁפָּטֶיךָ חַיֵּנִי. רַבִּים רֹדְפַי וְצָרָי, מֵעֵדְוֹתֶיךָ לֹא נָטִיתִי. רָאִיתִי בֹגְדִים וָאֶתְקוֹטָטָה, אֲשֶׁר אִמְרָתְךָ לֹא שָׁמָרוּ. רְאֵה כִּי פִקּוּדֶיךָ אָהָבְתִּי; יהוה, כְּחַסְדְּךָ חַיֵּנִי. רֹאשׁ דְּבָרְךָ אֱמֶת, וּלְעוֹלָם כָּל מִשְׁפַּט צִדְקֶךָ.

ש שָׂרִים רְדָפוּנִי חִנָּם, וּמִדְּבָרְךָ פָּחַד לִבִּי. שָׂשׂ אָנֹכִי עַל אִמְרָתֶךָ, כְּמוֹצֵא שָׁלָל רָב. שֶׁקֶר שָׂנֵאתִי וַאֲתַעֵבָה, תּוֹרָתְךָ אָהָבְתִּי. שֶׁבַע בַּיּוֹם הִלַּלְתִּיךָ, עַל מִשְׁפְּטֵי צִדְקֶךָ. שָׁלוֹם רָב לְאֹהֲבֵי תוֹרָתֶךָ, וְאֵין לָמוֹ מִכְשׁוֹל. שִׂבַּרְתִּי לִישׁוּעָתְךָ יהוה, וּמִצְוֹתֶיךָ עָשִׂיתִי. שָׁמְרָה נַפְשִׁי עֵדֹתֶיךָ, וָאֹהֲבֵם מְאֹד. שָׁמַרְתִּי פִקּוּדֶיךָ וְעֵדֹתֶיךָ, כִּי כָל דְּרָכַי נֶגְדֶּךָ.

ת *May my prayerful song approach Your Presence, HASHEM, that You grant me understanding in accordance with Your utterance. May my supplication come before You, rescue me in accordance with Your word. My lips will speak praise when You teach me Your statutes. My tongue shall proclaim Your word, because all Your commandments are righteous. Let Your hand be ready to assist me, for I have chosen Your precepts. I crave Your salvation, O HASHEM, and Your Torah is my preoccupation. Let my soul live and it shall praise You, and Your ordinances will assist me. I have strayed like a lost sheep — seek out Your servant; for I have not forgotten Your commandments.*

אָנָּא *We beg You! With the strength of Your right hand's greatness, untie the bundled sins. Accept the prayer of Your nation; strengthen us, purify us, O Awesome One. Please, O Strong One — those who foster Your Oneness, guard them like the pupil of the eye. Bless them, purify them, show them pity, may Your righteousness always recompense them. Powerful Holy One, with Your abundant goodness guide Your congregation. One and only Exalted One, turn to Your nation which proclaims Your holiness. Accept our entreaty and hear our cry, O Knower of mysteries. Blessed is the Name of His glorious kingdom for all eternity.*

ת תִּקְרַב רִנָּתִי לְפָנֶיךָ, יהוה; כִּדְבָרְךָ הֲבִינֵנִי. תָּבוֹא תְּחִנָּתִי לְפָנֶיךָ, כְּאִמְרָתְךָ הַצִּילֵנִי. תַּבַּעְנָה שְׂפָתַי תְּהִלָּה, כִּי תְלַמְּדֵנִי חֻקֶּיךָ. תַּעַן לְשׁוֹנִי אִמְרָתֶךָ, כִּי כָל מִצְוֹתֶיךָ צֶּדֶק. תְּהִי יָדְךָ לְעָזְרֵנִי, כִּי פִקּוּדֶיךָ בָחָרְתִּי. תָּאַבְתִּי לִישׁוּעָתְךָ, יהוה; וְתוֹרָתְךָ שַׁעֲשֻׁעָי. תְּחִי נַפְשִׁי וּתְהַלְלֶךָּ, וּמִשְׁפָּטֶךָ יַעְזְרֻנִי. תָּעִיתִי כְּשֶׂה אֹבֵד, בַּקֵּשׁ עַבְדֶּךָ; כִּי מִצְוֹתֶיךָ לֹא שָׁכָחְתִּי.

אָנָּא בְּכֹחַ גְּדֻלַּת יְמִינְךָ תַּתִּיר צְרוּרָה, קַבֵּל רִנַּת עַמְּךָ שַׂגְּבֵנוּ טַהֲרֵנוּ נוֹרָא, נָא גִבּוֹר דּוֹרְשֵׁי יִחוּדְךָ כְּבָבַת שָׁמְרֵם בָּרְכֵם טַהֲרֵם רַחֲמֵם צִדְקָתְךָ תָּמִיד גָּמְלֵם, חֲסִין קָדוֹשׁ בְּרֹב טוּבְךָ נַהֵל עֲדָתֶךָ, יָחִיד גֵּאֶה לְעַמְּךָ פְּנֵה זוֹכְרֵי קְדֻשָּׁתֶךָ, שַׁוְעָתֵנוּ קַבֵּל וּשְׁמַע צַעֲקָתֵנוּ יוֹדֵעַ תַּעֲלֻמוֹת, בָּרוּךְ שֵׁם כְּבוֹד מַלְכוּתוֹ לְעוֹלָם וָעֶד.

It is customary to recite supplications upon visiting the graves of one's parents. Although there are various customs in this regard, and one may surely pour out his heart expressing his needs in his own way, the following texts are used by many.

◄§ Upon Visiting the Grave of a Father

שָׁלוֹם *Peace upon you my master, my father, and my teacher; my glory, my splendor, and my majesty. It is my duty to honor you in your life as in your death, for I am flesh of your flesh, bone of your bone, and of your limb and blood, since you took part in my creation as I emerged on this world. The intention was for the good as, for the sake of His righteousness, Hashem built skin, flesh, and sinews upon my soul, to bring me upon the surface of His populated world in the hope that I would develop from it to influence the body to follow the soul, to become entirely like it, and to grant me the abundant, hidden good, where the lawgiver's portion is concealed.*

But because of the circumstances that cause anxiety over the source of gold, and other changing matters that cause the wheel of fortune to be overturned — and because of their abundance — I could not withstand the ambush that lurks in every chamber. It has built up against

שָׁלוֹם עָלֶיךָ, אֲדוֹנִי, אָבִי, וּמוֹרִי; הוֹדִי, זִיוִי, וַהֲדָרִי עָלַי מֻטָּל לְכַבֵּד אוֹתְךָ בְּחַיֶּיךָ וּבְמוֹתְךָ, כִּי אֲנִי בָּשָׂר מִבְּשָׂרְךָ, וְעֶצֶם מֵעֲצָמֶיךָ, וּמֵאֵיבָרֶיךָ וְדָמְךָ, אַחֲרֵי הֱיוֹתְךָ מְשֻׁתָּף בִּבְרִיאָתִי לָעוֹלָם הַזֶּה בְּצֵאתִי. אֲשֶׁר לְטוֹבָה הָיְתָה הַכַּוָּנָה כַּאֲשֶׁר עַל נִשְׁמָתִי עוֹר וּבָשָׂר וְגִידִים בָּנָה, יהוה חָפֵץ, לְמַעַן צִדְקוֹ, לַהֲבִיאֵנִי עַל פְּנֵי תֵבֵל אַרְצוֹ אוּלַי אֶבָּנֶה אָנֹכִי מִמֶּנָּה לְהַמְשִׁיךְ הַגּוּף אַחַר הַנְּשָׁמָה, לִהְיוֹת כָּל כְּמִינָה, וּלְזַכּוֹתִי לְרֹב טוֹב הַצָּפוּן אֲשֶׁר שָׁם חֶלְקַת מְחוֹקֵק סָפוּן.

אַךְ מִסִּבּוֹת מַטְרֵד בַּת מֵי זָהָב, וּשְׁאָר דְּבָרִים אֲשֶׁר מִסִּבּוֹת מִתְהַפֵּךְ וְגַלְגִּלָּא דְּיוֹמָא הוּא דְּהָדַר וְאֶת נָהַב אֵין אֲנִי יָכוֹל לַעֲמוֹד בְּהָאוֹרֵב הַיּוֹשֵׁב בְּהֶחָדֶר. וּבָנָה עָלַי

me and surrounded me with huge barricades, a fence on this side of me and a fence on that. I could not withstand it and my malodorous deed gave forth its scent while the King was yet on His throne. I corrupted my deeds and hampered my livelihood, such and such have I done! And now, after all that has occurred, the cause is surely ours — but not in rebellion and treachery have I done this. The causes of my degraded acts are obvious from my degraded acts [themselves].

But behold! — after my repentance I am remorseful. I have taken my deeds to heart, and after becoming aware [of my shortcomings], I slapped my thigh, saying to myself, "I have summoned you to curse my foe [i.e., the evil inclination], but behold you have blessed him." And now, my master, my father, and teacher, my tutor and parent — not myself alone have I harmed, but you as well have I betrayed, although I should have brought you merit, raised you to a higher level. This, not this [did I do]! What was lowly I raised aloft, and what was aloft I laid low. Of such as me has it been said, children whom I nurtured and raised have betrayed me.

Nevertheless, though this is true, a father retains his mercy toward his son. Let you and I seek mercy from Him Who is above all the exalted ones, Whose works are upright and pure, and in Whose Sanctuary all proclaim "Glory"; Who dwells with the downtrodden and the humble-spirited, to revive the heart of the downtrodden and those who walk bent over. May He be gracious to me and say, "Redeem him from descending to the Pit; may his bread not be diminished and may he not die [to go down] to the grave." For many are my groans because of the hindering pricks. Because of this my heart aches and all my nurtured organs ache.

But I anticipate the salvation of God; though I have fallen I shall arise. May God hear and respond, and say, "I have forgiven." The groaning and wailing of my soul — may He accept it in atonement for my sins, like an offering of bulls and rams, accompanied by trumpets and the sound of a flute.

Behold! I have raised my hand to Hashem. And you, too, heaven forfend that you refrain from praying for me, for great is a father's mercy upon a son. A father's mercy upon a son is such that he prepares him a staff as sturdy as a brick mold to support him.

Stand up from your bed and arouse your love as of old. Arouse as well the angel of my fortune to pray for me, and may he hasten to do it bit by bit, begging mercy for me from the God

וַיַּקֵּף מְצוֹדִים גְּדוֹלִים, גָּדֵר מִזֶּה וּמִזֶּה גָּדֵר. וְלֹא יָכֹלְתִּי לַעֲמוֹד בּוֹ וְנִרְדִּי נָתַן רֵיחוֹ עַד שֶׁהַמֶּלֶךְ בִּמְסִבּוֹ. וַהֲרֵעוֹתִי אֶת מַעֲשַׂי וְקִפַּחְתִּי אֶת פַּרְנָסָתִי, וְכָזֹאת וְכָזֹאת עָשִׂיתִי! וְעַתָּה, אַחֲרֵי כָל הַבָּא, וַדַּאי לָנוּ הַסִּבָּה אַךְ לֹא בְּמֶרֶד וּבְמַעַל פָּעֲלֻתִי פּוֹעַל. וְהַסִּבּוֹת יְדוּעוֹת מִמַּעֲשַׂי הַגְּרוּעוֹת.

וְהִנֵּה אַחֲרֵי שׁוּבִי נִחַמְתִּי. וּמִמַּעֲשַׂי לְלִבִּי שַׂמְתִּי וְאַחֲרֵי הַוָּדְעִי, סָפַקְתִּי עַל יָרֵךְ, בֵּאֱמוֹר לְנַפְשִׁי לָקוֹב אוֹיְבַי קְרָאתִיךְ וְהִנֵּה בֵּרַכְתָּ בָרֵךְ. וְעַתָּה אֲדוֹנִי אָבִי וּמוֹרִי, מַלְפְנִי וּמְעַבְּדֵנִי וְהוֹרִי לֹא לְנַפְשִׁי לְבַד הֲרֵעוֹתִי, אַךְ גַּם נֶגְדְּךָ פָּשַׁעְתִּי עֵקֶב אֲשֶׁר הָיָה לִי לְזַכּוֹתֶךָ, לְמַעֲלָה רָמָה לְהַעֲלוֹתֶךָ. זֹאת לֹא זֹאת. הַשְּׁפָלָה הִגְבַּהְתִּי, וְהַגְּבוֹהָה הִשְׁפַּלְתִּי. וְעָלַי נֶאֱמַר, פָּשְׁעוּ בִי בָּנִים גִּדַּלְתִּי וְרוֹמַמְתִּי.

אַךְ אָמְנָם כֵּן, עֲדַיִן רַחֲמֵי הָאָב עַל הַבֵּן, וַאֲנִי וְאַתָּה נְבַקֵּשׁ רַחֲמִים מֵרָם עַל רָמִים, וַזַךְ וְיָשָׁר פָּעֳלוֹ וּבְהֵיכָלוֹ כָּבוֹד אוֹמֵר כֻּלּוֹ שׁוֹכֵן אֶת דַּכָּא וּשְׁפַל רוּחַ לְהַחֲיוֹת לֵב נִדְכָּאִים וְהוֹלֵךְ שְׁחוֹחַ. יְחָנֵּנִי וְיֹאמַר פְּדָעֵהוּ מֵרֶדֶת שַׁחַת, וְלֹא יֶחְסַר לַחְמוֹ וְלֹא יָמוּת לַשַּׁחַת. כִּי רַבּוֹת מְאֹד אַנְחוֹתַי מִסִּבּוֹת הַמּוֹנְעוֹת. וְעַל זֶה דָוָה לִבִּי וְכָל אֵבָרַי מְטַפָּחוֹת וּמְעֻנּוֹת.

אַף לִישׁוּעַת יהוה קִוִּיתִי, כִּי נָפַלְתִּי קָמְתִּי. יִשְׁמַע אֵל וְיַעֲנֶה, וְיֹאמַר סָלַחְתִּי. וְנַפְשִׁי אֲשֶׁר גְּנוּחֵי גָנַח וְיִלּוּלֵי יְלִיל יִקַּח לְכַפָּרַת חַטָּאתִי, כְּהַקְרָבַת פָּרִים וְאֵילִים, בַּחֲצוֹצְרוֹת וְקוֹל חָלִיל.

וְהִנֵּה הֲרִימוֹתִי אֶל יהוה יָדִי. וְגַם אַתָּה, חָלִילָה לְךָ מֵחֲדוֹל מִלְהִתְפַּלֵּל בַּעֲדִי, בַּאֲשֶׁר עַד כַּאן רַחֲמֵי הָאָב עַל הַבֵּן. וְרַחֲמֵי דְּאַבָּא אַבָּרָא דְּאִית לֵיהּ לְהָכִין אוֹתוֹ לְסַעֲדוֹ בְּמִשְׁעַנְתּוֹ כְּמוֹ בְּמַלְבֵּן.

מִמִּשְׁכָּבְךָ עִמְדִי נָא וְאַהֲבָה הַיְשָׁנָה עוֹרְרָה נָא, וְגַם עוֹרֵר אֶת מַלְאַךְ מַזָּלִי לְהִתְפַּלֵּל בִּגְלָלִי, וִימַהֵר לַעֲשׂוֹת אוֹתוֹ קַמָּא קַמָּא, דְּמַטּוּ יְבַקֵּשׁ עָלַי רַחֲמִים מֵהָאֵל

Who can be trusted to keep His covenant. Proclaim now: "O Merciful and Compassionate God, Slow to anger, Preserver of kindness for thousands of generations, Master of all creatures, Who sees the outcome from the beginning, Who said and it came into being that the earth should produce a living being according to its specie; and that man, whose wisdom sings in the public, be born, built in His likeness, in his image, fruit of a tree of life in a partnership of man and woman, with the Divine Presence." Whoever leaves behind a son is as if his body is at rest, but not dead; it is one of the commandments of Hashem his God to produce him. Now behold! Your servant has found grace in your eyes, and your kindness that you did with me has grown to keep my soul alive and to make for me a remnant in the world, to be for me a great salvation from the hand of my accuser, my antagonist, to go free.

But I cannot escape lest the evil overtake me and I die a second death. When I see the bad fortune of my homeland, which is downtrodden and afflicted, and I cannot come to achieve the purpose of the [Divine] intention, upon whose foundation [man] was created to safeguard the path to the Tree of Life, for the labor was too much for them because of causes that hinder and cause anxiety.

Today, please descend ten descents, for behold! you are there and we are here. Let us call to Him Who rests with the downtrodden, may He remove the hindrance from us, thrust it away to a wilderness and wasteland and let it move away so that I will be able to serve Him wholeheartedly, from now and forever, so that I shall instruct my children and my household after me for the generations, that they may keep the way of Hashem, doing charity and justice.

May Hashem illuminate and set aflame the stars of heaven, and let Him not bring me up in the midst of my days. May I be among those who stay alive in Your hand for a lifetime, and until the last clod may I have peace upon the earth. May my light burst forth like the dawn, and may my cure soon sprout ; may He rescue me, deliver me, and save me from every travail and distress, sin and guilt, and from all who stand over me to harm me, and from evil people and libels, and from all evils that tumultuously come upon the world and its neighborhoods.

May He open my heart through His Torah and imbue my heart with His love and awe, and may He grant me grace, kindness, and mercy in His eyes and in the eyes of all who see me. May He strengthen and fortify my hand

הַנֶּאֱמָן בִּבְרִיתוֹ. וְאִמְרִי נָא, אֵל רַחוּם, וְחַנּוּן אֶרֶךְ אַפַּיִם, נוֹצֵר חֶסֶד לָאֲלָפִים, רִבּוֹן כָּל הַבְּרִיּוֹת, הַמַּבִּיט מֵרֵאשִׁית אַחֲרִית, וְהוּא אָמַר וַיְהִי תּוֹצֵא הָאָרֶץ נֶפֶשׁ חַיָּה לְמִינָהּ, וְאָדָם, אֲשֶׁר בַּחוּץ חָכְמָתוֹ תָרוֹנָה, לְהוֹלִיד בִּדְמוּתוֹ, בְּצַלְמוֹ זֶה מִזֶּה מִבְנֶה פְּרִי עֵץ חַיִּים, בְּשֻׁתָּפוּת אִישׁ וְאִשָּׁה עִם הַשְּׁכִינָה. וְכָל הַמַּנִּיחַ בֵּן נִקְרֵאת גְּוִיעָתוֹ שְׁכִיבָה וְלֹא מִיתָה, אַחַת מִמִּצְוֹת יהוה אֱלֹהָיו בַּעֲשׂוֹתָהּ, וְהִנֵּה נָא מָצָא עַבְדְּךָ חֵן בְּעֵינֶיךָ וַתַּגְדֵּל חַסְדְּךָ אֲשֶׁר עָשִׂיתָ עִמָּדִי לְהַחֲיוֹת אֶת נַפְשִׁי וְלָשׂוּם לִי שְׁאֵרִית בָּאָרֶץ, לִהְיוֹת לִי לִפְלֵיטָה גְדוֹלָה מִיַּד מְקַטְרִיגִי, וּבַעַל מִשְׁפָּטִי, לָצֵאת לַחָפְשִׁי.

וְאָנֹכִי לֹא אוּכַל לְהִמָּלֵט פֶּן תִּדְבָּקֵנִי הָרָעָה וָמַתִּי מִיתָה תִנְיָנָא. בִּרְאוֹתִי רָעוֹת מוֹלַדְתִּי אֲשֶׁר הוּא מְדֻכָּא וּמְעֻנֶּה, וְאֵינִי יָכוֹל לָבוֹא לְהַשִּׂיג תַּכְלִית הַכַּוָּנָה אֲשֶׁר יְסוֹדוֹ עָלָיו נִבְנָה לִשְׁמוֹר אֶת דֶּרֶךְ עֵץ הַחַיִּים, עַל כִּי הַמְּלָאכָה הָיְתָה רַבָּה מֵהֶם מִסִּבּוֹת הַמּוֹנְעוֹת וּמַטְרִידוֹת.

וְהַיּוֹם רַד מְאֹד עֲשֶׂר יְרִידוֹת, וְהִנֵּה, אַתָּה מֵהֵנָּה וַאֲנַן מֵהָכָא. נִקְרָא לְשׁוֹכֵן אֶת דַּכָּא, יָסִיר מִמֶּנִּי הַמּוֹנֵעַ, יַדִּיחֶנּוּ אֶל אֶרֶץ צִיָּה וּשְׁמָמָה וְנוֹעַ יָנוּעַ לְמַעַן אוּכַל לְעָבְדוֹ בְּלֵבָב שָׁלֵם, מֵעַתָּה וְעַד עוֹלָם, וּלְמַעַן אֲשֶׁר אֲצַוֶּה אֶת בָּנַי וְאֶת בֵּיתִי אַחֲרַי לְדוֹרוֹתָם, וְשָׁמְרוּ דֶּרֶךְ יהוה, צְדָקָה וּמִשְׁפָּט לַעֲשׂוֹתָם.

וְיָאֵר יהוה וְיָהֵל כּוֹכְבֵי שָׁמַיִם, וְאַל יַעֲלֵנִי בַּחֲצִי יָמָי. וְאֶהְיֶה מִמָּתִים יָדְךָ מֵחֶלֶד, וְעַד זְבוּלָא בַתְרַיְתָא לֶהֱוֵי לִי שְׁלָמָא עַל פְּנֵי חָלֶד. וְיִבָּקַע כַּשַּׁחַר אוֹרִי, וַאֲרוּכָתִי מְהֵרָה יַצְמִיחַ, וְיַצִּילֵנִי וִימַלְּטֵנִי, וִיפַלְּטֵנִי מִכָּל צָרָה וְצוּקָה, וְעָוֹן וְאַשְׁמָה, וּמִכָּל הָעוֹמְדִים עָלַי לְהַזִּיקֵנִי, וּמִבְּנֵי אָדָם הָרָעִים וּמַעֲלִילוֹת, וּמִכָּל שְׁעוֹת רָעוֹת הַמִּתְרַגְּשׁוֹת לָבֹא בָּעוֹלָם וּבִגְלִילוֹת.

וְיִפְתַּח לִבִּי בְּתוֹרָתוֹ וְיָשֵׂם בְּלִבִּי אַהֲבָתוֹ וְיִרְאָתוֹ וְיִתְּנֵנִי לְחֵן, וּלְחֶסֶד, וּלְרַחֲמִים בְּעֵינָיו וּבְעֵינֵי כָל רוֹאָי. וִיחַזֵּק וִיאַמֵּץ יָדִי

to perform His service and engage in His Torah. May He prepare my livelihood and the livelihood of the members of my household expansively, broadly, and with a flow to all who are loyal to His covenant. May my Torah be my preoccupation and may He give me a good heart, a good share, a good comrade, a humble soul and a lowly spirit. May His Name not be desecrated by me. May He not make me a topic of gossip among people. May [spiritual] excision not be my fate, and may my hope not be disillusioned. May He not make me needful of the gifts of human beings, whose gifts are few and whose disgraces are abundant, only of His hand, that is full, open, holy, and generous.

May He set my share in His Torah with those who do His will wholeheartedly, and privilege me to see and raise children and grandchildren who engage in the Torah and commandments. May they be filled with, and diligent, in the Torah, prosperity, and honor, without lacking anything. May He privilege me to see the building of His House, Temple, Sanctuary, and City with His majesty and splendor, quickly in our days. May He save us through His mercy and abundant kindness from every travail and distress.

You, too, bequeather of my heart, may HASHEM fulfill all your requests and your desire to elevate your soul as you wish. May you rest and rise up to your destiny at the end of days, and may my soul live because of you. Upon His judgment may a palace be built.

לַעֲבוֹד עֲבוֹדָתוֹ וְלַעֲסוֹק בְּתוֹרָתוֹ. וְיַזְמִין פַּרְנָסָתִי וּפַרְנָסַת אַנְשֵׁי בֵיתִי בְּרֶוַח, וּבְמִלּוּי, וּבְשֶׁפַע לְכָל הַנֶּאֱמָנִים בִּבְרִיתוֹ. וּתְהֵא תוֹרָתִי אֻמָּנוּתִי וְיִתֶּן לִי לֵב טוֹב, וְחֵלֶק טוֹב, וְחָבֵר טוֹב, וְנֶפֶשׁ שְׁפָלָה וְרוּחַ נְמוּכָה. וְאַל יִתְחַלֵּל בִּי שְׁמוֹ וְאַל יַעֲשׂוּנִי שִׂיחָה בְּפִי הַבְּרִיּוֹת. וְאַל תְּהִי אַחֲרִיתִי לְהַכְרִית, וְתִקְנָתִי לְמַפַּח נֶפֶשׁ. וְאַל יַצְרִיכֵנִי לִידֵי מַתְּנַת בָּשָׂר וָדָם, שֶׁמַתְּנָתָם מְעוּטָה וְחֶרְפָּתָם מְרֻבָּה, כִּי אִם לְיָדוֹ הַמְּלֵאָה, הַפְּתוּחָה, הַקְּדוֹשָׁה, וְהָרְחָבָה.

וְיִתֵּן חֶלְקִי בְּתוֹרָתוֹ עִם עוֹשֵׂי רְצוֹנוֹ בְּלֵבָב שָׁלֵם, וִיזַכֵּנִי לִרְאוֹת וּלְגַדֵּל בָּנִים וּבְנֵי בָנִים הָעוֹסְקִים בַּתּוֹרָה וּבְמִצְוֹת. וְיִהְיוּ מְמֻלָּאִים וּמְזֻרָזִים בַּתּוֹרָה, בְּעֹשֶׁר, וּבְכָבוֹד, בְּלִי שׁוּם מַחְסוֹר. וִיזַכֵּנִי לִרְאוֹת בְּנִין בֵּיתוֹ, וְהֵיכָלוֹ, וּמִקְדָּשׁוֹ, וְעִירוֹ, בְּהוֹדוֹ, וְתִפְאַרְתּוֹ, בִּמְהֵרָה בְיָמֵינוּ, וְיוֹשִׁיעֵנִי בְּרַחֲמָיו וַחֲסָדָיו הַמְרֻבִּים מִכָּל צָרָה וְצוּקָה. וְגַם אַתָּה אֲדוֹנִי מוֹרִי וְאָבִי, אֲשֶׁר אַתָּה מוֹרָשֵׁי לְבָבִי יְמַלֵּא יהוה כָּל מִשְׁאֲלוֹתֶיךָ וְתַאֲנָתֶךָ לְהַעֲלוֹת נִשְׁמָתְךָ כְּחֶפְצֶךָ. וְתָנוּחַ וְתַעֲמוֹד לְגוֹרָלְךָ לְקֵץ הַיָּמִין, וְחָיְתָה נַפְשִׁי בִּגְלָלֶךָ. יִבָּנֶה עַל מִשְׁפָּטוֹ אַרְמוֹן:

◄§ Upon Visiting the Grave of a Mother

שָׁלוֹם Peace upon you, my mother, my teacher, who nurtured and raised me from the womb, from conception and from birth; you who suffered over me without limit, like the corner [of a field, which is left for the poor], first-fruits, and the pilgrimage. You cared for me all your days; all my needs were on you and on your hands. You brought me to the study hall to read, you trained me to study, and you brought me to fear of heaven.

Now that you have gone on your way, no merciful pedagogue has remained for me, who was always ready to do good for me. Now, it is difficult

שָׁלוֹם לָךְ, אִמִּי, מוֹרָתִי, אֲשֶׁר טִפַּחַתְּ וְרִבִּית אוֹתִי מִבֶּטֶן, מֵהֵרָיוֹן וּמִלֵּדָה, וְנִצְטַעַרְתְּ עָלַי בְּלִי שִׁעוּר כְּפֵאָה וּכְבִכּוּרִים וְהָרֵאָיוֹן. וְנִטְפַּלְתְּ בִּי כָל יָמַיִךְ, וְכָל מַחְסוֹרַי עָלַיִךְ וְעַל יָדַיִךְ. וְלִמַּיְתֵי לְבֵי רַבָּנָן לְאַקְרוּיֵי, וְלְאַתְנוּיֵי הִדְרַכְתֵּנִי, וּלְיִרְאַת שָׁמַיִם הֲבֵאתַנִי.

וְעַתָּה אֲשֶׁר הָלַכְתְּ בַּדֶּרֶךְ, לֹא נִשְׁאַר לִי כָמוֹךְ פֵּדָגוֹג רַחֲמָן, אֲשֶׁר בְּכָל עֵת לְטוֹבָתִי הָיָה מְזֻמָּן. וְעַתָּה, כַּאֲשֶׁר צַר

for me, as I see my road, my quarter, and my path, and this is my share from all my travail. The actions of my circuits [in this world] are without measure. I said to my soul, "Be not silent, to lose the exertion that my mother exerted for me." So I went to the field of tears and where they offer consolation for departed ones until I arrived at the home of my mother and the chamber of my parent, my mistress and my princess. Behold! she is garbed in a shroud and her spirit has risen on high.

I say, peace upon you and peace upon your rest and upon your life-force, spirit, and soul. Above all the women in the tent are you blessed, and may one always say about you "Rise up and shine, for your light has come, and the glory of HASHEM shall shine upon you, as on [Abraham,] the mighty one of the east. May you never suffer in the grave from the distress of your children, because of any pain or any lack. May your mercy be aroused upon me, your servant, to pray for me to HASHEM. May He hear the sound of my supplication when I say, "Please, O Awesome and Holy One, multiply Your forgiveness, forgive my wantonness, overwhelm Your attributes."

May He grant me life after the two Temples with His mercy, He Who makes peace in His heights.

May He provide me from His heavens with produce, bread, and sustenance with His mercy, and may He not be deaf to my tears when I call from the depths, like one who is poor and destitute. May He be gracious to me and say, "Redeem him that he not descend to the Pit, and may he not lack his bread and not die [going] to the grave."

May He privilege me to see children and grandchildren engaged in the Torah and commandments. May they not cease all day from fear of heaven and may they be people of the commandments, good reputations, and righteous people; free of any sin or guilt, and may they spend their days with good. Upon my knees may three and four generations be born, and may their hope and nature spread throughout the world. May You see from among the entire people who emerge from my loins God-fearing men of accomplishment, who merit the highest of all levels.

May your soul dwell in the shelter of the Garden of Eden near the upright ones, with the holy and pure Matriarchs, and may you

לִי, בִּרְאוֹתִי אָרְחִי, וְרִבְעִי, וּשְׁבִילִי, וְזֶה חֶלְקִי מִכָּל עֲמָלִי. לֹא נִתְּנוּ עֲלִילוֹת מַעְגָּלִי. אָמַרְתִּי לְנַפְשִׁי, אַל תִּדְמִי לְאַבֵּד הַיְגִיעָה שֶׁיָּגְעָה בִּי אִמִּי. וְהָלַכְתִּי שְׂדֵה בוֹכִים וּלְבֵית מַרְזֵחַ סְרוּחִים עַד שֶׁבָּאתִי אֶל בֵּית אִמִּי וּלְחֶדֶר הוֹרָתִי רַבָּתִי וְשָׂרָתִי. וְהִנֵּה הִיא לוּטָה בַשִּׂמְלָה וְרוּחָהּ הִיא הָעוֹלָה לְמָעְלָה.

וְאָמַרְתִּי שָׁלוֹם לָךְ וְשָׁלוֹם לִמְנוּחָתֵךְ, וּלְרוּחֵךְ, וּלְנַפְשֵׁךְ, וּלְנִשְׁמָתֵךְ. מִנָּשִׁים בָּאֹהֶל תְּבֹרָךְ, וְתָמִיד יֹאמַר עָלַיִךְ, קוּמִי אוֹרִי כִּי בָא אוֹרֵךְ, וּכְבוֹד יהוה עָלַיִךְ יִזְרָח, כְּאֵיתָן הָאֶזְרָח. וְלֹא תִצְטַעֲרִי לְעוֹלָם בְּצָרַת בָּנַיִךְ בַּקֶּבֶר מֵחֲמַת שׁוּם צַעַר וְחֶסְרוֹן שׁוּם דָּבָר. וְלִי, אֲנִי עַבְדֵּךְ, יֶהֱמוּ נָא עָלַי רַחֲמַיִךְ לְהִתְפַּלֵּל בַּעֲדִי אֶל יהוה. יִשְׁמַע קוֹל תַּחֲנוּנַי בְּאָמְרִי, אָנָּא נוֹרָא קָדוֹשׁ, תַּרְבֶּה מְחִילָתֶךָ, פְּשָׁעַי סְלוֹחַ, תְּגַלְגֵּל מִדּוֹתֶיךָ.

וִיחַיֵּנִי מִיּוֹמַיִם בְּרַחֲמָיו, עוֹשֶׂה שָׁלוֹם בִּמְרוֹמָיו.

וְיַסְפִּיק לִי מִשָּׁמָיו בָּר, וָלֶחֶם, וּמָזוֹן בְּרַחֲמָיו, וְאֶת דִּמְעָתִי אַל יֶחֱרַשׁ בְּקָרְאִי מִן הַמֵּצַר כְּעָנִי וָרָשׁ. יְחָנֵּנִי וְיֹאמַר, פְּדָעֵהוּ מֵרֶדֶת שַׁחַת, וְלֹא יֶחְסַר לַחְמוֹ וְלֹא יָמוּת לַשָּׁחַת.

וִיזַכֵּנִי לִרְאוֹת בָּנִים וּבְנֵי בָנִים עוֹסְקִים בַּתּוֹרָה וּבְמִצְוֹת, עוֹסְקִים בְּיִרְאַת יהוה כָּל הַיּוֹם וְלֹא יִהְיוּ פוֹסְקִים וְיִהְיוּ בַּעֲלֵי מִצְוֹת, וְשֵׁם טוֹב, וְצַדִּיקִים, וּמִכָּל עָוֹן וְאַשְׁמָה מְנֻקִּים, וּבְטוּב יְכַלּוּ יְמֵיהֶם. וְעַל בִּרְכַּי יֻלְּדוּ שְׁלֵשִׁים וְרִבֵּעִים וּבְכָל הָאָרֶץ יֵצֵא קַוָּם וְטִבְעָם. וְאַתָּה תֶחֱזֶה מִכָּל הָעָם יוֹצְאֵי חֲלָצַי אַנְשֵׁי חַיִל, יִרְאֵי אֱלֹהִים, זוֹכִים לְמַעֲלוֹת גְּבוֹהוֹת מֵעַל גְּבוֹהִים.

וְנִשְׁמָתֵךְ תִּשְׁכּוֹן בְּצֵל עֲצֵי עֵדֶן אֵצֶל יְשָׁרוֹת, עִם הָאִמָּהוֹת הַקְּדוֹשׁוֹת וְהַטְּהוֹרוֹת,

merit to stand up in life with the other tranquil women and the devout men and women of high caliber, and may you stand up to your destiny at the end of Days.

    May the God, HASHEM, *say this. Amen.*

וְתִזְכִּי לַעֲמֹד לִתְחִיָה עִם שְׁאָר נָשִׁים שַׁאֲנַנּוֹת וַחֲסִידִים וַחֲסִידוֹת בְּנֵי עֲלִיָה, וְתַעֲמְדִי לְגוֹרָלֵךְ לְקֵץ הַיָמִין. כֵּן יֹאמַר הָאֵל יהוה אָמֵן:

ON EREV ROSH HASHANAH AND EREV YOM KIPPUR AT THE GRAVES OF PARENTS AND FOREBEARS

צַדִּיקֵי O righteous ones, pillars of the world, may it be His will that you rest in honor. May the merit of your Torah study and good deeds stand by me, my household, all Jews who are attached to me, and the entire House of Israel. May it be your will, O God of mercy and supplications, King over all the world, that Your abundant mercies and kindnesses overwhelm Your attributes. May we be remembered

צַדִּיקֵי יְסוֹדֵי עוֹלָם, יְהִי רָצוֹן שֶׁתְּהֵא מְנוּחַתְכֶם בְּכָבוֹד. וּזְכוּת תַּלְמוּד תּוֹרַתְכֶם וּמַעֲשֵׂיכֶם הַטּוֹבִים יַעֲמָד לִי, וּלְבֵיתִי, וּלְכָל יִשְׂרָאֵל הַנִּלְוִים לִי, וּלְכָל בֵּית יִשְׂרָאֵל. יְהִי רָצוֹן לְפָנֶיךָ, אֱלֹהֵי הָרַחֲמִים וְהַסְּלִיחוֹת, מֶלֶךְ עַל כָּל הָאָרֶץ, שֶׁיִּתְגּוֹלְלוּ רַחֲמֶיךָ וַחֲסָדֶיךָ הַמְרֻבִּים עַל מִדּוֹתֶיךָ וְנִזָּכֵר

on Erev Rosh Hashanah:
    and inscribed before You
    on this Rosh Hashanah

on Erev Rosh Hashanah:
וְנִכָּתֵב לְפָנֶיךָ בְּזֶה רֹאשׁ הַשָּׁנָה

on Erev Yom Kippur:
    and sealed before You
    on this Yom Kippur

on Erev Yom Kippur:
וְנֵחָתֵם לְפָנֶיךָ בְּזֶה יוֹם הַכִּפּוּרִים

for forgiveness and pardon, and to atone on it for all our errors, transgressions, and wanton sins, and for a good and perfected year, for good life, peace, livelihood, sustenance; for satiety, for blessing; for a year of redemption and salvation; a year of blessing and success in all our handiwork; a year of relief and rescue, tranquility and contentment from every terror and confusion, mishap and evil decree. May we merit wealth and honor; and may Satan and the evil inclination have no dominion over us.

    May we find grace and good understanding in Your eyes and in the eyes of all who see us. O Merciful and Compassionate One Who hears prayers, incline to us in all this that we have requested of You, for the sake of Your abundant mercies and kindnesses, for the sake of all these righteous people and the merit of all the righteous and devout ones of the world. Do not turn us away from You empty-handed, for You are the One Who hears prayer.

לִסְלִיחָה וְלִמְחִילָה, וּלְכַפֵּר בּוֹ עַל כָּל חַטֹּאתֵינוּ, וַעֲוֹנוֹתֵינוּ, וּפִשְׁעֵינוּ, וּלְשָׁנָה טוֹבָה וּמְתֻקֶּנֶת, לְחַיִּים טוֹבִים, וּלְשָׁלוֹם, לְפַרְנָסָה, וּלְכַלְכָּלָה, לְשָׂבַע, וְלִבְרָכָה, וּלְשְׁנַת גְּאֻלָּה וִישׁוּעָה, וּשְׁנַת בְּרָכָה וְהַצְלָחָה בְּכָל מַעֲשֵׂה יָדֵינוּ, וּשְׁנַת רֶוַח וְהַצָּלָה, הַשְׁקֵט וּמְנוּחָה מִכָּל פַּחַד וּבֶהָלָה, מִכָּל תַּקָּלָה וּגְזֵרָה רָעָה. וְשֶׁנִּזְכֶּה לְעֹשֶׁר וְכָבוֹד, וְאַל יִשְׁלָט בָּנוּ שָׂטָן וְיֵצֶר הָרָע.

וְנִמְצָא חֵן וְשֵׂכֶל טוֹב בְּעֵינֶיךָ וּבְעֵינֵי כָל רוֹאֵינוּ. רַחוּם וְחַנּוּן, שׁוֹמֵעַ תְּפִלָּה, הַעֲתֵר לָנוּ עַל כָּל זֹאת שֶׁבִּקַּשְׁנוּ לְפָנֶיךָ, לְמַעַן רַחֲמֶיךָ וַחֲסָדֶיךָ הַמְרֻבִּים, וּלְמַעַן זְכוּת הַצַּדִּיקִים הָאֵלּוּ וּזְכוּת כָּל צַדִּיקֵי וַחֲסִידֵי עוֹלָם. וְאַל תְּשִׁיבֵנִי רֵיקָם מִלְּפָנֶיךָ, כִּי אַתָּה שׁוֹמֵעַ תְּפִלָּה:

◄§ Keil Malei Rachamim

אֵל O God, full of mercy, Who dwells on high, grant proper rest on the wings of the Divine Presence — in the lofty levels of the holy and the pure ones, who shine like the glow of the firmament — for the soul of (deceased's Hebrew name) the [son/daughter] of (deceased's father's name) who went on to [his/her] world, because they will contribute to charity in remembrance of [his/her] soul. May [his/her] resting place be in the Garden of Eden — therefore may the Master of mercy shelter [him/her] in the shelter of His wings for eternity; and may He bind [his/her] soul in the Bond of Life. HASHEM is [his/her] heritage, and may [he/she] repose in peace on [his/her] resting place. Now let us respond: Amen.

אֵל מָלֵא רַחֲמִים שׁוֹכֵן בַּמְּרוֹמִים הַמְצֵא מְנוּחָה נְכוֹנָה עַל כַּנְפֵי הַשְּׁכִינָה בְּמַעֲלוֹת קְדוֹשִׁים וּטְהוֹרִים כְּזֹהַר הָרָקִיעַ מַזְהִירִים אֶת נִשְׁמַת (שם הנפטר/הנפטרת) [בֶּן/ בַּת] (שם אבי הנפטר/הנפטרת) [שֶׁהָלַךְ לְעוֹלָמוֹ/ שֶׁהָלְכָה לְעוֹלָמָהּ] בַּעֲבוּר שֶׁנָּדְבוּ צְדָקָה בְּעַד הַזְכָּרַת [נִשְׁמָתוֹ/נִשְׁמָתָהּ] בְּגַן עֵדֶן תְּהֵא [מְנוּחָתוֹ/מְנוּחָתָהּ] לָכֵן בְּעַל הָרַחֲמִים [יַסְתִּירֵהוּ/יַסְתִּירֶהָ] בְּסֵתֶר כְּנָפָיו לְעוֹלָמִים וְיִצְרוֹר בִּצְרוֹר הַחַיִּים אֶת [נִשְׁמָתוֹ/נִשְׁמָתָהּ] יהוה הוּא [נַחֲלָתוֹ/ נַחֲלָתָהּ] [וְיָנוּחַ/וְתָנוּחַ] עַל [מִשְׁכָּבוֹ/ מִשְׁכָּבָהּ] בְּשָׁלוֹם וְנֹאמַר אָמֵן:

◄§ Mourner's Kaddish

The male mourners recite the following Kaddish [a transliteration of this Kaddish appears on page 469]:

יִתְגַּדַּל May His great Name grow exalted and sanctified (Cong.— Amen.) in the world that He created as He willed. May He give reign to His kingship, [Nusach Sefard: and cause his salvation to sprout, and bring near His Messiah (Cong. — Amen)] in your lifetimes and in your days, and in the lifetimes of the entire Family of Israel, swiftly and soon. Now respond: Amen. (Cong. — Amen)

יִתְגַּדַּל וְיִתְקַדַּשׁ שְׁמֵהּ רַבָּא. (.Cong — אָמֵן.) בְּעָלְמָא דִי בְרָא כִרְעוּתֵהּ. וְיַמְלִיךְ מַלְכוּתֵהּ, [נוסח ספרד: וְיַצְמַח פֻּרְקָנֵהּ וִיקָרֵב מְשִׁיחֵהּ.)[(.Cong — אָמֵן.)] בְּחַיֵּיכוֹן וּבְיוֹמֵיכוֹן וּבְחַיֵּי דְכָל בֵּית יִשְׂרָאֵל, בַּעֲגָלָא וּבִזְמַן קָרִיב. וְאִמְרוּ: אָמֵן. (.Cong — אָמֵן.)

Cong., then mourner:
May His great Name be blessed forever and ever.

Cong., then mourner:
יְהֵא שְׁמֵהּ רַבָּא מְבָרַךְ לְעָלַם וּלְעָלְמֵי עָלְמַיָּא.

Mourner continues: Blessed, praised, glorified, exalted, extolled, mighty, upraised, and lauded be the Name of the Holy One, Blessed is He (Cong. — Blessed is He) — (from Rosh Hashanah to Yom Kippur add: exceedingly) beyond any blessing and song, praise and consolation that are uttered in the world. Now respond: Amen. (Cong. — Amen)

Mourner continues:
יִתְבָּרַךְ וְיִשְׁתַּבַּח וְיִתְפָּאַר וְיִתְרוֹמַם וְיִתְנַשֵּׂא וְיִתְהַדָּר וְיִתְעַלֶּה וְיִתְהַלָּל שְׁמֵהּ דְּקֻדְשָׁא בְּרִיךְ הוּא (.Cong — בְּרִיךְ הוּא.) — לְעֵלָּא מִן כָּל — from Rosh Hashanah to Yom Kippur) לְעֵלָּא וּלְעֵלָּא מִכָּל] בִּרְכָתָא וְשִׁירָתָא תֻּשְׁבְּחָתָא וְנֶחֱמָתָא, דַּאֲמִירָן בְּעָלְמָא. וְאִמְרוּ: אָמֵן. (.Cong — אָמֵן.)

May there be abundant peace from Heaven, and (good) life, upon us and upon all Israel. Now respond: Amen. (Cong. — Amen)

יְהֵא שְׁלָמָא רַבָּא מִן שְׁמַיָּא, וְחַיִּים (טוֹבִים) עָלֵינוּ וְעַל כָּל יִשְׂרָאֵל. וְאִמְרוּ: אָמֵן. (.Cong — אָמֵן.)

Take three steps back. Bow left and say, 'He Who makes peace . . .'; bow right and say, 'may He . . .'; bow forward and say, 'and upon all Israel . . .'

He Who makes [from Rosh Hashanah to Yom Kippur some add: the] peace in His heights, may He make peace upon us, and upon all Israel. Now respond: Amen. (Cong. — Amen.)

from Rosh Hashanah to Yom) עֹשֶׂה שָׁלוֹם Kippur some substitute — הַשָּׁלוֹם) בִּמְרוֹמָיו, הוּא יַעֲשֶׂה שָׁלוֹם עָלֵינוּ, וְעַל כָּל יִשְׂרָאֵל. וְאִמְרוּ: אָמֵן. (.Cong — אָמֵן.)

◆§ Study of Mishnah In Memory of the Deceased

It is customary to study Mishnah in memory of the deceased. Many study the following chapter (*Mikvaos* ch. 7) because the first letters of *mishnayos* 4-7 spell the word נְשָׁמָה, *soul,* (see 16:33; 40:17,18; 44:13).

[1] Some [substances] complete a mikveh and [certainly] do not invalidate [it]; [some] invalidate [a mikveh] and do not complete [it]; [and some] neither complete nor invalidate [it].

These complete and do not invalidate: snow, hail, sleet, ice, salt and liquid mud. Said Rabbi Akiva: 'Rabbi Yishmael argued with me saying: 'Snow cannot complete a mikveh.' " But the citizens of Meidva testified in his [i.e., Rabbi Yishmael's] name that he said to them, "Go and bring snow and make a mikveh from the beginning.' Rabbi Yochanan ben Nuri says: Hailstones are like water.

In what instance do they complete and not invalidate? If a mikveh contains forty se'ah less one and a se'ah of [one of] these [substances] falls into it, it has completed [the mikveh]; thus they complete but do not invalidate.

[2] These [substances] invalidate [a mikveh] and do not complete [it]: water, whether contaminated or not contaminated; water in which fruits or vegetables have been soaked; water in which fruits and vegetables have been cooked; and marc-wine which has not yet fermented.

In what instance do they invalidate and not complete? If a mikveh contains forty se'ah less one kortov and a kortov of [one of] these [substances] falls into it, it has not completed [the mikveh], but it invalidates, with three log.

But other liquids, fruit juices, fish-water, fish-oil, and marc-wine which has fermented, sometimes complete [a mikveh], and sometimes do not complete [a mikveh]. In what instances? If a mikveh contains forty se'ah less one and a se'ah of [one of] these [substances] falls into it, it has not completed [the mikveh]. If [the mikveh] contained forty se'ah, and he put in a se'ah [of one of these substances], then removed a se'ah, it [the mikveh] is valid.

[3] If one rinsed olive baskets or grape baskets in it [a valid mikveh] thus changing its color, it is valid. Rabbi Yose says: Dye-water invalidates [a mikveh] if there are three log, but does not invalidate it by change of color.

[א] יֵשׁ מַעֲלִין אֶת הַמִּקְוֶה וְלֹא פוֹסְלִין, פוֹסְלִין וְלֹא מַעֲלִין, לֹא מַעֲלִין וְלֹא פוֹסְלִין.

אֵלּוּ מַעֲלִין וְלֹא פוֹסְלִין: הַשֶּׁלֶג, וְהַבָּרָד, וְהַכְּפוֹר, וְהַגְּלִיד, וְהַמֶּלַח, וְהַטִּיט הַנָּרוֹק. אָמַר רַבִּי עֲקִיבָא: הָיָה רַבִּי יִשְׁמָעֵאל דָּן כְּנֶגְדִּי לוֹמַר: הַשֶּׁלֶג אֵינוֹ מַעֲלֶה אֶת הַמִּקְוֶה. וְהֵעִידוּ אַנְשֵׁי מֵידְבָא מִשְּׁמוֹ, שֶׁאָמַר לָהֶם: צְאוּ וְהָבִיאוּ שֶׁלֶג וַעֲשׂוּ מִקְוֶה בַּתְּחִלָּה. רַבִּי יוֹחָנָן בֶּן נוּרִי אוֹמֵר: אֶבֶן הַבָּרָד כְּמָיִם.

כֵּיצַד מַעֲלִין וְלֹא פוֹסְלִין? מִקְוֶה שֶׁיֵּשׁ בּוֹ אַרְבָּעִים סְאָה חָסֵר אַחַת, נָפַל מֵהֶם סְאָה לְתוֹכוֹ, וְהֶעֱלָהוּ, נִמְצְאוּ – מַעֲלִין וְלֹא פוֹסְלִין.

[ב] אֵלּוּ פוֹסְלִין וְלֹא מַעֲלִין: הַמַּיִם בֵּין טְמֵאִים בֵּין טְהוֹרִים, וּמֵי כְבָשִׁים, וּמֵי שְׁלָקוֹת, וְהַתֶּמֶד עַד שֶׁלֹּא הֶחֱמִיץ.

כֵּיצַד פוֹסְלִין וְלֹא מַעֲלִין? מִקְוֶה שֶׁיֵּשׁ בּוֹ אַרְבָּעִים סְאָה חָסֵר קוֹרְטוֹב, וְנָפַל מֵהֶן קוֹרְטוֹב לְתוֹכוֹ – לֹא הֶעֱלָהוּ; פּוֹסְלוֹ בִּשְׁלֹשָׁה לֻגִּין.

אֲבָל שְׁאָר הַמַּשְׁקִין, וּמֵי פֵרוֹת, וְהַצִּיר, וְהַמֻּרְיָס, וְהַתֶּמֶד מִשֶּׁהֶחֱמִיץ – פְּעָמִים מַעֲלִין וּפְעָמִים שֶׁאֵינָן מַעֲלִין. כֵּיצַד? מִקְוֶה שֶׁיֵּשׁ בּוֹ אַרְבָּעִים סְאָה חָסֵר אַחַת נָפַל לְתוֹכוֹ סְאָה מֵהֶם – לֹא הֶעֱלָהוּ. הָיוּ בּוֹ אַרְבָּעִים סְאָה, נָתַן סְאָה וְנָטַל סְאָה, הֲרֵי זֶה כָּשֵׁר.

[ג] הֵדִיחַ בּוֹ סַלֵּי זֵיתִים וְסַלֵּי עֲנָבִים, וְשִׁנּוּ אֶת מַרְאָיו – כָּשֵׁר. רַבִּי יוֹסֵי אוֹמֵר: מֵי הַצֶּבַע פּוֹסְלִין אוֹתוֹ בִּשְׁלֹשָׁה לֻגִּין, וְאֵינָן פּוֹסְלִין אוֹתוֹ בְּשִׁנּוּי מַרְאֶה.

If wine or olive-water fell into it [the mikveh] and changed its color, it is invalid. What should one do? One should wait until rain falls and restores its color to the color of water. If it contained forty se'ah, he may draw [water, carry it] on his shoulder and place it into it [the mikveh], until its color returns to the color of water.

[4] If wine or olive-water fell into it [a mikveh] and changed the color of part [of the mikveh], if there are no longer forty se'ah with the color of water, one may not immerse in it.

[5] If three log of water — into which a kortov of wine had fallen and their color became like the color of wine — fell into a mikveh, they did not invalidate it.

If three log less a kortov of water — into which a kortov of milk had fallen and their color was like the color of water — fell into a mikveh, they did not invalidate it. Rabbi Yochanan ben Nuri says: Everything follows the color.

[6] If a mikveh contained exactly forty se'ah and two people immersed in it one after the other, the first is cleansed but the second [remains] contaminated. Rabbi Yehudah says: If the feet of the first were [still] touching the water, even the second is cleansed.

If one immersed a thick cloth in it [a mikveh of exactly forty se'ah] and lifted it out, [as long as] part of it touches the water [one who immerses in the mikveh] is cleansed. [If a mattress or a cushion of leather [is immersed in such a mikveh], as soon as one lifts their edges from the water, the water within them is she'uvin. What should one do? One should immerse them and remove them holding their bottoms upward.

[7] If one immersed a bed in it, then even if the legs sink into the thick mud it is cleansed, because the water comes first.

A mikveh of shallow water: he may press down [material on one side of the mikveh], even bundles of wood, even bundles of reeds, to raise the water [level], then he goes down and immerses.

If a needle was placed on the steps of a cave and one moved the water to and fro, as soon as a wave passes over it [the needle] is cleansed.

נָפַל לְתוֹכוֹ יַיִן וּמֹחַל, וְשִׁנּוּ אֶת מַרְאָיו — פָּסוּל. כֵּיצַד יַעֲשֶׂה? יַמְתִּין לוֹ עַד שֶׁיֵּרְדוּ גְשָׁמִים, וְיַחְזְרוּ מַרְאֵיהֶן לְמַרְאֵה הַמָּיִם. הָיוּ בוֹ אַרְבָּעִים סְאָה, מְמַלֵּא בְכָתֵף וְנוֹתֵן לְתוֹכוֹ, עַד שֶׁיַּחְזְרוּ מַרְאֵיהֶן לְמַרְאֵה הַמָּיִם.

[ד] **נָ**פַל לְתוֹכוֹ יַיִן אוֹ מֹחַל, וְשִׁנּוּ מִקְצָת מַרְאָיו: אִם אֵין בּוֹ מַרְאֵה מַיִם אַרְבָּעִים סְאָה, הֲרֵי זֶה לֹא יִטְבֹּל בּוֹ.

[ה] **שְׁ**לֹשָׁה לֻגִּין מַיִם, וְנָפַל לְתוֹכָן קֻרְטוֹב יַיִן, וַהֲרֵי מַרְאֵיהֶן כְּמַרְאֵה הַיַּיִן, וְנָפְלוּ לַמִּקְוֶה, לֹא פְסָלוּהוּ.

שְׁלֹשָׁה לֻגִּין מַיִם חָסֵר קֻרְטוֹב, וְנָפַל לְתוֹכָן קֻרְטוֹב חָלָב, וַהֲרֵי מַרְאֵיהֶן כְּמַרְאֵה הַמָּיִם, וְנָפְלוּ לַמִּקְוֶה — לֹא פְסָלוּהוּ. רַבִּי יוֹחָנָן בֶּן נוּרִי אוֹמֵר: הַכֹּל הוֹלֵךְ אַחַר הַמַּרְאֶה.

[ו] **מִ**קְוֶה שֶׁיֵּשׁ בּוֹ אַרְבָּעִים סְאָה מְכֻוָּנוֹת, יָרְדוּ שְׁנַיִם וְטָבְלוּ זֶה אַחַר זֶה — הָרִאשׁוֹן טָהוֹר, וְהַשֵּׁנִי טָמֵא. רַבִּי יְהוּדָה אוֹמֵר: אִם הָיוּ רַגְלָיו שֶׁל רִאשׁוֹן נוֹגְעוֹת בַּמַּיִם, אַף הַשֵּׁנִי טָהוֹר. הִטְבִּיל בּוֹ אֶת הַסָּגוֹס וְהֶעֱלָהוּ, מִקְצָתוֹ נוֹגֵעַ בַּמַּיִם — טָהוֹר.

הַכַּר וְהַכֶּסֶת שֶׁל עוֹר, כֵּיוָן שֶׁהִגְבִּיהַּ שִׂפְתוֹתֵיהֶם מִן הַמַּיִם — הַמַּיִם שֶׁבְּתוֹכָן שְׁאוּבִין. כֵּיצַד יַעֲשֶׂה? מַטְבִּילָן וּמַעֲלֶה אוֹתָן דֶּרֶךְ שׁוּלֵיהֶם.

[ז] **הִ**טְבִּיל בּוֹ אֶת הַמִּטָּה, אַף עַל פִּי שֶׁרַגְלֶיהָ שׁוֹקְעוֹת בְּטִיט הֶעָבֶה — טְהוֹרָה, מִפְּנֵי שֶׁהַמַּיִם מְקַדְּמִין.

מִקְוֶה שֶׁמֵּימָיו מְרֻדָּדִין, כּוֹבֵשׁ אֲפִלּוּ חֲבִילֵי עֵצִים, אֲפִלּוּ חֲבִילֵי קָנִים, כְּדֵי שֶׁיִּתְפְּחוּ הַמַּיִם, וְיוֹרֵד וְטוֹבֵל.

מַחַט שֶׁהִיא נְתוּנָה עַל מַעֲלוֹת הַמְּעָרָה, הָיָה מוֹלִיךְ וּמֵבִיא בַּמַּיִם, כֵּיוָן שֶׁעָבַר עָלֶיהָ הַגַּל — טְהוֹרָה.

◆§ The Rabbis' Kaddish

If a *minyan* is present, the mourners recite the Rabbi's *Kaddish* after the study of Mishnah.
[A transliteration of this *Kaddish* appears on page 470.]

יִתְגַּדַּל May His great Name grow exalted and sanctified (Cong. — *Amen.*) in the world that He created as He willed. May He give reign to His kingship, [*Nusach Sefard:* and cause his salvation to sprout, and bring near His Messiah (Cong. — *Amen*)] in your lifetimes and in your days, and in the lifetimes of the entire Family of Israel, swiftly and soon. Now respond: *Amen.* (Cong. — *Amen*)

Cong., then mourner:
May His great Name be blessed forever and ever.

Mourner continues: *Blessed, praised, glorified, exalted, extolled, mighty, upraised, and lauded be the Name of the Holy One, Blessed is He (Cong. — Blessed is He) — (from Rosh Hashanah to Yom Kippur add: exceedingly) beyond any blessing and song, praise and consolation that are uttered in the world. Now respond: Amen. (Cong. — Amen)*

Upon Israel, upon the teachers, their disciples and all of their disciples and upon all those who engage in the study of Torah, who are here or anywhere else; may they and you have abundant peace, grace, kindness, and mercy, long life, ample nourishment, and salvation from before their Father Who is in Heaven (and on earth). Now respond: Amen. (Cong. — Amen)

May there be abundant peace from Heaven, and (good) life, upon us and upon all Israel. Now respond: Amen. (Cong. — Amen)

Take three steps back. Bow left and say, '*He Who makes peace . . .*'; bow right and say, '*may He . . .*'; bow forward and say, '*and upon all Israel . . .*'

He Who makes [From Rosh Hashanah to Yom Kippur some add: *the*] *peace in His heights, may He, in His compassion make peace upon us, and upon all Israel. Now respond: Amen. (Cong. — Amen)*

Mourner remains standing in place for a few moments, then take three steps forward.

יִתְגַּדַּל וְיִתְקַדַּשׁ שְׁמֵהּ רַבָּא. (Cong. — אָמֵן.) בְּעָלְמָא דִּי בְרָא כִרְעוּתֵהּ. וְיַמְלִיךְ מַלְכוּתֵהּ, [נוסח ספרד: וְיַצְמַח פֻּרְקָנֵהּ וִיקָרֵב מְשִׁיחֵהּ. (Cong. — אָמֵן.)] בְּחַיֵּיכוֹן וּבְיוֹמֵיכוֹן וּבְחַיֵּי דְכָל בֵּית יִשְׂרָאֵל, בַּעֲגָלָא וּבִזְמַן קָרִיב. וְאִמְרוּ: אָמֵן. (Cong. — אָמֵן.)

Cong., then mourner:
יְהֵא שְׁמֵהּ רַבָּא מְבָרַךְ לְעָלַם וּלְעָלְמֵי עָלְמַיָּא.

Mourner continues:

יִתְבָּרַךְ וְיִשְׁתַּבַּח וְיִתְפָּאַר וְיִתְרוֹמַם וְיִתְנַשֵּׂא וְיִתְהַדָּר וְיִתְעַלֶּה וְיִתְהַלָּל שְׁמֵהּ דְּקֻדְשָׁא בְּרִיךְ הוּא (Cong. — בְּרִיךְ הוּא.) — from Rosh Hashanah to Yom Kippur) לְעֵלָּא מִן כָּל — לְעֵלָּא וּלְעֵלָּא מִכָּל) בִּרְכָתָא וְשִׁירָתָא תֻּשְׁבְּחָתָא וְנֶחֱמָתָא, דַּאֲמִירָן בְּעָלְמָא. וְאִמְרוּ: אָמֵן. (Cong. — אָמֵן.)

עַל יִשְׂרָאֵל וְעַל רַבָּנָן, וְעַל תַּלְמִידֵיהוֹן וְעַל כָּל תַּלְמִידֵי תַלְמִידֵיהוֹן, וְעַל כָּל מָאן דְּעָסְקִין בְּאוֹרַיְתָא, דִּי בְאַתְרָא הָדֵין וְדִי בְכָל אֲתַר וַאֲתַר. יְהֵא לְהוֹן וּלְכוֹן שְׁלָמָא רַבָּא, חִנָּא וְחִסְדָּא וְרַחֲמִין, וְחַיִּין אֲרִיכִין, וּמְזוֹנֵי רְוִיחֵי, וּפֻרְקָנָא, מִן קֳדָם אֲבוּהוֹן דִּי בִשְׁמַיָּא וְאַרְעָא. וְאִמְרוּ: אָמֵן. (Cong. — אָמֵן.)

יְהֵא שְׁלָמָא רַבָּא מִן שְׁמַיָּא, וְחַיִּים (טוֹבִים) עָלֵינוּ וְעַל כָּל יִשְׂרָאֵל. וְאִמְרוּ: אָמֵן. (Cong. — אָמֵן.)

from Rosh Hashanah to Yom) עֹשֶׂה שָׁלוֹם Kippur some substitute —הַשָּׁלוֹם) בִּמְרוֹמָיו, הוּא בְּרַחֲמָיו יַעֲשֶׂה שָׁלוֹם עָלֵינוּ, וְעַל כָּל יִשְׂרָאֵל. וְאִמְרוּ: אָמֵן. (Cong. — אָמֵן.)

৺ Prayer After Mishnah

It is customary to recite this prayer whenever mishnayos are studied in memory of a deceased.

אָנָּא יהוה מָלֵא רַחֲמִים, אֲשֶׁר בְּיָדְךָ נֶפֶשׁ כָּל חַי, וְרוּחַ כָּל בְּשַׂר אִישׁ. יִהְיֶה נָא לְרָצוֹן לְפָנֶיךָ תּוֹרָתֵנוּ וּתְפִלָּתֵנוּ בַּעֲבוּר נִשְׁמַת [שם הנפטר(ת)] בֶּן/בַּת [שם אמו/ אמה] וּגְמוֹל נָא עִמָּה בְּחַסְדְּךָ הַגָּדוֹל, לִפְתּוֹחַ לָה שַׁעֲרֵי רַחֲמִים וָחֶסֶד, וְשַׁעֲרֵי גַּן עֵדֶן. וּתְקַבֵּל אוֹתָה בְּאַהֲבָה וּבְחִבָּה, וְשָׁלַח לָה מַלְאָכֶיךָ הַקְּדוֹשִׁים וְהַטְּהוֹרִים, לְהוֹלִיכָה וּלְהוֹשִׁיבָה תַּחַת עֵץ הַחַיִּים, אֵצֶל נִשְׁמַת הַצַּדִּיקִים וְהַצִּדְקָנִיּוֹת, חֲסִידִים וַחֲסִידוֹת, לֵהָנוֹת מִזִּיו שְׁכִינָתָךְ, לְהַשְׂבִּיעָהּ מִטּוּבְךָ הַצָּפוּן לַצַּדִּיקִים. וְהַגּוּף יָנוּחַ בַּקֶּבֶר בִּמְנוּחָה נְכוֹנָה, בְּחֶדְוָה וּבְשִׂמְחָה וְשָׁלוֹם, כְּדִכְתִיב: יָבֹא שָׁלוֹם, יָנוּחוּ עַל מִשְׁכְּבוֹתָם, הֹלֵךְ נְכֹחוֹ. וּכְתִיב: יַעְלְזוּ חֲסִידִים בְּכָבוֹד, יְרַנְּנוּ עַל מִשְׁכְּבוֹתָם. וּכְתִיב: אִם תִּשְׁכַּב לֹא תִפְחָד, וְשָׁכַבְתָּ וְעָרְבָה שְׁנָתֶךָ. וְתִשְׁמוֹר [אוֹתוֹ/אוֹתָהּ] מֵחִבּוּט הַקֶּבֶר, וּמֵרִמָּה וְתוֹלֵעָה. וְתִסְלַח וְתִמְחוֹל [לוֹ/לָהּ] עַל כָּל [פְּשָׁעָיו/פְּשָׁעֶיהָ], כִּי אָדָם אֵין צַדִּיק בָּאָרֶץ, אֲשֶׁר יַעֲשֶׂה טוֹב וְלֹא יֶחֱטָא. וּזְכוֹר [לוֹ זְכִיּוֹתָיו וְצִדְקוֹתָיו/לָהּ זְכִיּוֹתֶיהָ וְצִדְקוֹתֶיהָ] אֲשֶׁר [עָשָׂה/עָשְׂתָה.] וְתַשְׁפִּיעַ [לוֹ מִנִּשְׁמָתוֹ/לָהּ מִנִּשְׁמָתָהּ] לְדַשֵׁן [עַצְמוֹתָיו/עַצְמוֹתֶיהָ] בַּקֶּבֶר מֵרֹב טוֹב הַצָּפוּן לַצַּדִּיקִים, דִּכְתִיב: מָה רַב טוּבְךָ אֲשֶׁר צָפַנְתָּ לִּירֵאֶיךָ. וּכְתִיב: שֹׁמֵר כָּל עַצְמֹתָיו, אַחַת מֵהֵנָּה לֹא נִשְׁבָּרָה. [וְיִשְׁכּוֹן/וְתִשְׁכּוֹן] בֶּטַח בָּדָד וְשַׁאֲנַן מִפַּחַד רָעָה, וְאַל [יִרְאֶה/תִּרְאֶה] פְּנֵי גֵיהִנֹּם. [וְנִשְׁמָתוֹ/וְנִשְׁמָתָהּ] תְּהֵא צְרוּרָה בִּצְרוֹר הַחַיִּים, [וּלְהַחֲיוֹתוֹ/וּלְהַחֲיוֹתָהּ] בִּתְחִיַּת הַמֵּתִים עִם כָּל מֵתֵי עַמְּךָ יִשְׂרָאֵל בְּרַחֲמִים. אָמֵן.

אָנָּא Please, O HASHEM, full of mercy, for in Your hand is the soul of all the living and the spirit of every human being, may You find favor in our Torah study and prayer for the soul of

(deceased's Hebrew name)

son/daughter of

(father's Hebrew name)

and do with it according to Your great kindness to open for it the gates of mercy and kindness and the gates of the Garden of Eden. Accept it with love and affection and send it Your holy and pure angels to lead it and to settle it under the Tree of Life near the souls of the righteous and devout men and women, to enjoy the radiance of Your Presence, to satiate it from Your good that is concealed for the righteous. May the body repose in the grave with proper contentment, pleasure, gladness and peace, as it is written: 'Let him enter in peace, let them rest on their beds — everyone who has lived in his proper way.' And it is written: 'Let the devout exult in glory, let them sing joyously upon their beds.' And it is written: 'If you lay down, you will not fear; when you lay down, your sleep will be sweet.' And protect [him/her] from the tribulations of the grave and from worms and maggots. Forgive and pardon [him/her] for all [his/her] sins, for there is no man so wholly righteous on earth that he does good and never sins. Remember for [him/her] the merits and righteous deeds that [he/she] performed, and cause a spiritual flow from [his/her] soul to keep [his/her] bones fresh in the grave from the abundant good that is concealed for the righteous, as it is written: 'How abundant is Your goodness that You have concealed for Your reverent ones,' and it is written: 'He guards all his bones, even one of them was not broken.' May it rest secure, alone, and serene, from fear of evil and may it not see the threshold of Gehinnom. May [his/her] soul be bound in the Bond of Life. And may it be brought back to life with the Resuscitation of the Dead with all the dead of Your people Israel, with mercy. Amen.

◄§ *Kaddish HaGadol* /*Kaddish* After Burial

Transliterated with Ashkenazic pronunciation

Yisgadal v'yiskadash sh'mei rabbaw (Cong. – Amein).
   B'allmaw dee hu awsid l'ischadawsaw,
u'l'achayawsaw meisayaw,
u'l'asawkaw yaws'hon l'chayei allmaw,
u'l'mivnei kartaw dee yerushleim,
u'l'shachlawlaw heichlei b'gavaw,
u'l'me'kar paelchawnaw nuchraw'aw min ar'aw,
u'l'asawvaw pawlchawnaw dee sh'mayaw l'asrei,
v'yamlich kudshaw b'rich hu b'malchusei veekawrei,
[Nusach Sefard – V'yatzmach purkanei v'kareiv m'shichei
(Cong. – Amein)].
b'chayeichon, uv'yomeichon, uv'chayei d'chol beis yisroel,
ba'agawlaw u'vizman kawriv, u'imru: Amein.
(Cong. – Amein. Y'hei sh'mei rabbaw m'vawrach l'allam u'l'allmei
allmayaw.)

Y'hei sh'mei rabbaw m'vawrach, l'allam u'l'allmei allmayaw.
Yis'bawrach, v'yishtabach, v'yispaw'ar, v'yisromam, v'yis'nassei,
v'yish'hador, v'yis'aleh, v'yis'halawl
sh'mei d'kudshaw b'rich hu (Cong. – b'rich hu).
L'aylaw min kol [From Rosh Hashanah to Yom Kippur substitute: ul'aylaw mikol]
bir'chawsaw v'shirawsaw,
tush'b'chawsaw v'nechemawsaw,
da'ami'rawn b'allmaw, v'imru: Amein (Cong. – Amein).

Y'hei shlawmaw rabbaw min sh'mayaw,
v'chayim [Nusach Sefard – tovim] awleinu v'al kol yisroel,
v'imru: Amein (Cong. – Amein).

> Take three steps back, bow left and say, 'Oseh. . .';
> bow right and say, 'hu b'rachamawv ya'aseh. . .';
> bow forward and say, 'v'al kol yisroel v'imru: Amein.'

Oseh shawlom bim'ro'mawv,
hu ya'aseh shawlom awleinu,
v'al kol yisroel v'imru: Amein (Cong. – Amein).

Remain standing in place for a few moments, then take three steps forward.

⌁ Mourner's *Kaddish*

Transliterated with Ashkenazic pronunciation

Yisgadal v'yiskadash sh'mei rabbaw (Cong. – Amein).
B'allmaw dee v'raw chir'usei v'yamlich malchusei,
[*Nusach Sefard* – V'yatzmach purkanei v'kareiv m'shichei
(Cong. – Amein)].
b'chayeichon, uv'yomeichon, uv'chayei d'chol beis yisroel,
ba'agawlaw u'vizman kawriv, u'imru: Amein.
(Cong. – Amein. Y'hei sh'mei rabbaw m'vawrach
l'allam u'l'allmei allmayaw.)

Y'hei sh'mei rabbaw m'vawrach, l'allam u'l'allmei allmayaw.
Yis'bawrach, v'yishtabach, v'yispaw'ar, v'yisromam, v'yis'nassei,
v'yis'hador, v'yis'aleh, v'yis'halawl
sh'mei d'kudshaw b'rich hu (Cong. – b'rich hu).
L'aylaw [From Rosh Hashanah to Yom Kippur substitute: ul'aylaw mikol]
bir'chawsaw v'shirawsaw,
tush'b'chawsaw v'nechemawsaw,
da'ami'rawn b'allmaw, v'imru: Amein (Cong. – Amein).

Y'hei shlawmaw rabbaw min sh'mayaw,
v'chayim [*Nusach Sefard* – tovim] awleinu v'al kol yisroel,
v'imru: Amein (Cong. – Amein).

> Take three steps back, bow left and say, 'Oseh. . .';
> bow right and say, 'hu b'rachamavv ya'aseh. . .';
> bow forward and say, 'v'al kol yisroel v'imru: Amein.'

Oseh shawlom bim'ro'mawv,
hu ya'aseh shawlom awleinu,
v'al kol yisroel v'imru: Amein (Cong. – Amein).

> Remain standing in place for a few moments, then take three steps forward.

⇜ The Rabbis' Kaddish/*Kaddish D'rabbanan*
Transliterated with Ashkenazic pronunciation

Yisgadal v'yiskadash sh'mei rabbaw (Cong. – Amein).
 B'allmaw dee v'raw chir'usei v'yamlich malchusei,
[*Nusach Sefard* – V'yatzmach purkanei v'kareiv m'shichei
(Cong. – Amein)].
b'chayeichon, uv'yomeichon, uv'chayei d'chol beis yisroel,
ba'agawlaw u'vizman kawriv, u'imru: Amein.
(Cong. – Amein. Y'hei sh'mei rabbaw m'vawrach
l'allam u'l'allmei allmayaw.)

Y'hei sh'mei rabbaw m'vawrach, l'allam u'l'allmei allmayaw.
Yis'bawrach, v'yishtabach, v'yispaw'ar, v'yisromam, v'yis'nassei,
v'yish'hador, v'yis'aleh, v'yis'halawl
sh'mei d'kudshaw b'rich hu (Cong. – b'rich hu).
L'aylaw [From Rosh Hashanah to Yom Kippur substitute: ul'aylaw mikol]
bir'chawsaw v'shirawsaw,
tush'b'chawsaw v'nechemawsaw,
da'ami'rawn b'allmaw, v'imru: Amein (Cong. – Amein).

Al yisroel v'al rabaw'nawn v'al talmidei'hon,
v'al kol talmidei salmidei'hon, v'al kol mawn d'awskin b'oray'saw,
dee v'as'raw haw'dain, v'dee b'chol asar va'asar.
Y'hei l'hon u'l'chon shlaw'maw rabbaw,
chee'naw v'chisdaw v'rachamin,
v'chayin arichin, u'm'zonei r'vichei, u'furkawnaw
min kaw'dawm a'vu'hone dee vi'sh'ma'yaw [Nusach Sefard – v'araw]
v'imru: Amein (Cong. – Amein).

Y'hei shlawmaw rabbaw min sh'mayaw,
v'chayim [Nusach Sefard – tovim] awleinu v'al kol yisroel,
v'imru: Amein (Cong. – Amein).

> Take three steps back, bow left and say, 'Oseh...';
> bow right and say, 'hu b'rachamawv ya'aseh...';
> bow forward and say, 'v'al kol yisroel v'imru: Amein.'

Oseh shawlom bim'ro'mawv,
hu b'rachamawv ya'aseh shawlom awleinu,
v'al kol yisroel v'imru: Amein (Cong. – Amein).

Remain standing in place for a few moments, then take three steps forward.

Index

✑ Index

D

L

N

O

U

Z

Family Records

Relation	Name/Father's Name	Born	Died

This volume is part of
THE ARTSCROLL SERIES®
an ongoing project of
translations, commentaries and expositions
on Scripture, Mishnah, Talmud, Halachah,
liturgy, history, the classic Rabbinic writings,
biographies, and thought.

For a brochure of current publications
visit your local Hebrew bookseller
or contact the publisher:

Mesorah Publications, ltd.

4401 Second Avenue
Brooklyn, New York 11232
(718) 921-9000